Rebour
The Bicycle Illustrations of Daniel Rebour

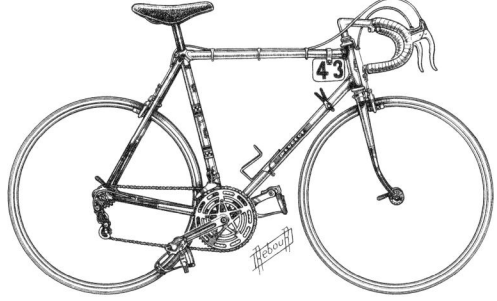

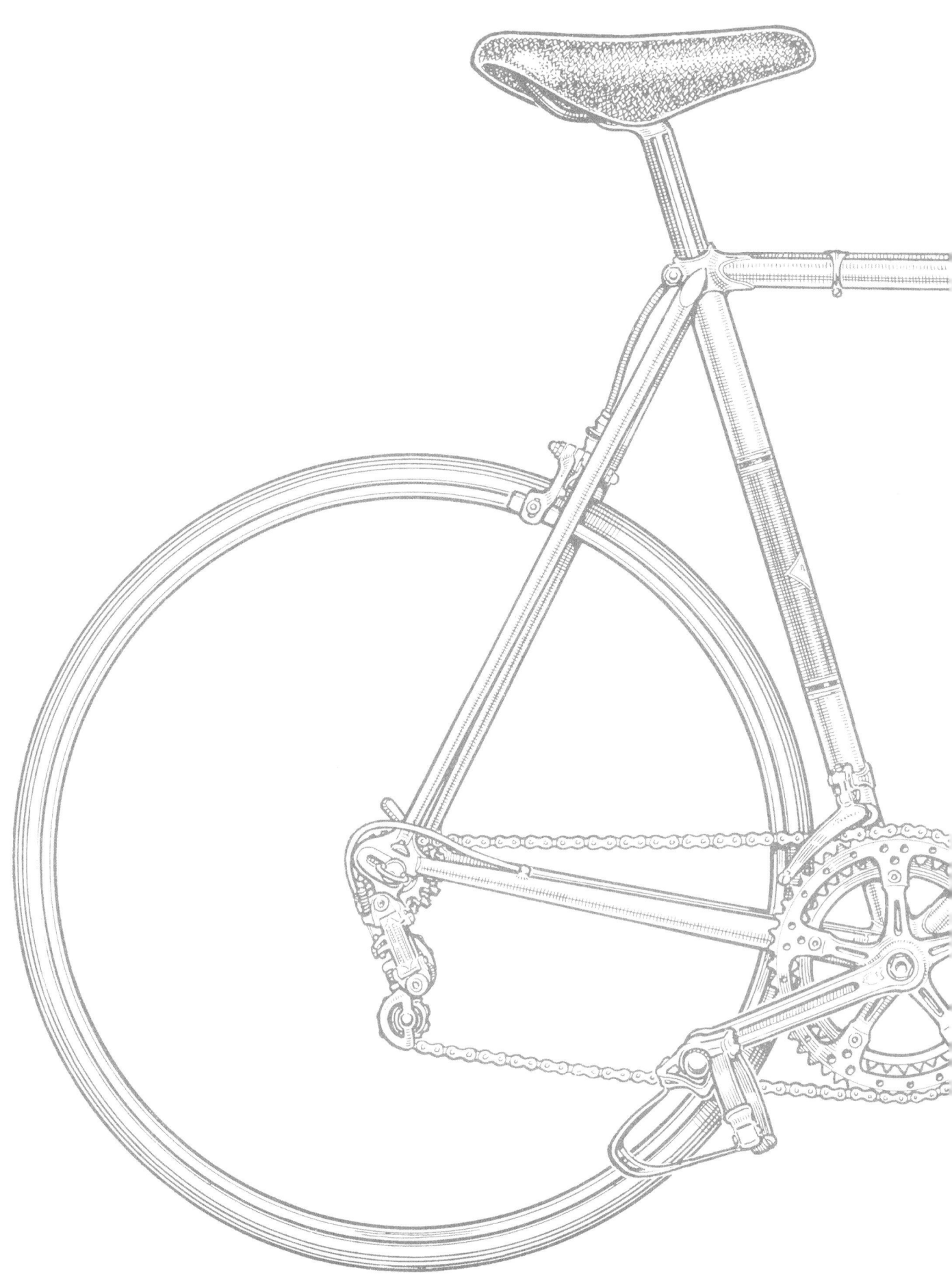

REBOUR

THE BICYCLE ILLUSTRATIONS OF DANIEL REBOUR

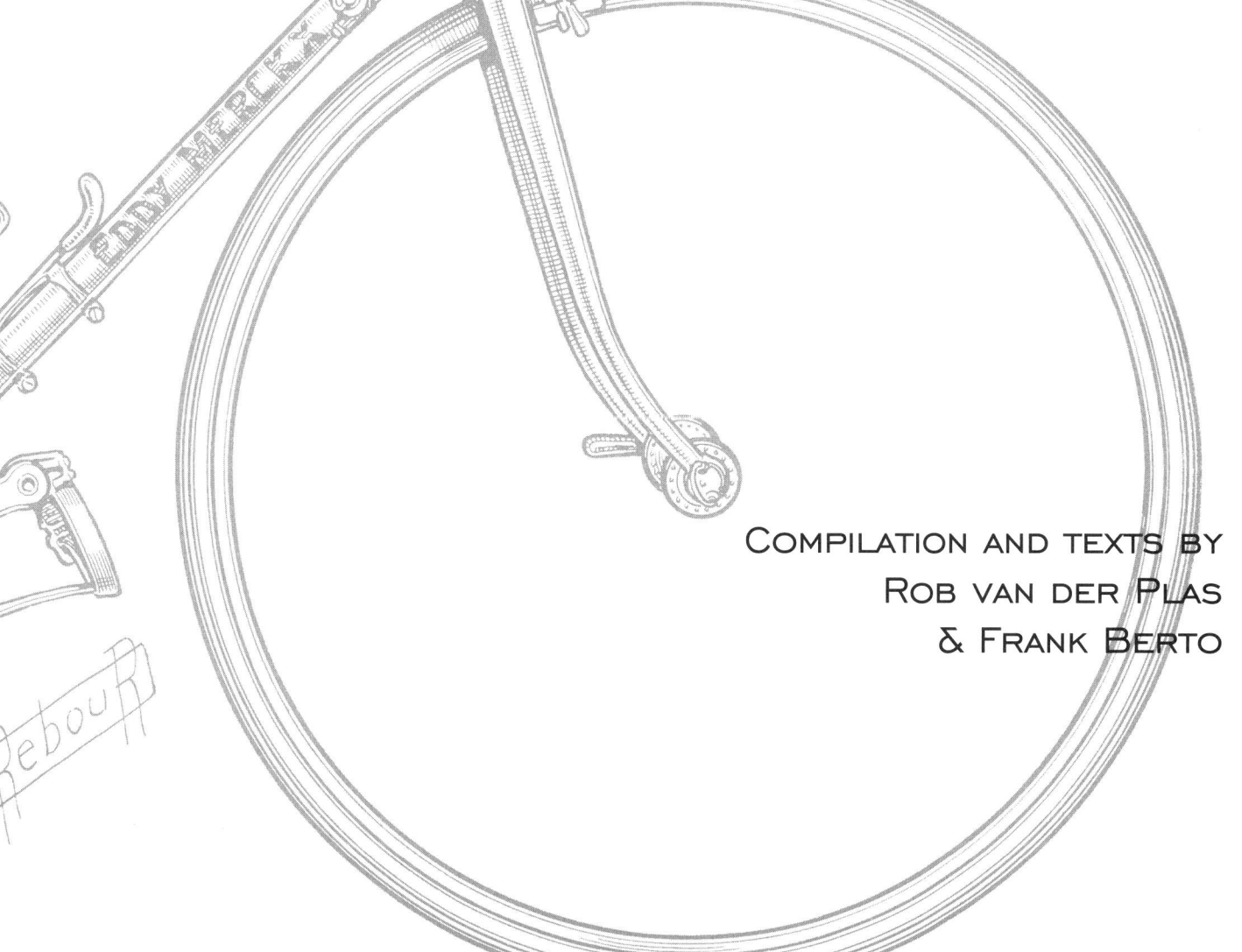

Compilation and texts by
Rob van der Plas
& Frank Berto

Cycle Publishing / Van der Plas Publications, San Francisco

Text copyright © 2013 Rob van der Plas. All rights reserved

Printed in the USA on acid-free paper

Publisher's information:
Cycle Publishing / Van der Plas Publications
1282 7th Avenue
San Francisco, CA 94122, USA
http://www.cyclepublishing.com

Distributed or represented to the book trade by:
USA: Midpoint Trade Books
UK: Orca Book Services /Chris Lloyd Sales and Marketing Services
Australia: Bicycling Australia

Cover design: TandemCreative.com / Ben Hopfer, based on a Daniel Rebour illustration of a BSA loaded-touring bicycle displayed at the 1951 London bicycle trade show and depicted in *Le Cycle* of 24 November 1951.

Frontispiece: Daniel Rebour illustration of Eddy Merckx' 1969 Tour de France bicycle, published in the August-September 1969 issue of *Le Cycle*.

Half-title page illustration: Daniel Rebour illustration of Bernard Thévènet's bicycle in the 1972 Tour de France.

Publisher's Cataloging in Publication Data:
van der Plas, Rob, 1938—, and Frank Berto, 1929—
Rebour: The Bicycle Illustrations of Daniel Rebour
1. Bicycles and bicycling—handbooks and manuals.
2. Illustration technique.
28 cm. Bibliography: p. Includes index
I. Title: The Bicycle Illustrations of Daniel Rebour
II. Authorship: Frank Berto, contributor.
Library of Congress Control Number: 2013900073
ISBN 978-1-892495-71-6

Acknowledgments

Our special thanks to David Herlihy for lending us some of the Rebour materials he had collected, and to Jan Heine for allowing us to reprint some of the materials on Rebour by Jean-Pierre Pradères and Mark Lawrence previously published in *(Vintage) Bicycle Quarterly*. Also our posthumous thanks to Fred DeLong, whose collection of French periodicals, left by him to Frank Berto, formed the basis and inspiration for this book. And finally to Daniel Rebour himself, for offering, when asked about permission to use his drawings, "use anything you like, as long as you don't omit my signature."[*]

---

[*] We have adhered to this request wherever either his initials or his full signature appeared in the original drawing, though some drawings were not signed, and therefore also appear in this book unsigned. In a few cases, we've taken the liberty to move the signature to a different location in the drawing to fit the available space.

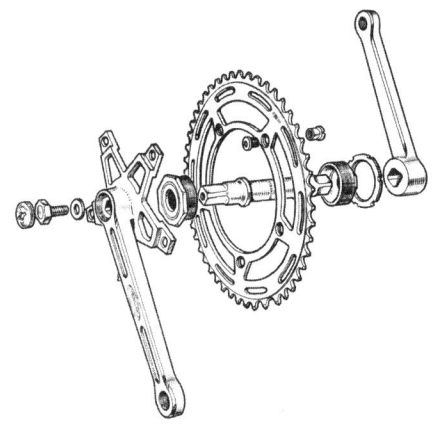

Table of Contents

Introduction: Who Was Daniel Rebour? 9

Chapter 1. Historic Bicycle Drawings. 15

Chapter 2. Frame Details. 19

Chapter 3. Derailleur Gearing 41

Chapter 4. Drivetrain Components. 74

Chapter 5. Pedals and Toeclips. 98

Chapter 6. Rim Brakes 106

Chapter 7. Regular Wheel Hubs 120

Chapter 8. Gear and Brake Hubs 130

Chapter 9. Rims, Tires, and Spokes 139

Chapter 10. Steering Components 146

Chapter 11. Seat and Seatpost. 161

Chapter 12. Component Gruppos. 169

Chapter 13. Luggage Carrying Equipment. . 180

Chapter 14. Lighting Equipment 192

Chapter 15. Other Accessories 200

Chapter 16. Product Overviews. 214

Chapter 17. Tandem Bicycles 222

Chapter 18. Folding and Parting Bikes ... 233

Chapter 19. Children's Bikes 239

Chapter 20. Suspension Systems 241

Chapter 21. Trailers and Sidecars 245

Chapter 22. Alternate Drives 247

Chapter 23. Bicycle Derivatives 250

Chapter 24. Motorized Bicycles. 252

Chapter 25. Tools and Equipment 257

Chapter 26. Bicycle Clothing 260

Chapter 27. Original Scans 262

Chapter 28. Captions to Selected Illustrations 269

Appendix 1. Pierre-Georges Hugaud 273

Appendix 2. Rodolphe Rebour 274

Appendix 3. George Retseck 275

Bibliography 277

Index 279

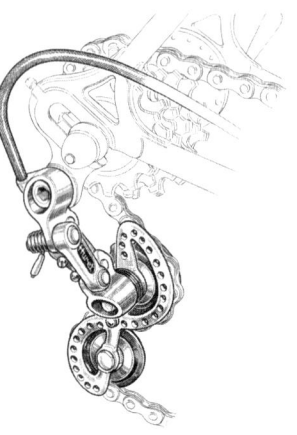

Introduction: Who Was Daniel Rebour?

Looking at cycling books and magazines from the mid-1940s through the mid-1970s, one can't help but be impressed by the technical illustrations used during this period, which were so much clearer than the photographs used in later years. Many of those drawings are signed with the initials "DR" or "D Rebour." This book is devoted to the art of cycling illustrations as much as it is to the man who created them, Daniel Rebour.

Rebour was without a doubt the most prolific illustrator of the period that might be described as the "golden age of technical illustration" or just as aptly, "the golden age of bicycle development"—the three decades following World War II. His amazingly clear line drawings appeared in the French cycling press, as well as in manufacturers' catalogues and cycling books.

Born in the port city of Le Havre in 1908 or 1909[*], his family moved to Paris, where he studied illustration at the Paris École Nationale Supérieure des Arts Décoratifs, where also his elder brother Rodolphe had been educated. After graduation in 1928, Daniel was hired in 1930 as test rider and illustrator for *Moto-Revue*, where he further developed his skill as a technical illustrator and got his feet wet in technical journalism.

---

[*] Accounts vary. Raymond Henri and David Herlihy both report 1909 as his birth year, whereas Jean-Pierre Pradères, who interviewed Rebour's wife Simone, reports it as 1908.

His career, as that of so many of his generation, was interrupted by World War II, during which time he worked for Técalémit, a manufacturer of motorcar parts, producing their catalogues. He moved to Biarritz when the company relocated there in 1940, and it was there that he met his future wife, Simone.

After the war, he was approached by his friend Claude Tillet to join him as an illustrator and technical writer for his newly founded periodical *Le Cycle*, the first issue of which appeared in September 1945. This was a time of austerity, and *Le Cycle* was printed on whatever paper was available, and that was usually neither very white, nor smooth, nor durable, which explains why it is today hard to find surviving early issues of *Le Cycle*. It also means that some of the early illustrations were not reproduced in the same clear black-and-white as they were drawn, and that will be evident in some of the pages of this book.

Le Cycle initially saw its circulation increase, but this was also a time when the bicycle trade expanded into motorized bicycles, and by 1960 the title had been "updated" to include "*Motos, Cyclomoteurs, Scooters*" in the masthead, and for a while in the early 1970s even the word "*Karting*" (referring to go-carts, motorized or not) was added. Consequently, there were also many Rebour drawings of motor cycles, mopeds, and scooters,

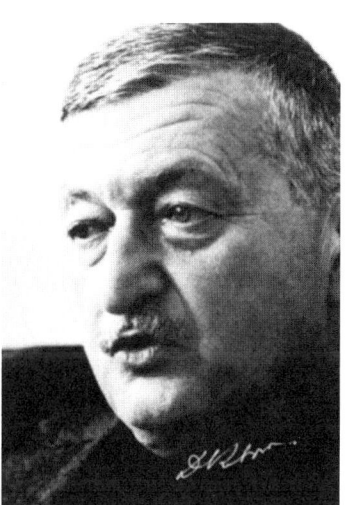

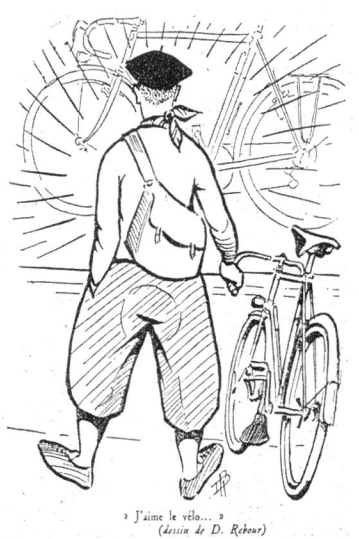

Left: This signed 1976 portrait of Rebour appeared in the 1976 Japanese-language book *Le Monde de Daniel Rebour*.

Right: The first Rebour drawing to appear in *Le Cycle* was not a technical illustration but this cartoon, published in the 5th issue, December 1945.

and indeed some go-carts, and it is striking with what attention to detail those drawings were executed, a few of which have been included in this work under a separate heading. His drawings also appeared in *Le Cycliste*, the magazine for cycle tourists founded by Vélocio, and other publications.

One of the few people in the U.S. to know about *Le Cycle* at the time was Fred DeLong, a mechanical engineer with a lifelong passion for the bicycle and its technology. For many years, he was technical editor for several U.S. cycling periodicals, and it was his collection, which was passed on to Frank Berto upon his death in 1995, that forms the basis for this compilation. In addition, we have made use of other publications in which his drawings appeared, notably his three books, *La Pratique du Vélo* (1949), *Cycle: Compétition, Cyclotourisme* (1962), and *Cycles de Competition et Randonneuses* (1975), as well as the catalogues of VAR tools and of Cycles Bertin.

There is one previous book devoted to Daniel Rebour's drawings, *Le Monde de Daniel Rebour*, published in Japan in 1976 by BERO Publishing Company. Despite the French title, all texts are in Japanese. The book does contain some interesting comments, including a brief introduction by Rebour himself.

Another originally Japanese book in which many of Rebour's drawings were included was called *'83 The Data Book*, published in 1983 by Mr. Tsunezo Terashima, of the Joto Ringyo bicycle component distributors, as a New-Year's present to his friends and business associates. This book was republished in the U.S. in 1998 under the title *The Data Book: 100 Years of Bicycle Component and Accessory Design*.

Finally, Frank Berto, in his epic *The Dancing Chain: History and Development of the Derailleur Bicycle*, includes quite a number of Rebour illustrations, including useful captions that explain in some detail how things—especially drivetrain components—work.

Reading some of the articles Rebour wrote for the magazine and the books he authored, one can't help but be impressed with his insight into technical matters. Though he never seems to have received a formal engineering education, he nevertheless had a keen understanding of technical issues, and a remarkable ability to clarify them in terms that could be understood by regular cyclists.

Daniel Rebour was no mean cyclist himself, and his name can be found amongst the participants of many of the French Rondonnées (long-distance touring rides) of the period. When he married his wife Simone in September 1948, the newlyweds spent their honeymoon riding their tandem in Paris–Brest–Paris, winning the mixed-tandem category in 61 hours and 56 minutes, despite a 4-hour delay due to a broken crank.

Left: Newlyweds Daniel and Simone Rebour on the tandem with which they won the mixed tandem category of Paris–Brest–Paris in 1948.

Below: How Rebour signed his work. The initials only were mainly used up to 1950; after that the full signature usually appeared.

In the mid-1970s, after the American 10-speed bicycle boom had ended, the French cycle industry was soon eclipsed by the Japanese manufacturers, and *Le Cycle* suffered the same fate as the famed French component manufacturers, who seemed no longer to be the innovators they had been before. Circulation of *Le Cycle*, and the volume of each issue as well as the number of Rebour drawings, went into a tailspin, until the last issue of *Le Cycle* appeared December 1975.

The following year, some of the former *Le Cycle* editors started a new periodical, *L'Officiel du Cycle*. Initially some of Rebour's drawings and writings appeared there, in a few issues he's even listed as "Honorary Editor in Chief," but soon his drawings were replaced by photographs, which were not as clear, but quicker and cheaper to make and reproduce. Instead, most of Rebour's work was now published in catalogues, such as those for André Bertin's Milremo mail order company, René Herse's specialty bike business, and the VAR tool company. Bertin was the importer of several Japanese component makers, including Shimano and Sakae Ringyo (SR), and consequently there are some very fine Rebour drawings of Shimano's and other Japanese components all the way up to 1983, many of which are included in this volume.

During the last few years at *Le Cycle,* Rebour had trained a younger illustrator, Pierre-Georges Hugaud, and his drawings, reminiscent of Rebour's style, also appeared in *L'Officiel du Cycle*, where Hugaud became technical editor. For reference, we have included some of Hugaud's illustrations in the Appendix. Rebour died in 1991, and was survived by his wife Simone and his elder brother Rodolphe.

Rodolphe also worked for *Le Cycle*, and his work is often signed "Ro Rebour." His specialties were advertising and the human form, much more so than technical illustrating. In the appendix, we have also included a few of his ads and drawings to make that point.

Surprisingly little has been published about the man Daniel Rebour himself. There is not a word about him, nor about *Le Cycle*, in the French version of Wikipedia, nor in any other French on-line sources we could find.

Several years after Rebour's death, the American bicycle historian David Herlihy wrote an article about

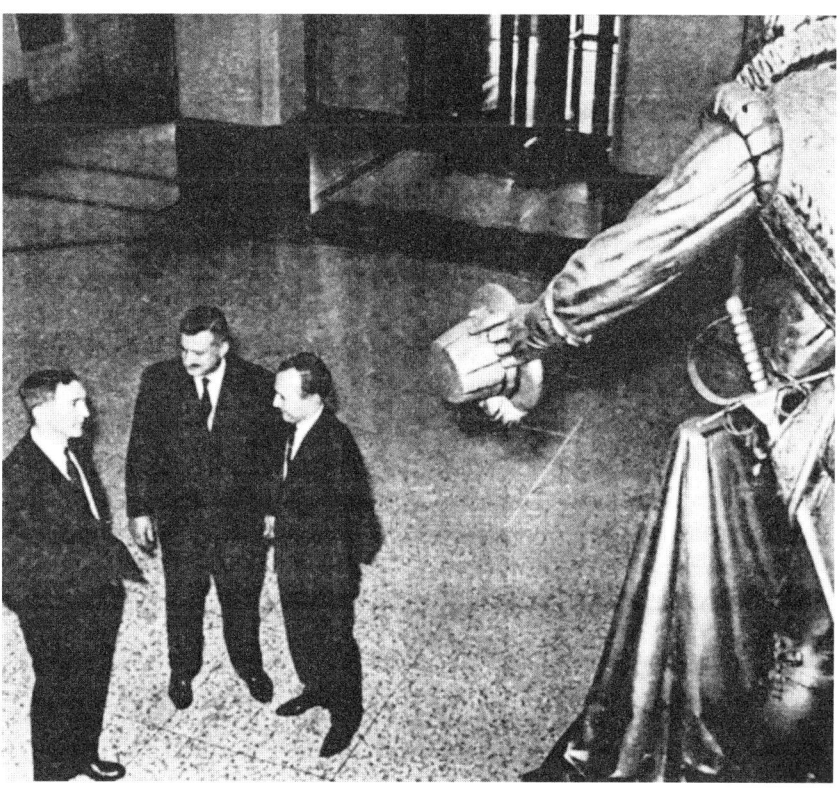

Above: Daniel Rebour with Eddy Merckx at the 1976 Paris bicycle trade show.

Right: Daniel Rebour with Claude Richardet and Raleigh's Director D. P. Harris at the Raleigh plant in Nottingham, 1961.

Rebour and his work, based on an interview with Daniel Rebour's elder brother Rodolphe, slightly different versions of which were published in the March 1995 issue of *Bicycle Guide* magazine, and in the 1993 U.S. Bridgestone catalogue.

Daniel Rebour's Technique
told by Ken Taylor

[Ed: I have wondered why original Rebour drawings were on photo paper, rather than on drafting paper. Ken Taylor told Mark Lawrence the secret.]

I was a "camera man" at the time, and I had a Leica camera. I used to see all these Daniel Rebour drawings that he did in all the catalogues and the French cycling magazines. When he came to our stand and photographed all our carriers and stems, and all the things we'd made on the bikes, I showed him everything we did.

I asked him how he did the drawings. He explained that he took the photograph with his camera, processed the negative, and then made a print from the negative in the normal way, but he only took the print to a certain stage. Then he stopped it, put it on the table, and drew over the faint outline of the subject. After he'd done the drawing with indelible ink, he'd wash the photograph out, and he was left with just his drawing, which he'd done on top of the print. It was a good process, because he had everything in perspective. And I thought: "Well, that's brilliant."

At the 1995 International Cycle History Conference, in Stellenbosch, South Africa, a paper by Raymond Henri was presented about Daniel Rebour and his work.

Jean-Pierre Pradères wrote an article based on his interview with Rebour's widow for *Vintage Bicycle Quarterly* in 2004. These three articles together form the most comprehensive information about Rebour himself (although there are some contradictions between them—see footnote on page 9).

In 2009, *Bicycle Quarterly* published an article by Mark Lawrence about Daniel Rebour's work. It included an account by Ken Taylor, one of the founders and owners of the English frame building company Jack Taylor Cycles, of the way Rebour created many of his drawings, reproduced below.

Rebour and the French Bicycle

The period covered in this book, i.e. the period of Rebour's illustrative input, was one of significant technical development, and much of that development took place in France.

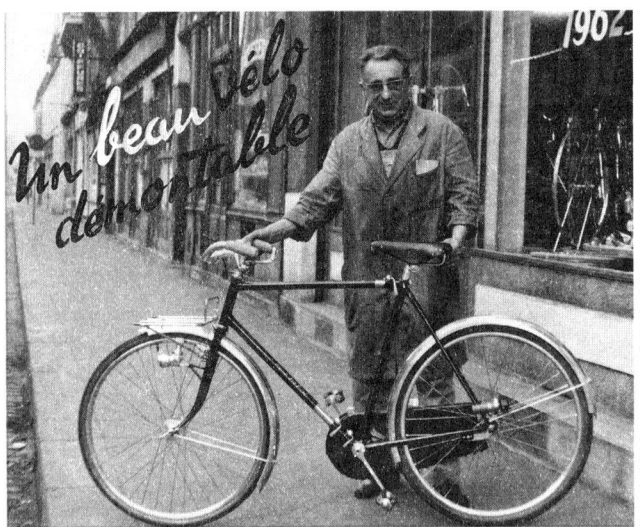

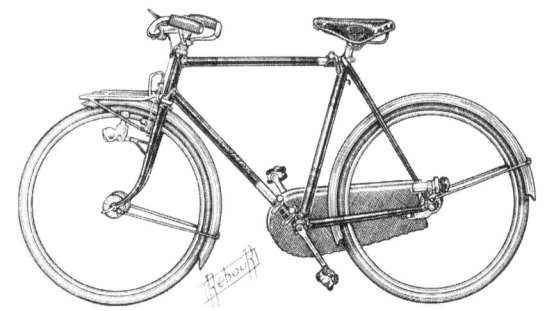

The drawing of the René Herse Démontable (from *Le Cycliste* Jan./Feb. 1964) exactly matches the unpublished photo from Daniel Rebour's files.

Left: Reprinted with permission from *Bicycle Quarterly*, Vol. 7, No. 4, Summer 2009. Ken Taylor's explanation of Rebour's drawing technique. Although the article explains well enough how drawings of assembled bikes and components were created, it leaves one question unanswered: how *did* he create those lovely exploded views of many components included in this book?

Right: Cover of the 1976 revised second printing of Rebour's third book *Cycles de Compétition et Randonneuses*.

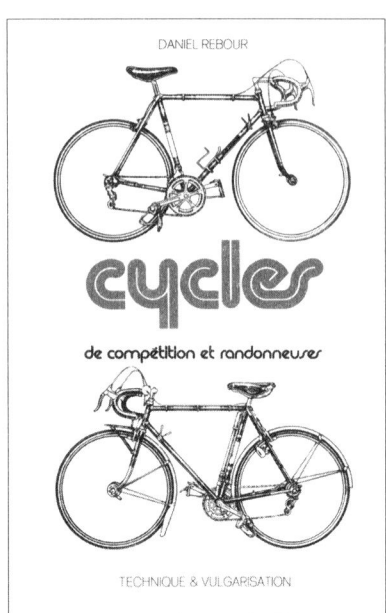

In France, more so than in neighboring countries, not to mention the U.S. and Canada, the bike trade had long been one of many small, and often innovative manufacturers. There were big bicycle manufacturers, but there were also numerous smaller operations specializing either in complete bicycles, in special-purpose framebuilding, or in the development and manufacture of specialized components.

Thus, between the wars, a culture of high-quality bicycles and bicycle components was alive, parallel to the world of plain utilitarian bicycles for the working class. Numerous small frame builders offered frames built for *coureurs* (bicycle racers) as well as for demanding *cyclosportifs* (sporting cyclists), *cyclocampeurs* (bicycle campers) and *cyclotouristes* (bicycle tourists), the latter also referred to as *randonneurs*.

Unlike the *coureur*s who tended to come from the working class, these latter category riders tended to be from the middle class (in the original sense of the word, i.e. independent professionals, artisans, and owners of small- to medium-size businesses). These people had disposable income, and were prepared to pay a premium for sophisticated bicycles and components.

The industry that catered to their needs included manufacturers who were willing to develop products for a limited but demanding clientele. Products like derailleur gearing systems and sophisticated brake systems, initially introduced for limited use by these bicycle connoisseurs, were eventually also accepted by bicycle racers. Thus, high-quality derailleur systems had been in use by *cyclotouristes* for many years, and were constantly being tested and improved, long before they found acceptance on the racing circuit.

The Second World War, though not as disruptive in France as in neighboring countries, temporarily put a stop to these developments. However, no sooner was peace restored, or cyclists started to resume their interest in qualitatively superior equipment. Companies such as

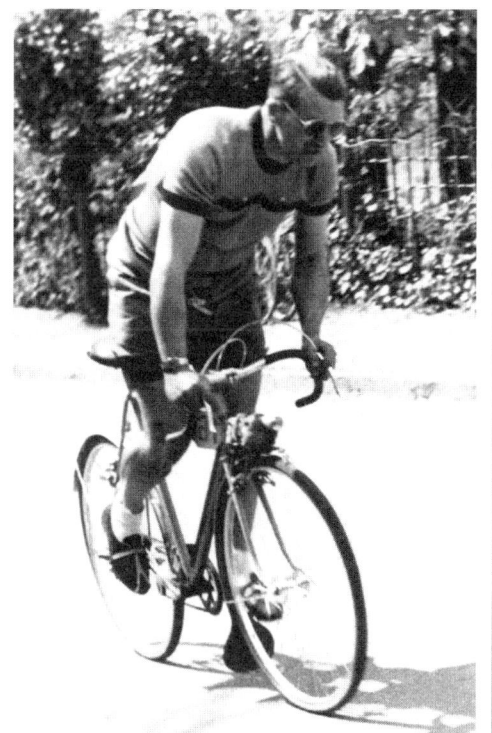
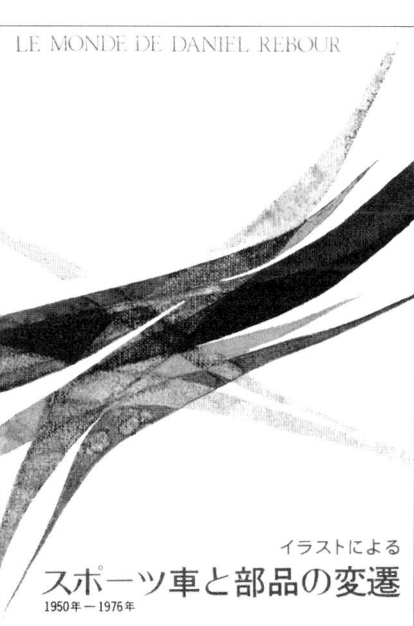
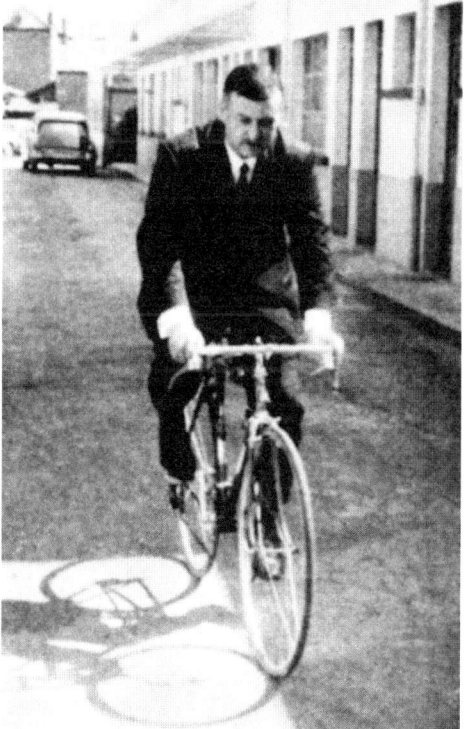

Left: Daniel Rebour in action. This photograph from Rebour's private collection was probably taken in the early 1950s.
Center: Cover of the Japanese book *Le Monde de Daniel Rebour*, published 1976 by BERO Publishing Company, Tokyo, publishers of the Japanese-language magazine NYUU SAIKURINGU (New Cycling).
Right: This photo, first published in the May 1967 issue of *Le Cycle*, shows Daniel Rebour test-riding a bicycle with Simplex' new top-tube shift lever at the Simplex factory. Judging by his outfit, it wasn't going to be a long test ride.

Simplex, TA, Stronglight, Huret, Maillard, Mafac, CLB, and many others went back to producing and refining their components. Similarly, frame-builders and small-scale bicycle manufacturers resumed production.

It is against this background that Rebour's friend and fellow randonneur Claude Tillet launched his magazine *Le Cycle*, addressing not only the bike trade, but also quality-conscious cyclists. Initially published weekly, then twice-monthly, and after mid 1960 monthly, the issues of *Le Cycle* paint a clear portrait of the state of the art in the world of sophisticated bicycle product development.

Rebour was hired in 1946, and soon became technical editor as well as chief illustrator, recording with his drawing pen as with his clear writing style all the developments of the post-war decades. Although this book concentrates exclusively on his drawings, some of his writings were remarkably revealing, and he did not hesitate to point out fallacies wherever they appeared, clearly explaining why certain things worked the way they did and others didn't.

Arrangement of This Book

For this project, we had collected some 3,000 images from Rebour's vast output, mainly those first published in *Le Cycle* and various manufacturer's catalogues. To do justice to this vast oeuvre, we have selected a more manageable number of images on the basis of several criteria: historical significance, image quality, and context.

We have made the decision to use nearly all the illustrations of whole bicycles, regardless of their reproduction quality, and run those full-width at the bottom of almost every page throughout the book. The other images have been divided into a number of distinct categories, as shown in the Table of Contents on page 7. The upper portion of the pages with a bicycle illustration at the bottom, and the full page area of pages without, are devoted to these subject matters.

In a few cases, this arrangement breaks down, such as when we have detail drawings available for a bicycle depicted. There we try to show those details on the same page as the bicycle, regardless of the subject heading within the book. We trust that the accompanying captions are sufficient to shed light on this matter, avoiding any confusion.

As for the illustrations themselves, most of them have been reproduced as is, with only minor touch-up corrections. In some cases, though, in order to fit an illustration to the available space, we have rearranged the elements, perhaps bringing side-by-side details that were originally arranged vertically, or bringing details closer together when needed. Chapter 27, contains images scanned directly from Rebour's original art-boards.

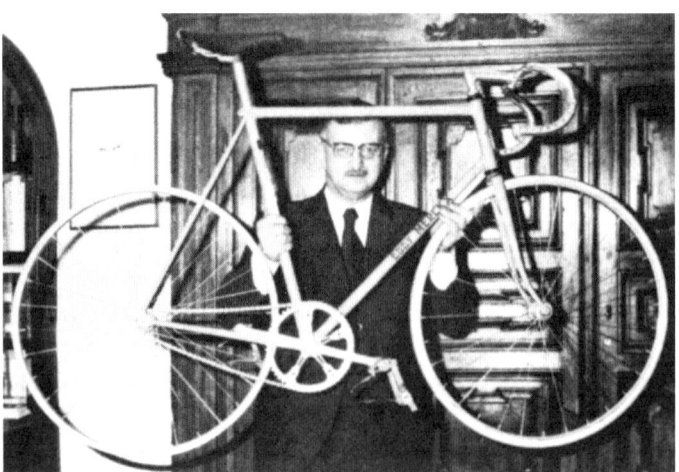

Above: Rebour with the bicycle with which Eddy Merckx broke the World Hour record in Mexico City, 1972. The bike, with steel frame, weighed in at 5.75 kg. *Le Cycle*, April 1973.

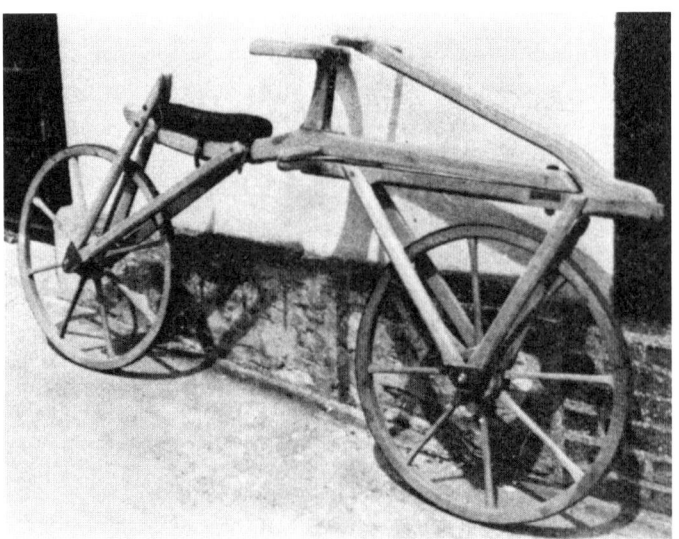

Left: Photograph of a replica 1817 Draisine which Rebour built in 1976. *L'Officiel du Cycle*, 1976.

Chapter 1. Historic Bicycle Drawings

Daniel Rebour's first book, *La Pratique du Vélo*, published in 1948, contains a first chapter devoted to the historic development of the bicycle. It was typical of the writings about cycle history of the time: based largely on xenophobic myths rather than facts, the text should not be taken seriously. However, there are some fine drawings that showcase Rebour's skill. Some of these are represented in this chapter, together with other drawings of historic bicycles.

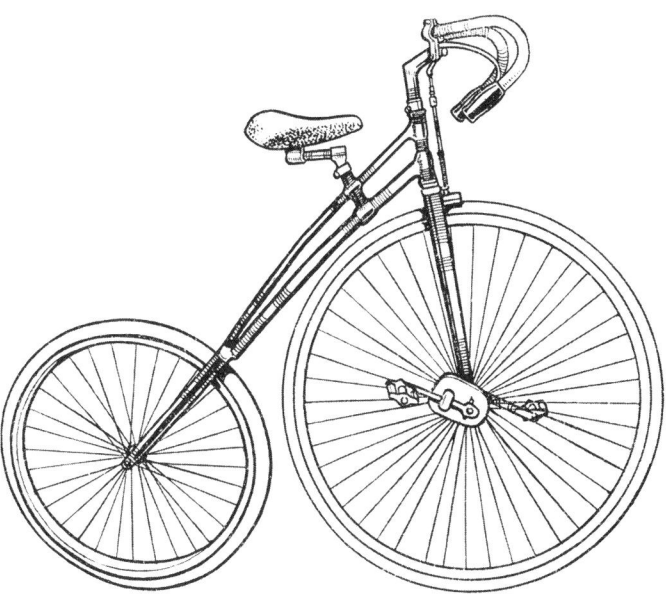

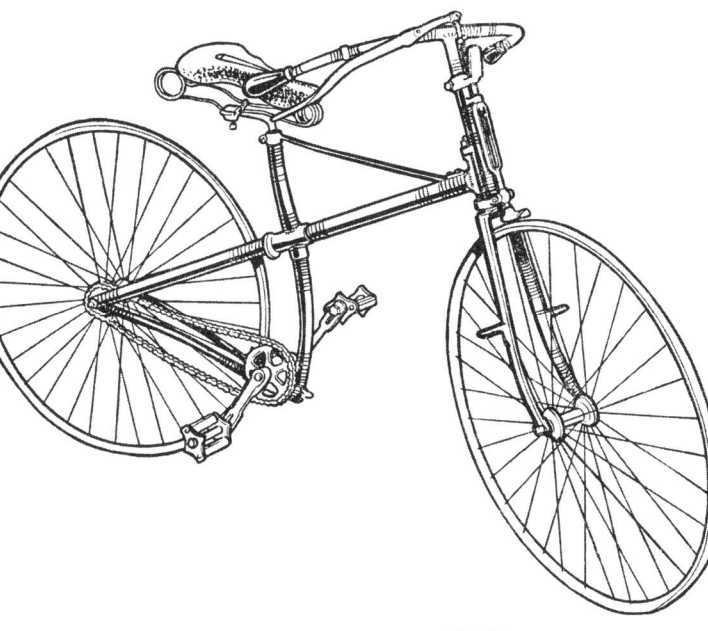

Left and above: two drawings from Rebour's first book, *Pratique du Vélo*.

Left: 1886 Pioneer cross-frame safety bicycle.

Above: 1890 Kangaroo-style bicycle with geared-up front wheel.

Below: 1869 Sargent treadle-drive bicycle, first published in *Le Cycle*, June 1961.

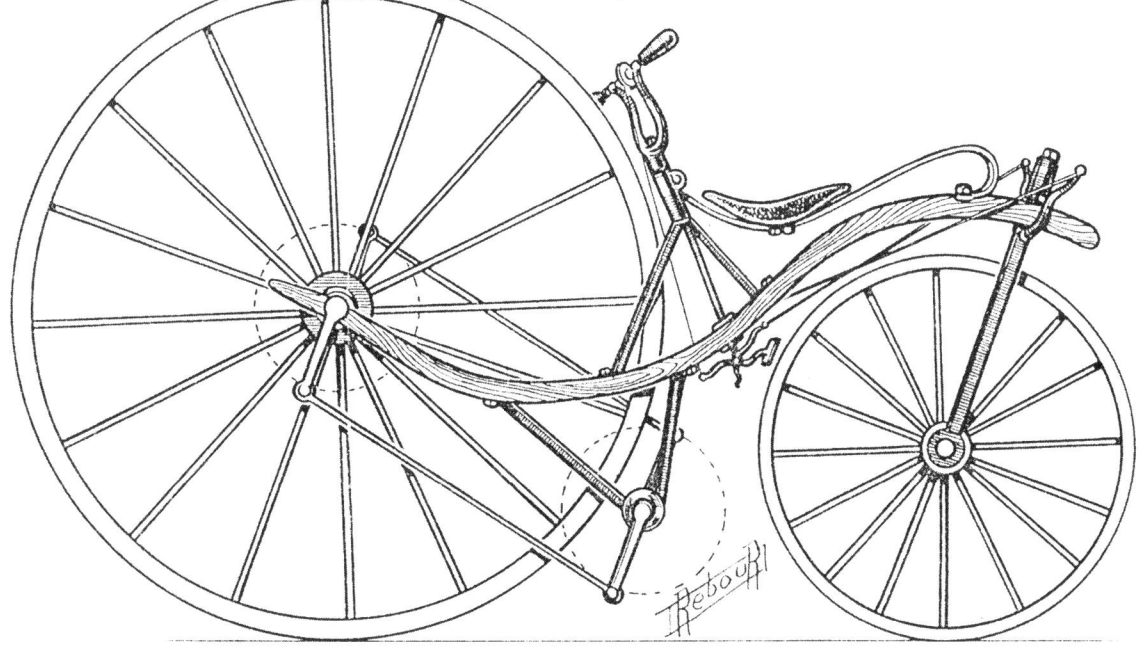

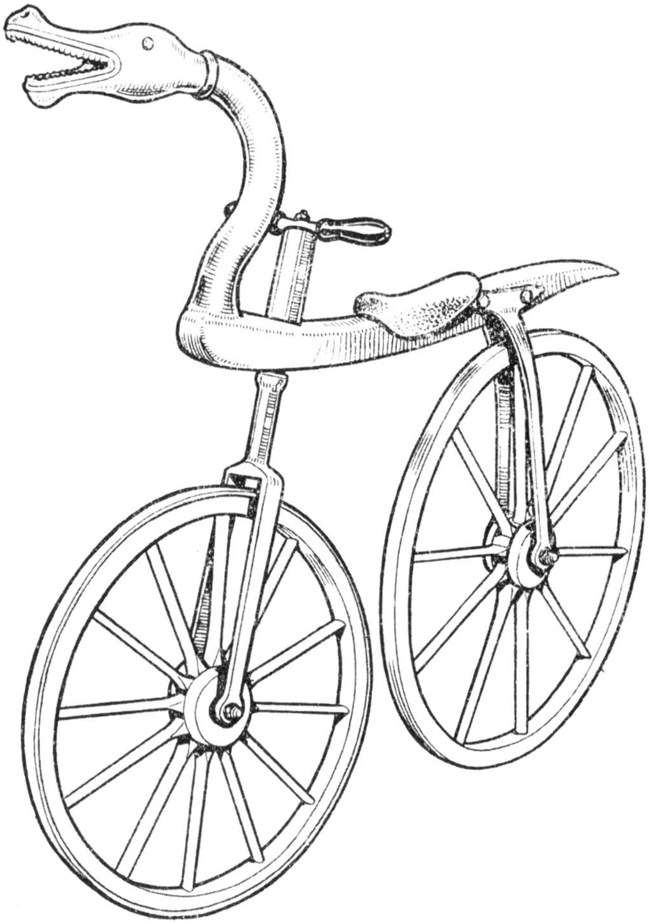

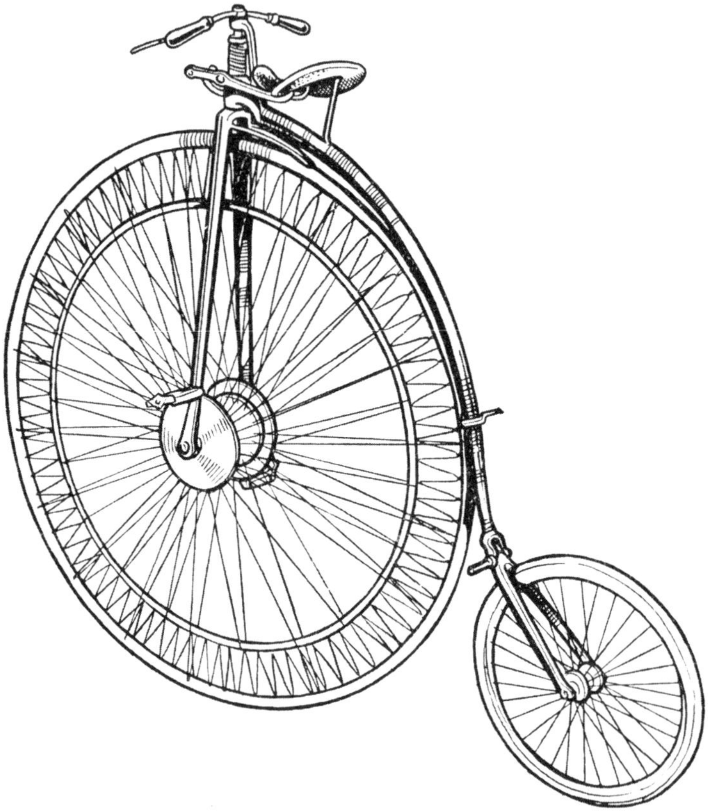

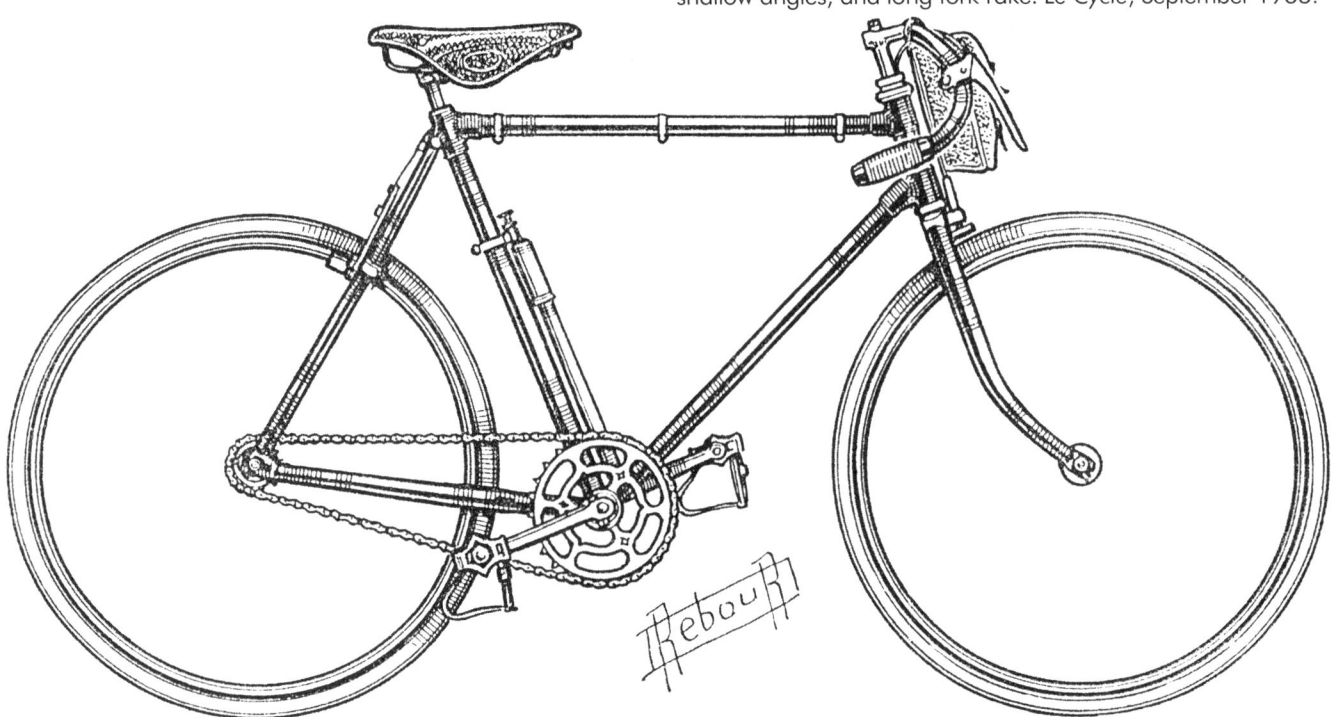

Above: 1877 high-wheel bicycle, with a special "suspension-wheel," also from *Pratique du Vélo*.

Left: Fanciful, and probably not realistic, drawing of a Draisine, the first type of bicycle, invented by Von Drais in 1817, published in *Pratique du Vélo*.

Below: 1909 Tour de France bicycle. Note the long chainstays, shallow angles, and long fork rake. *Le Cycle*, September 1963.

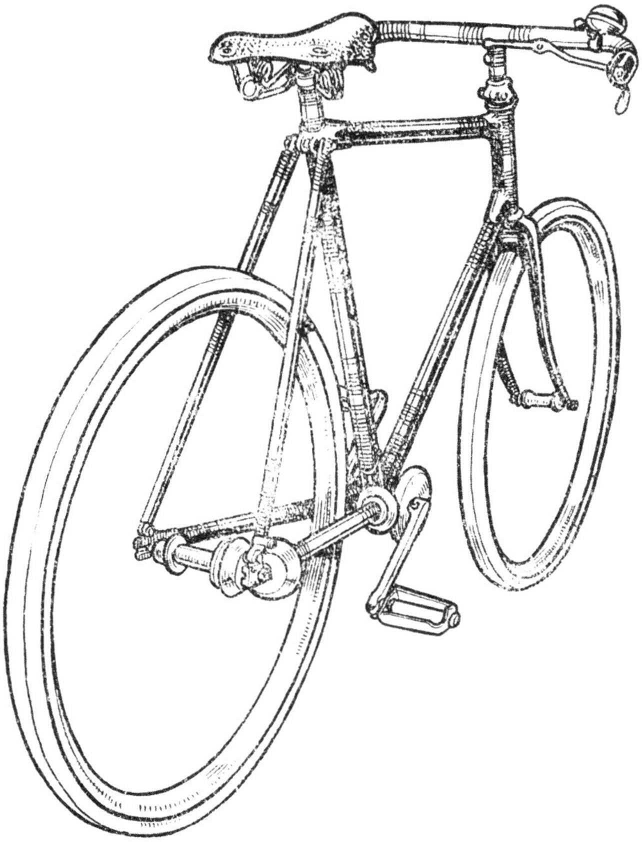

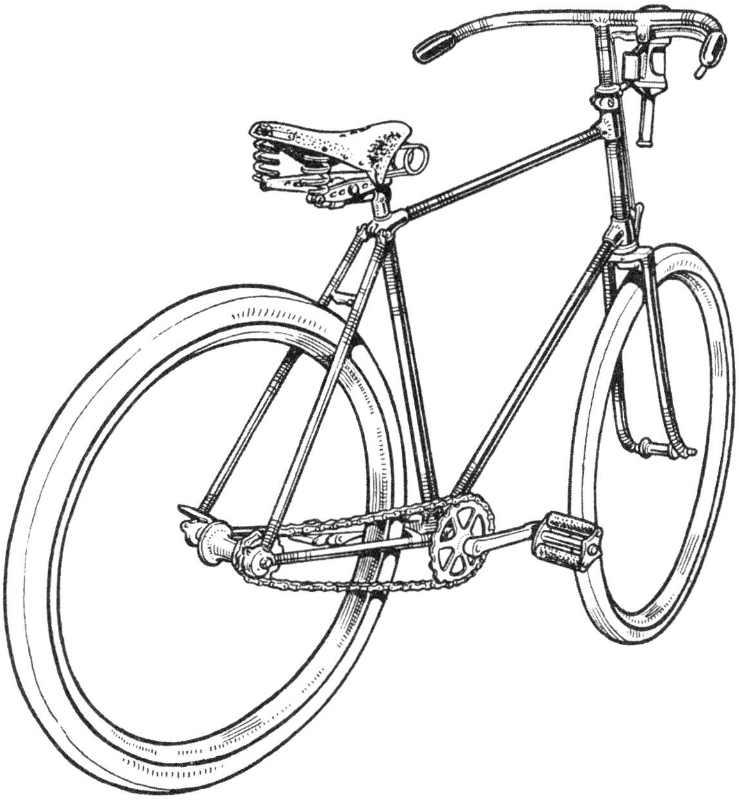

Chapter 1. Historic Bicycle Drawings

Above left: 1988 chainless, or "Acatène" bicycle, first published in *Pratique du Vélo*.
Above right: Typical early 1900s roadster bicycle, with block chain and candle lantern.
Below: Typical Tour de France bicycle as used around 1920. First shown in *Le Cycle* of February 1971, this illustration was also used in several subsequent issues, variously dating it to 1919, 1921, and 1922.

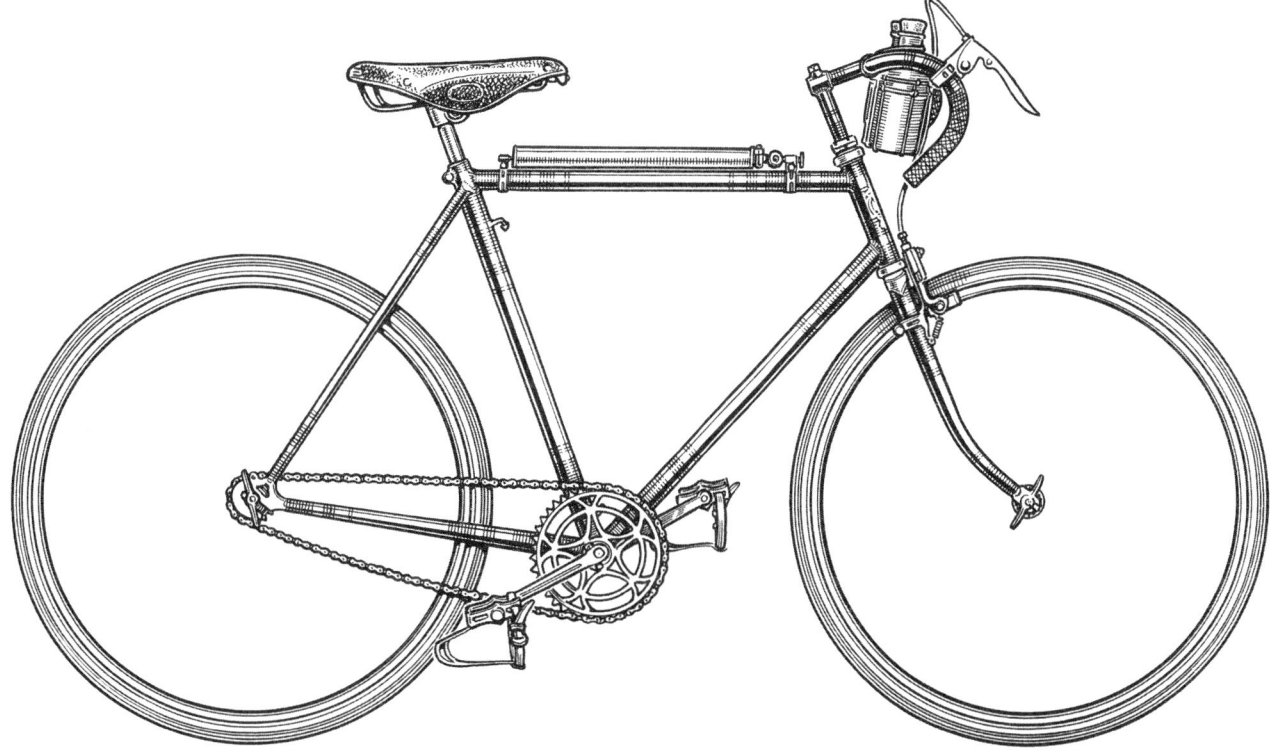

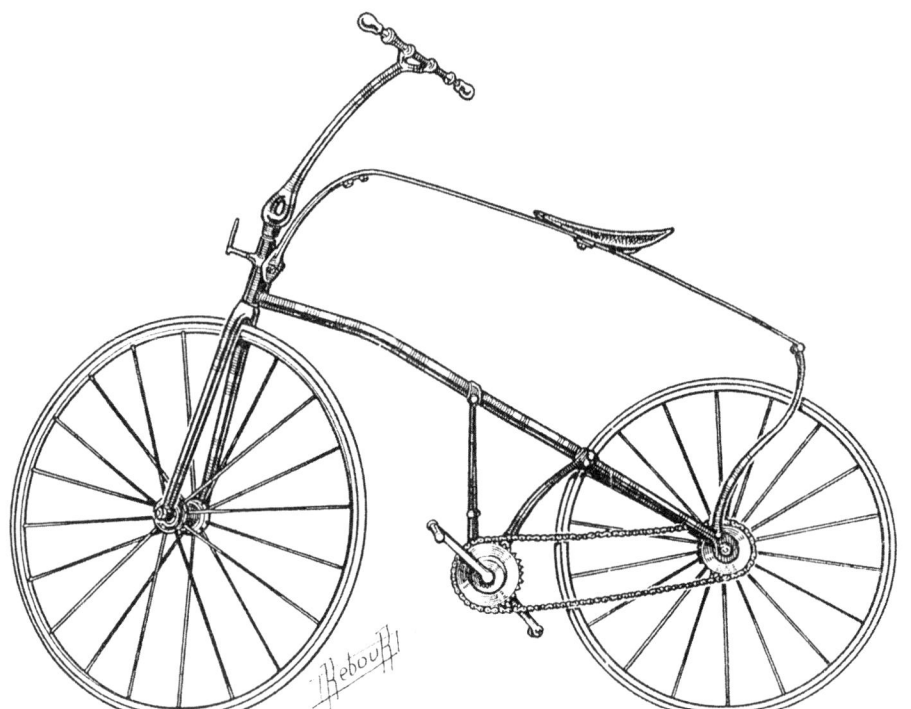

Left: Considered by most of today's cycle historians to be the true precursor of the modern safety bicycle, introduced 1869, this rear chain-drive bicycle resulted from a collaboration between bicycle maker Meyer and clockmaker Guilleaume. This drawing first appeared in the June 1961 issue of *Le Cycle*.

Below: Viking track racing bicycle, from England. A rather dumb design, with its lowered chainstays and extended downtube, seen at the 1951 London bicycle trade show, first published in the 12 December 1951 issue of *Le Cycle*.

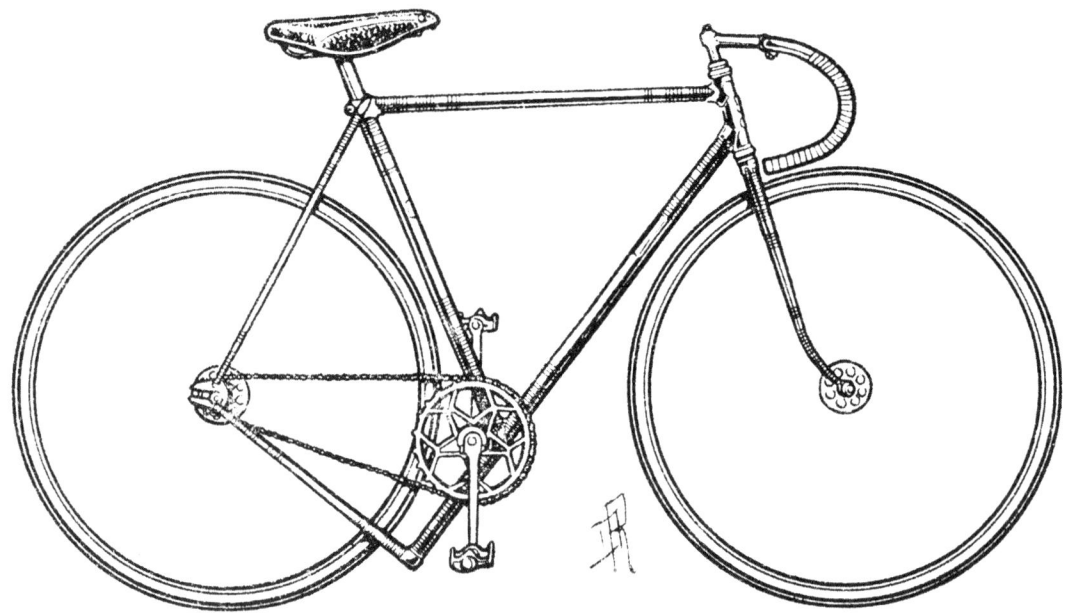

Chapter 2. Frame Details

This and the following chapters, are devoted to the individual component groups of the bicycle. Nevertheless, at the bottom of most pages is a drawing of a complete bicycle, arranged in roughly chronological order based on the date each one was first published.

In this chapter, we have assembled a number of drawings representing details of bicycles frames and their details. Also included here are some images of frame components, as well as some details that just didn't fit into any specific component group category.

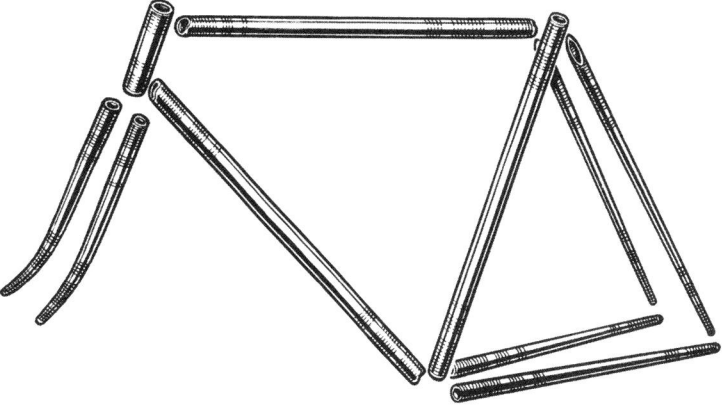

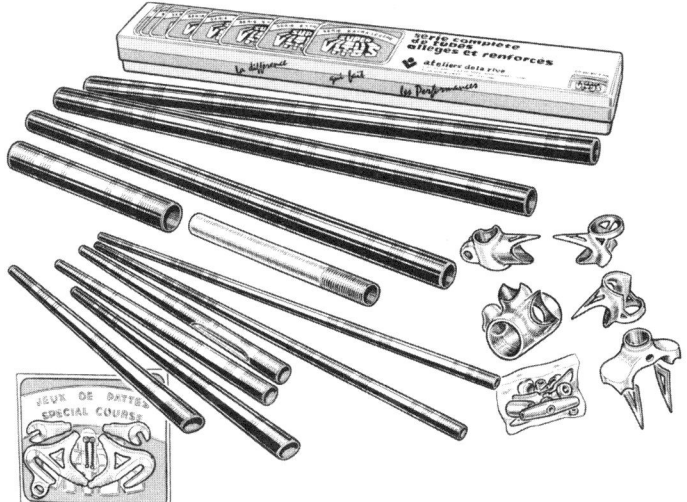

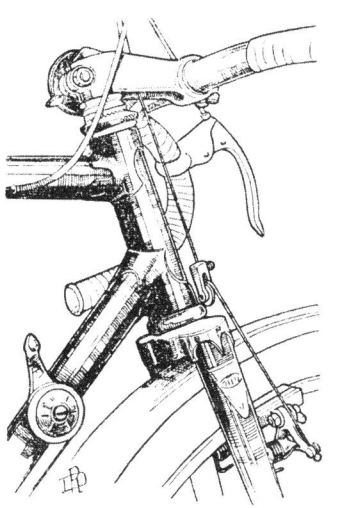

Upper right. Frame tube configuration using thin-wall double butted Super Vitus 971 tubing. *Le Cycle*, April 1972, scanned from original.

Left: Vitus frame tube and lug set. 1979 Milremo catalogue.

Right: Front-end detail of René Herse bike. *Le Cycle*, 20 April 1946.

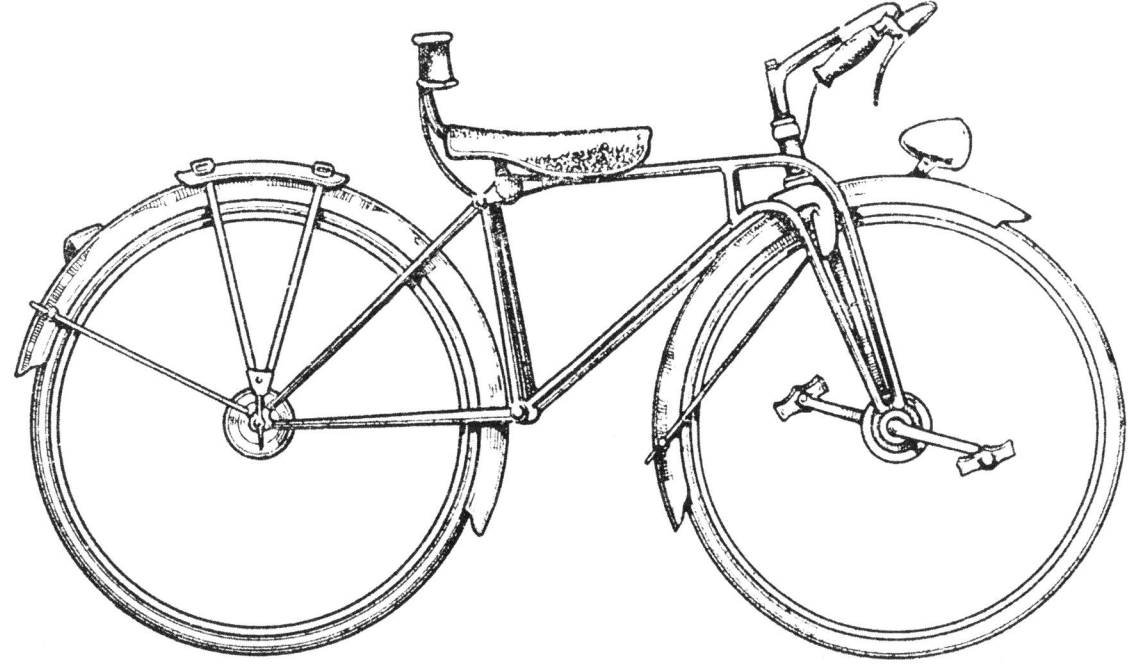

Right: This curious front-drive bicycle by Merlin-Garin & Debuit, said to weigh only 8.8 kg, has a main frame built up from twin small-diameter tubes instead of single larger-diameter tubes. It is not clear from the illustration how the front fork pivoted. *Le Cycle*, 28 December 1951.

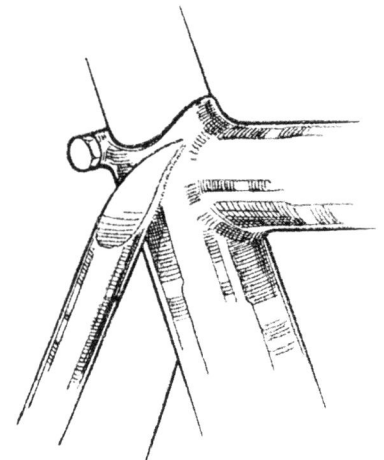

Left and right: Two details of a lugless stainless steel bicycle frame built by René Herse in 1946. Both images from *Le Cycle*, 26 January 1947.

Left: seat tube cluster. Right: fork crown and head tube to down tube joint.

Below: Frame with encased rear dropout, and external hub bearings, displayed at the 1946 Milan trade show. *Le Cycle*, 28 December 1946.

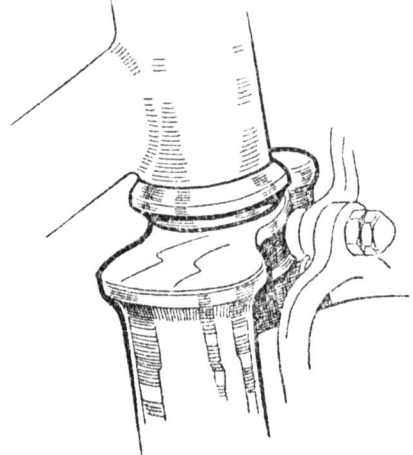

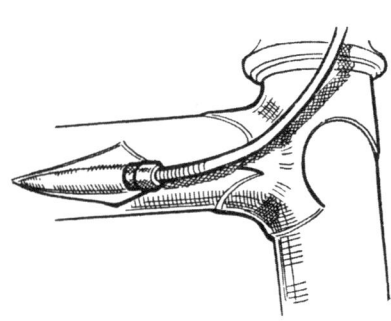

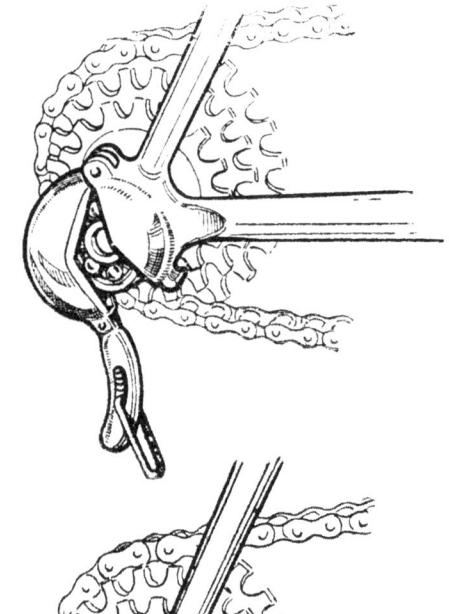

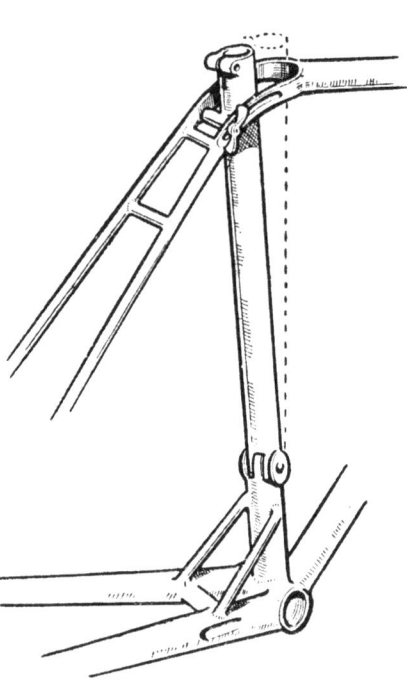

Above: Detail of internal cable routing, with an adjuster where the cable enters the frame at the top tube. See the drawing on the facing page 21 for a partial cut-away view of such an arrangement. *Pratique du Vélo*, 1948,

Below: Example of lugged frame joint. *Pratique du Vélo*.

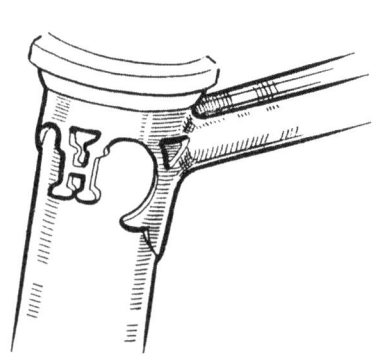

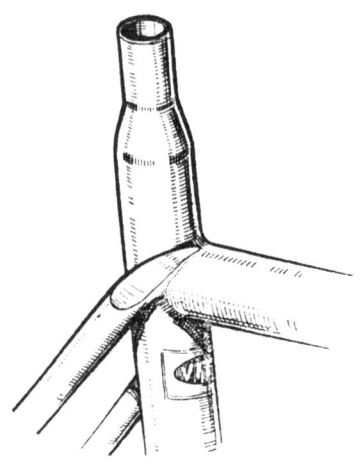

Above: Curious frame on which the seat tube angle could be adjusted, moving the seat backward or forward as appropriate for the terrain—forward for climbing, back for descending. *Le Cycle*, 18 December 1948.

Left: Vitus frame detail with integrated seat post, for a rider who is quite sure of his or her preferred seat height, saving some weight in the process. *Le Cycle*, 24 March 1948.

Chapter 2. Frame Details

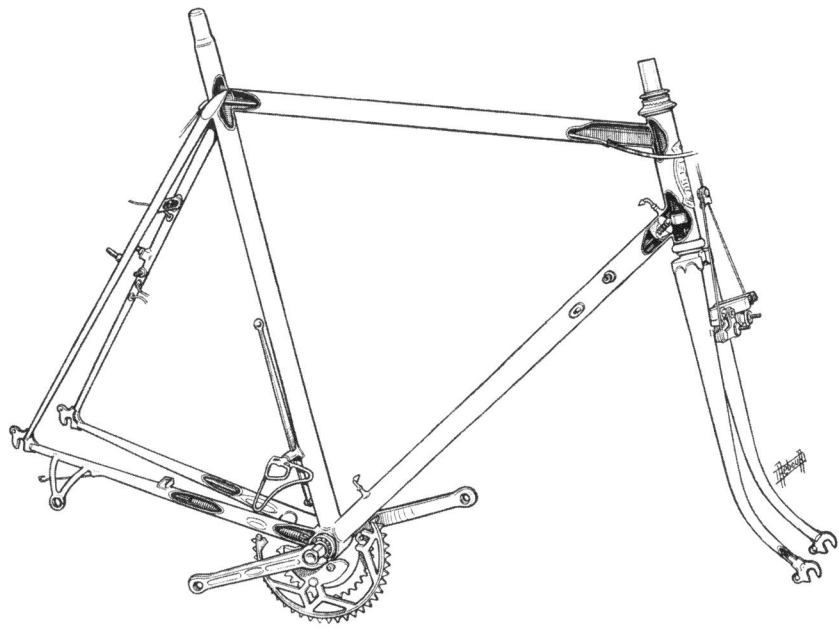

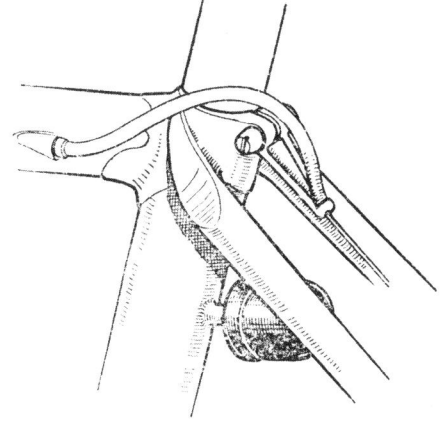

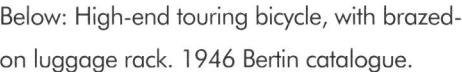

Above: High-end randonneur frame, with an integrated seatpost, showing details, including internal cable routing for rear brake and derailleur, and dynamo lighting. *Le Cycle*, 17 July 1948.

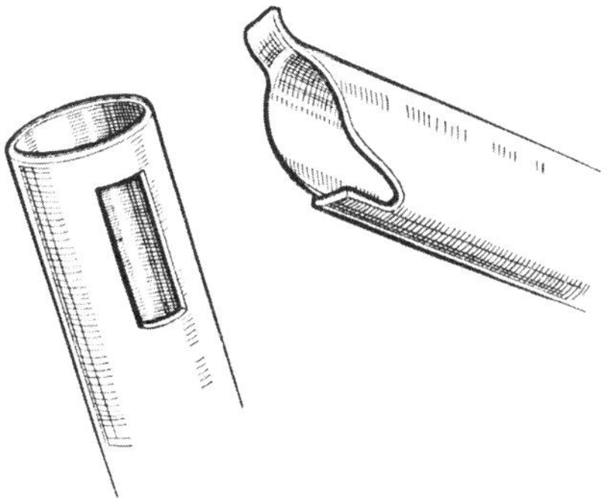

Below: High-end touring bicycle, with brazed-on luggage rack. 1946 Bertin catalogue.

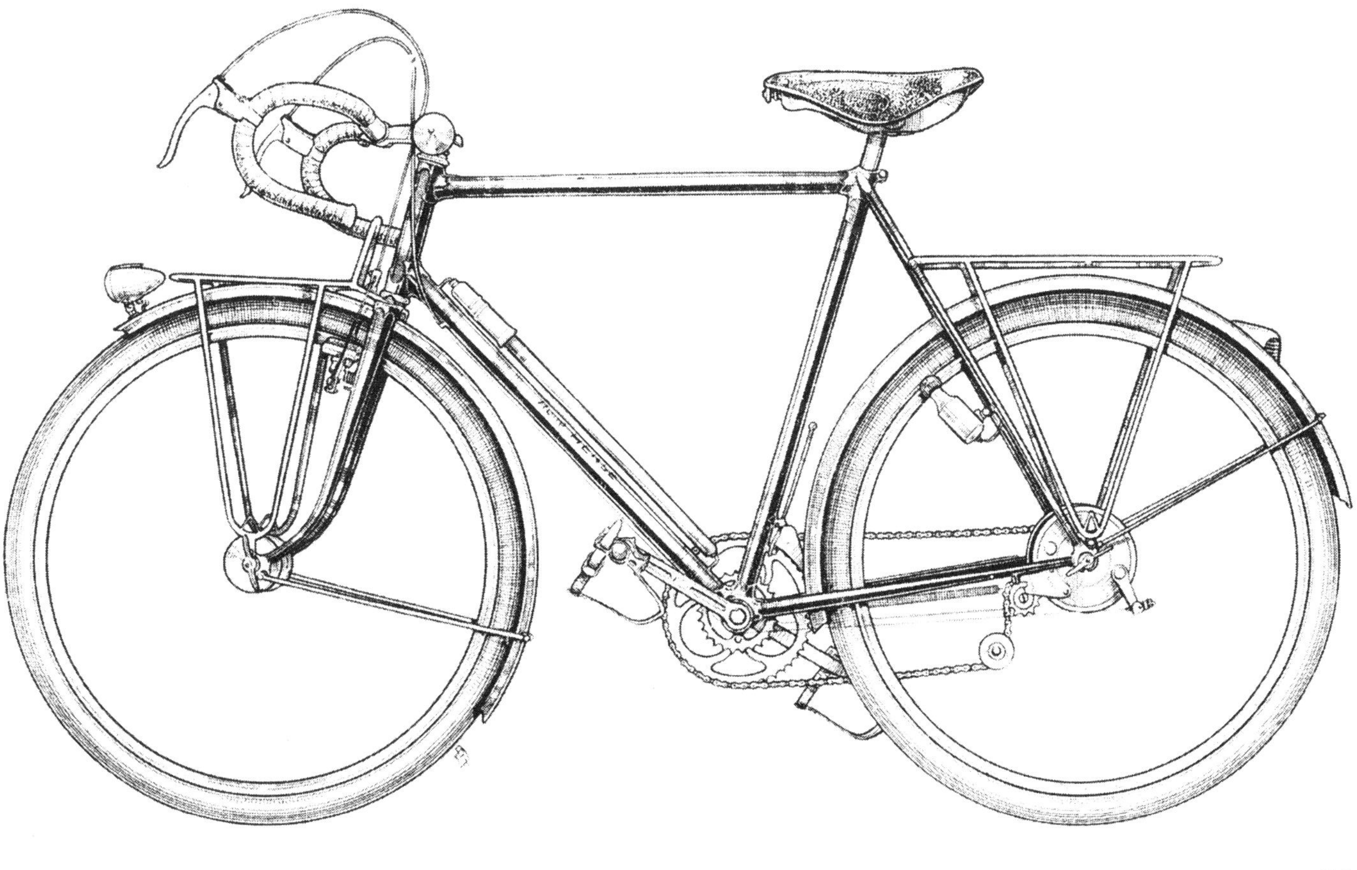

Above: Cable routing detail on René Herse frame with internal cables for brakes and rear derailleur. *Le Cycle*, January 1948.

Left: Frame tube forming details for a lugless frame. *Le Cycle*, 18 December 1948.

Below: Frame joint detail on a Genty-Jolly women's frame. *Le Cycle*, 26 January 1947.

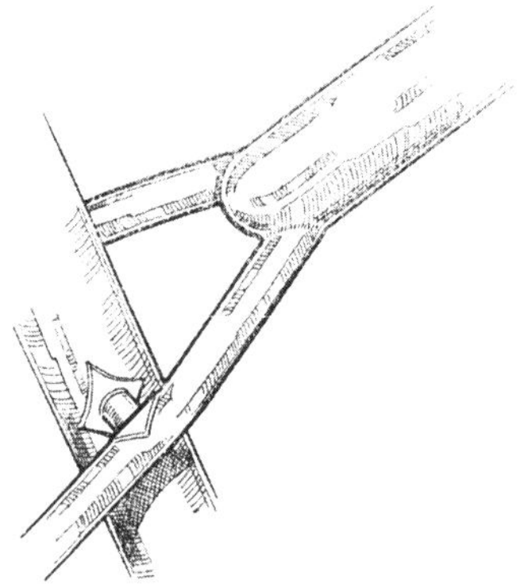

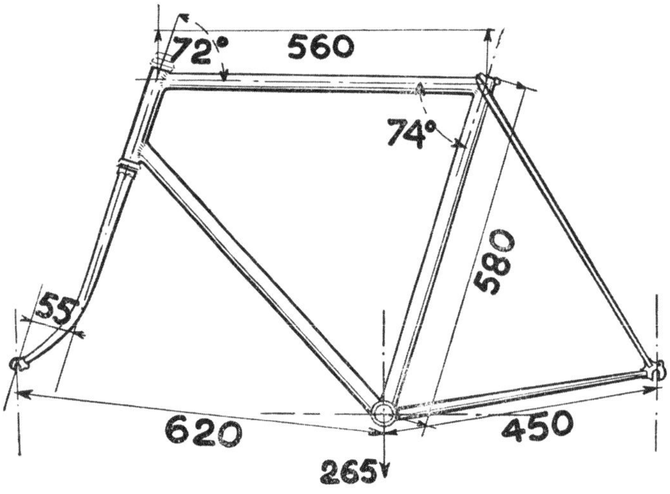

Left: Frame geometry drawing for a road bike. Note the shallower angle of the steerer tube, compared to the 74º seat tube, and the longer chainstays than on today's bikes. From Rebour's first book, *Pratique du Vélo*.

Right: Overall view of another Genty-Jolly modified mixte frame. *Le Cycle*, 26 January 1947.

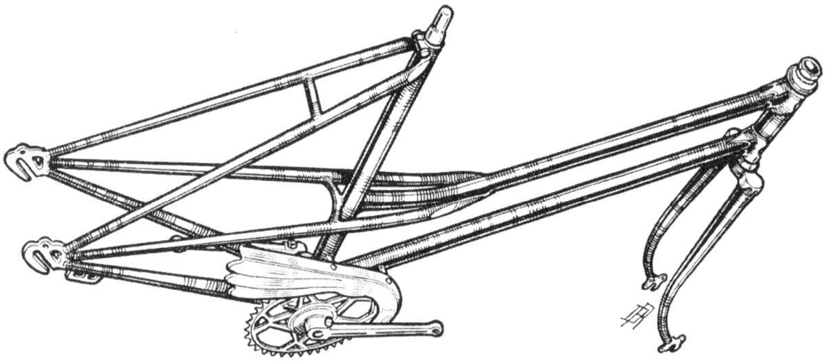

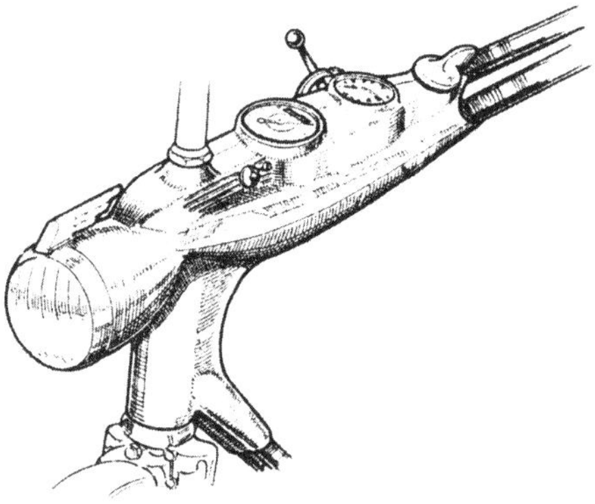

Below and detail to right: Stella Grossjean Aero bicycle, advertised as "in American style," first depicted in the 22 March 1947 issue of *Le Cycle*.

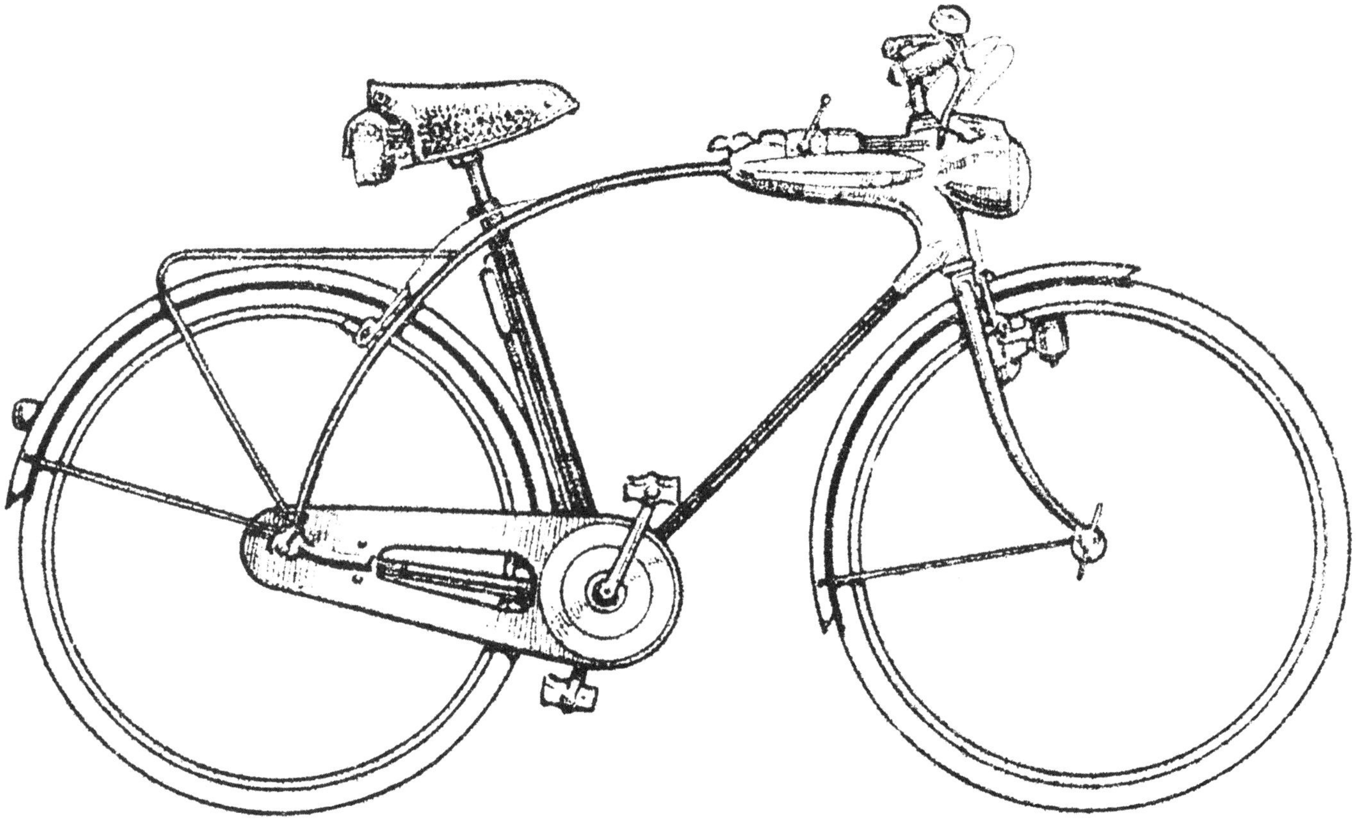

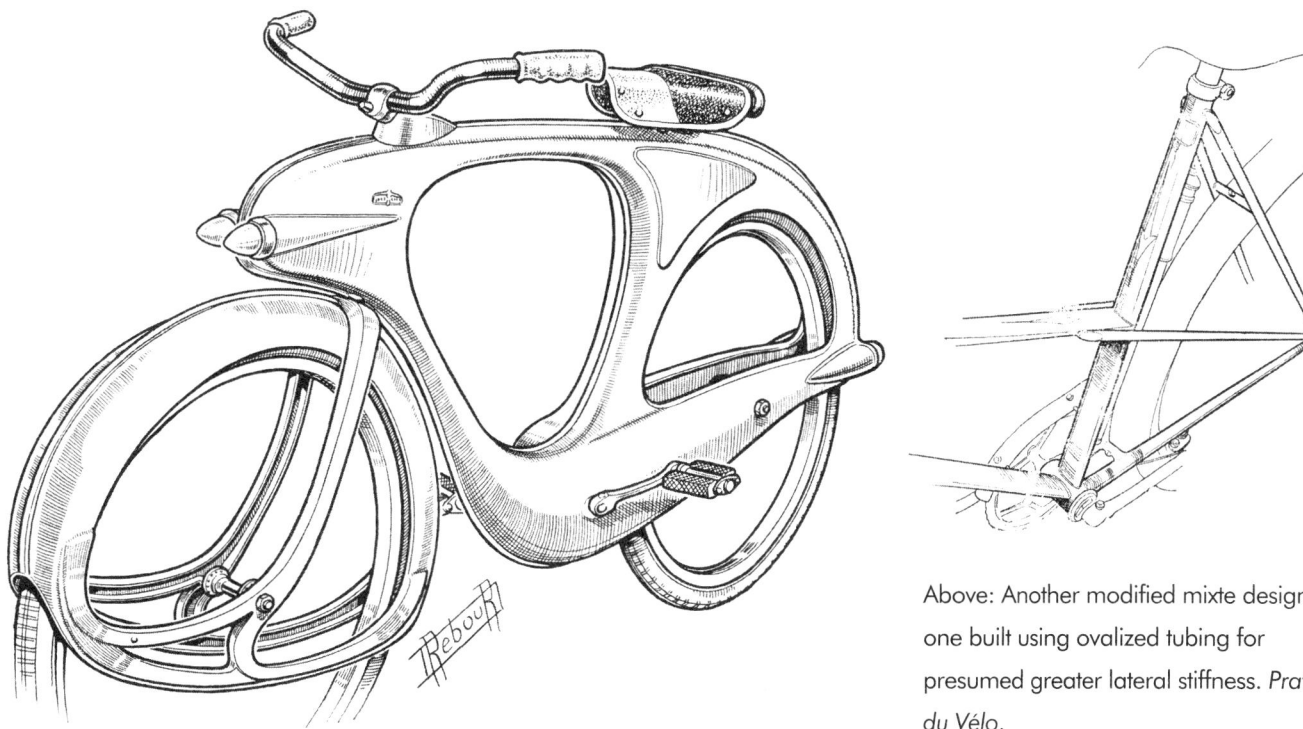

Above: Another modified mixte design, this one built using ovalized tubing for presumed greater lateral stiffness. *Pratique du Vélo.*

Below and above: Prototype Bowden plastic bicycle of 1947. *Le Cycle*, 12 January 1947. The lower illustration shows what is probably a design study rather than a prototype, since it doesn't even include cranks and pedals. The more detailed rendering above was published in *Le Cycle* of September 1960, when this bicycle went into production in the U.S. under the name Bowden Spacelander. It is now a sought-after collector's item.

Right: Liberia seat cluster detail, showing brake-cable anchor. *Le Cycle*, 20 October 1951.

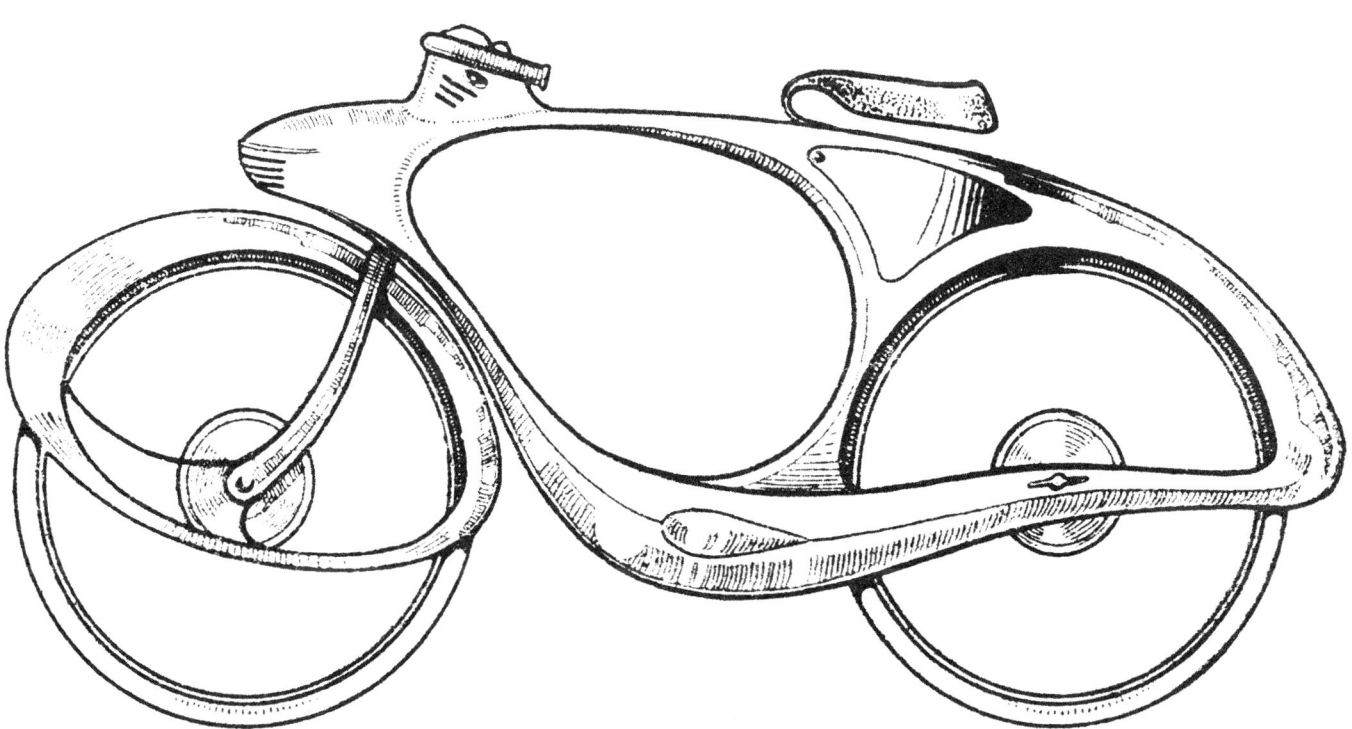

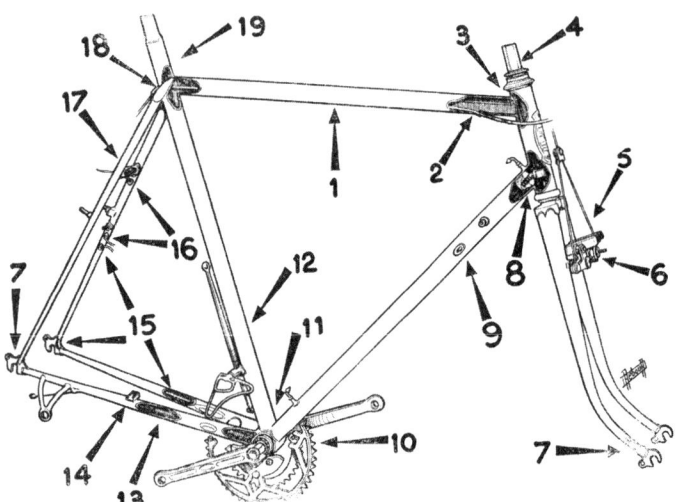

1) Tubes légers.
2) Câble de frein à l'intérieur du tube.
3) Soudobrasure.
4) Dépassant de la fourche pour potence à pince.
5) Freins cantilever.
6) Vis de fixation du porte-sac de guidon.
7) Pattes profondément encastrées.
8) Eclairage par fils intérieurs.
9) Câbles de dérailleur dans le tube.
10) Double plateau en métal léger.
11) Roulement de pédalier par roulements annulaires.
12) Dérailleur de pédalier.
13) Ressort de dérailleur dans la base.
14) Porte-patin évitant à la chaine de heurter la base.
15-16) Fil d'éclairage dans la base et le hauban.
17) Entretoise de fort diamètre.
18-19) Sortie du câble entre les haubans, avec tige de selle sans réglage.

Left: Bicycle component nomenclature, in French. This illustration from *Pratique du Vélo* is actually based on the same illustration of a partially cut-away view of a randonneur frame shown on page 21. *Pratique du Vélo*.

Below: Frame joint detail of a lugless fame built with flared and overlapped tube ends. *Pratique du Vélo*.

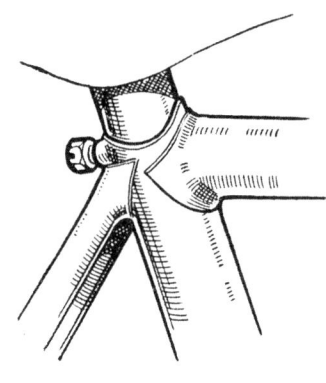

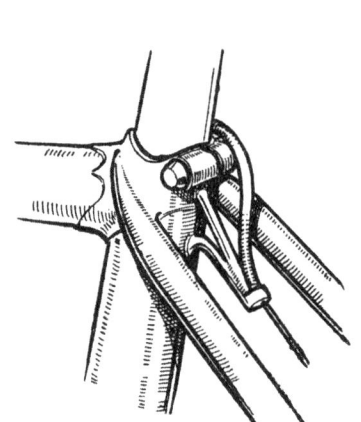

Above: A labor-intensive seat cluster detail with a labor-intensive integrated rear brake cable anchor. *Pratique du Vélo*.

Below: Comparison of two types of rear dropouts. The one on the left is designed for rear derailleur mounting. *Le Cycle*, 9 July 1949.

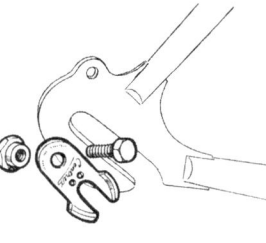

Right: Centrix wheel axle stop to place in dropout. *Le Cycle*, 23 April 1949.

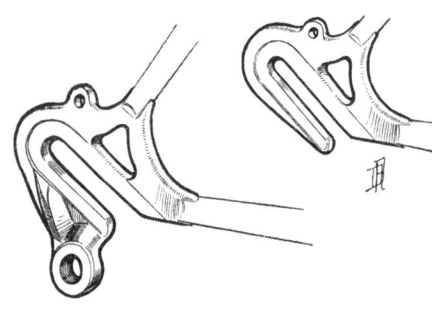

Above: Details of Vitus frame with lugged front end and lugless seat cluster with integrated seat post, as shown on page 20. *Le Cycle*, 24 September 1949.

Right: Detail of mixte frame, showing the installation of cantilever brakes on the bracing tubes and a Simplex direct-lever-operated front derailleur. *Pratique du Vélo*.

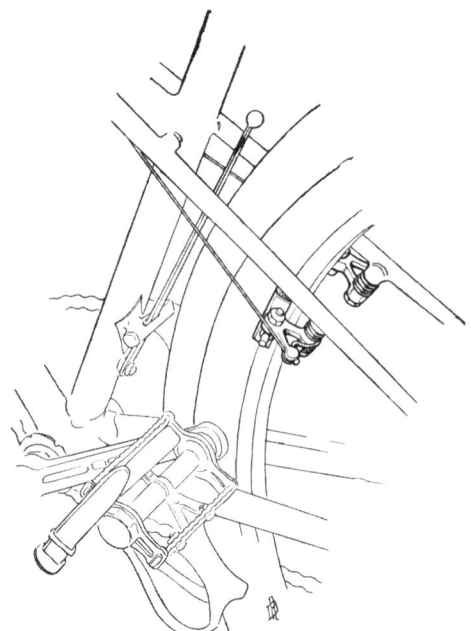

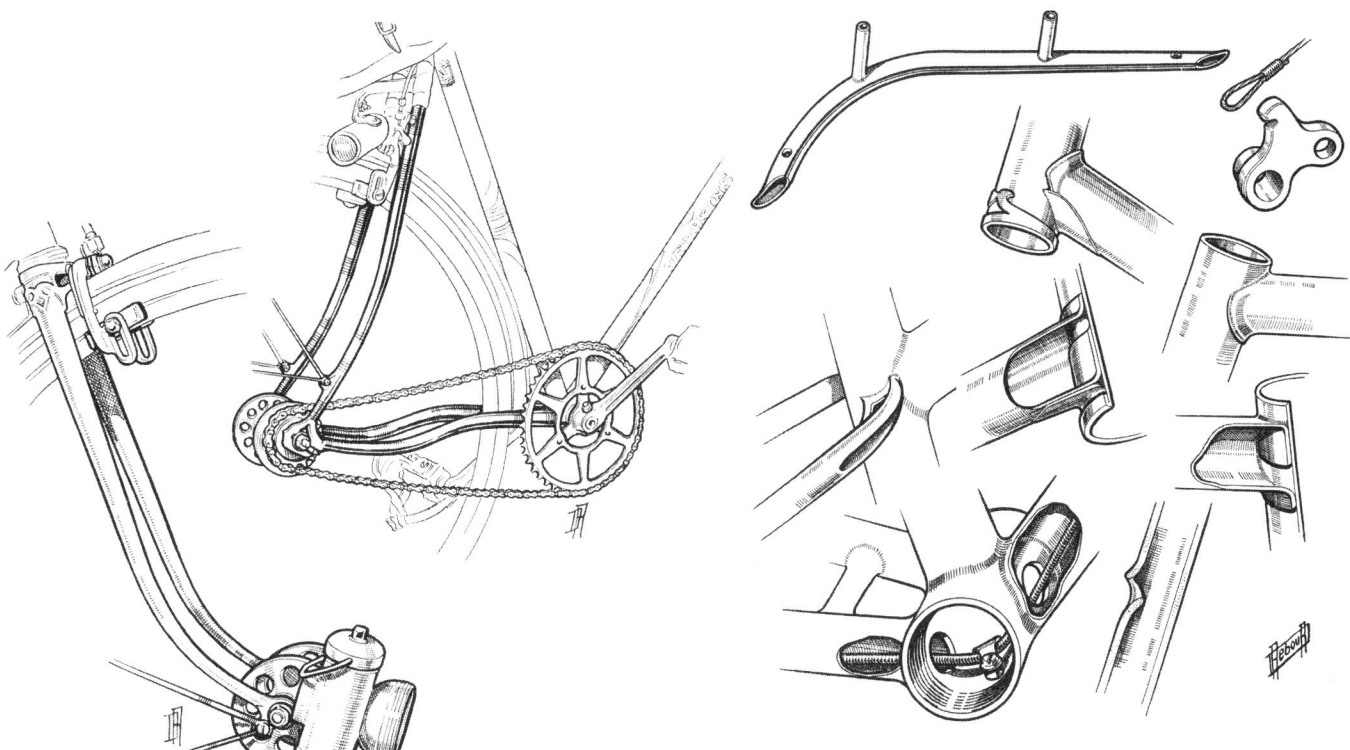

English touring bike details, showing "curly" rear stays typical of Hetchins frames (top), typical English battery lantern, and rear hub detail (right). *Le Cycle*, 13 August 1949.

Above: Brasobloc frame construction details, using the manufacturer's proprietary brazing method. Also shown are cut-away sections revealing hidden cable routing, etc. *Le Cycle*, 8 January 1949.

Right: Dil Claudio bicycle with curved monotube frame, advertised as "light and very flexible." A women's version with lowered top tube was also available. Both were actually *heavier* than standard bikes. *Le Cycle*, 23 June 1947.

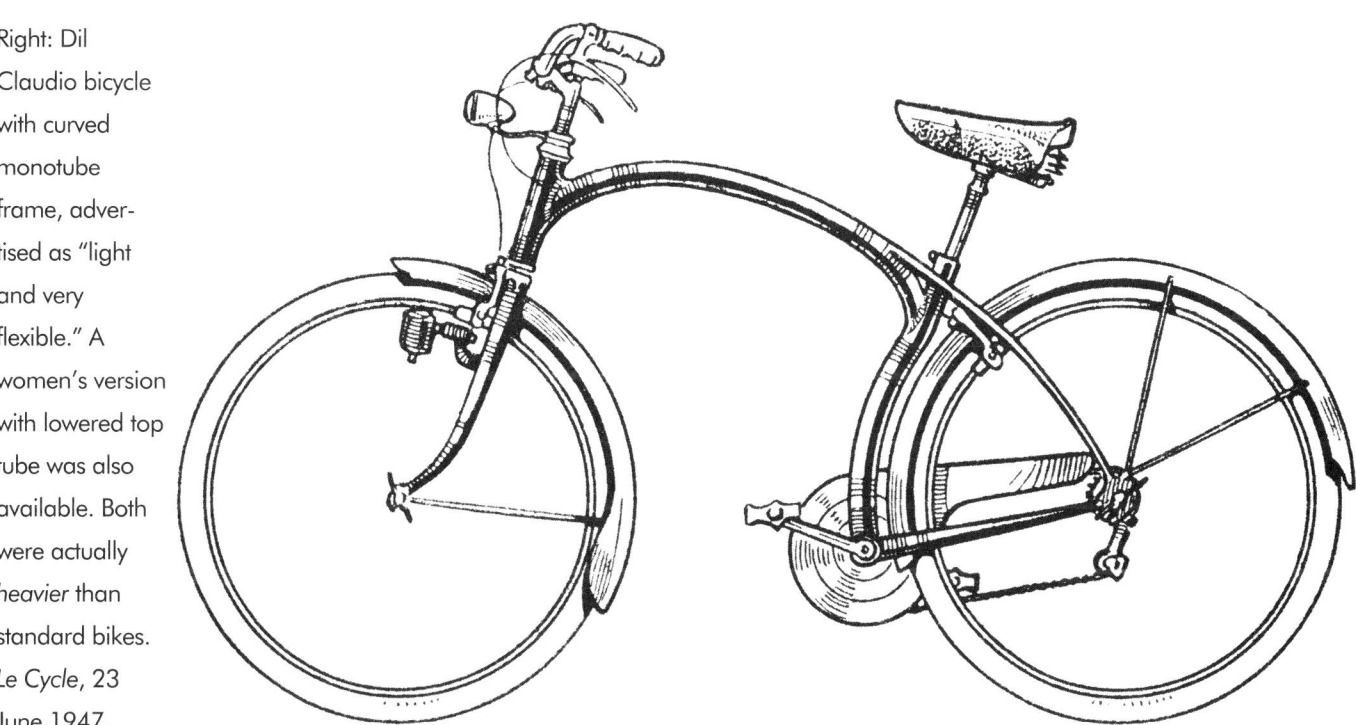

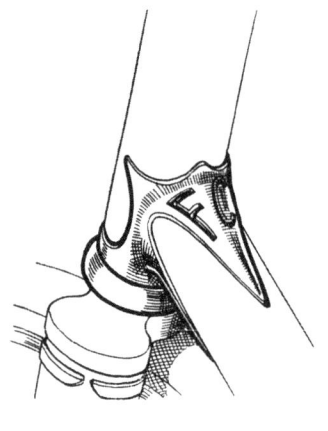

Left: Details of Fausto Coppi's Tour de France bike, made by Paulo Delay, with interesting dropout design. *Le Cycle*, 7 January 1950.

Right: Amalgam fillet-brazed frame details. *Le Cycle*, 6 February 1950.

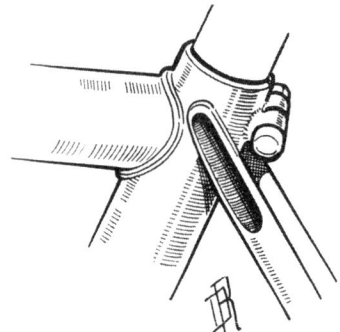

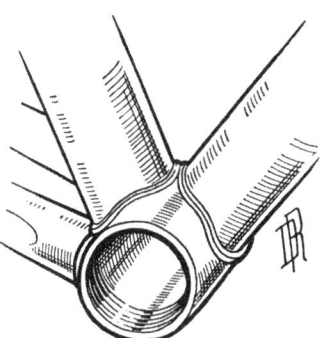

Below, top to bottom: French-made Italian-style head lug (top), and Italian-made Agrati fork crown and seat cluster lug. *Le Cycle*, 13 January 1951 and 10 March 1951.

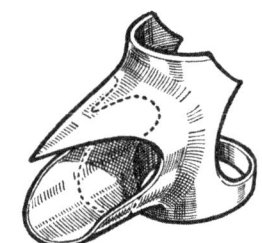

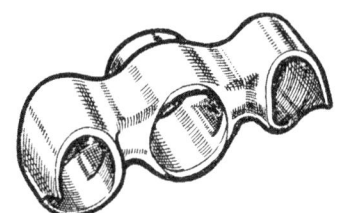

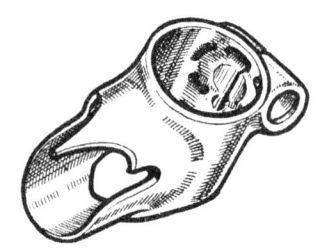

In August 1947, Rebour predicted that some of the features incorporated in this drawing would be amongst the design details that would be shown in next year's Concours des Inventeurs, at Lépine. *Le Cycle*, 30 August 1947.

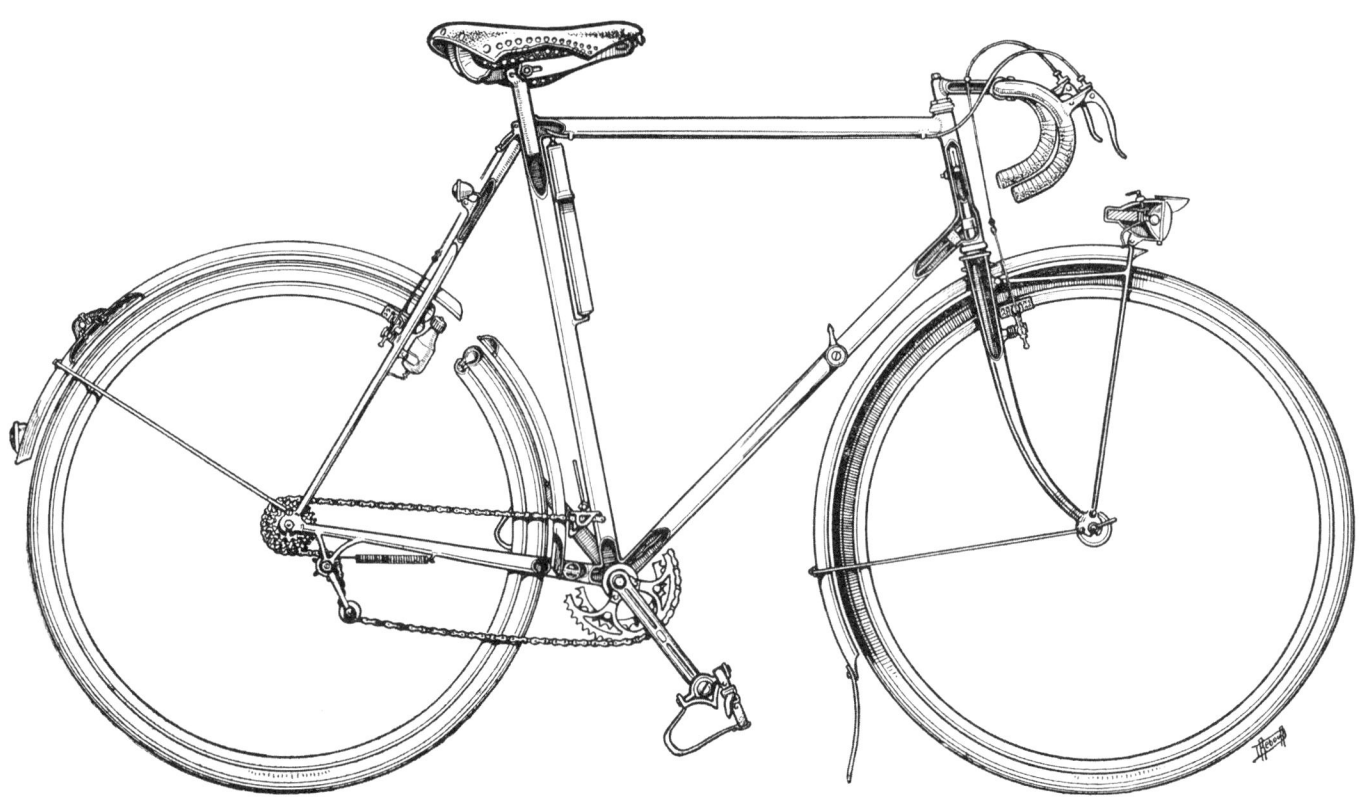

Chapter 2. Frame Details

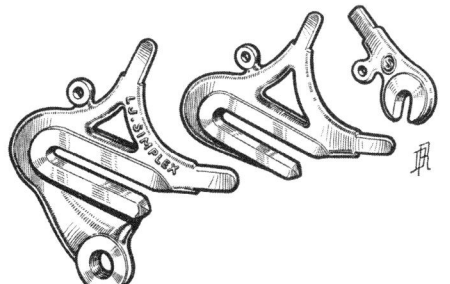

Left: Simplex investment-cast dropouts, for use with Simplex derailleur. *Le Cycle*, 24 February 1951.

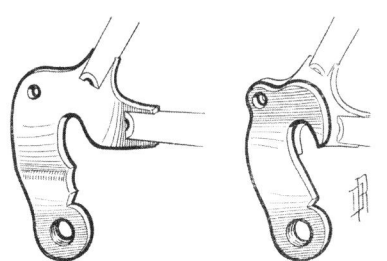

Above: Spirax stamped steel dropouts. *Le Cycle*, 26 May 1951.

Below: Paris–Brest–Paris bicycle, fully equipped and dimensioned, as first published in the 25 September 1948 issue of *Le Cycle* and in *Pratique du Vélo*, published the following year. **

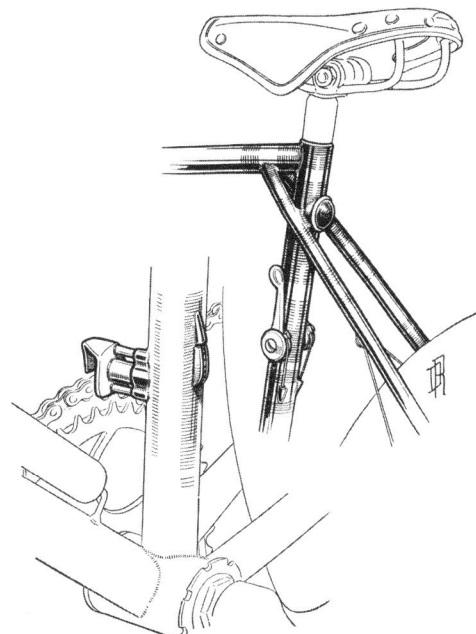

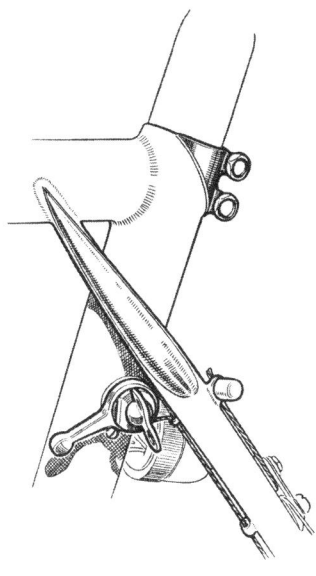

Above: Detail of Ferdinand lugless frame showing seat stays crossing the seat tube. *Le Cycle*, 22 September 1951.

Left: Rouby-Lombardy frame detail, showing front derailleur control through the seat tube. *Le Cycle*, 5 May 1951.

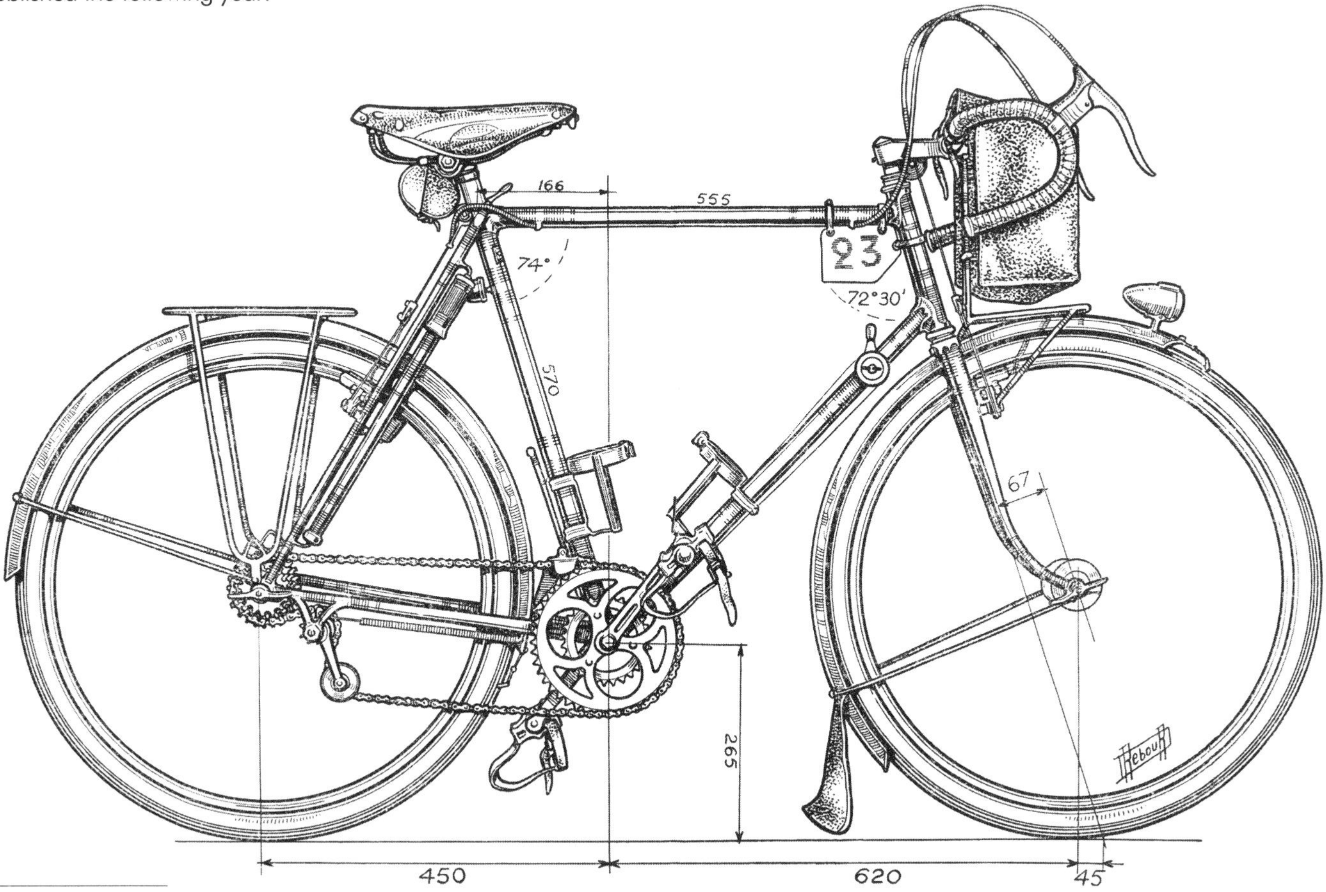

** See pages 269–271 for expanded caption text.

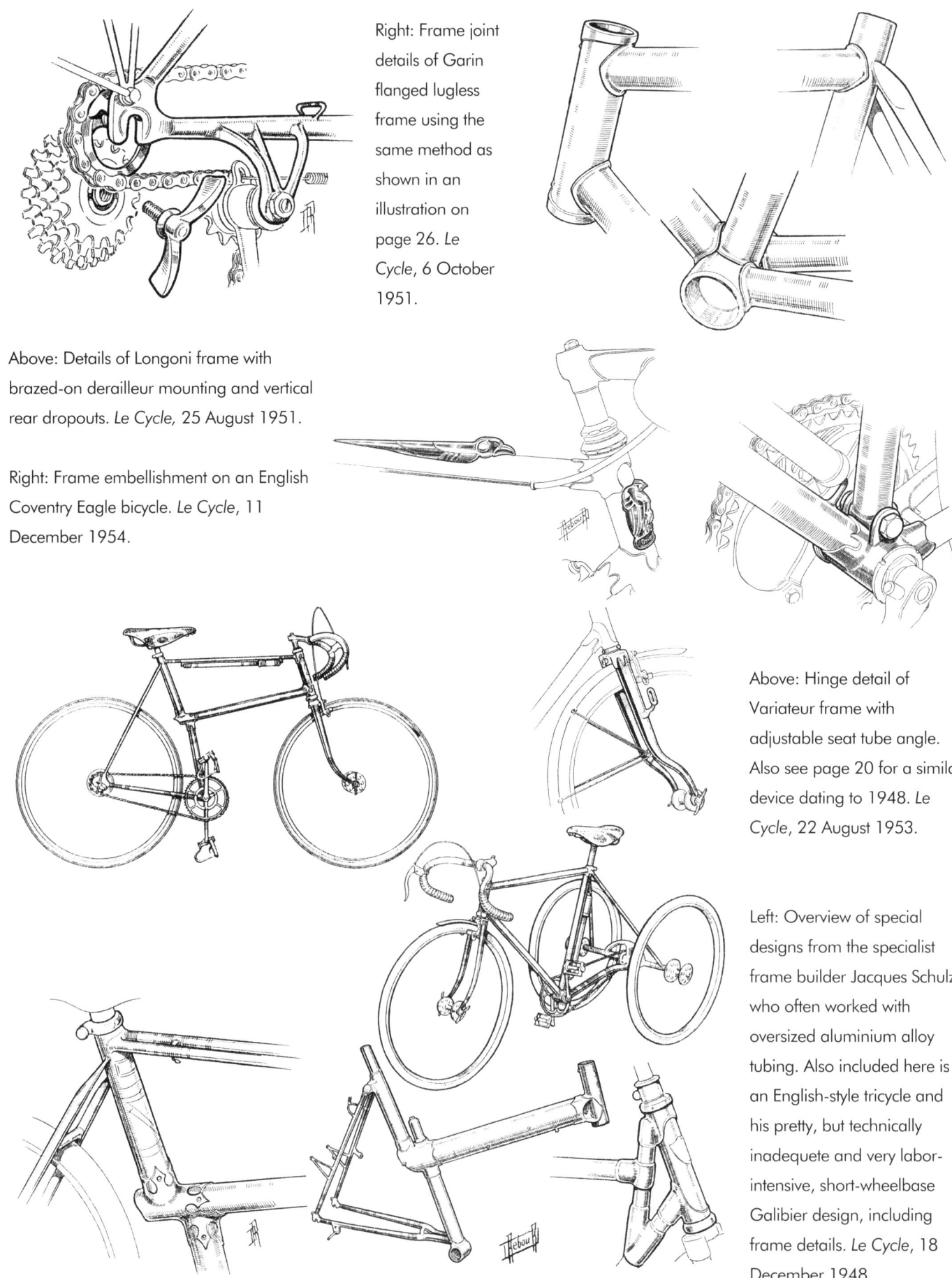

Right: Frame joint details of Garin flanged lugless frame using the same method as shown in an illustration on page 26. *Le Cycle*, 6 October 1951.

Above: Details of Longoni frame with brazed-on derailleur mounting and vertical rear dropouts. *Le Cycle,* 25 August 1951.

Right: Frame embellishment on an English Coventry Eagle bicycle. *Le Cycle*, 11 December 1954.

Above: Hinge detail of Variateur frame with adjustable seat tube angle. Also see page 20 for a similar device dating to 1948. *Le Cycle*, 22 August 1953.

Left: Overview of special designs from the specialist frame builder Jacques Schulz, who often worked with oversized aluminium alloy tubing. Also included here is an English-style tricycle and his pretty, but technically inadequete and very labor-intensive, short-wheelbase Galibier design, including frame details. *Le Cycle*, 18 December 1948.

CHAPTER 2. FRAME DETAILS

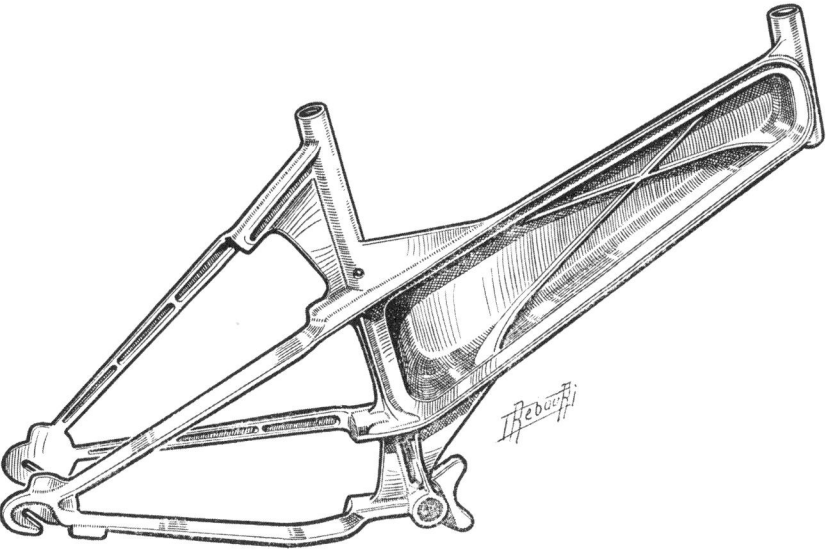

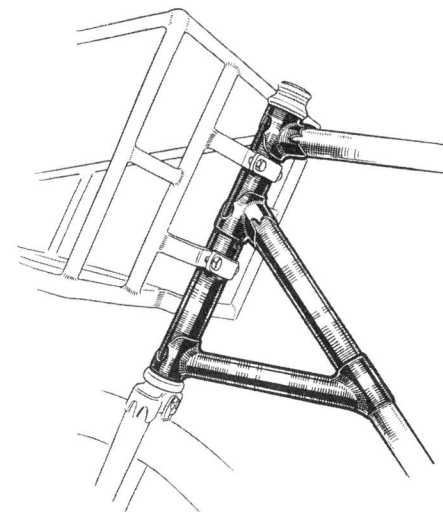

Below: Reinforced frame for carrier bicycle. *Le Cycle*, 9 October 1953.

Above: M. Ponceblanc stamped cast aluminium alloy frame. It was used on a moped, but its bicycle-design origins are clearly visible. *Le Cycle*, 18 October 1952.

Right: Campagnolo road dropouts. *Le Cycle*, 21 February 1953.

Below: Colomb high-end city bicycle, with 4-speed rear derailleur. Colomb ad in *Le Cycle*, 9 October 1948.

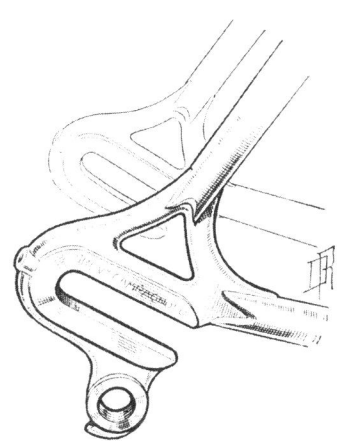

Right: Campagnolo front and rear track dropouts. *Le Cycle*, 18 April 1959.

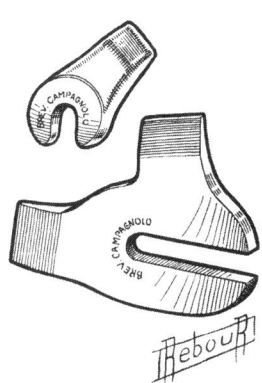

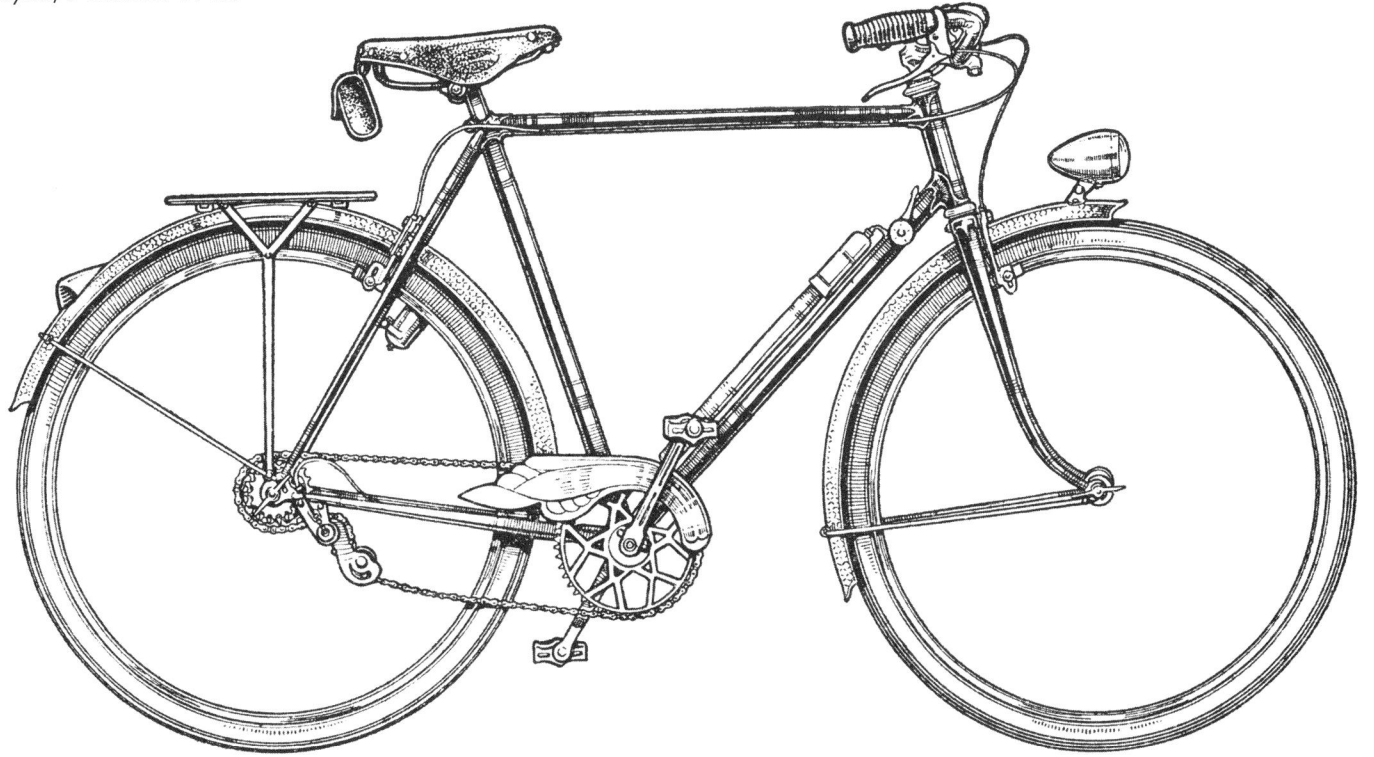

Right and below: Hercules glass-fiber-reinforced plastic frame tubing, as a precursor of carbon frame tubing. *Le Cycle*, 27 November 1954.

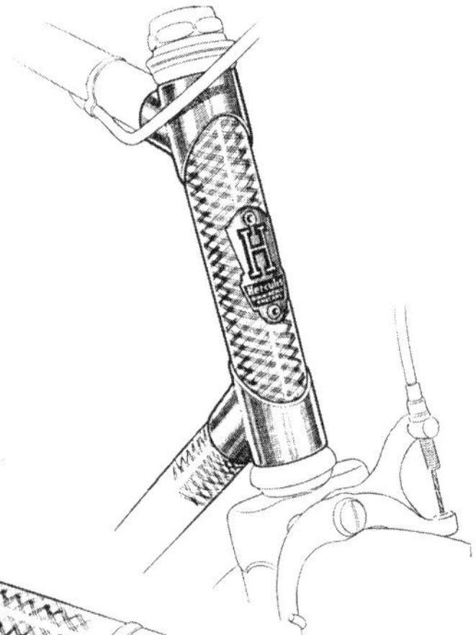

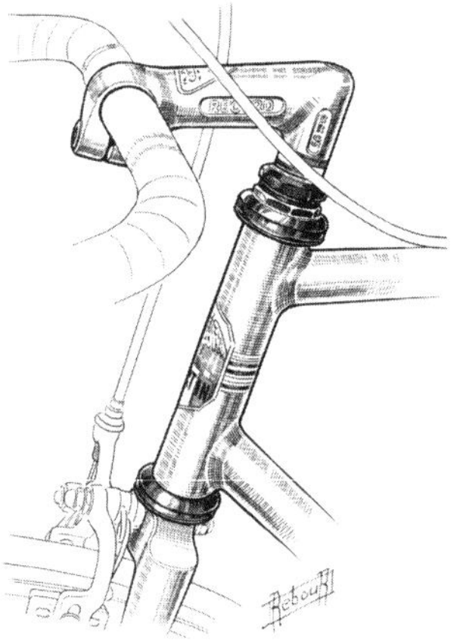

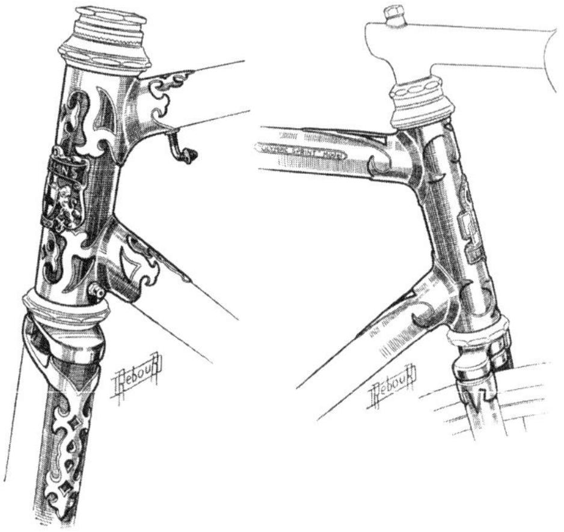

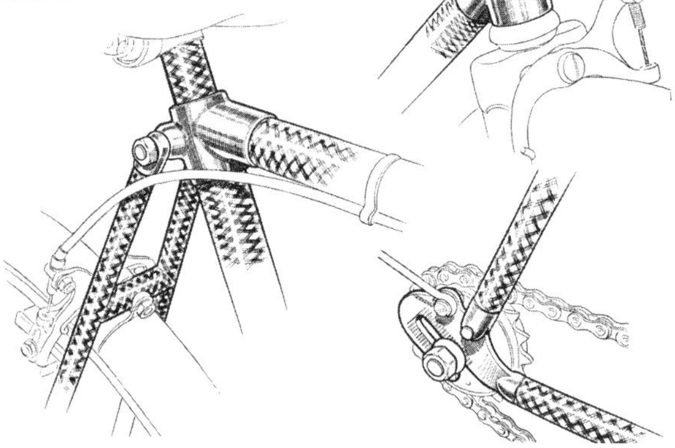

Above center: Front end of Bertin titanium bike, based on Speedwell frame. *Le Cycle*, November 1973.

Above right: Hetchins frame details. *Le Cycle*, 11 December 1954.

Right: Cast aluminium frame, from Germany. *Le Cycle*, 7 September 1957.

Below: Typical post-war utility bike. Note the "*porteur*"-style front rack, dynamo (but no lights installed), oilcloth chainguard, coaster brake, and no front brake. *Pratique du Vélo*.

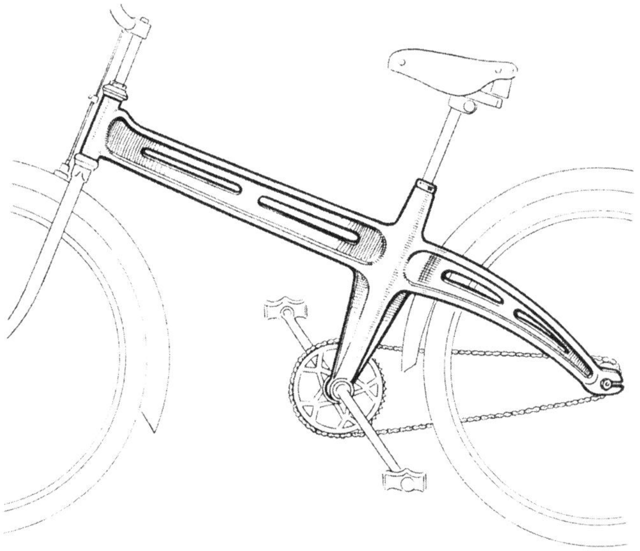

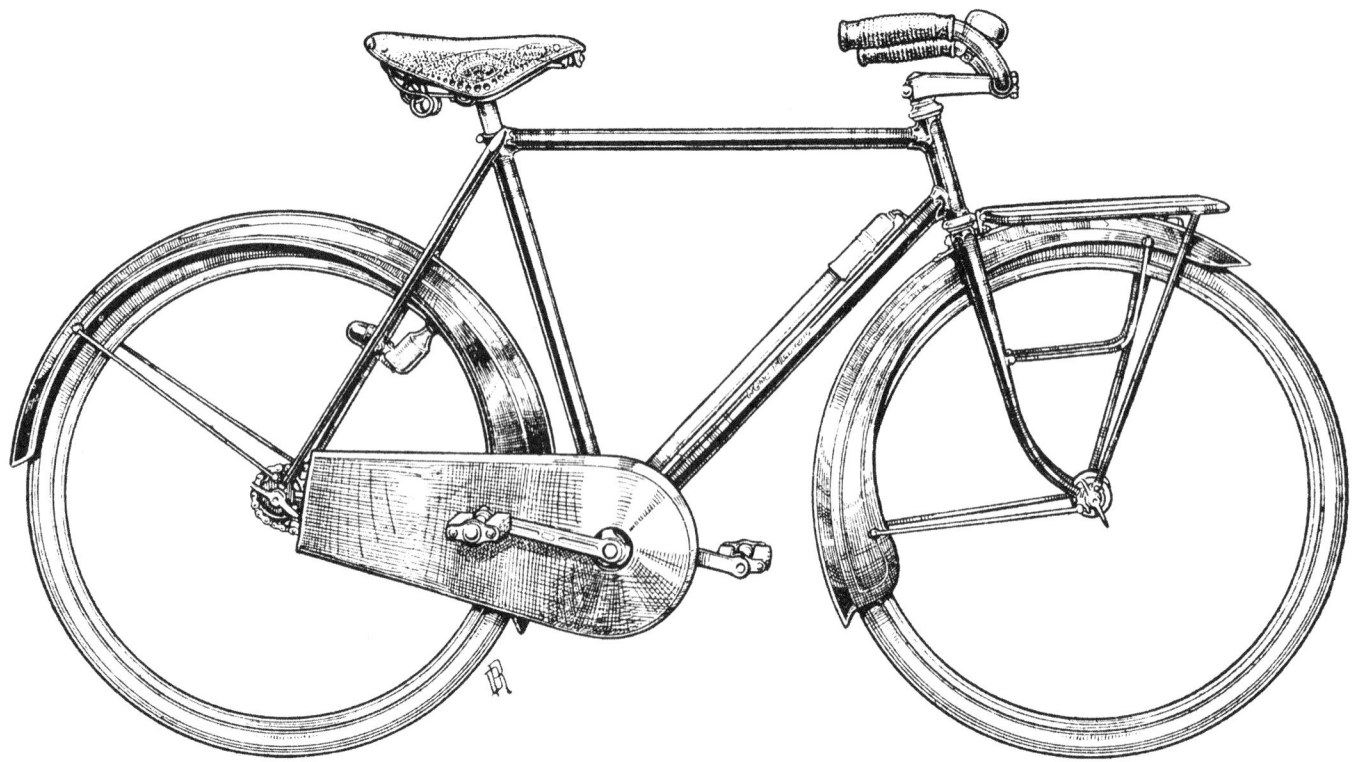

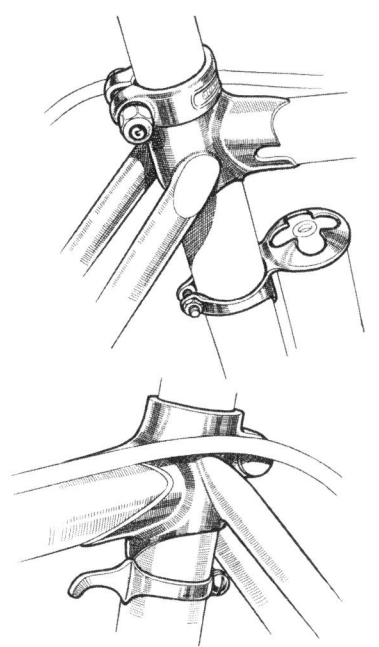
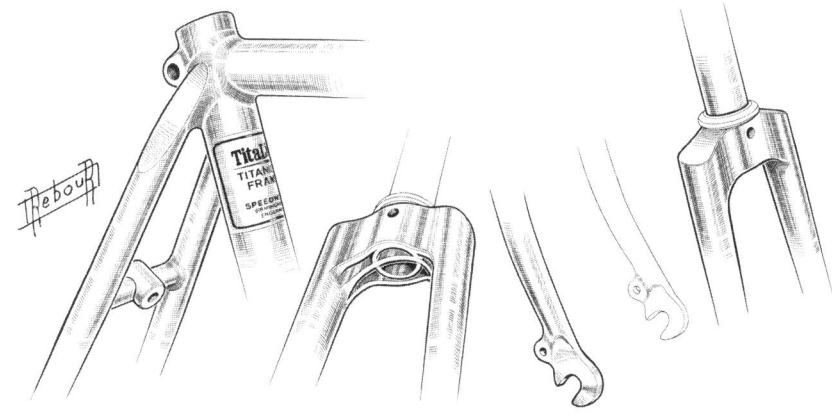
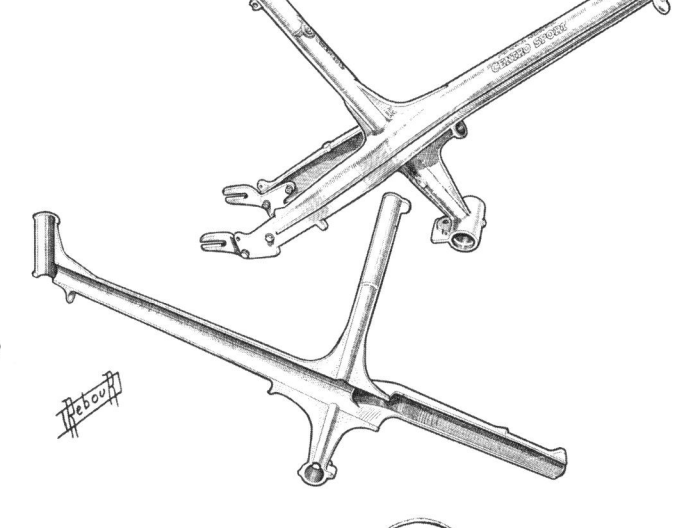

Above: Learco-Guerra Bianchi frame details. *Le Cycle*, 28 July 1956.

Top right: Speedwell titanium welded frame details. *Le Cycle*, July 1973.

Right: Centro Sports cast aluminium alloy monocoque cross-frame, introduced at the 1954 Brussels trade show. *Le Cycle*, 29 January 1955.

Below: 1948 Narcise road racing machine, shown in *Pratique du Vélo*.

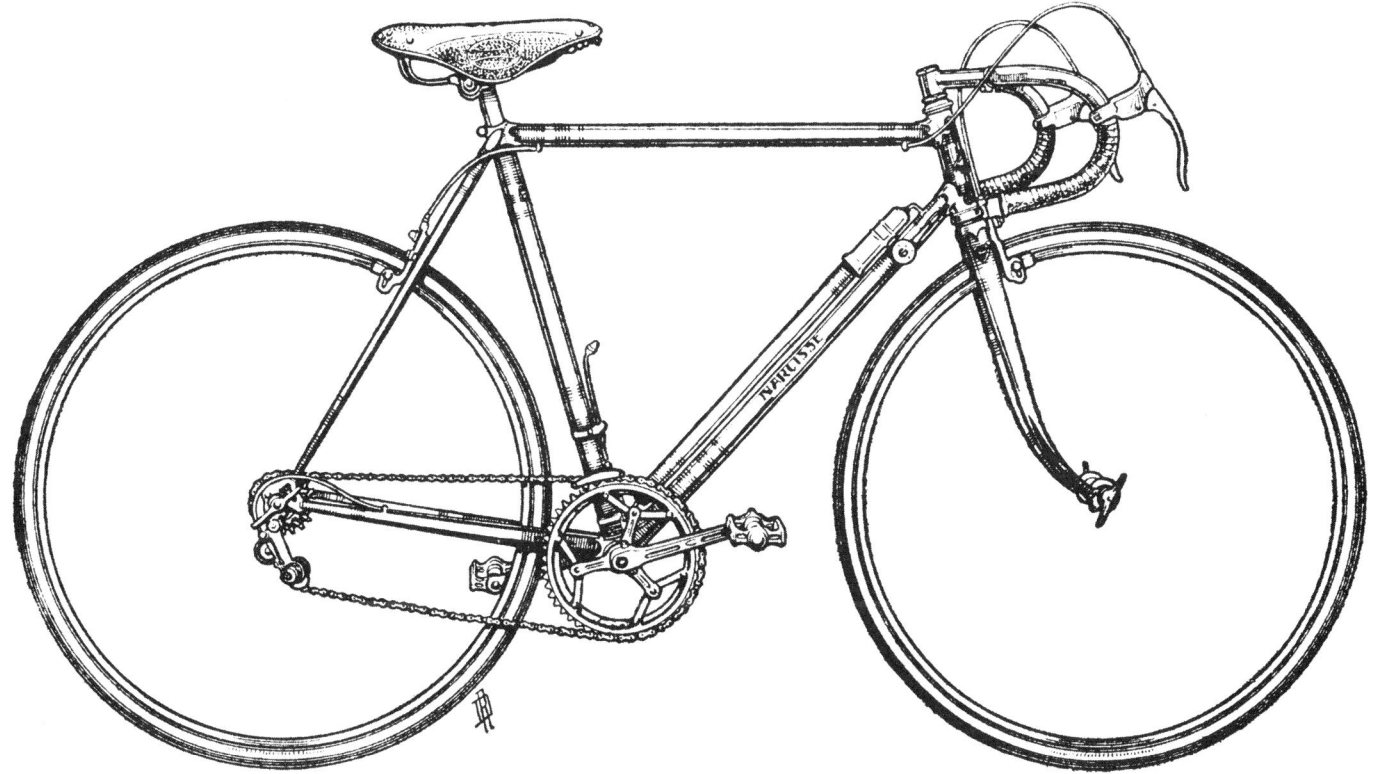

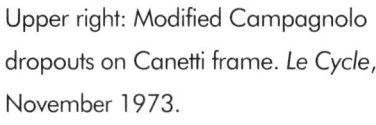

Upper right: Modified Campagnolo dropouts on Canetti frame. *Le Cycle*, November 1973.

Lower right: Rear dropout details on Speedwell titanium frame. *Le Cycle*, November 1973.

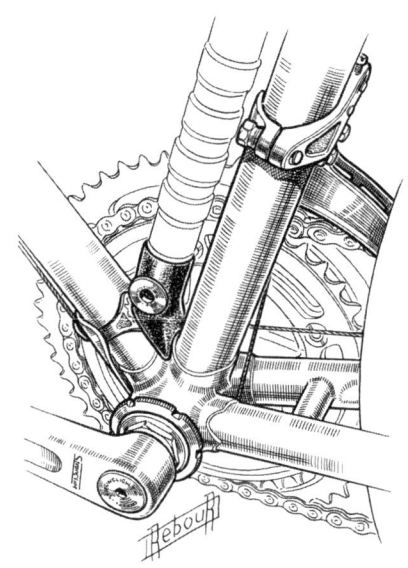

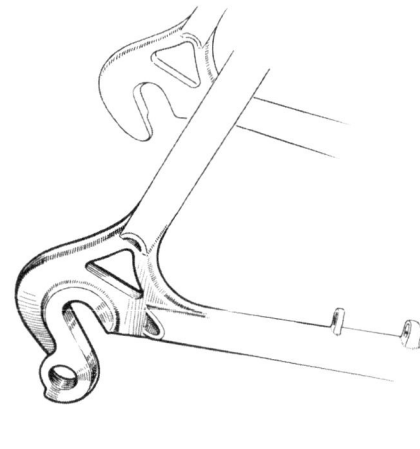

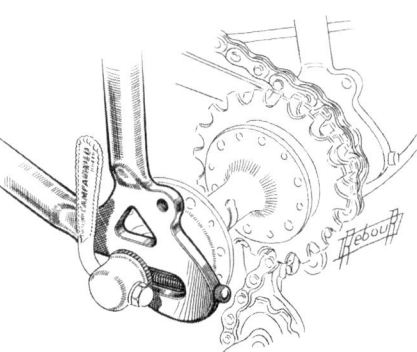

Above: Frame details at bottom bracket on Bertin frame. *Le Cycle*, April 1973.

Right: Front end details of a Dutch Kaptein city bicycle with lowered twin-top tubes. *Le Cycle*, 9 March 1957.

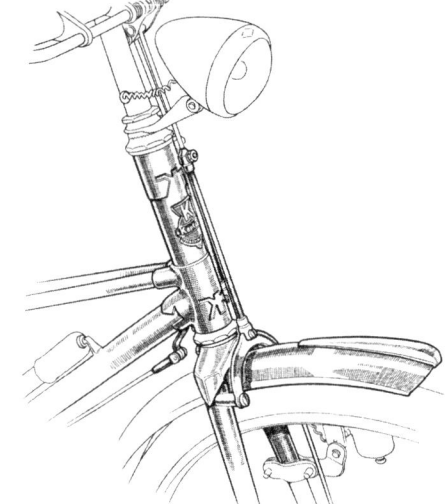

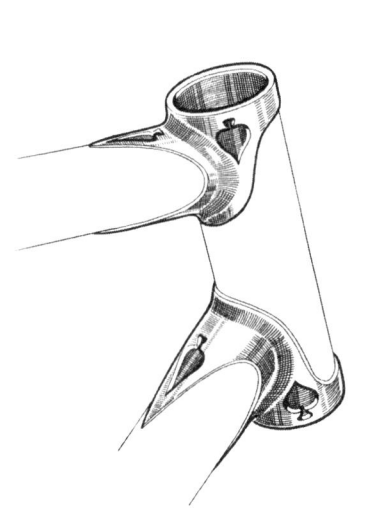

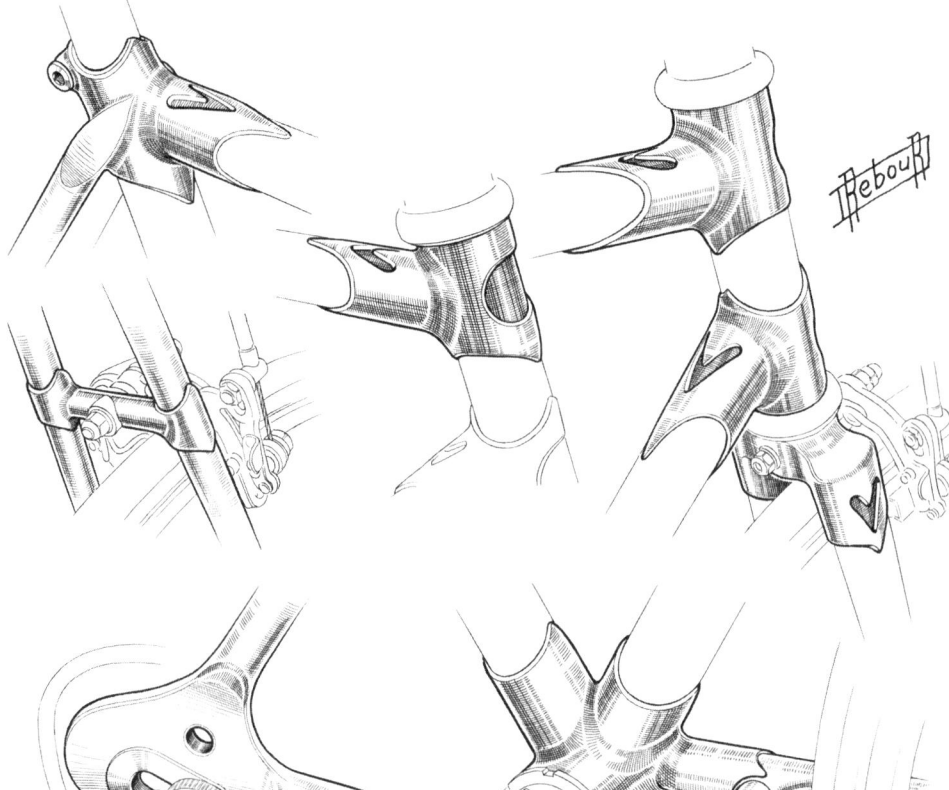

Above: Details of head lugs with cut-outs on Canetti frame. *Le Cycle*, November 1973.

Right: Details of Dagedur aluminium alloy frame with screwed and bonded lugs. *Le Cycle*, July 1973.

Chapter 2. Frame Details

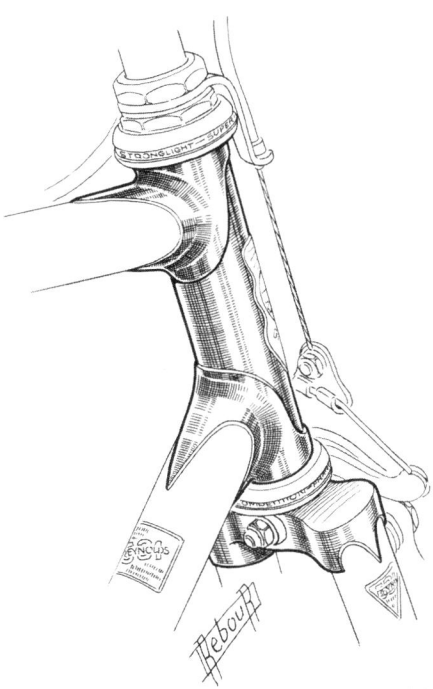

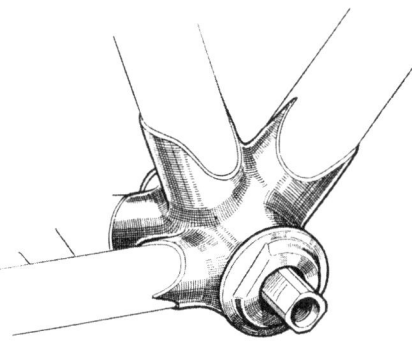

Above: Oversize tubing and special bottom bracket shell on 1956 René Herse bike. *Le Cycle*, 5 May 1956.

Below: Canetti bottom bracket shell details. *Le Cycle*, November 1973.

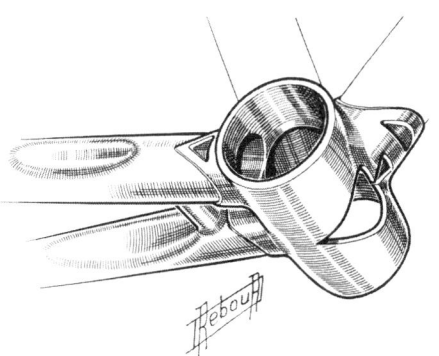

Above: Front end detail of Liberia frame. *Le Cycle*, November 1973.

Below: Jo Routens touring bike, with frame stiffened by chainstays attached to seat tube and top tube. Note the wide-range gearing obtained with the big difference in front chainrings. *Pratique du Vélo*.

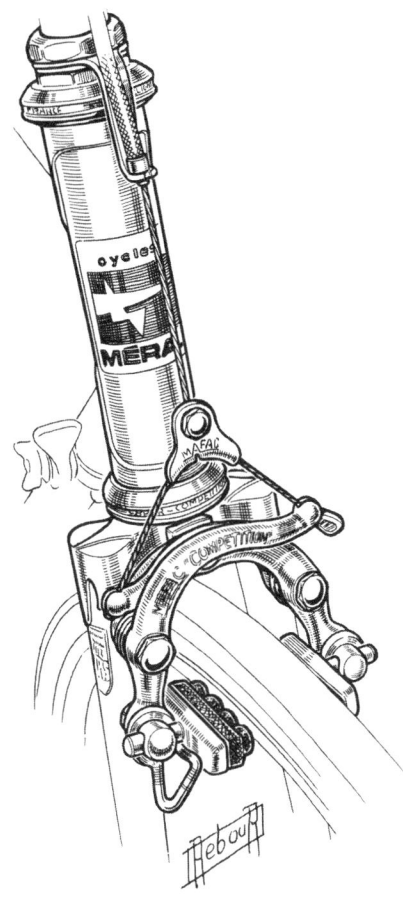

Above: Front-end details of Meral frame. *Le Cycle*, November 1973.

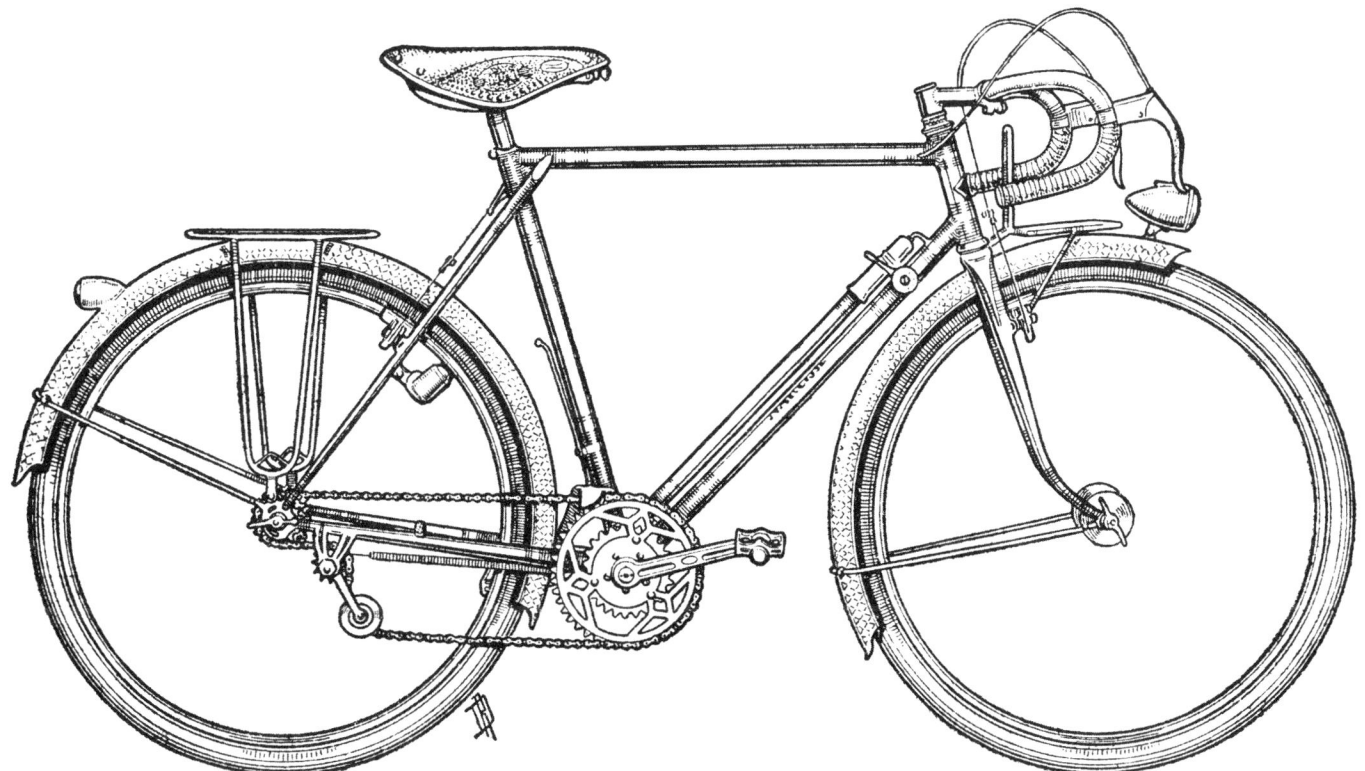

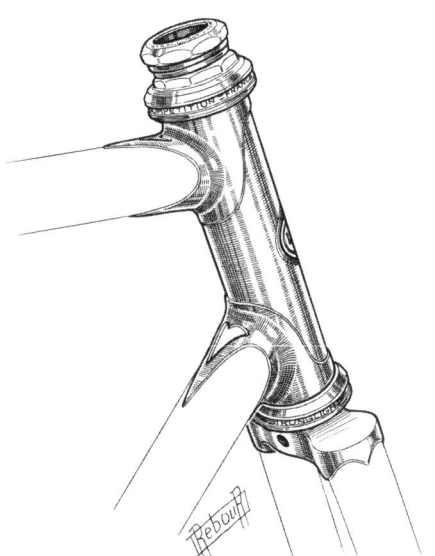
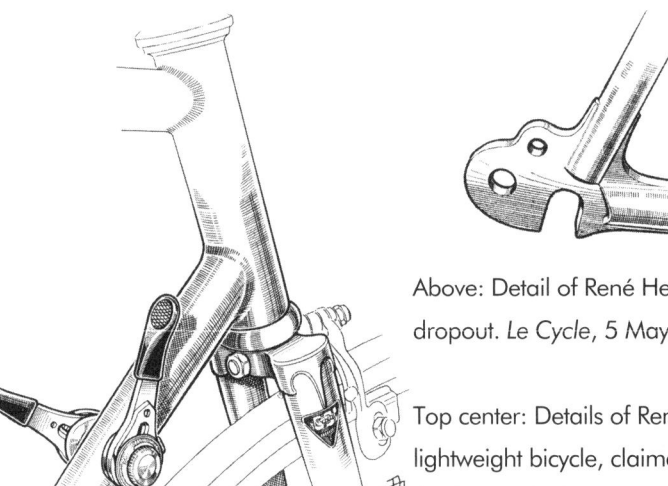

Above: Detail of René Herse vertical dropout. *Le Cycle*, 5 May 1956.

Top center: Details of René Herse lightweight bicycle, claimed to weigh only 6.8 kg. *Le Cycle*, December 1973.

Above: Front-end details of a Lejeune road racing frame. *Le Cycle*, December 1973.

Right: Lower head-lug area detail of Ocaña's 1973 Motobécane frame. *Le Cycle*, December 1973.

Below: Continuously bent rear triangle detail on a 1962 Flandria. *Cycle:*

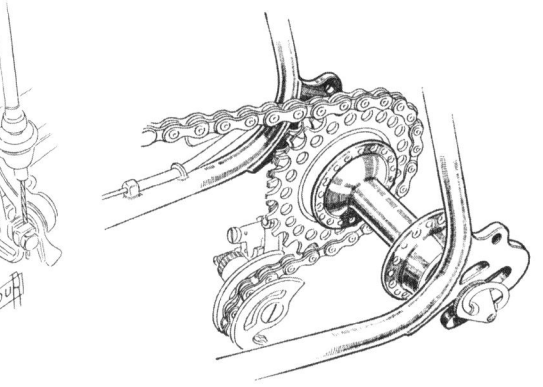

Below: René Herse 1948 mixte-frame ladies' touring bicycle, also with wide-range derailleur gearing. *Pratique du Vélo*.

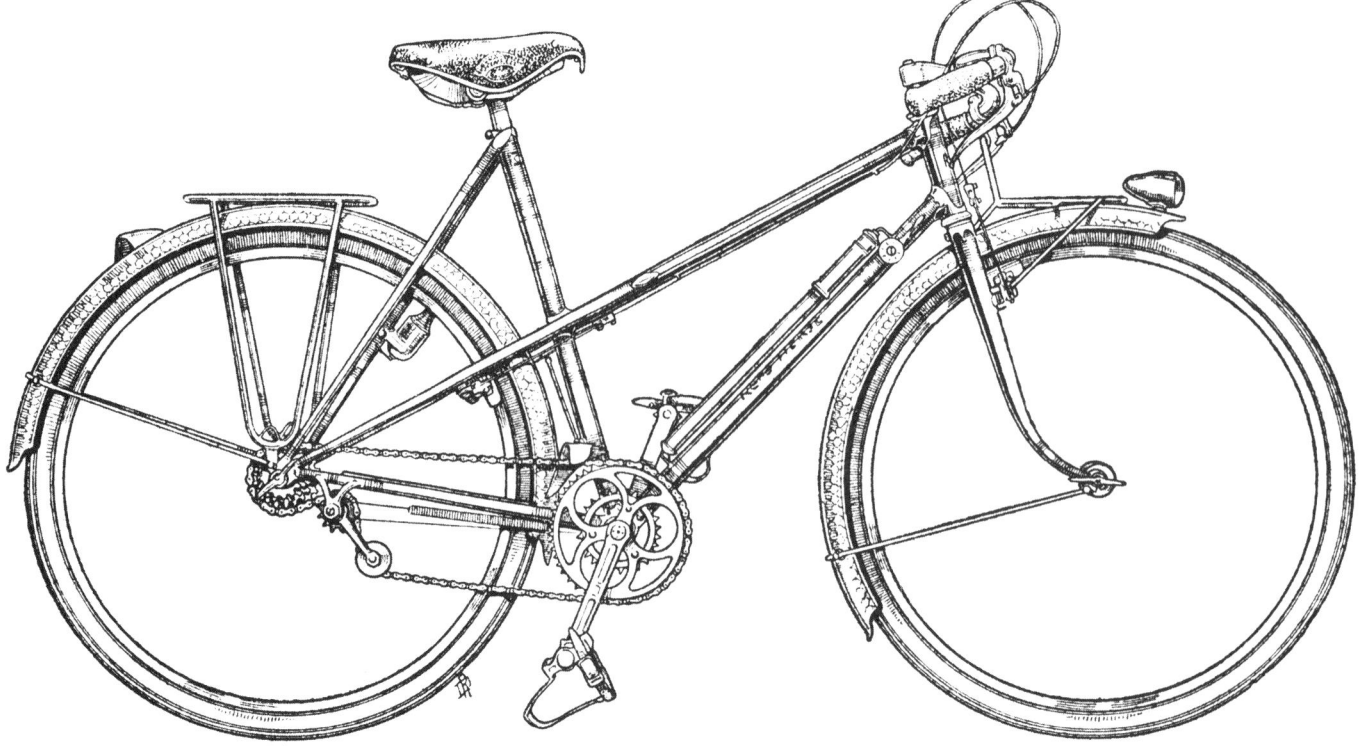

Chapter 2. Frame Details

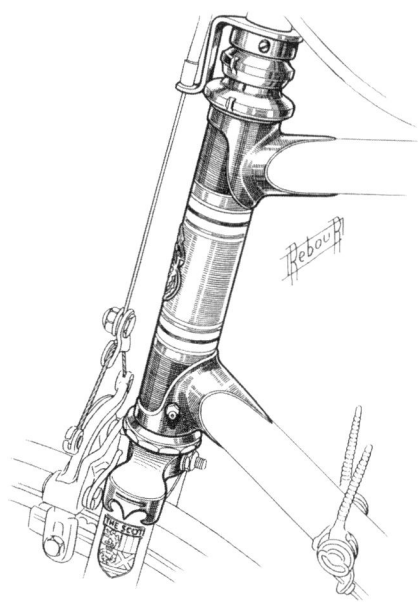

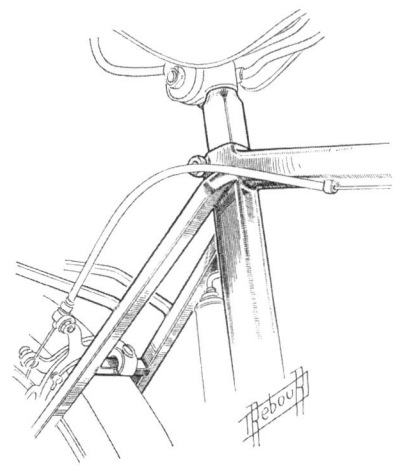

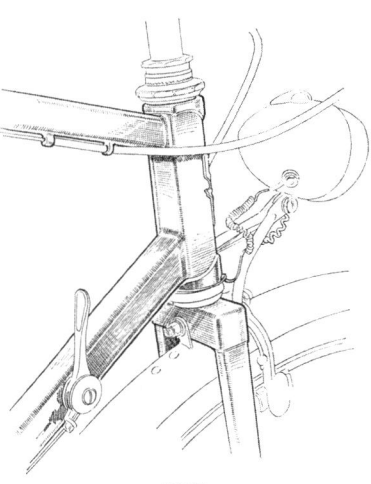

Above: Frame details of a Flying Scot bicycle. *Le Cycle*, November 1961.

Right: Detail of bottom bracket shell and tube joints on a Gitane frame with lugless joints. *Le Cycle*, February 1961

Below: Narcise ladies' bike—similar, but not quite. Not a modified version of the same basic drawings, but different details, also from *Pratique du Vélo*.

Above center and right: Details of a Novy bicycle frame with square tubing, displayed in Brussels. *Le Cycle*, April 1965.

Right: Detail of René Herse frame with oversize tubing. *Le Cycle*, 5 May 1956.

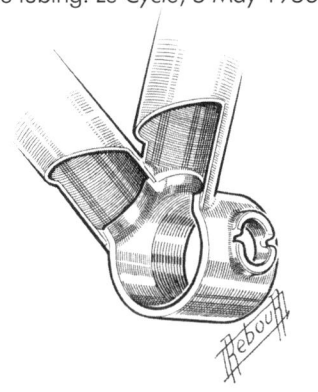

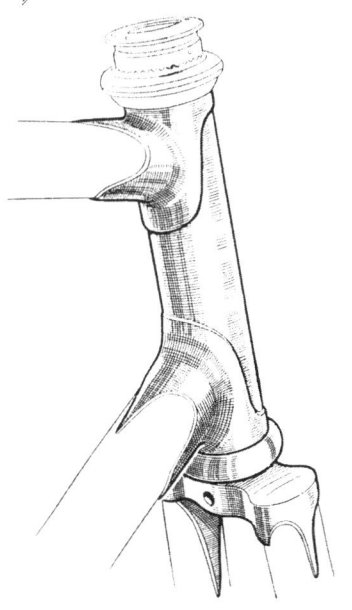

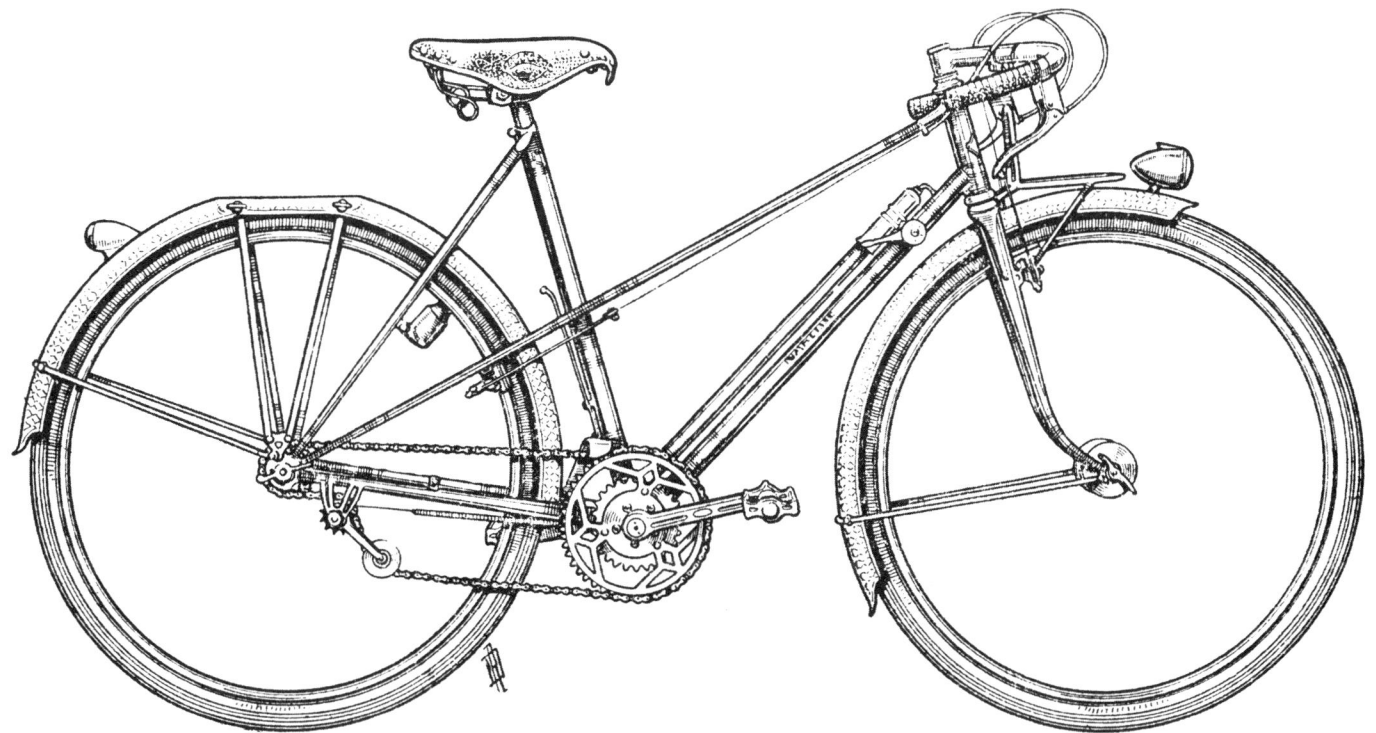

35

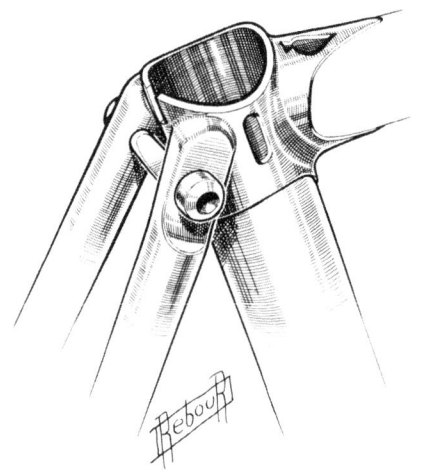

Left: Italian style "fastback" seat lug detail. *Cycles de Compétition et Randonneuses*.

Right: Cut-out Italian fork crown on 1974 Colnago bicycle. *Cycles de Compétition et Randonneuses*.

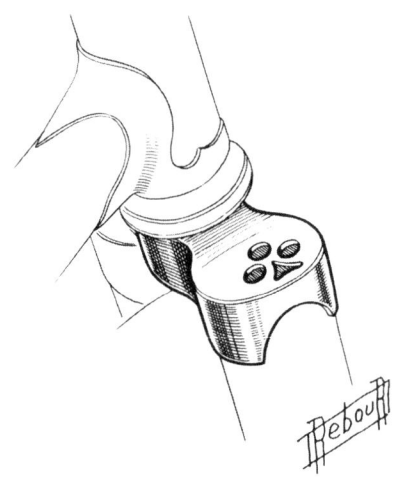

Below: Top and bottom Italian head-lug details with cutouts on an Italian frame by Canetti. *Cycles de Compétition et*

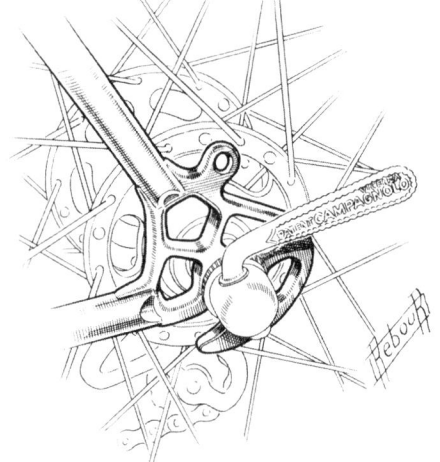

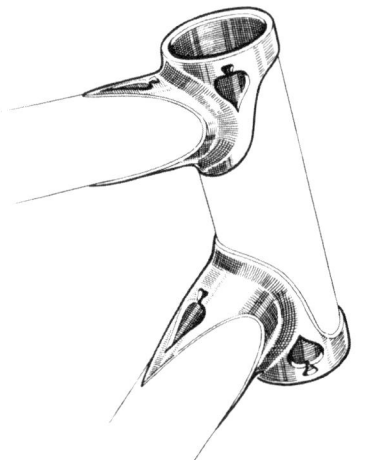

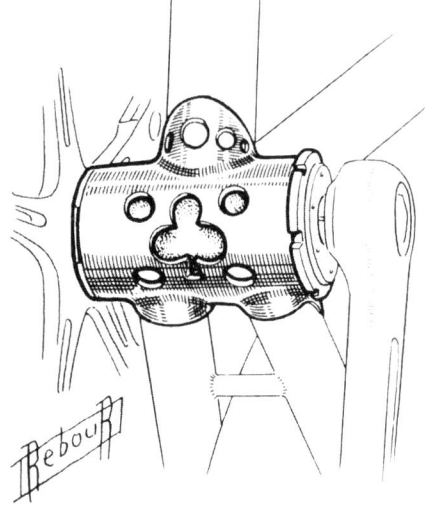

Above: Colnago cut-out bottom bracket detail. *Cycles de Compétition et Randonneuses*.

Above: Finely worked dropouts on a special 1975 Gitane frame. *Cycles de Compétition et Randonneuses*.

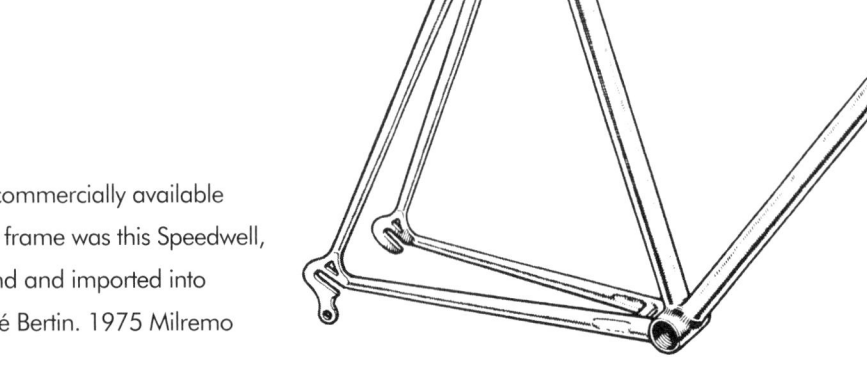

Right: The first commercially available titanium bicycle frame was this Speedwell, made in England and imported into France by André Bertin. 1975 Milremo catalogue.

CHAPTER 2. FRAME DETAILS

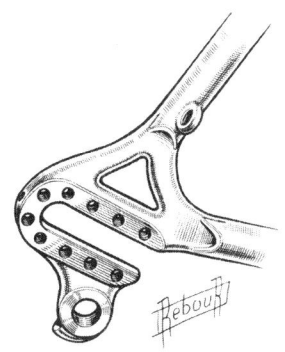
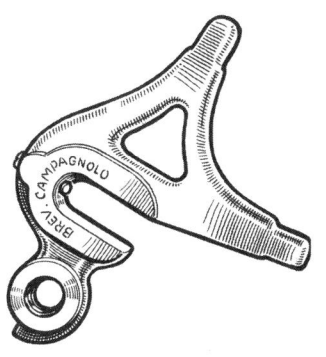
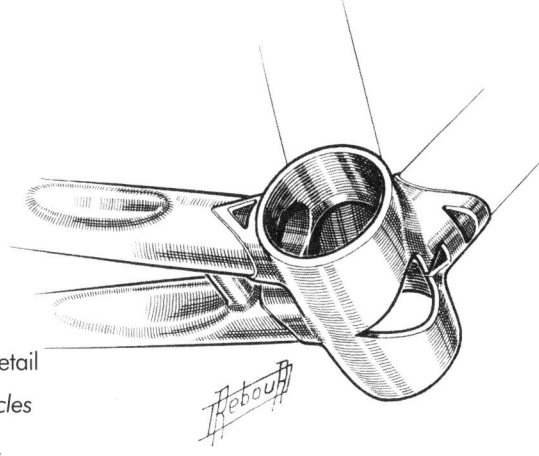

Above left and center: Special drilled-out Campagnolo dropouts on a Lejeune frame; new Campagnolo dropouts at the 1975 Paris bicycle trade show.
Right: Front and rear Milremo road bike dropouts.
All three images from *Cycles de Compétition et Randonneuses*.
Far right: Seat lug area detail with "fastback"-style seatstays on Raleigh bicycle. *Le Cycle*, April 1973.

Below: Usually bikes are shown from the right, or "chocolate side." But here is a typical 1948 Randonneur bike seen from the left, as shown in *Pratique du Vélo*.

Top right: Bottom bracket area detail on Limongi or Canetti frame. *Cycles de Compétition et Randonneuses*.

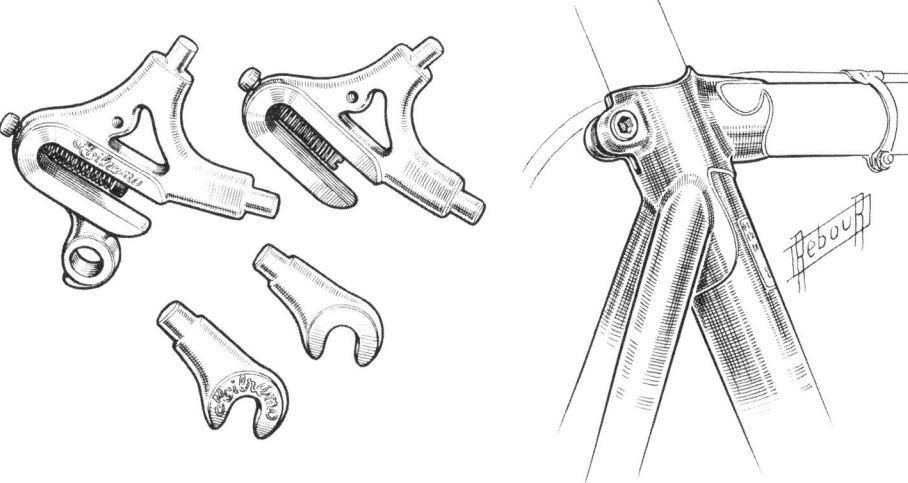

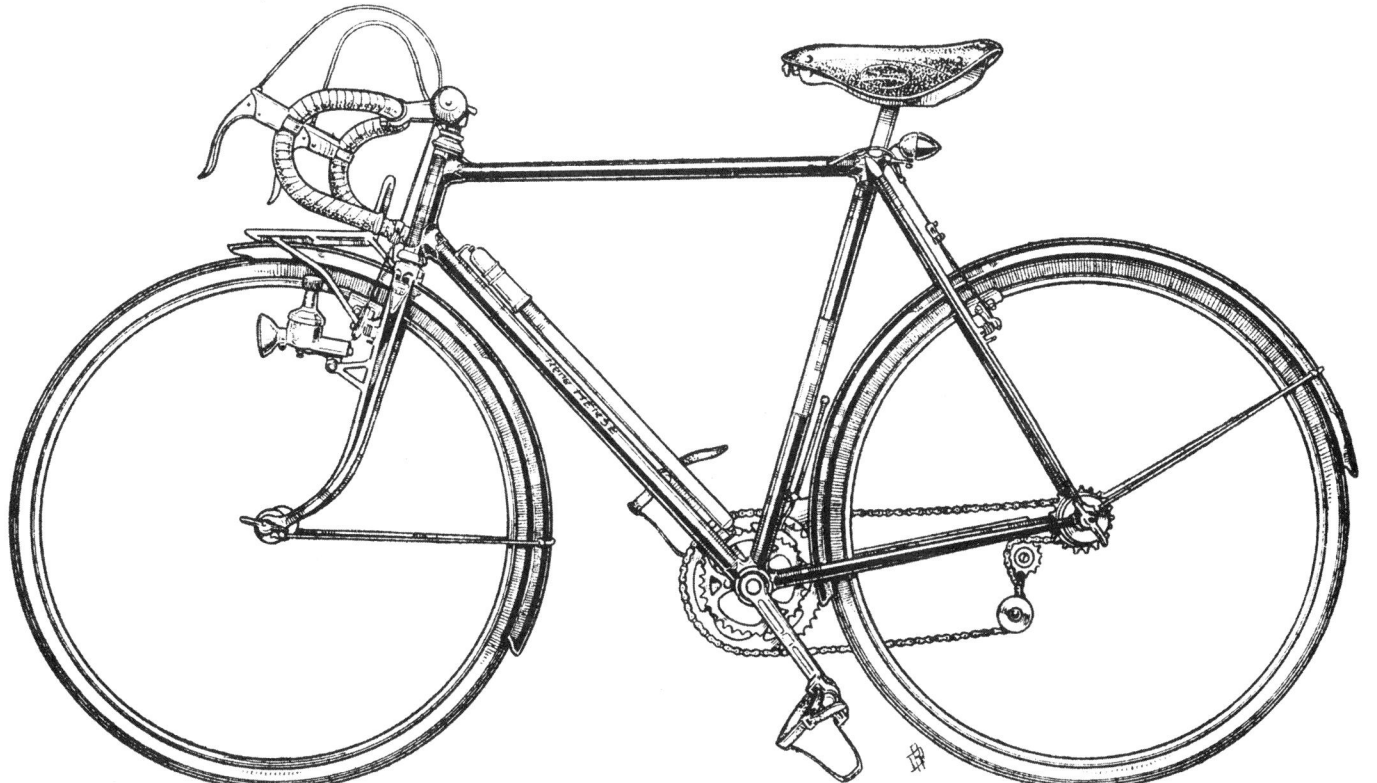

37

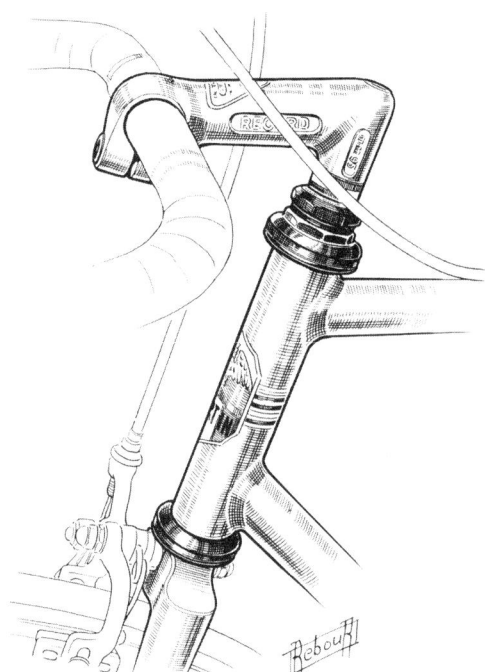

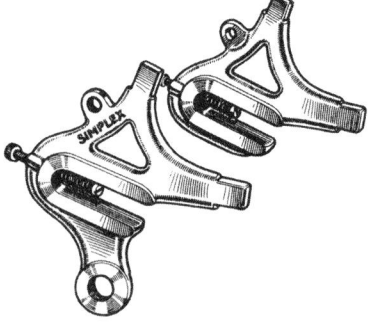

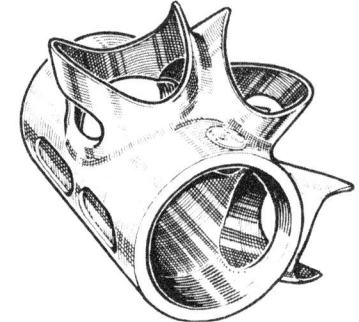

Above: Simplex investment cast drop-outs with non-threaded derailleur eye.
Top right: Roto investment cast bottom bracket.
Below: Roto investment cast fork crown.
All three images from *Cycles de Compétition et Randonneuses*.

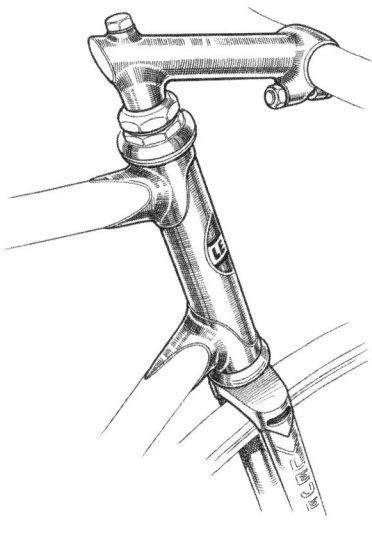

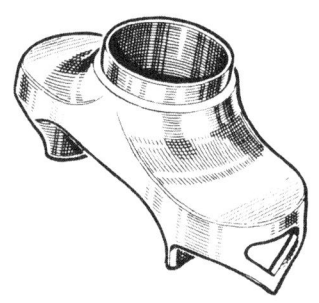

Above: Lightweight Campagnolo headset detail on a bike built up with the Speedwell titanium frame. *Cycles de Compétition et Randonneuses*.

Below: 1948 Urago road racing bike, from *Pratique du Vélo*.

Above: Front end detail of Lejeune track bike. *Le Cycle*, December 1970.

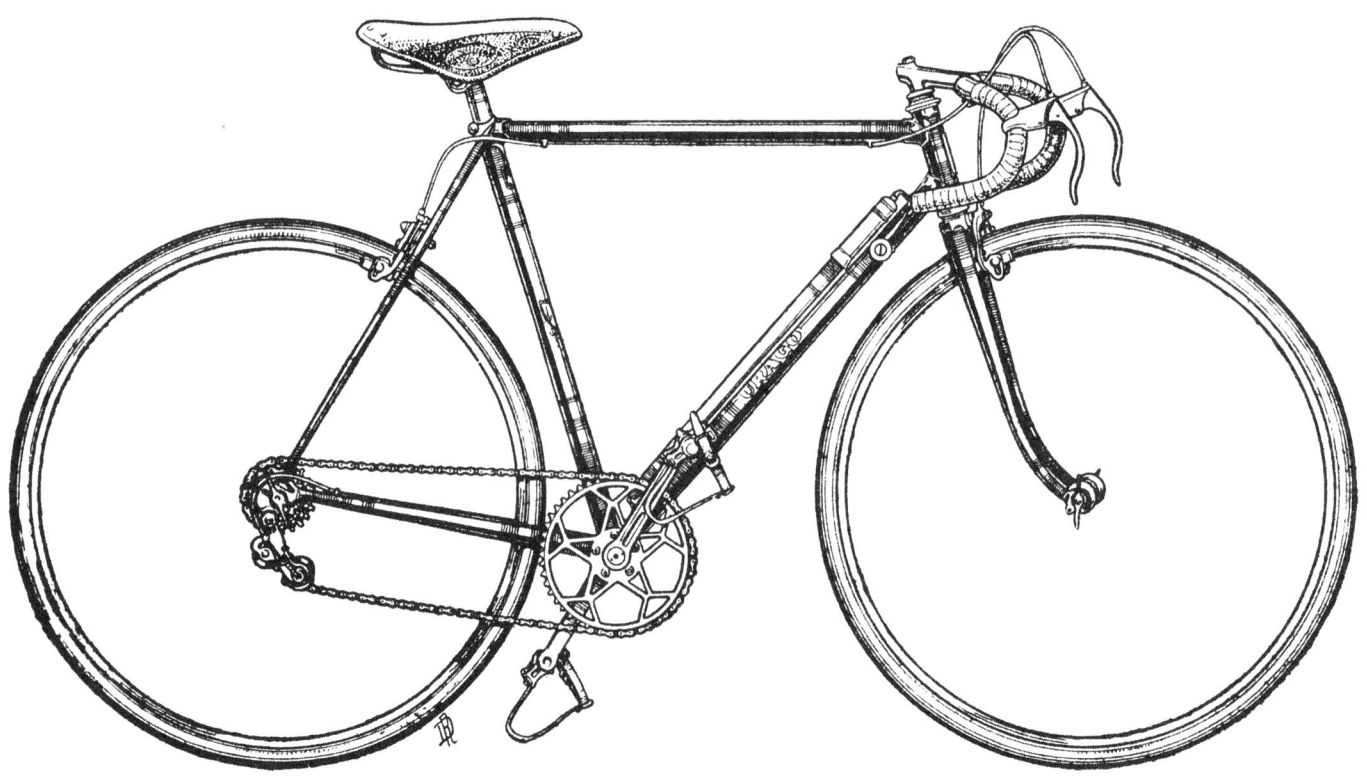

CHAPTER 2. FRAME DETAILS

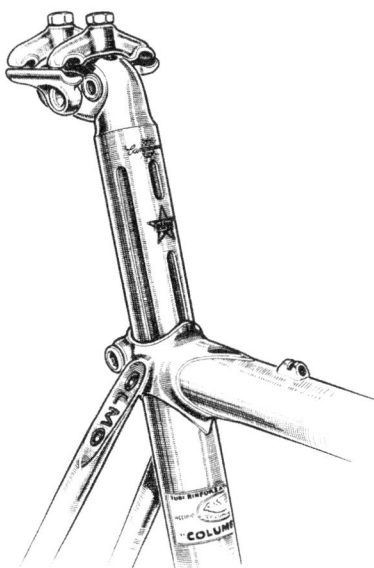

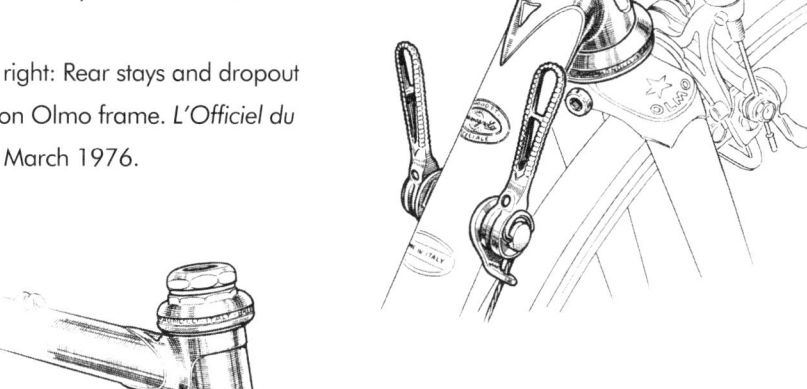

Upper right: Front end details with braze-ons for shifters on Olmo frame. *L'Officiel du Cycle*, March 1976.

Lower right: Rear stays and dropout detail on Olmo frame. *L'Officiel du Cycle*, March 1976.

Above: Seat cluster detail and Campagnolo seat post on Olmo frame. *L'Officiel du Cycle*, March 1976.

Right: Head detail on 1976 Olmo frame. *L'Officiel du Cycle*, March 1976.

Below: 1948 René Herse touring bike, from *Pratique du Vélo*.

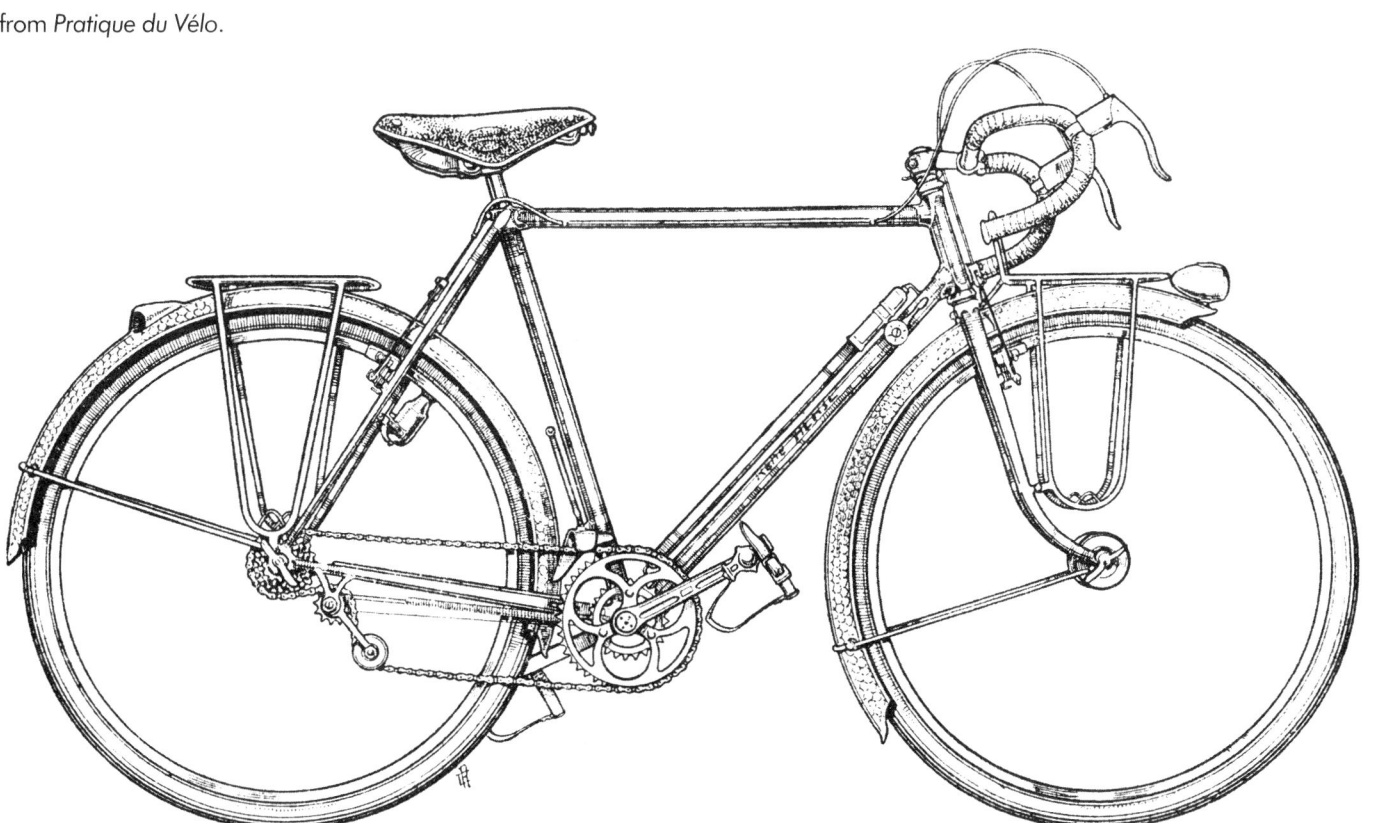

39

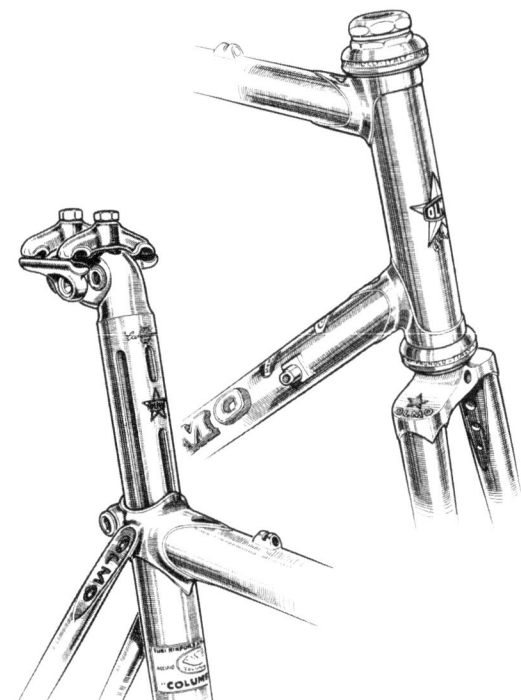
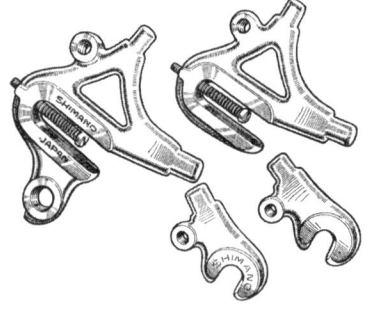
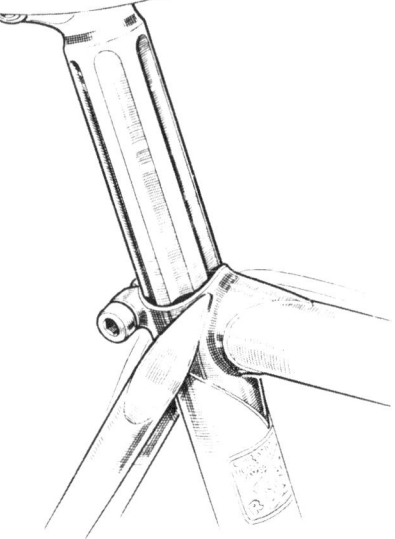

Above: Shimano dropouts and fork-ends. 1980 Milremo catalogue.

Right: Seat cluster detail on Olmo frame. *L'Officiel du Cycle*, March 1976.

Above: Front and rear frame details on Olmo frame. *L'Officiel du Cycle*, March 1976.

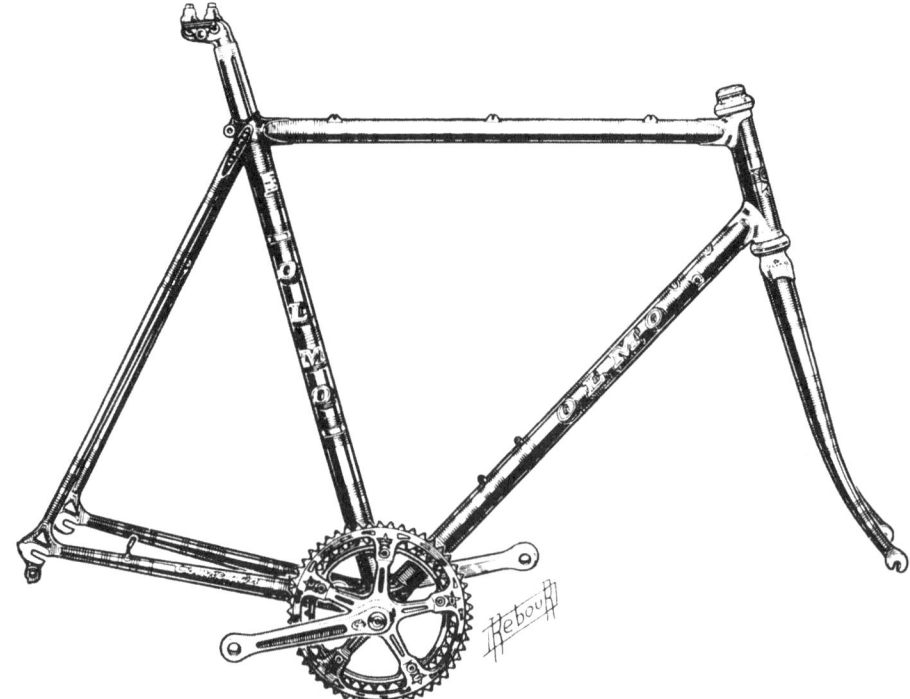

Right: Overview of the same Olmo frame with fork, headset, seatpost, and crankset installed. *L'Officiel du Cycle*, March 1976.

Chapter 3. Derailleur Gearing

At the time Rebour's first bicycle drawings were published, derailleur gearing was used extensively only by racers and randonneurs, i.e. French long-distance touring cyclists. Since those days, significant progress was made in all components that work together for effective derailleur gearing: front and rear derailleurs, shifters, and the tooth shapes on cogs and chainrings. By the time of the last drawings in this collection, from the 1983 Bertin catalogue, derailleur gearing had evolved significantly, and hardly a bicycle was sold for adult use, at least in France, but equally so in the U.S., without derailleur gearing. This chapter gives an overview of derailleur developments during this period.

Below: Left-side view of 1948 René Herse touring bike. Typical for randonneur and touring bicycles of the period, it had 650 B tires, giving a comfortable and stable ride. The long chainstays allowed for the long rear rack. The derailleur is a Cyclo chainstay-mounted unit, and there is a rear drum brake. *Pratique du Vélo*.

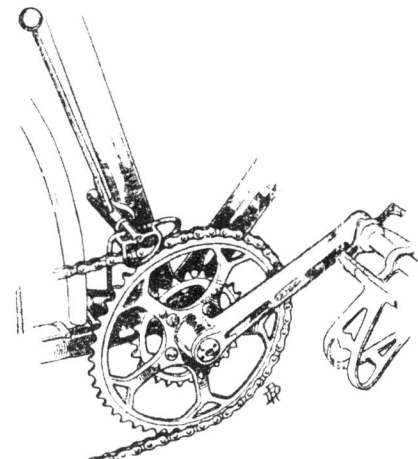

Left: The first derailleur drawing to appear in *Le Cycle*, 16 March 1946, was this lightweight Daudon front derailleur.

Below: Souhart bar-end shifter, or "*passe-vitesse.*" *Le Cycle*, 22 June 1946.

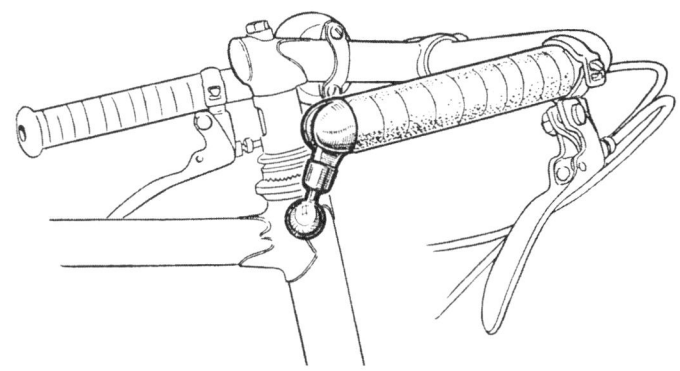

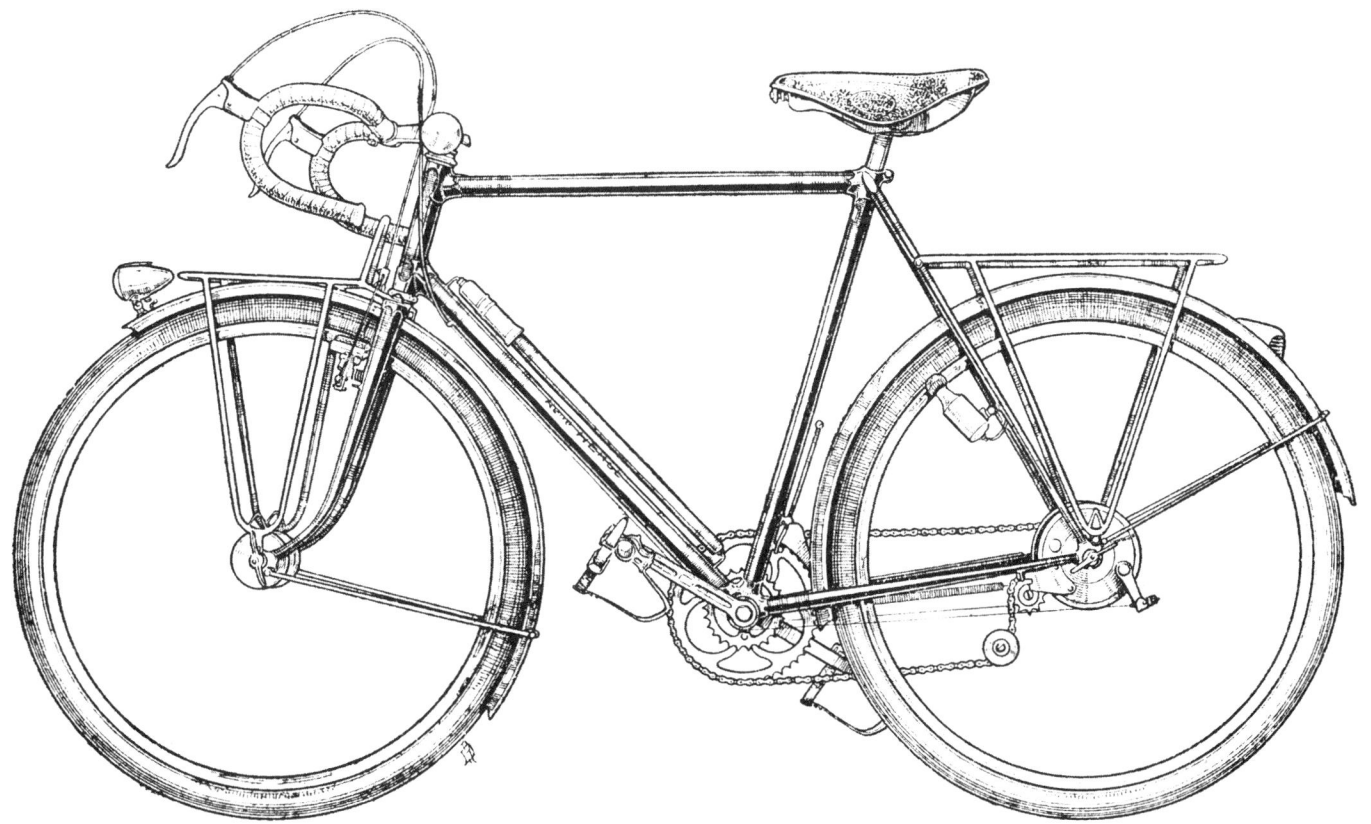

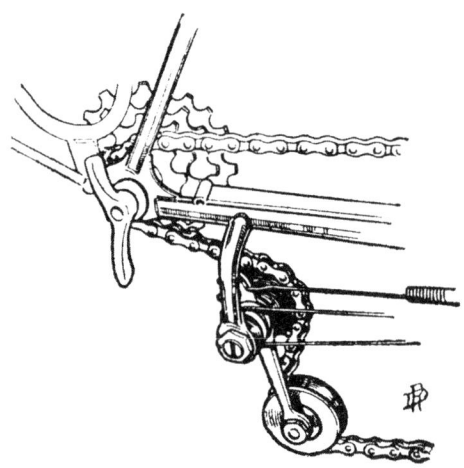 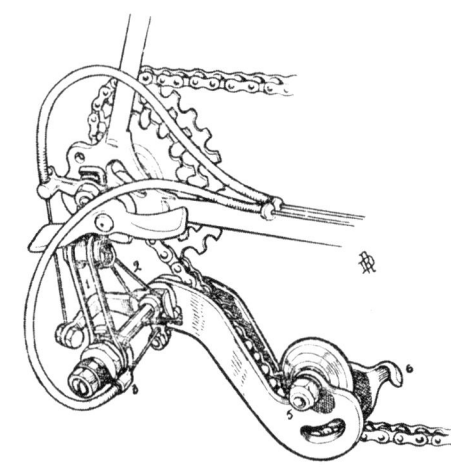

Left and below: Two different Huret rear derailleurs with "piano-wire" mounting to a bracket on the right-side chainstay, showing capacity to take up chain slack with the chain between the small and the large front chainring. The one on the left is a single-pulley design, the one below a double-pulley design. *Le Cycle*, 19 August 1946.

Above: Detail of Mauré machine with 2-cable Cyclo rear derailleur mounted on a brazed-on bracket on the right-side chainstay. *Le Cycle*, 20 April 1946.

Right: Super Leader rear derailleur. *Le Cycle*, 30 October 1950.

Below: 1948 Urago ladies' bike, with Berceau type frame (i.e. a mixte variant with curved and lowered twin diagonal tubes). *Pratique du Vélo*.

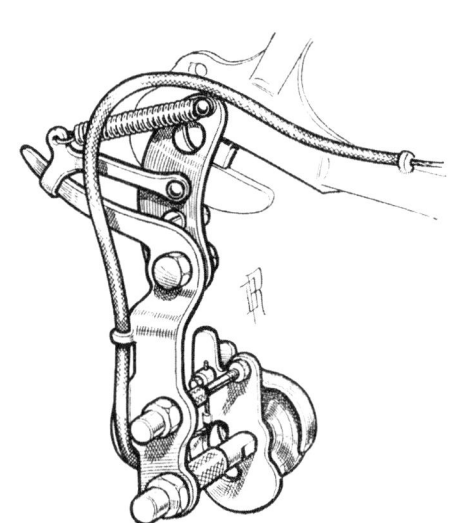 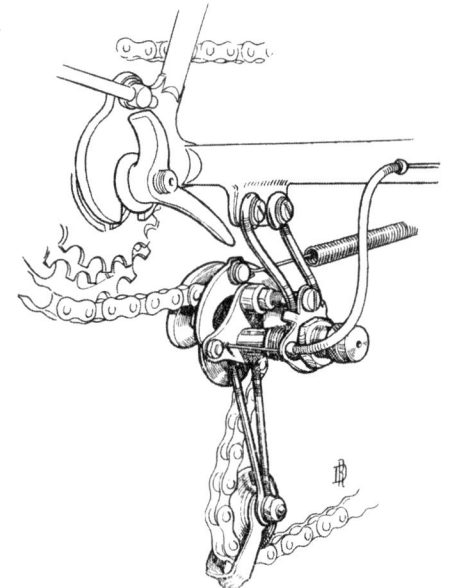

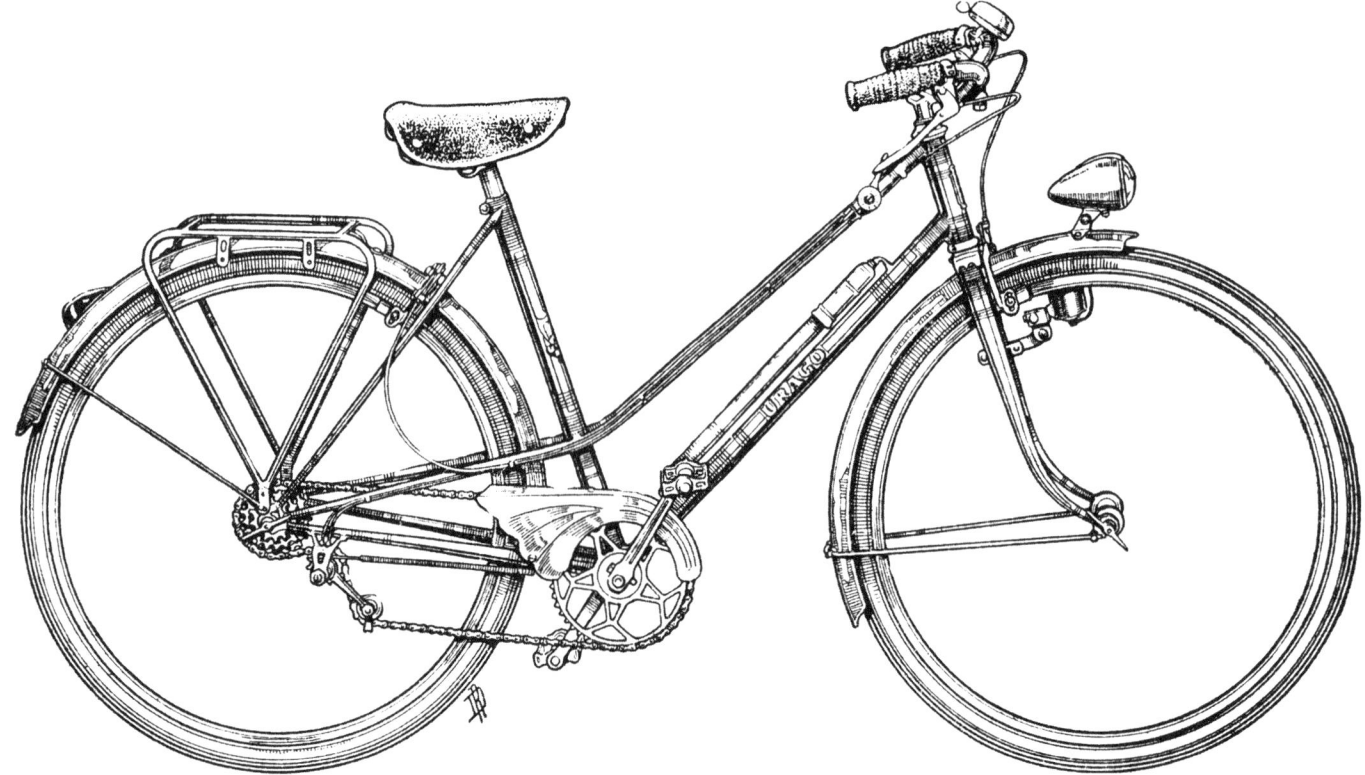

Chapter 3. Derailleur Gearing

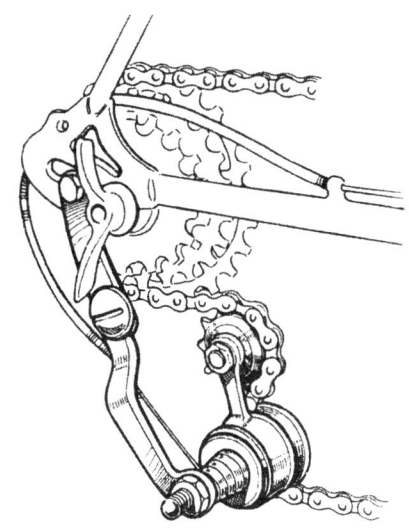 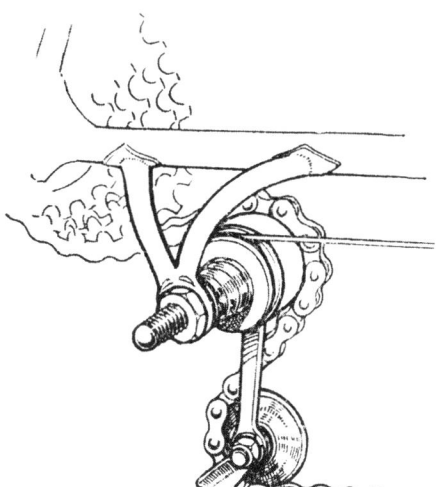

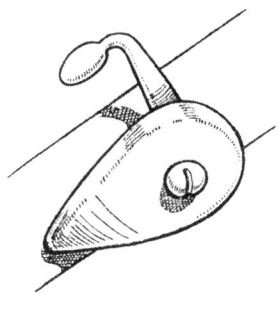

Below: Downtube-mounted single-lever shifter for Metevier-Laurent derailleur. *Le Cycle,* 26 January 1947.

Above and above center: BON derailleurs in racing version (left) and touring version (right).
Both images from *Le Cycle*, 26 January 1947.

Below: The Frejus bicycle on which Ferdi Kübler, of Switzerland, won the 1950 Tour de France. The very narrow-range gearing suggests he may have used a different bike on mountain stages. *Le Cycle*, 12 August 1950.**

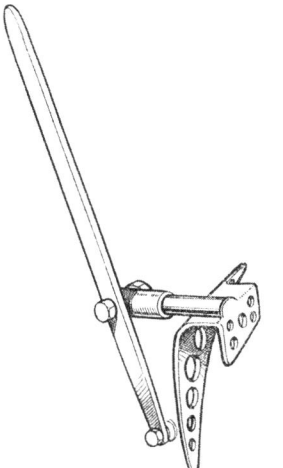

Left and right: The 1940s was the time of direct-lever-operated front derailleurs (if used at all). Dardenne (left) and Derche (right).
Both images from *Le Cycle*, 26 January 1947.

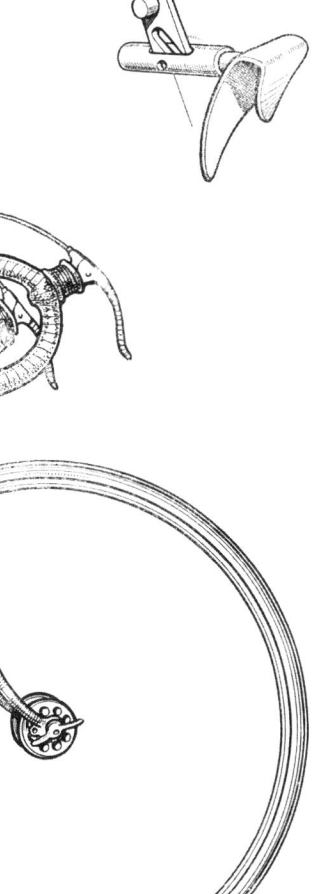

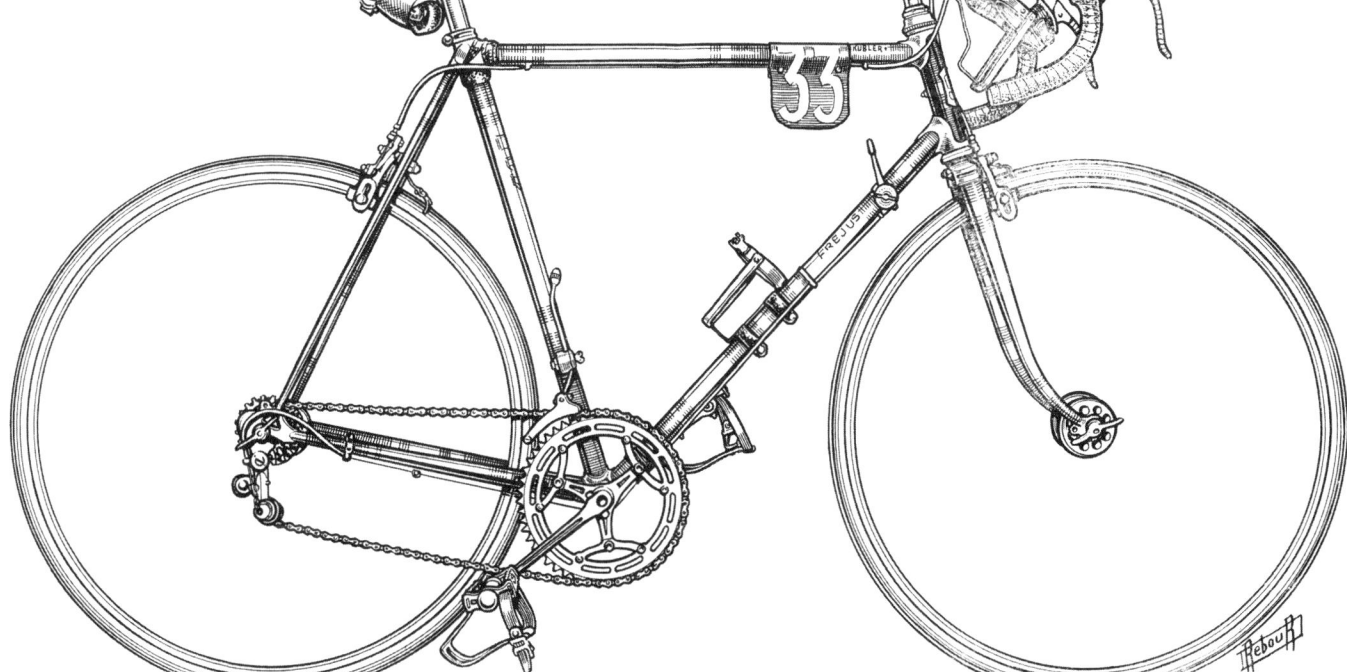

** See pages 269–271 for expanded caption text.

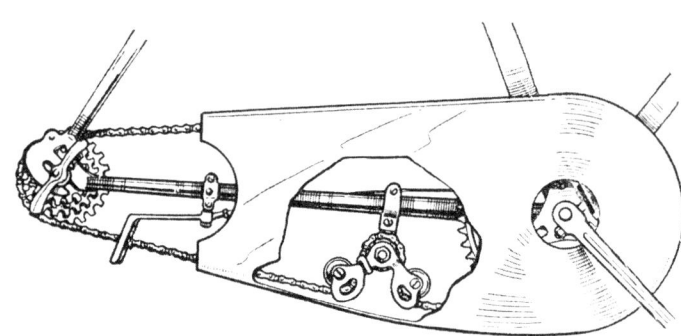

Right: Dante Gianello in-line derailleur with separate chain-wrap unit mounted to the chain stay. *Le Cycle*, 31 May 1947.

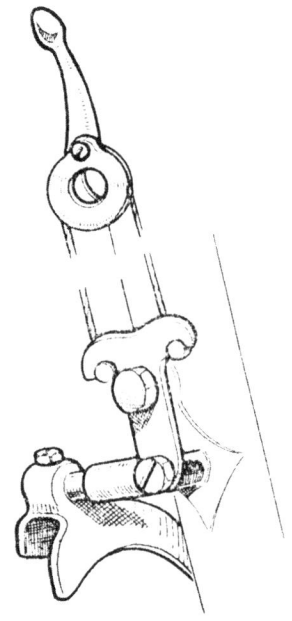

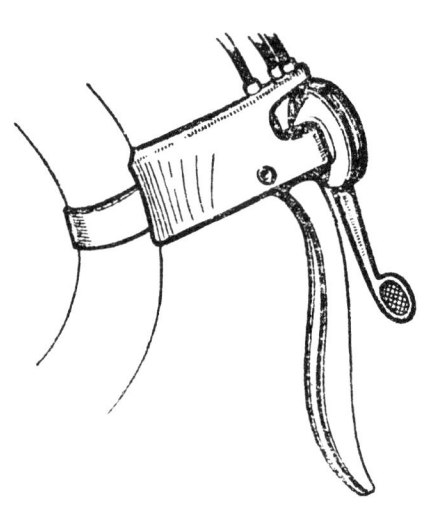

Right: Alfredo Cardinali Sport derailleur. *Le Cycle*, 23 June 1947.

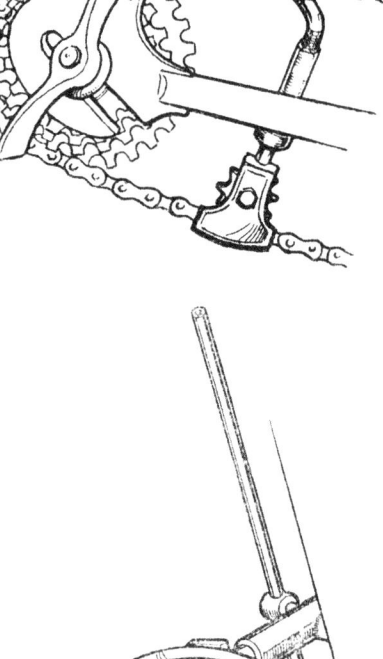

Above: Fletcher cable-operated front derailleur, with the shift lever mounted on the seat tube. *Le Cycle*, 26 January 1947.

Right: George Navet integrated brake-shift lever, which can be considered a precursor of today's popular brake-shift levers. *Le Cycle*, 27 October 1948.

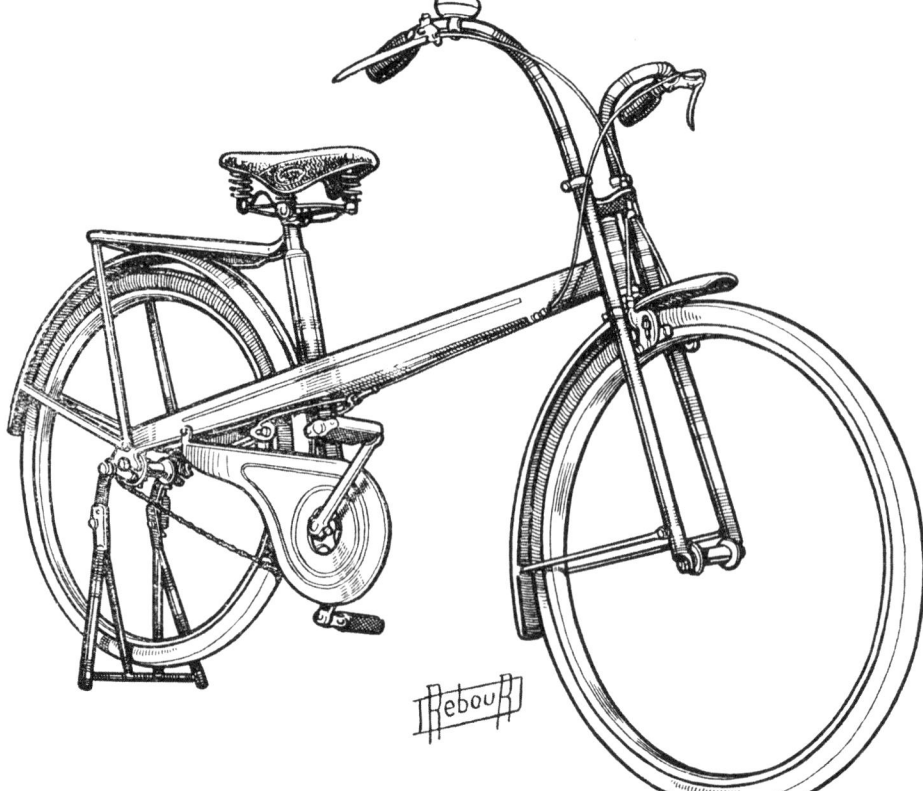

Above: Pittard lightweight direct-lever-operated front derailleur. *Le Cycle*, 26 January 1947.

Left: Japanese DuJee city bike with aluminium monocoque cross-frame, a curious front-fork and handlebar arrangement, and cantilever brakes. *Le Cycle*, 5 January 1952.

Chapter 3. Derailleur Gearing

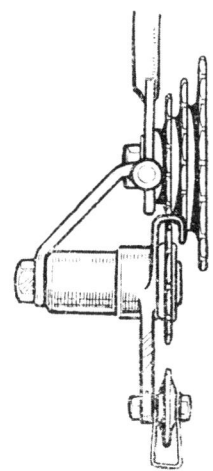
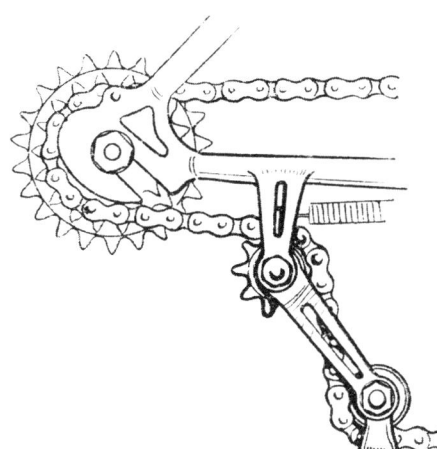

Left: 1946 New Lewis rear derailleur
Right: Renalb Lux "automatic" (pedaling-operated) rear derailleur, with split rear wheel hub. Both images from *Le Cycle*, 21 July 1947.

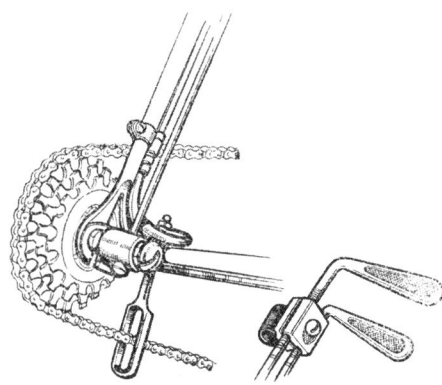

Below: Gasparetto and Monviso rear derailleurs. *Le Cycle*, 22 May 1948.

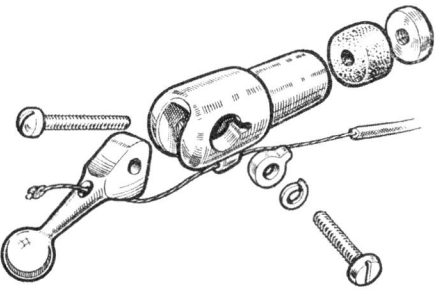
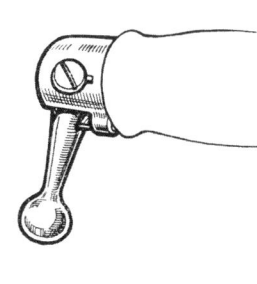

Left and right: Exploded and installed views of Souhart *passe vitesse* bar-end shifter. *Le Cycle*, 23 October 1948.

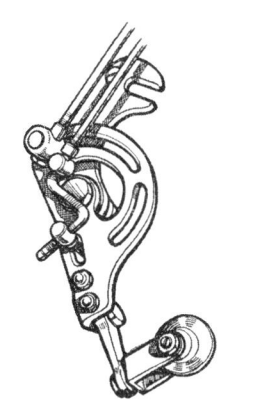

Below: The Metropole bike on which Raphaël Géminiani rode the 1952 Tour de France, from *Le Cycle*, 4 August 1951.

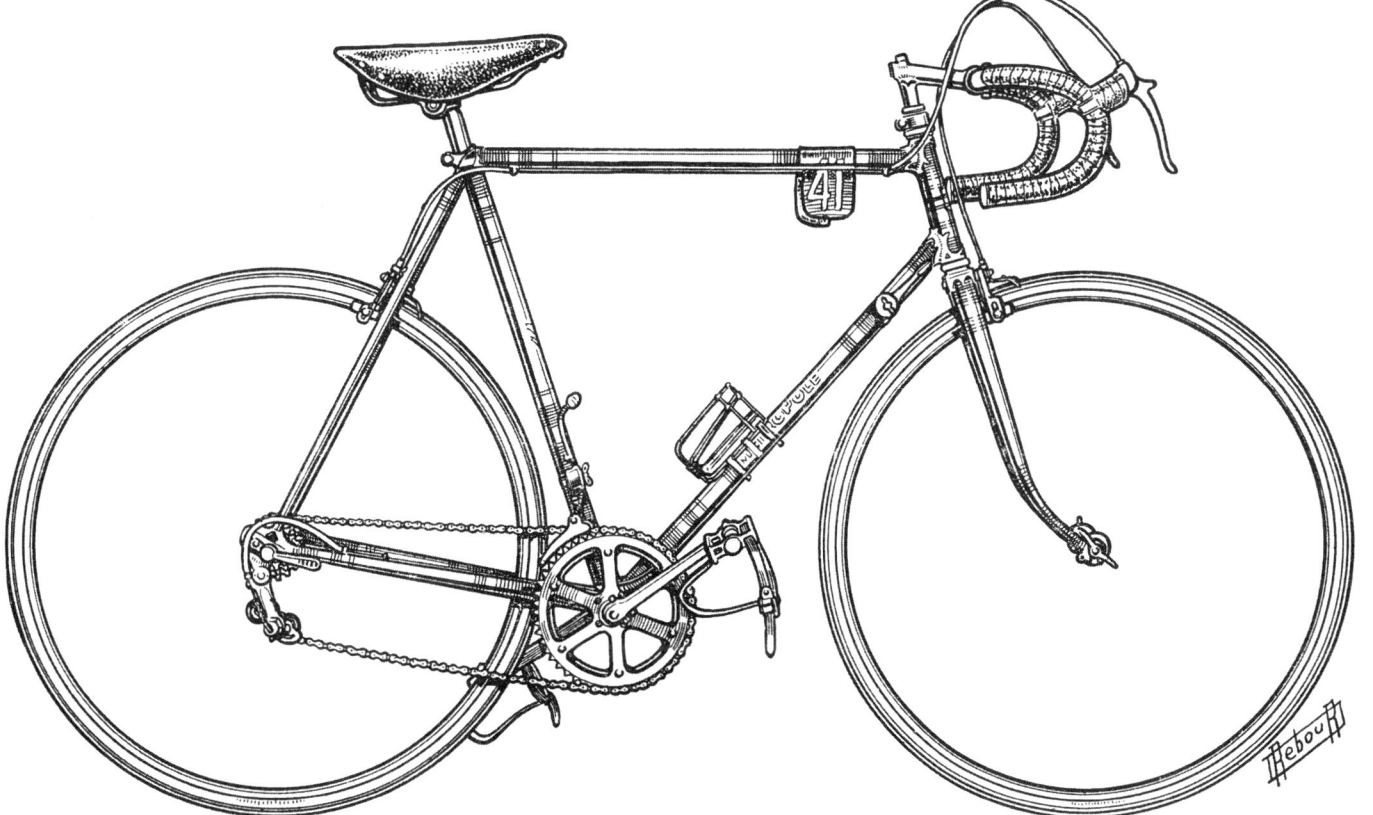

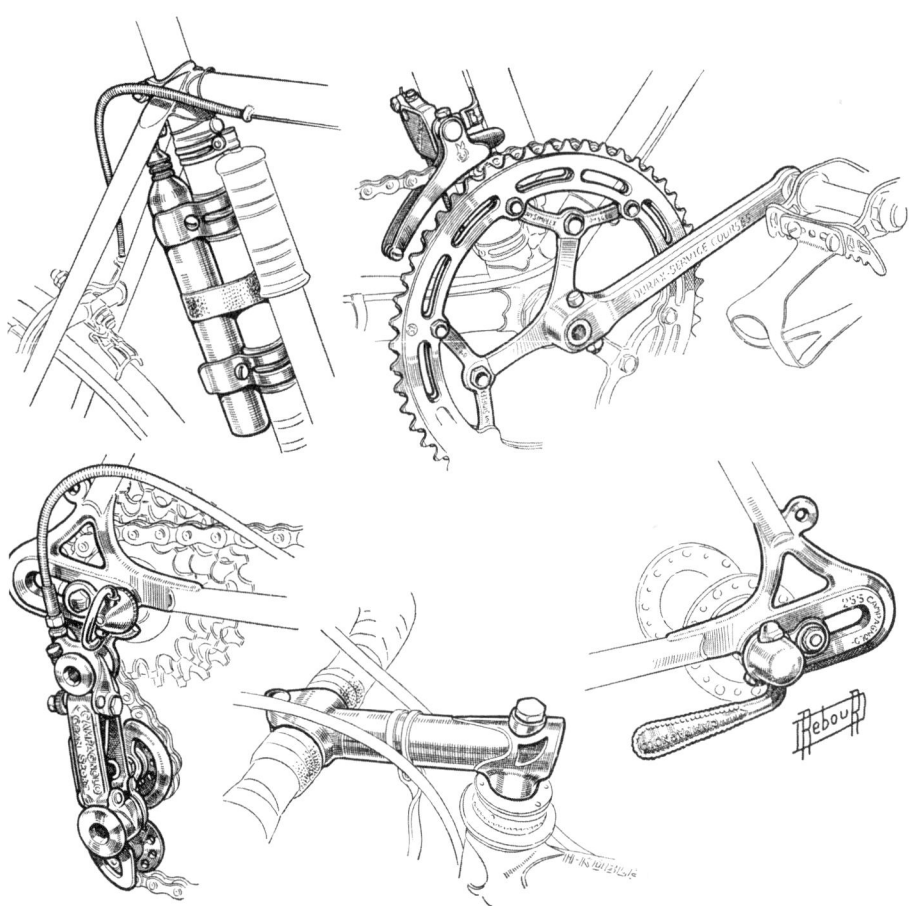
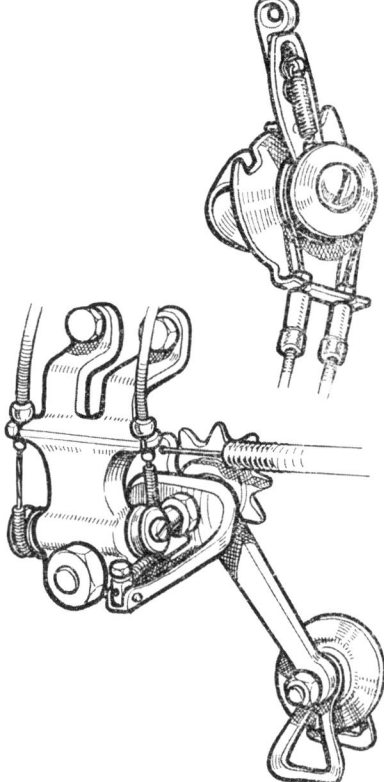

Below: Huet (no, that's not a typo) twin-cable-operated rear derailleur and spring-loaded shift lever. *Le Cycle*, 23 October 1948.

Below and above: The La Perle bicycle on which Hugo Koblet, of Switzerland, won the 1951 Tour de France. Note the Campagnolo Gran Sport derailleur. *Le Cycle*, 4 August 1951.**

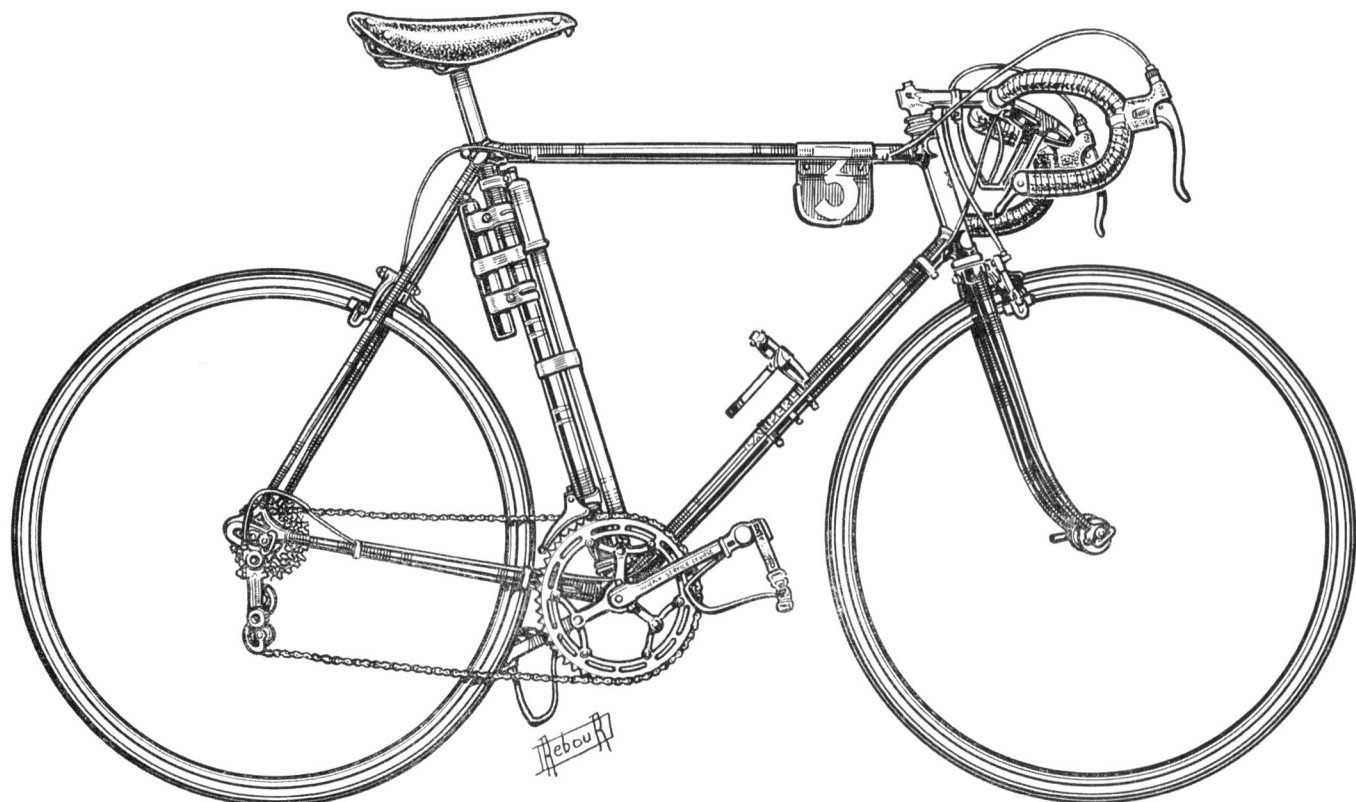

** See pages 269–271 for expanded caption text.

Chapter 3. Derailleur Gearing

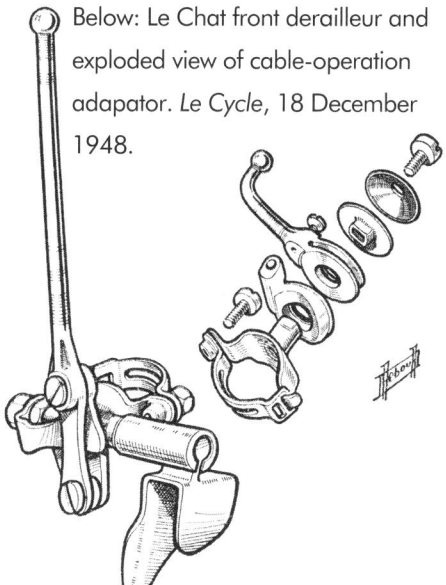

Below: Le Chat front derailleur and exploded view of cable-operation adapator. *Le Cycle*, 18 December 1948.

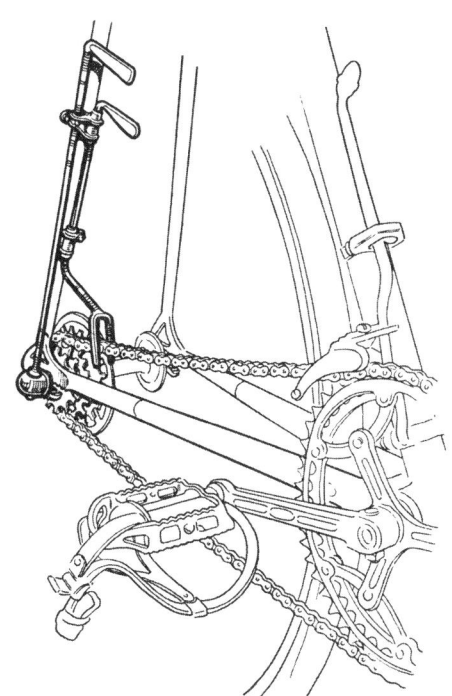

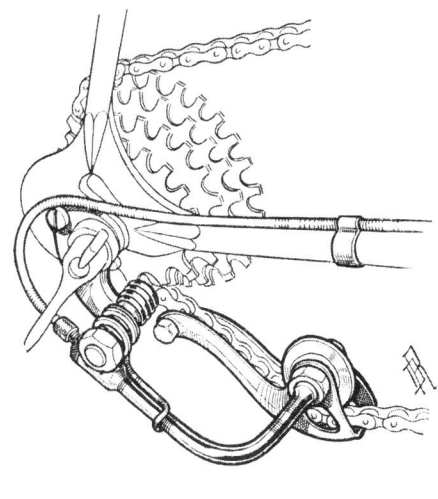

Above: BSA 4-speed derailleur, from England. *Le Cycle*, 4 December 1948.

Above: Campagnolo Corsa derailleur as of 1948. The upper lever loosens the quick-release, allowing the wheel to be repositioned to shift. *Pratique du Vélo*. Below: Quite a bit shorter than Koblet, Biquet rode this Colomb bicycle in the 1952 Tour de France. *Le Cycle*, 2 August 1952.

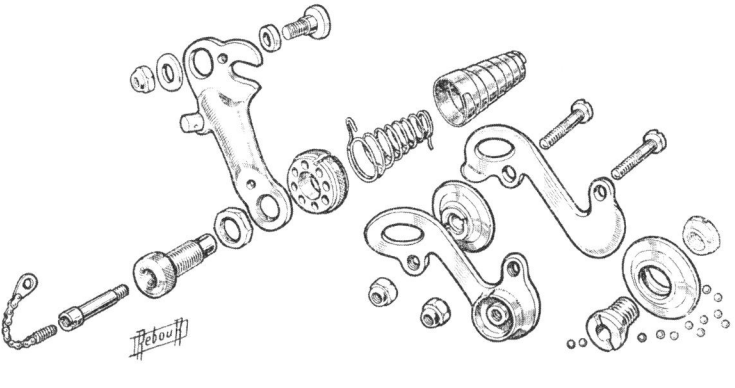

Left: Exploded view of 1948 Huret rear derailleur. *Le Cycle*, 26 November 1949.

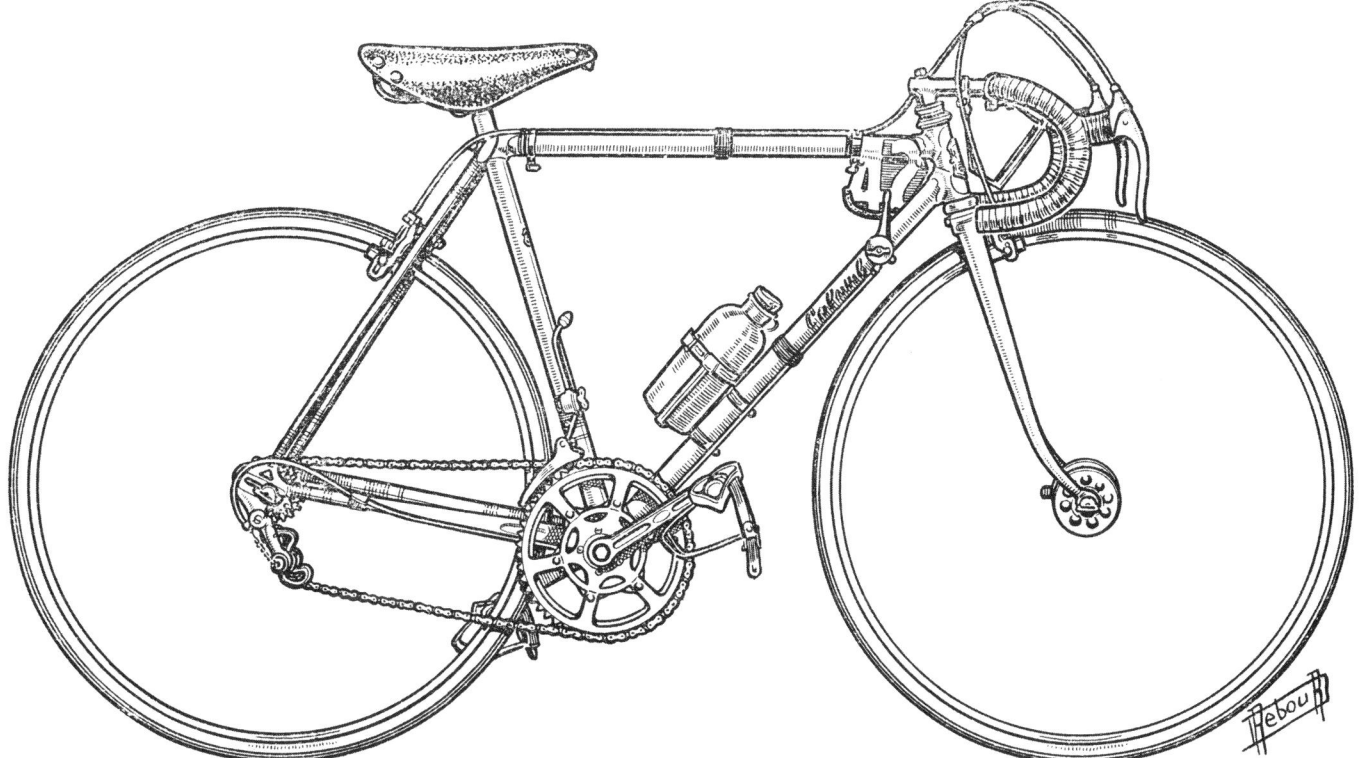

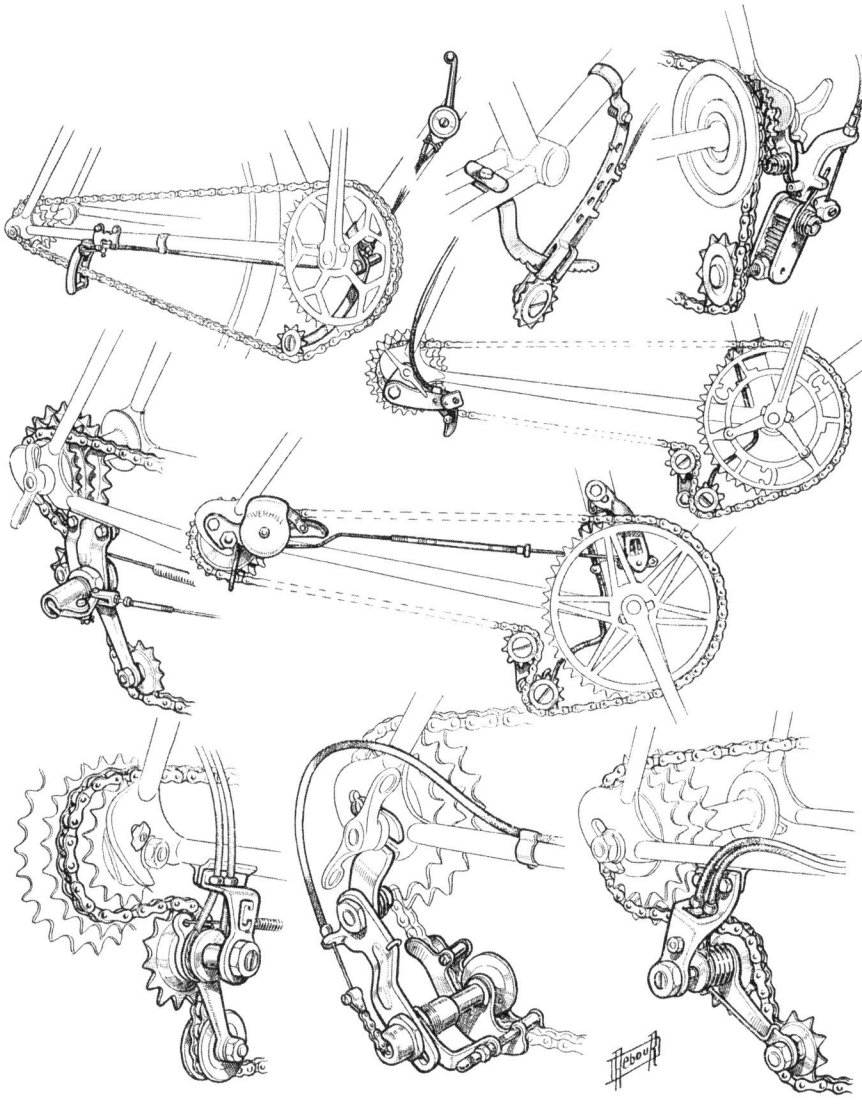

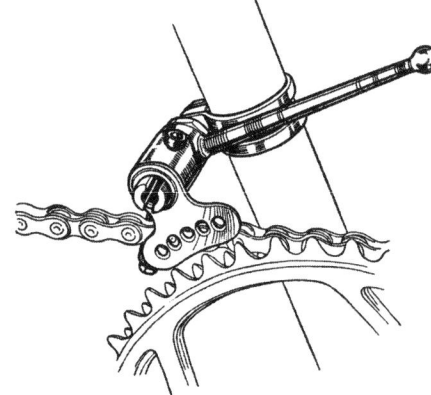

Left: Summary of English derailleurs at the 1948 Earls Court cycle show in London. *Le Cycle*. 4 December 1948.

Above and below: Huret direct-lever-operated front derailleur in positions for inner and outer chainring. *Pratique du Vélo*.

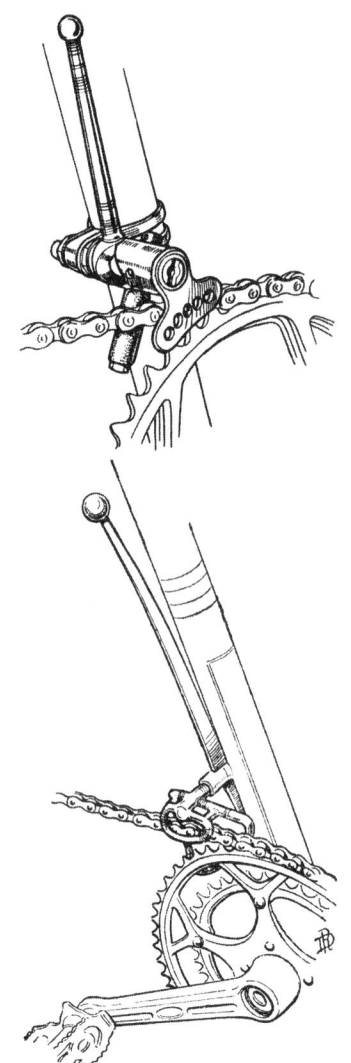

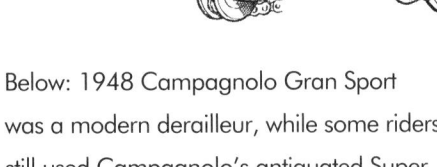

Below: 1948 Campagnolo Gran Sport was a modern derailleur, while some riders still used Campagnolo's antiquated Super Corsa. *Pratique du Vélo*.

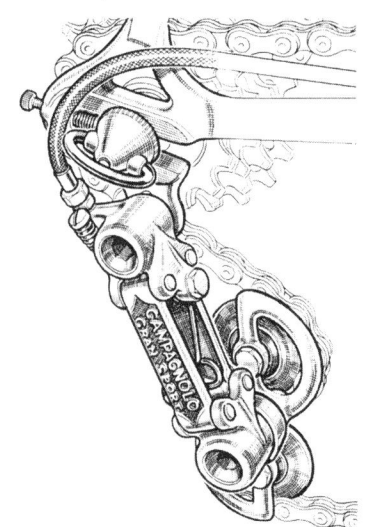

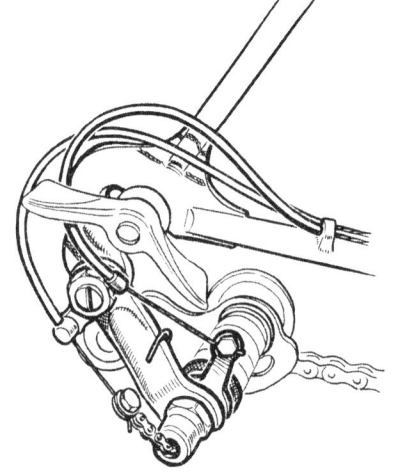

Above: Simplex double-cable derailleur on René Herse bicycle. *Pratique du Vélo*.

Right: Daudon direct-lever-operated front derailleur. *Pratique du Vélo*.

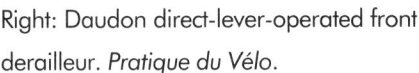

Chapter 3. Derailleur Gearing

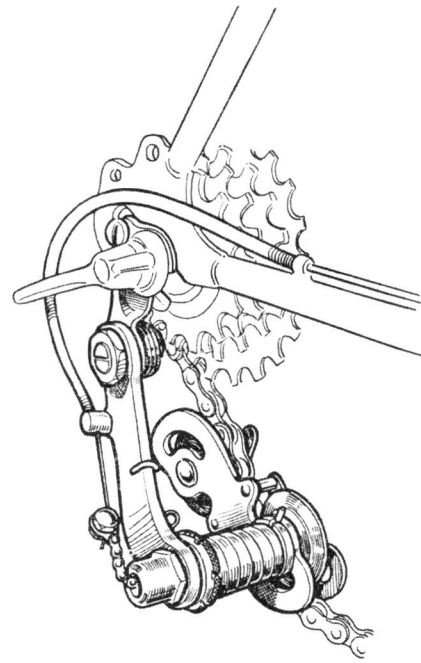

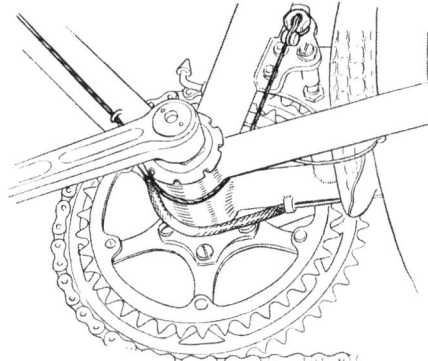

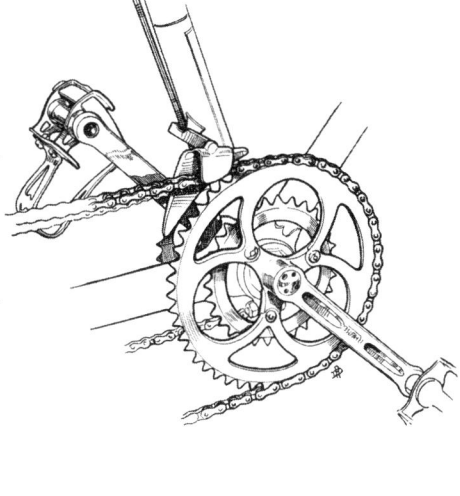

Right: René Herse lever-operated front derailleur. *Le Cycle*, 2 December 1949.

Below: Hervé front derailleur and cable routing detail. *Le Cycle*, 12 February 1949.

Above: 1948 Simplex Professional derailleur. *Pratique du Vélo*.

Below: Fausto Coppi rode this Bianchi bicycle to victory in the 1952 Tour de France, *Le Cycle*, 2 August 1952.**

Left: Exploded view of Cyclo shift lever, showing twin-cable control. *Pratique du Vélo*.

Right: Auto-Moto cable-operation of front derailleur from a seat-tube-mounted lever. *Le Cycle*, 8 January 1949.

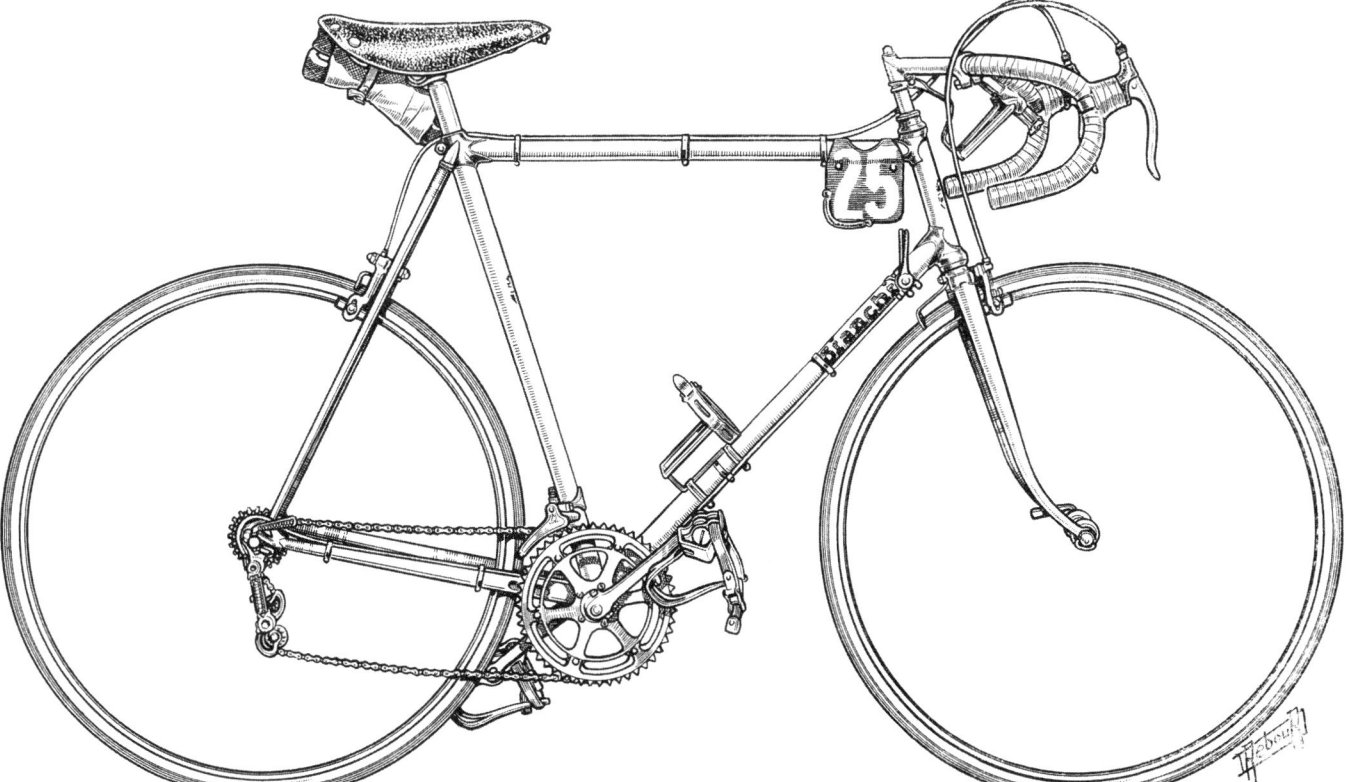

_____
** See pages 269–271 for expanded caption text.

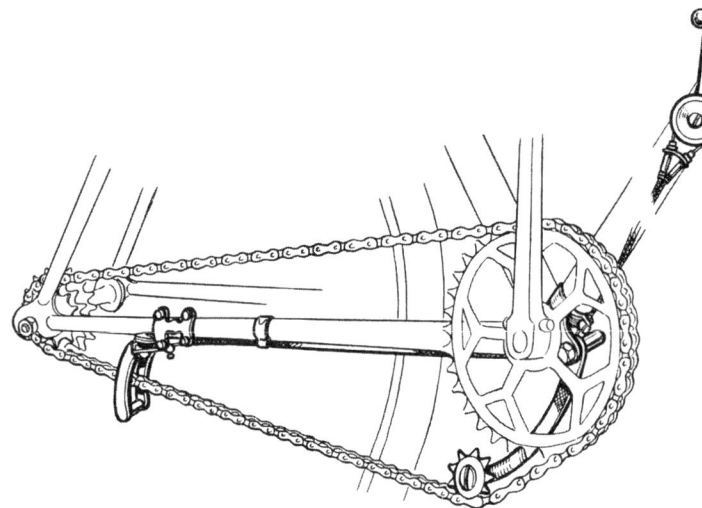

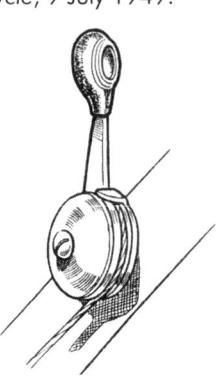

Below: Amadei Comfor downtube shifter. *Le Cycle*, 9 July 1949.

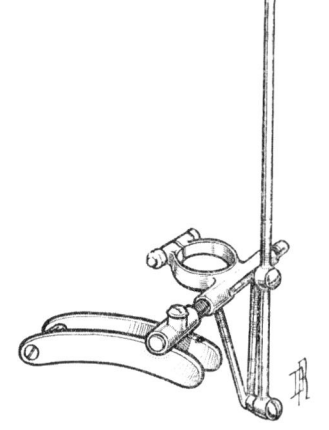

Above: 1948 Super Champion derailleur. At the time, systems like this, with little chain wrap-up and a single pulley were favored by racers because they thought single pulleys had less resistance than dual-pulley systems. *Pratique du Vélo*.

Right: Brisseay rear derailleur, mounted on the chainstay. *Le Cycle*, 23 April 1949.

Below: The Peugeot of 2nd-placed Stan Ockers, of Belgium, in the 1952 Tour de France. *Le Cycle*, 2 August 1952.

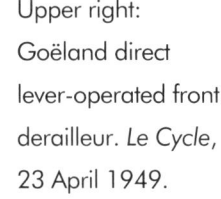

Upper right: Goëland direct lever-operated front derailleur. *Le Cycle*, 23 April 1949.

Right: Direct-lever-operated front derailleur modified to allow operation via a cable from a bar-end shifter. *Le Cycle*, 9 July 1949.

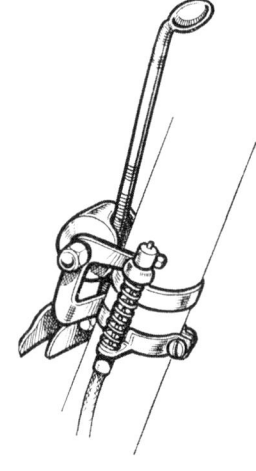

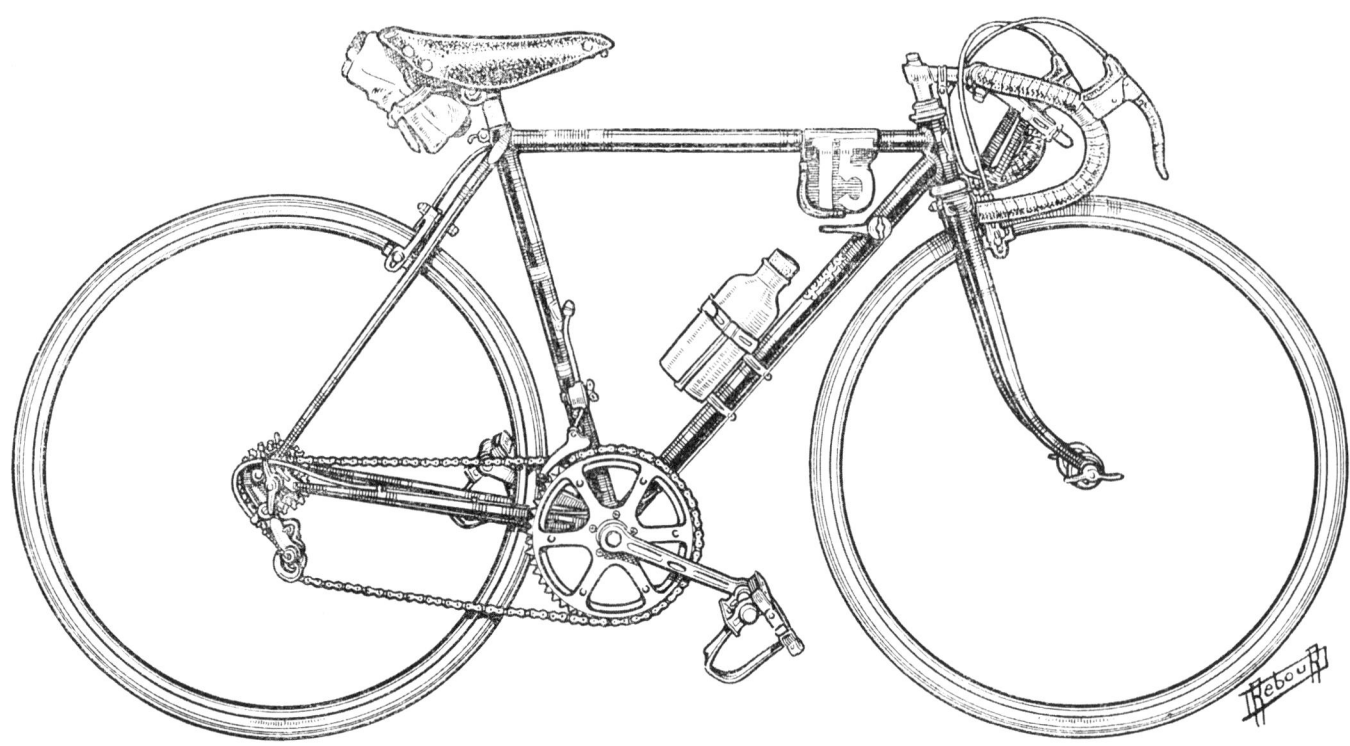

Chapter 3. Derailleur Gearing

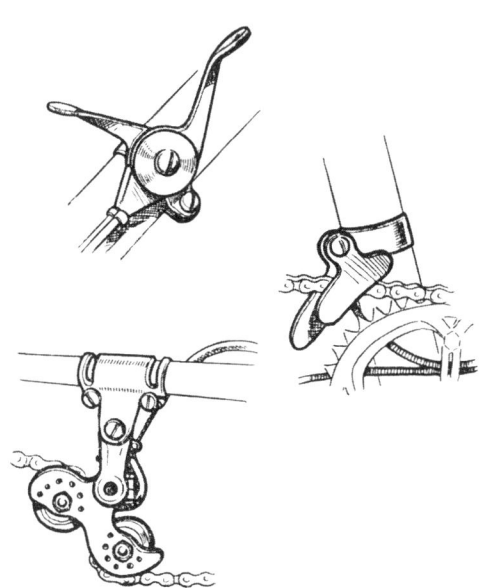

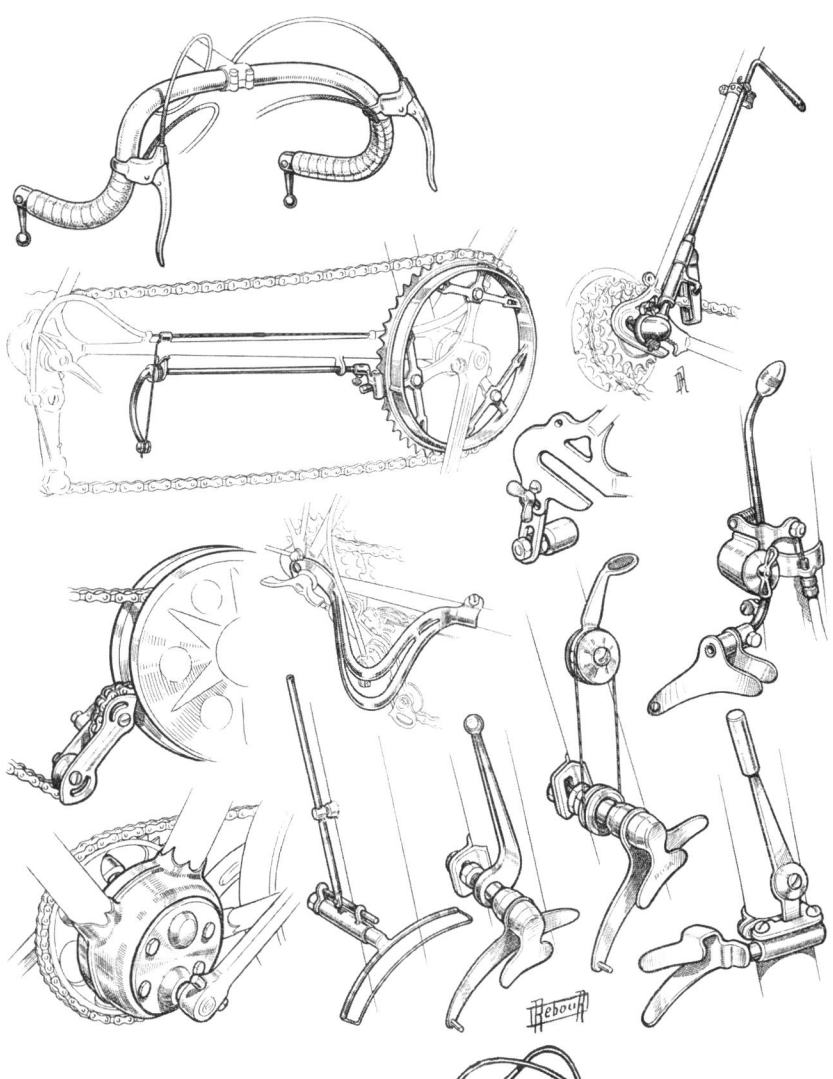

Above: Thomasso Nieddu Italsport derailleurs and shifters. *Le Cycle*, 10 September 1949.

Right: General bicycle gearing overview, including both derailleurs and other gearing options. *Le Cycle*, 26 January 1949.

Below: The La Perle bicycle of Bernardo Ruiz, of Spain, who placed 3rd in the 1952 Tour de France. *Le Cycle*, 2 August 1952.

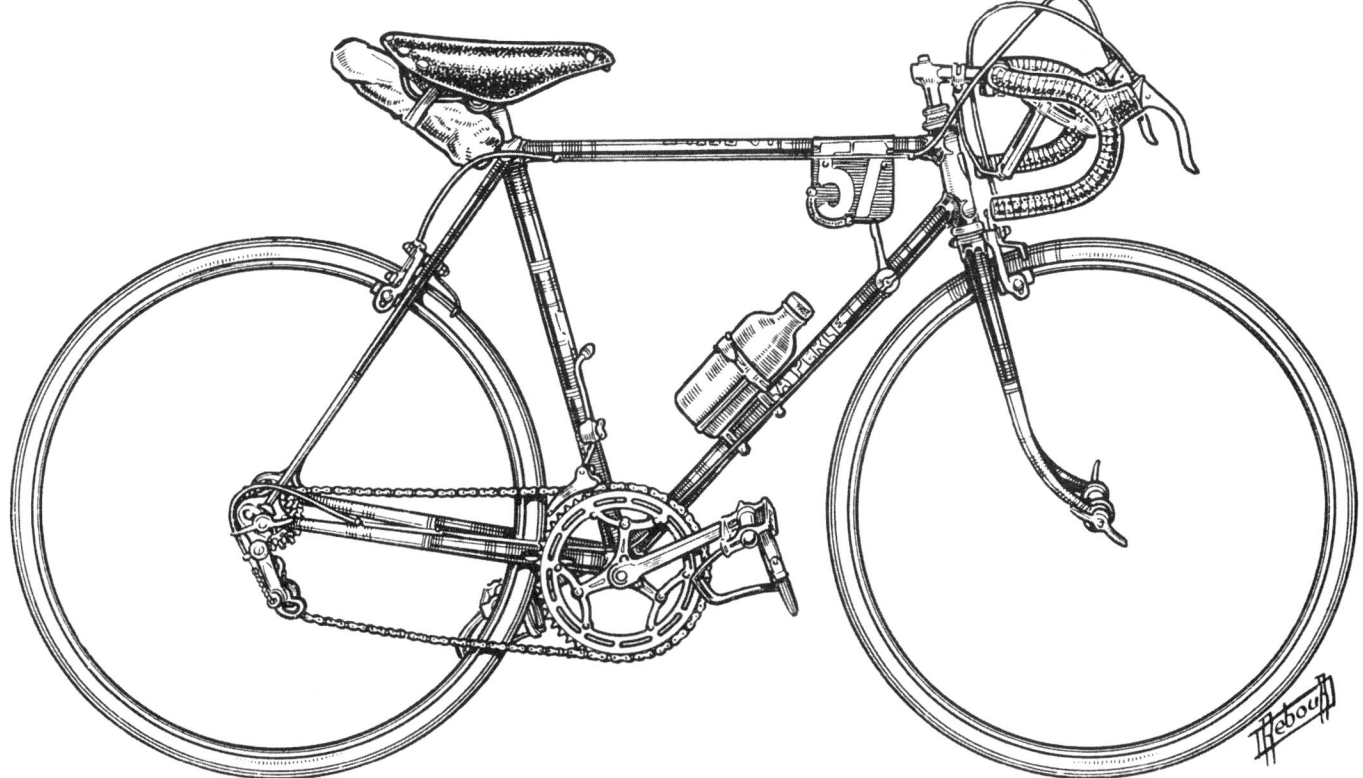

Right: English Cyclo Benelux rear derailleur. *Le Cycle,* October 1949, special issue.

Far right: Modified Cyclo derailleur and split hub. *Le Cycle*, 12 August 1950.

Below: English Hercules Herailleur rear derailleur. *Le Cycle*, 9 July 1949.

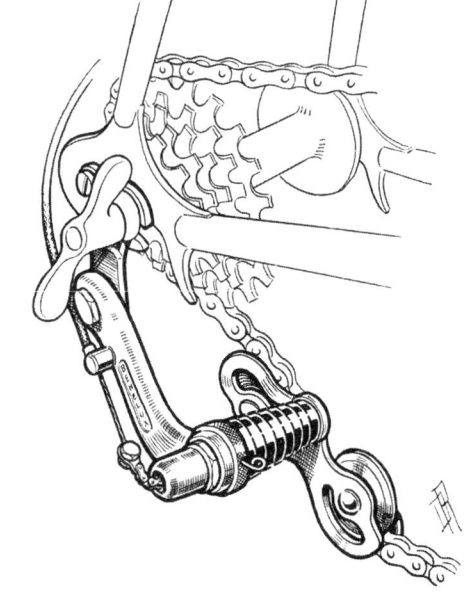

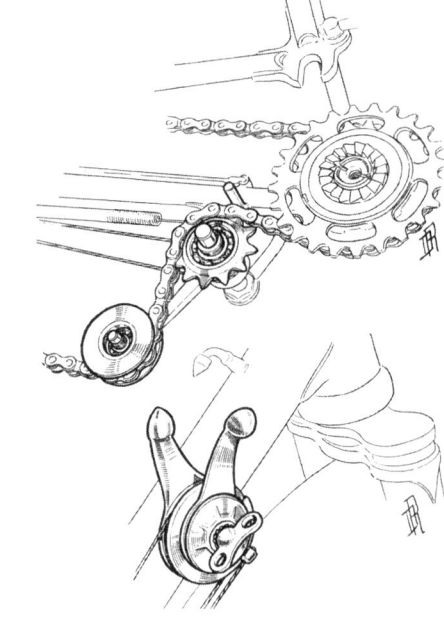

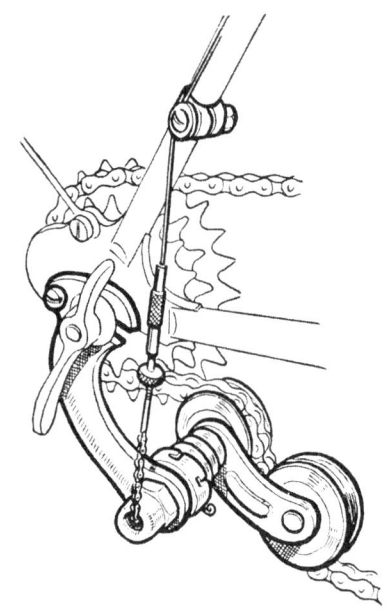

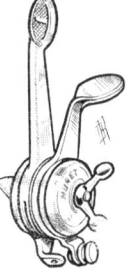

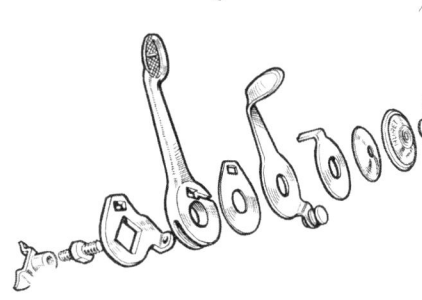

Left: Huret derailleur control shifter with chain tension control, as installed and exploded view. *Le Cycle*, 23 October 1949.

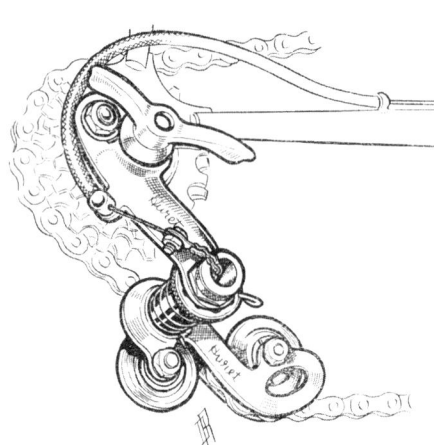

Left and right: 1950 versions of Huret rear and front derailleurs.

Below left: Simplex details, including front derailleur with integrated chainguard, quick-release, and twist-grip derailleur control. **

Bottom right: Cyclo rear derailleur.

All three images from *Le Cycle*, 23 October 1949.

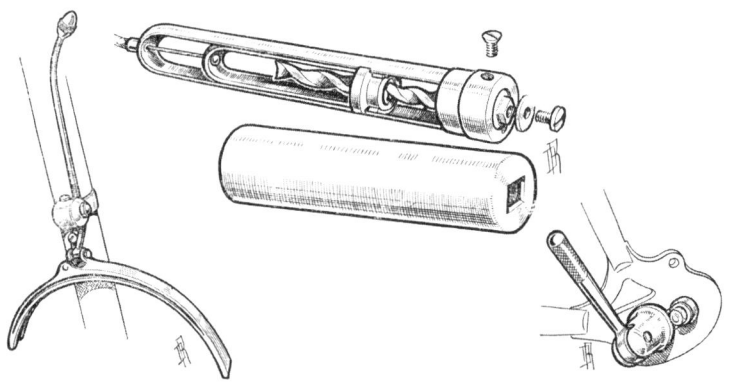

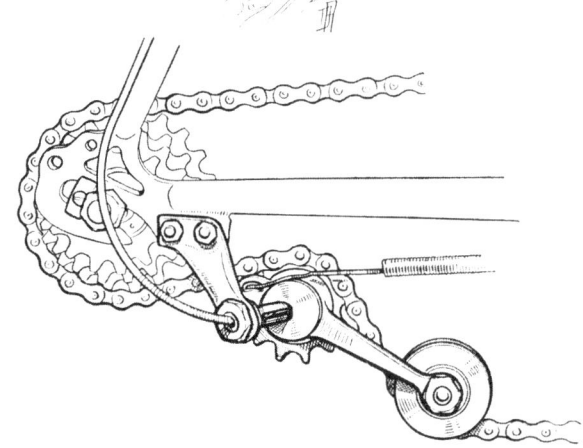

** See pages 269–271 for expanded caption text.

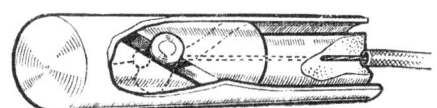
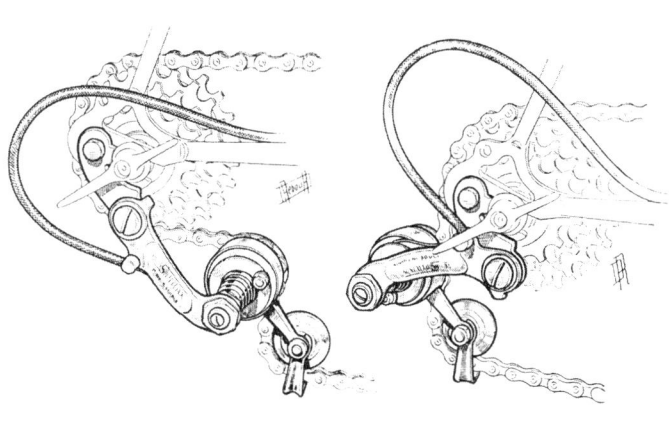
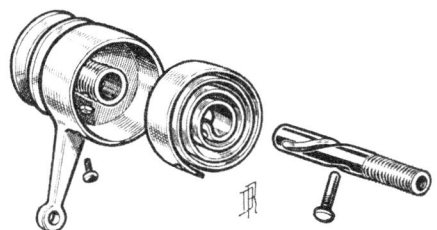

Upper left: Rotating twist-grip derailleur control. *Le Cycle*, 23 October 1949.**

Lower left and right: Another rotary shifter mechanism and Spirax rear derailleur in low and retracted positions. *Le Cycle*, 25 March 1950.**

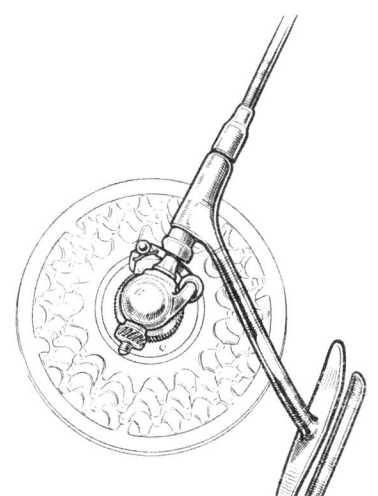

Left: Even for the 1950 model year, Campagnolo still offered the cumbersome Super Corsa, which required moving the rear wheel to shift gears, as well as its modern Gran Sport 2-pulley derailleur (see page 48).

Right: Huret Randonneur rear derailleur, mounted to brazed-on chainstay brackets. *Le Cycle*, 23 October 1950.

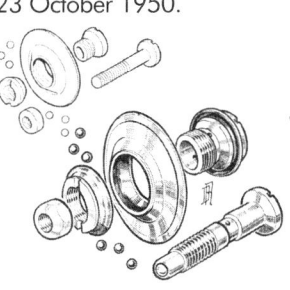

Below: Exploded view of Volo ball-bearing derailleur pulley. *Le Cycle*, 23 October 1950.

Right: 1952 DeLange carrier bike, with reinforced frame and a frame-supported front rack and basket, used by delivery men for items such as bread in much of France at the time. *Le Cycle*, 18 October 1952.

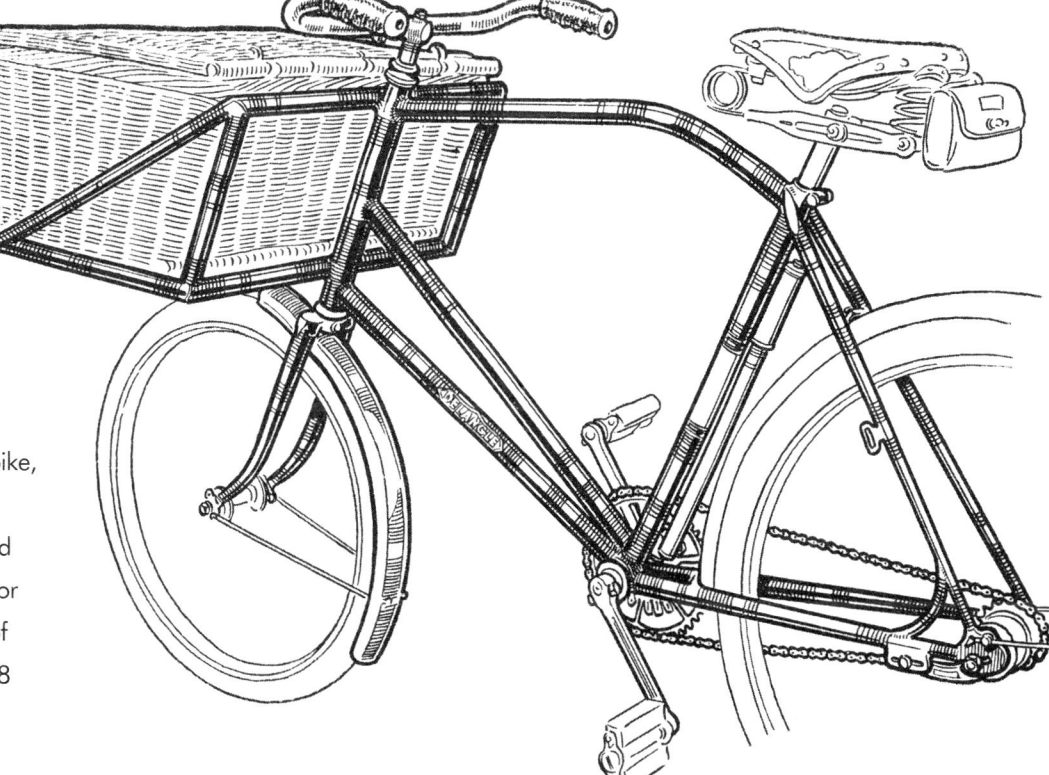

** See pages 269–271 for expanded caption texts.

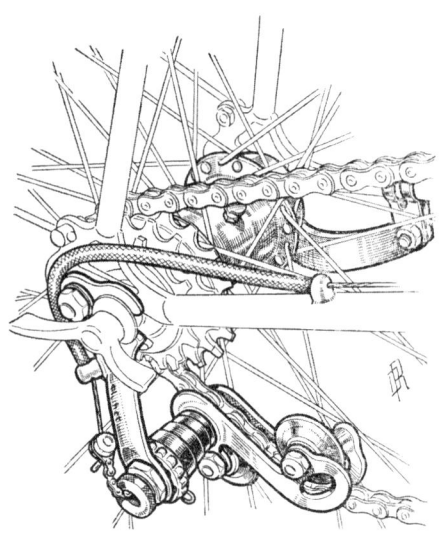

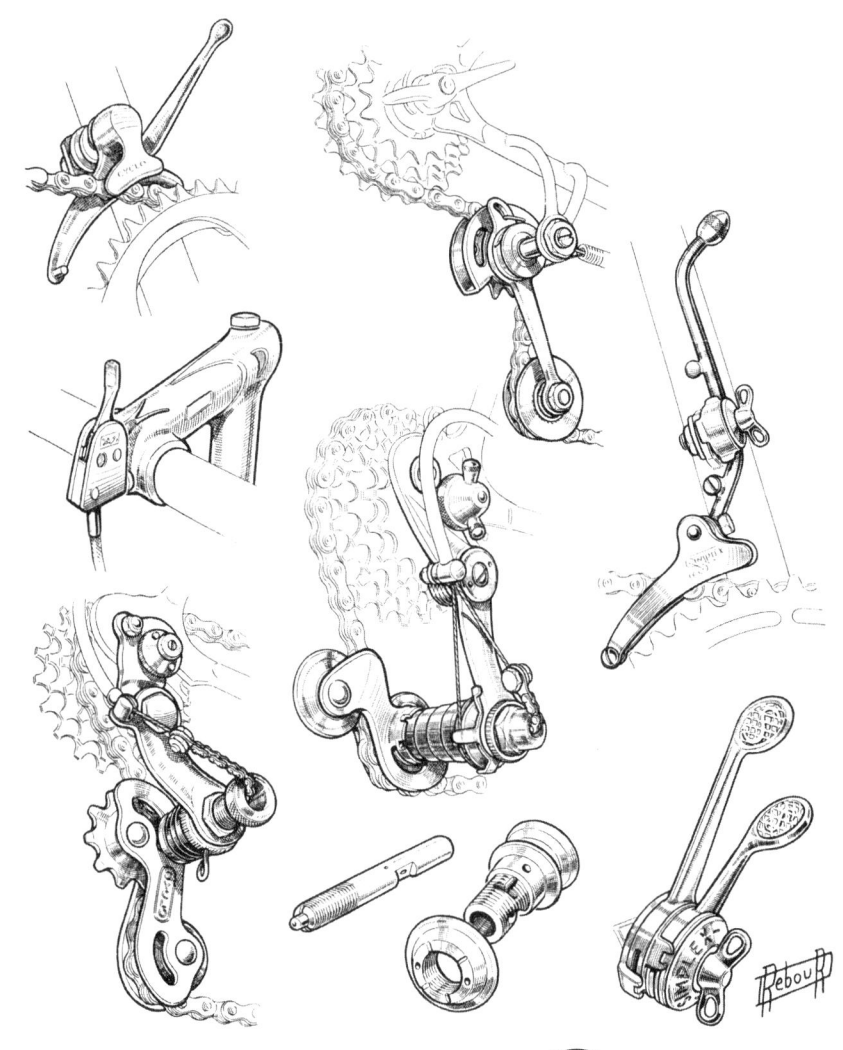

Above: Cyclo rear derailleur version for use with coaster brakes for the German market. *Le Cycle*, 23 October 1950.

Right: Overview of derailleurs and their controls at the 1950 Paris bicycle trade show. *Le Cycle*, 11 November 1950.

Below: The bike of Jean Ducheron, winner of the 1952 Tour de France mountains classification. *Le Cycle*, 8 August 1953.

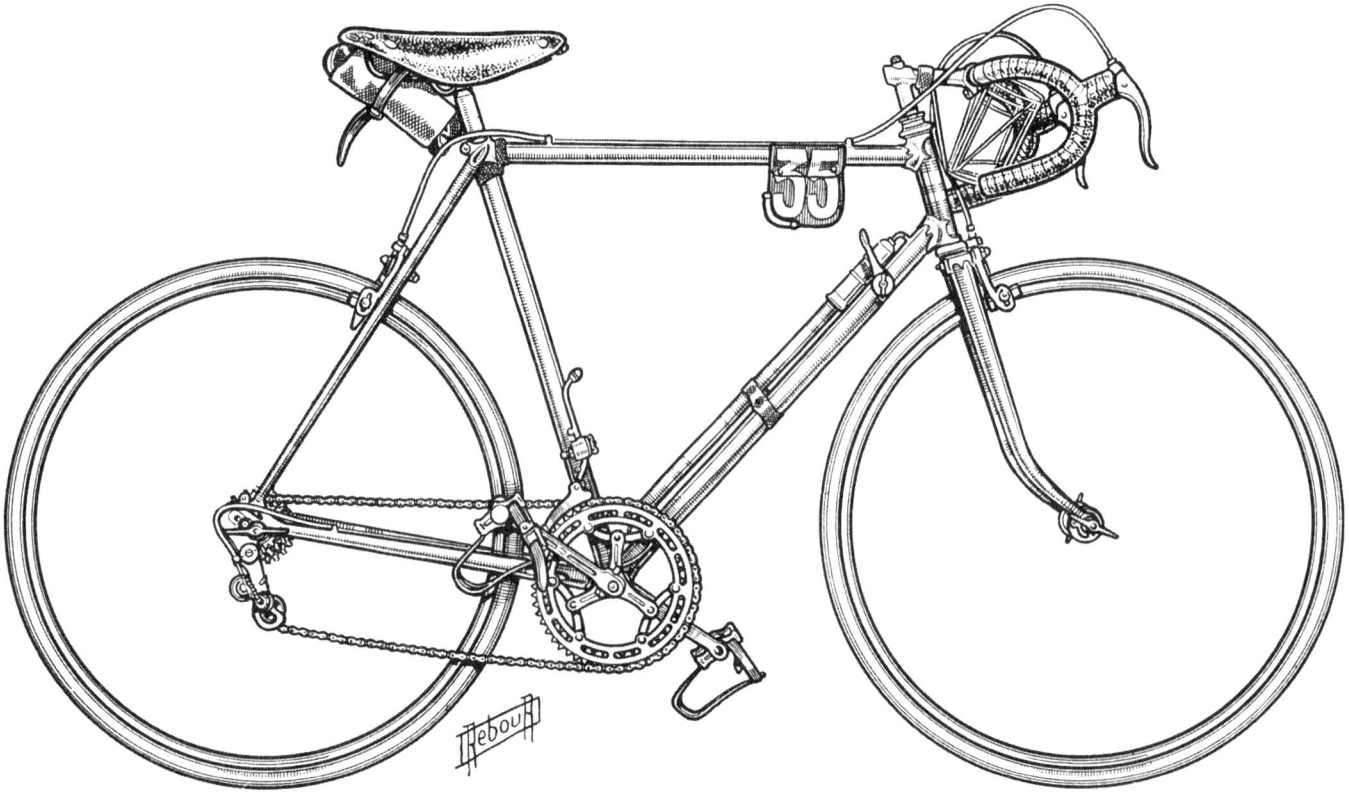

Chapter 3. Derailleur Gearing

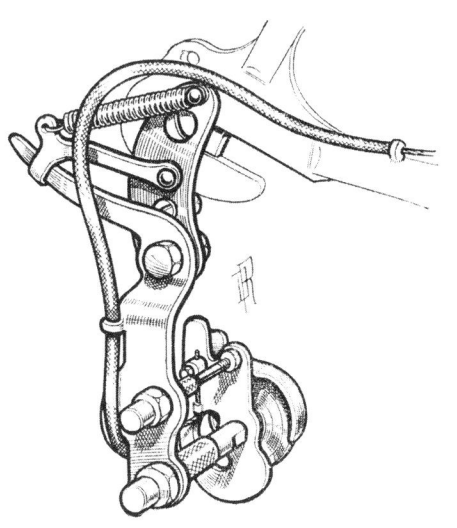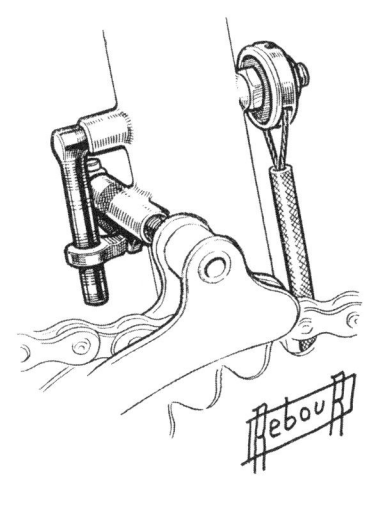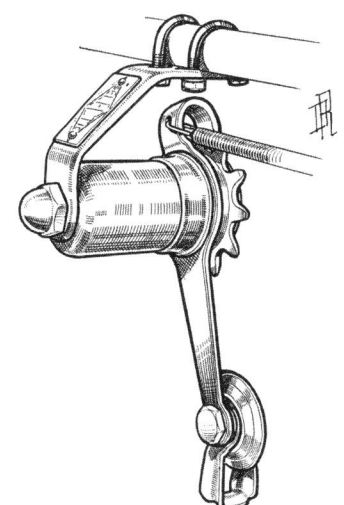

Above left: Super Leader rear derailleur. *Le Cycle*, 30 October 1951.

Above center: Liberia cable-operated front derailleur. *Le Cycle*, 22 September 1951.

Above right: Selectic 2-speed backpedal-operated derailleur. *Le Cycle*, 5 May 1951.

Right: Transalpino rear derailleur with clamp-on chainstay mounting. *Le Cycle*, 10 February 1951.

Below: The Stella bicycle of 1953 Tour winner Louison Bobet. *Le Cycle*, 8 August 1953.**

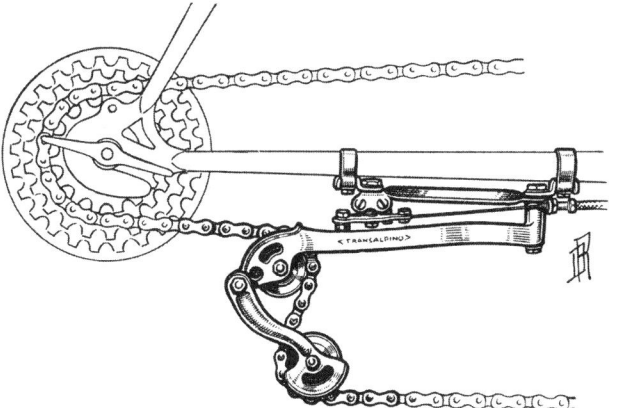

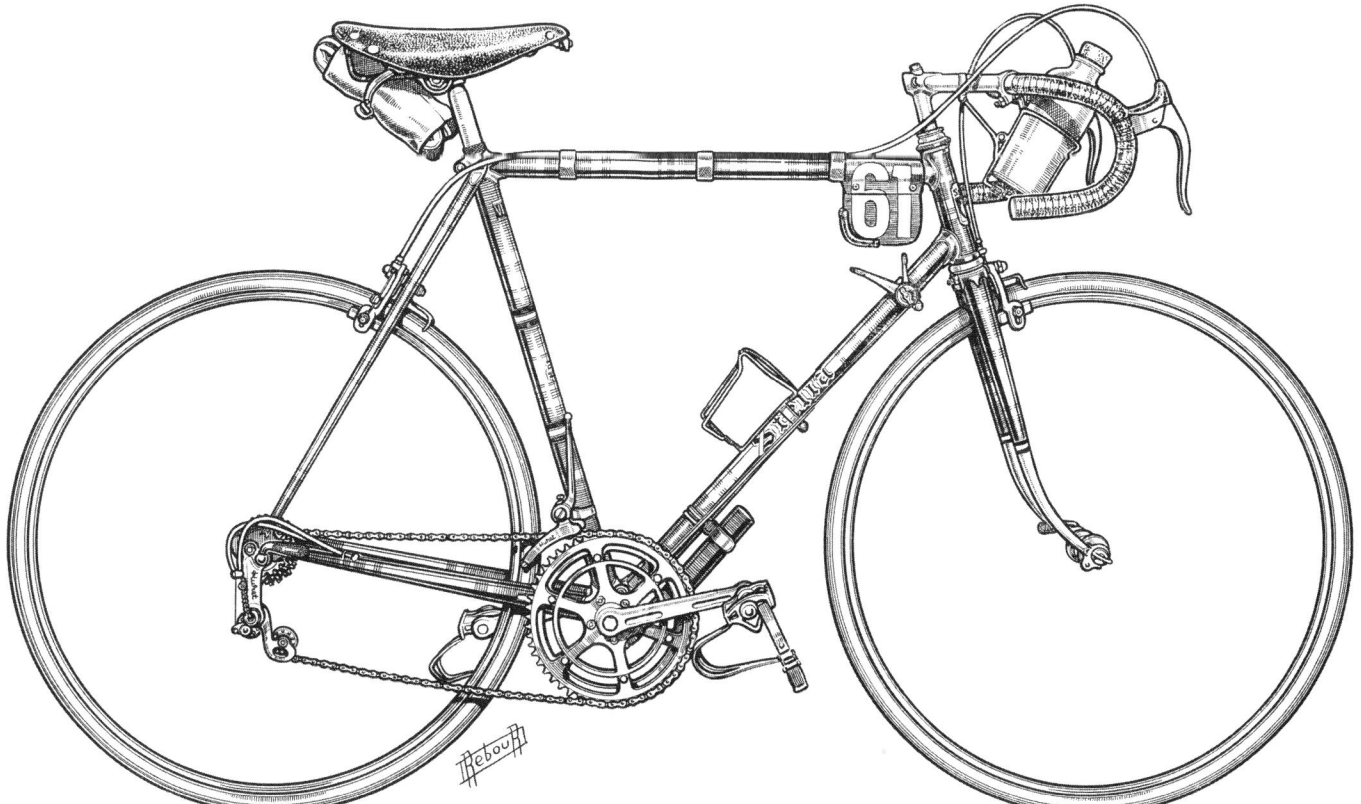

** See pages 269–271 for expanded caption texts.

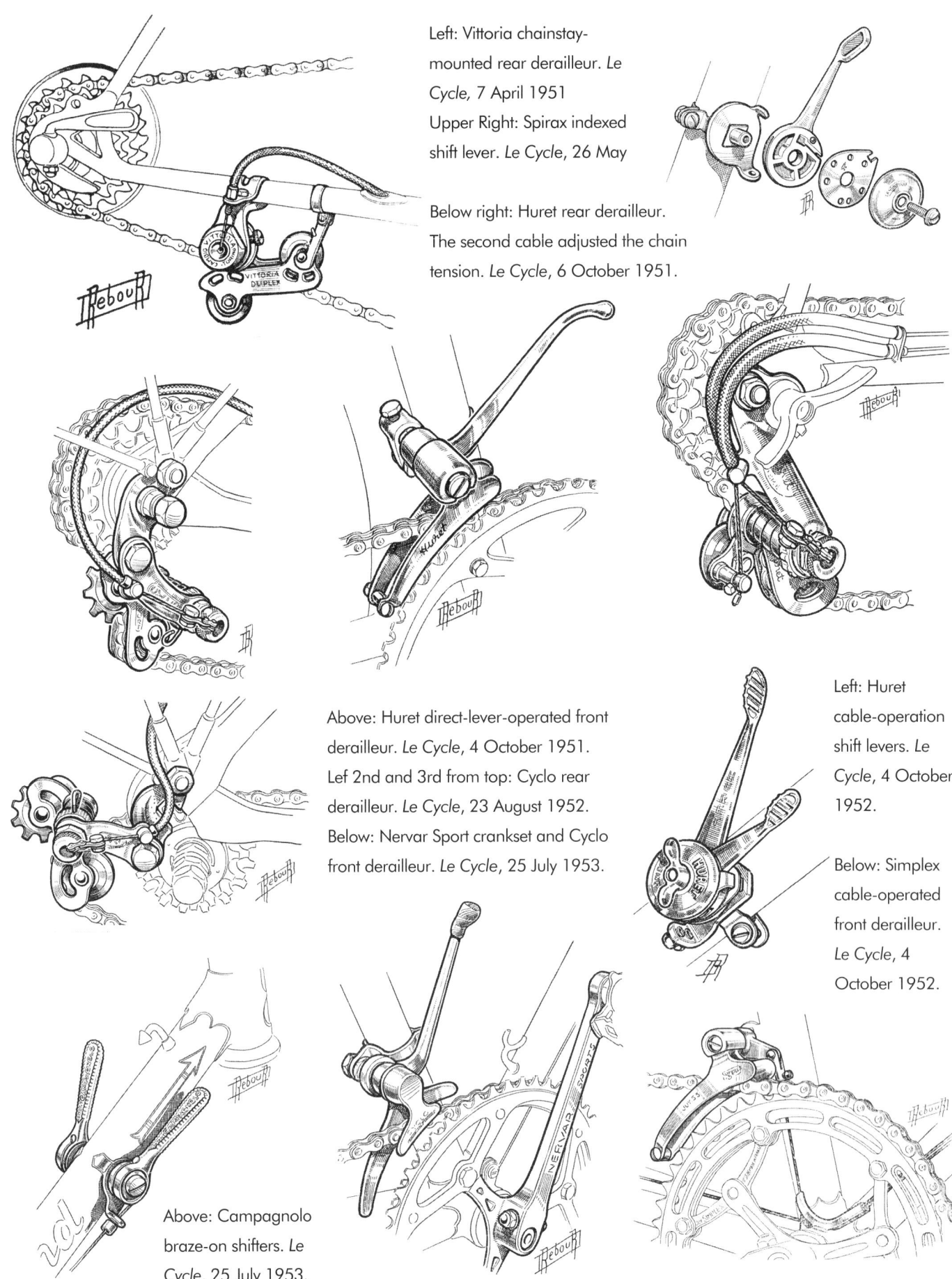

Left: Vittoria chainstay-mounted rear derailleur. *Le Cycle*, 7 April 1951

Upper Right: Spirax indexed shift lever. *Le Cycle*, 26 May

Below right: Huret rear derailleur. The second cable adjusted the chain tension. *Le Cycle*, 6 October 1951.

Above: Huret direct-lever-operated front derailleur. *Le Cycle*, 4 October 1951.
Lef 2nd and 3rd from top: Cyclo rear derailleur. *Le Cycle*, 23 August 1952.
Below: Nervar Sport crankset and Cyclo front derailleur. *Le Cycle*, 25 July 1953.

Left: Huret cable-operation shift levers. *Le Cycle*, 4 October 1952.

Below: Simplex cable-operated front derailleur. *Le Cycle*, 4 October 1952.

Above: Campagnolo braze-on shifters. *Le Cycle*, 25 July 1953.

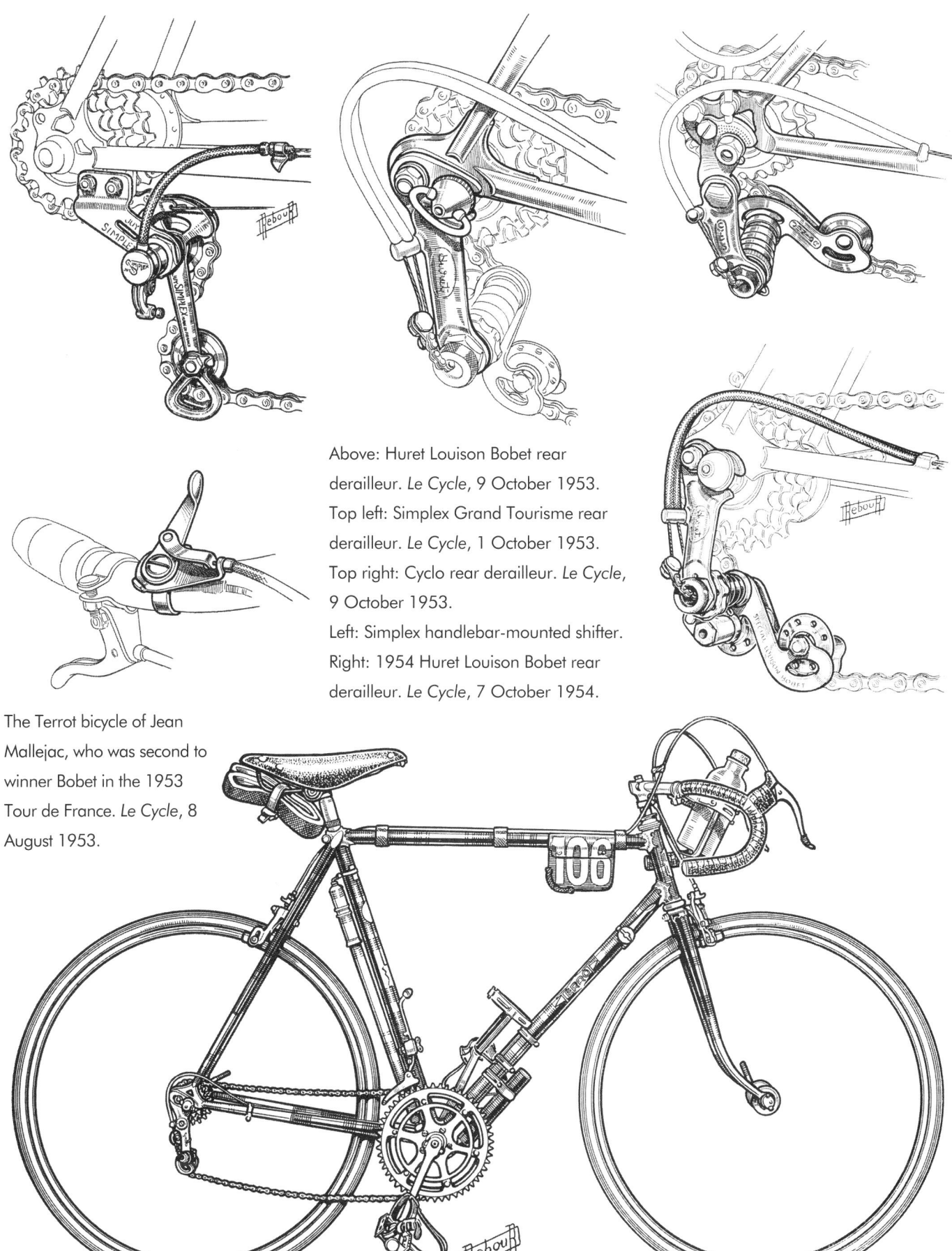

Above: Huret Louison Bobet rear derailleur. *Le Cycle*, 9 October 1953.
Top left: Simplex Grand Tourisme rear derailleur. *Le Cycle*, 1 October 1953.
Top right: Cyclo rear derailleur. *Le Cycle*, 9 October 1953.
Left: Simplex handlebar-mounted shifter.
Right: 1954 Huret Louison Bobet rear derailleur. *Le Cycle*, 7 October 1954.

The Terrot bicycle of Jean Mallejac, who was second to winner Bobet in the 1953 Tour de France. *Le Cycle*, 8 August 1953.

The "Poly de Chanteloup"

Held annually throughout the 1940s until the 1960s, these were technical trials held to evaluate the various derailleur designs and other technical improvements that were being developed at the time of intense technical development in France. The photo on the facing page 59 gives some idea of the remarkably strong public interest in these events.

Right: Overview of prominent derailleur systems used at the 1954 Poly de Chanteloup technical trials. *Le Cycle*, 15 May 1954.

Below: Atala bicycle of 3rd placed rider Giancarlo Astrua, of Italy, in the 1953 Tour de France. *Le Cycle*, 8 August 1953.

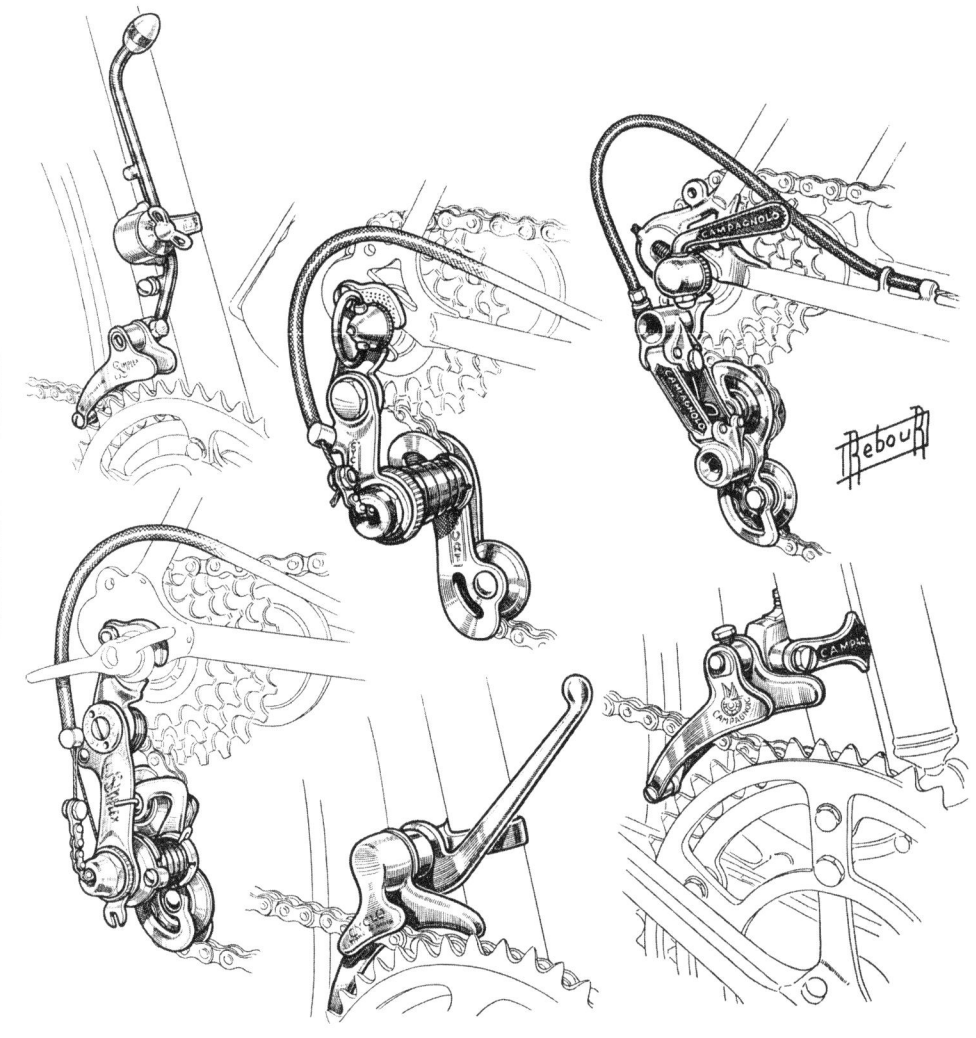

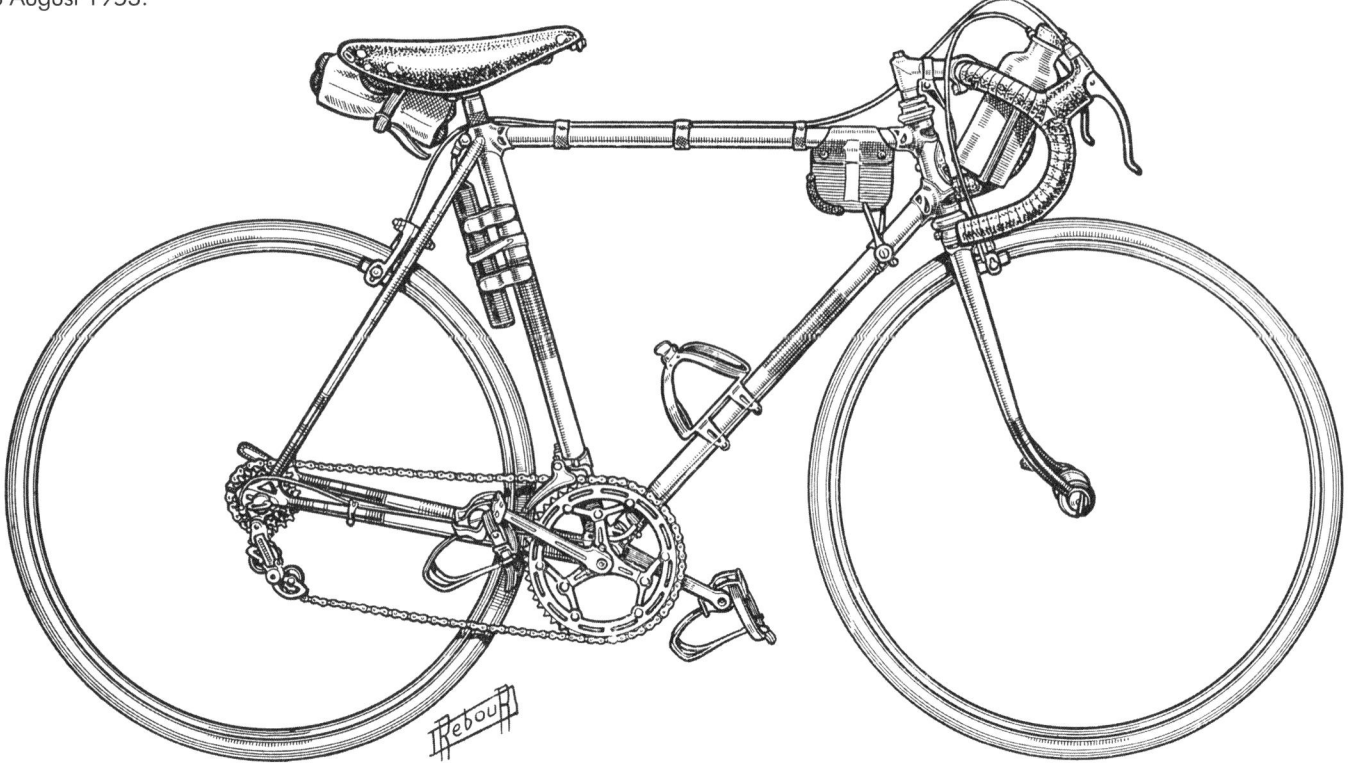

Chapter 3. Derailleur Gearing

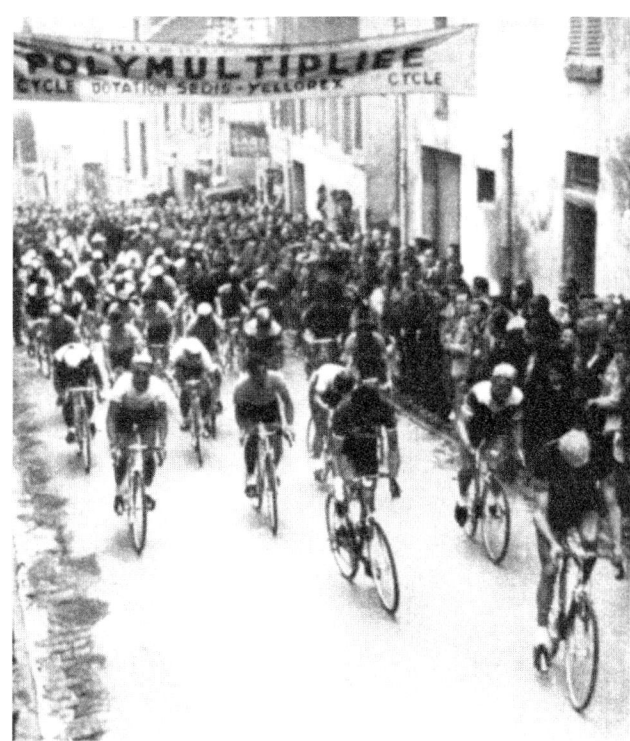

Above: Start of the 1953 "Poly" (short for Polymultipliée) de Chanteloup technical hill-climbing trials. See explanation on facing page 58.

Below: Mondia bicycle of Fritz Schaer, of Switzerland, winner of the points classification of the 1953 Tour de France. *Le Cycle*, 8 August 1953.

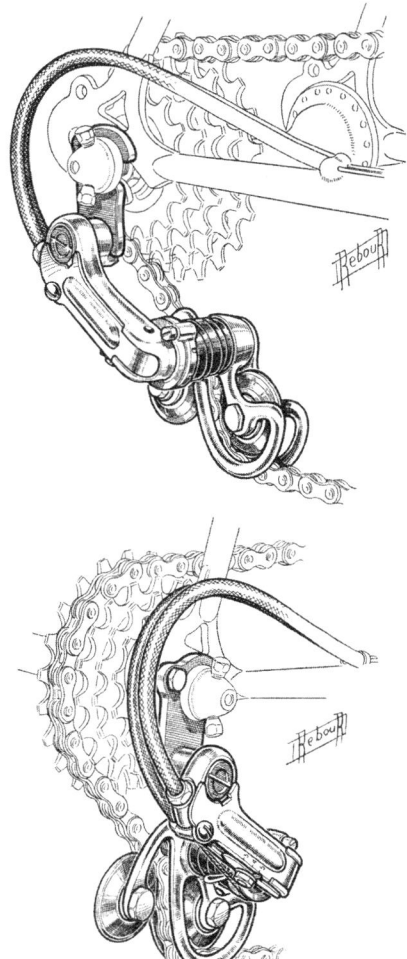

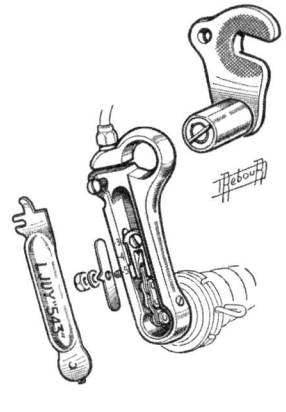

Left and above: Simplex Juy 543 derailleur, which derived its name from its adaptability to either 3-, 4- or 5-speed freewheels, shown here in the position for the highest gear (smallest cog) and a low gear (larger cog), and the internal mechanism (above). This has become a very collectible item. *Le Cycle*, 16 October 1954.

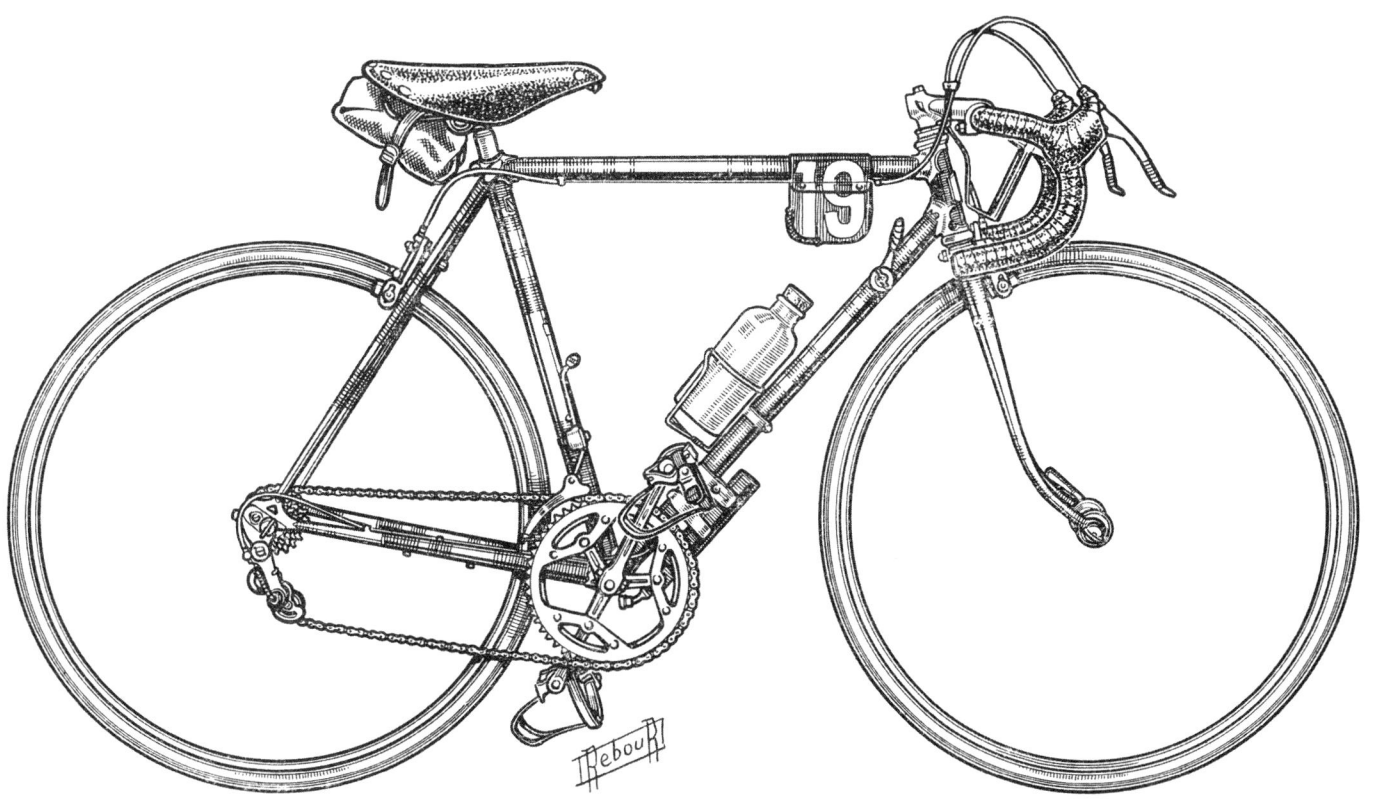

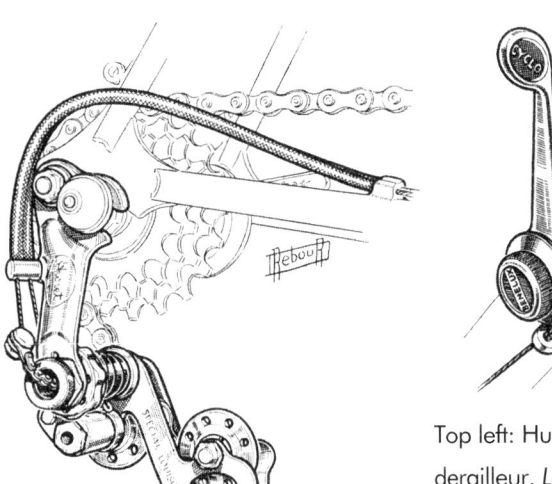
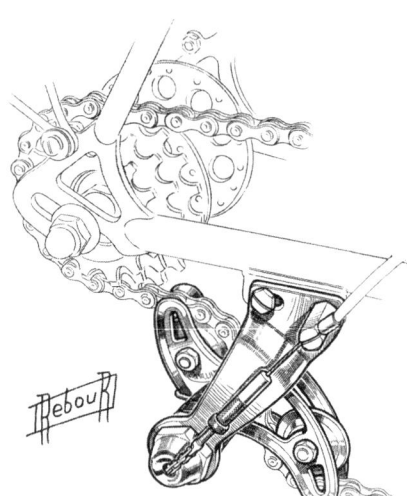

Left: English Cyclo Benelux downtube shifter.
Right: Phillips chainstay-mounted rear derailleur. Both images from London bicycle trade show article in *Le Cycle*, 27 November 1954.

Top left: Huret rear derailleur. *Le Cycle*, 7 October 1954.

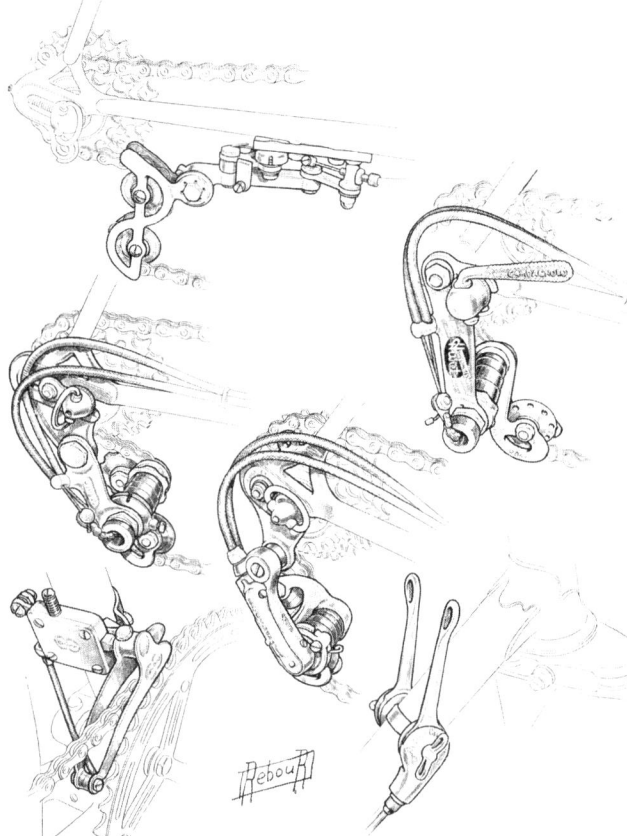

Above: 1956 Tour de France derailleur components, as recorded before the start of the race. *Le Cycle*, 23 July 1956.

Right: English Rigidex rear derailleur, with protective guard. *Le Cycle*, 8 February 1958.

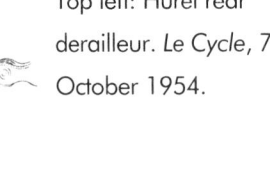

Above: After the 1956 Tour de France, Rebour did another overview of derailleurs. *Le Cycle*, 11 August 1956.

Chapter 3. Derailleur Gearing

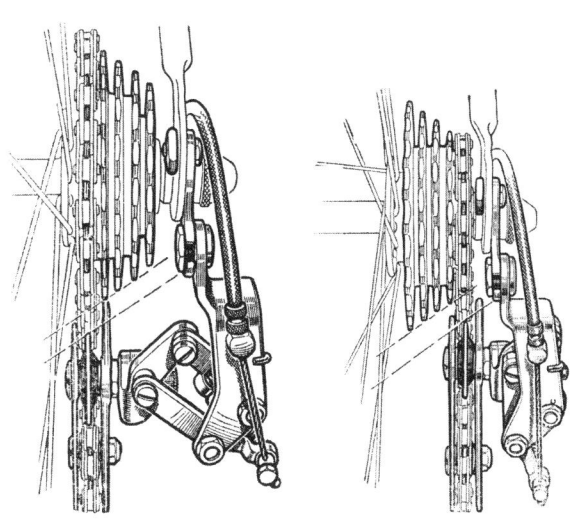

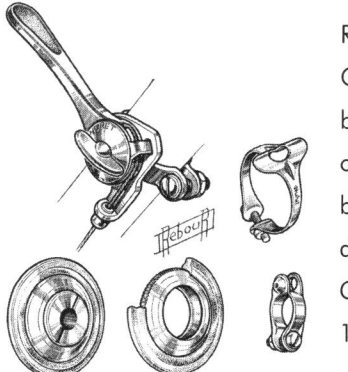

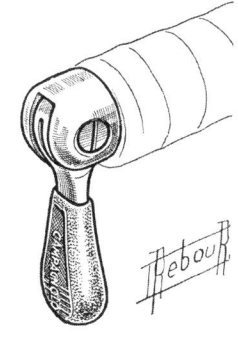

Right: Campagnolo bar-end shifter on a 1959 Atala bike at the Tour de France. *Le Cycle*, 22 July 1959.

Above: Huret shifter and other details. *Le Cycle*, 21 February 1959.

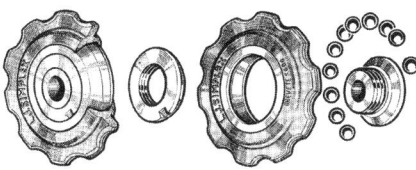

Above: Shifting pattern of the Huret Allvit rear derailleur, showing how the chain gap remains constant. *Le Cycle*, 7 February 1959.

Right: Fichtel & Sachs derailleur used by the 1959 German Tour de France team. *Le Cycle*, 22 July 1959.

Below: This 1953 Riva Sport roadster was France's most successful export bicycle at the time (though not to the U.S.). *Le Cycle*, 9 October 1953.

Above: Simplex ball-bearing derailleur pulley. *Le Cycle*, 10 October 1969.

Below: Magura twist-grip shifter, actually designed for moped use. *Le Cycle*, April 1960.

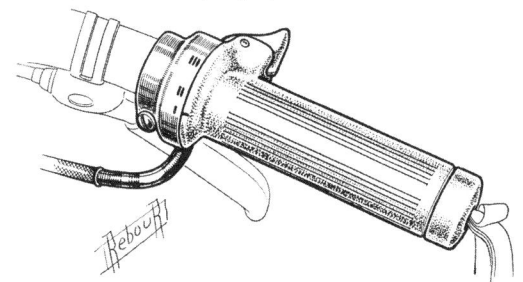

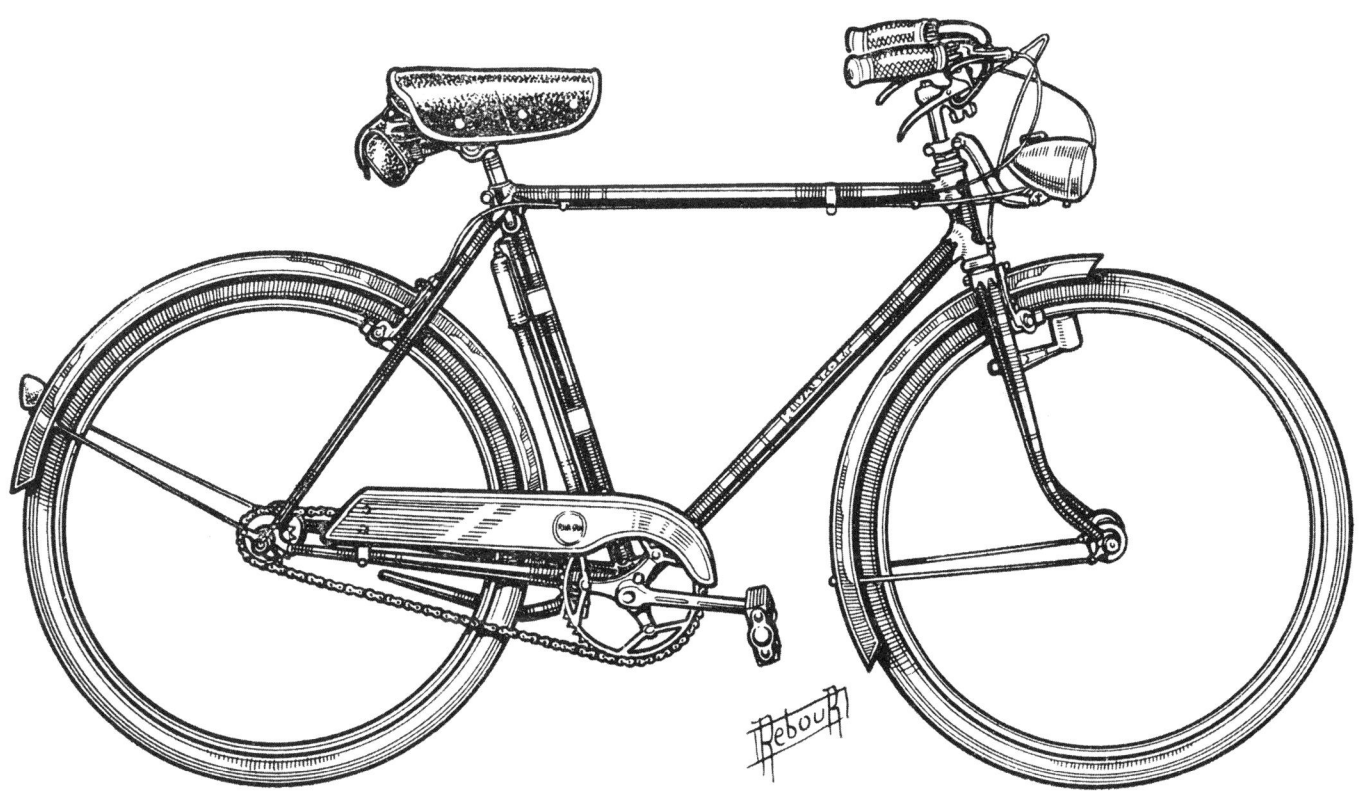

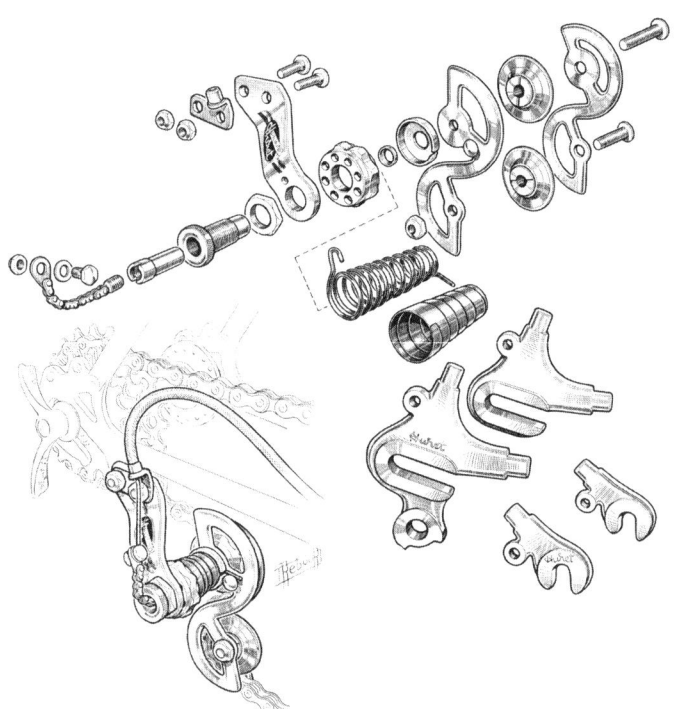

Above: Huret chainstay-mounted derailleur. Exploded view and other details. *Le Cycle*, September 1960.

Upper right: Huret front derailleur and exploded view of Huret Allvit derailleur. *Le Cycle*, October 1961.

Below: Simplex overview, showing front and rear derailleurs, shifters, and other details. *Le Cycle*, October 1961.

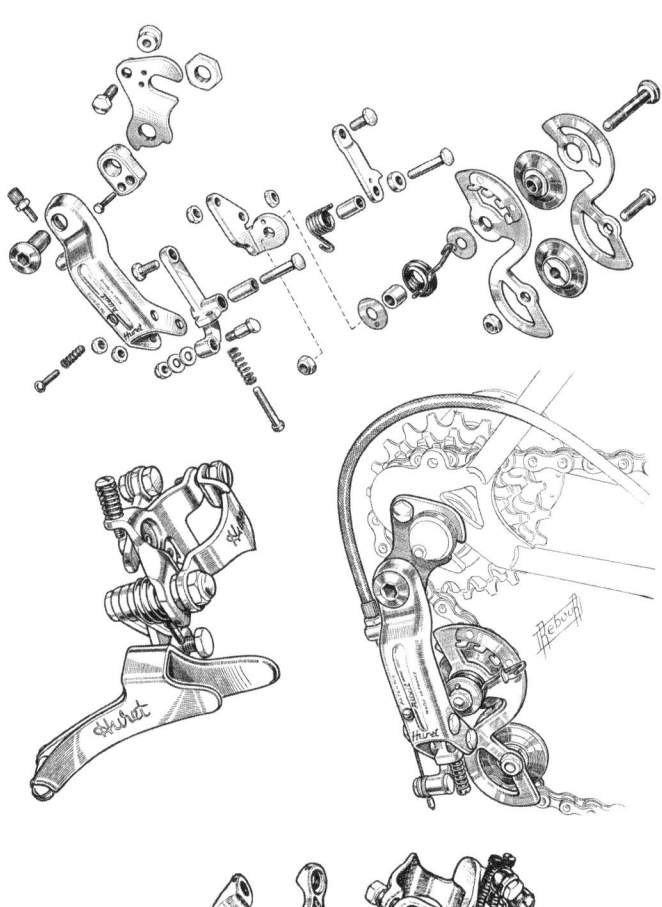

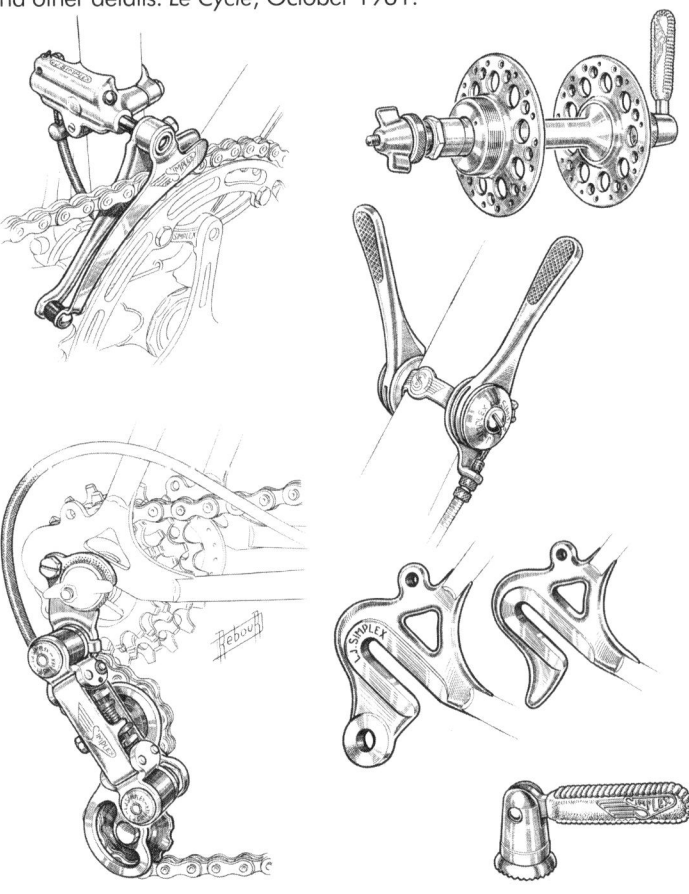

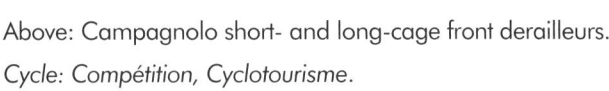

Above: Campagnolo short- and long-cage front derailleurs. *Cycle: Compétition, Cyclotourisme*.

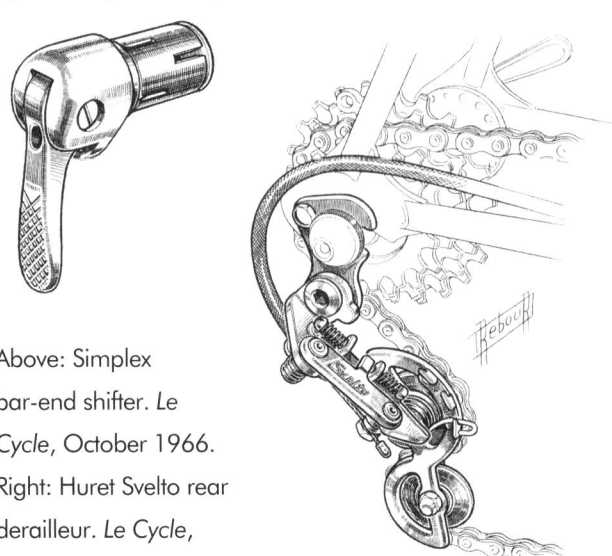

Above: Simplex bar-end shifter. *Le Cycle*, October 1966.
Right: Huret Svelto rear derailleur. *Le Cycle*, March 1963.

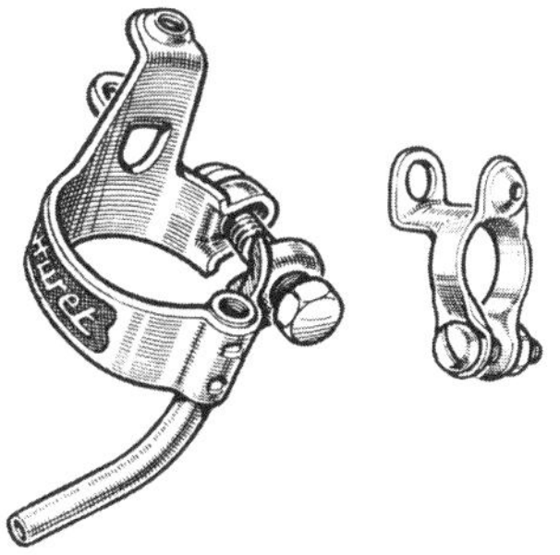

Left: Huret derailleur cable guides. *Le Cycle*, May 1967.

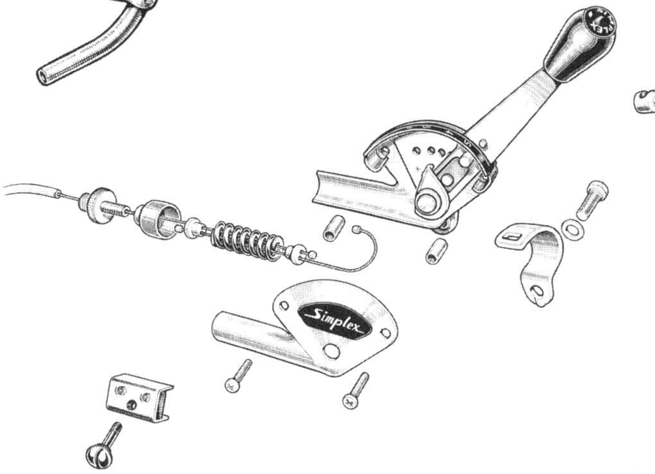

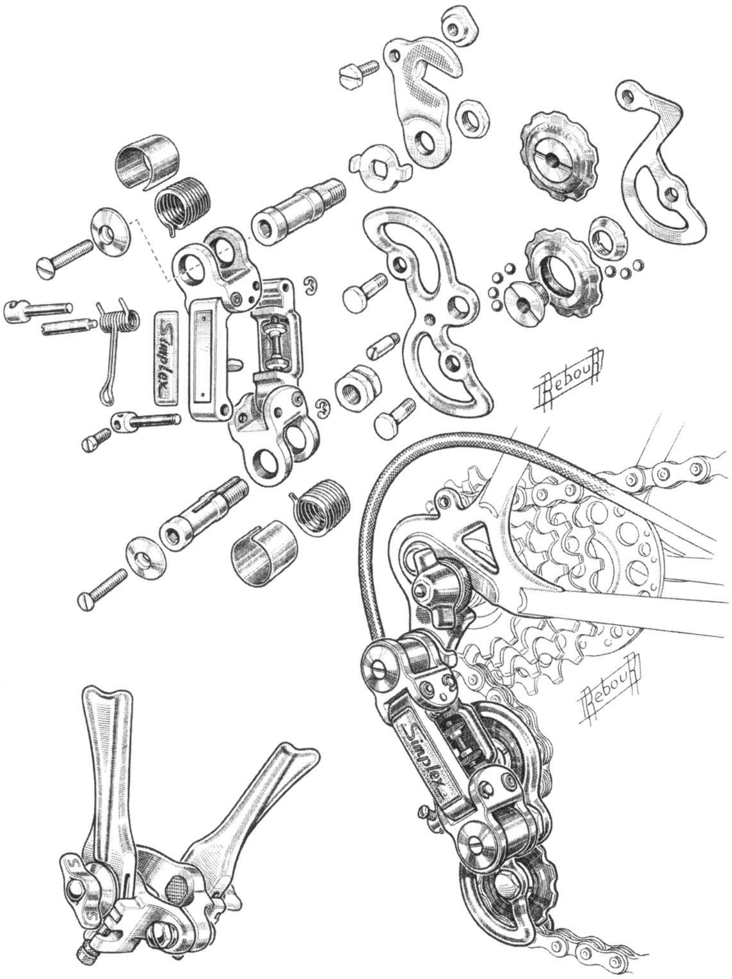

Above: Exploded view of Simplex indexed stick-shift. *Le Cycle*, December 1968.

Right: Exploded view of Simplex Prestige derailleur and Delrin plastic downtube shifters. *Le Cycle*, October 1963.

Below: This Sauvage Atomic single-speed roadster was the cheapest bike displayed at the September 1953 Paris bicycle trade show. *Le Cycle*, 9 October 1953.

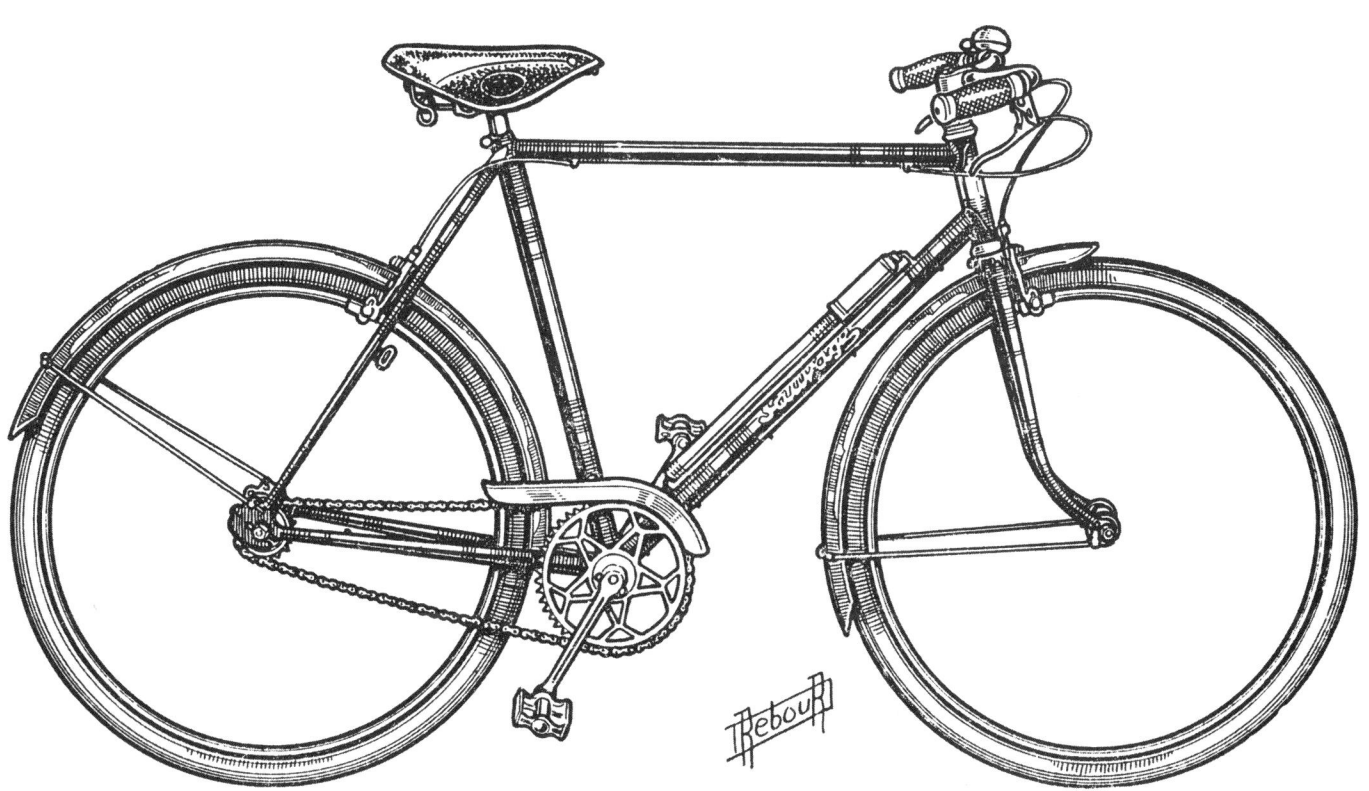

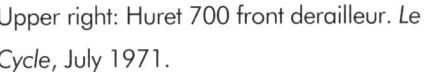

Upper right: Huret 700 front derailleur. *Le Cycle*, July 1971.

Lower right: Huret Jubilee rear derailleur. *Le Cycle*, July 1972.

Below: The Campagnolo Gran Turismo long-cage rear derailleur was too heavy and hard to shift, and never became a success. *Le Cycle*, January 1971.

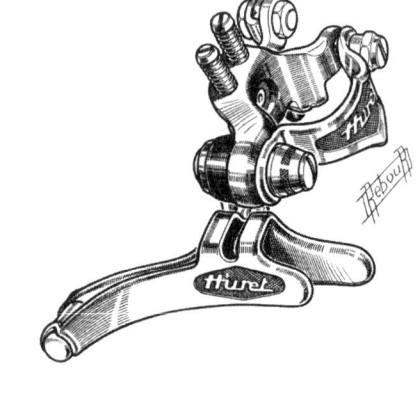

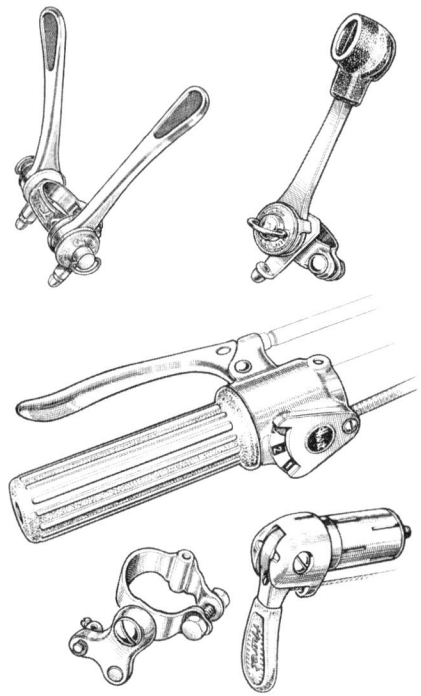

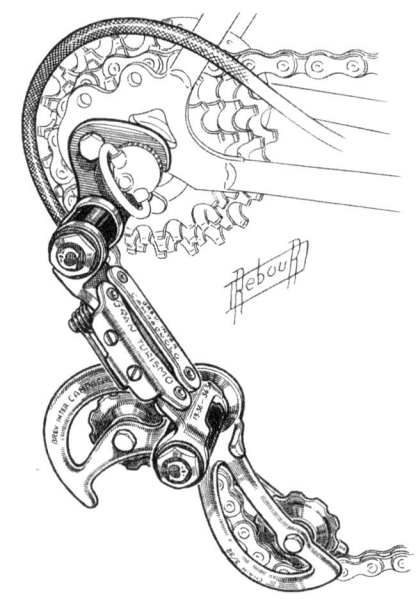

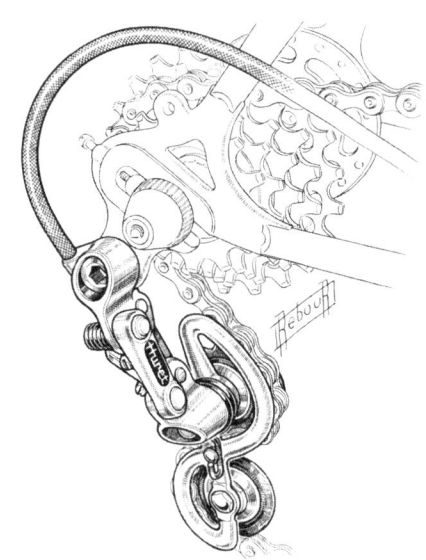

Above: Huret shifter collection at Brussels bicycle trade show. *Le Cycle*, March 1968.

Below: The Stella bicycle on which Louison Bobet won the 1954 Tour de France. *Le Cycle*, 7 August 1954.

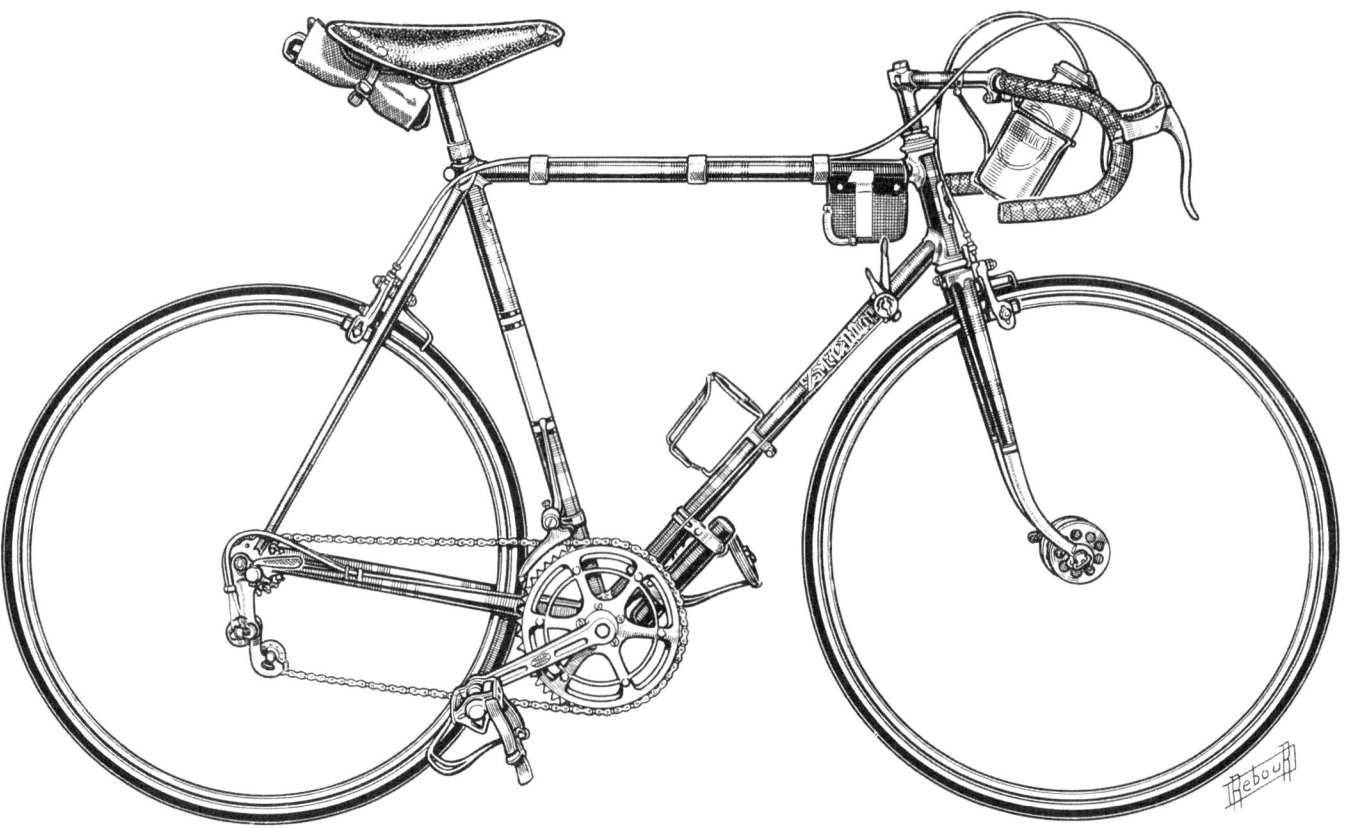

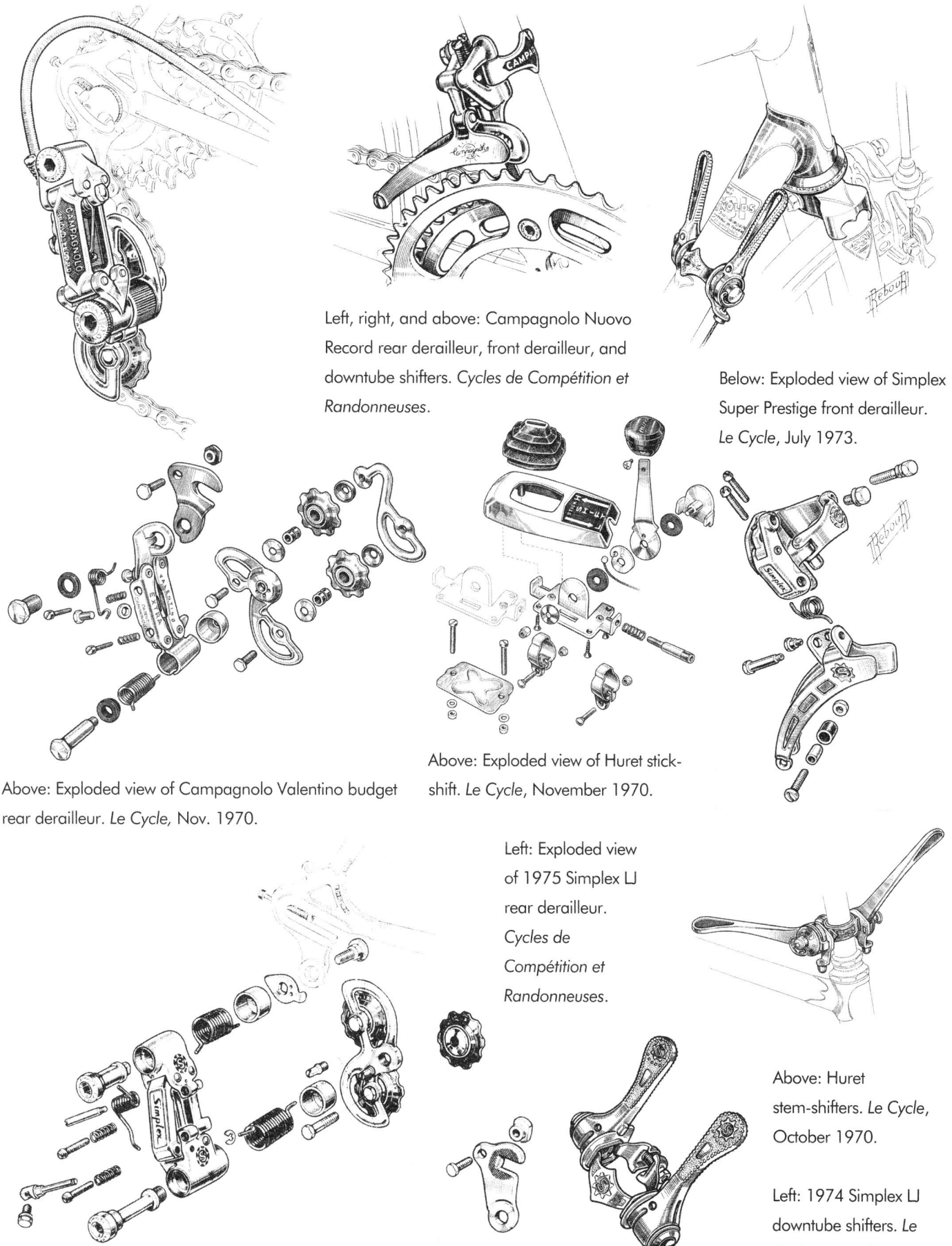

Left, right, and above: Campagnolo Nuovo Record rear derailleur, front derailleur, and downtube shifters. *Cycles de Compétition et Randonneuses.*

Below: Exploded view of Simplex Super Prestige front derailleur. *Le Cycle,* July 1973.

Above: Exploded view of Campagnolo Valentino budget rear derailleur. *Le Cycle,* Nov. 1970.

Above: Exploded view of Huret stick-shift. *Le Cycle,* November 1970.

Left: Exploded view of 1975 Simplex LJ rear derailleur. *Cycles de Compétition et Randonneuses.*

Above: Huret stem-shifters. *Le Cycle,* October 1970.

Left: 1974 Simplex LJ downtube shifters. *Le Cycle,* December 1973.

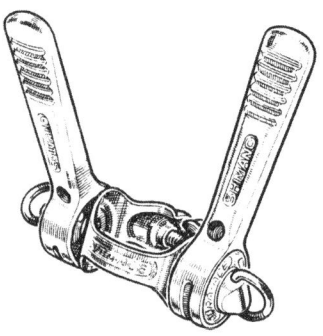

Above: 1976 Downtube shifters for Shimano's Crane and Dura-Ace derailleurs. *Le Monde de Daniel Rebour.*

Right: 1976 Shimano Crane rear derailleur, Dura-Ace front derailleur, and derailleur cable guide. *Le Monde de Daniel Rebour.*

Below: Fédérico Bahamontès won the mountain category in the 1954 Tour de France on this Splendid bicycle. *Le Cycle,* 7 August 1954.

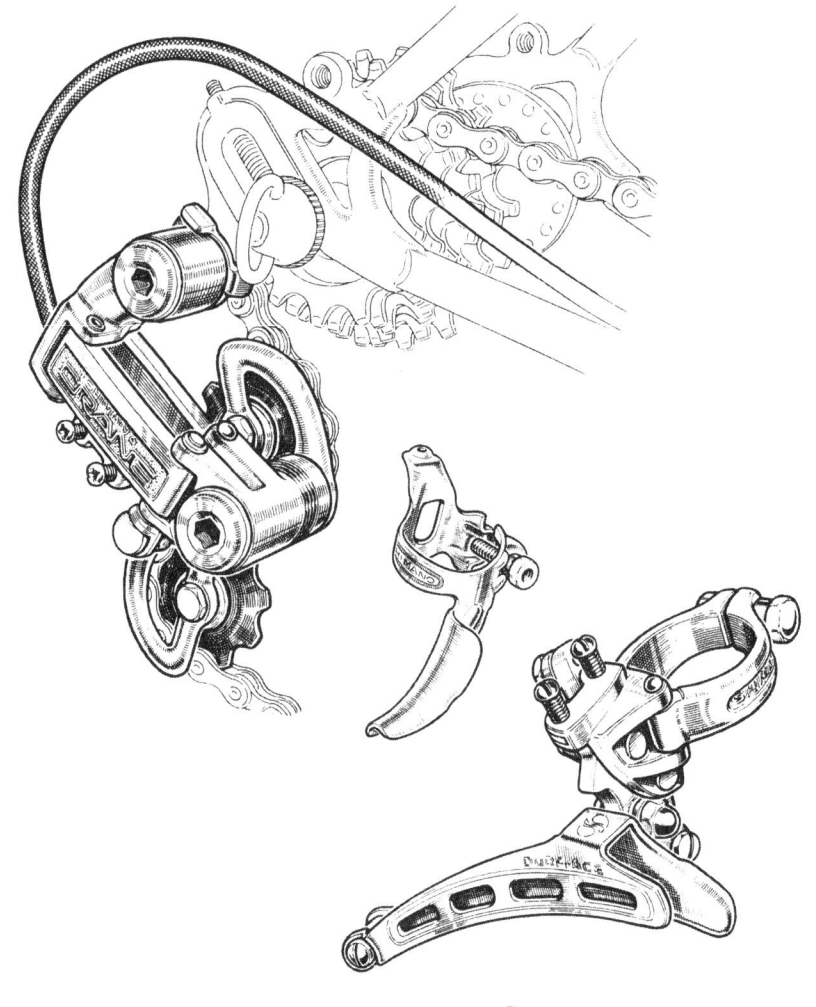

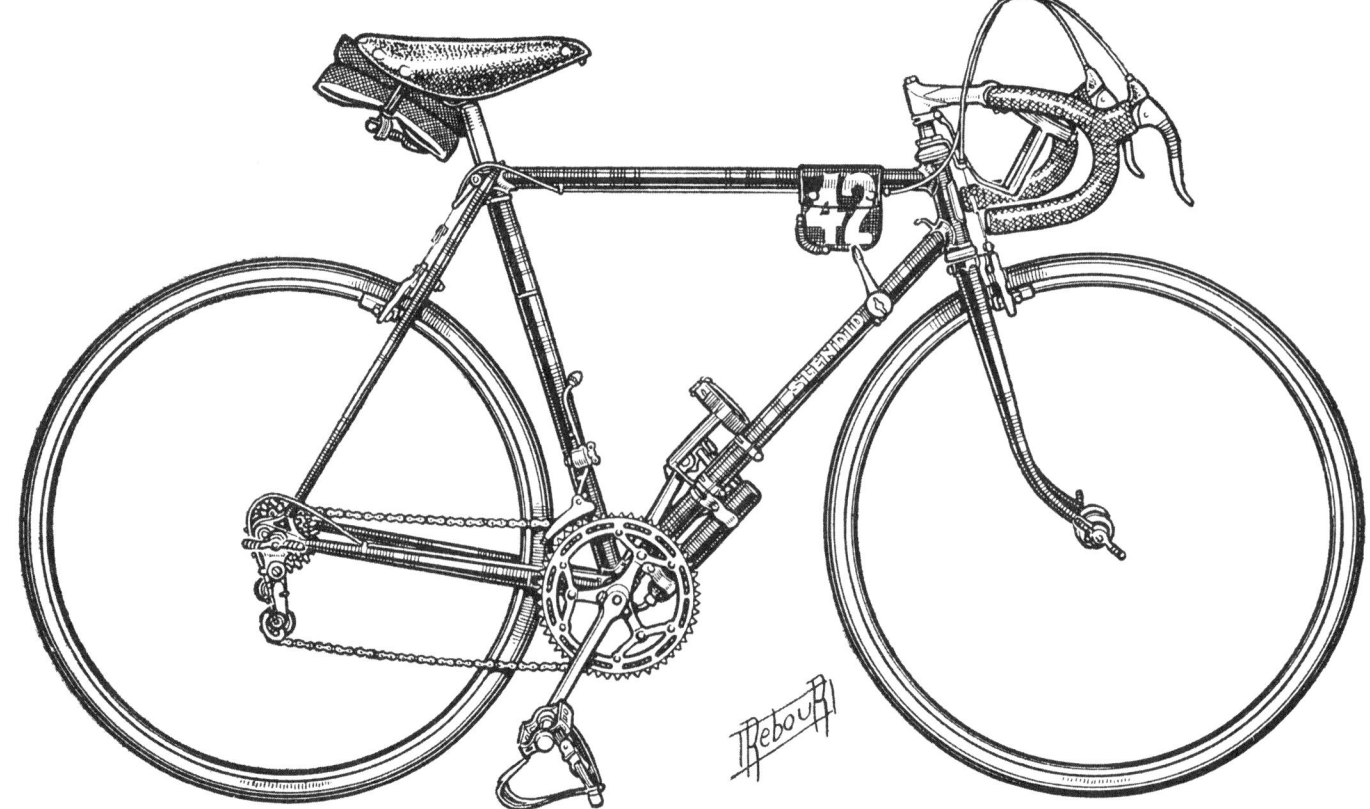

Chapter 3. Derailleur Gearing

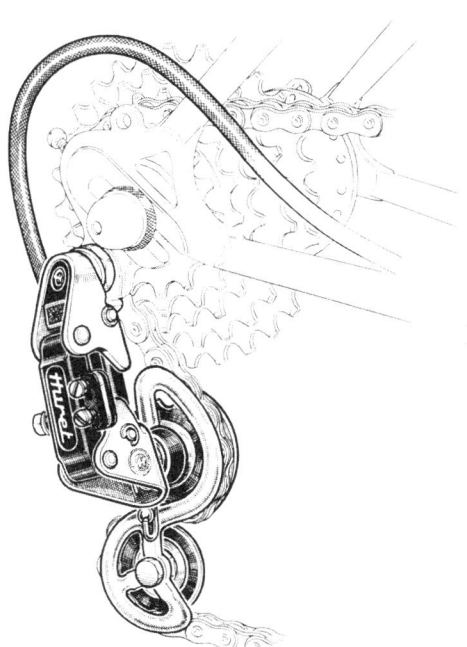

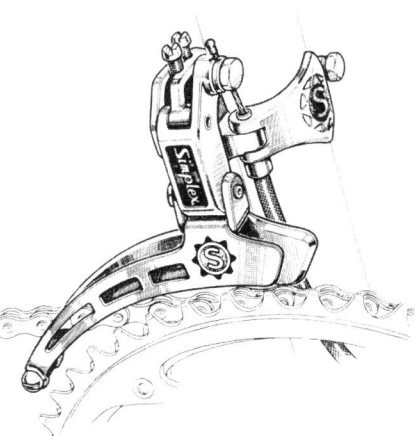

Left: 1975 Simplex Super Prestige front derailleur.
Below: Simplex Super Prestige rear derailleur, installed on a frame with Simplex dropouts.
Both images from *Cycles de Compétition et Randonneuses*.

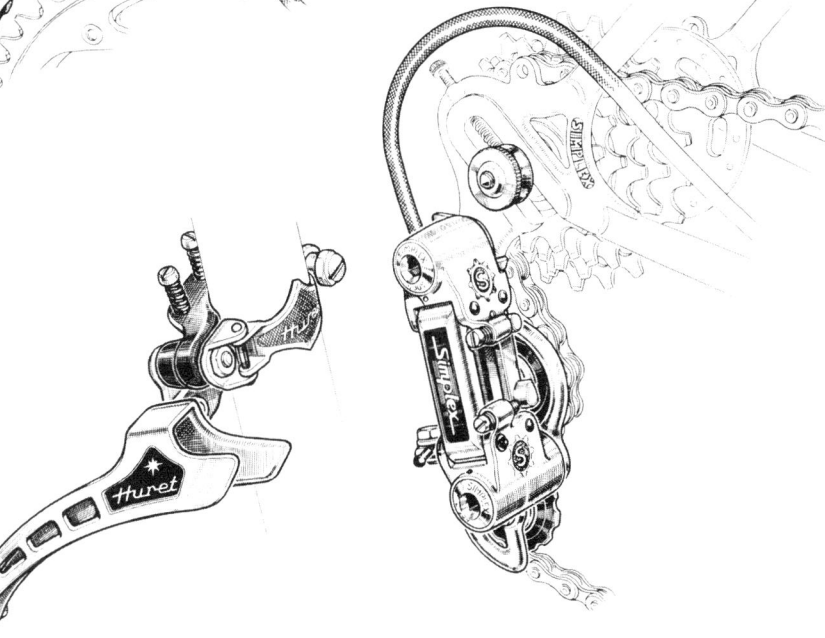

Above: 1975 Huret Success rear derailleur.
Right: 1975 Huret Success front derailleur.
Both images from *Cycles de Compétition et Randonneuses*.

Below: 4th placed Jean Dotto in the 1954 Tour de France rode this Magnat-Debon bicycle. *Le Cycle*, 7 August 1954.

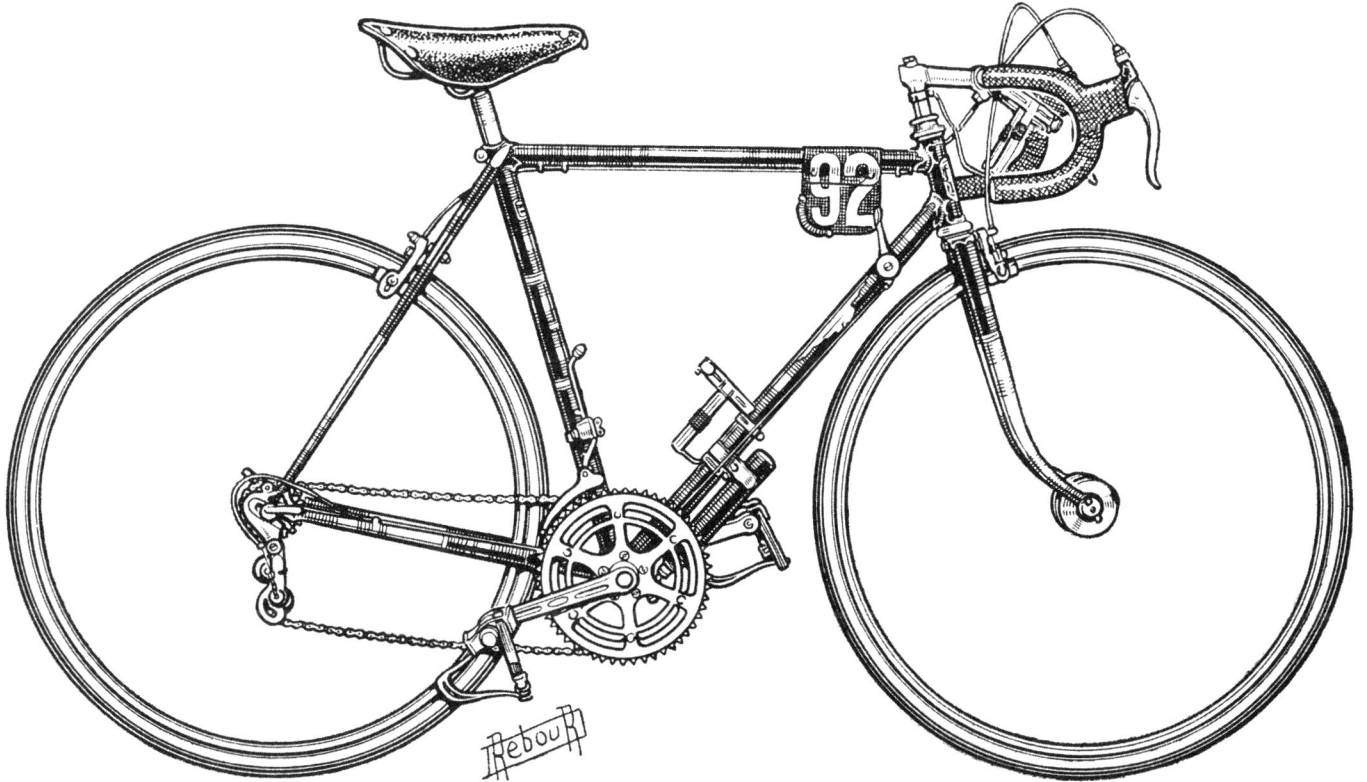

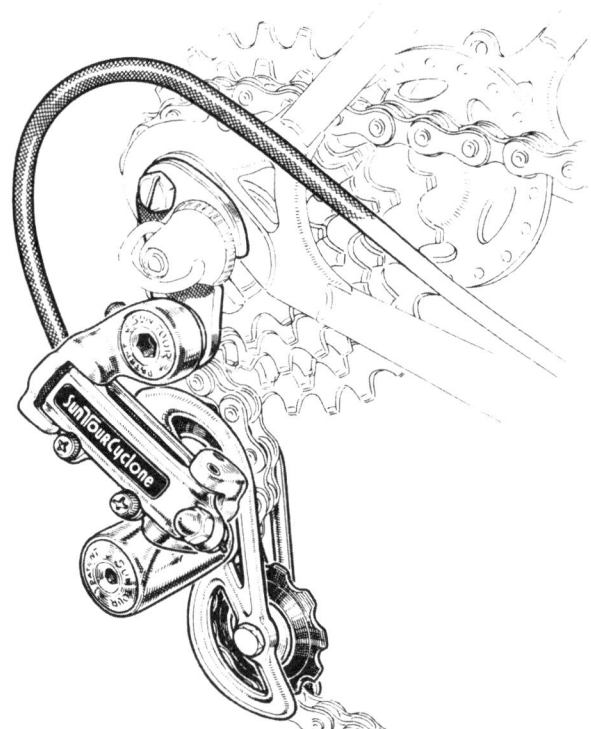
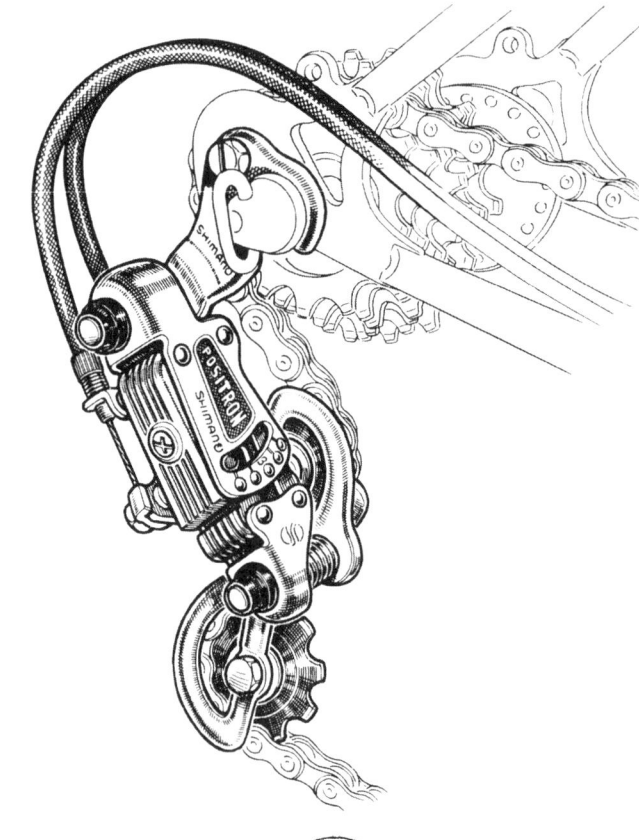

Left: SunTour's very successful Cyclone rear derailleur.
Below: The Positron was Shimano's first successful modern index-shifting rear derailleur. Both images from *Le Monde de Daniel Rebour*.

Below: 2nd placed Ferdi Kübler rode this bicycle in the 1954 Tour de France. Note the long Ambrosio handlebar stem and a mix of TA, Simplex, and Campagnolo components. Also note the generous use of handlebar tape around the bike. *Le Cycle*, 7 August 1954.

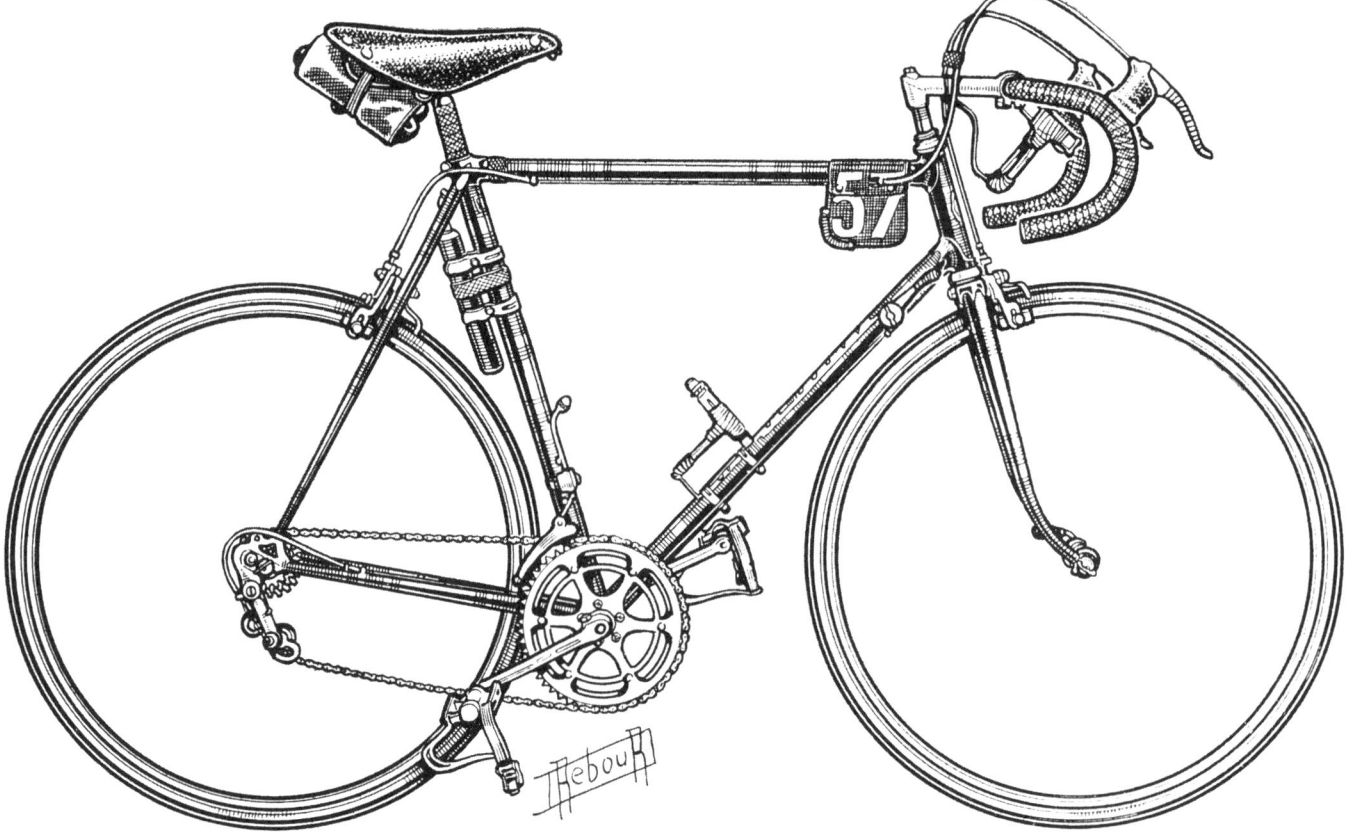

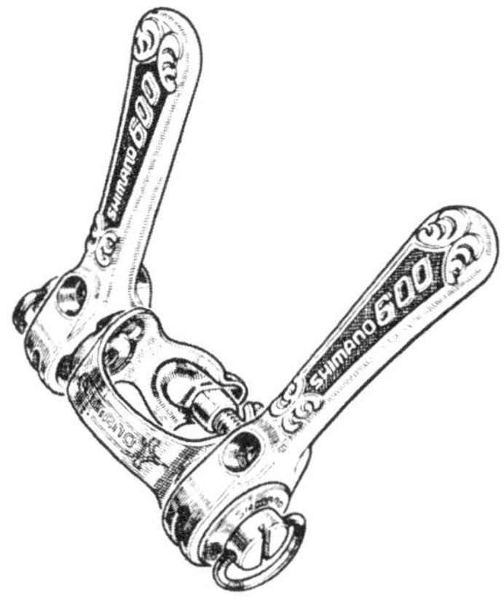

Chapter 3. Derailleur Gearing

Left: The 1980 Shimano 600 downtube shifters were rather ornately embellished.

Right: The 1980 Shimano 600 rear derailleur.

Both images from 1980 Milremo catalogue.

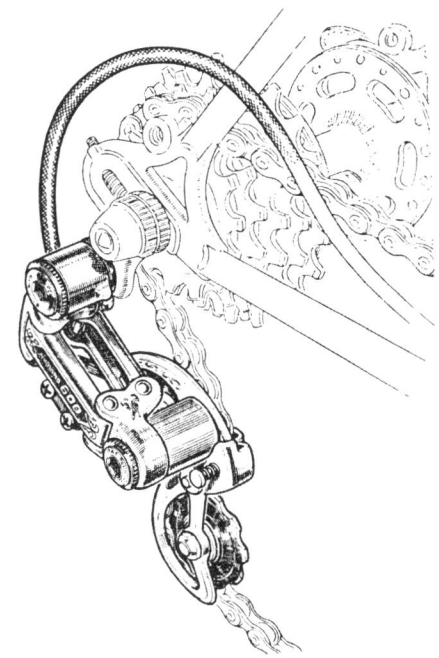

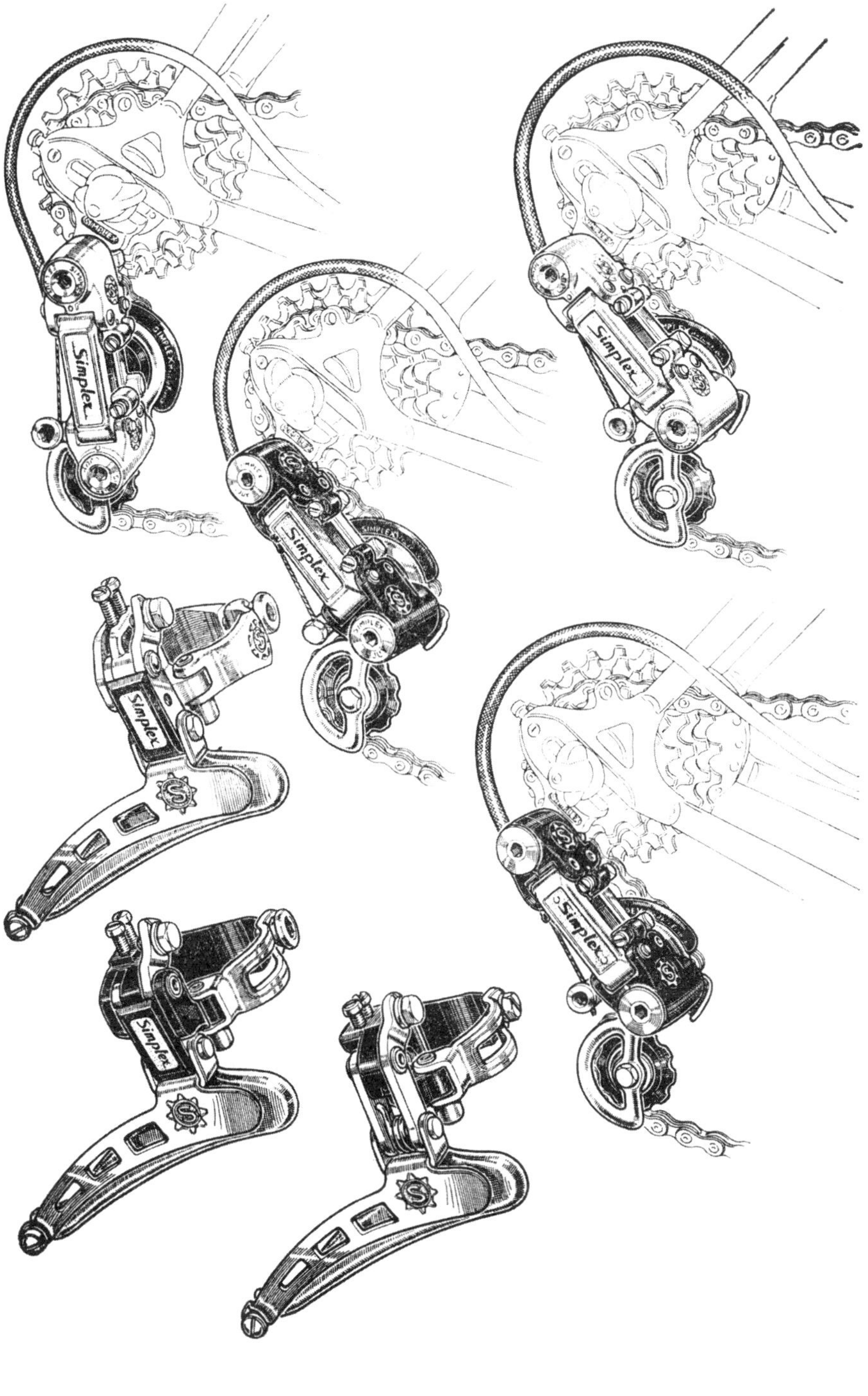

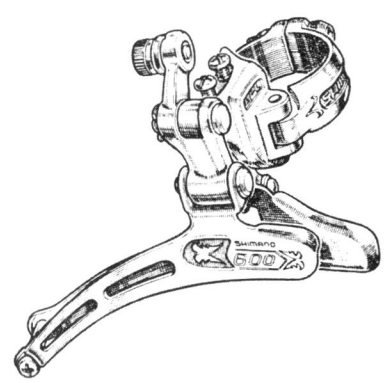

Above: 1980 Shimano 600 front derailleur. 1980 Milremo catalogue.

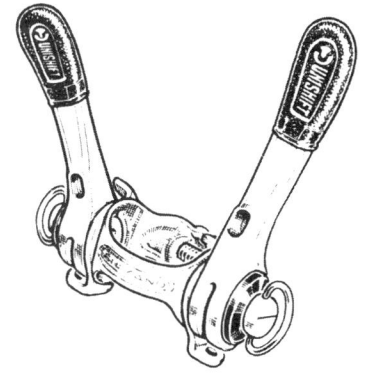

Above: 1976 Shimano Unishift downtube shifters. *Le Monde de Daniel Rebour*.

Left: The 1980 Simplex derailleur range. 1980 Milremo catalogue.

69

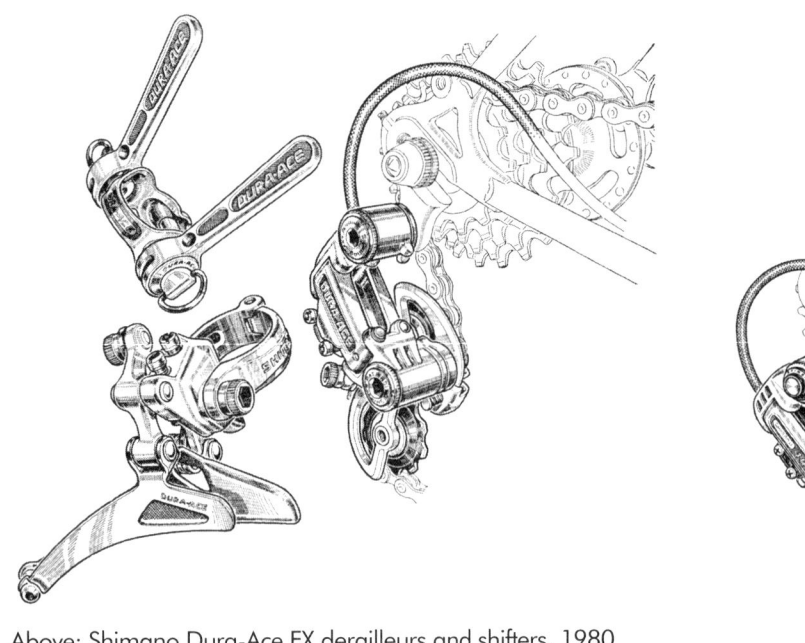
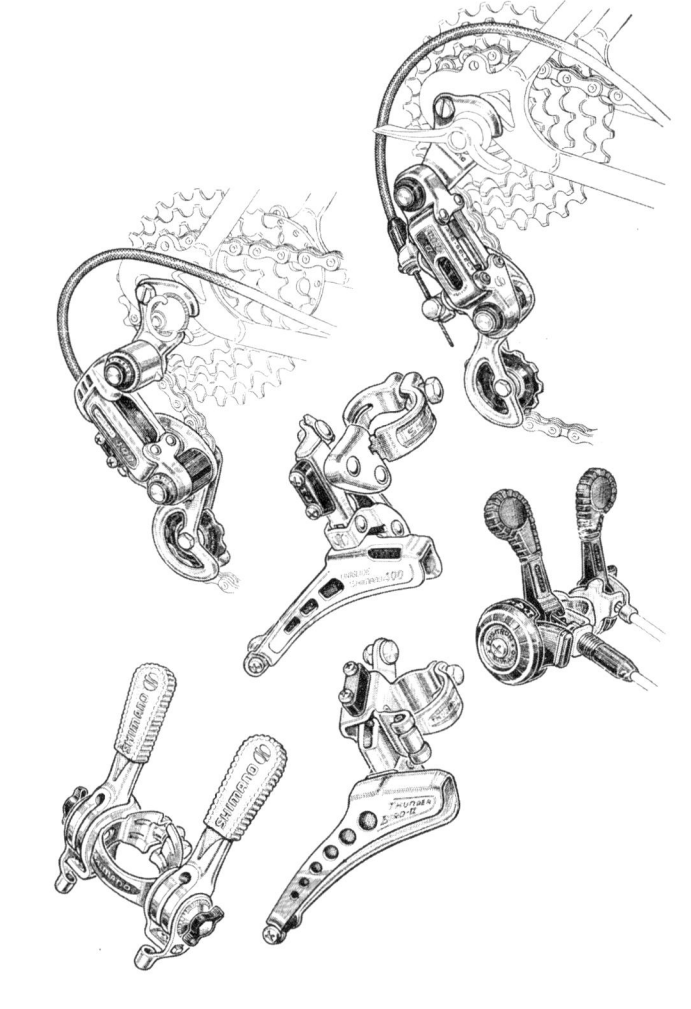

Above: Shimano Dura-Ace EX derailleurs and shifters. 1980 Milremo catalogue.

Right: Shimano Altus friction-shifting (left) and Position indexed shifting (right) rear derailleurs and other components. 1980 Milremo catalogue.

Below: Jean Mallejac's 1954 Terrot bicycle had a short stem, Beborex brakes, and the same mix of drivetrain components as on Kübler's bike, shown on page 68. *Le Cycle*, 7 August 1954.

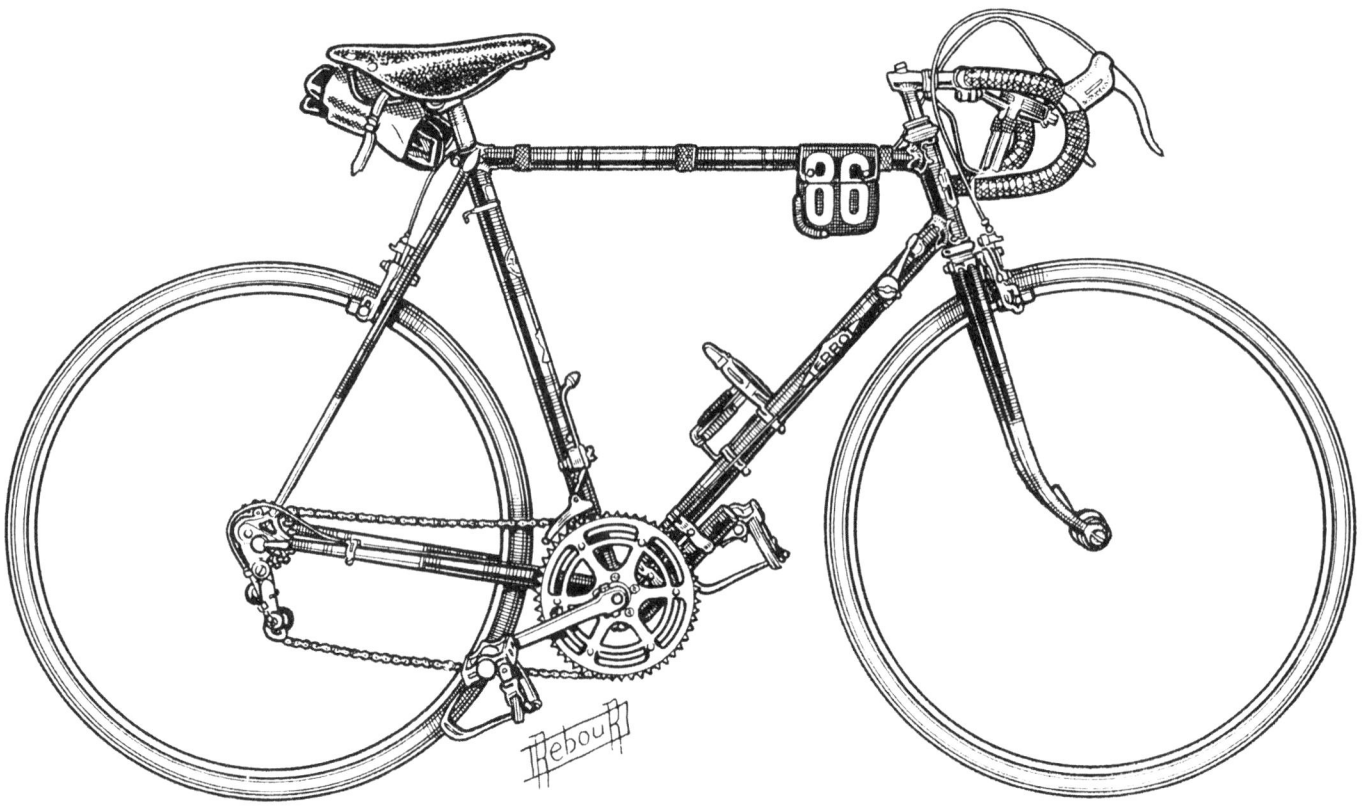

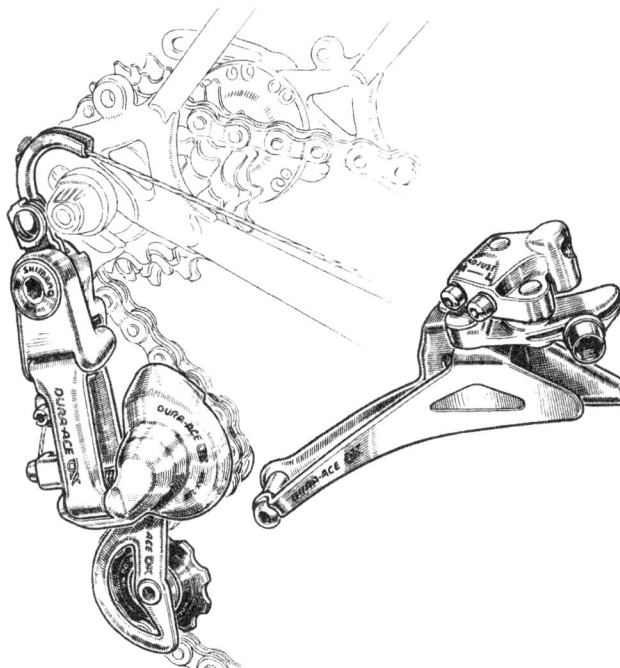

Right: Campagnolo Super Record rear derailleur. 1981 Milremo catalogue.

Above: 1981 Shimano Dura-Ace AX aero front and rear derailleurs. introduced together with other aero components at the October 1980 Cologne bicycle trade show.

Below: Gilbert's René Herse randonneur bicycle at the 1955 Poly de Chanteloup technical trials. *Le Cycle*, 7 May 1955.**

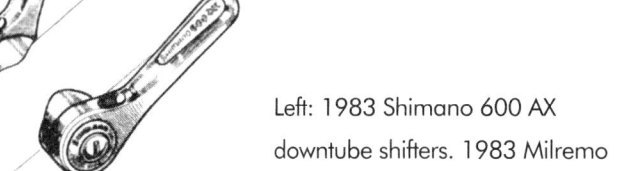

Left: 1983 Shimano 600 AX downtube shifters. 1983 Milremo catalogue.

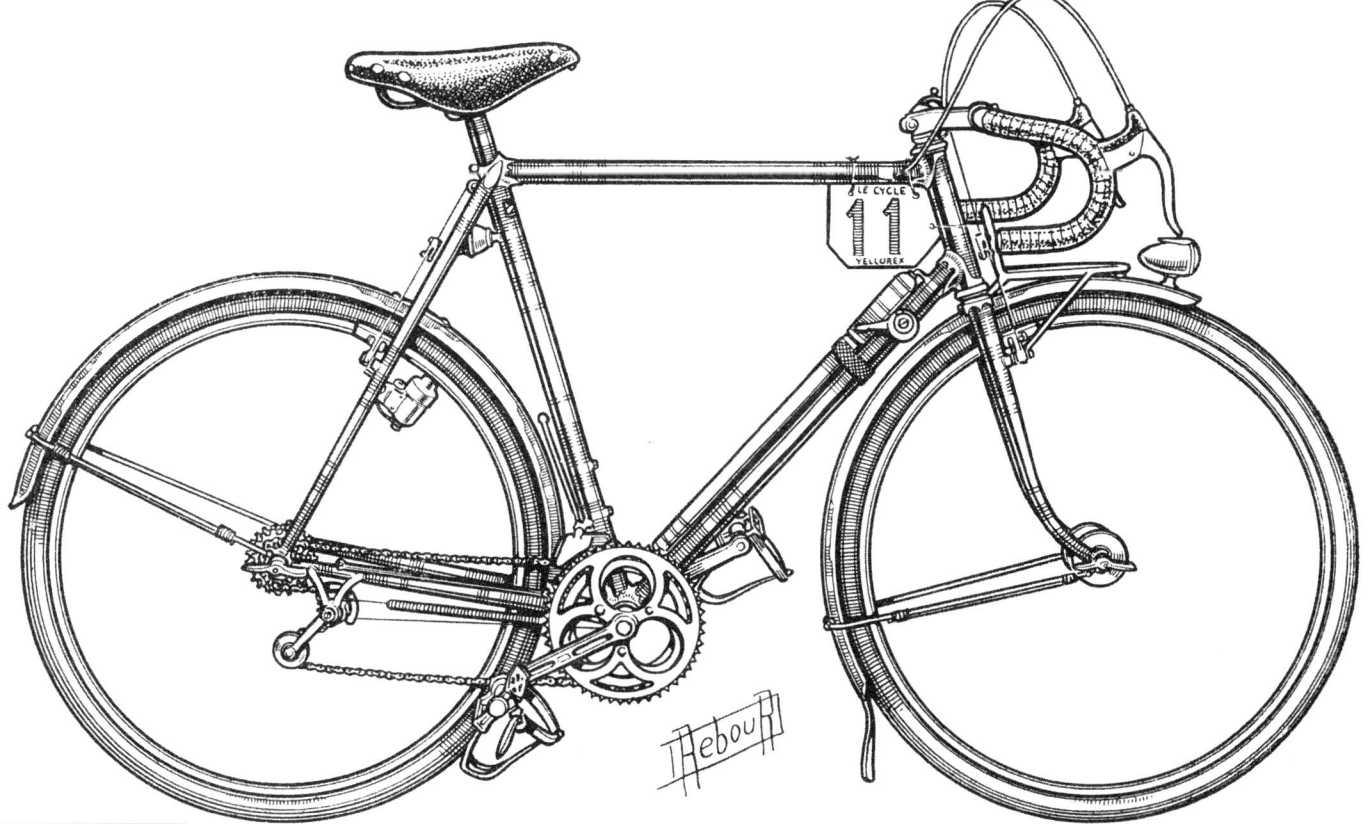

** See pages 269–271 for expanded caption text.

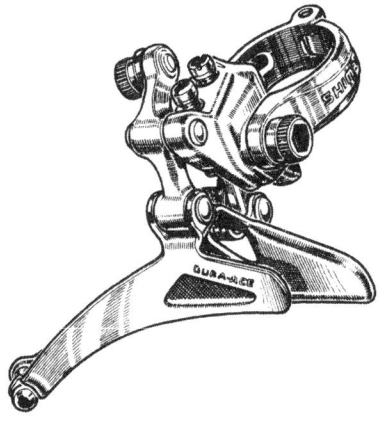

Top left: 1983 Shimano Dura-Ace front derailleur. 1983 Milremo catalogue.

Right: The 1980 Simplex derailleur range was still dominated by variants of the old hanging parallelogram design. 1980 Milremo catalogue.

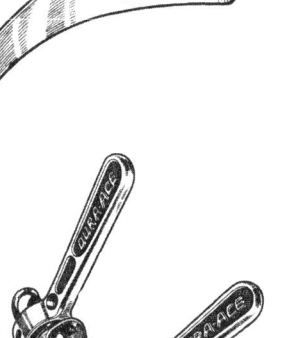

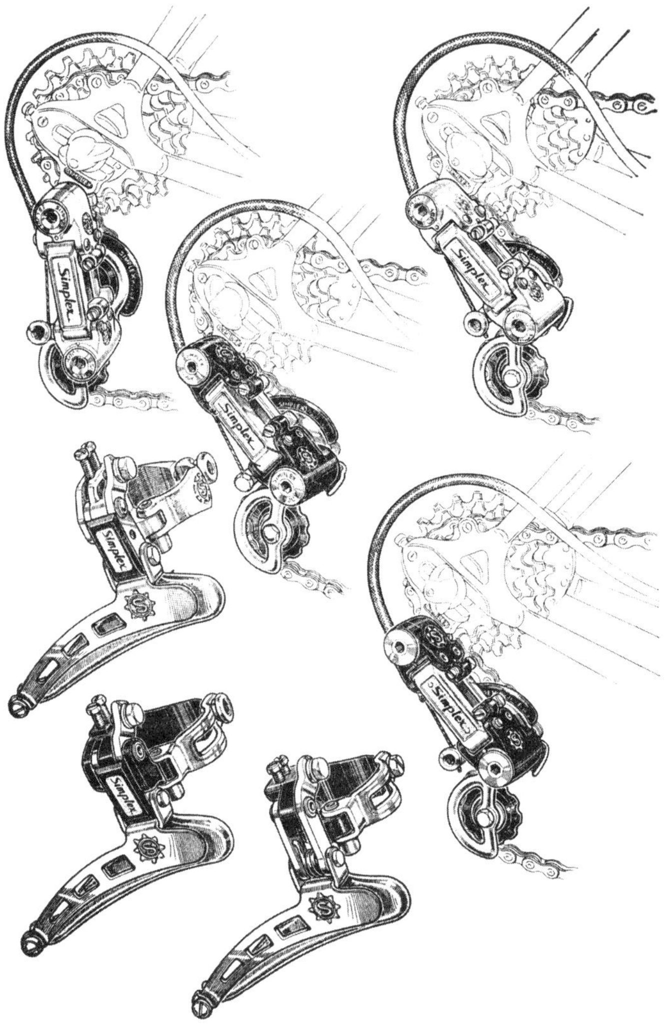

Above: Shimano Dura-Ace downtube shifters. 1983 Milremo catalogue.

Below: Valentin Huot's Rochet bicycle at the 1955 Poly de Chanteloup technical trials. *Le Cycle*, 7 May 1955.

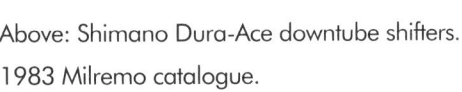

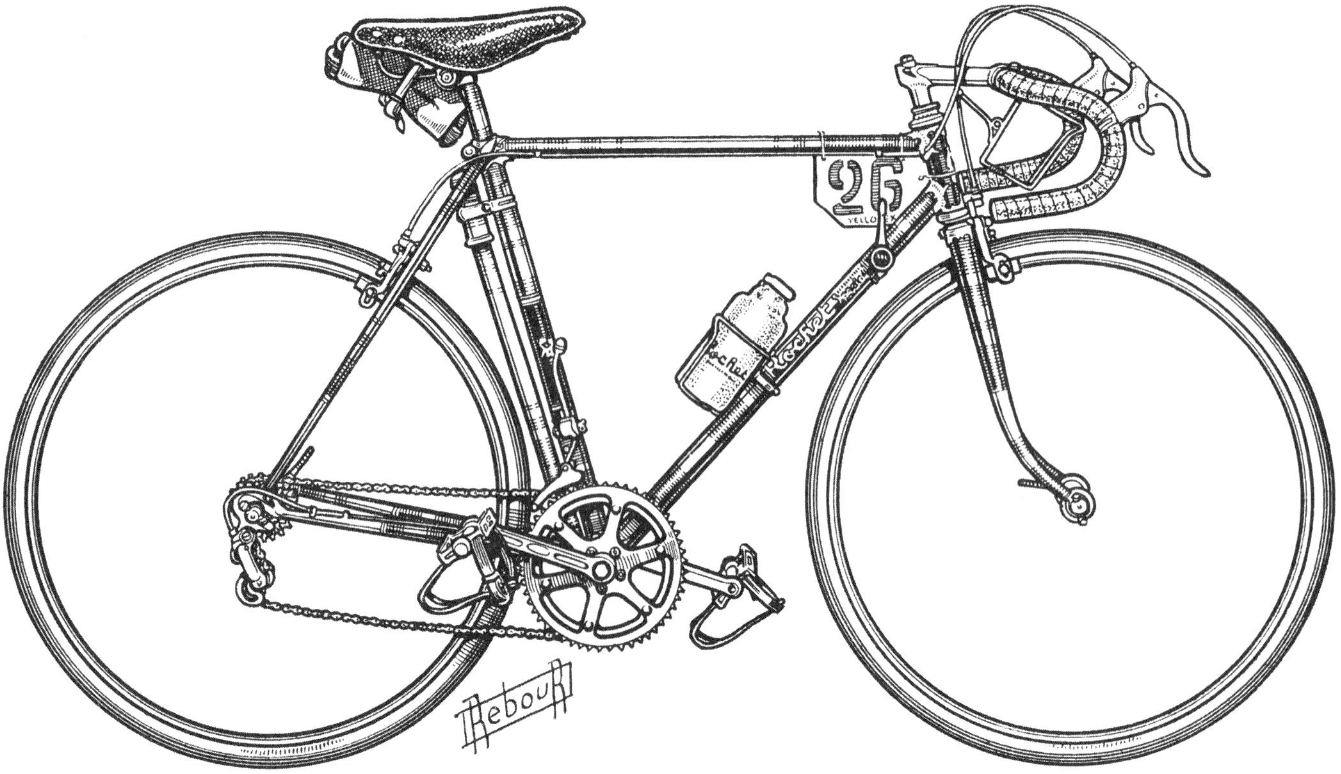

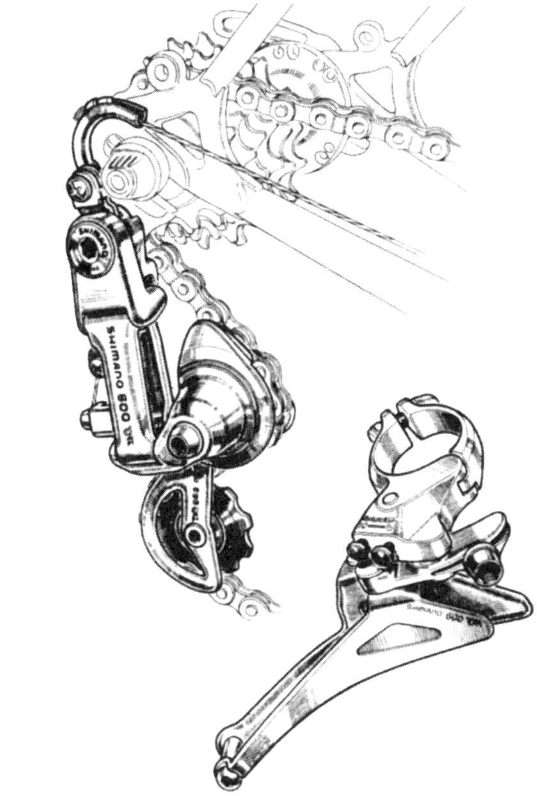

Left: 1983 Shimano 600 AX front and rear derailleurs.
Right: Campagnolo Nuevo Record front derailleur.
Below: Campagnolo Nuevo Record downtube shifters.
Lower right: Simplex stem-mounted shifters.
All images on this page 1981 and 1983 Milremo catalogue.

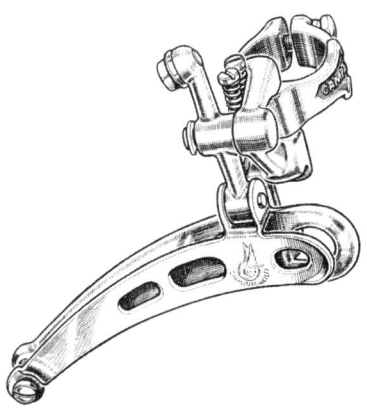

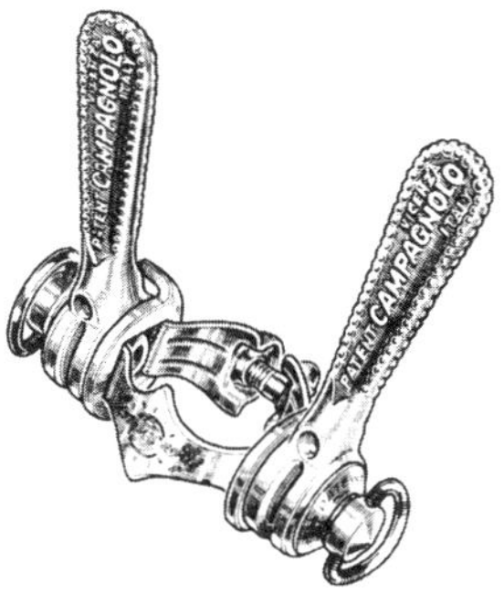

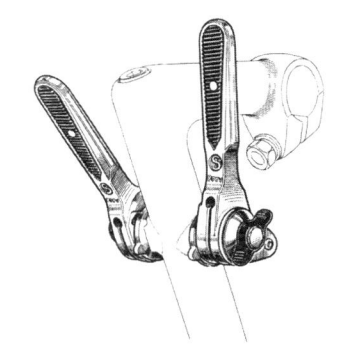

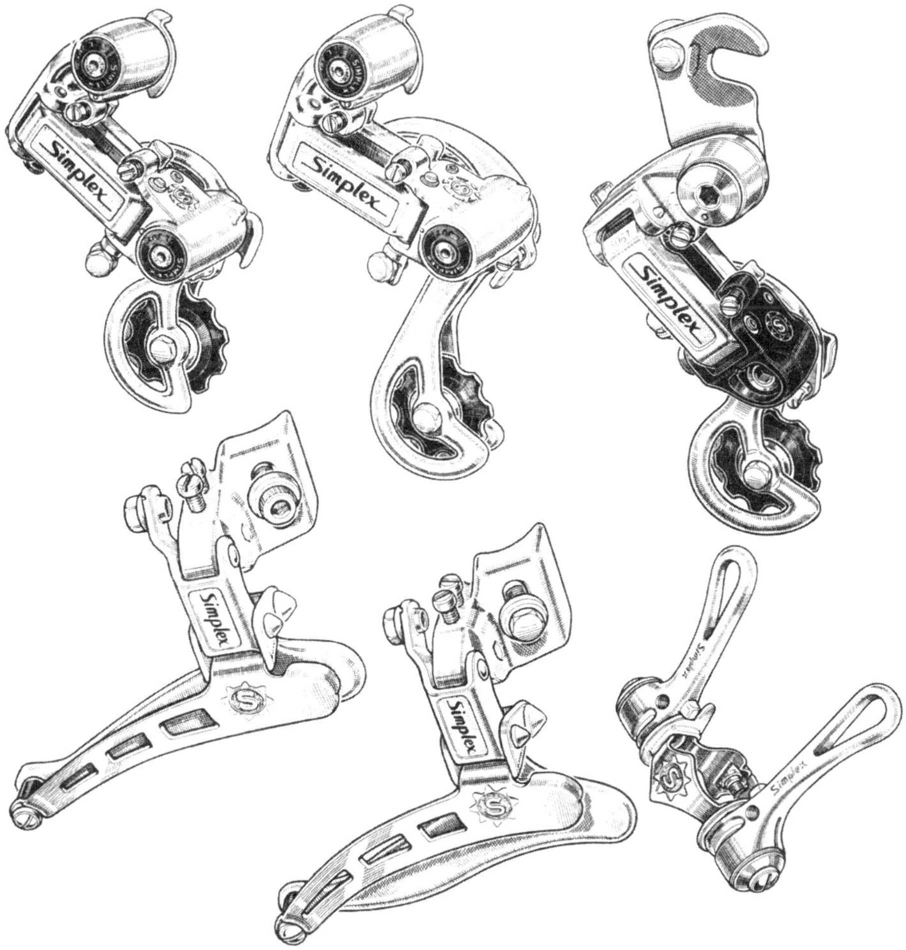

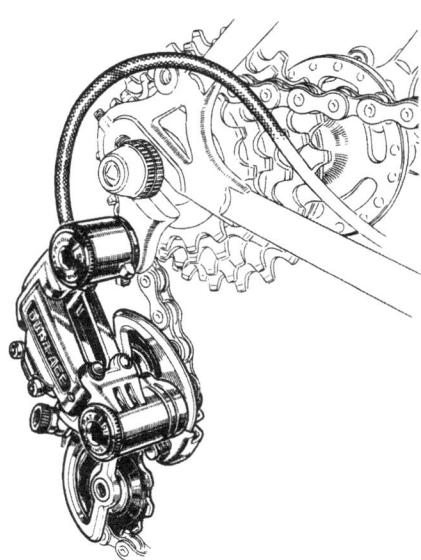

Above: Shimano Dura Ace rear derailleur. 1983 Milremo catalogue.
Left: The 1983 Simplex range of "Japanese-style" derailleurs. Top row from left to right: SLJ 6600-T, SLJ 6600-GT, and S 061-T rear derailleurs. Bottom row from left to right: SLJA 422 and SLJA 223 front derailleurs, and SLJ 5057 downtube shifters. 1983 Milremo catalogue.

Chapter 4. Drivetrain Components

This chapter is devoted to the major drivetrain components—crankset, bottom bracket, freewheel, and chain. The following chapter 5 will deal with pedals and toeclips.

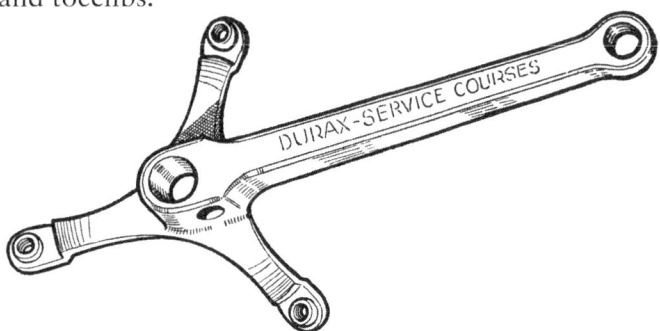

Above: Durax cottered aluminium alloy crank. *Le Cycle*, 28 August 1948.

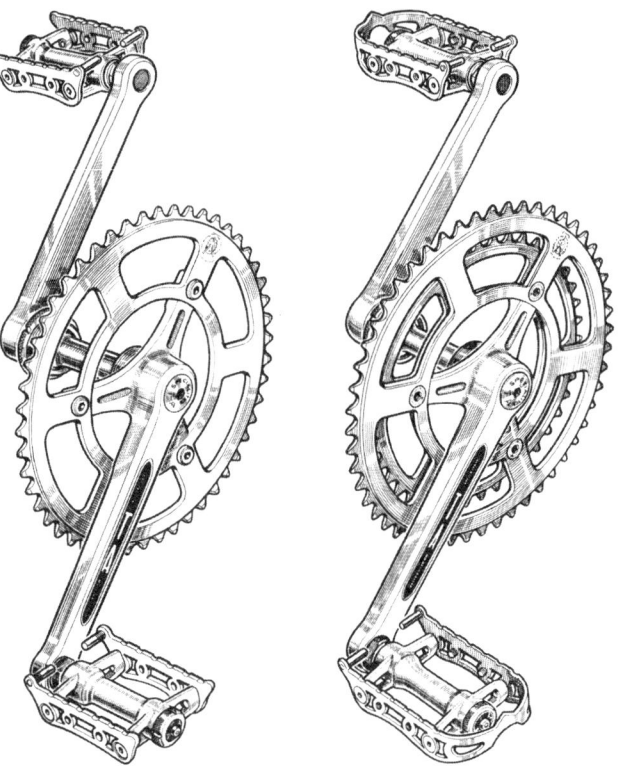

Right: 1970s TA cotterless cranksets with single (left) and double chainrings. TA advertisement in *Le Cycle*, 1973, scanned from original art.

Below: Louison Bobet rode this Mercier bicycle to victory in the 1955 Tour de France. *Le Cycle*, 13 August, 1955.

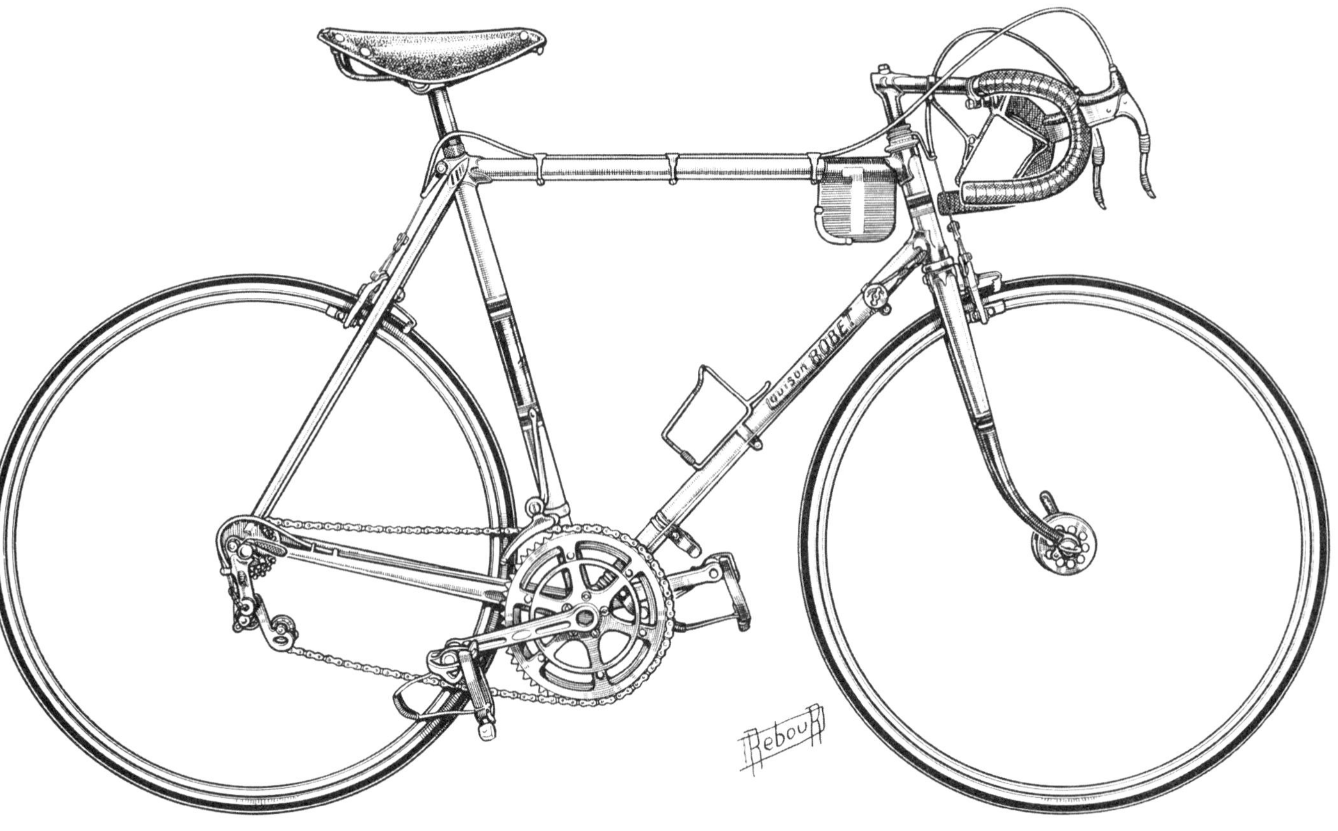

Chapter 4. Drivetrain Components

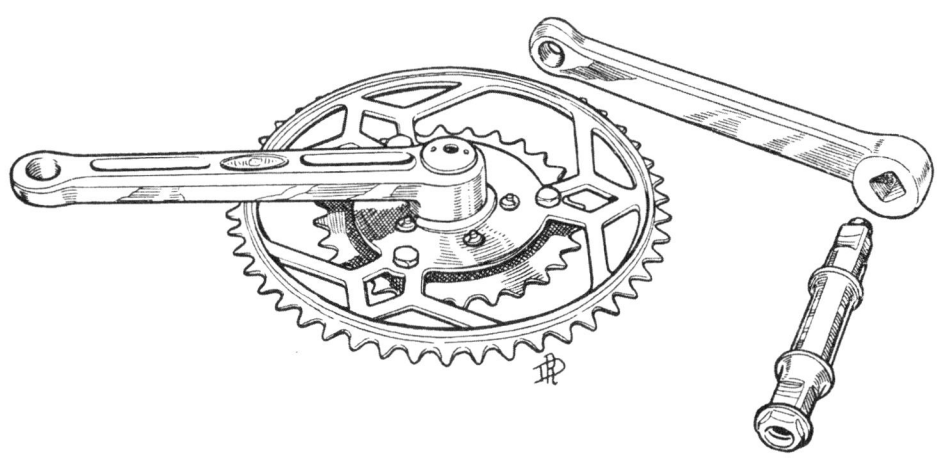

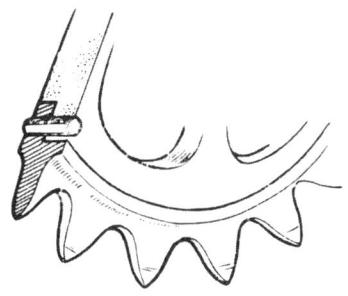

Above: Alex Singer 2-part chainring detail. *Le Cycle*, 22 June 1946.

Above: Stronglight Super Touriste crankset with cotterless cranks. *Le Cycle*, 1 December 1945.

Right: René Herse bottom bracket with sealed bearings and cotterless cranks. *Le Cycle*, 26 January 1947.

Below: 2nd place finisher in the 1955 Tour de France, Jean Brankart, of Belgium, rode this Elve-Peugeot bicycle with taped-on cables. *Le Cycle*, 13 August 1955.

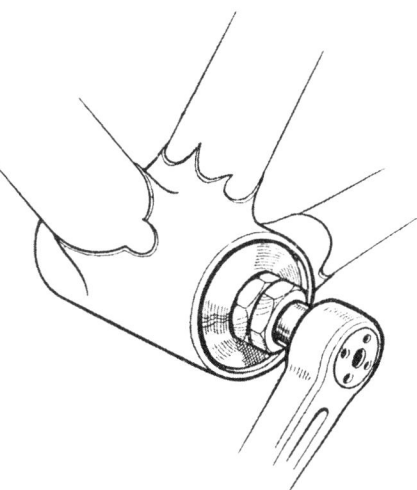

Right: Unidentified 4-speed freewheel. *Pratique du Vélo*.

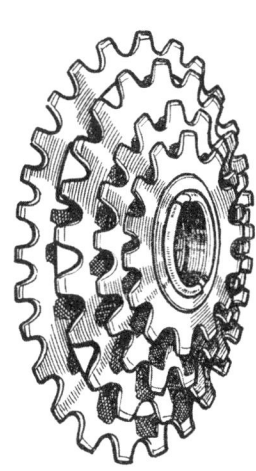

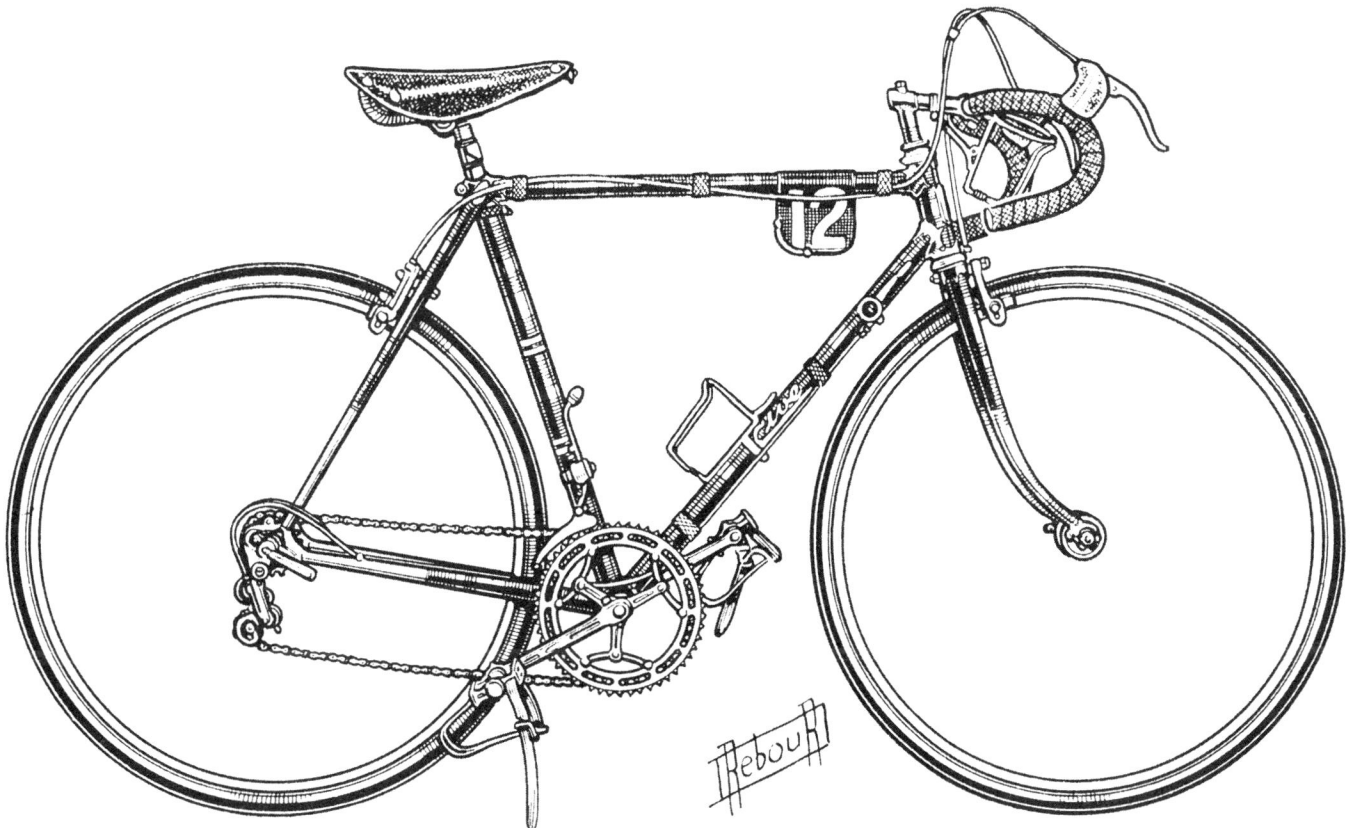

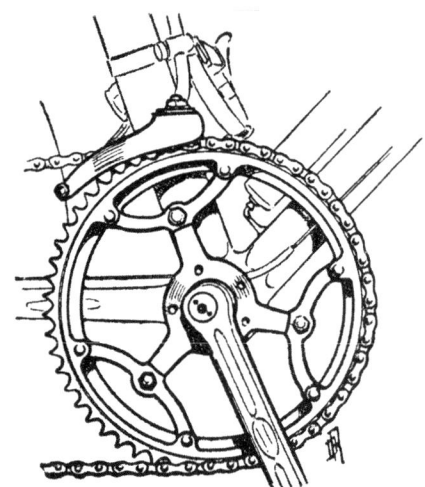
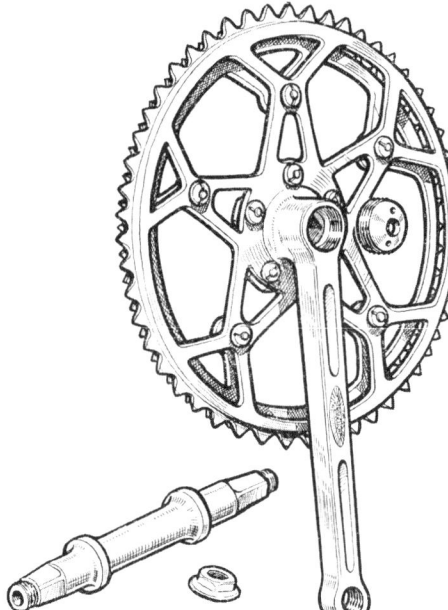
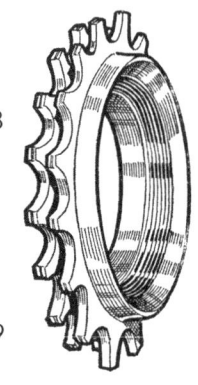

Right: Additional 5th cog on 4-speed freewheel. *Le Cycle*, 28 August 1948.

Below: Gnutti spliced and splined crank attachment. *Le Cycle*, 9 October 1950.

Above: Stronglight 3-arm crankset. *Le Cycle*, 24 January 1948.

Above center Stronglight 5-arm crankset. *Le Cycle*, 9 October 1948.

Right: Pelladini cassette hub with splined connection and hollow axle. *Le Cycle*, 31 May 1947.

Below: Charly Gaul, 3rd place finisher in the 1955 Tour de France, rode this Magnat-Debon bicycle, also with taped-on cables. *Le Cycle*, 13 August 1955,

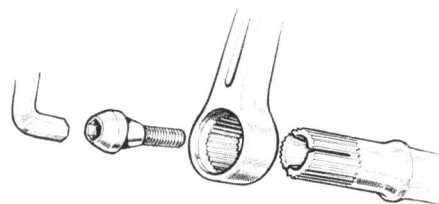
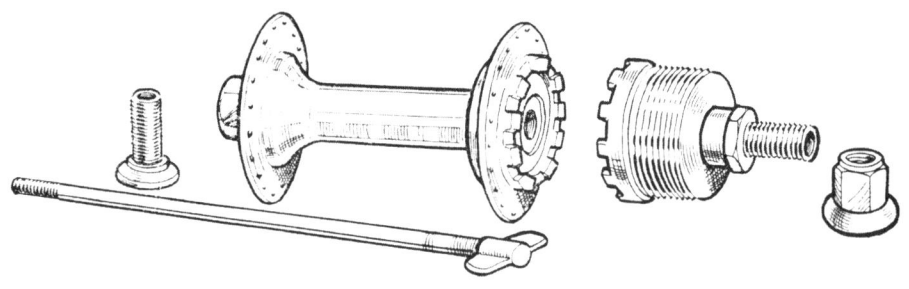
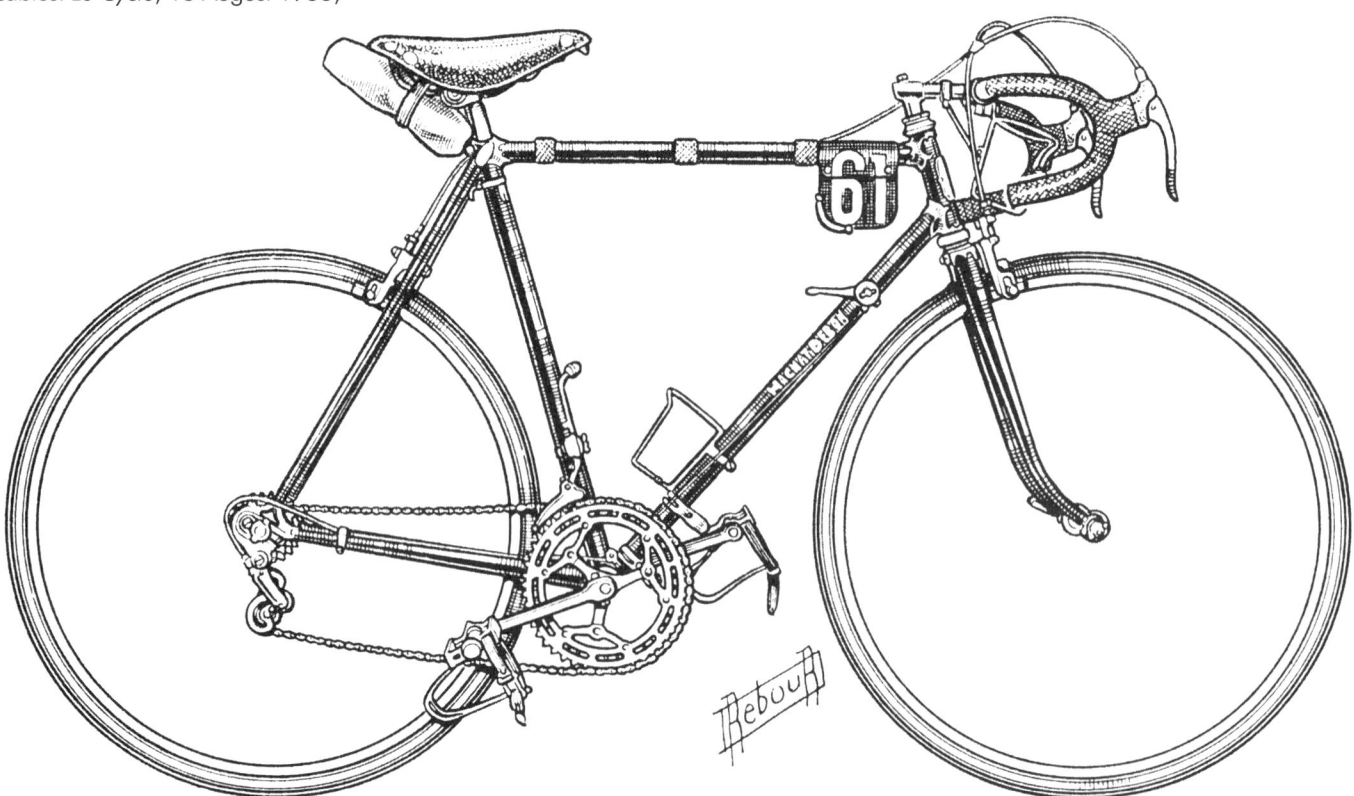

CHAPTER 4. DRIVETRAIN COMPONENTS

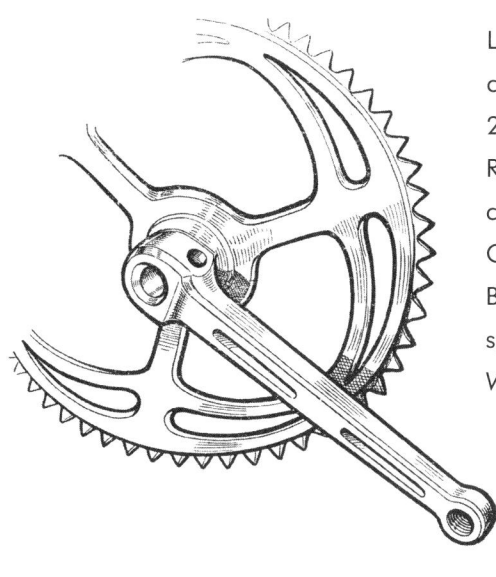
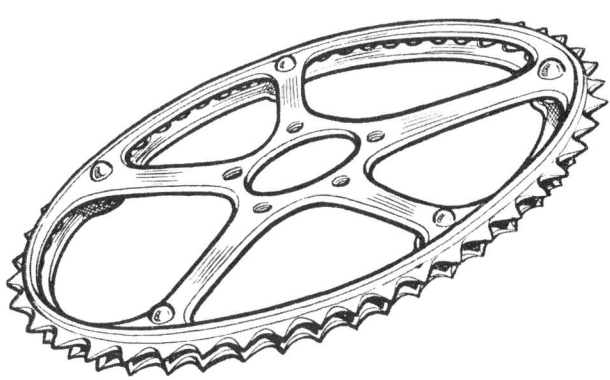

Left: Forged crank and chainring unit. *Le Cycle*, 23 October 1948.
Right: Rosa double chainrings. *Le Cycle*, 23 October 1948.
Below: Chain running on sprockets. *Pratique du Vélo*.

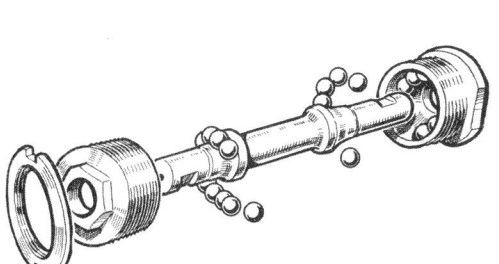
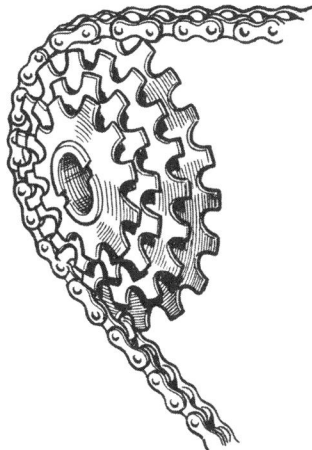
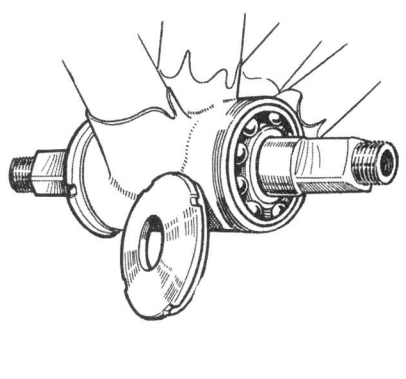

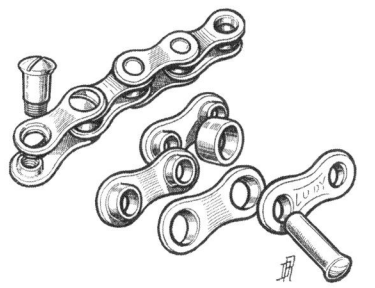
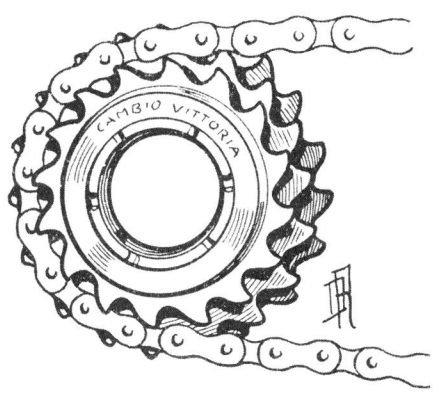

Above left: Exploded view of bottom bracket for cottered cranks. *Pratique du Vélo*.
Left: Exploded view of Ludy bushingless chain. *Le Cycle*, 12 March 1949.
Above right: Sealed-bearing bottom bracket for cotterless crankset. *Pratique du Vélo*.
Right: Vittoria freewheel with shaped sprocket teeth. *Le Cycle*, 7 January 1950.

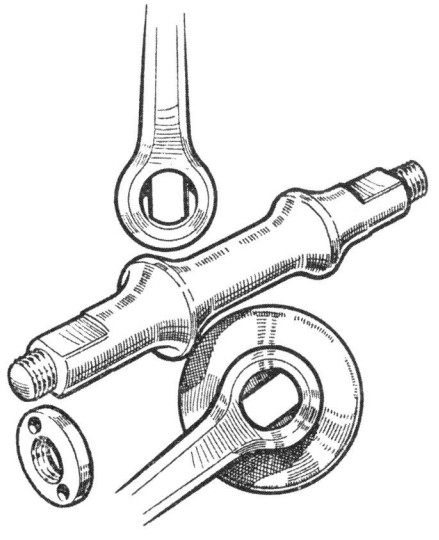
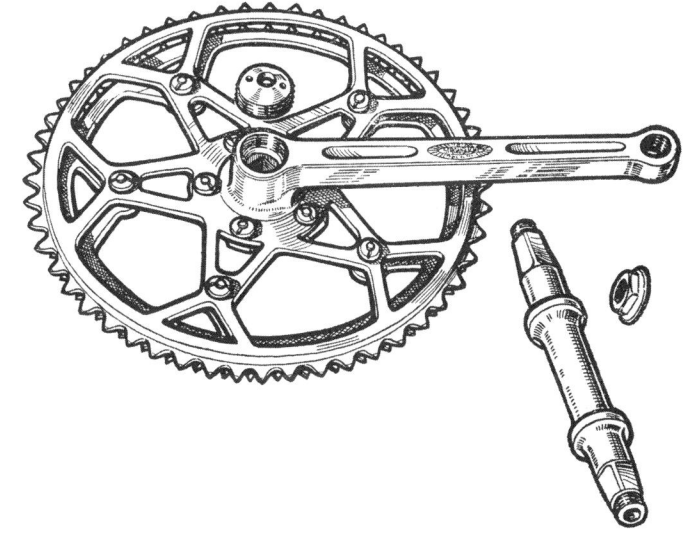

Left: Rochet cotterless cranks with flat-surfaces on round spindle ends. *Le Cycle*, 12 February 1949.
Right: Stronglight cotterless crankset with hollow spindle and tapered square spindle ends. *Pratique du Vélo*.

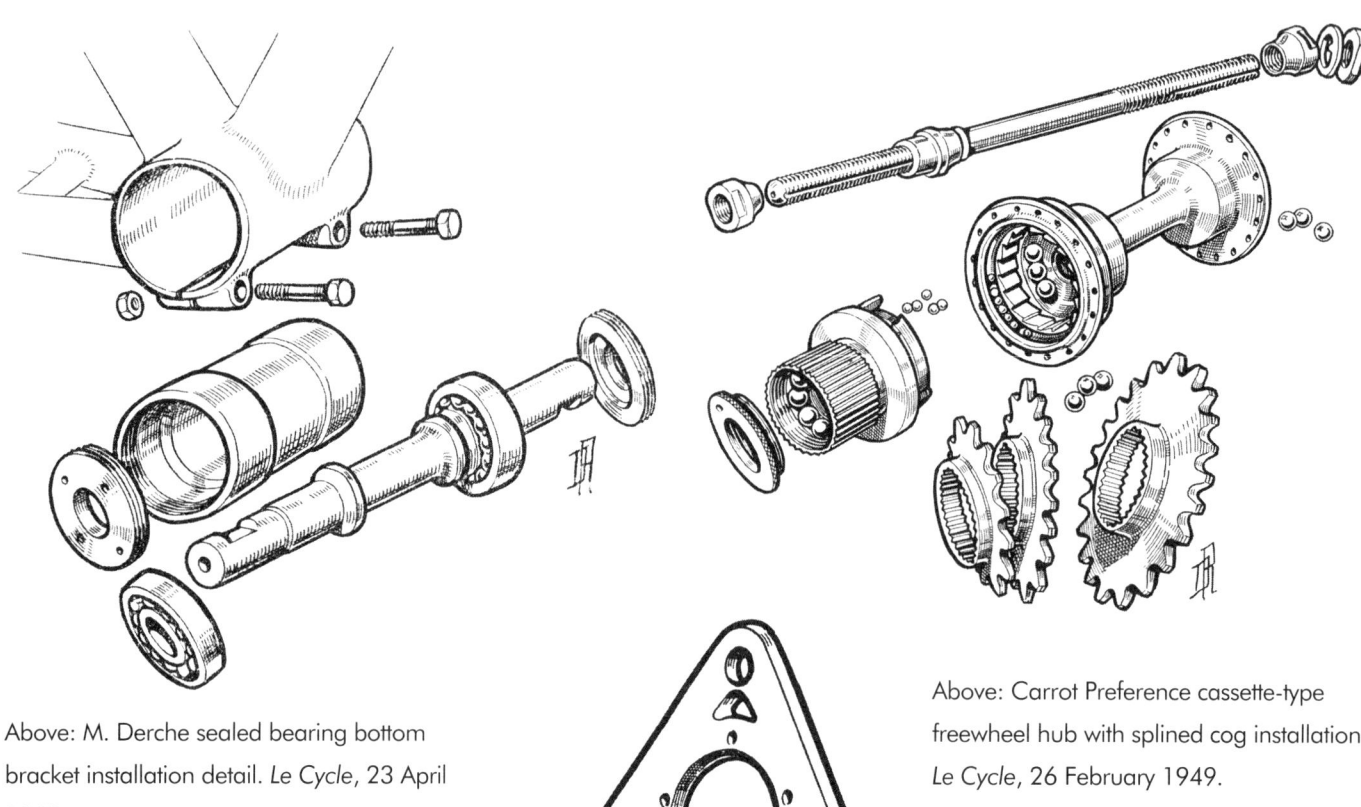

Above: M. Derche sealed bearing bottom bracket installation detail. *Le Cycle*, 23 April 1949.

Below: 6th place finisher Raphaël Géminiani rode this Jeunet machine in the 1955 Tour de France. *Le Cycle*, 13 August 1955.

Above: Carrot Preference cassette-type freewheel hub with splined cog installation. *Le Cycle*, 26 February 1949.

Left: Amadel 3- to 5-pin chainring attachment converter. *Le Cycle*, 12 February 1949.

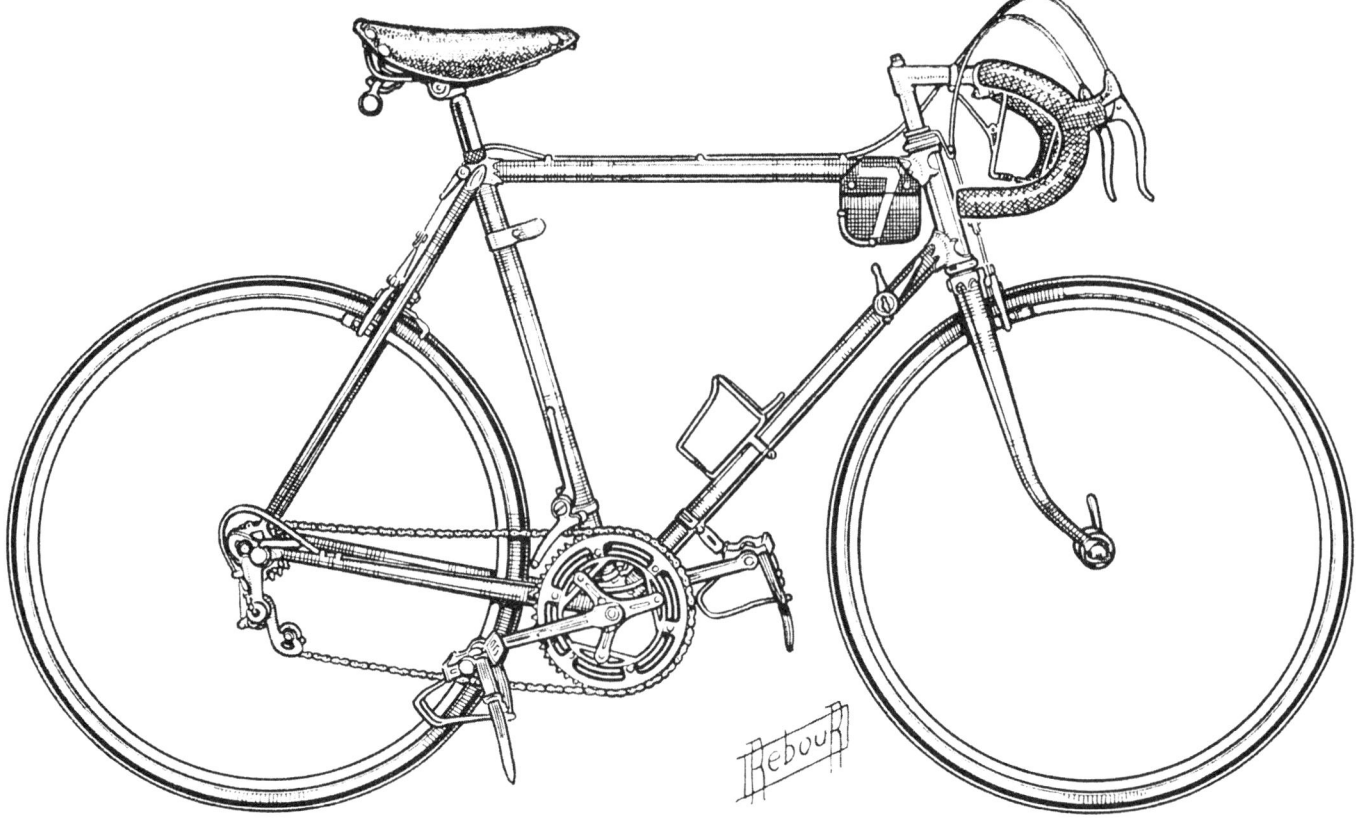

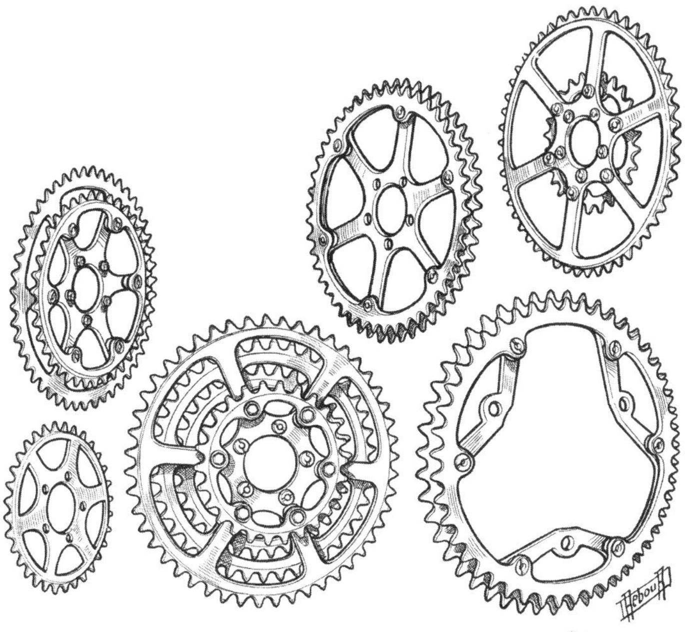

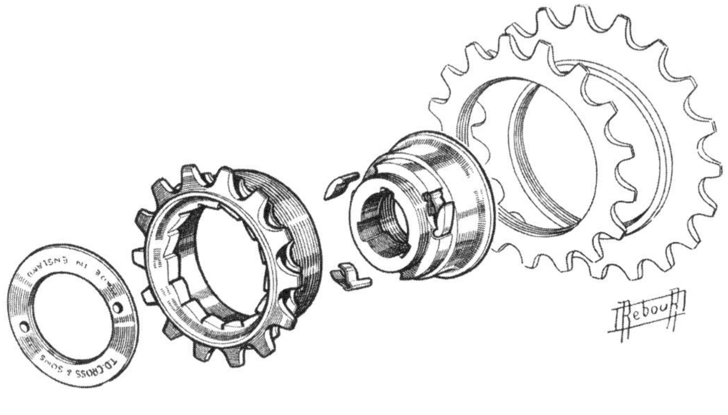

Chapter 4. Drivetrain Components

Above: Exploded view of Cross freewheel, from England. *Le Cycle*, 9 January 1954.

Above: Assortment of TA chainring combinations. *Le Cycle*, 9 July 1949.

Right: Ravat lightweight cottered crankset and chainrings. *Le Cycle*, 20 October 1951.

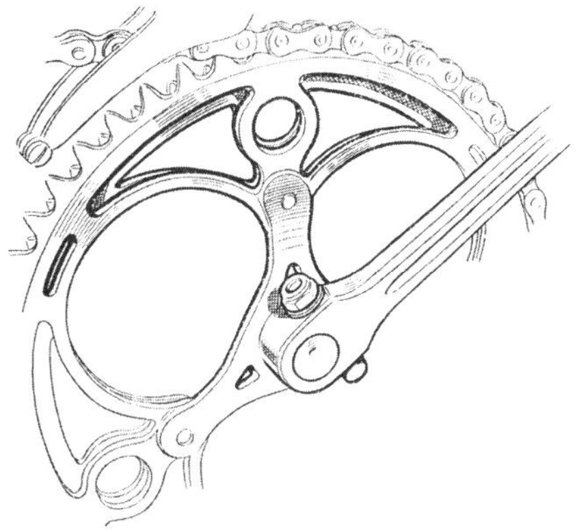

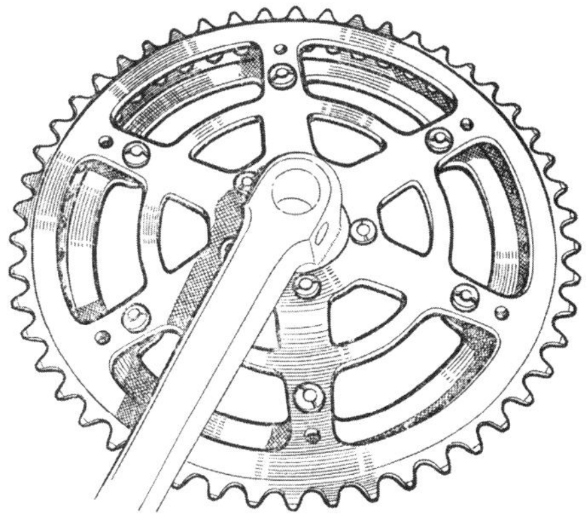

Below: The Elve-Peugeot bicycle of 2nd place finisher Stan Ockers in the 1955 Tour de France. *Le Cycle*, 13 August 1955.

Above: Huret right-side crank and chainrings. *Le Cycle*, 6 October 1951.

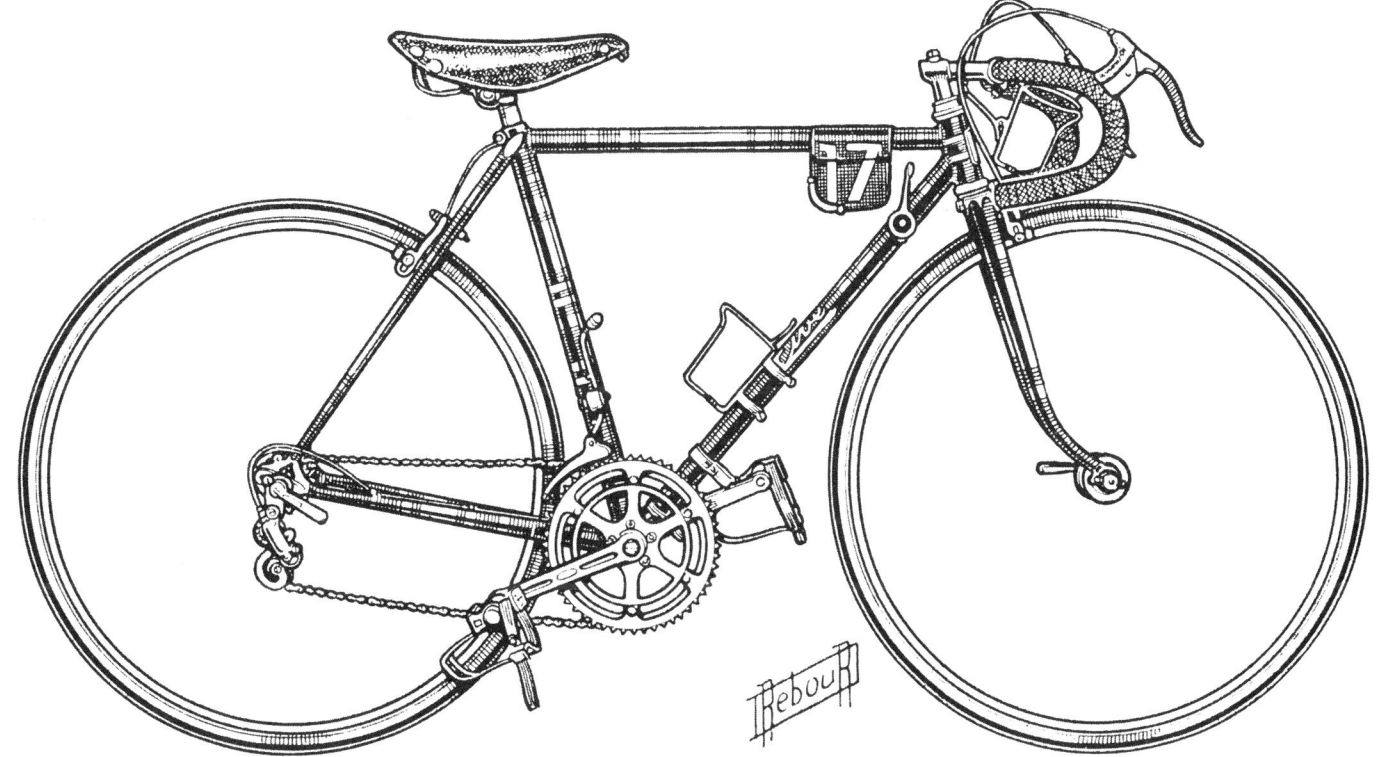

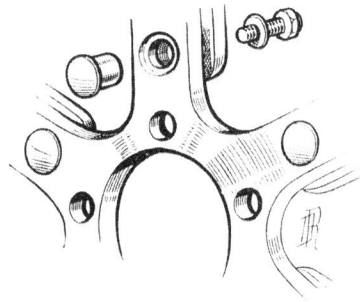

Left: TA 6-arm chainring attachment detail. *Le Cycle*, 1 October 1953.

Right: Exploded view of Cyclo freewheel. *Le Cycle*, 24 April 1954.

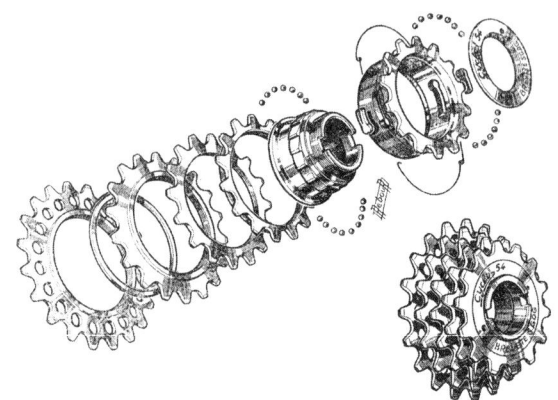

Right A.M. chain with external pins and matching chainring. *Le Cycle*, 9 October 1953.

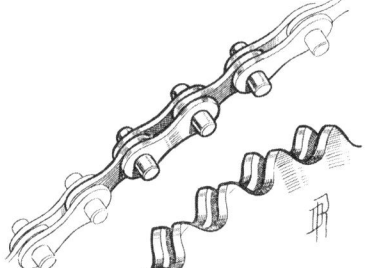

Right: Exploded view of Stronglight 99 cotterless crankset and bottom bracket parts. *Le Cycle*, 5 October 1956.

Below: Richard Van Geechten's Peugeot bicycle at the 1956 Poly de Chanteloup technical trials, with beautifully chrome-plated lugs, fork-ends, and rear dropouts. *Le Cycle*, 5 May 1956.

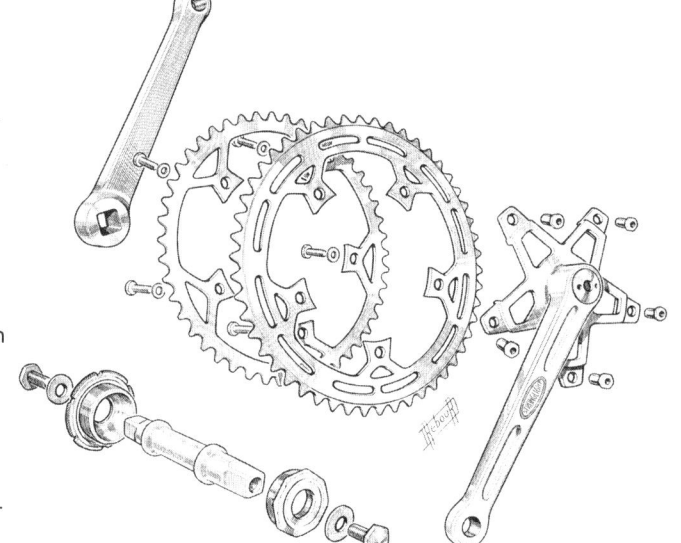

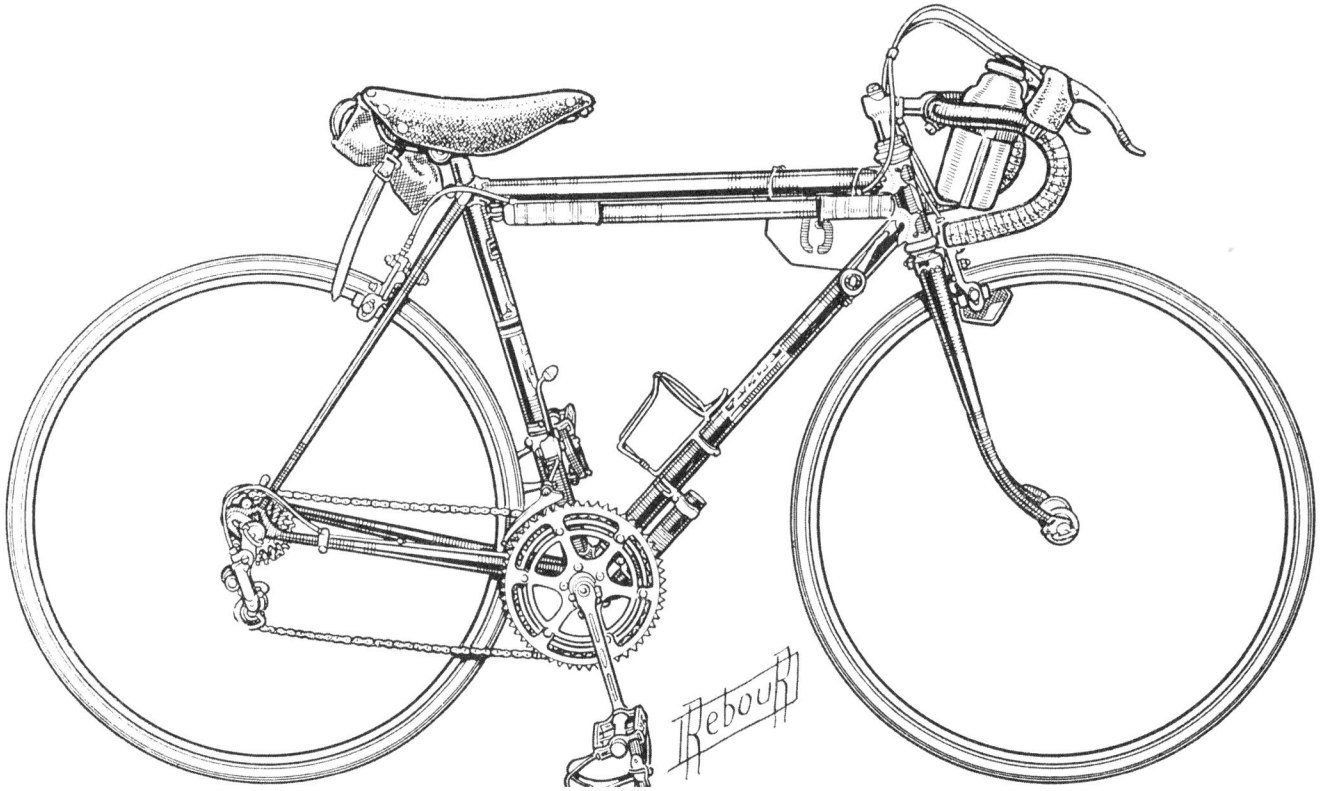

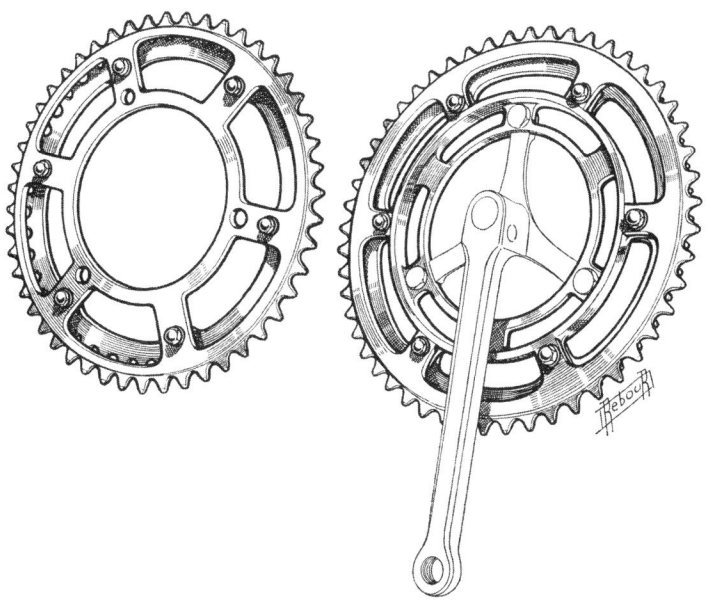
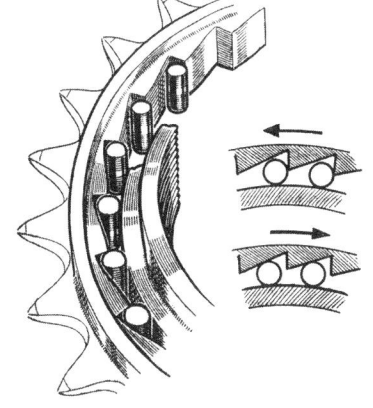

Left: New TA crankset and chainrings for 1955. *Le Cycle*, 12 June, 1954.

Right: Préférence freewheel with frictionless roller engagement. *Le Cycle*, 15 October 1955.

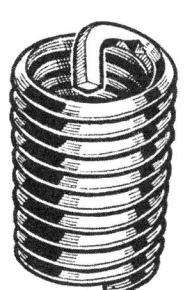
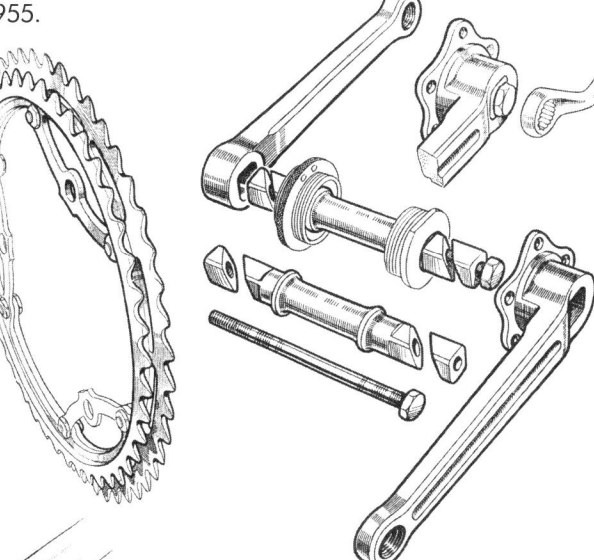

Left: Helicoil insert, designed to be used when the threaded pedal attachment in an aluminium alloy crank is damaged. *Le Cycle*, 25 February 1956.

Right: Stronglight double chainring combination. *Le Cycle*, 11 February 1956.

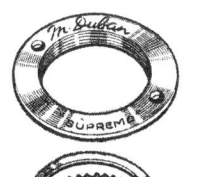
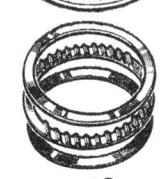
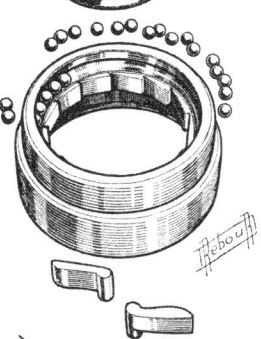
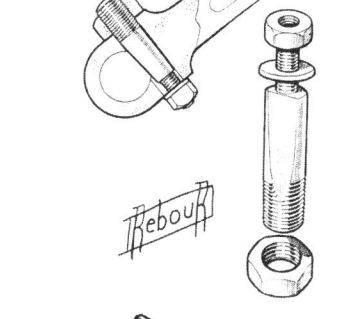
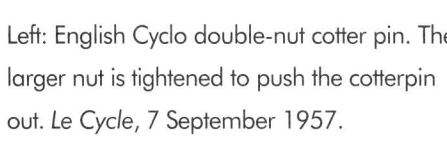
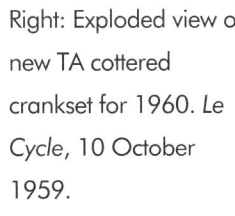
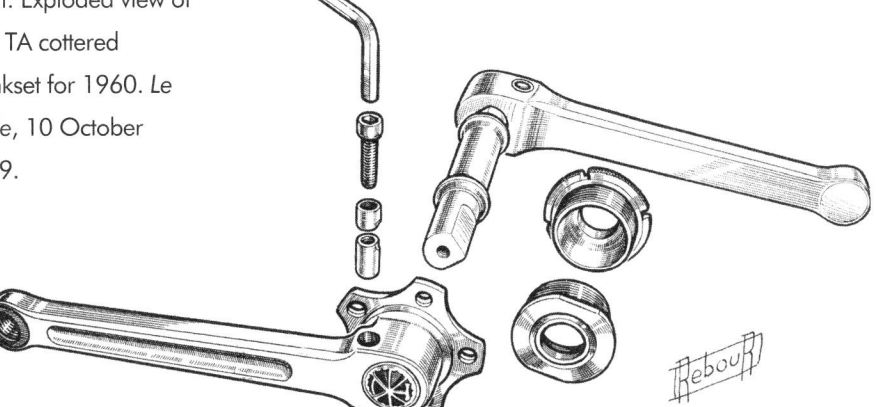

Left: Exploded view of M. Duban freewheel assembly. *Le Cycle*, 3 October 1958.

Right: Exploded view of new TA cottered crankset for 1960. *Le Cycle*, 10 October 1959.

Above: Cycle Trading crankset with wedge joints to spindle, from England. *Le Cycle*, 3 October 1958.

Left: English Cyclo double-nut cotter pin. The larger nut is tightened to push the cotterpin out. *Le Cycle*, 7 September 1957.

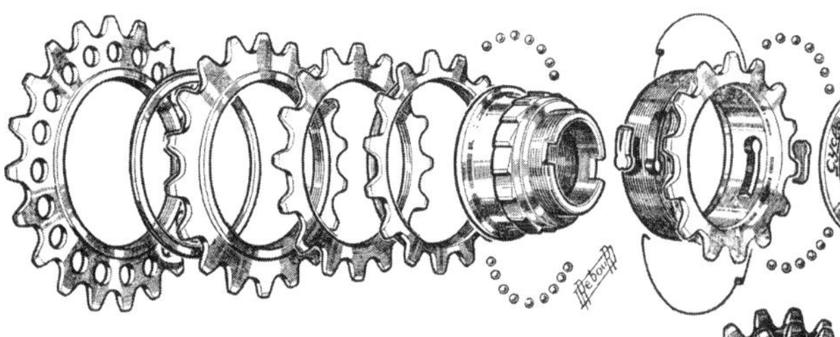

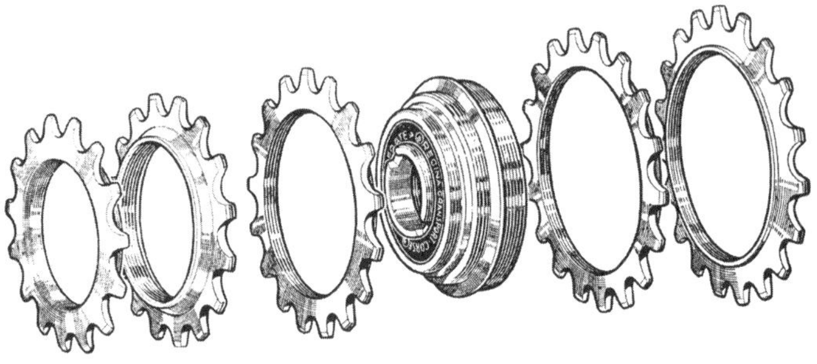

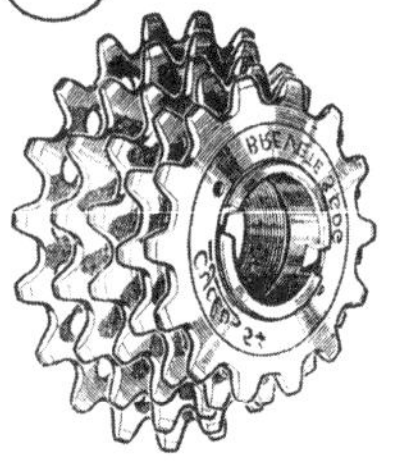

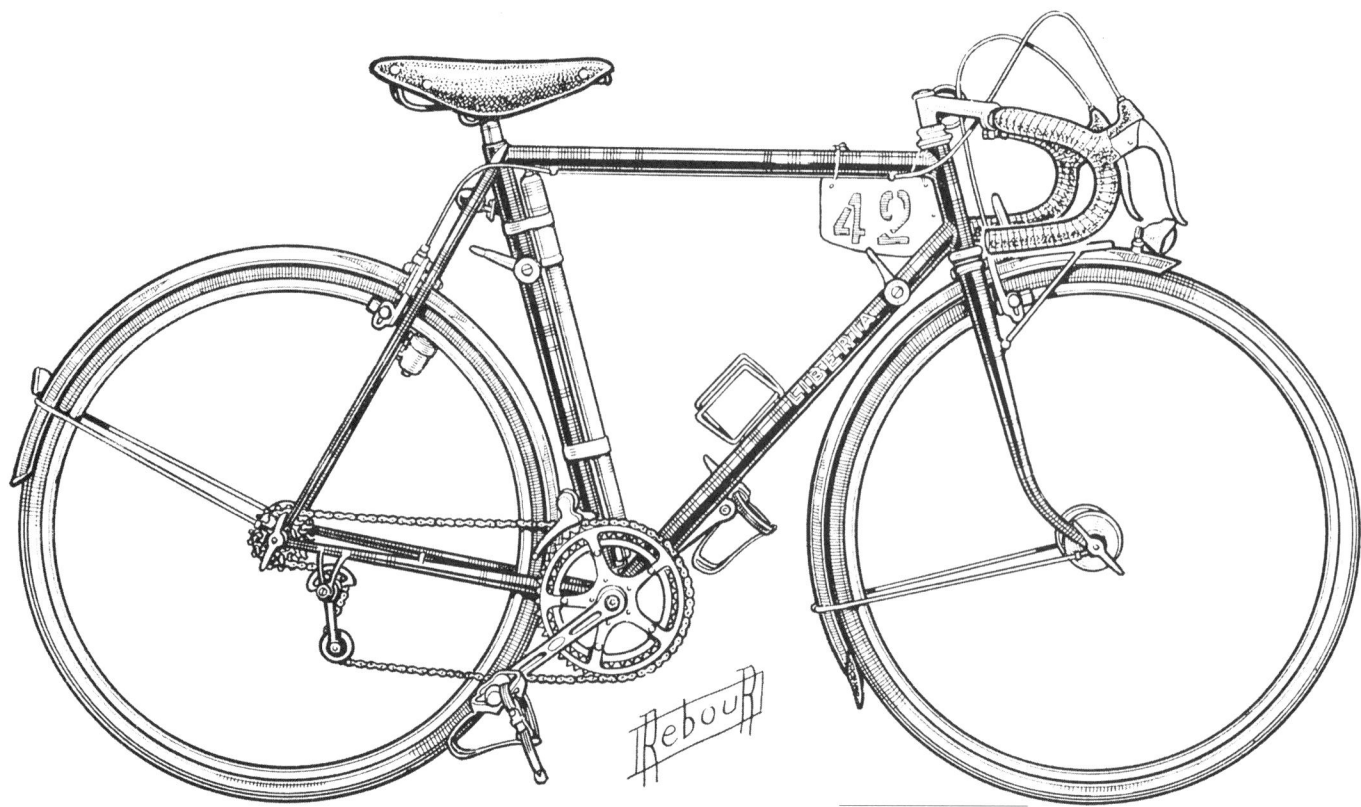

Above left: Exploded view of Cyclo Compétition freewheel. *Le Cycle*, 10 October 1959.

Above right: Exploded view of Regina freewheel. *Le Cycle*, 7 February 1959.

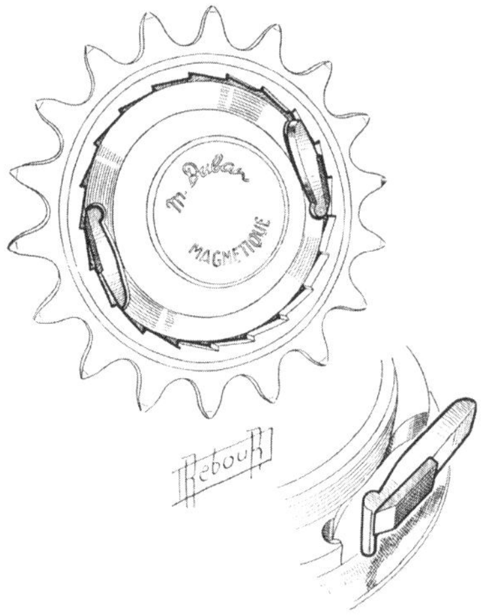

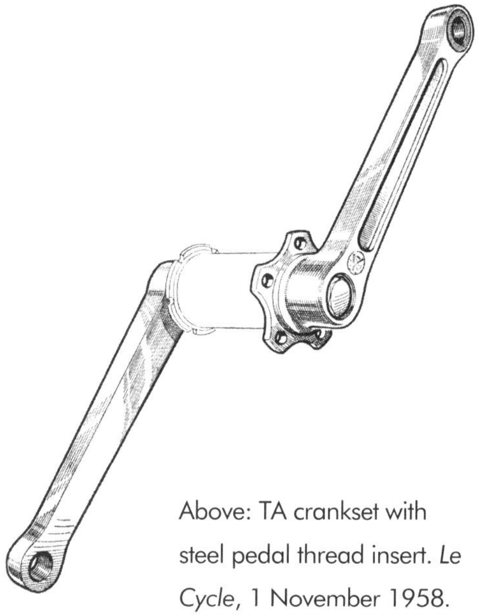

Right: Duban freewheel detail with magnetic pawl engagement. *Le Cycle*, 11 October 1958.

Below: Jacquelin's Liberia randonneur bicycle at the 1956 Chanteloup technical trials. *Le Cycle*, 5 May 1956.**

Above: TA crankset with steel pedal thread insert. *Le Cycle*, 1 November 1958.

** See pages 269–271 for expanded caption text.

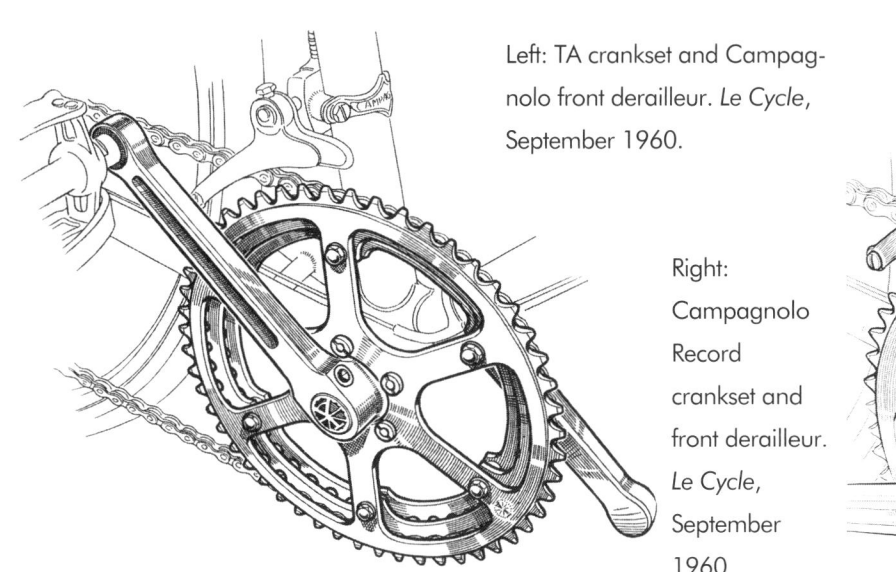

Left: TA crankset and Campagnolo front derailleur. *Le Cycle*, September 1960.

Right: Campagnolo Record crankset and front derailleur. *Le Cycle*, September 1960.

Right: Stronglight bottom bracket spindle and bearing cup. *Le Cycle*, 1 March 1960.

Far right: Atom freewheel. *Le Cycle*, November 1961.

Below: The Masi track bike on which Jacques Anquetil set a new World Hour record on 29 June 1956. *Le Cycle*, 14 July 1956.**

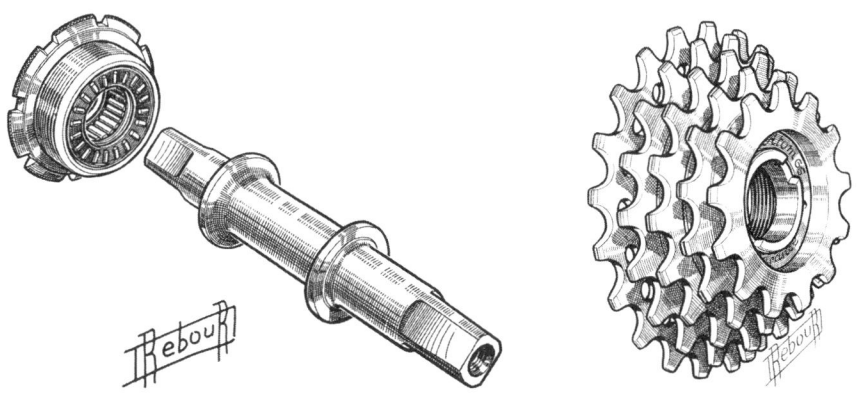

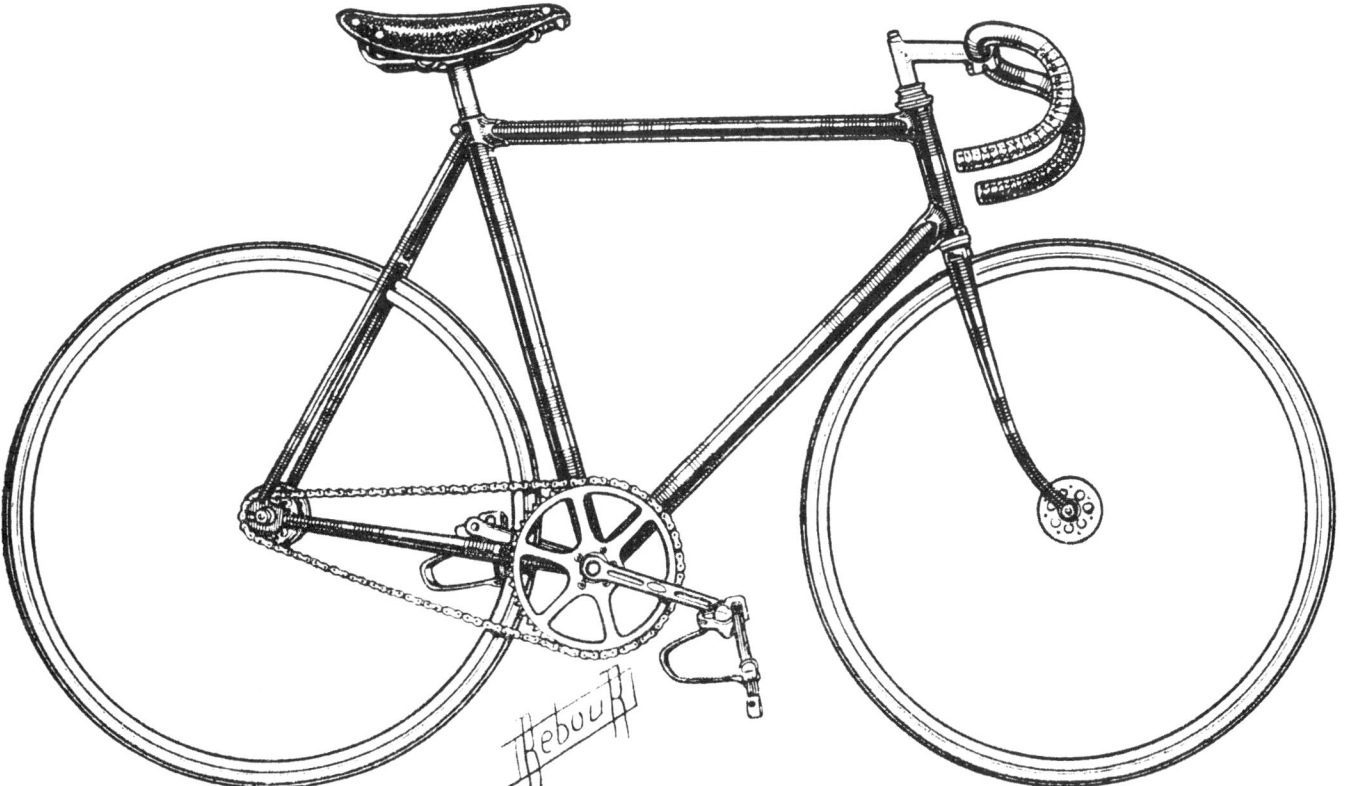

** See pages 269–271 for expanded caption text.

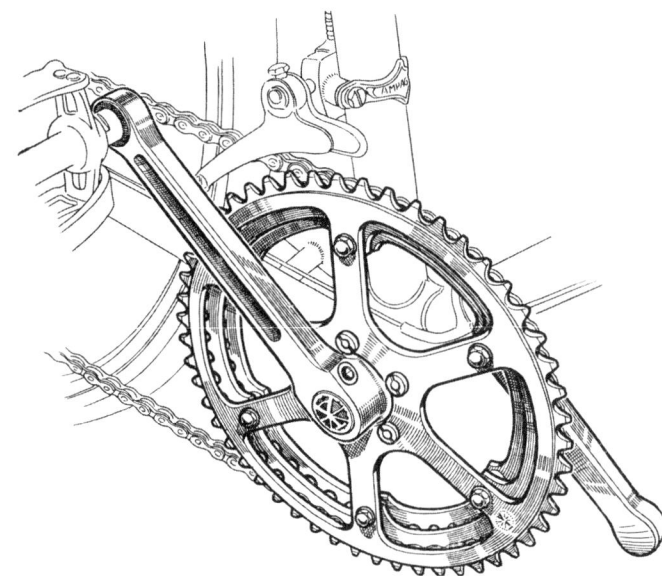

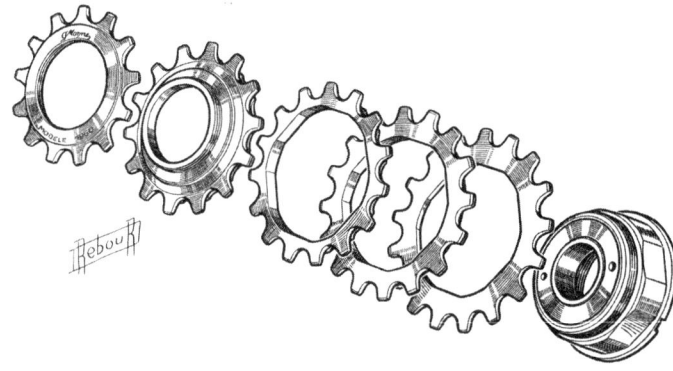

Above: Partially exploded view of J. Moyne monobloc freewheel and sprockets. *Le Cycle*, September 1960.

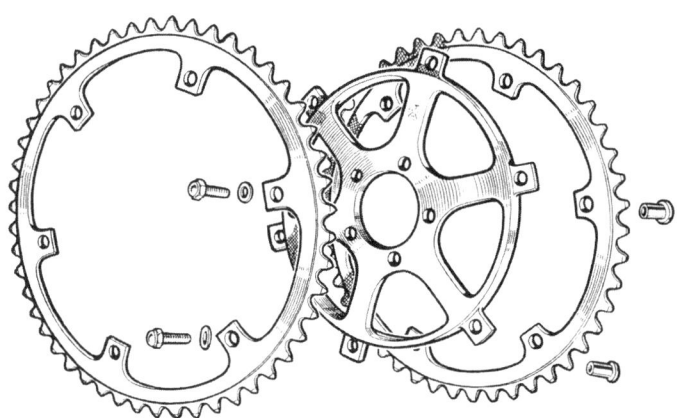

Above: TA triple crankset. *Le Cycle*, November 1961.

Right: TA double chainring set and installation details. *Le Cycle*, September 1960.

Below: The Mercier bicycle of 1956 French road champion Bernard Gautier. *Le Cycle*, 14 July 1956.

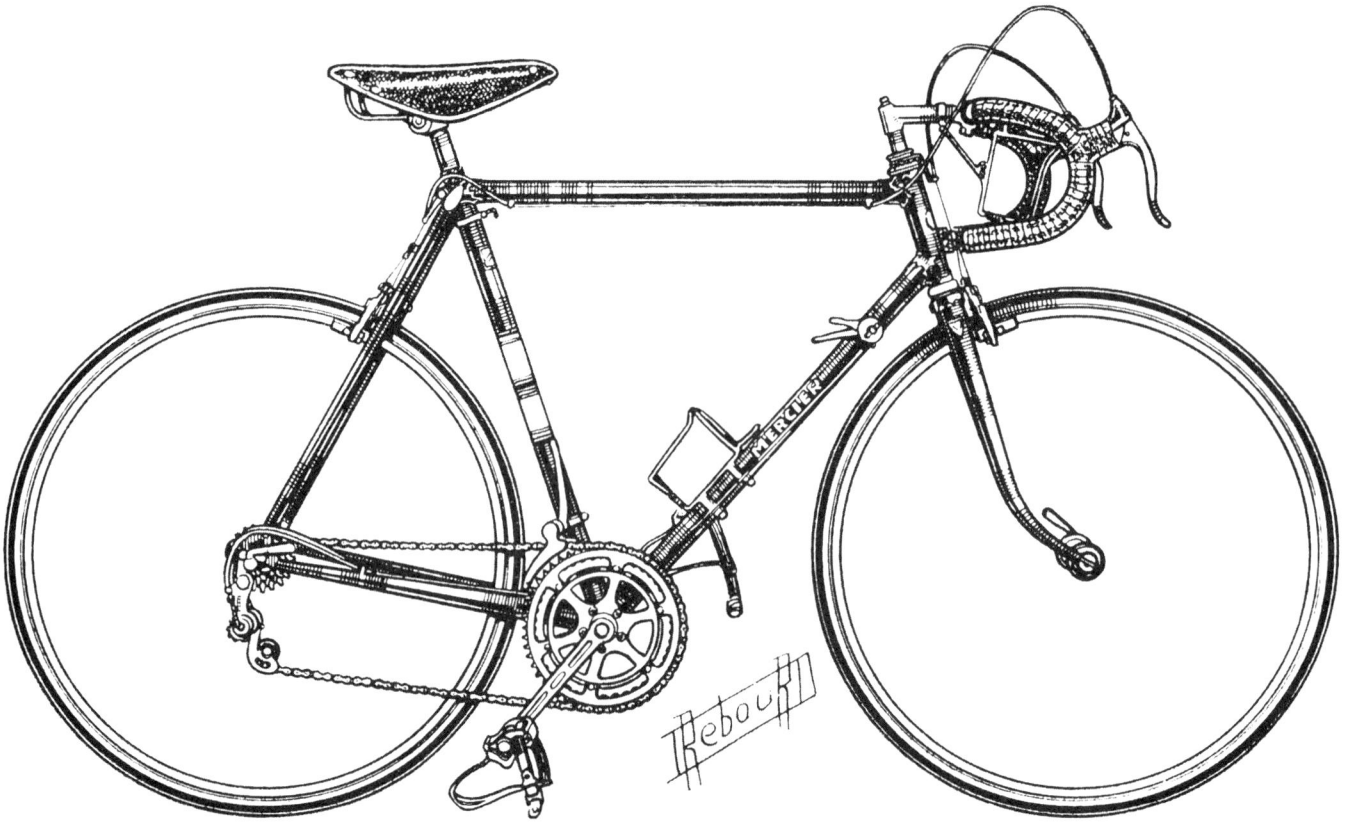

Chapter 4. Drivetrain Components

Below: TA cyclo-cross chainring detail. *Le Cycle*, Oct. 1960.

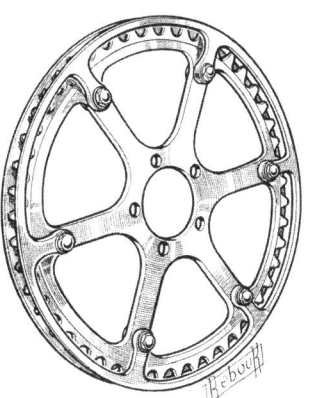

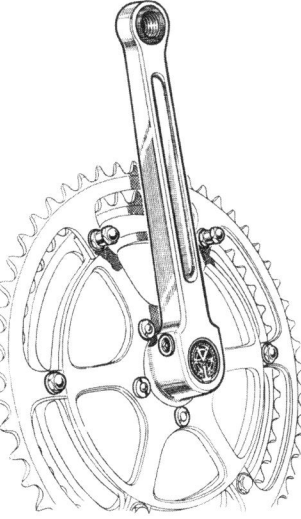

Left: TA crank and chainring installation detail.
Right: TA crankset and Huret front derailleur. *Le Cycle*, Oct. 1961.

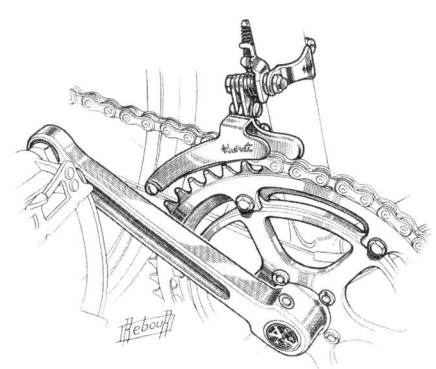

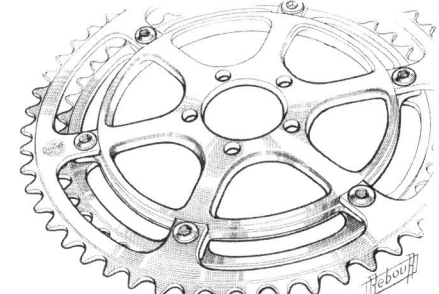

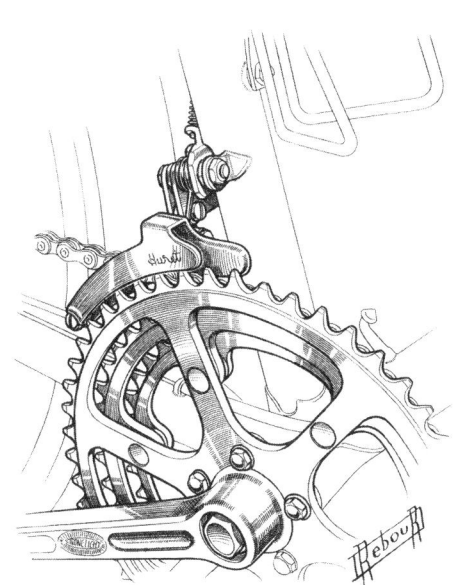

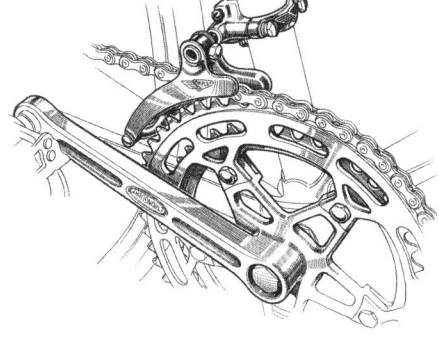

Above: Stronglight crankset with Simplex front derailleur. *Le Cycle,* Oct. 1961.
Left: René Herse chairings on Stronglight crankset. *Le Cycle*, May 1961.
Right: Stronglight Super Compétition crankset. *Le Cycle*, October 1961.
Below left: Magistroni crankset. *Le Cycle*, October 1961.
Below center: Campagnolo triple crankset. *Le Cycle*, Jan. 1962.
Below right: TA triple crankset. *Le Cycle*, November 1961.

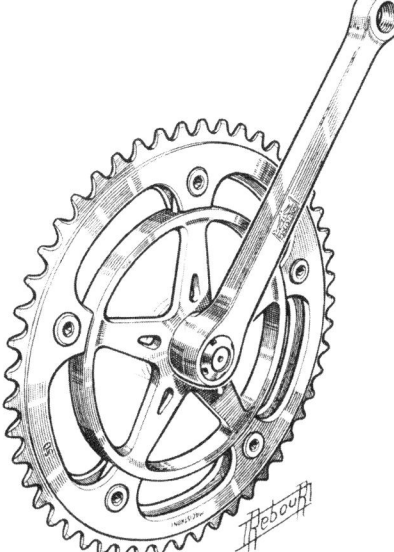

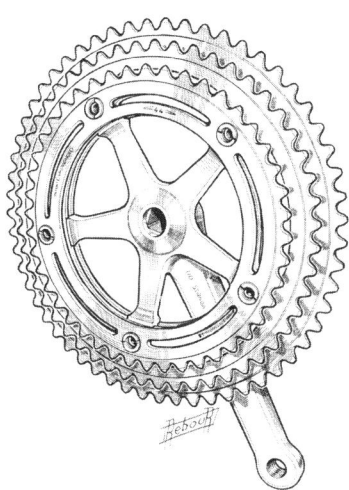

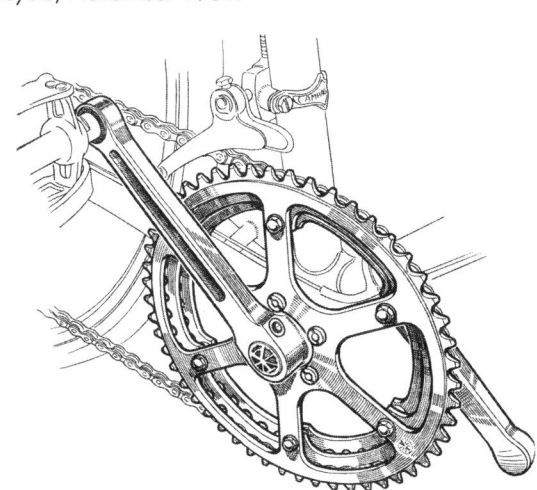

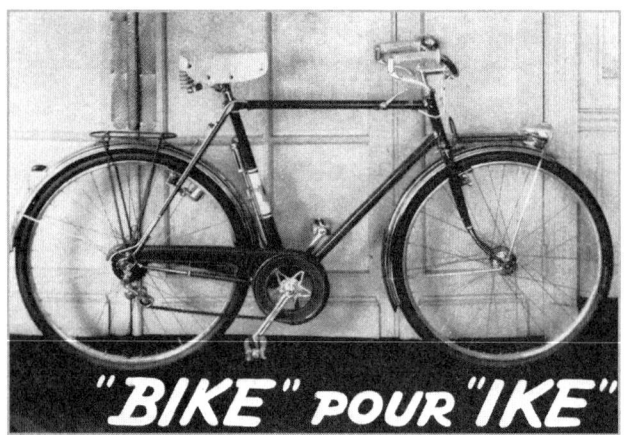

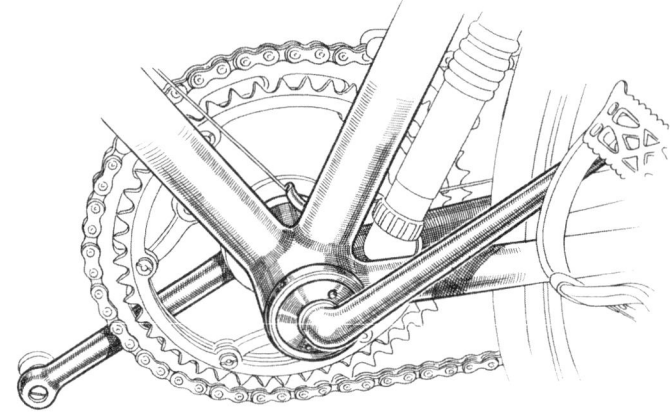

Above: Photograph of the bicycle depicted in the drawing below, as presentation to American President Dwight Eisenhower. *Le Cycle,* 28 July 1956.**

Below: The bicycle presented to President Dwight Eisenhower by the French cycling federation, after his doctor, Paul Dudley White, had recommended cycling to prevent further heart attacks. Ike took up golf instead. He lived another 12 years, but died of congestive heart failure in 1969 at age 79. *Le Cycle,* 28 July 1956.**

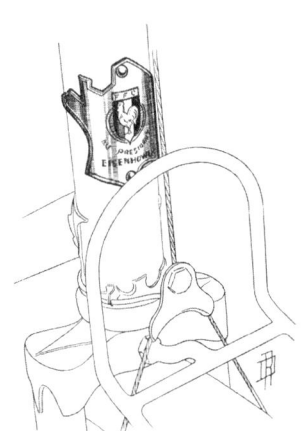

Above right and right: Details of Fauber-type one-piece crankset (known as one-piece or Ashtabula cranks in the U.S.). *Le Cycle,*

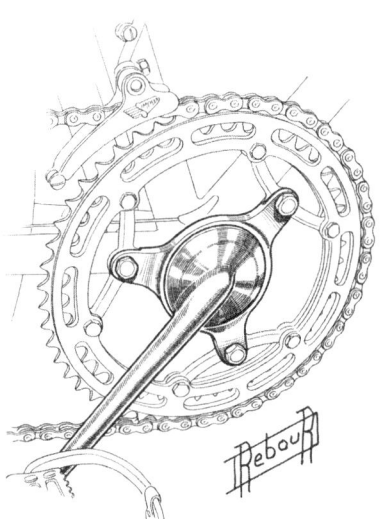

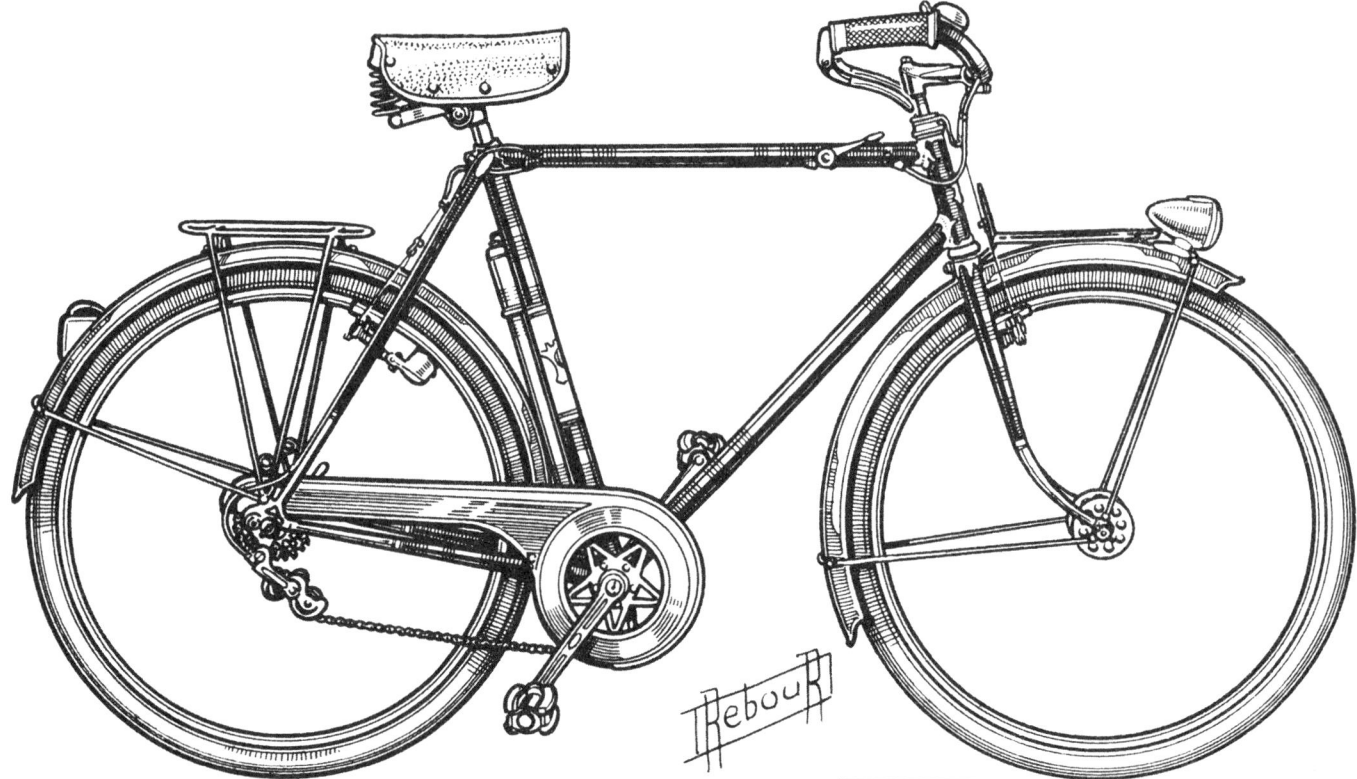

** See pages 269–271 for expanded caption texts.

Chapter 4. Drivetrain Components

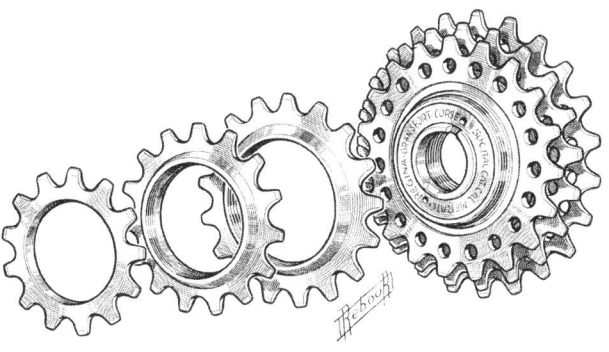

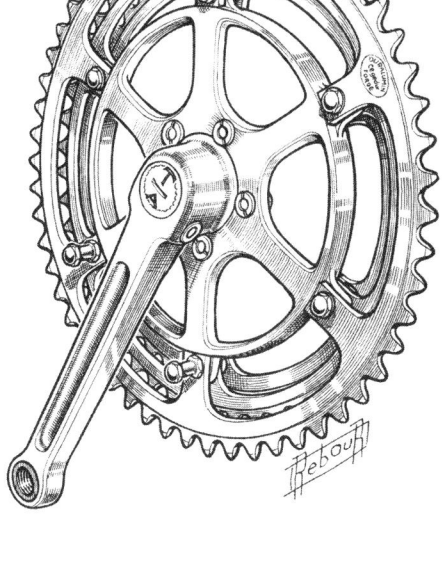

Left: Regina 6-speed freewheel, introduced at Milan, 1962.
Right: TA triple-chainring crankset, also introduced at Milan, 1962.
Both images from *Le Cycle*, September 1962.

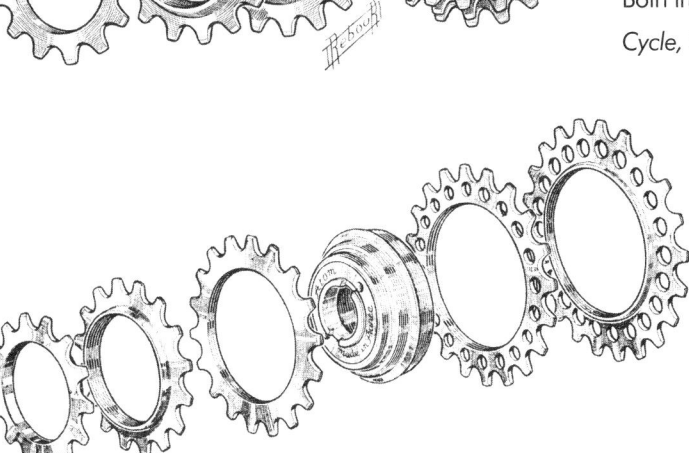

Left: Atom freewheel and sprockets. *Le Cycle*, September 1962.

Right: Unidentified 1962 cartridge bearing bottom bracket spindle and bearings unit. *Cycle: Compétition, Cyclotourisme*.

Below: The Mercier bicycle ridden by Jean Adriaenssens, 3rd in the 1956 Tour de France. *Le Cycle*, 11 August 1956.**

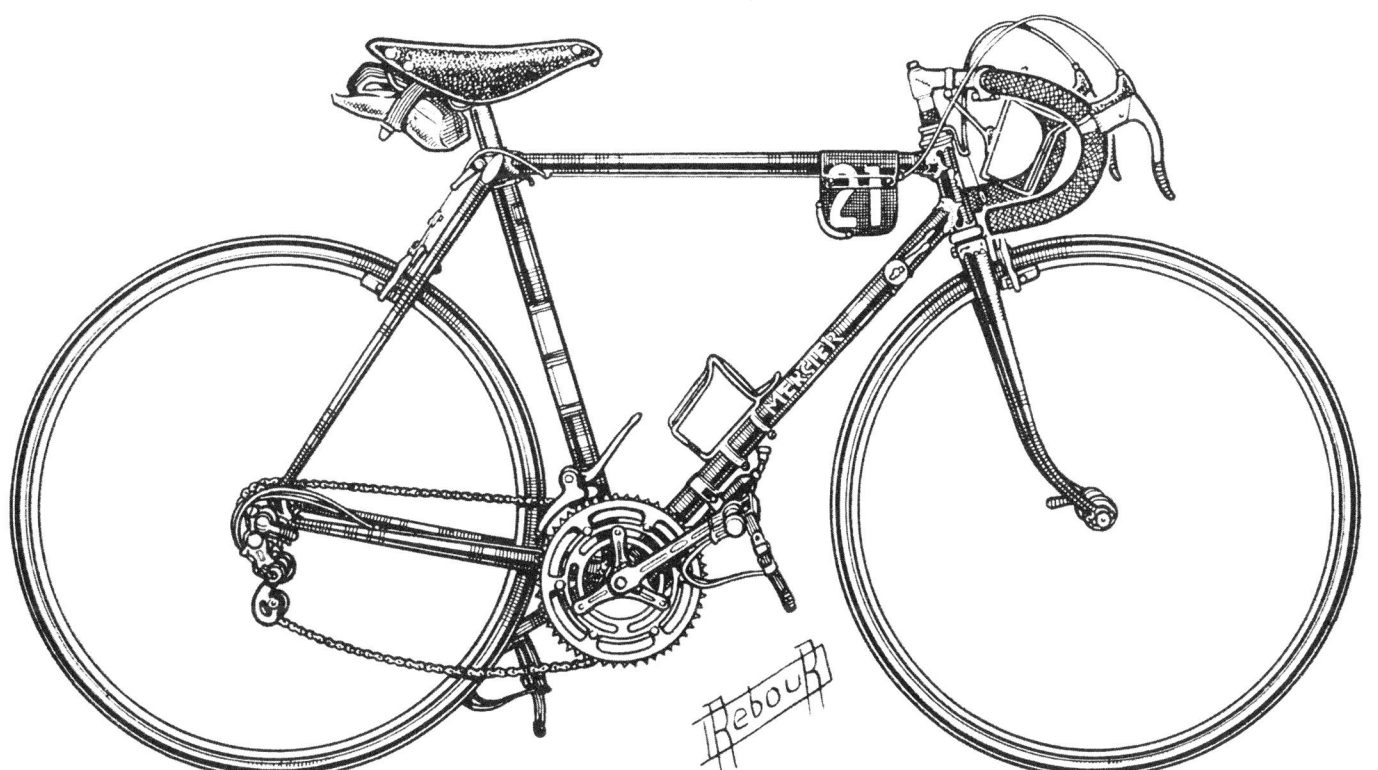

** See pages 269–271 for expanded caption text.

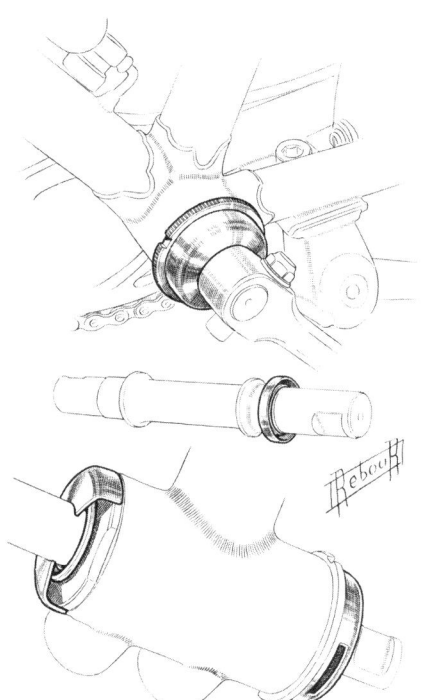

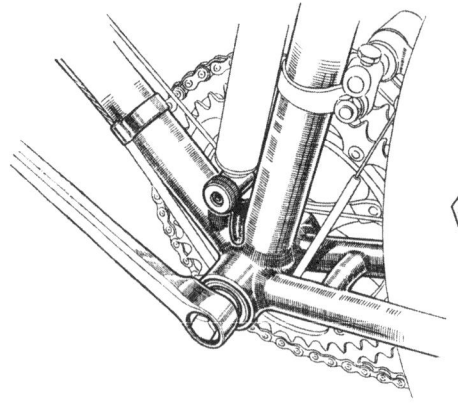

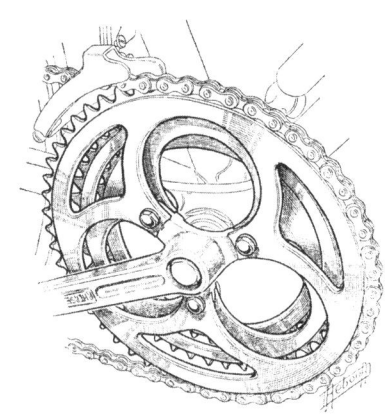

Above: Stronglight needle-bearing bottom bracket. *Cycle: Compétition, Cyclotourisme.*

Above: Bottom bracket detail on Flandria bicycle. *Cycle: Compétition, Cyclotourisme.*

Below: One-piece crank and double chainring on Schwinn Superior. *Le Cycle*, January 1963.

Above: Cartridge-bearing bottom bracket on a Mondia bicycle, from Switzerland. *Le Cycle*, January 1962.

Below: A small rider, 2nd-placed Gilbert Bauvin, of France, used this bike, painted sky blue, in the 1956 Tour. *Le Cycle*, 11 August 1956.

Above: René Herse proprietary triple crankset. *Cycle: Compétition, Cyclotourisme.*

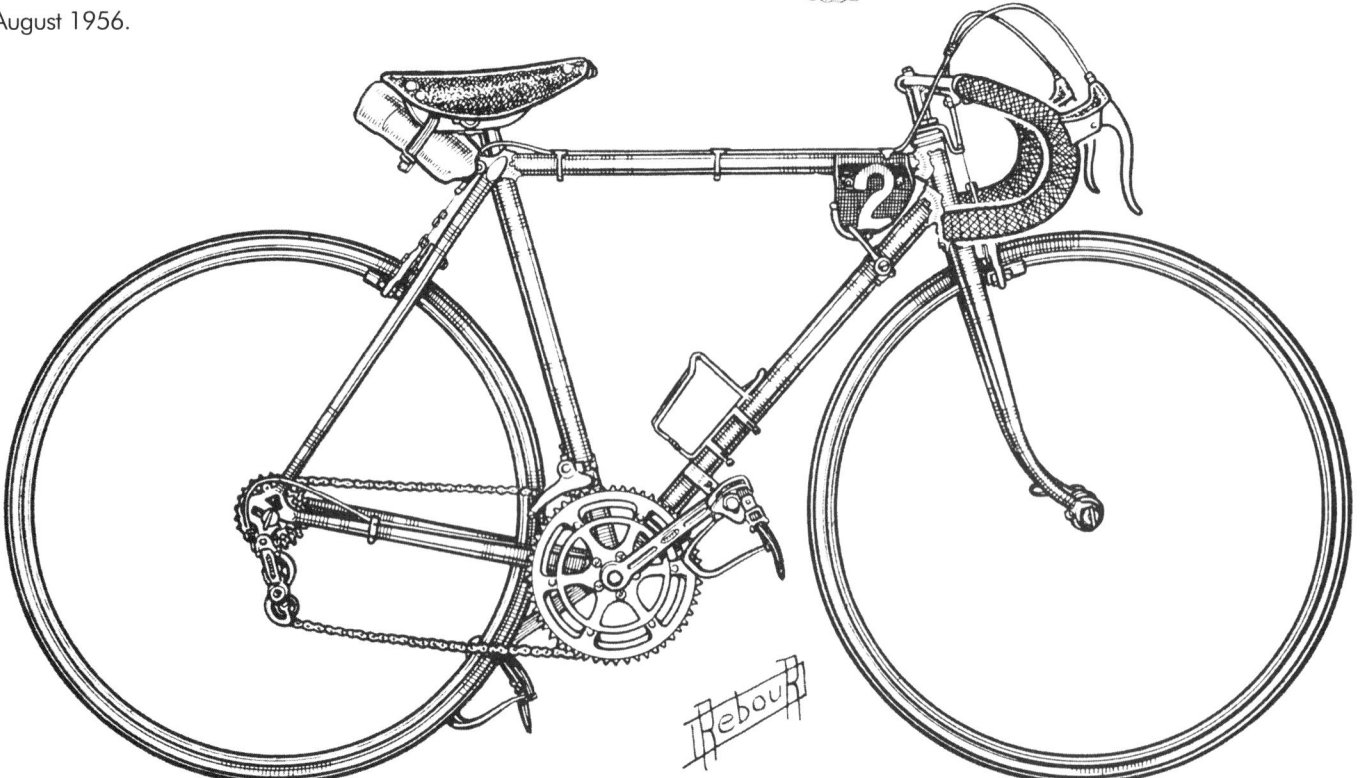

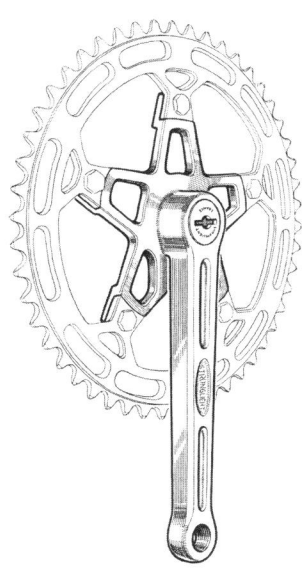

Left: Stronglight single-chainring crankset. *Le Cycle*, May 1964.

Right: TA chainrings. *Cycle: Compétition, Cyclotourisme.*

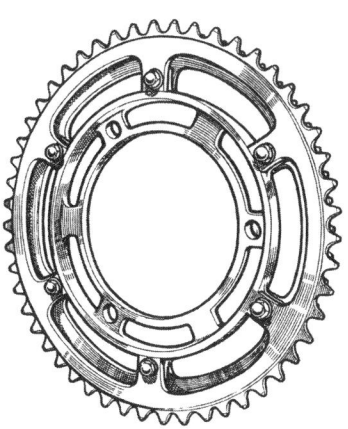

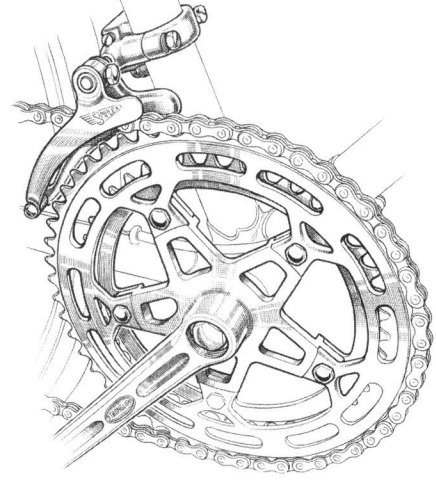

Right: TA chainrings and attachment. *Le Cycle*, May 1964.

Below: Maillard freewheel and removal tool. *Le Cycle*, November 1964.

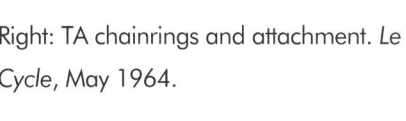

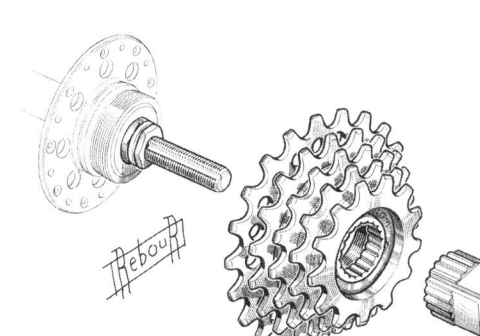

Above: Stronglight crankset and Simplex front derailleur. *Le Cycle*, May 1964.

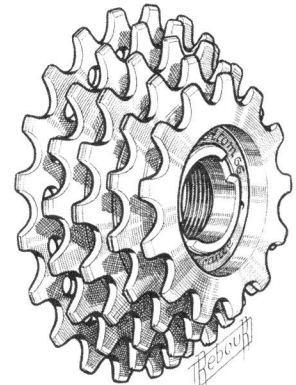

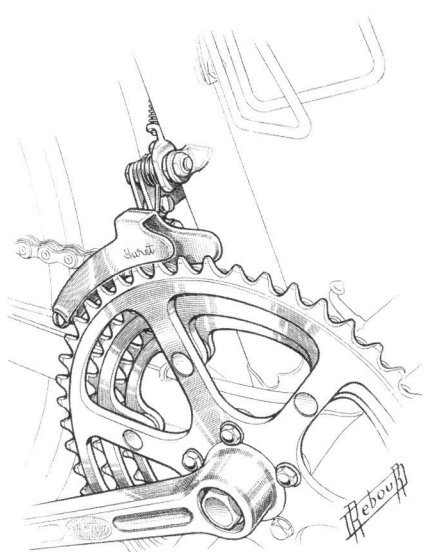

Above: Atom 5-speed freewheel. *Le Cycle*, October 1964.

Above right: TA triple crankset and Huret front derailleur. *Le Cycle*, May 1964.

Left: Stronglight triple crankset. *Le Cycle*, October 1964.

Right: New 5-pin, 6-arm TA triple-chainring crankset, introduced at the 1964 Paris bicycle trade show. *Le Cycle*, October 1964.

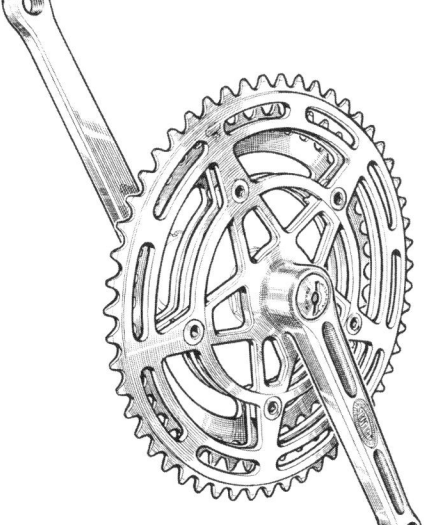

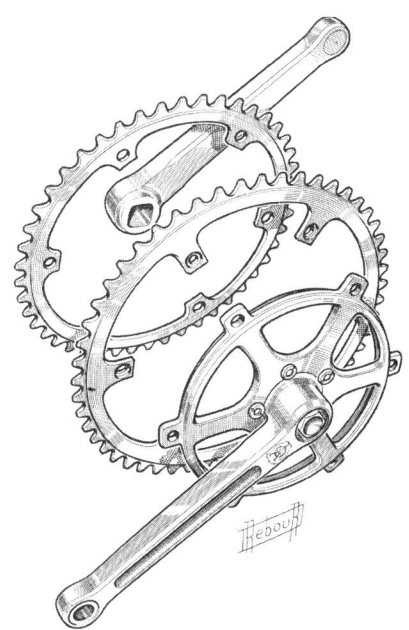

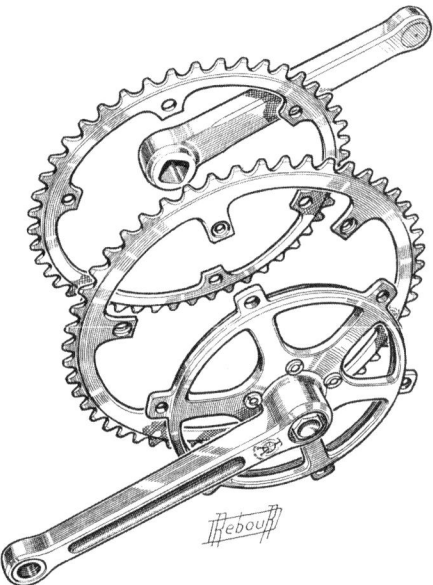
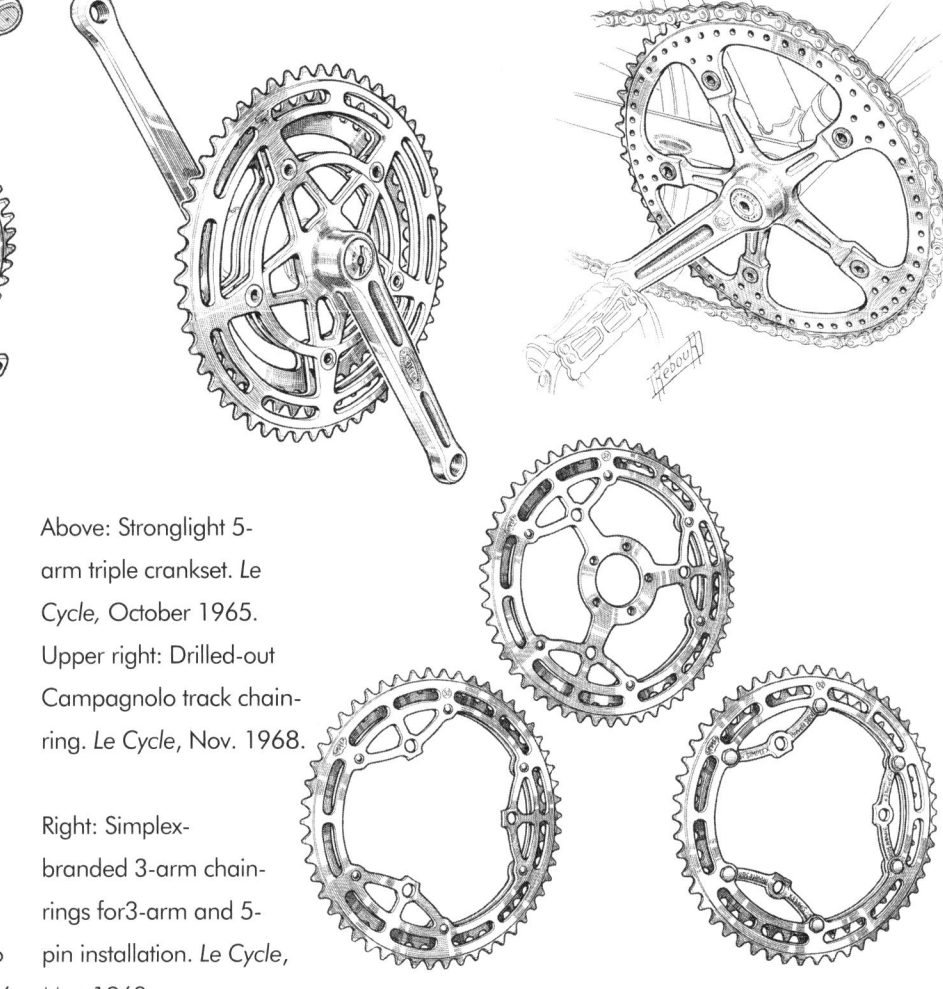

Above: Exploded view of the same TA crankset depicted on page 89. *Le Cycle,* October 1965.

Below: Charly Gaul, of Luxembourg, winner of the 1956 Tour de France mountains classification, rode this Learco Guerra bicycle. *Le Cycle,* 11 August 1956.

Above: Stronglight 5-arm triple crankset. *Le Cycle,* October 1965.
Upper right: Drilled-out Campagnolo track chainring. *Le Cycle,* Nov. 1968.

Right: Simplex-branded 3-arm chainrings for 3-arm and 5-pin installation. *Le Cycle,* May 1968.

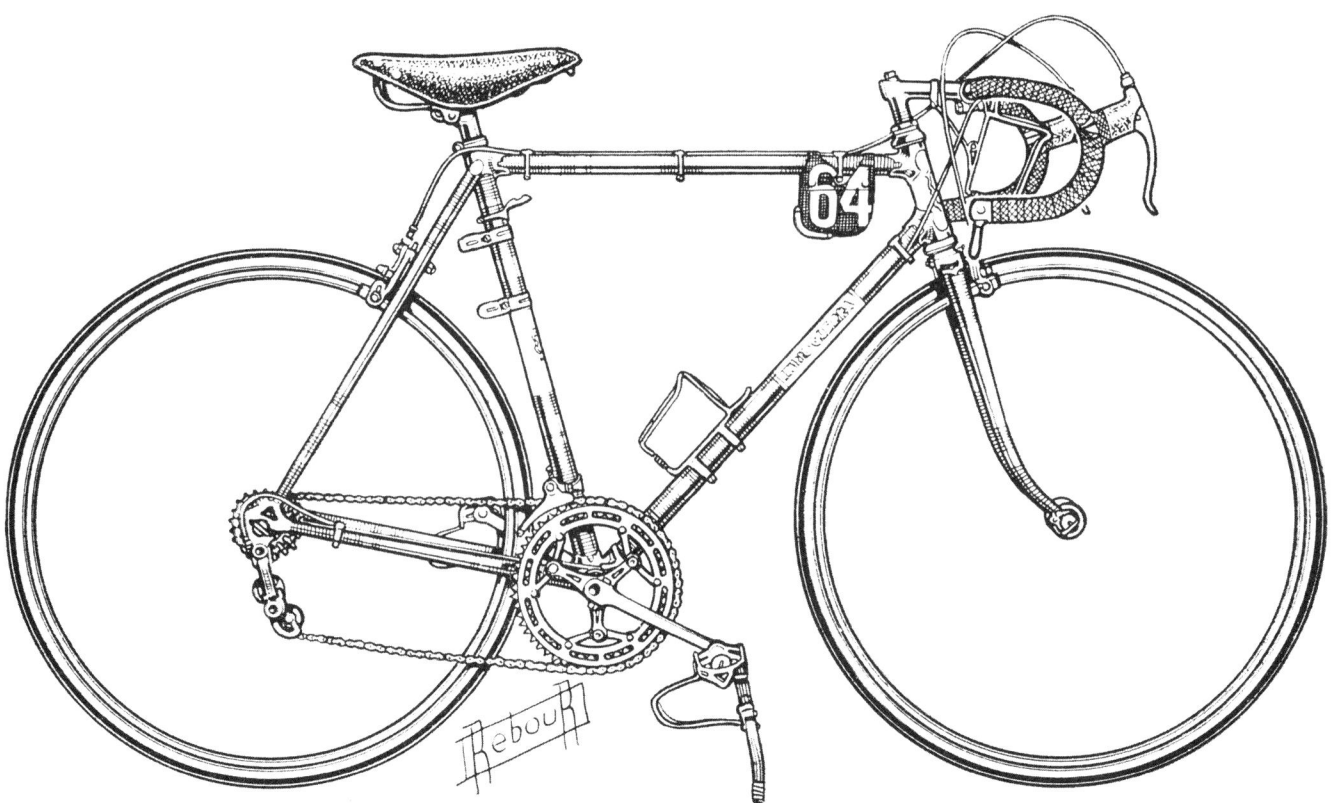

CHAPTER 4. DRIVETRAIN COMPONENTS

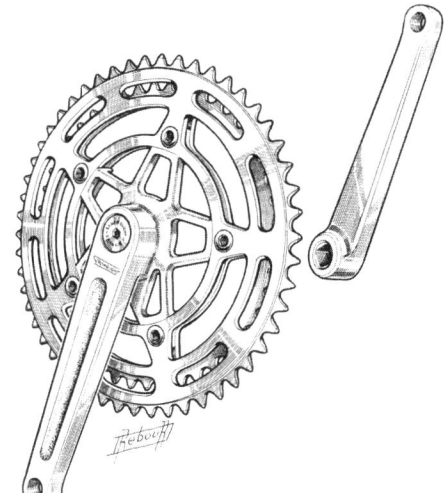

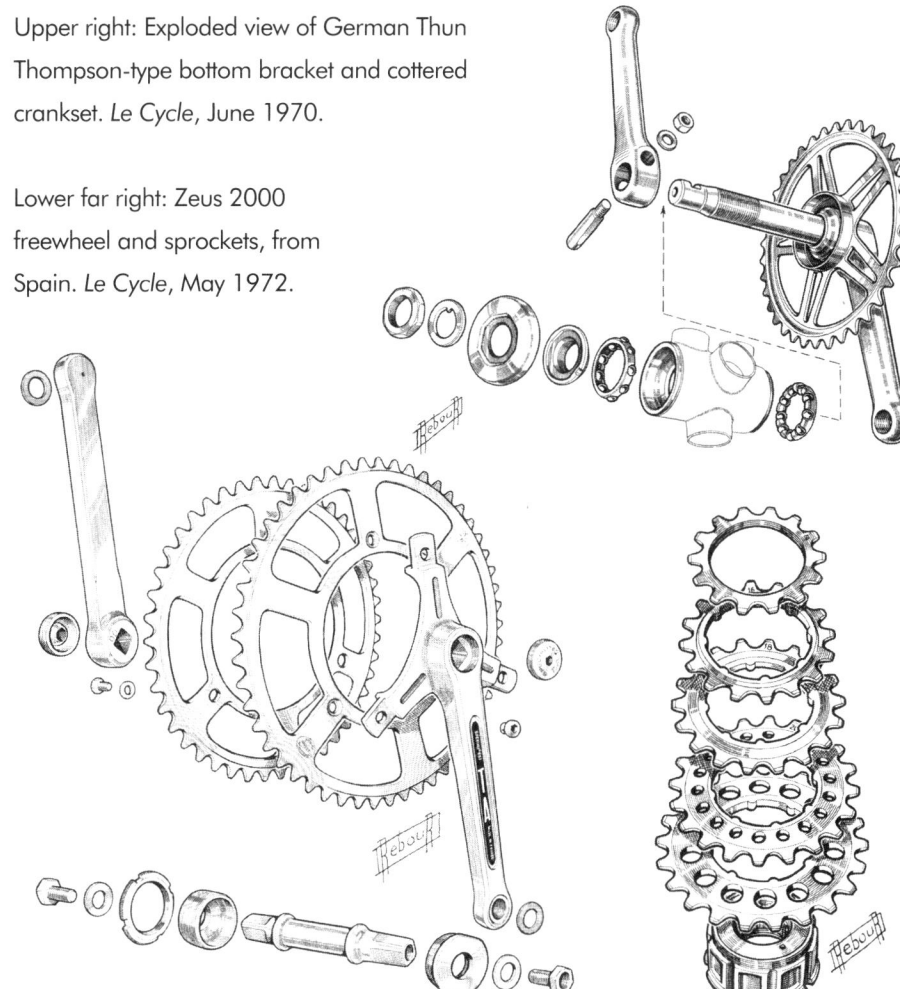

Upper right: Exploded view of German Thun Thompson-type bottom bracket and cottered crankset. *Le Cycle*, June 1970.

Lower far right: Zeus 2000 freewheel and sprockets, from Spain. *Le Cycle*, May 1972.

Above: Stronglight Model 93 5-arm crankset. *Le Cycle*, October 1968.

Right: Exploded view of TA 3-arm crankset and bottom bracket. *Le Cycle*, October 1968.

Below: The Peugeot-Elve bicycle ridden by Stan Ockers, winner of the points classification of the 1956 Tour de France. *Le Cycle*, 11 August 1956.

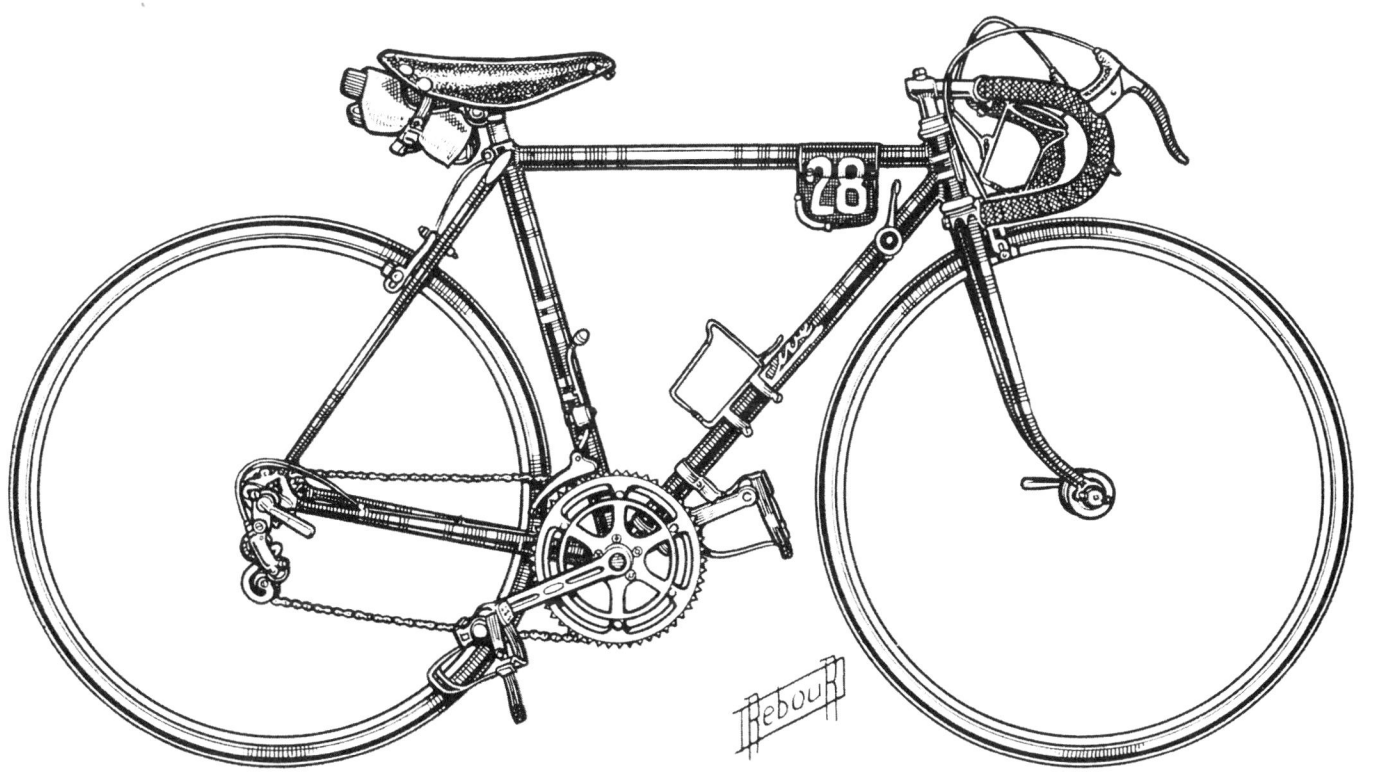

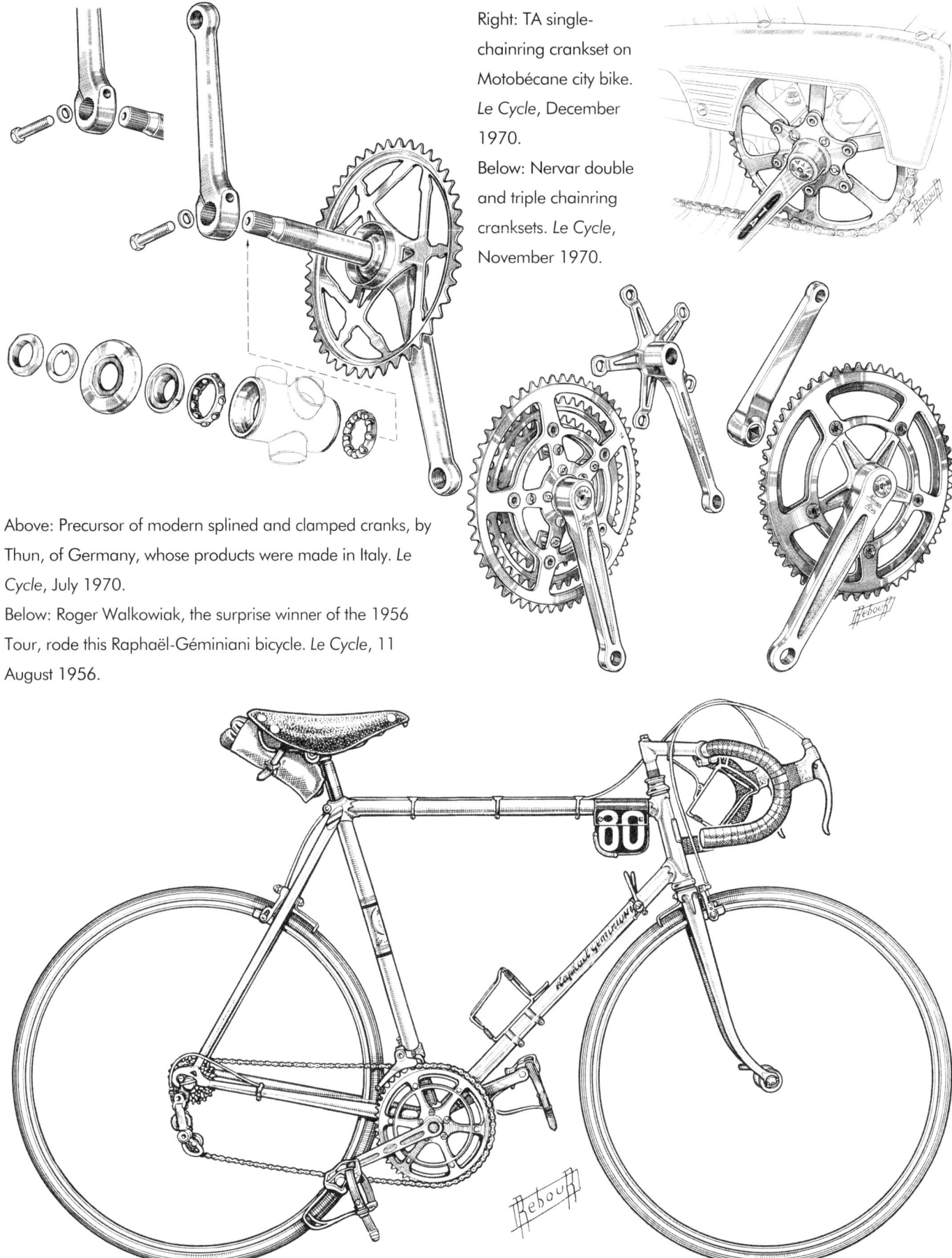

Right: TA single-chainring crankset on Motobécane city bike. *Le Cycle*, December 1970.

Below: Nervar double and triple chainring cranksets. *Le Cycle*, November 1970.

Above: Precursor of modern splined and clamped cranks, by Thun, of Germany, whose products were made in Italy. *Le Cycle*, July 1970.

Below: Roger Walkowiak, the surprise winner of the 1956 Tour, rode this Raphaël-Géminiani bicycle. *Le Cycle*, 11 August 1956.

Chapter 4. Drivetrain Components

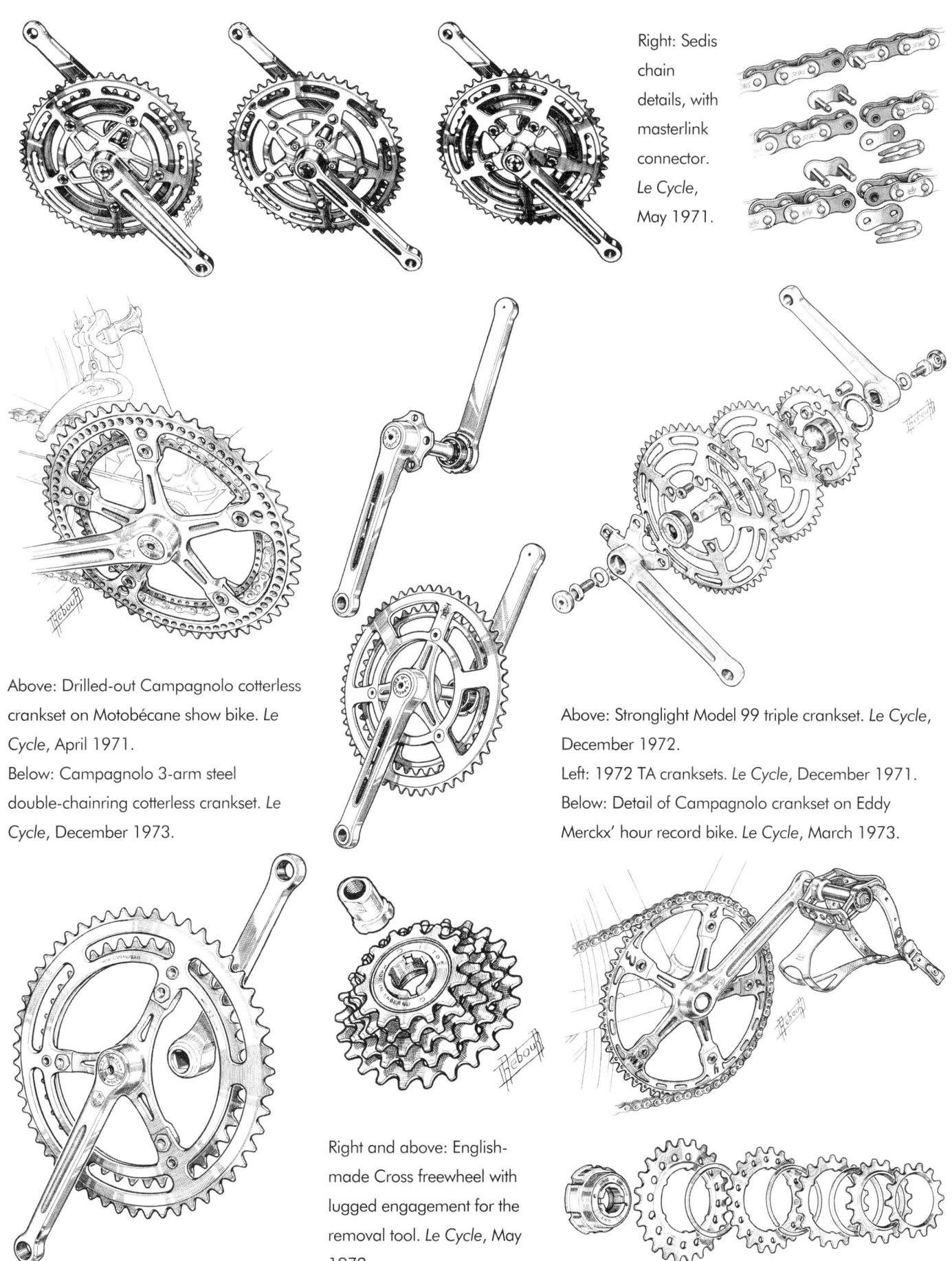

Right: Sedis chain details, with masterlink connector. *Le Cycle*, May 1971.

Above: Drilled-out Campagnolo cotterless crankset on Motobécane show bike. *Le Cycle*, April 1971.
Below: Campagnolo 3-arm steel double-chainring cotterless crankset. *Le Cycle*, December 1973.

Above: Stronglight Model 99 triple crankset. *Le Cycle*, December 1972.
Left: 1972 TA cranksets. *Le Cycle*, December 1971.
Below: Detail of Campagnolo crankset on Eddy Merckx' hour record bike. *Le Cycle*, March 1973.

Right and above: English-made Cross freewheel with lugged engagement for the removal tool. *Le Cycle*, May 1972.

93

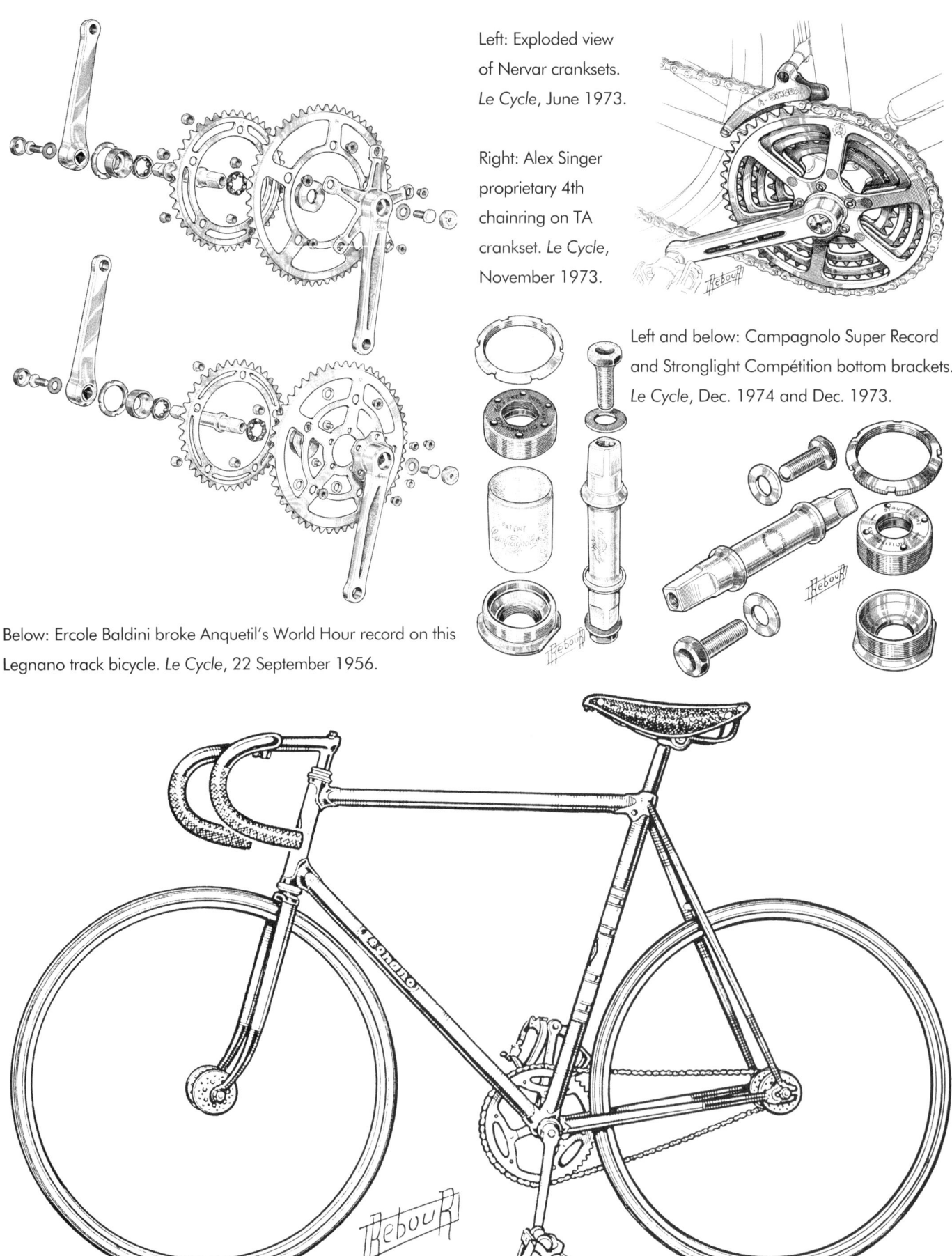

Left: Exploded view of Nervar cranksets. *Le Cycle*, June 1973.

Right: Alex Singer proprietary 4th chainring on TA crankset. *Le Cycle*, November 1973.

Left and below: Campagnolo Super Record and Stronglight Compétition bottom brackets. *Le Cycle*, Dec. 1974 and Dec. 1973.

Below: Ercole Baldini broke Anquetil's World Hour record on this Legnano track bicycle. *Le Cycle*, 22 September 1956.

Chapter 4. Drivetrain Components

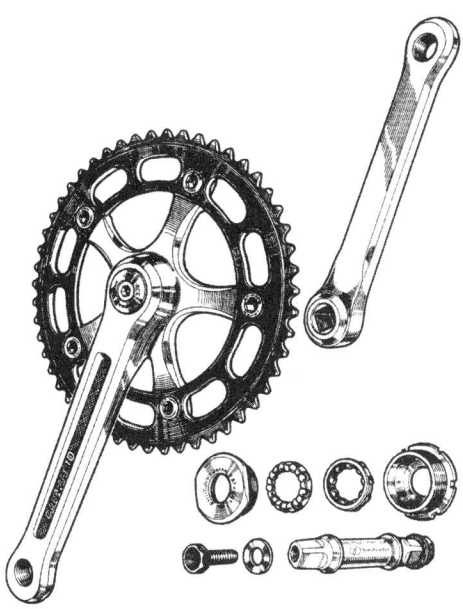

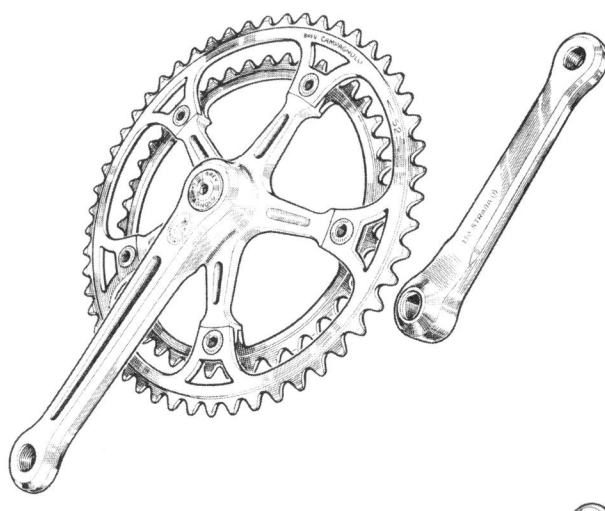

Left: Shimano 10 mm pitch Keirin (track) crankset. 1983 Milremo catalogue.

Right: Campagnolo Record crankset and chainrings. 1981 Milremo catalogue.

Right: Shimano 105 crankset and bottom bracket bearings. 1983 Milremo catalogue.

Right: Shimano Dura-Ace freewheel cassette. 1983 Milremo catalogue.

Below: The Follis bicycle entered by Fernandes in the 1956 Eastern regional technical trials, at Lyons. *Le Cycle*, 22 September 1956.

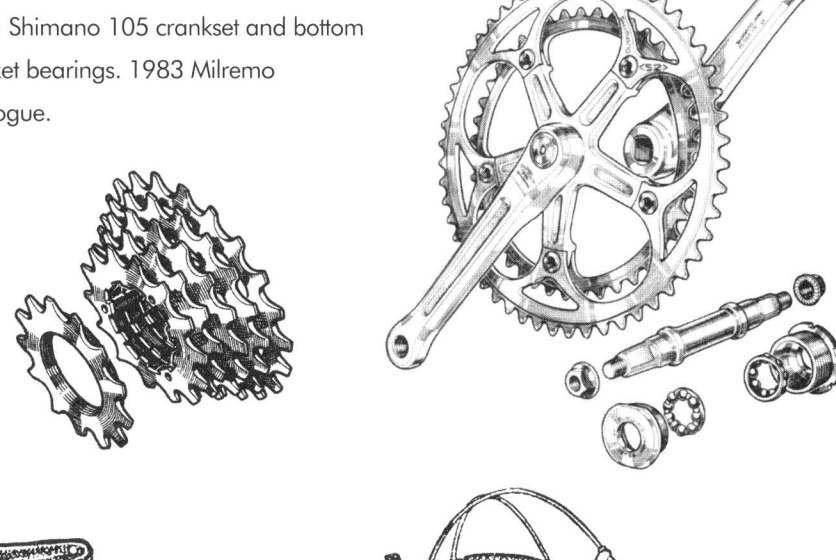

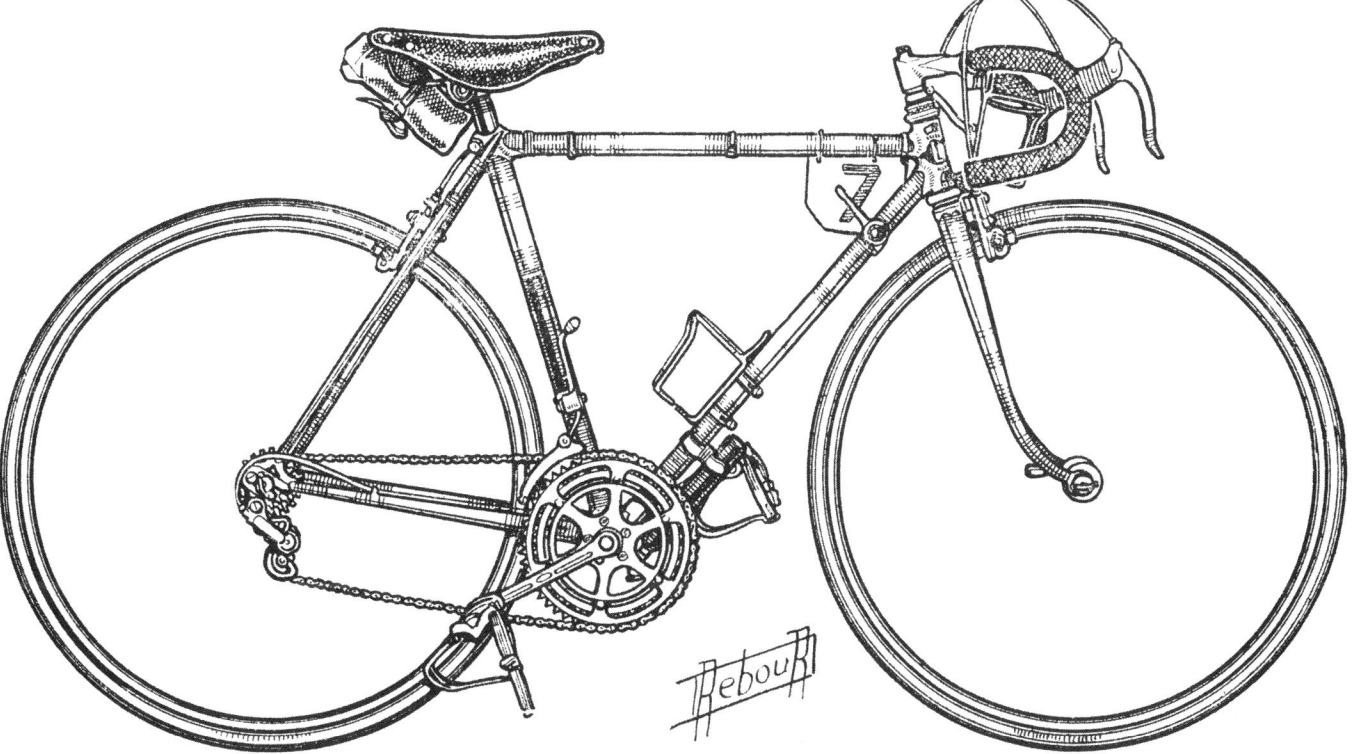

95

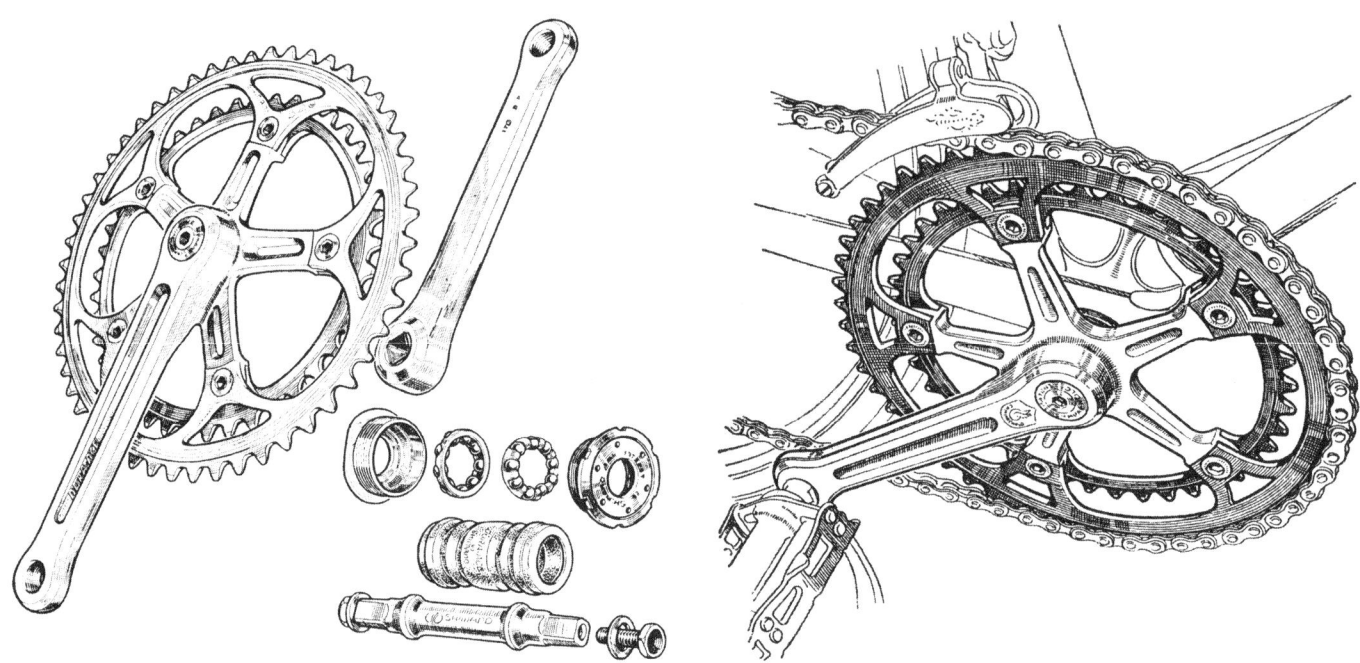

Above: Shimano Dura-Ace EX crankset and bottom bracket bearings. 1980 Milremo catalogue.

Below: The Jo Routens randonneur bike with which Thalia came in first at the 1956 Paris–Brest–Paris. *Le Cycle*, 22 September 1956.

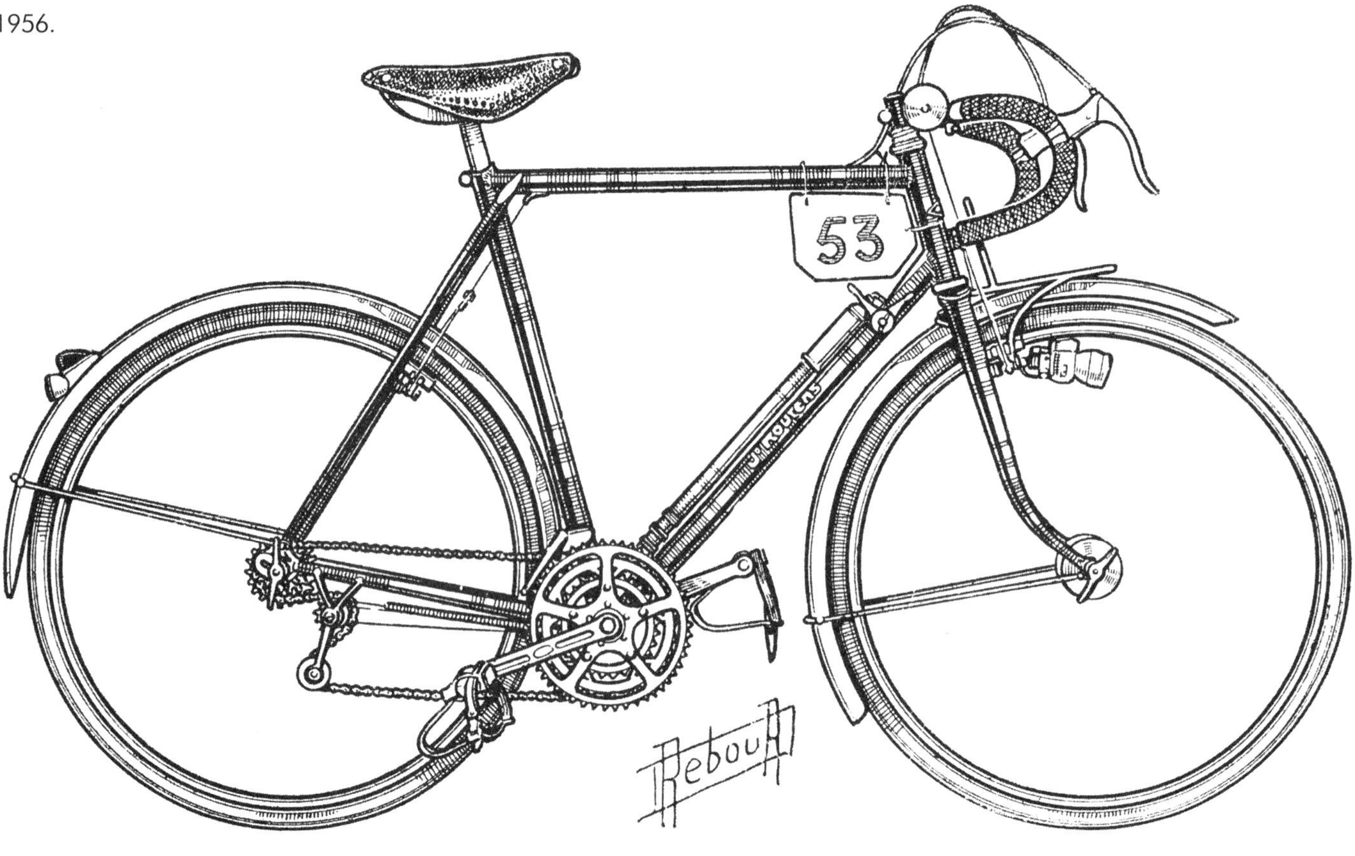

Above: Campagnolo Super Record crankset. 1980 Milremo catalogue.

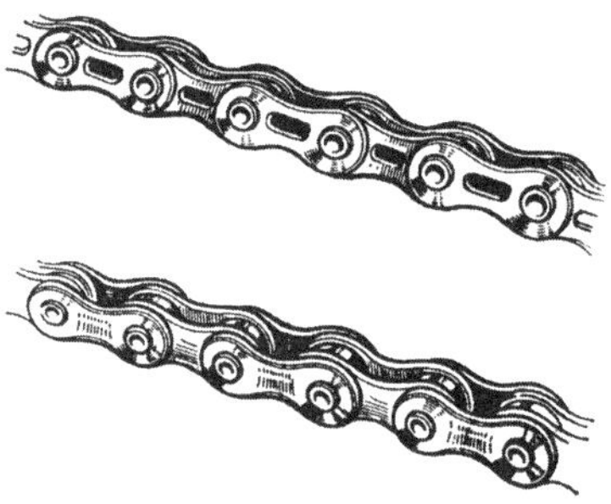

Left: Chain details, showing Everest Superlight chain (top) and regular DID chain. 1980 Milremo catalogue.

Chapter 4. Drivetrain Components

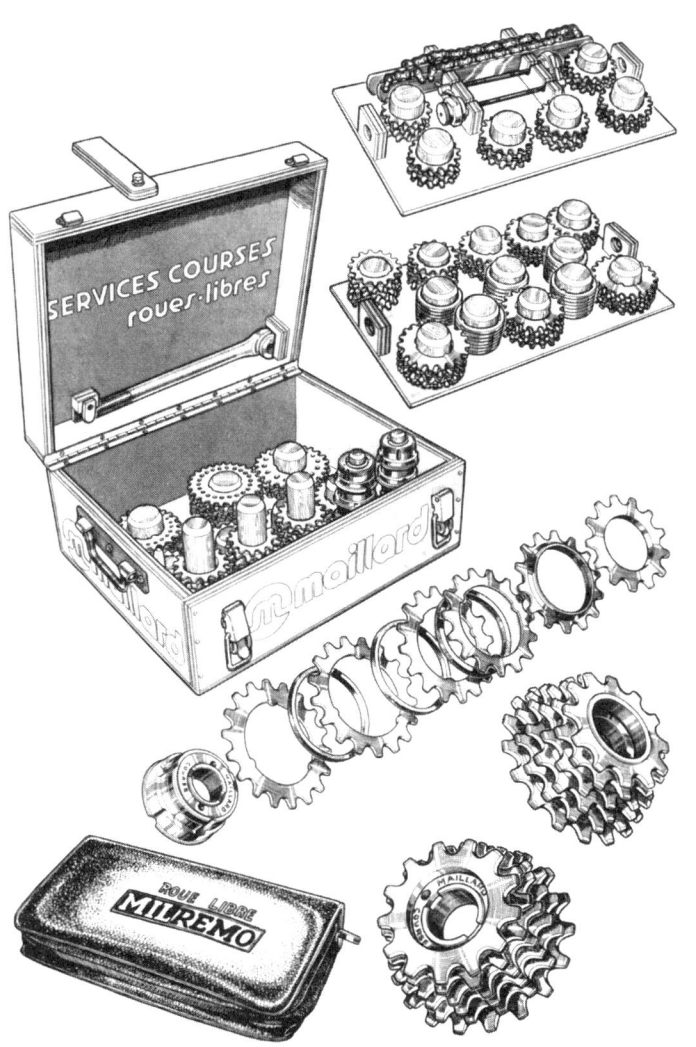

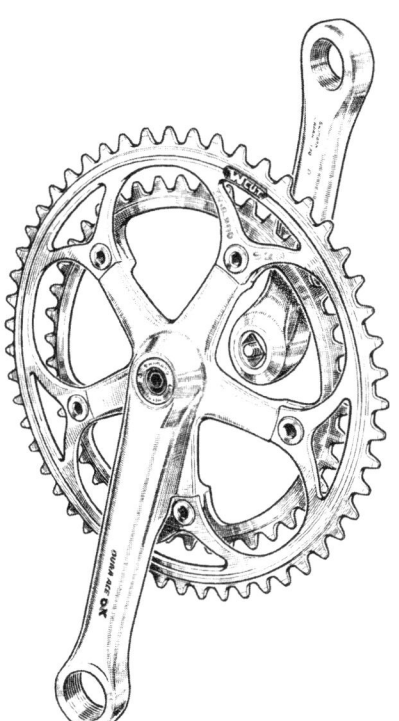

Above: Shimano Ultra-Glide bushingless chain. 1981 Milremo catalogue.

Left: Maillard freewheel and sprocket set. 1983 Milremo catalogue.

Right: Shimano Dura-Ace AX aerodynamic crankset. 1981 Milremo catalogue.

Bottom right: Stronglight cranksets. 1981 Milremo catalogue.

Below: Campagnolo Super Record bottom bracket parts. 1980 Milremo catalogue.

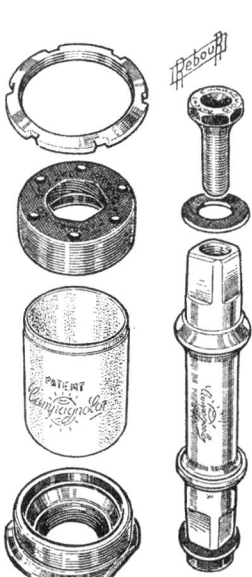

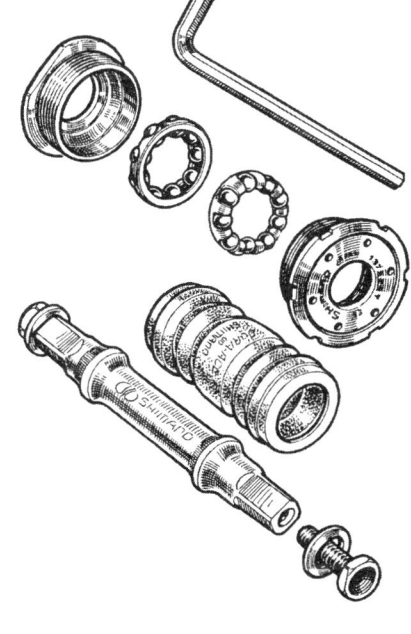

Above: Shimano Dura-Ace bottom bracket bearings. 1980 Milremo

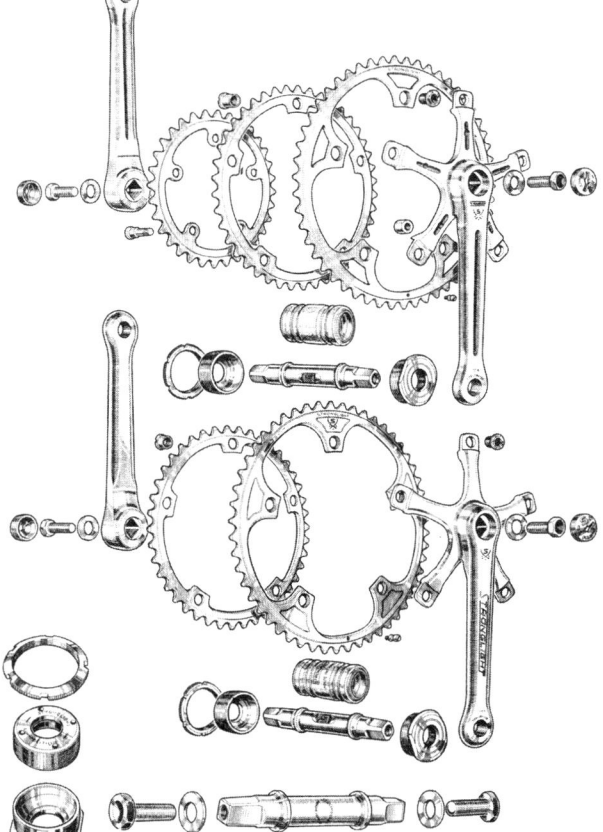

97

Chapter 5. Pedals and Toeclips

This chapter is devoted to the pedals and toeclips, as they were used universally before the widespread introduction of clipless pedals. Although you will find at least one example of clipless pedals, namely the F-71 made by Cinelli from 1971 on, these were used in track races only. In fact, they were sometimes referred to as "suicide clips," due to the difficulty of dislodging the shoes to dismount, at times causing the rider to fall.

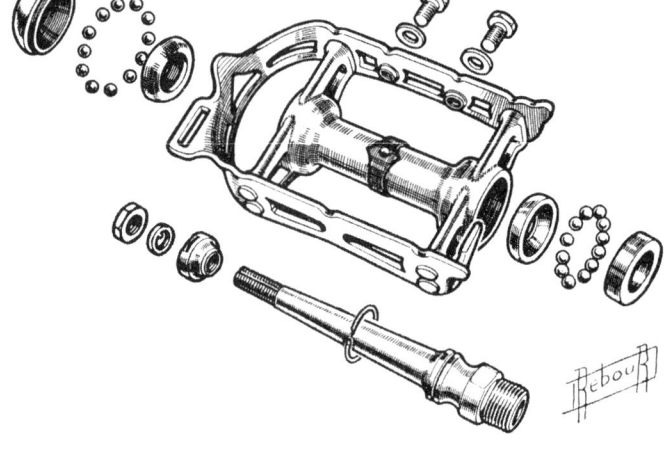

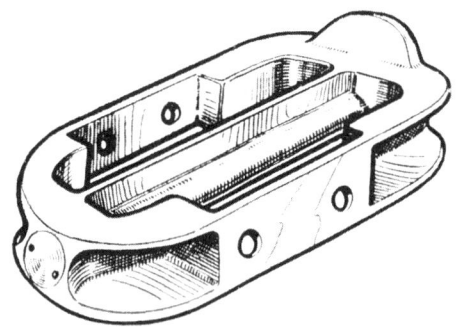

Left: Drawing showing Rebour's own platform pedal design, which does not appear to have gone into production. *Le Cycle*, 20 December 1947.

Above: Exploded view of a Campagnolo Record pedal, showing all the parts of a conventional high-quality pedal found on touring and racing bikes until the introduction of clipless pedals in the late 1980s. *Le Cycle*, 28 July 1956.

Below: The René Herse bicycle built for Bauman, a very tall rider, in the 1956 Paris–Brest–Paris. *Le Cycle*, 22 September 1956.**

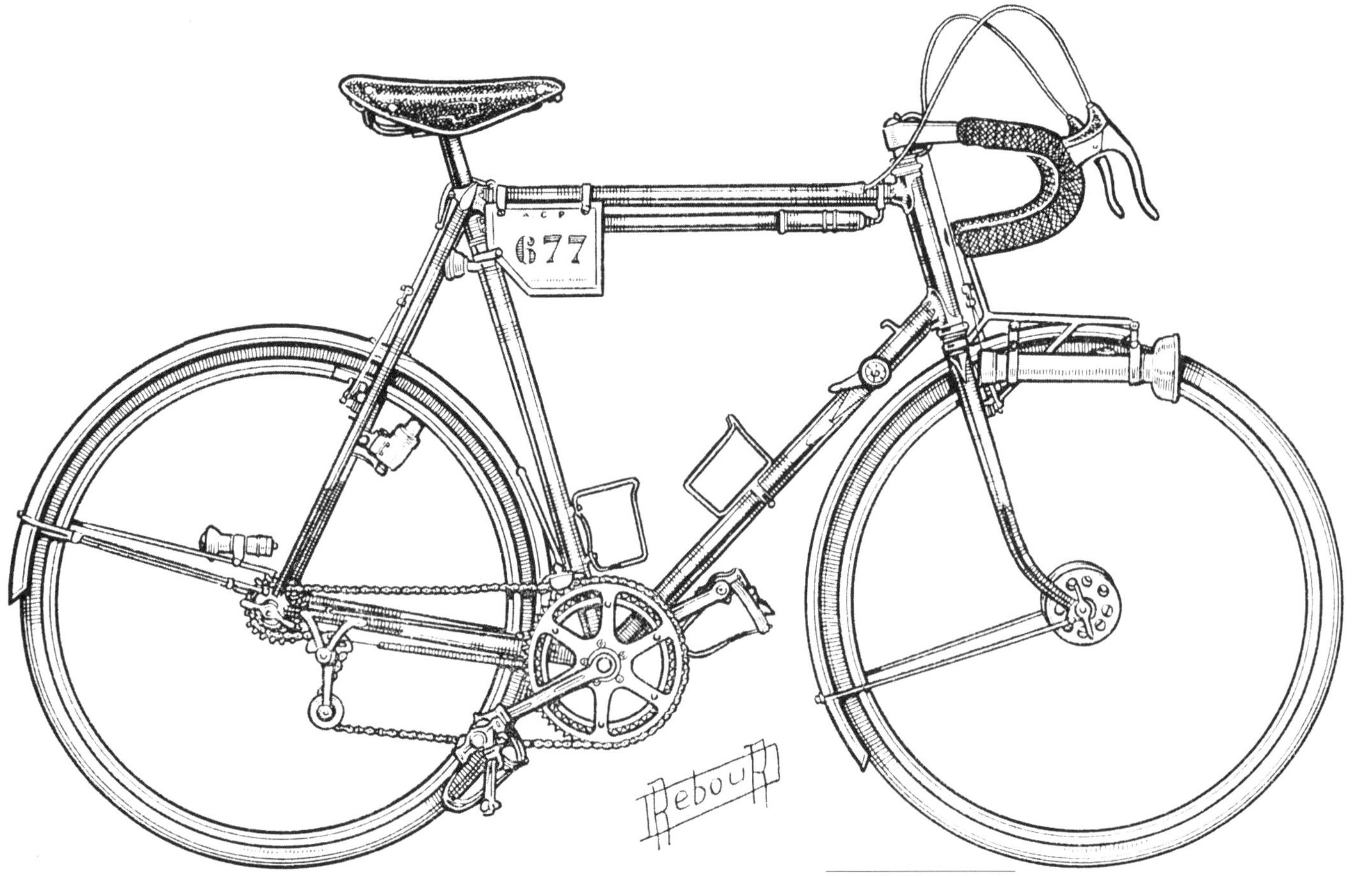

** See pages 269–271 for expanded caption text.

98

Chapter 5. Pedals and Toeclips

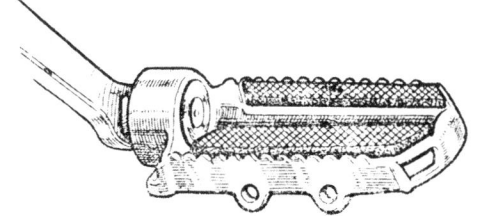
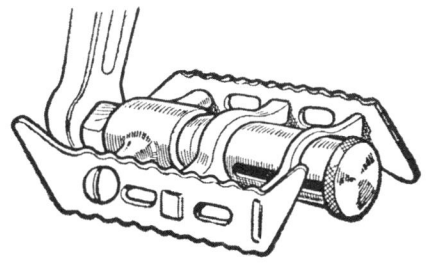
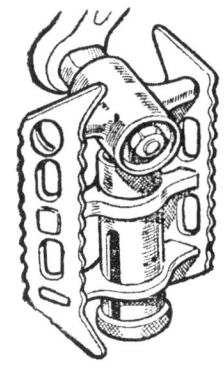

Left: Souhart drop-platform pedal, an idea later adapted in Shimano AX pedals. *Le Cycle*, 22 June 1946.

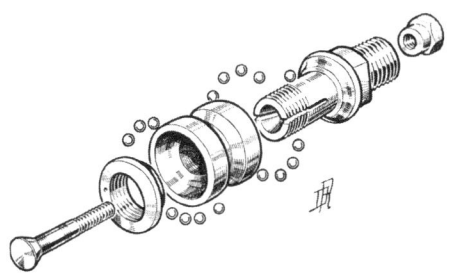

Above right: Folding pedal, for use on folding bicycles. *Le Cycle*, 24 Feb. 1947.

Below: ISO hanging platform pedal. *Le Cycle*, 24 April 1948.

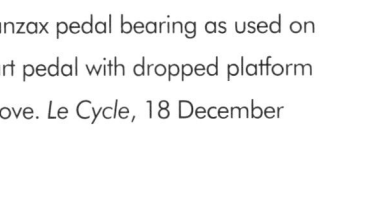

Above: Sanzax pedal bearing as used on the Souhart pedal with dropped platform shown above. *Le Cycle*, 18 December 1948.

Below: Dufour's René Herse machine entered in the 1957 Poly de Chanteloup technical trials. *Le Cycle*, 11 May 1957.

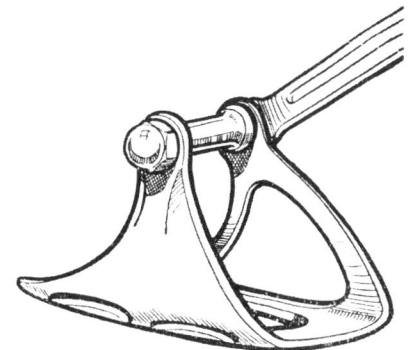
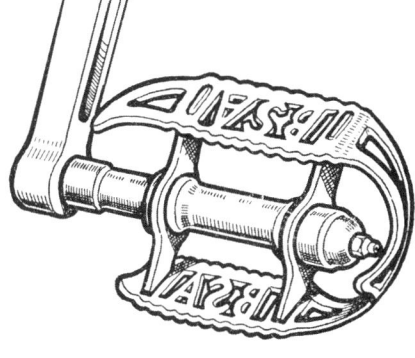

Above: English BSA touring pedal, a holdover from pre-World-War-II days. *Pratique du Vélo*.

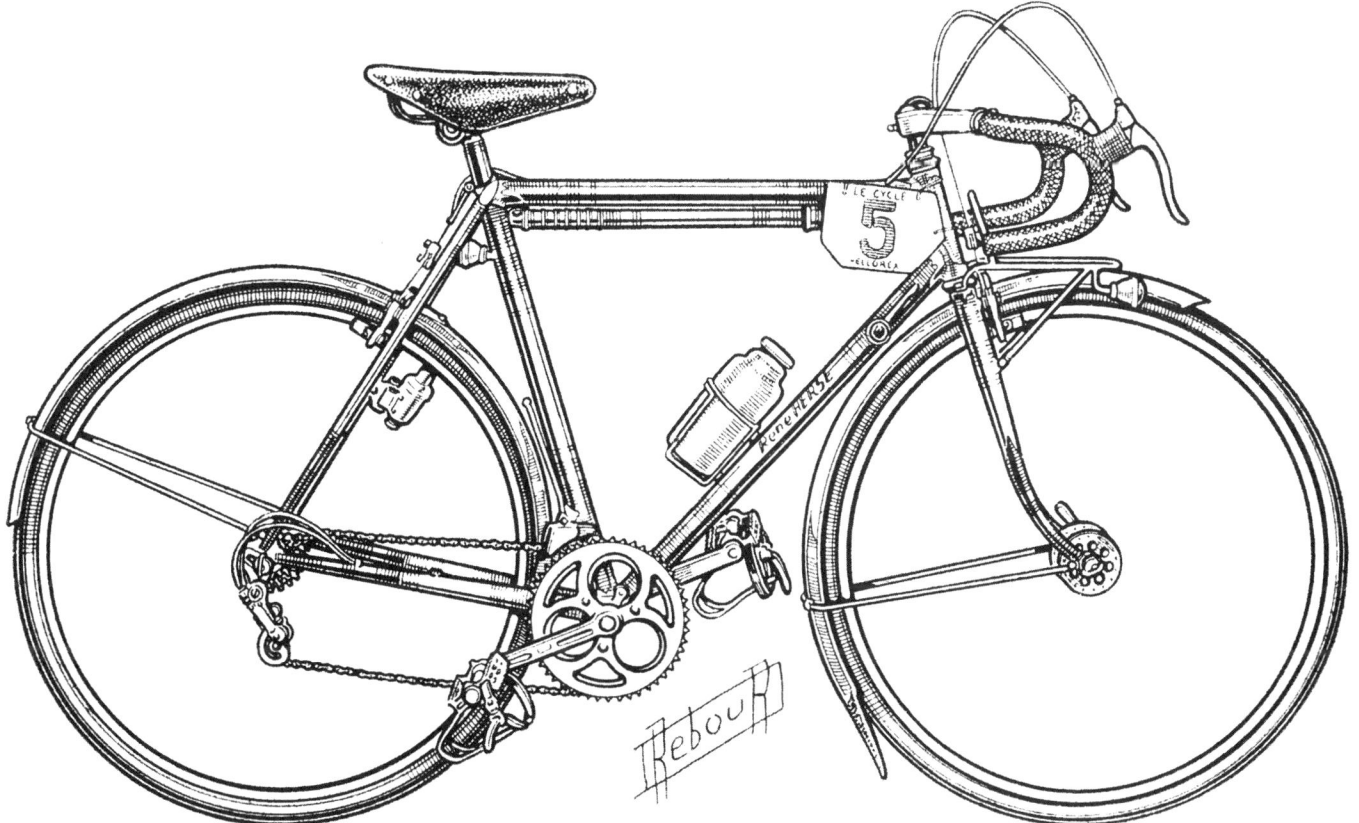

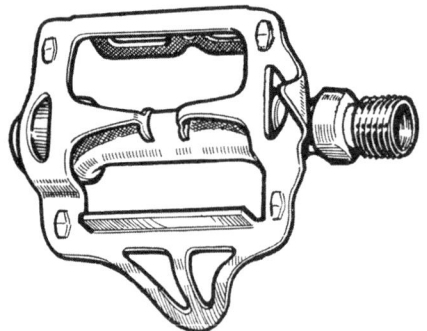

Left: Berthet-designed platform pedal, made by Lyotard. *Pratique du Vélo*.

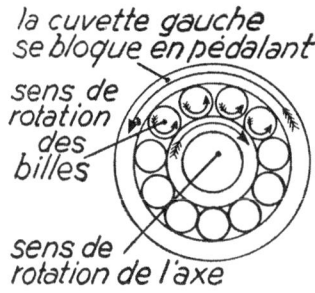

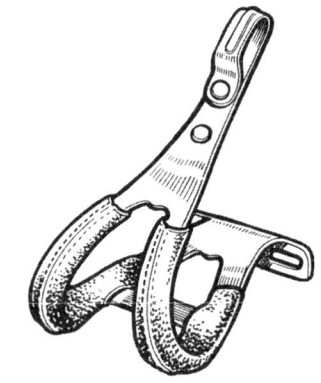

Left: Typical toeclip, with leather sleeves to protect the shoe from damage. *Pratique du Vélo*.

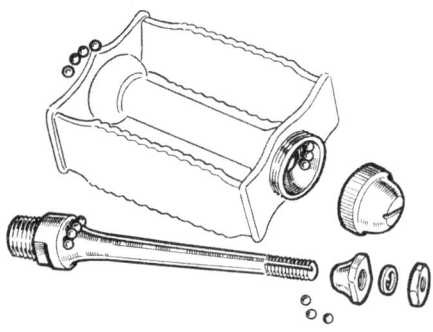

Above: Rebour's explanation of the reason for left pedals to have left-hand thread. *Le Cycle*, 9 July 1949.

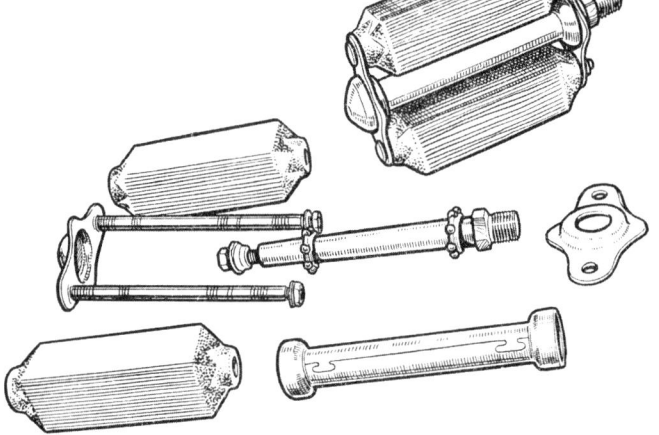

Above: Exploded view of rattrap-type pedal. *Pratique du Vélo*.

Right: Exploded view of a rubber-block pedal, as used on most European city bikes at the time. *Le Cycle*, 12 February 1949.

Below: The Raphaël-Géminiani bicycle ridden in the 1957 Poly de Chanteloup trials by the winner of the climbing category, Louis Bergaud. *Le Cycle*, 11 May 1957.

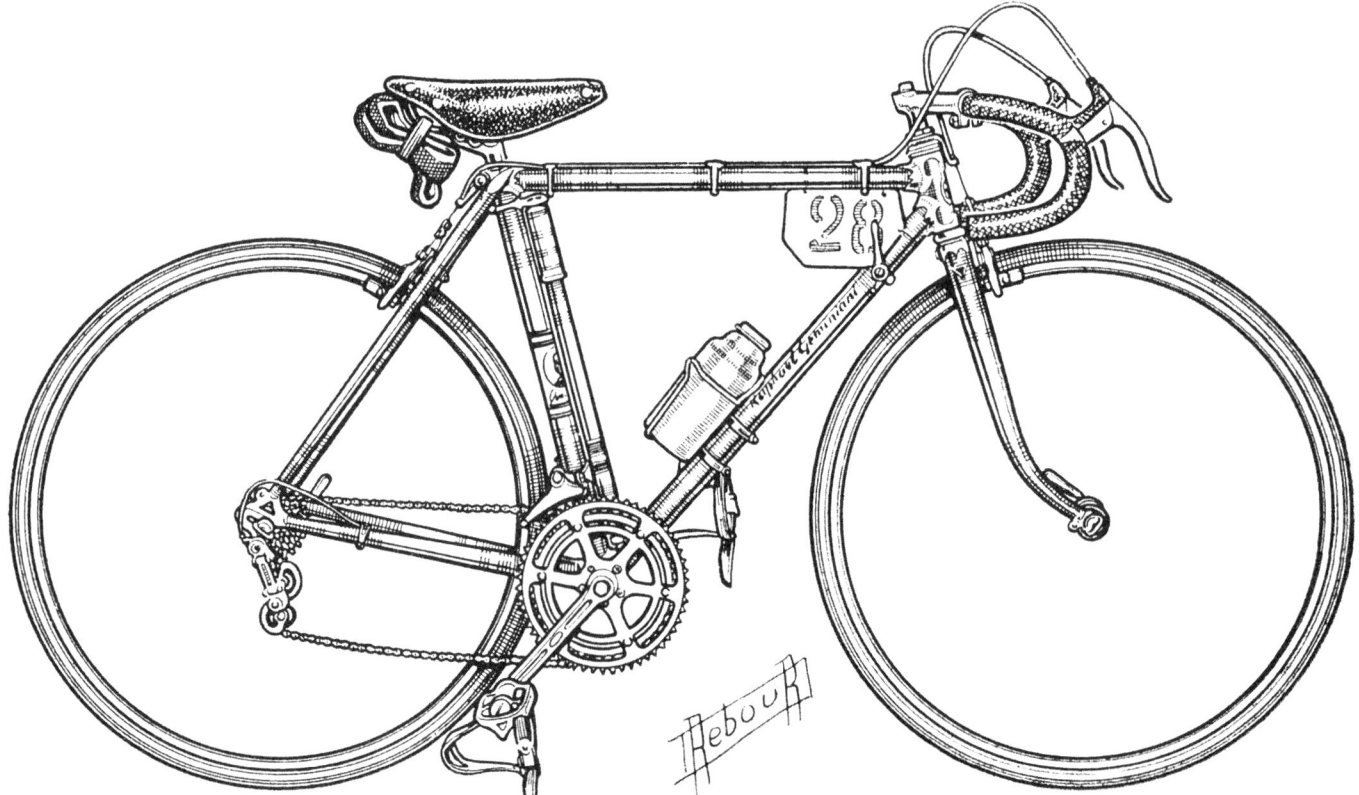

CHAPTER 5. PEDALS AND TOECLIPS

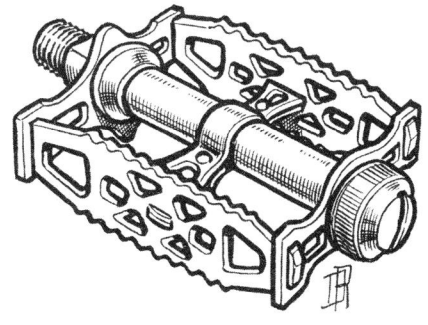

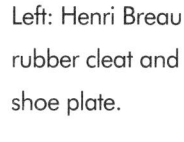

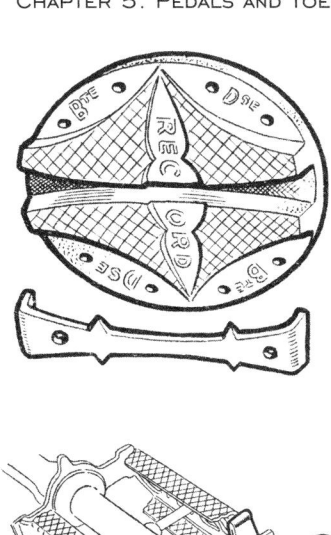

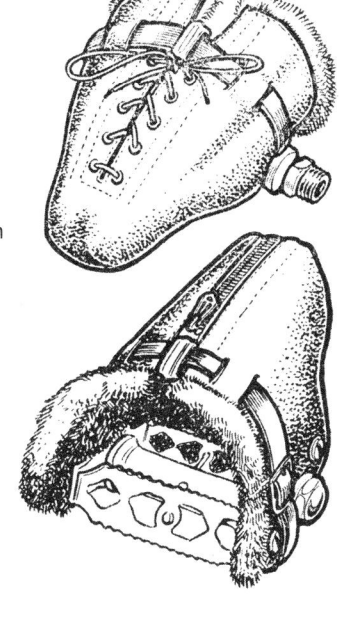

Above: LDC rattrap pedal. *Le Cycle*, 30 July 1949.

Right: Pedal-reflectors. *Le Cycle*, 11 November 1950.

Below: Promax Sansomax dropped platform pedal. *Le Cycle*, 6 May 1950.

Left: Henri Breau rubber cleat and shoe plate.

Right: Fur-lined shoe covers. Both images from *Le Cycle*, 7 January 1950.

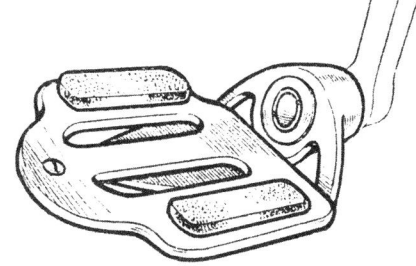

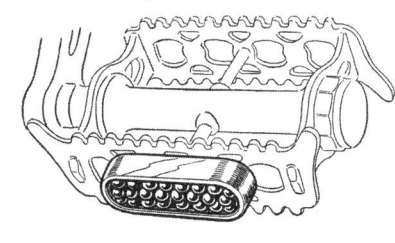

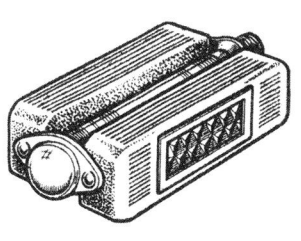

Right: Campagnolo pedal spindle and seals. *Le Cycle*, 27 October 1956.

Far right: TA pedal with needle bearings. *Le Cycle*, 6 October 1951.

Left: Union rubber-block pedal with reflectors. *Le Cycle*, 24 Feb. 1952.

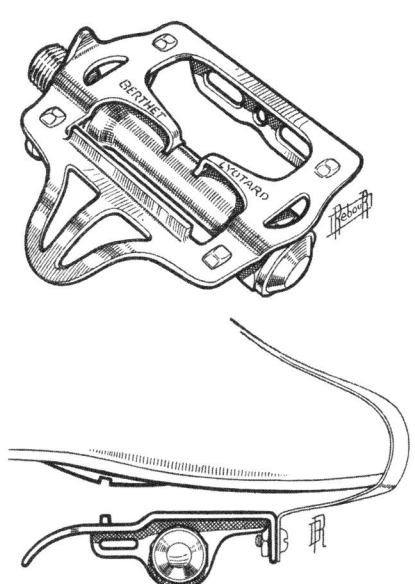

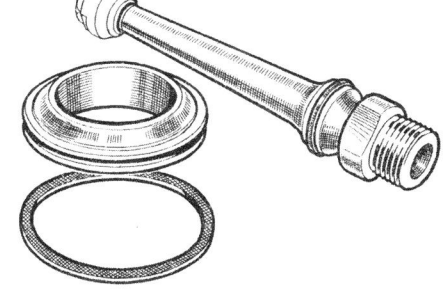

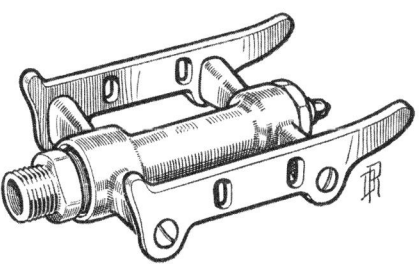

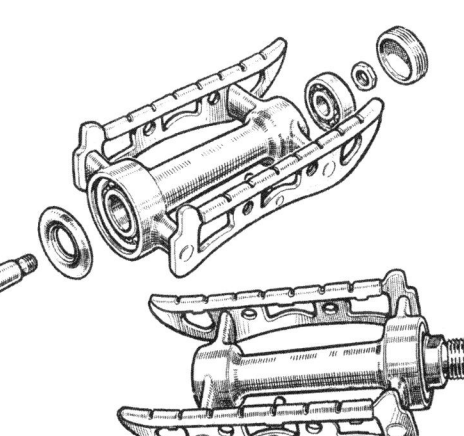

Left: Lyotard Berthet platform pedal and toeclip installation. *Le Cycle*, 21 July 1951. Note how much more detailed this drawing is than the one on facing page 100.

Right: Exploded view of Follis aluminium quill pedal with cartridge bearings. *Le Cycle*, 21 April 1951.

101

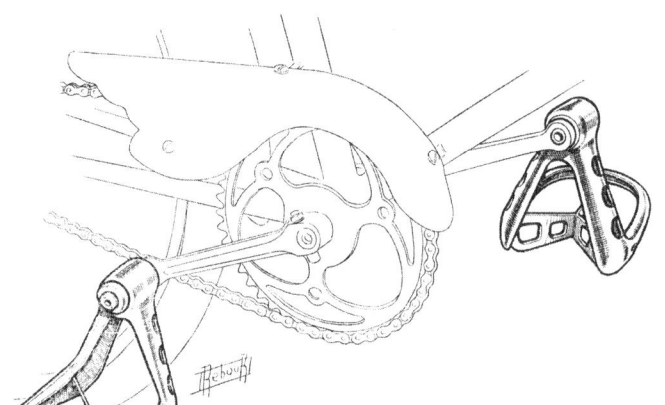

Left: ISO hanging pedals installed. *Le Cycle*, 7 August 1954.

Right: Lightweight cleat from TA, weighing 15 grams each. *Le Cycle*, 21 February 1953.

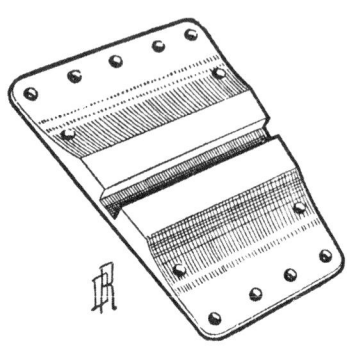

Below: English Cyclo shoe-guide, to ease entering the shoe onto the pedal with the toeclip up. *Le Cycle*, 7 September 1957.

Below: Lyotard Model 46 rattrap-style pedal. *Le Cycle*, 10 October 1959.

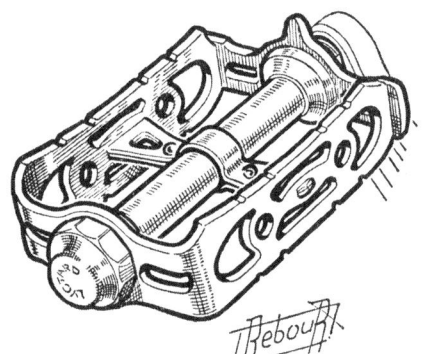

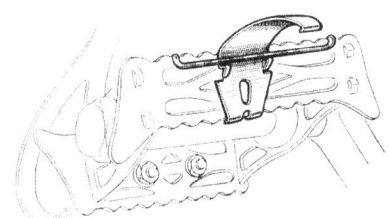

Above: TA needle bearing pedal details. *Le Cycle*, 18 October 1952.

Right: Rochet men's touring bicycle at the 1957 Poly de Chanteloup technical trials. With its balloon tires and derailleur gearing (though without front derailleur), it presaged the early California mountain bikes of the late 1970s. However, unlike the early mountain bikes, it was equipped for touring, with fenders, lights, and luggage racks. Rochet advertisement in *Le Cycle*, 11 May 1957.

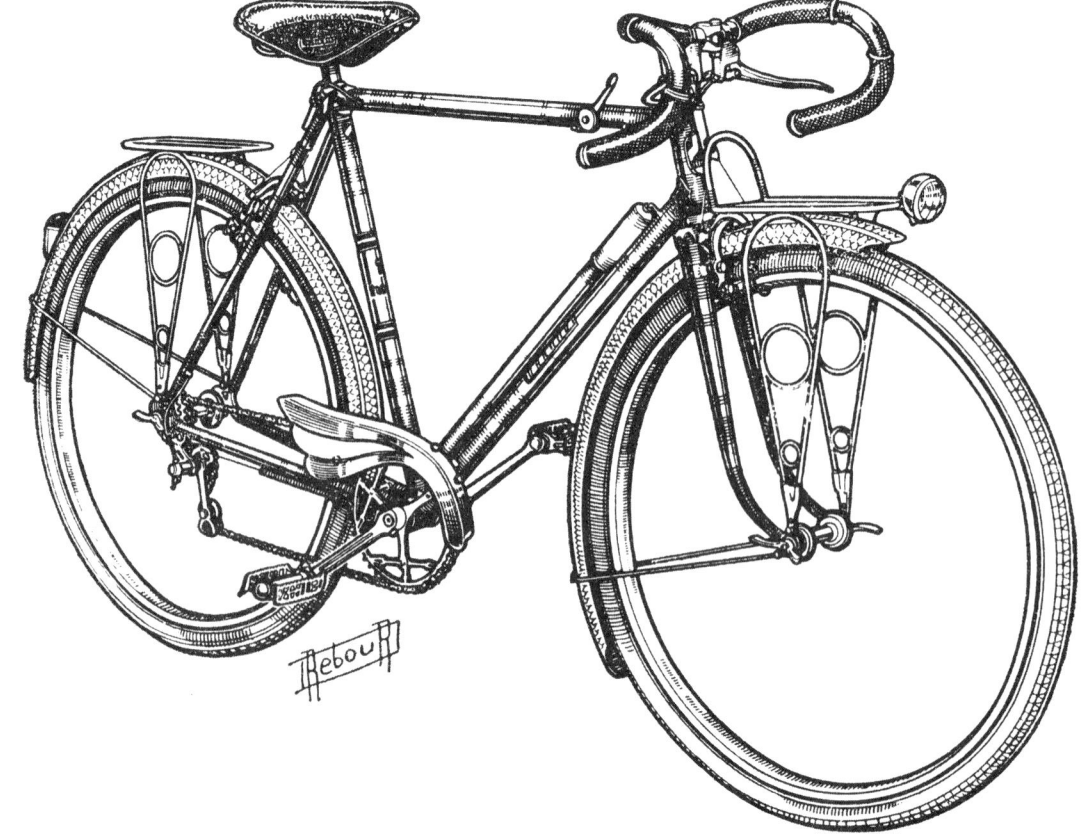

Chapter 5. Pedals and Toeclips

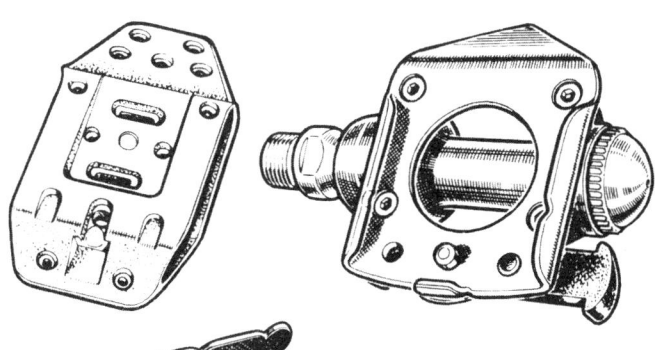

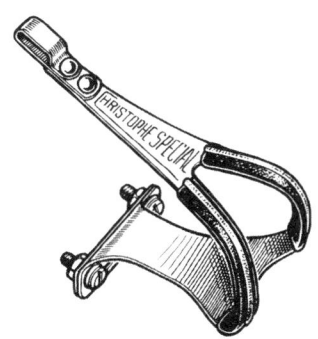

Left: Cinelli F-71 clipless "suicide" track pedal and matching cleat. *Cycles de Compétition et Randonneuses.*
Below: Maillard 700 Road racing pedal. *Le Cycle,* November 1973.

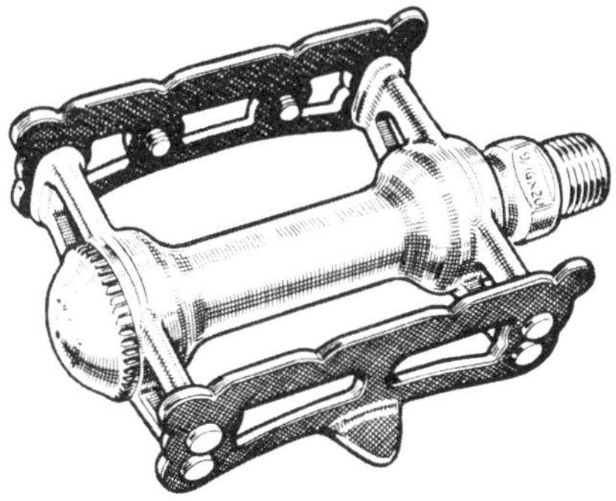

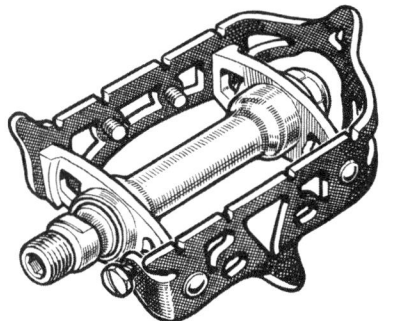

Above and below: Christophe regular toeclips for use with straps and Poutrait-Morin short clips without straps. *Le Cycle,* December 1973.

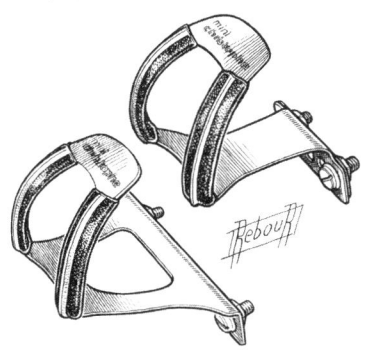

Above: Campagnolo track pedal. *Cycles de Compétition et Randonneuses.*
Right: Lapize toestrap. *Cycles de Compétition et Randonneuses.*

Below: Jacques Anquetil's bicycle for the 1957 Tour de France. *Le Cycle,* 27 July 1957.

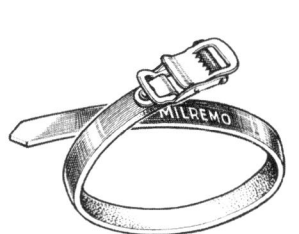

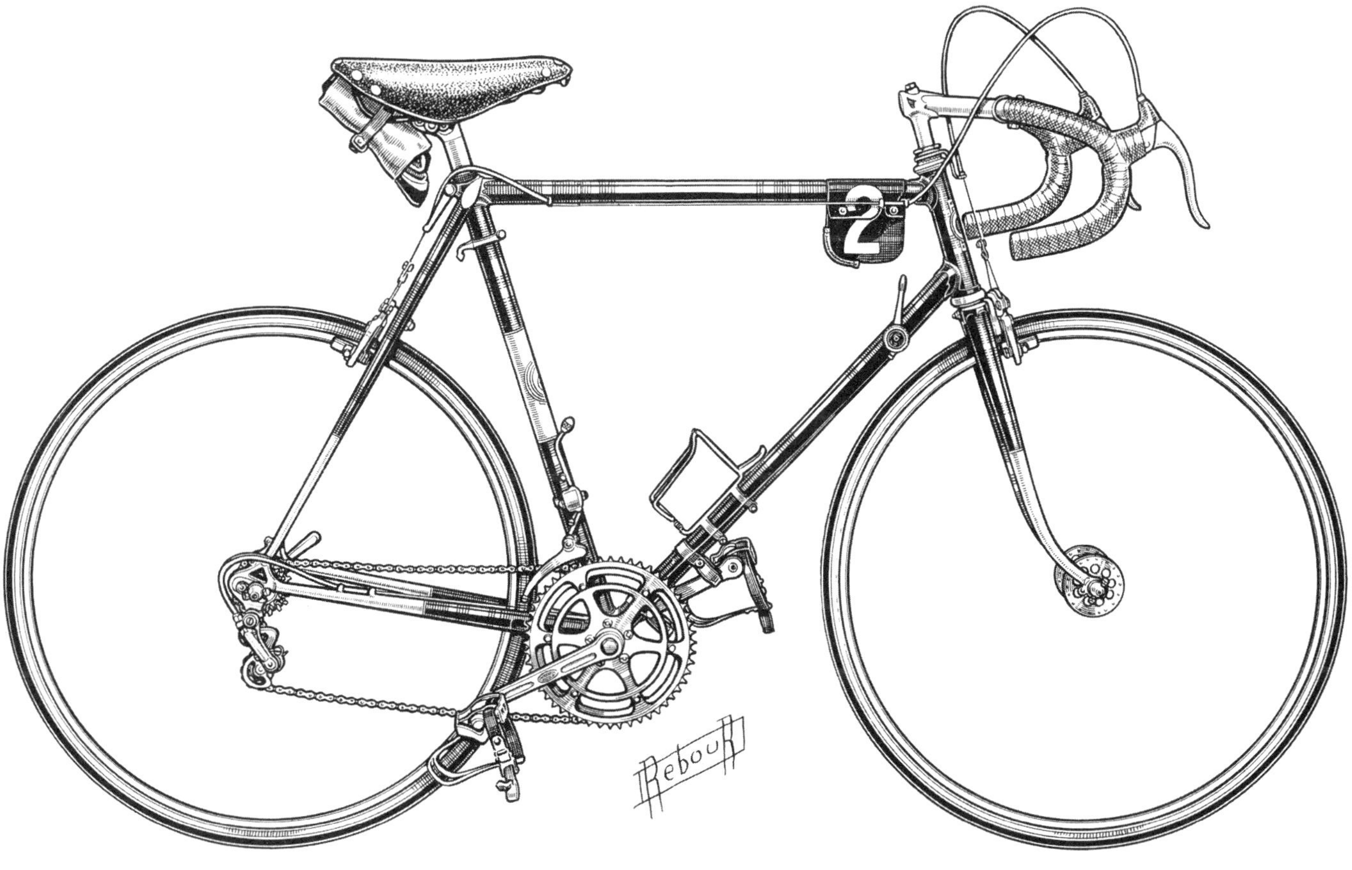

103

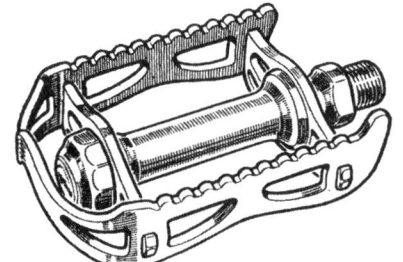

Left: Standard French road racing quill pedal. 1980 Milremo catalogue.

Below: Still popular in 1980: Berthet platform pedal. 1980 Milremo catalogue.

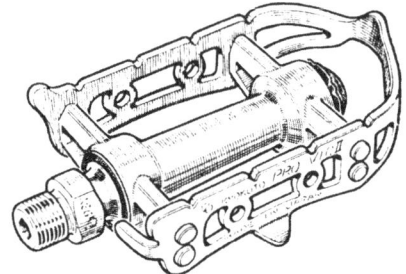

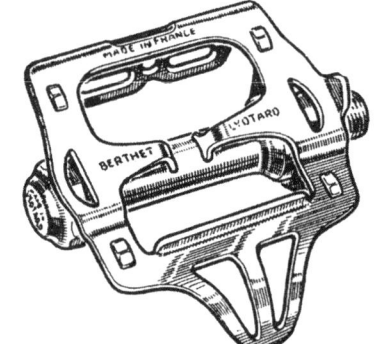

Above: Shimano Dura-Ace AX aero pedal, with toeclip and strap. 1980 Milremo catalogue.

Above and right: 1980 Shimano 600 EX and Dura-Ace road racing pedals, which were actually made by KyoKuTo (KKT), and corresponded to KKT's own models Pro Vic II and Pro Ace. 1980 Milremo catalogue.

Below: The Cardinale machine that Gastone Nencini rode to victory in the mountains classification of the 1957 Tour de France. *Le Cycle*, 27 July 1957.**

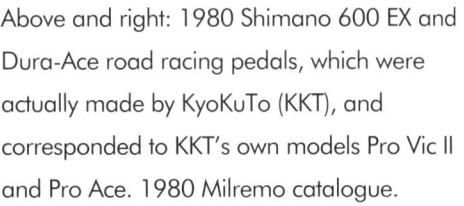

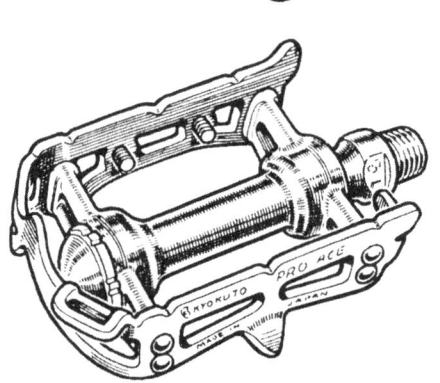

Above: Early budget clipless pedal, made by La Font. 1983 Milremo catalogue.

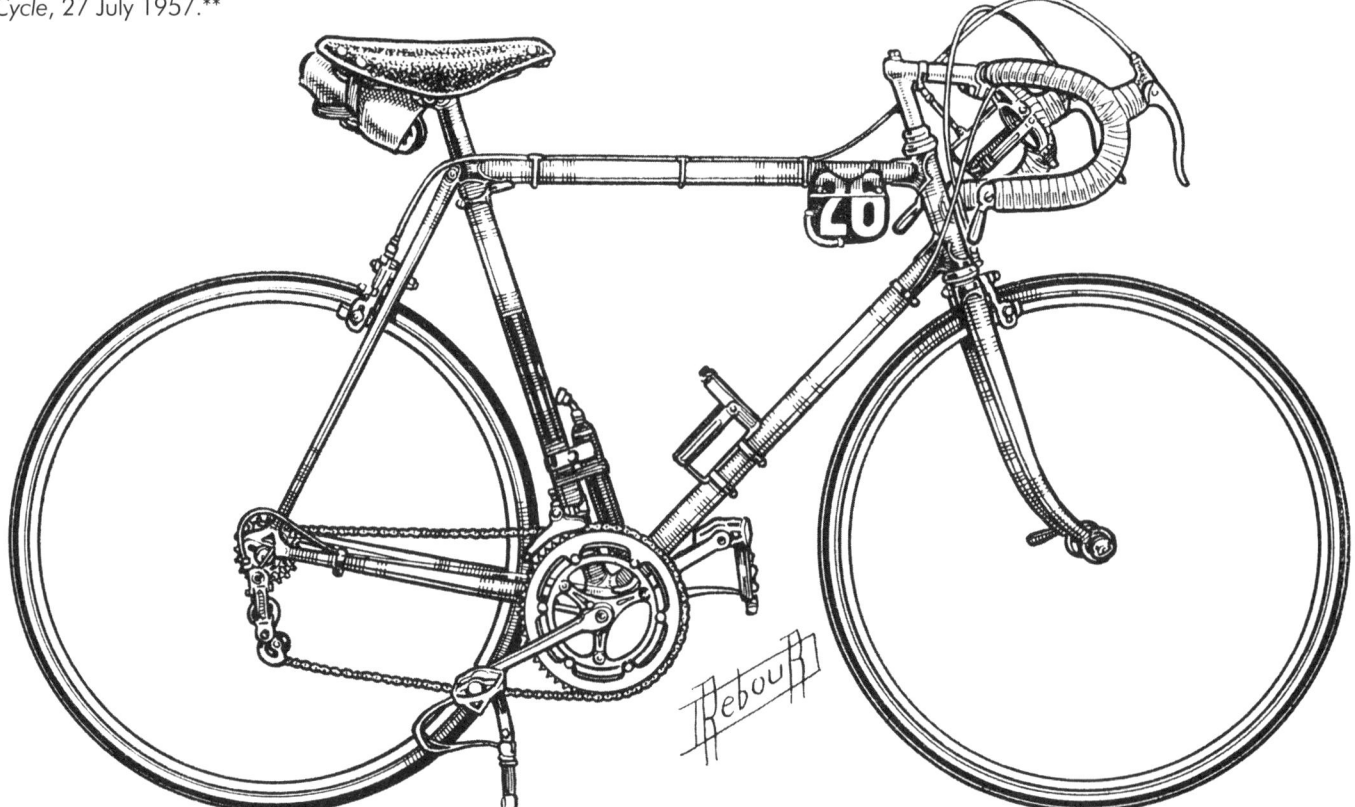

** See pages 269–271 for expanded caption text.

Chapter 5. Pedals and Toeclips

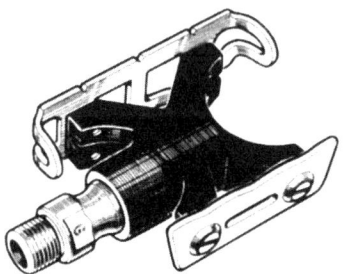

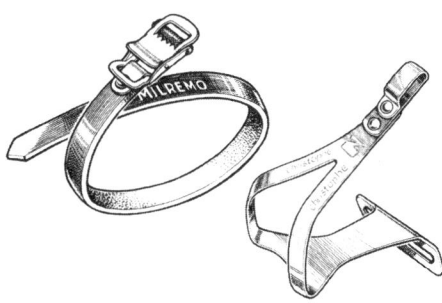

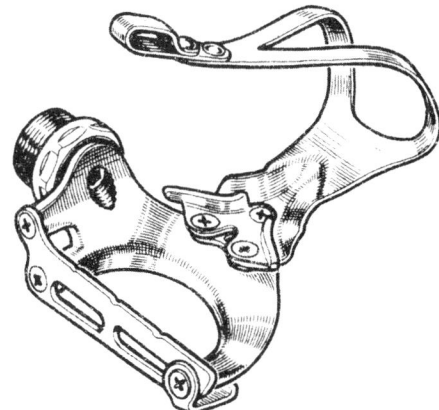

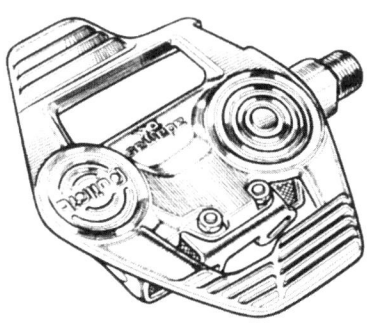

Above: Milremo toeclips and toe straps. 1983 Milremo catalogue.

Upper right: Shimano AX road racing pedal. Like the 1947 Souhart pedal, it had the platform below the short spindle. 1981 Milremo catalogue.

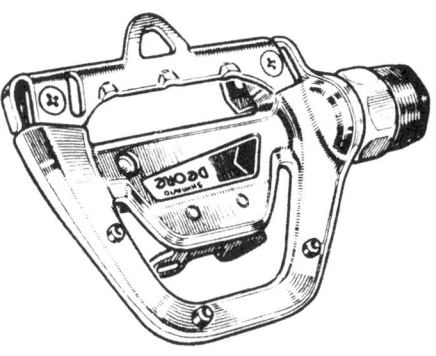

Above: André Bertin pedals for track (top) and touring (bottom). 1983 Milremo catalogue.

Right: Campagnolo Super Record pedal. 1981 Milremo catalogue, scanned from original art.

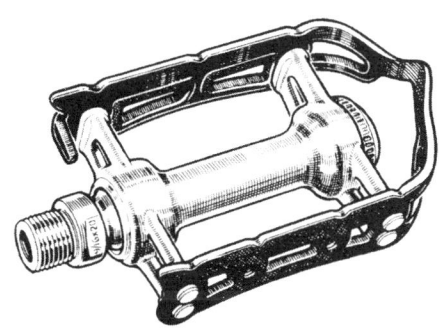

Shimano DeOre platform touring pedal, like the AX pedal, it has a single large-diameter needle bearing and a short spindle. 1981 Milremo catalogue.

Chapter 6. Rim Brakes

This chapter is devoted to the brakes, and specifically the rim brakes used almost universally on sports bikes at the time. Other kinds of brakes were rarely used in France, being more popular in some neighboring countries, especially Germany and Holland, as well as in the U.S. Such other brakes—coaster brakes (operated by back-pedaling), drum brakes, and even some early examples of disk brakes—will be covered separately in Chapter 8. In that same chapter we will present some Rebour drawings of hub gears, which were also much less popular in France than they were in e.g. Germany, Holland, and England at the time.

Below: The Coppi bicycle on which Adolf Christian, of Switzerland, took 3rd place in the 1957 Tour de France. *Le Cycle*, 27 July 1957.

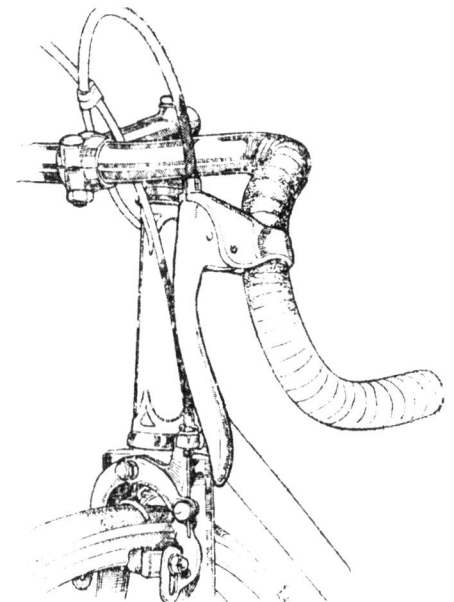

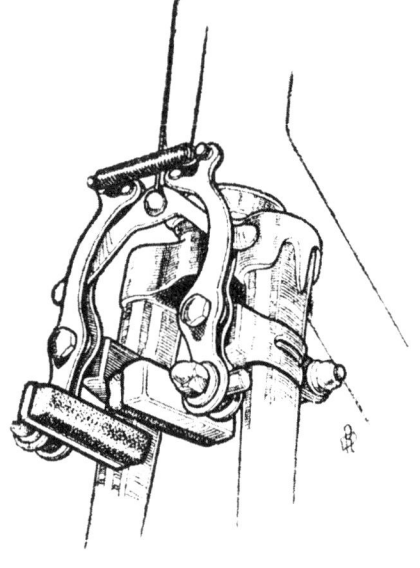

Above: Jeay cam-operated brake. *Le Cycle*, 16 February 1946.

Left: LAM sidepull brake and controls. *Le Cycle*, 16 February 1946.

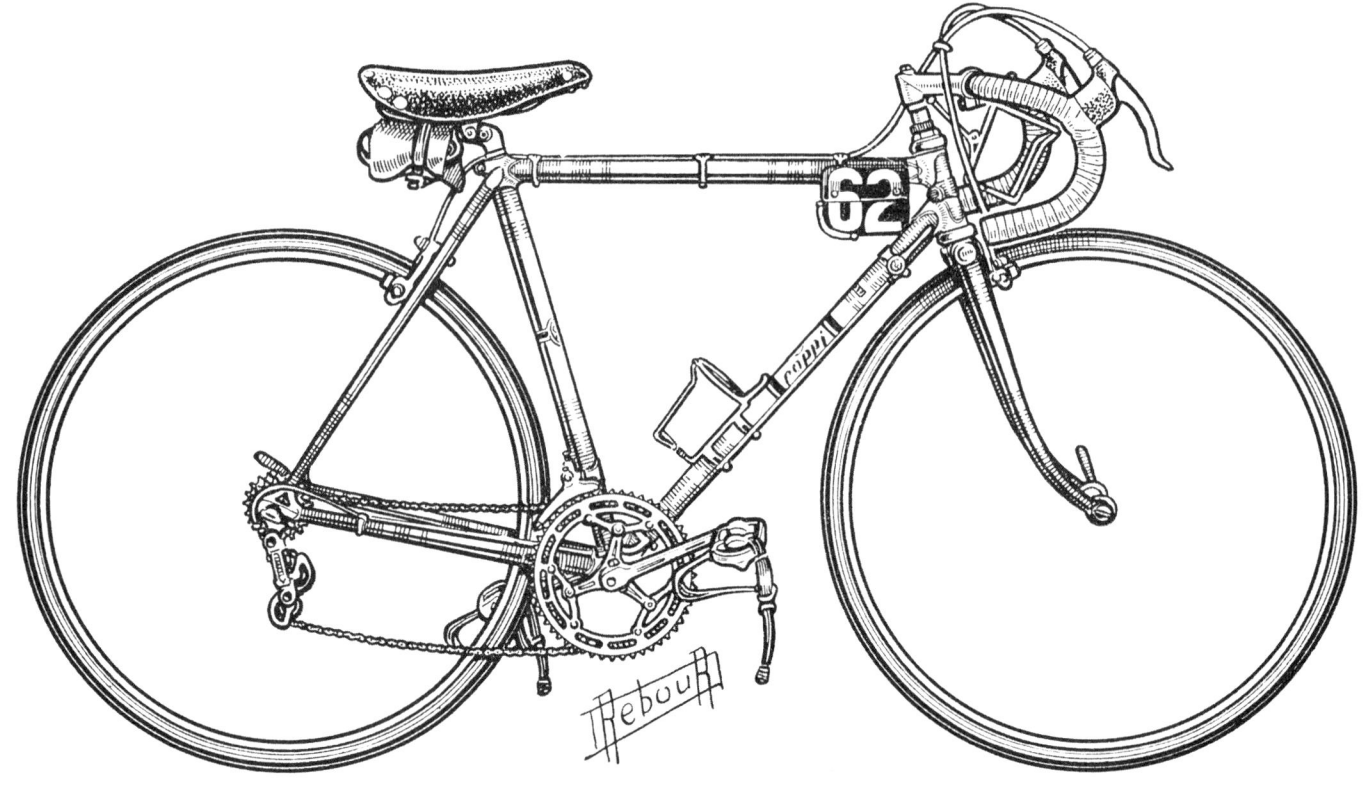

Chapter 6. Rim Brakes

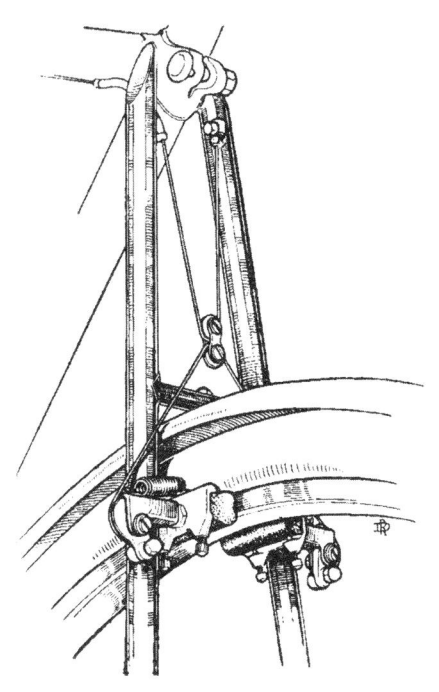

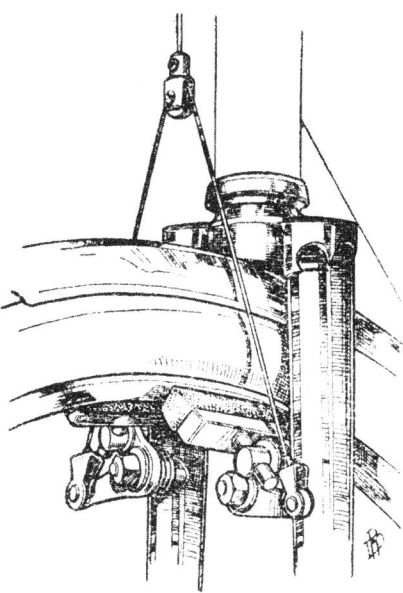

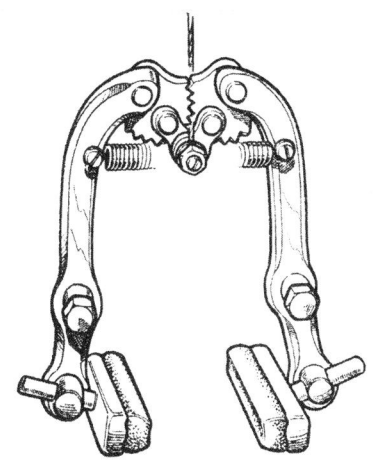

Left: Lewis cantilever brake. *Le Cycle*, 16 March 1946.

Below: Follis brake. *Le Cycle*, 28 December 1946.

Above: Singer cantilever brake and special cable routing. *Le Cycle*, 1 April 1946.

Below: 1957 Tour de France green jersey winner Jean Forestier's Helyett-Essor bicycle. *Le Cycle*, 27 July 1957.

Below: Brake lever orientation and hand positions. *Le Cycle*, 20 April 1946.

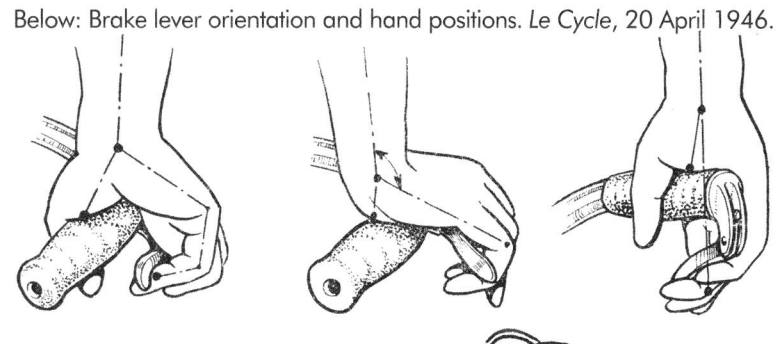

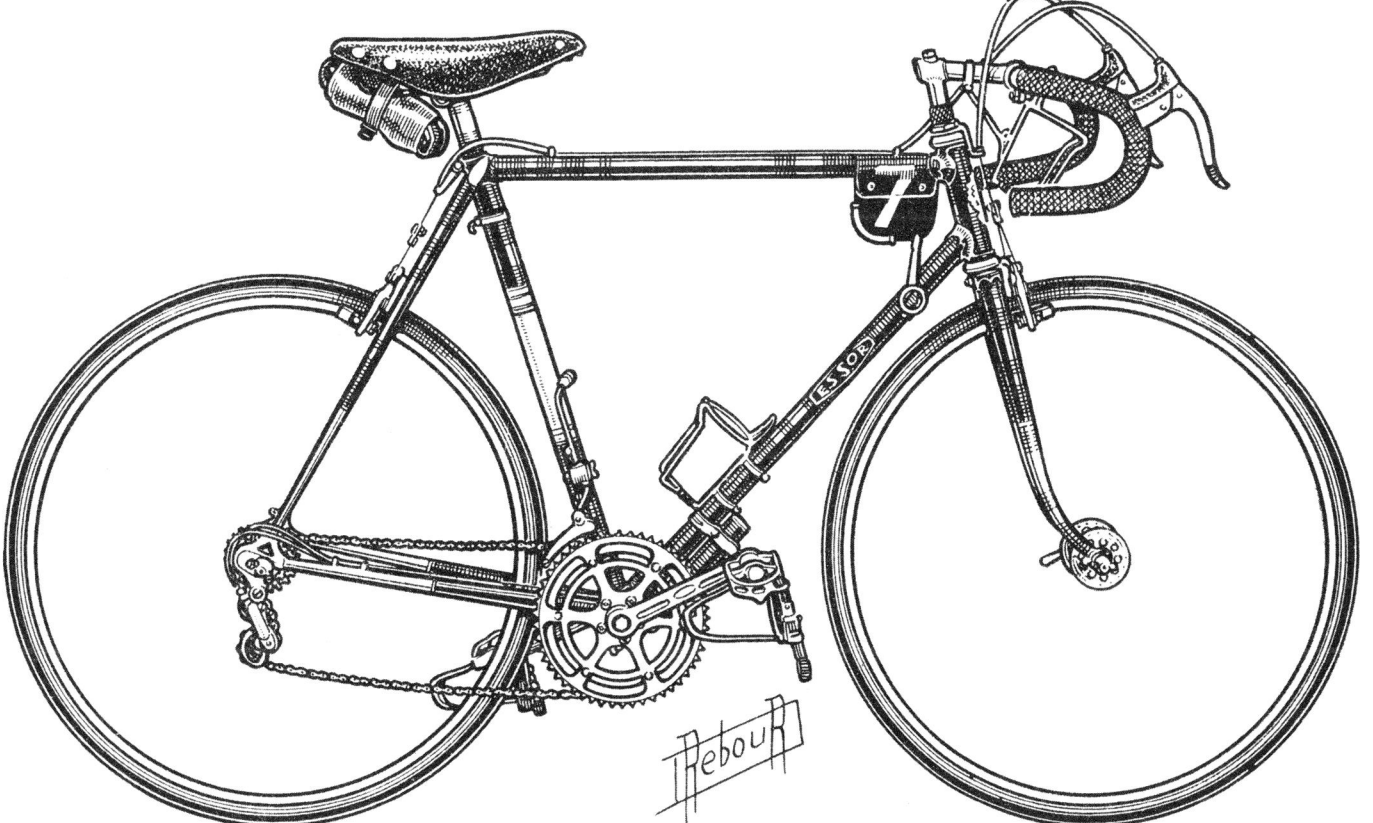

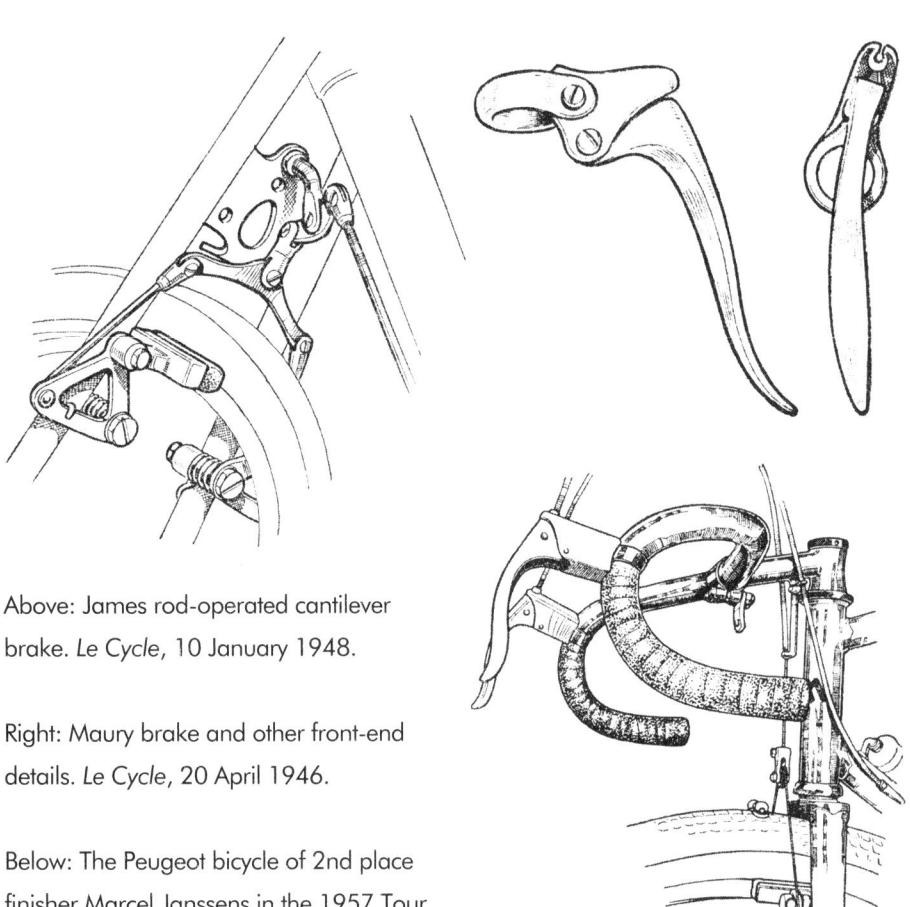

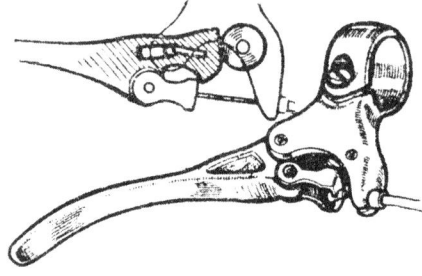

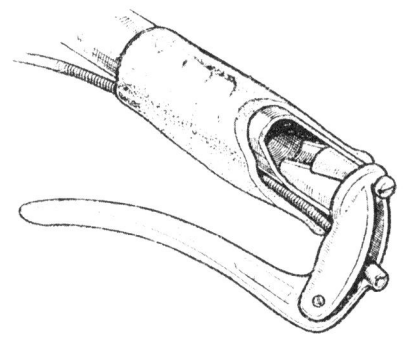

Above: James rod-operated cantilever brake. *Le Cycle*, 10 January 1948.

Right: Maury brake and other front-end details. *Le Cycle*, 20 April 1946.

Below: The Peugeot bicycle of 2nd place finisher Marcel Janssens in the 1957 Tour de France. *Le Cycle*, 27 July 1957.

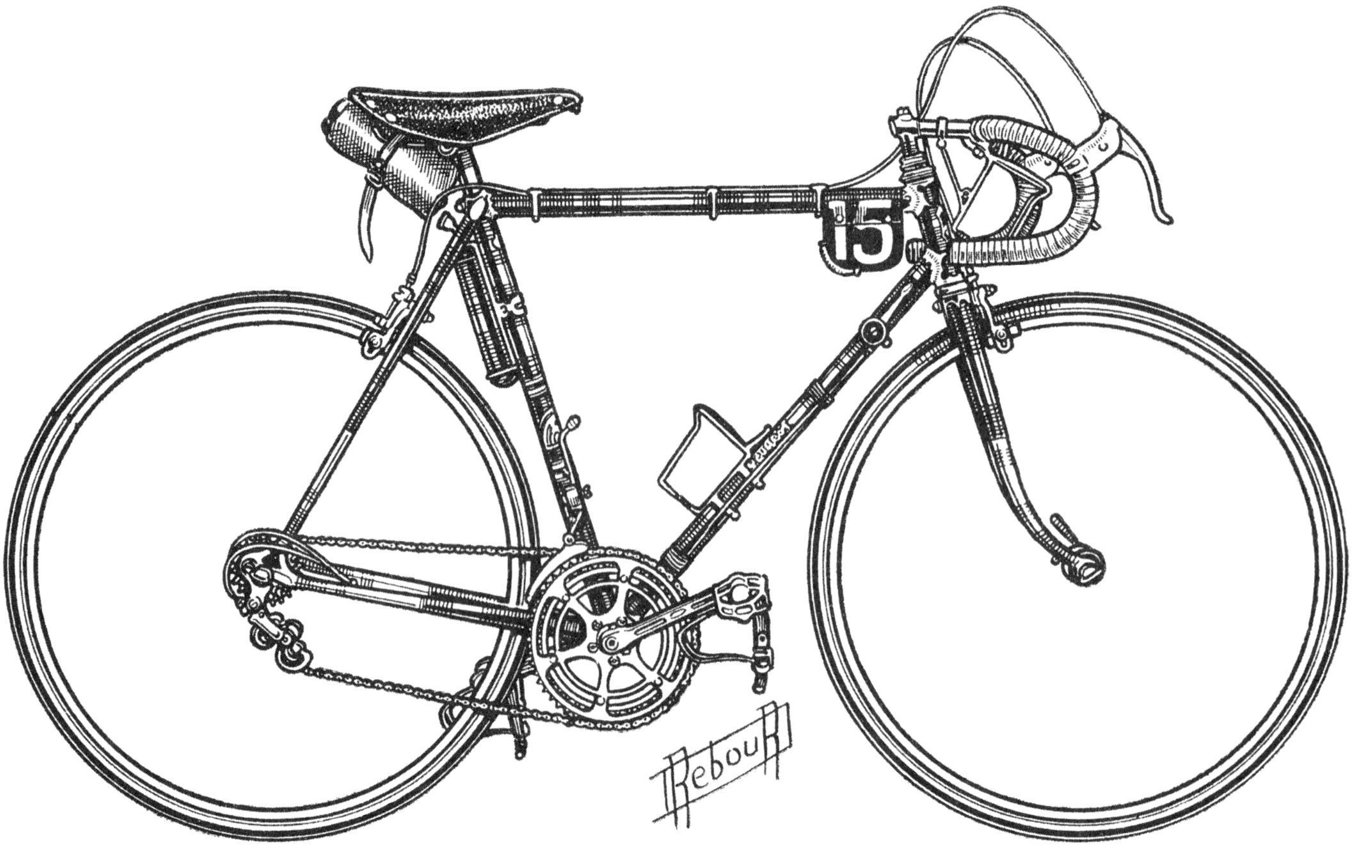

Above: Minimax brake lever. *Le Cycle*, 18 October 1947.

Above left: CLB brake levers. *Le Cycle*, 29 March 1947.

Below: Frexel brake lever with internal cable routing. *Le Cycle*, 29 March 1947.

Chapter 6. Rim Brakes

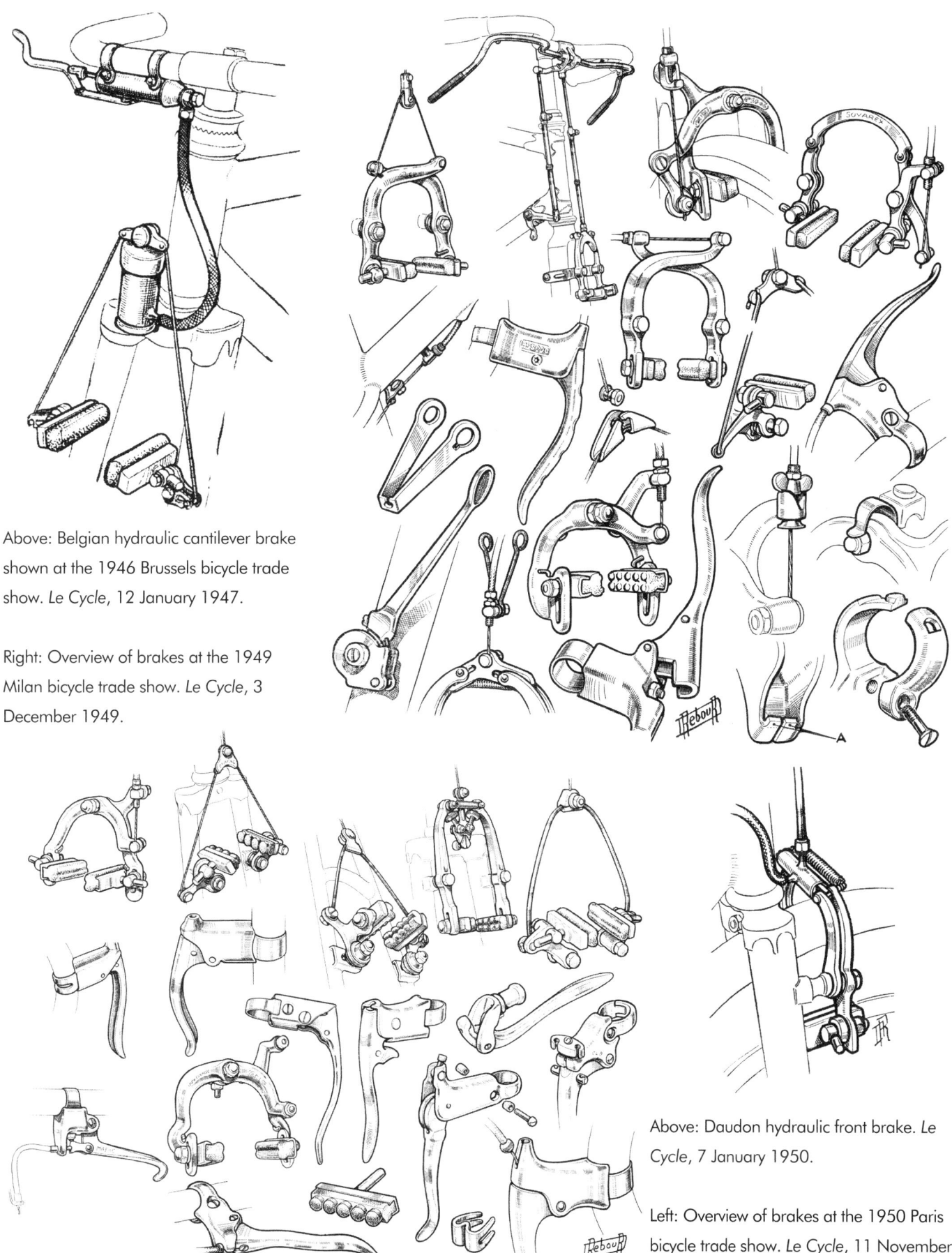

Above: Belgian hydraulic cantilever brake shown at the 1946 Brussels bicycle trade show. *Le Cycle*, 12 January 1947.

Right: Overview of brakes at the 1949 Milan bicycle trade show. *Le Cycle*, 3 December 1949.

Above: Daudon hydraulic front brake. *Le Cycle*, 7 January 1950.

Left: Overview of brakes at the 1950 Paris bicycle trade show. *Le Cycle*, 11 November 1950.

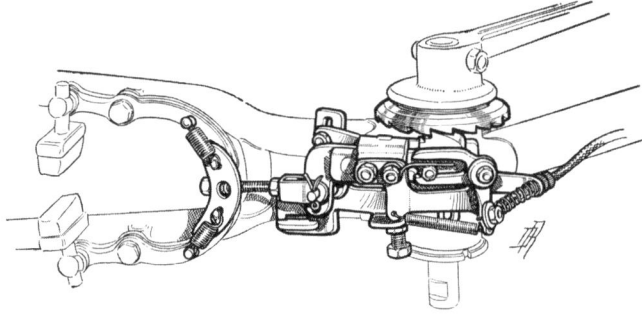

Left: Sanspeine foot-operated rear brake. *Le Cycle*, 26 May 1951.

Below: M. Bourgeois 3-cable brake lever for tandem use. *Le Cycle*, 6 October 1951.

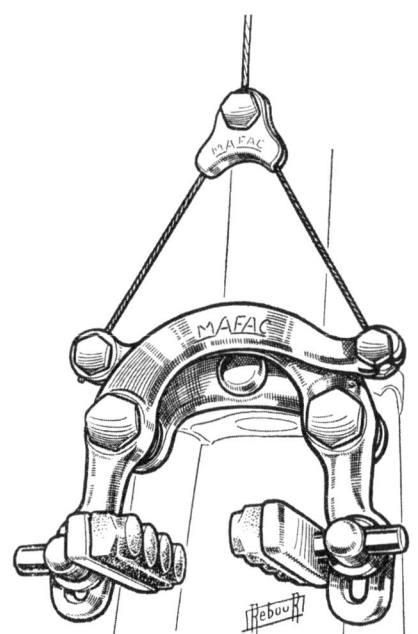

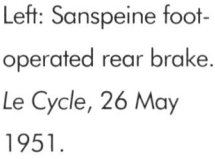

Below: Exploded view of Mafac cantilever brake, extensively used on cyclo-cross and tandem bikes. *Le Cycle*, 26 May 1951.

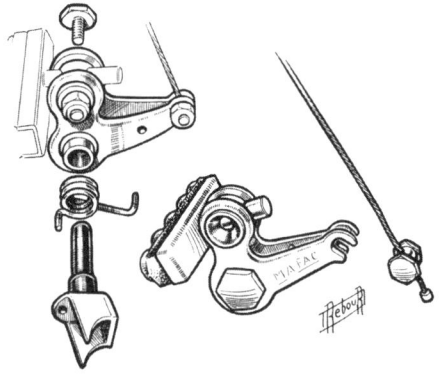

Above: Mafac Racer centerpull brake, long the most popular brake on road racing bikes. *Le Cycle*, 27 October 1951.

Below: 1957 Tour de France for *cyclosportives* winner Gaillard's bicycle, built by Jo Routens. *Le Cycle*, 29 September 1957.

Right: Belestibeau brake adjusting detail. *Le Cycle*, 22 December 1951.

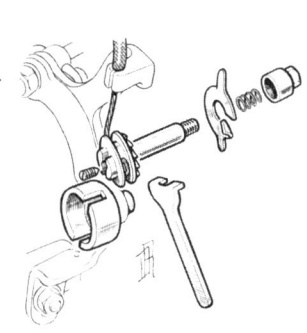

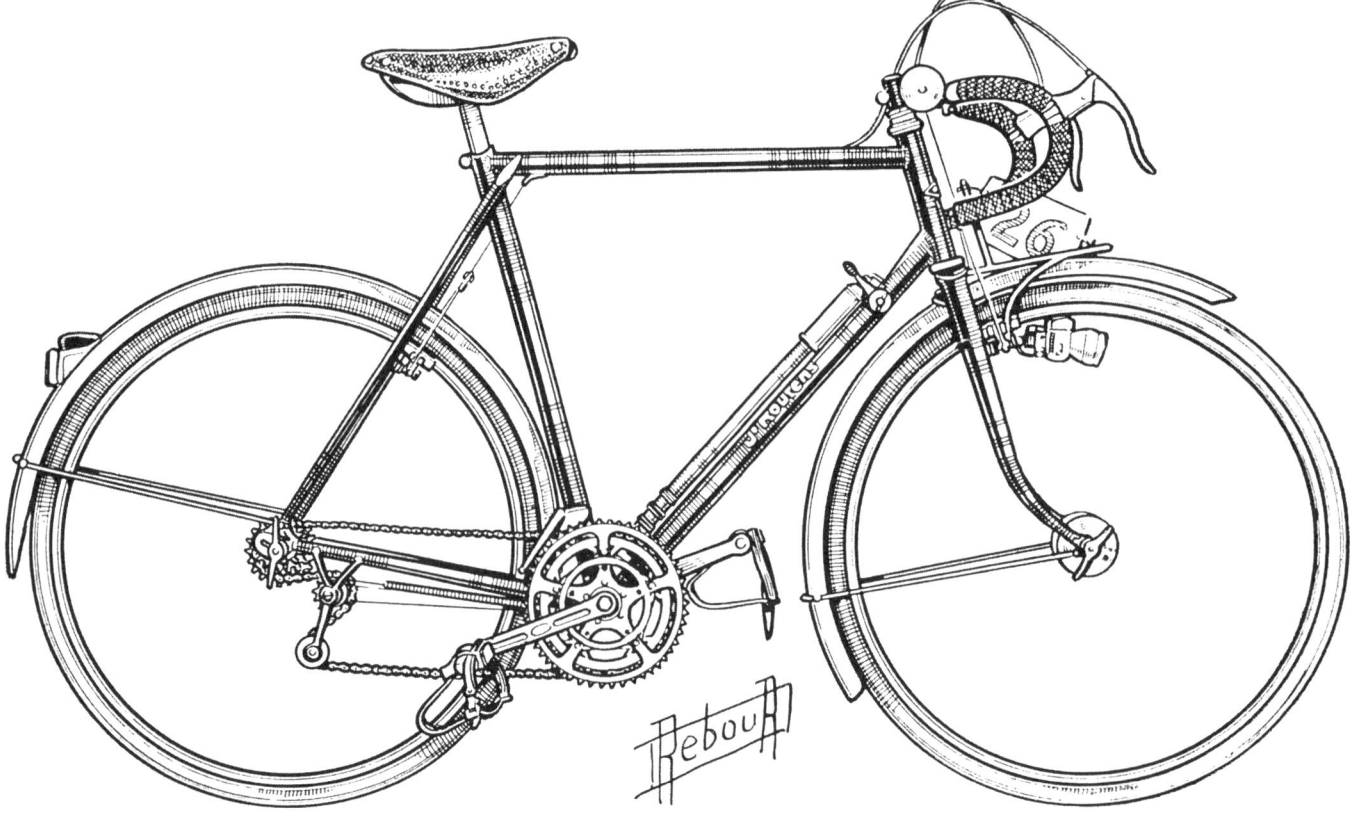

Chapter 6. Rim Brakes

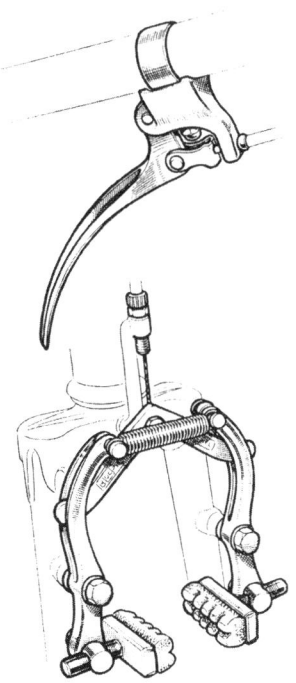

Above: Locpil cam-operated brake and lever. *Le Cycle*, 24 April 1954.

Below: The Liberia bicycle of Agut, first-place finisher in the 1957 Eastern regional technical trials, at Lyons. *Le Cycle*, 29 September 1957.

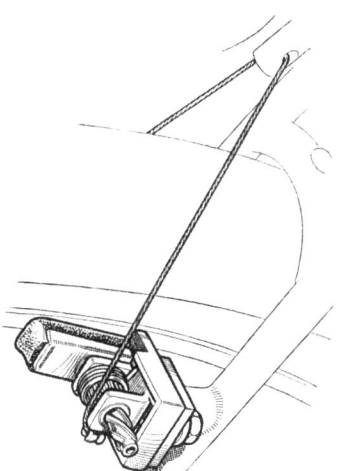

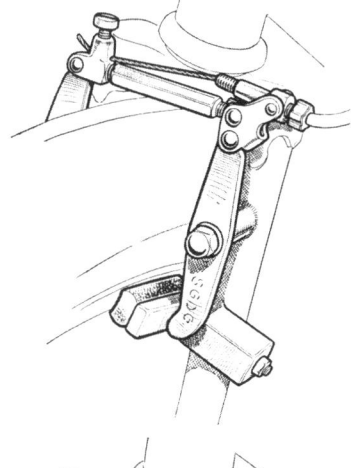

Left: KIT spindle-operated brake. *Le Cycle*, 29 May 1954.

Right: J. Morin inverse linear-pull brake. *Le Cycle*, 12 June 1955.

Below: Handlebar-controlled brake. *Le Cycle*, 4 January 1952.

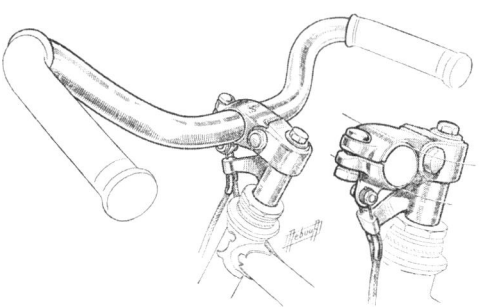

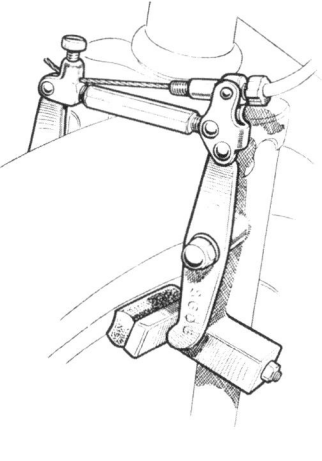

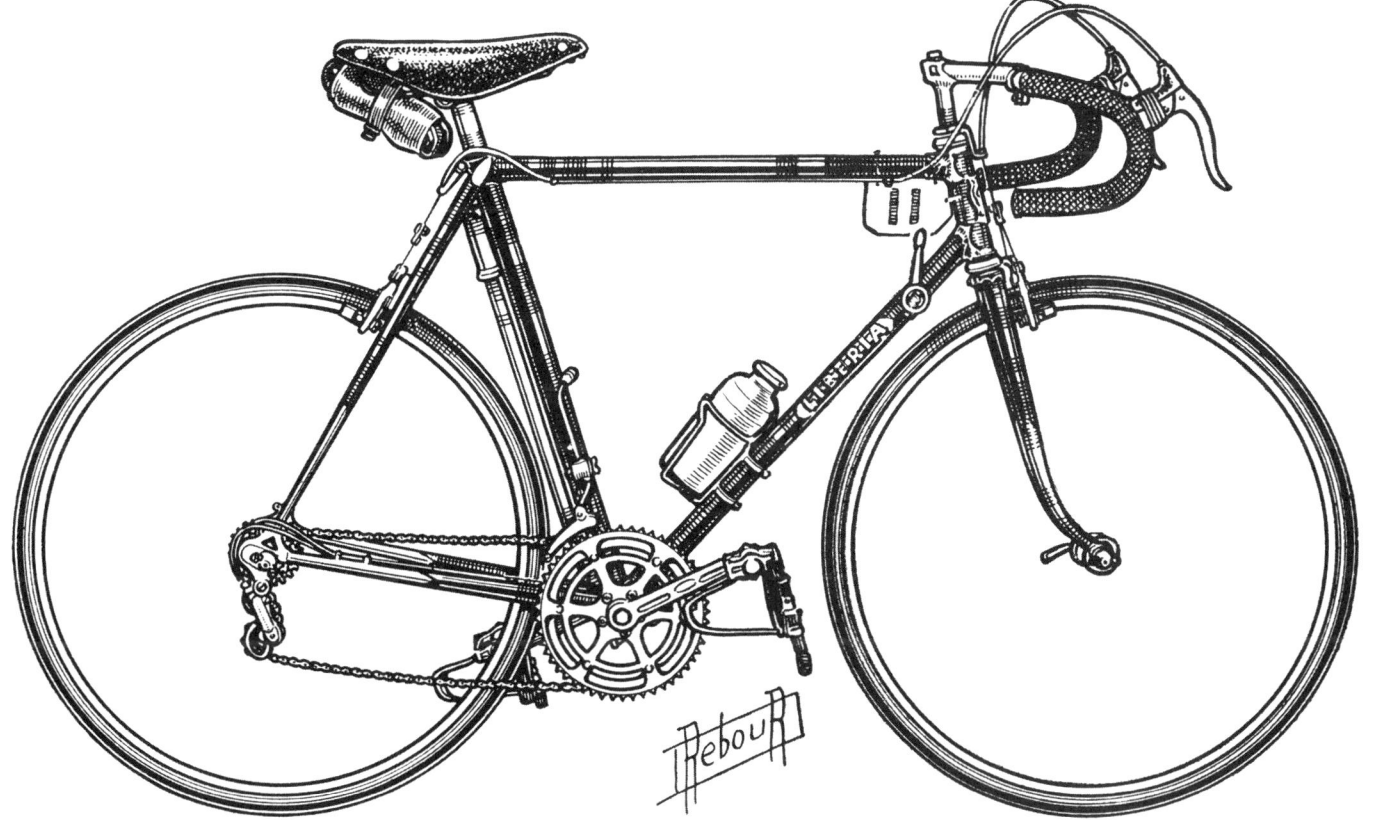

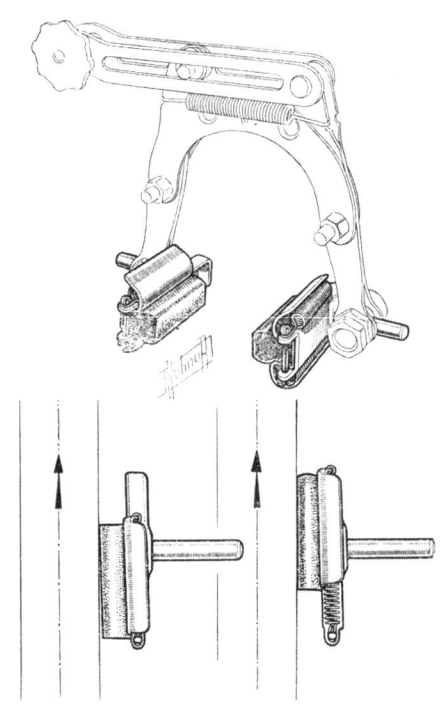
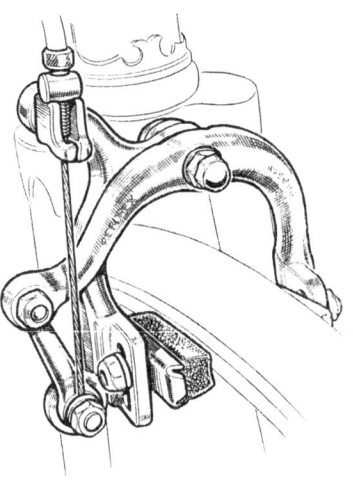
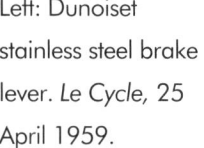
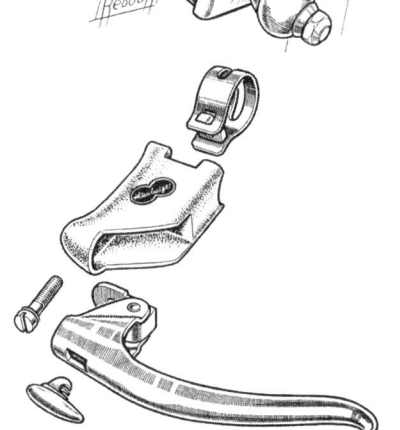

Left: English Beborex sidepull brake. *Le Cycle*, 13 November 1954.

Right: Mafac Tiger low-end centerpull brake. *Le Cycle*, Sept. 1960.

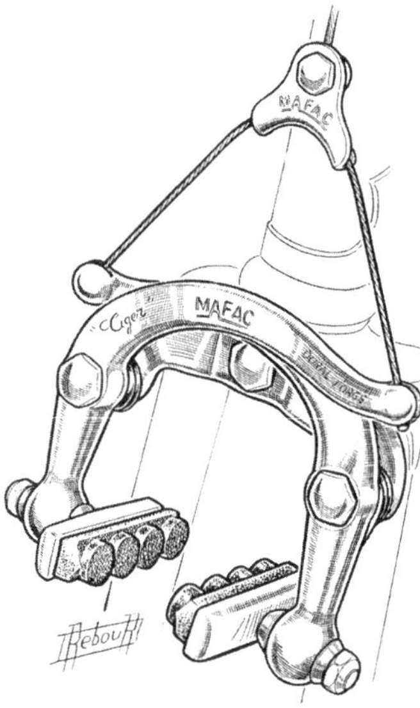

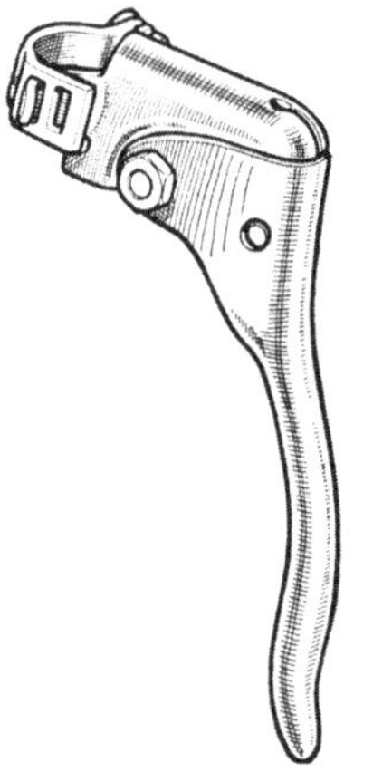

Left: Dunoiset stainless steel brake lever. *Le Cycle*, 25 April 1959.

Right: Exploded view of Altenburger brake lever. *Le Cycle*, September 1960.

Above: Hernandez self-energizing brake. *Le Cycle*, 28 July 1956.

Below: The René Herse track bicycle used by Leulhier to set a new 24-hour record at 668.33 km. *Le Cycle*, 29 September 1957.**

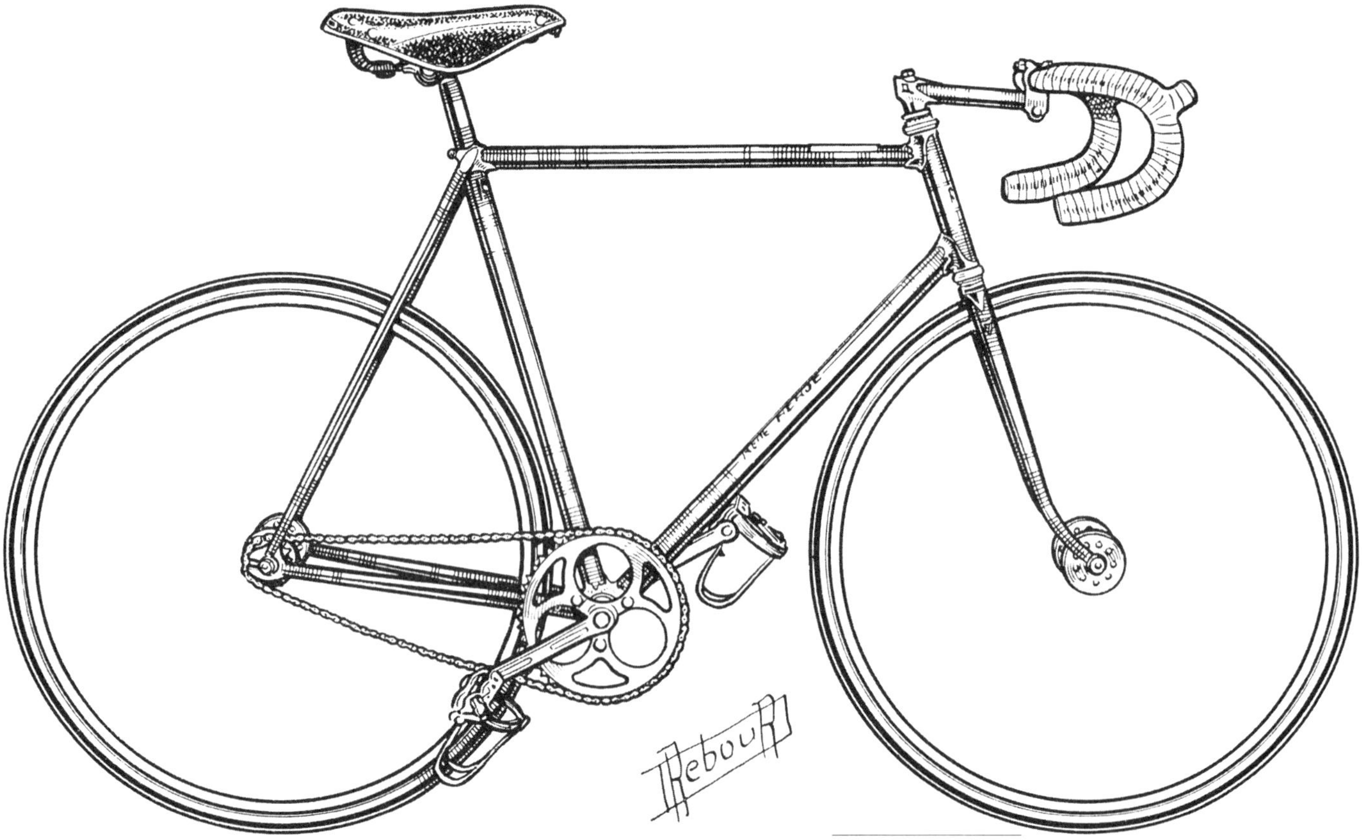

** See pages 269–271 for expanded caption text.

Chapter 6. Rim Brakes

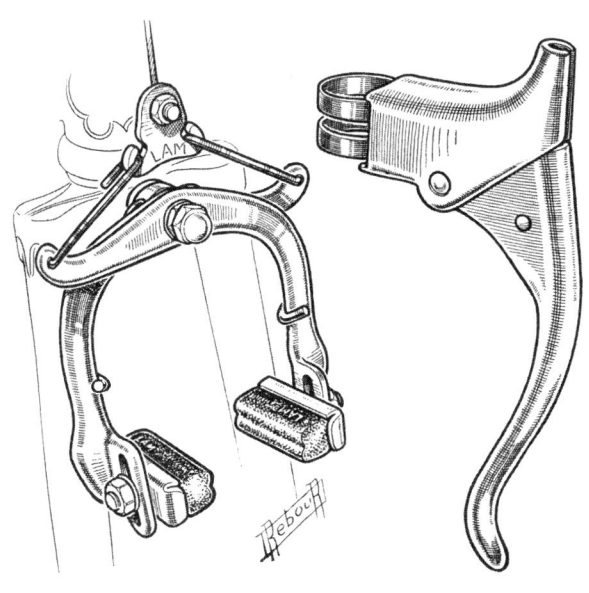

Left: LAM solid-link centerpull brake and lever. *Le Cycle*, September 1960.

Right: Front brake and cable routing on the René Herse bike ridden by Lily Herse in the 1961 French road racing championships. *Le Cycle*, November 1961.

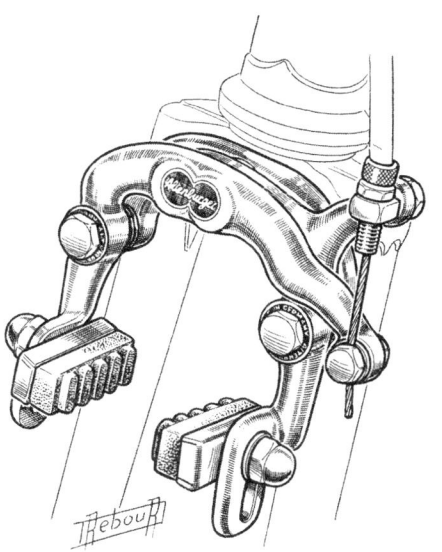

Left: Altenburger Sychron dual-pivot sidepull brake, precursor of the currently popular dual-pivot brakes. *Le Cycle*, November 1961.

Right and below: Regular and exploded views of Milremo centerpull brake and lever. *Le Cycle*, December 1960.

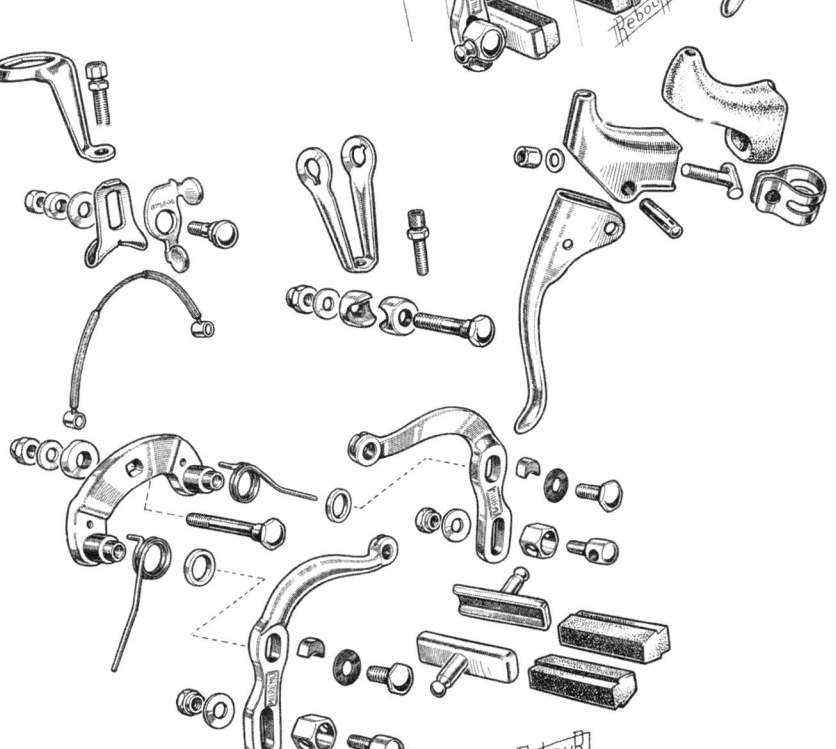

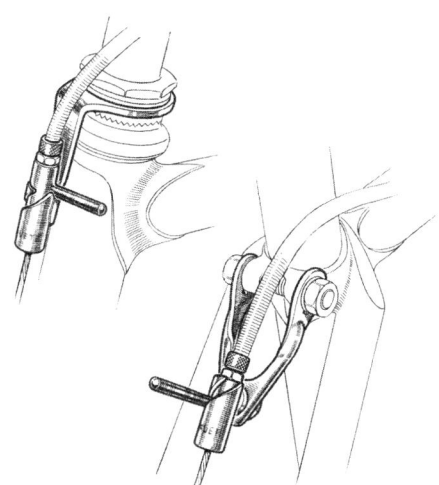

Above: CLB quick-release brake cable tensioner for front and rear brakes. *Le Cycle*, September 1962.

113

Exploded view of Altenburger Synchron dual-pivot brake. *Le Cycle*, June 1962.

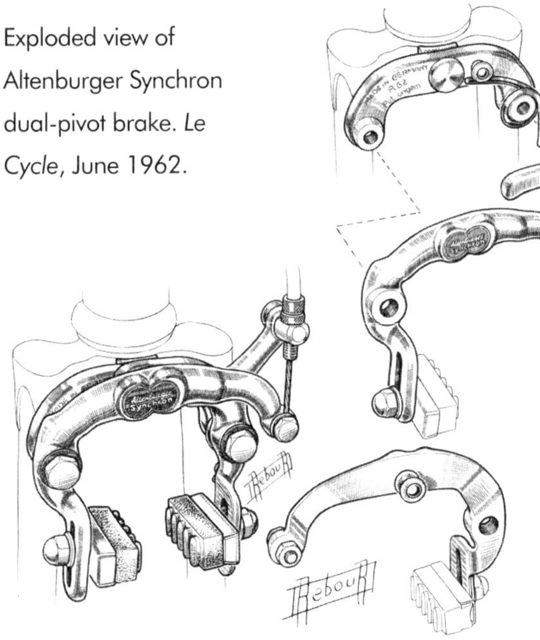

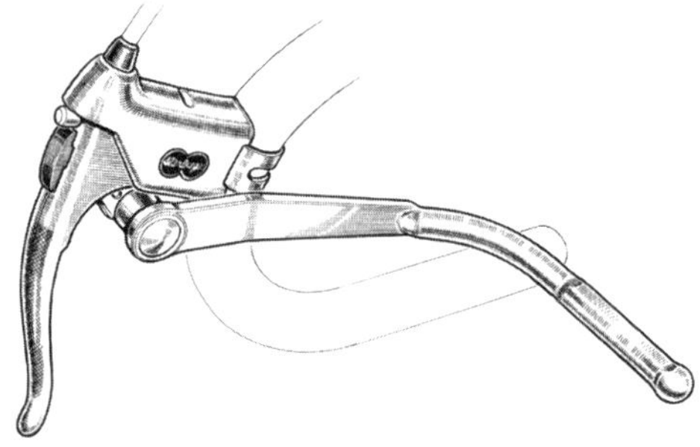

Left: Altenburger brake extension lever, a type that was popular during the U.S. 10-speed boom. *Le Cycle*, December 1972.

Right: Weinmann Symmetric dual-pivot sidepull brake, with close pivot spacing. *Le Cycle*, December 1973.

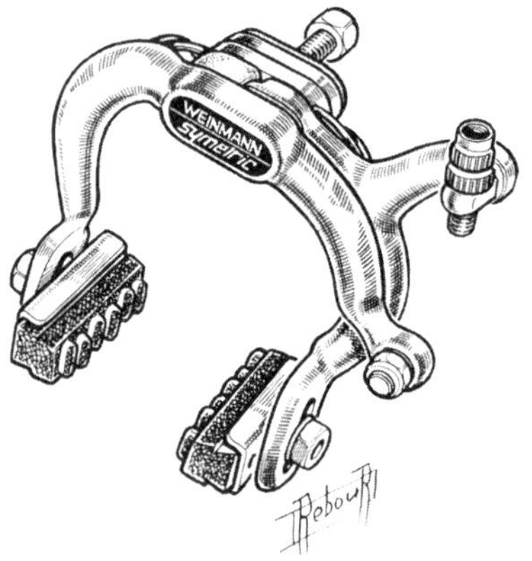

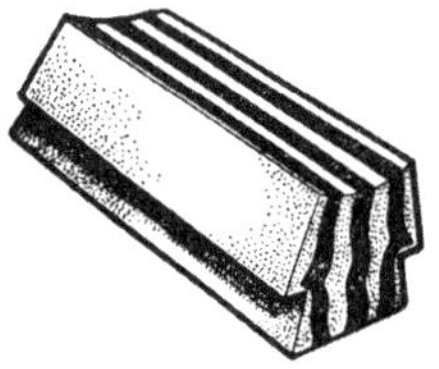

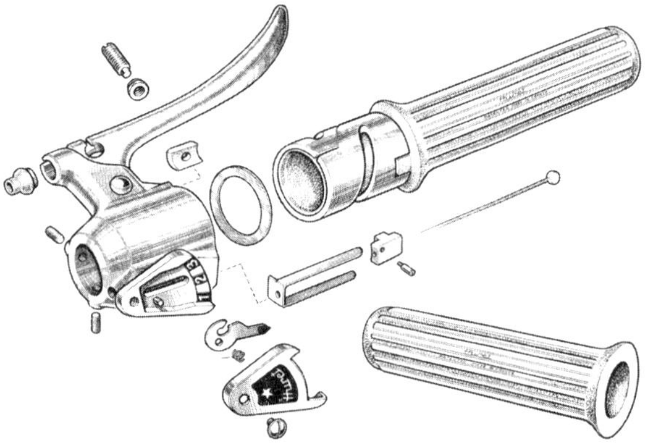

Above: CLB laminated brake pad. *Cycles de Compétition et Randonneuses*.

Left: Huret combined brake-shift lever for flat handlebars. *Le Cycle*, December 1968.

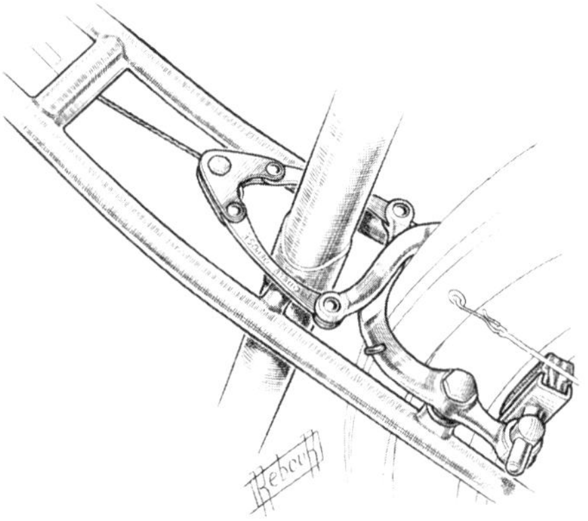

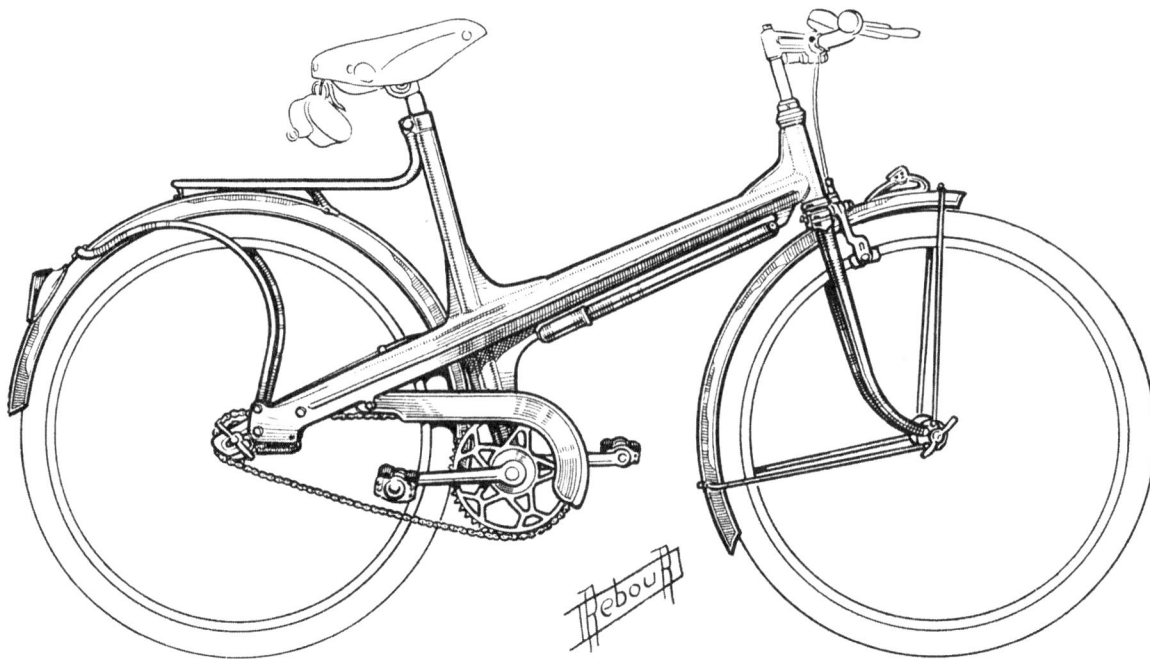

Above: BeBo brake, with solid linkage, and cable routing detail, installed on a Peugeot mixte frame. *Le Cycle*, October 1962.

Left: Hercules monocoque cross-frame bicycle, from Germany. *Le Cycle*, 4 October 1957.

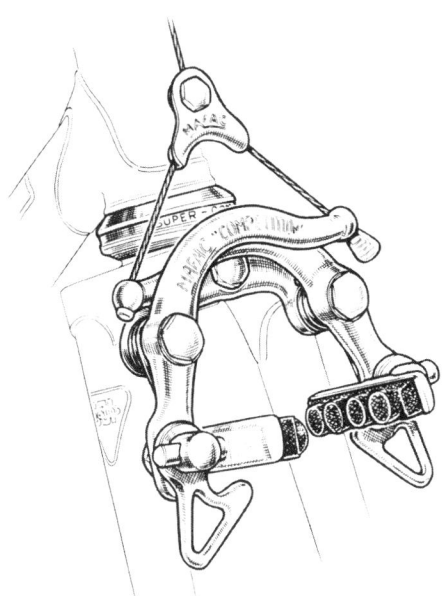 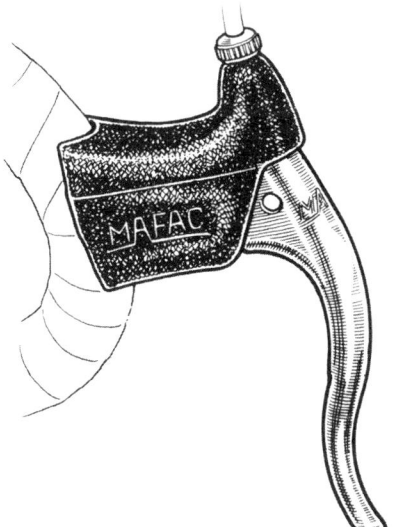 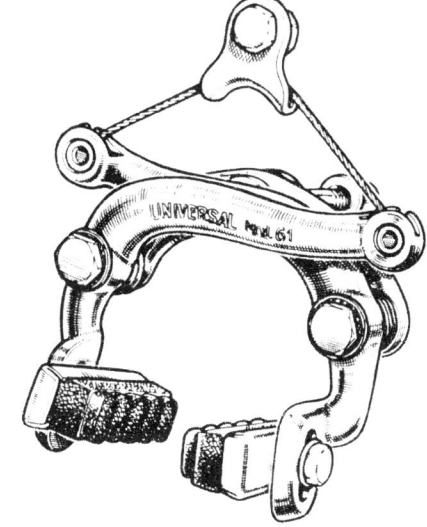

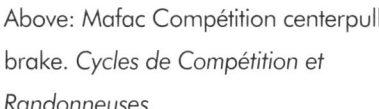 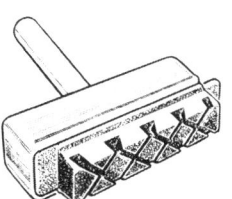 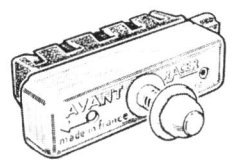

Above: Mafac Compétition centerpull brake. *Cycles de Compétition et Randonneuses.*

Below: The track bike on which Roger Rivière set a new World Hour record at 46.923 km on the Vigorelli track in Milan. *Le Cycle,* 4 October 1957.

Above left: Mafac brake lever, with cable-tension adjuster.
Above right: 1975 Universal centerpull brake.
Left and right: Mafac self-energizing brake pads.
All four images from *Cycles de Compétition et Randonneuses.*

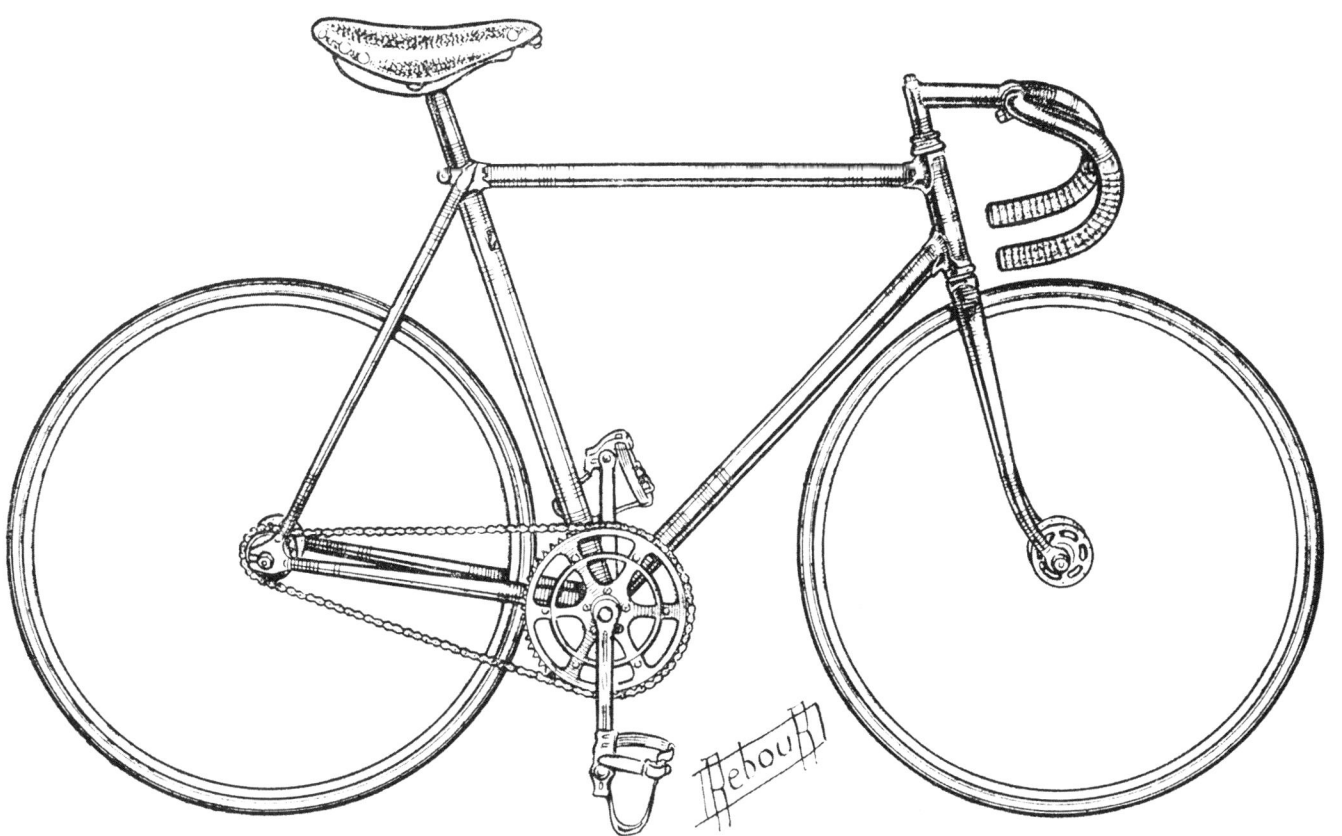

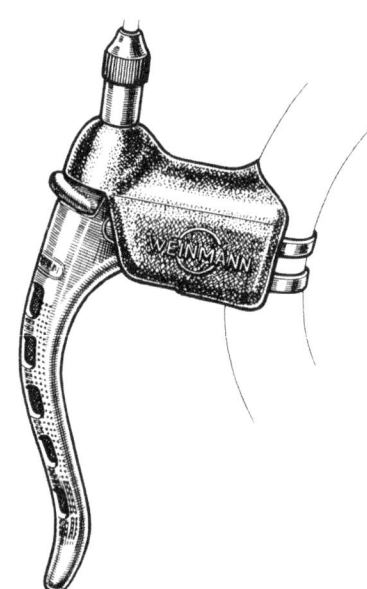
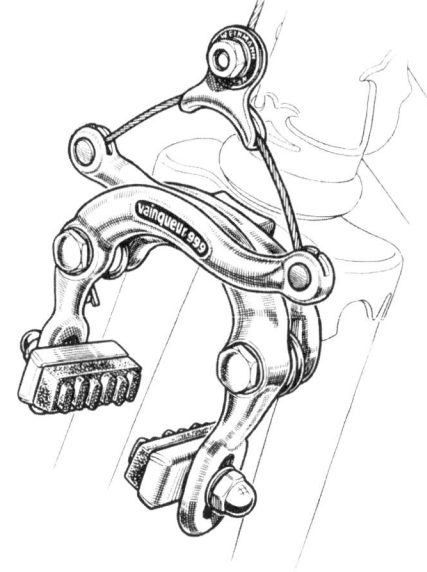
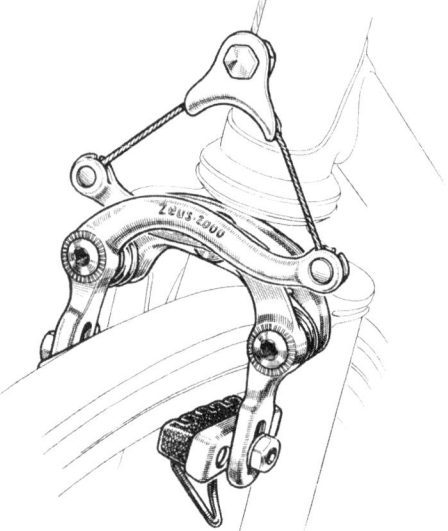

Left: Weinmann Vainqueur front centerpull brake, made in Switzerland. *Cycles de Compétition et Randonneuses.*

Above: Weinmann Vainqueur brake lever with cable tension quick-release and cable adjuster. *Cycles de Compétition et Randonneuses.*

Above: 1975 Zeus 2000 front centerpull brake, from Spain. *Cycles de Compétition et Randonneuses.*

Below: Louis Bergaud rode this Raphaël-Géminiani bicycle in the 1958 Poly de Chanteloup technical trials. *Le Cycle*, 10 May 1958.

Left: TA brake cable anchor and seat binder bolt combination. *Cycles de Compétition et Randonneuses.*

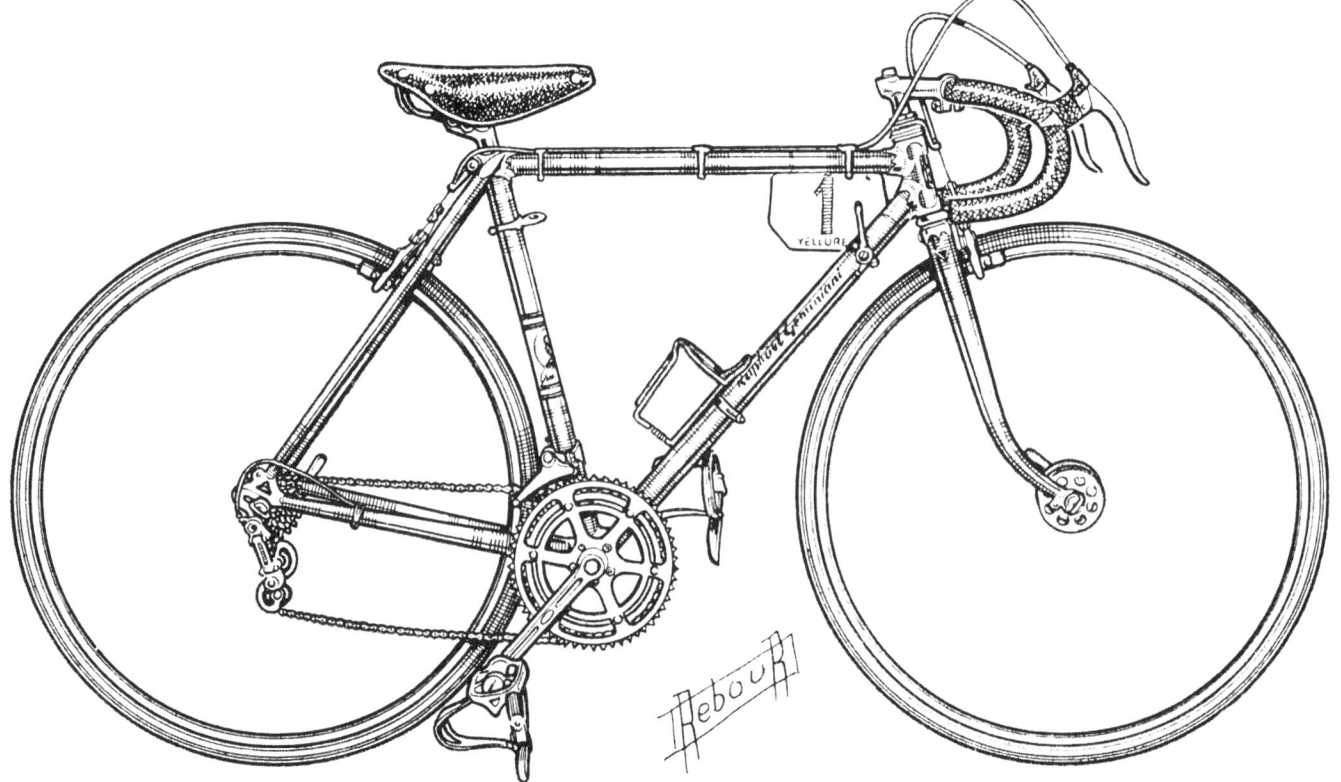

Chapter 6. Rim Brakes

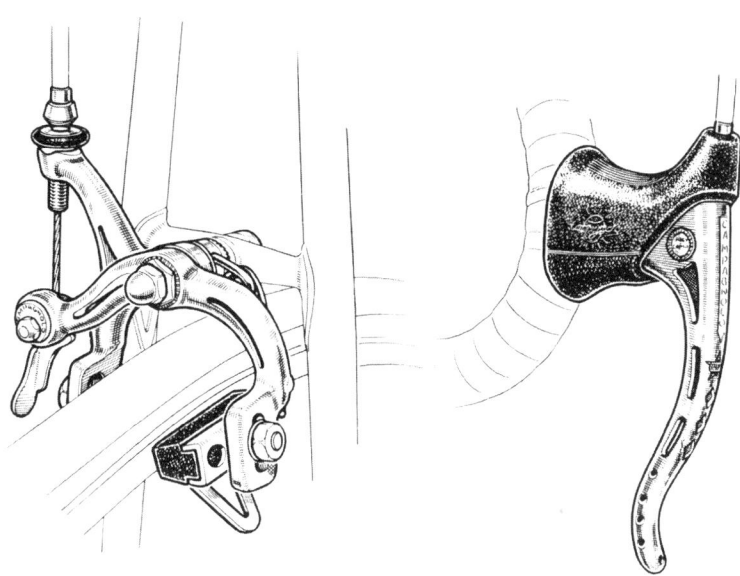
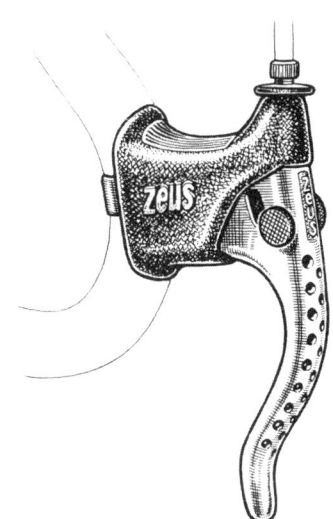

Left: Campagnolo Super Record brake and lever, with cutouts. *L'Officiel du Cycle*, March 1976.

Right: 1975 Zeus 2000 drilled-out brake lever. *Cycles de Compétition et Randonneuses*.

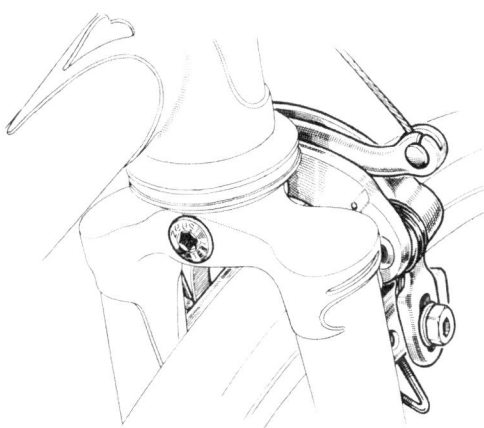
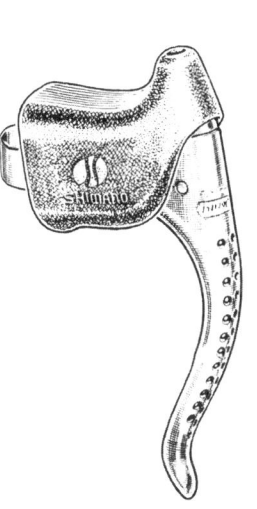
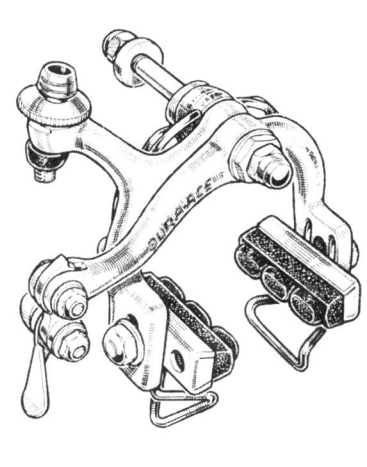

Left: Mounting detail of Zeus 2000 centerpull brake. *Le Monde de Daniel Rebour*.

Right: Shimano Dura-Ace sidepull brake and lever. 1976 Milremo catalogue.

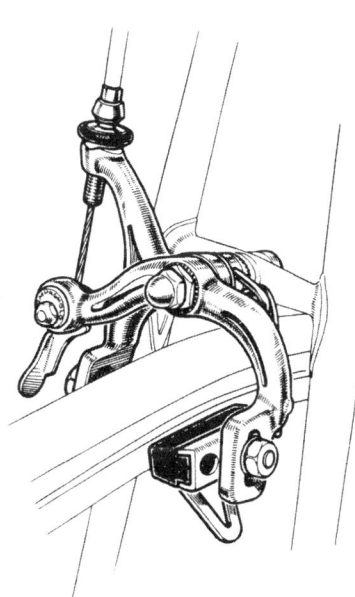
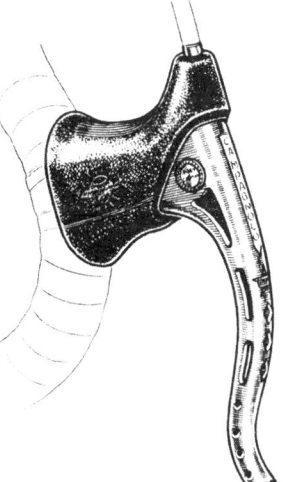
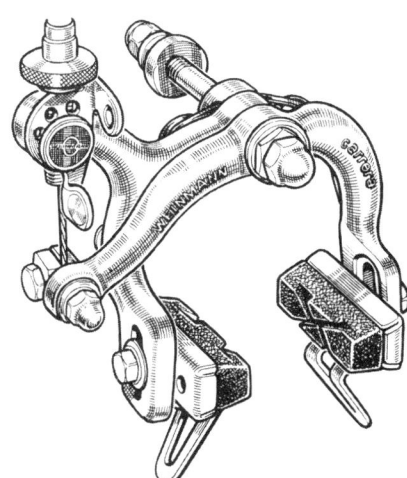

Left and right: Campagnolo Super Record brake and lever, as mounted on an Olmo bicycle. *L'Officiel du Cycle*, March 1976.

Far right: Weinmann Carerra sidepull brake. *L'Officiel du Cycle*, February 1976.

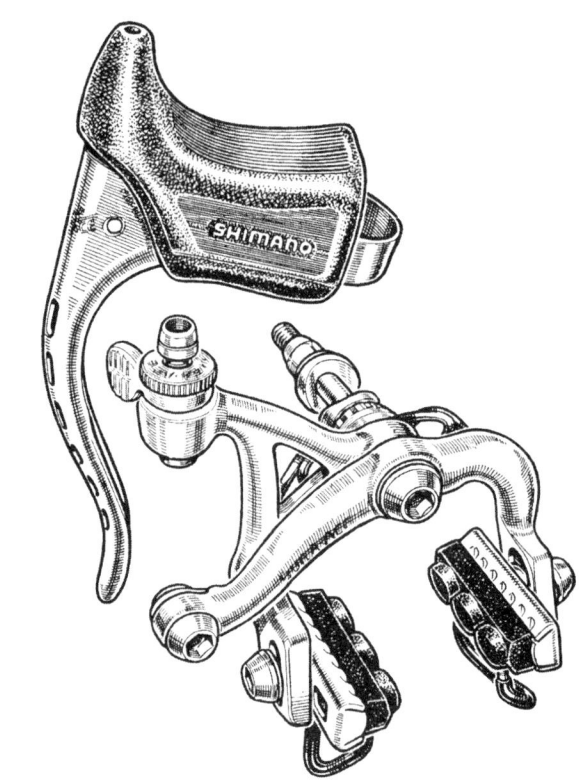

Below: 1980 Shimano Dura-Ace sidepull brake and conventional (i.e., non-aero) brake lever. 1981 Milremo catalogue.

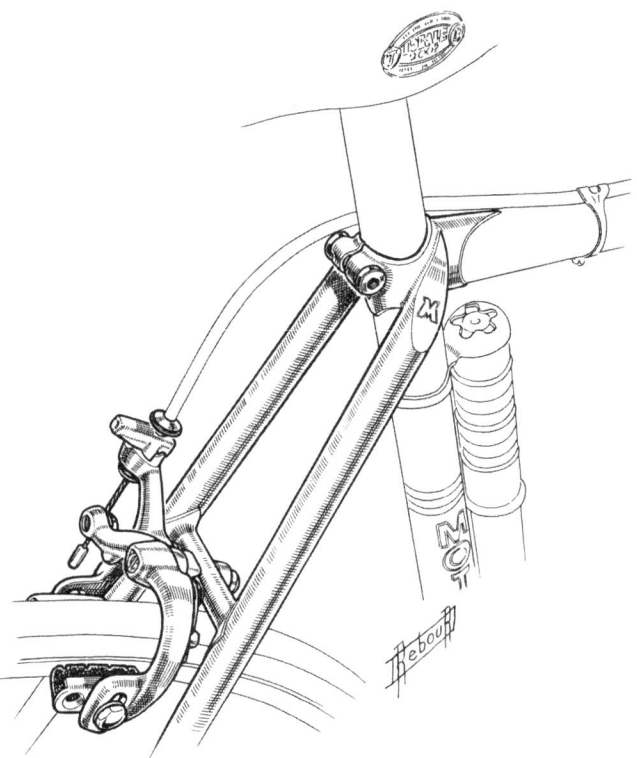

Above: CLB rear brake, shown at the 1976 Salon Motobécane. *L'Officiel du Cycle*, December 1976.

Below: Gaillard's Jo Routens bicycle at the 1958 Poly de Chanteloup technical trials. *Le Cycle*, 10 May 1958.**

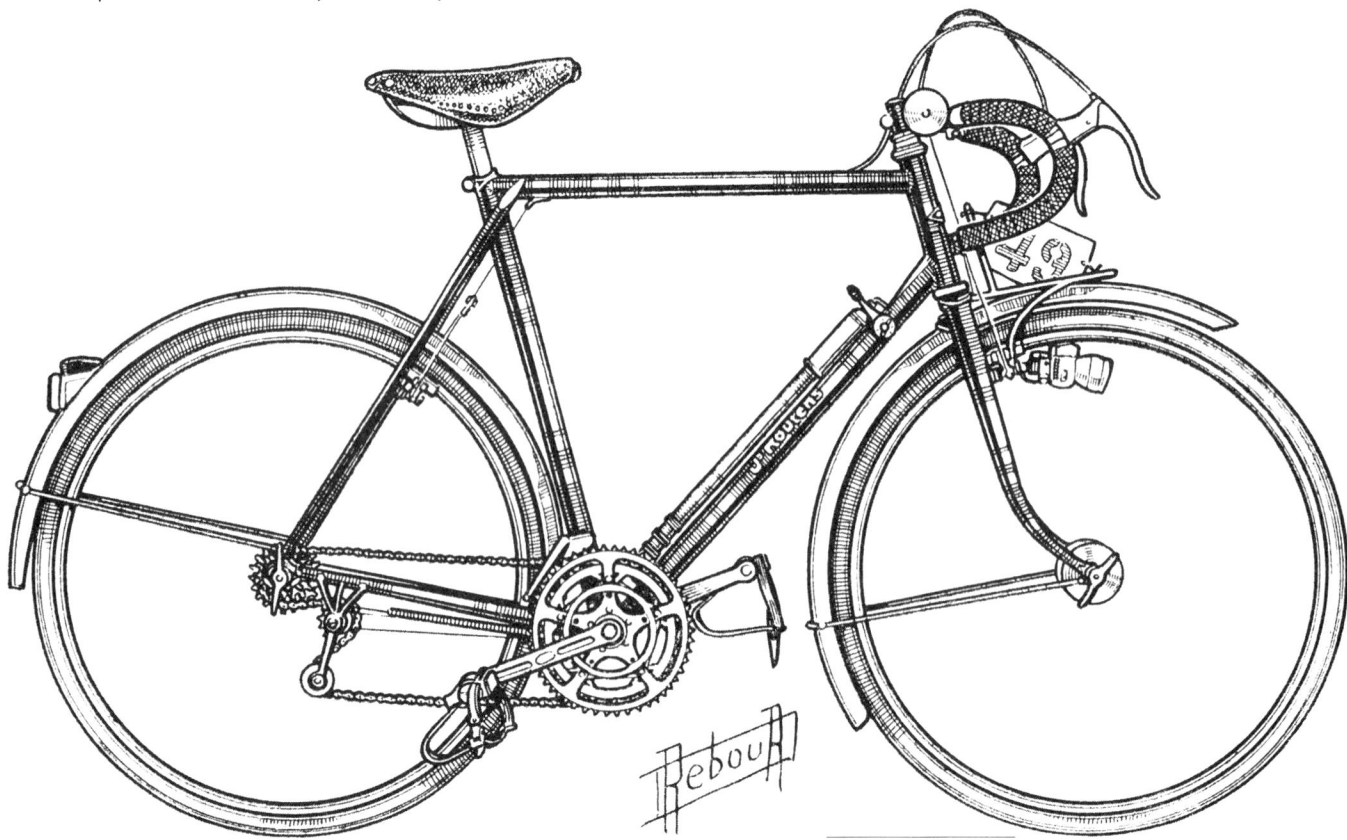

** See pages 269–271 for expanded caption text.

Chapter 6. Rim Brakes

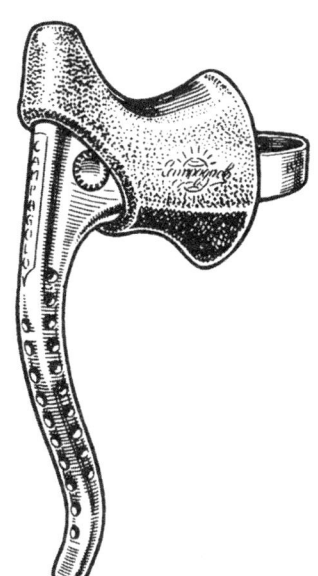

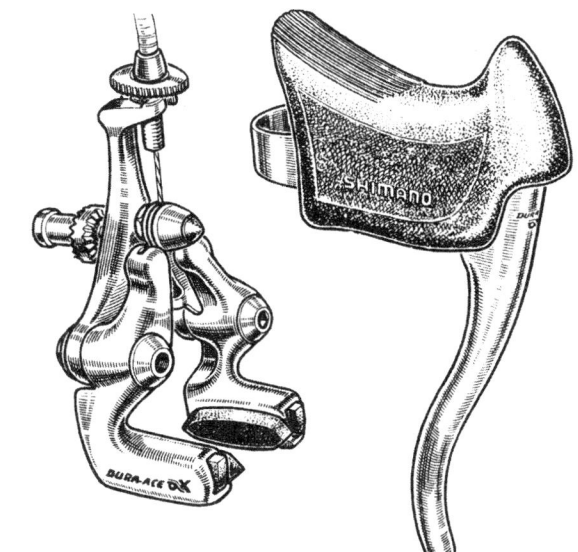

Left: Campagnolo Super Record brake lever. This was still a conventional lever, with exposed cable. 1981 Milremo catalogue.

Right: Shimano AX brake lever and Parapull cam-operated caliper brake. This was one of the first "aero" brake levers, with the cable routed along the handlebars. 1981 Milremo catalogue.

Right: Campagnolo Record sidepull brake. 1981 Milremo catalogue.

Below: 2nd place finisher in the 1958 Tour de France, Vito Favero's Atala bicycle. *Le Cycle*, 9 August 1958.

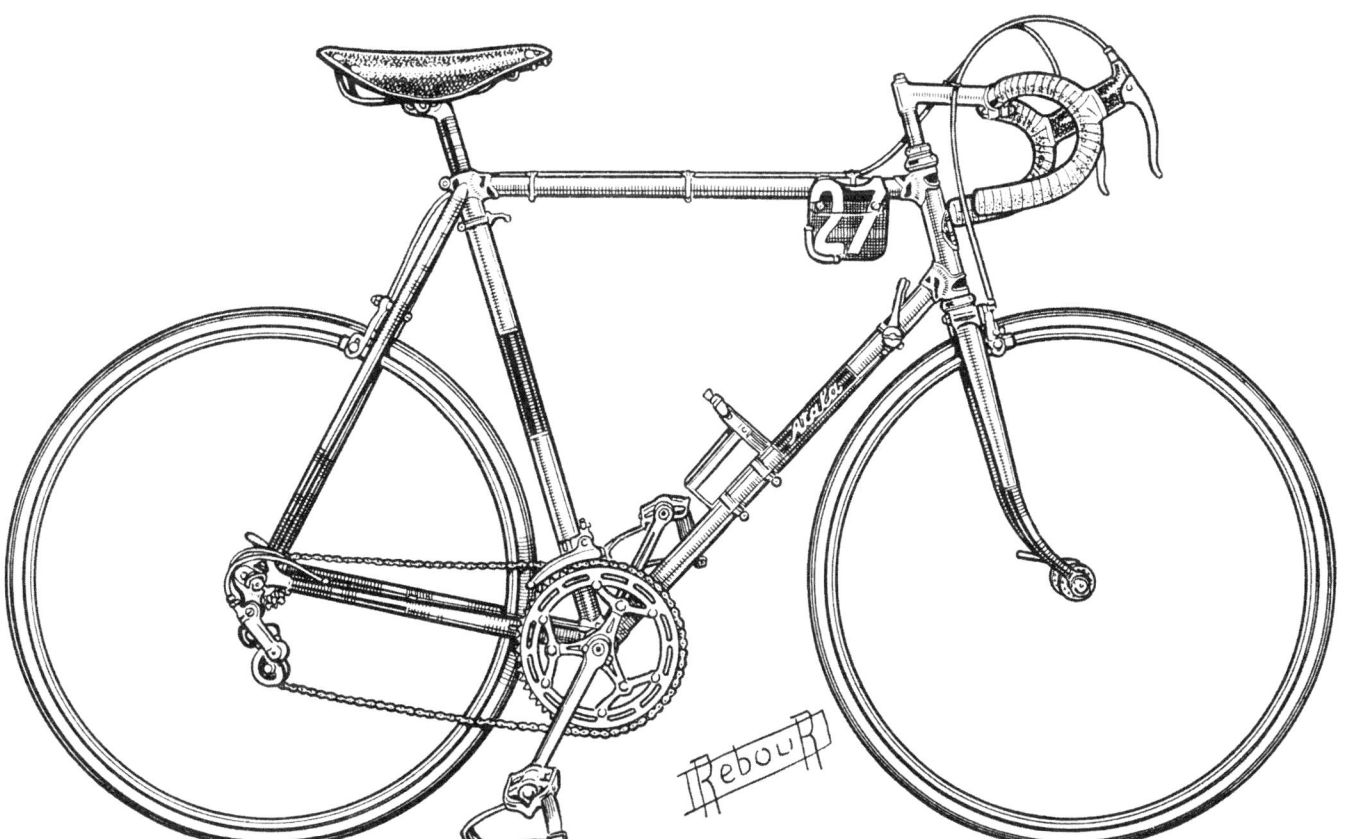

119

Chapter 7. Wheel Hubs

In this chapter we have collected a number of Rebour drawings that show various wheel hubs. Included are both front and rear hubs, with or without freewheel cassettes, and with or without quick-releases. Other hub types, such as those with built-in gears, brakes, or generators, will be covered separately in Chapter 8.

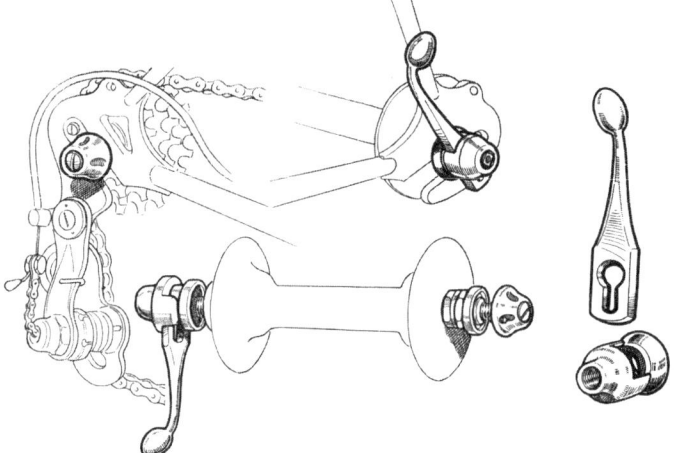

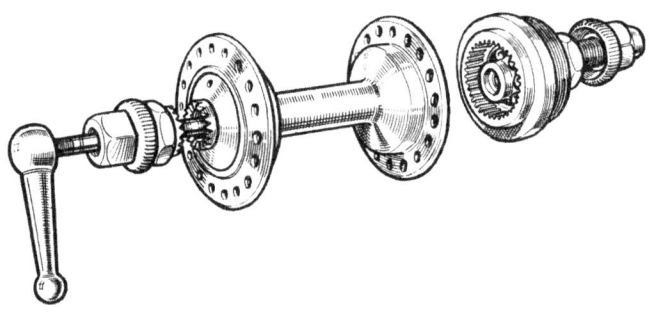

Above: Chioda cassette rear hub with quick-release. *Le Cycle*, 20 February 1950.

Below: The Helyett bicycle of Louis Graczyk, winner of the points classification in the 1958 Tour de France. *Le Cycle*, 9 August 1958.

Above: Details of solid-axle Simplex quick-release mechanism. *Le Cycle*, 9 October 1948.

Left: Aluminium wing nut for use with a hub with solid axle, which was quite common throughout the 1940s and early 1950s, even amongst racers. *Pratique du Vélo*.

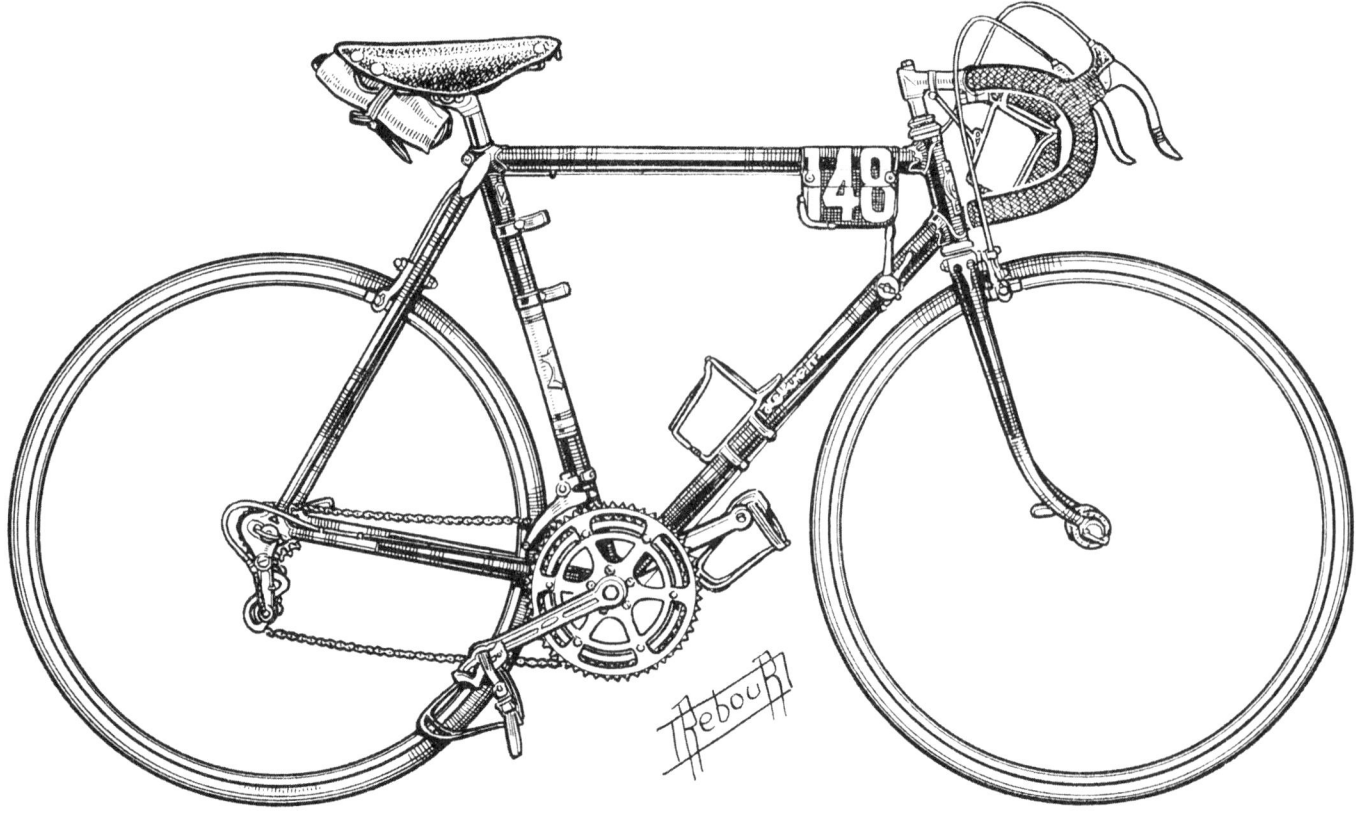

Chapter 7. Wheel Hubs

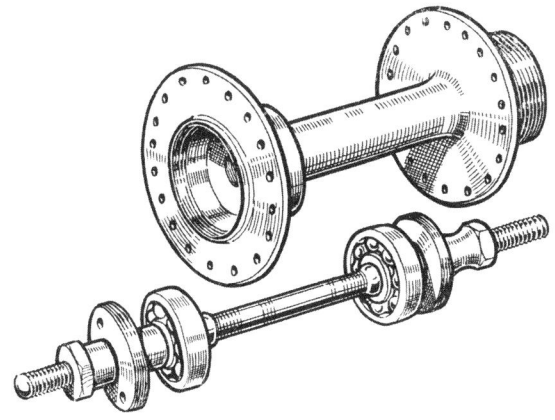

Above: Cartridge bearing hub with Hoffman sealed bearings. *Le Cycle*, 12 February 1949.

Above right: Cassette-type rear hub with 3-speed cassette freewheel with splined-on cogs. *Pratique du Vélo*.

Left: Exeltoo sealed-bearing split rear hub. *Le Cycle*, October 1949.

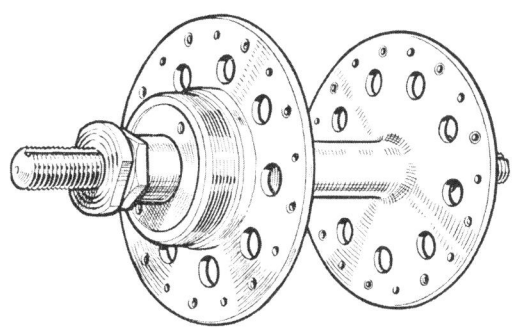

Right: Italian-made split rear hub with through-axle. *Pratique du Vélo*.

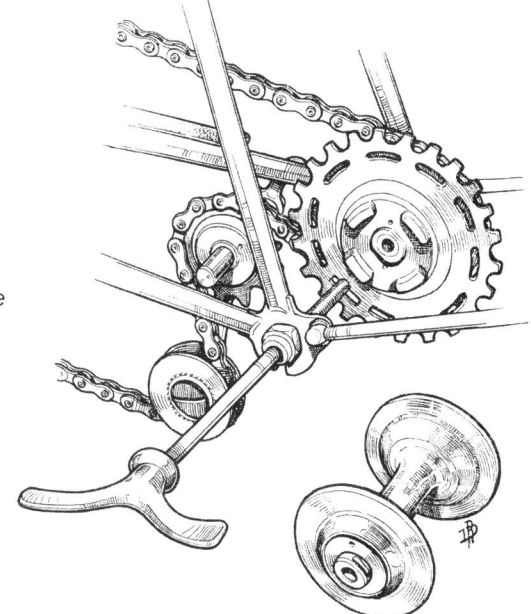

Above: Through-axle split rear hub installation detail. *Pratique du Vélo*.

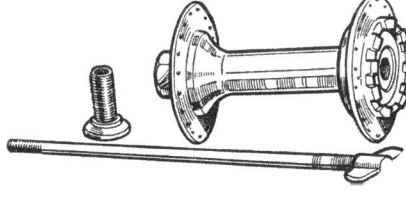

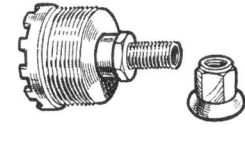

Left: Préférence split rear hub. *Le Cycle*, 9 October 1950.

Left: Rear hub with large drive-side hub flange to ease spoke replacement. *Le Cycle*, 7 January 1950.

Below: GB ergonomic wing nut. *Le Cycle*, 7 January 1950.

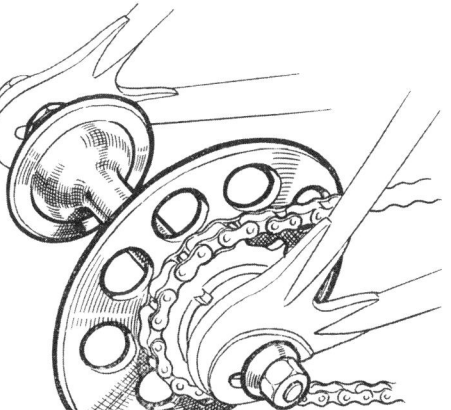

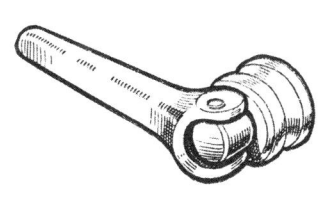

Left: Huret solid-axle quick-release. *Le Cycle*, 12 February 1949.

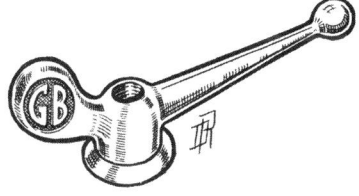

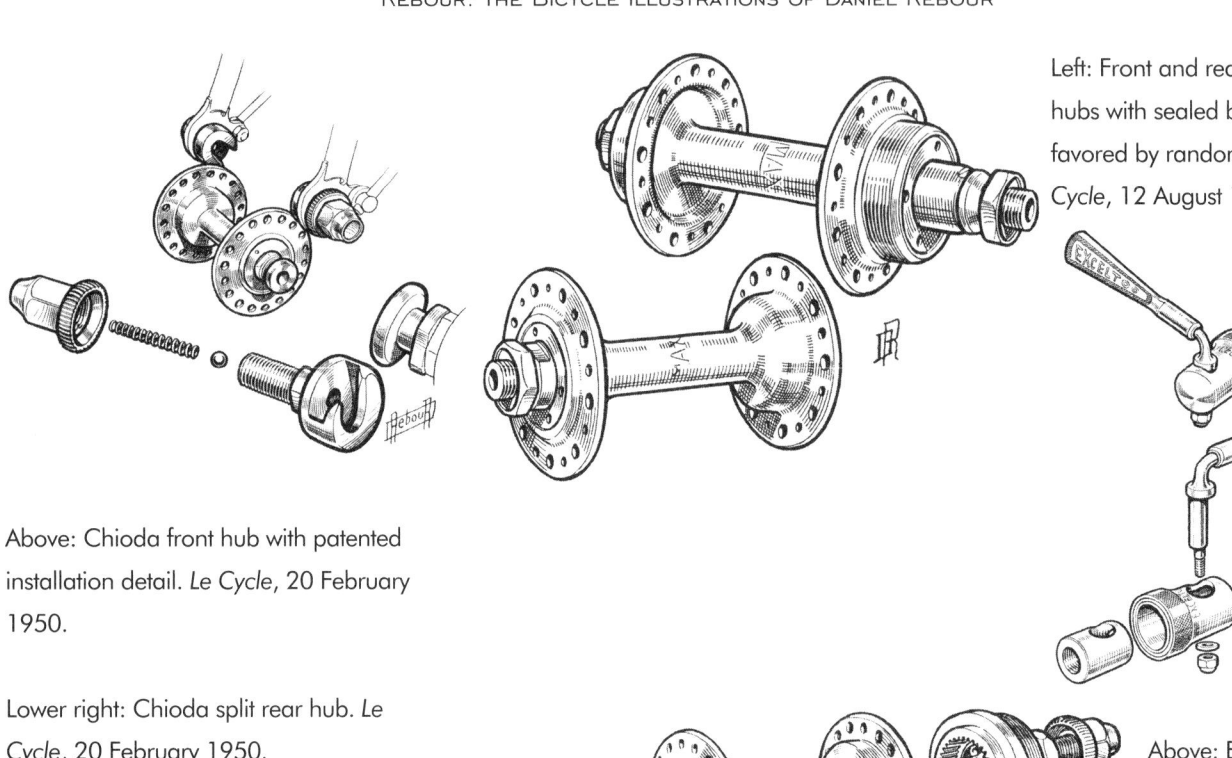

Left: Front and rear Maxi-Car hubs with sealed bearings, favored by randonneurs. *Le Cycle*, 12 August 1950.

Above: Chioda front hub with patented installation detail. *Le Cycle*, 20 February 1950.

Lower right: Chioda split rear hub. *Le Cycle*, 20 February 1950.

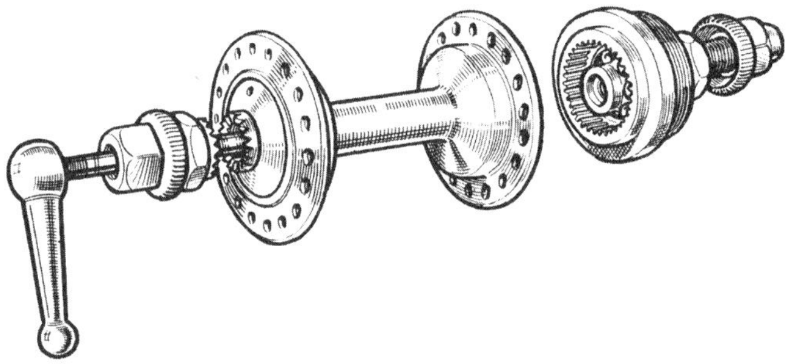

Above: Exploded view of Exceltoo quick-release mechanism. *Le Cycle*, 11 March 1950.

Below: Fédérico Bahamontès won the mountains classification of the 1958 Tour de France on this Learco-Guerra bicycle. *Le Cycle*, 9 August 1958.

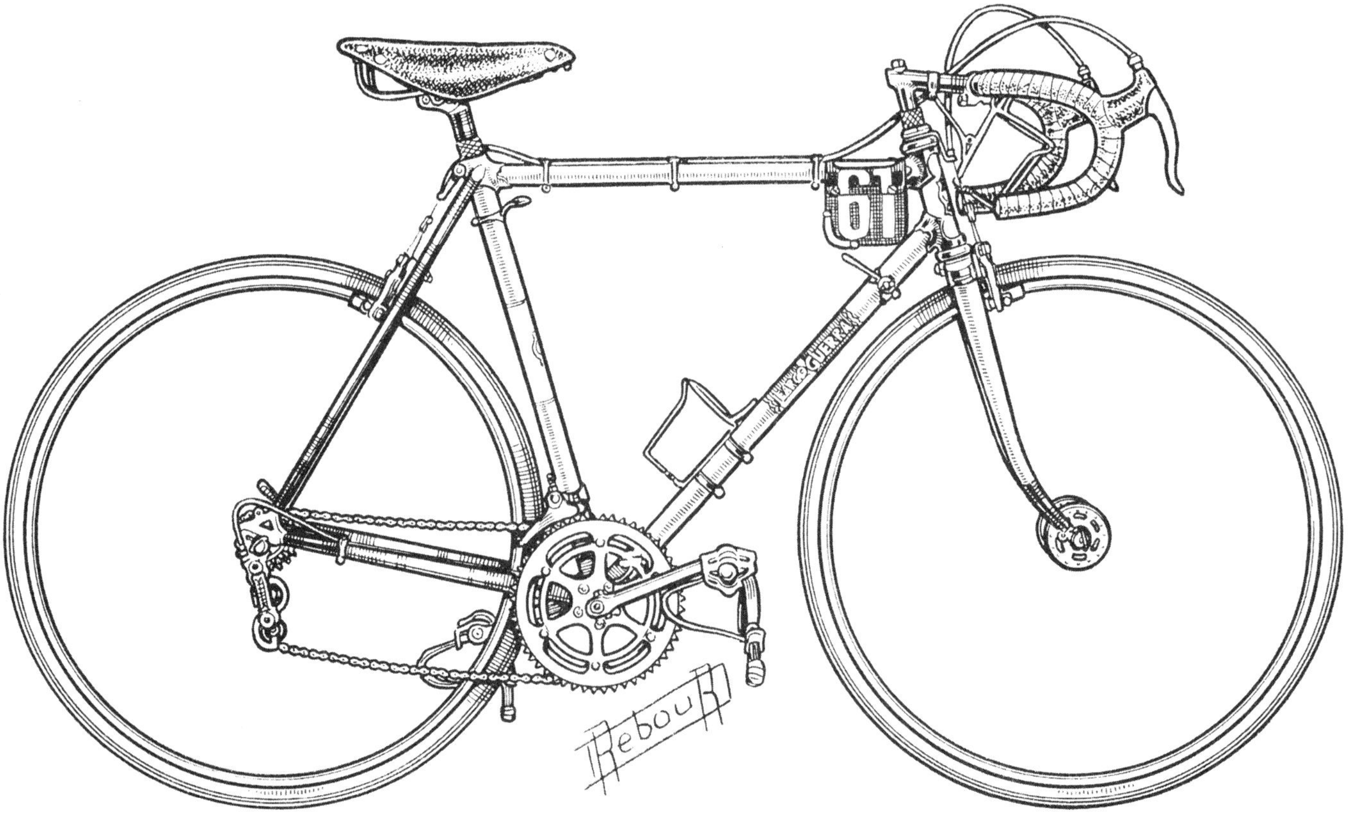

Chapter 7. Wheel Hubs

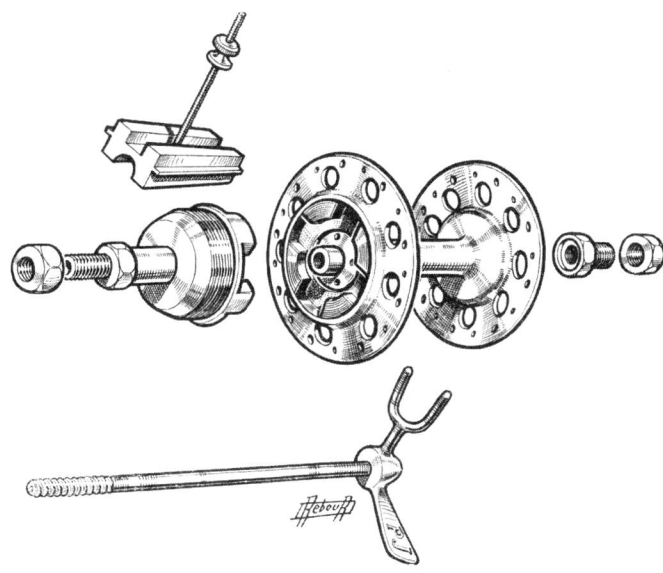

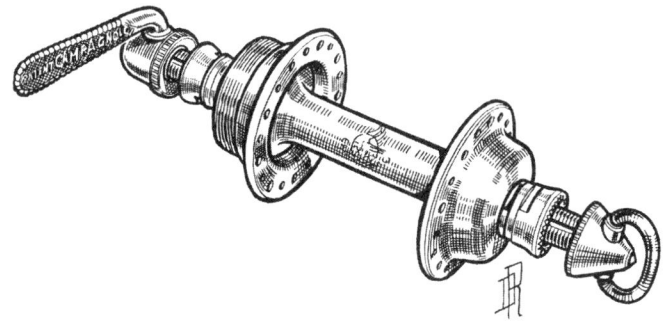

Above: Campagnolo Record steel rear hub with quick-release. *Le Cycle*, 4 October 1952.

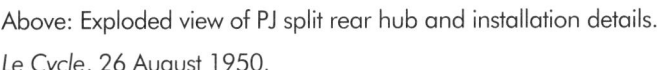

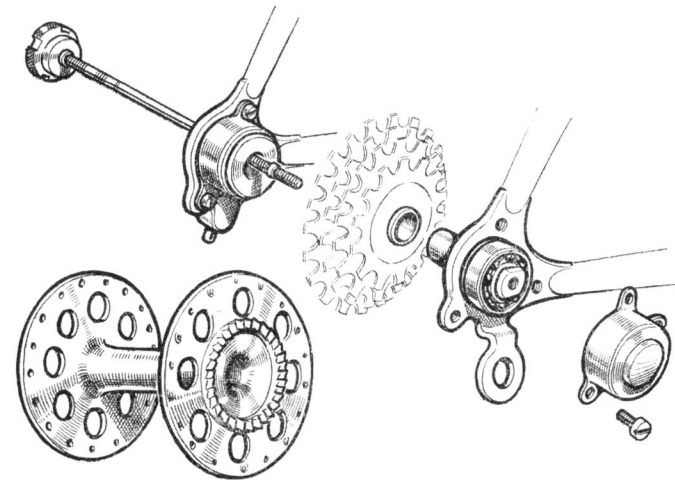

Above: Exploded view of PJ split rear hub and installation details. *Le Cycle*, 26 August 1950.

Right: Exploded view of Préférence spilt rear hub and installation details. *Le Cycle*, 30 October 1950.

Below: Overal winner of the 1958 Tour de France, Charly Gaul, of Luxembourg, also rode a Learco-Guerra machine. *Le Cycle*, 9 August 1958.

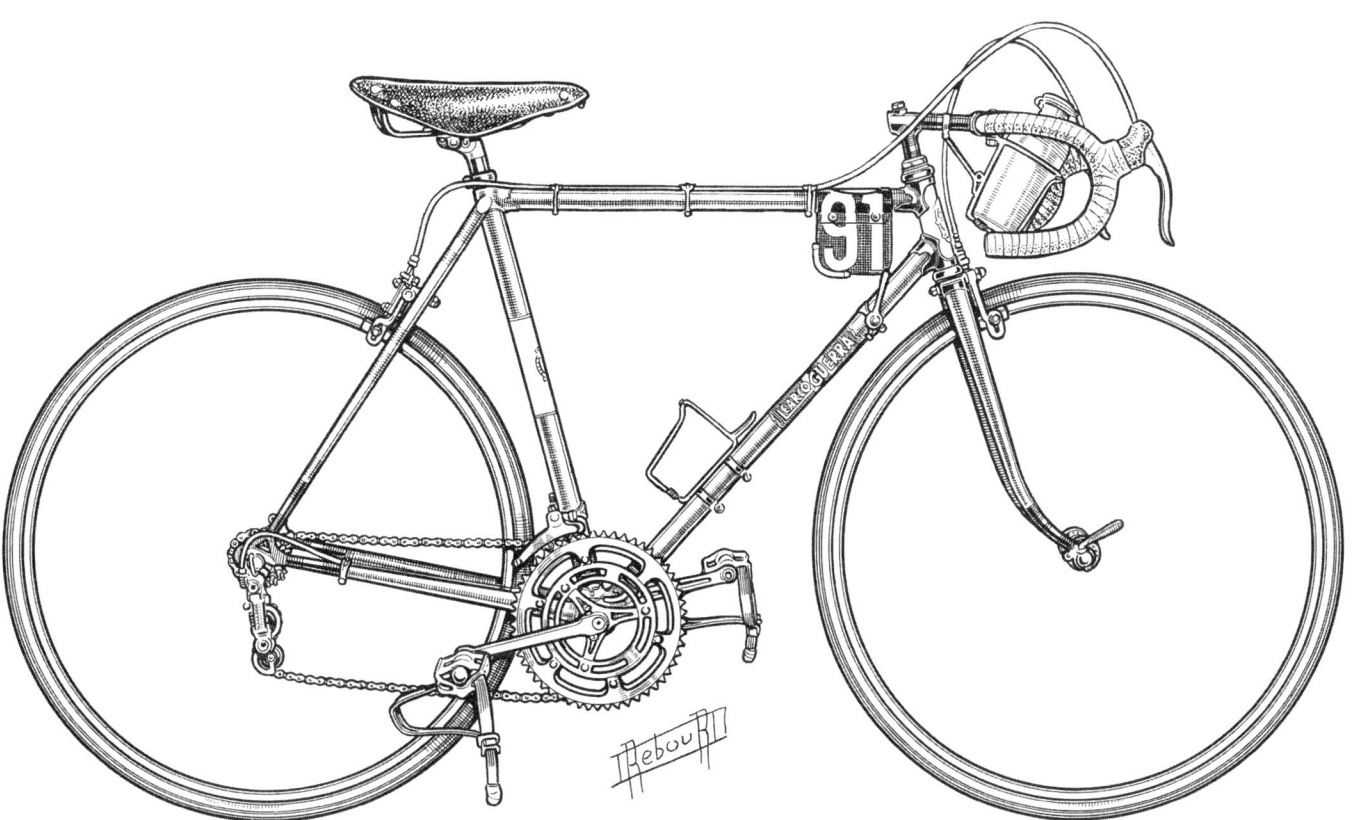

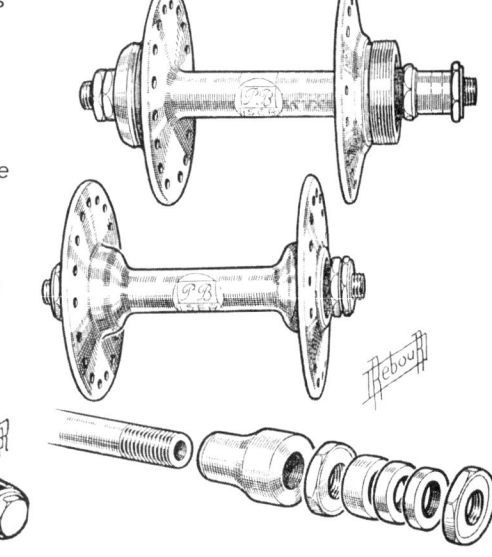

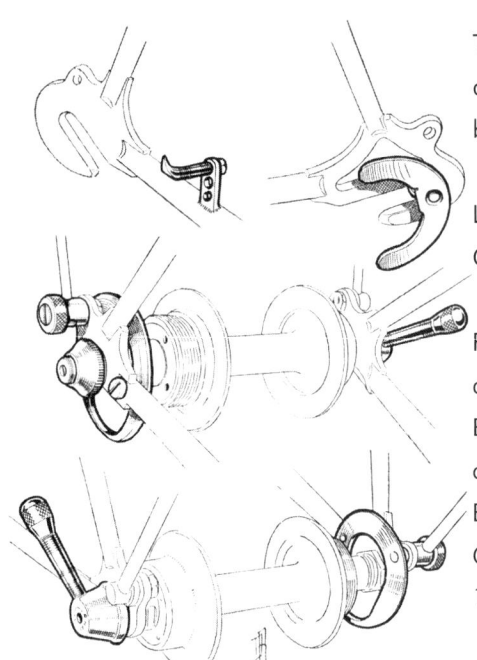

Top right: Paul Barbier high-flange hubs and exploded view of their adjustable bearing. *Le Cycle*, 13 August 1955.

Lower right: Simplex Juy-Record hubs. *Le Cycle*, 10 October 1959.

Right: Giu-Beste quick-release.
Below: Lampo quick-release. Both images from *Le Cycle*, 25 November 1950.

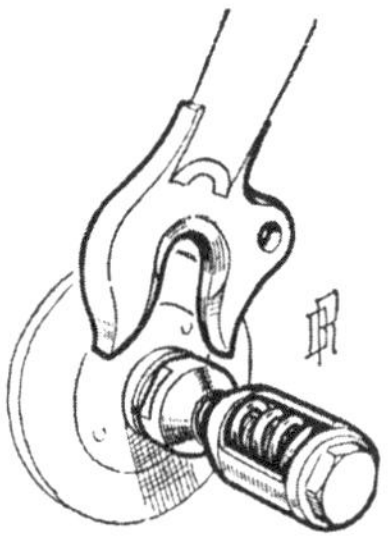

Above: Cyclo-Rapid rear hub installation details. *Le Cycle*, 23 October 1950.

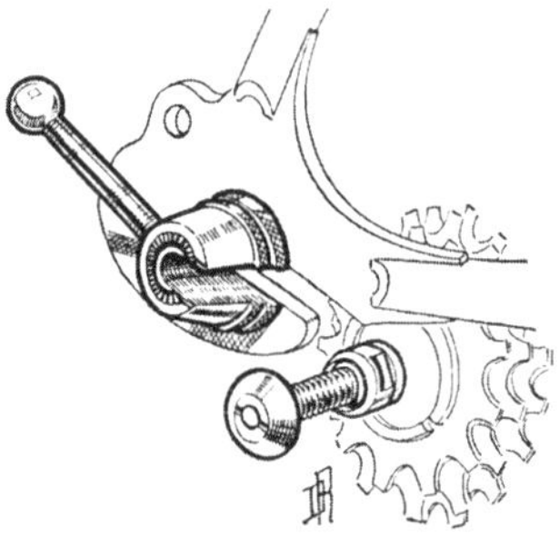

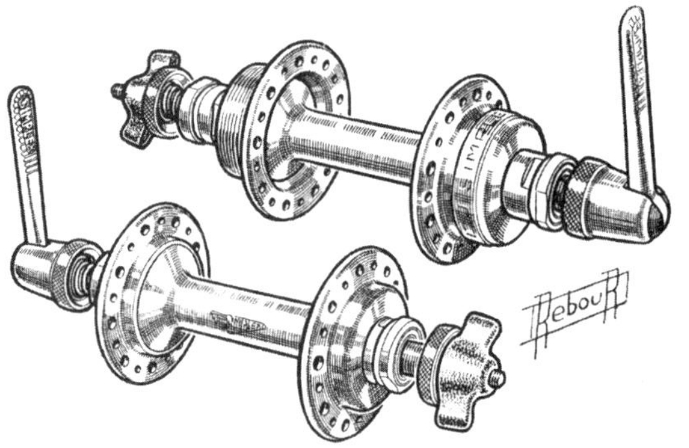

Below: 1958 Tour de France 3rd place finisher Géminiani's Raphaël-Géminiani-branded bicycle. *Le Cycle*, 9 August 1958.

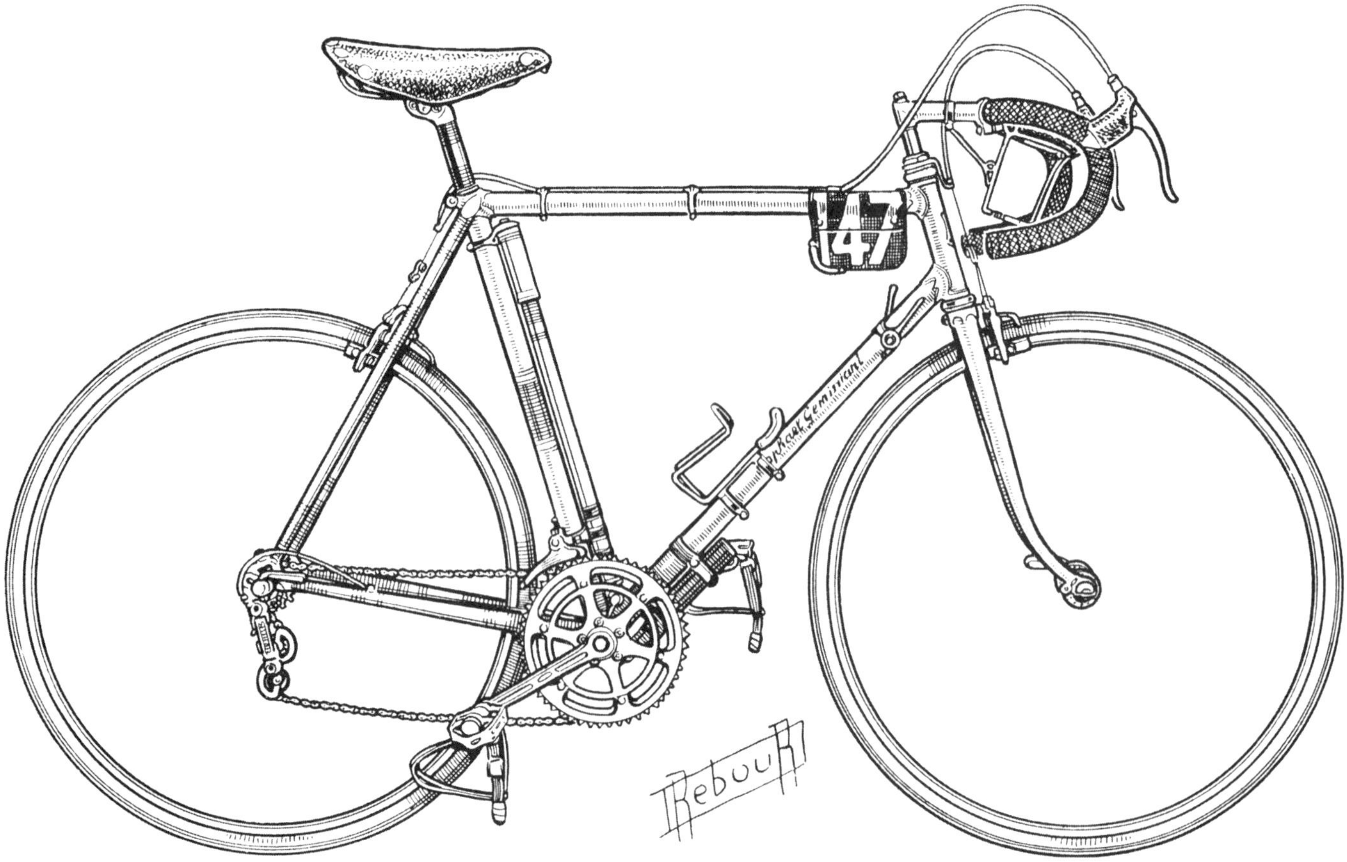

Chapter 7. Wheel Hubs

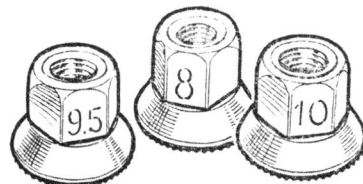
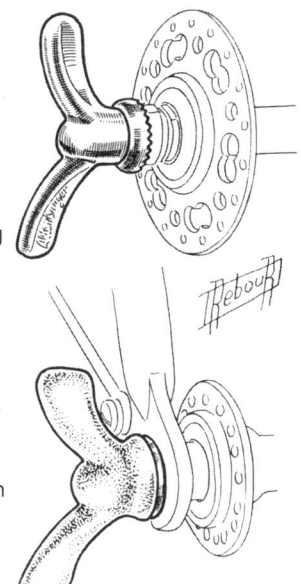
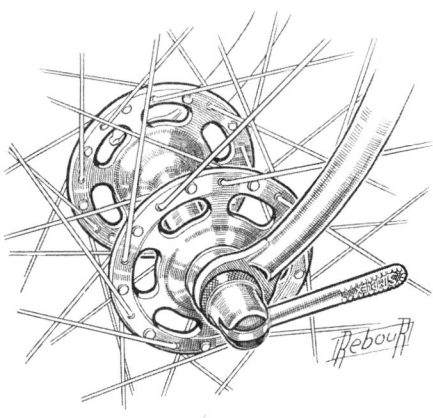

Top left: Collection of Huret hub nuts for solid axle hubs. *Le Cycle*, 1 October 1953.
Lower left: Singer wing nut. *Le Cycle*, 4 October 1957.
Right: Two types of Altenburger wing nuts. *Le Cycle*, April 1960.
Below: Atom hubs with quick-release. *Le Cycle*, September 1960.

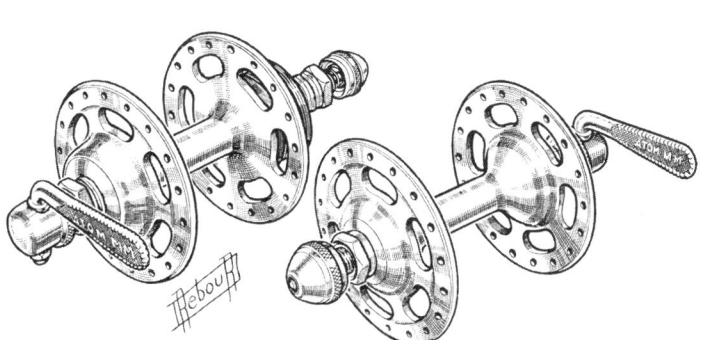

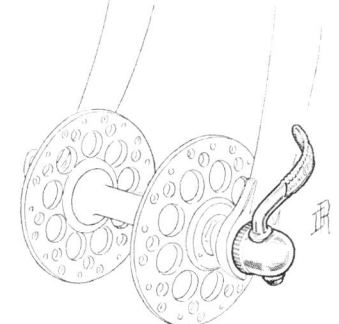

Top right: Simplex quick-release detail on Anquetil's Helyett bike. *Le Cycle*, 22 August 1959.
Right: Campagnolo high-flange hubs. *Le Cycle*, 25

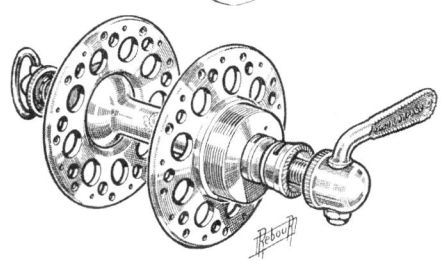

Right: Simplex quick-release parts. *Le Cycle*, June 1964.
Below: New Star steel high- and low-flange hubs. *Le Cycle*, November 1960.

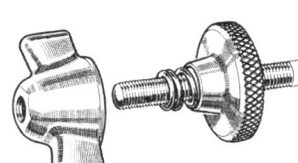

Right: Simplex quick-release hubs. *Le Cycle*, November 1960.

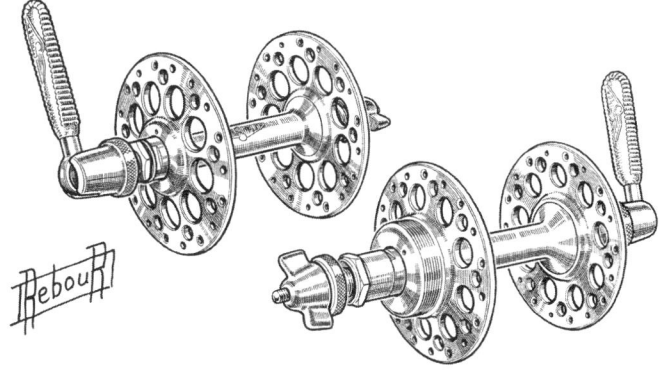

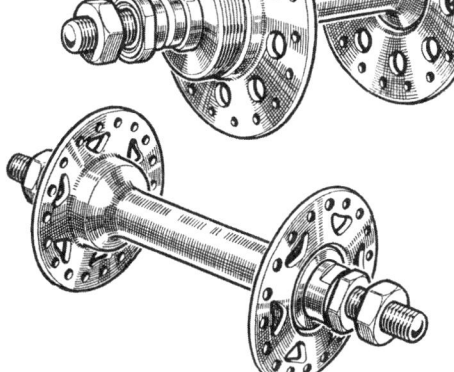
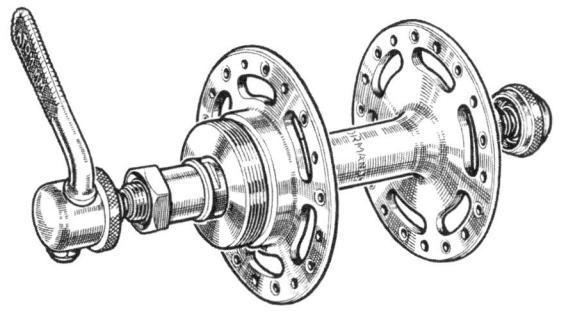

Left: Maillard Normandy high-flange rear hub with Atom-branded quick-release. *Le Cycle*, July-August 1962.

125

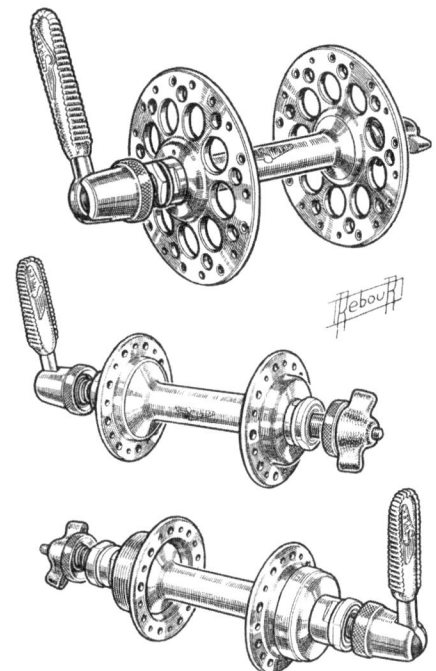

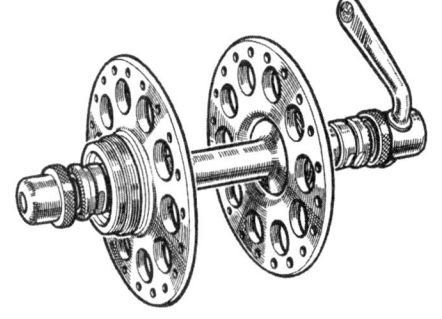

Above: Spanish-made BH high-flange hub, shown at the London bicycle trade show. *Le Cycle*, November 1960.

Below: German Sachs Torpedo freewheel hub. *Le Cycle*, November 1961.

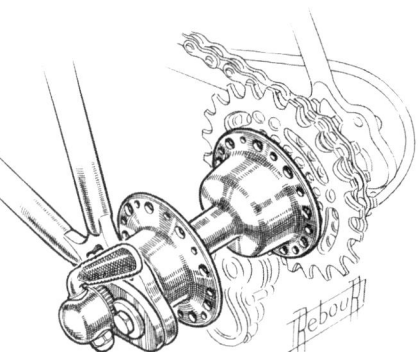

Above: Simplex high- and low-flange quick-release hubs. *Le Cycle*, November 1961.

Below: The bicycle ridden by the first-placed amateur in the 1958 Eastern regional technical trials, at Lyons. *Le Cycle*, 20 September 1958.

Above: Unidentified 1950 front and rear hubs and installation details. *Le Monde de Daniel Rebour*.

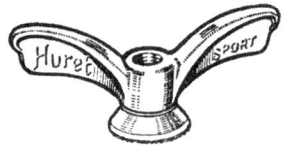

Above: 1960s Huret wing nut. *Cycle: Compétition, Cyclotourisme*.

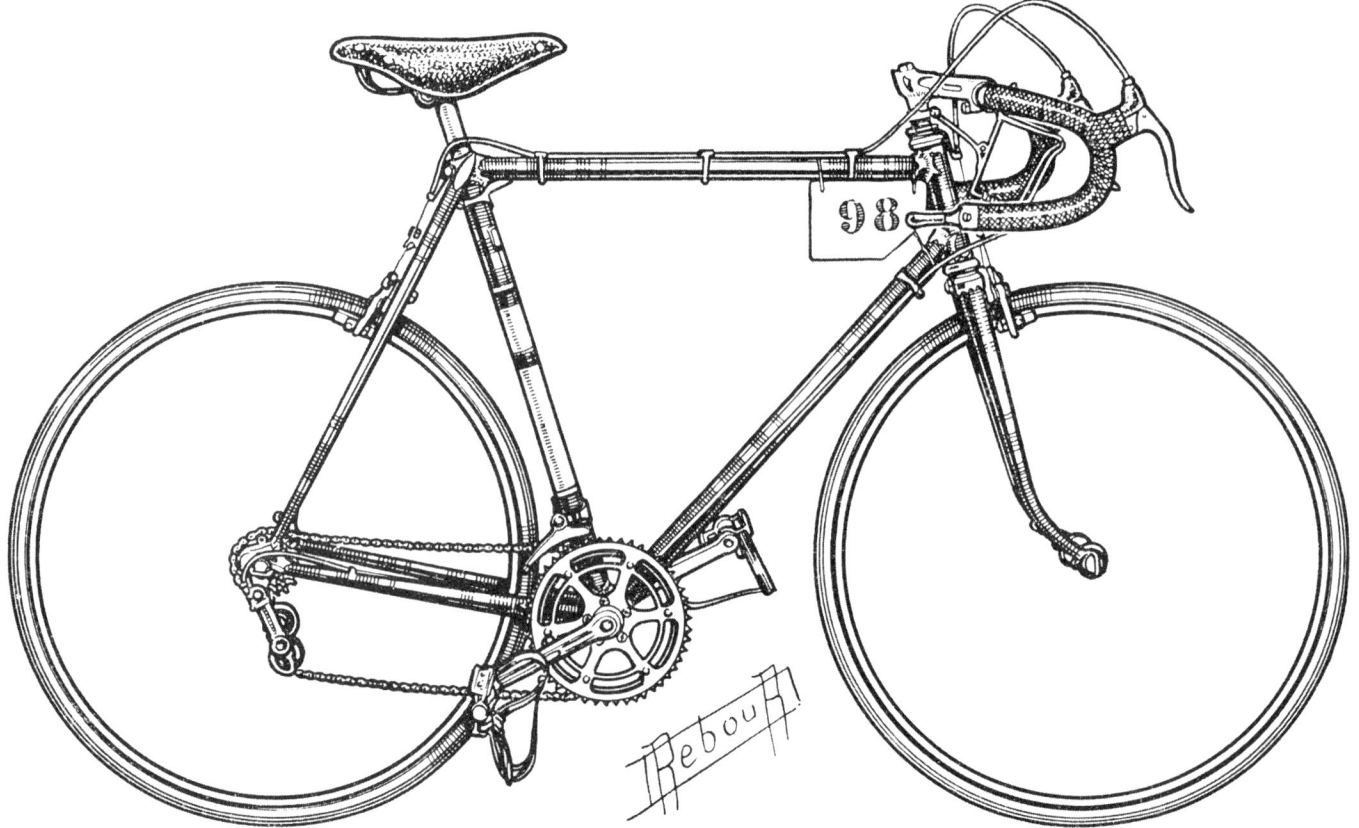

Chapter 7. Wheel Hubs

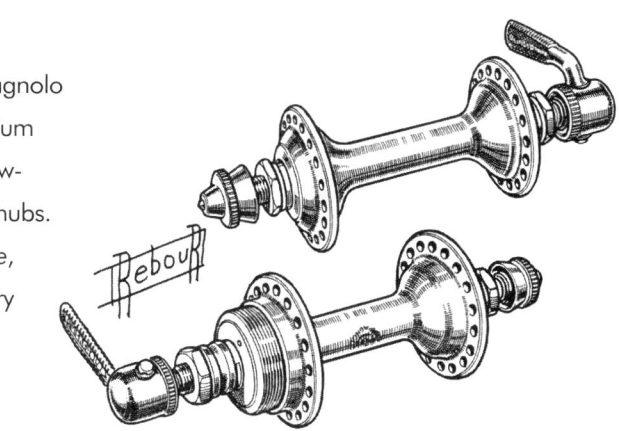

Right: Campagnolo aluminium alloy low-flange hubs. *Le Cycle,* February 1966.

Below: Exploded view of Normandy high-flange quick-release front hub. *Le Cycle,* October 1963.

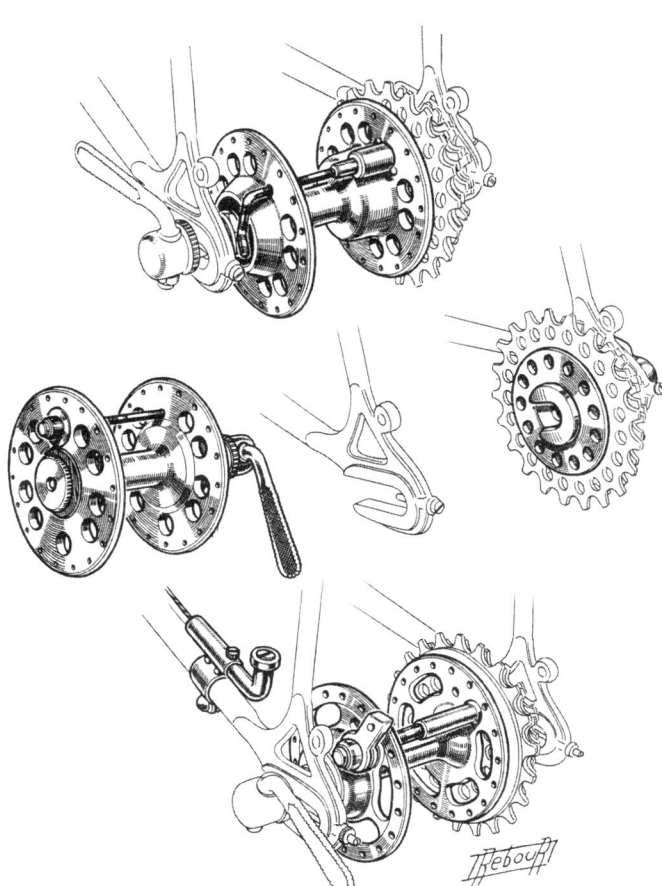

Above: D'Allessandro split rear hub and installation details. *Le Cycle,* February 1966.
Below: Small Urago bicycle entered in the 1958 Eastern regional technical trials, at Lyons. *Le Cycle,* 20 September 1958.**

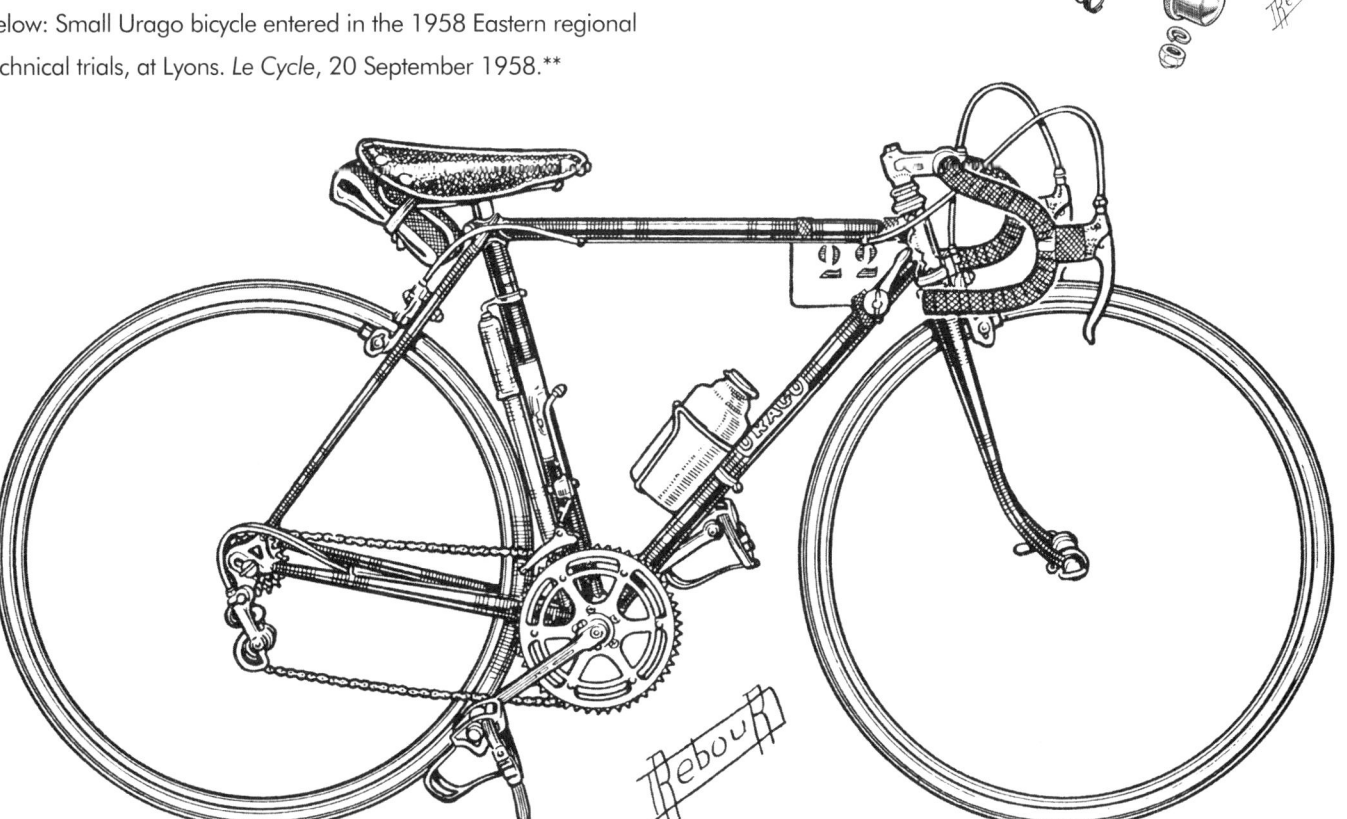

** See pages 269–271 for expanded caption text.

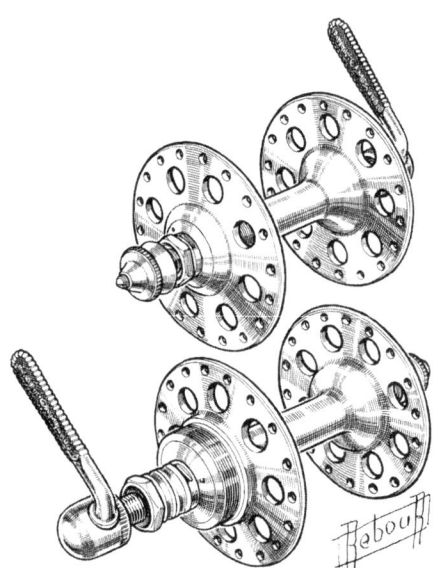

Right: Joffre split-axle hub details. *Le Cycle*, December 1972.

Below: Milremo high flange quick-release hubs. *Le Cycle*, October 1972.

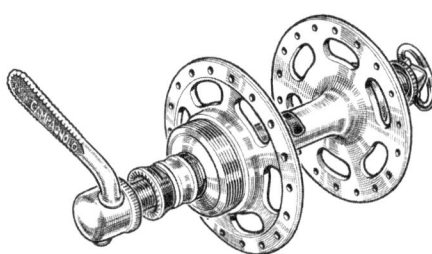

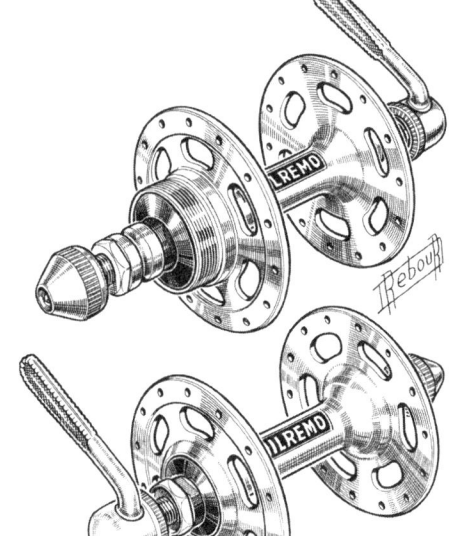

Above: Campagnolo Sport high-flange quick-release hubs. *Le Cycle*, November 1966.

Below: The Sabliere machine that won the randonneur category at the 1958 Eastern regional technical trials, at Lyons. *Le Cycle*, 20 September 1958.

Above: Campagnolo Nuovo Record high-flange hub. *Le Cycle*, December 1972.
Below: Corbelleta solid-axle quick-release. *Le Cycle*, December 1973.

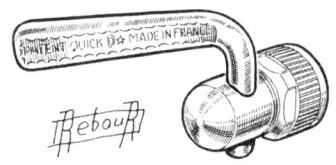

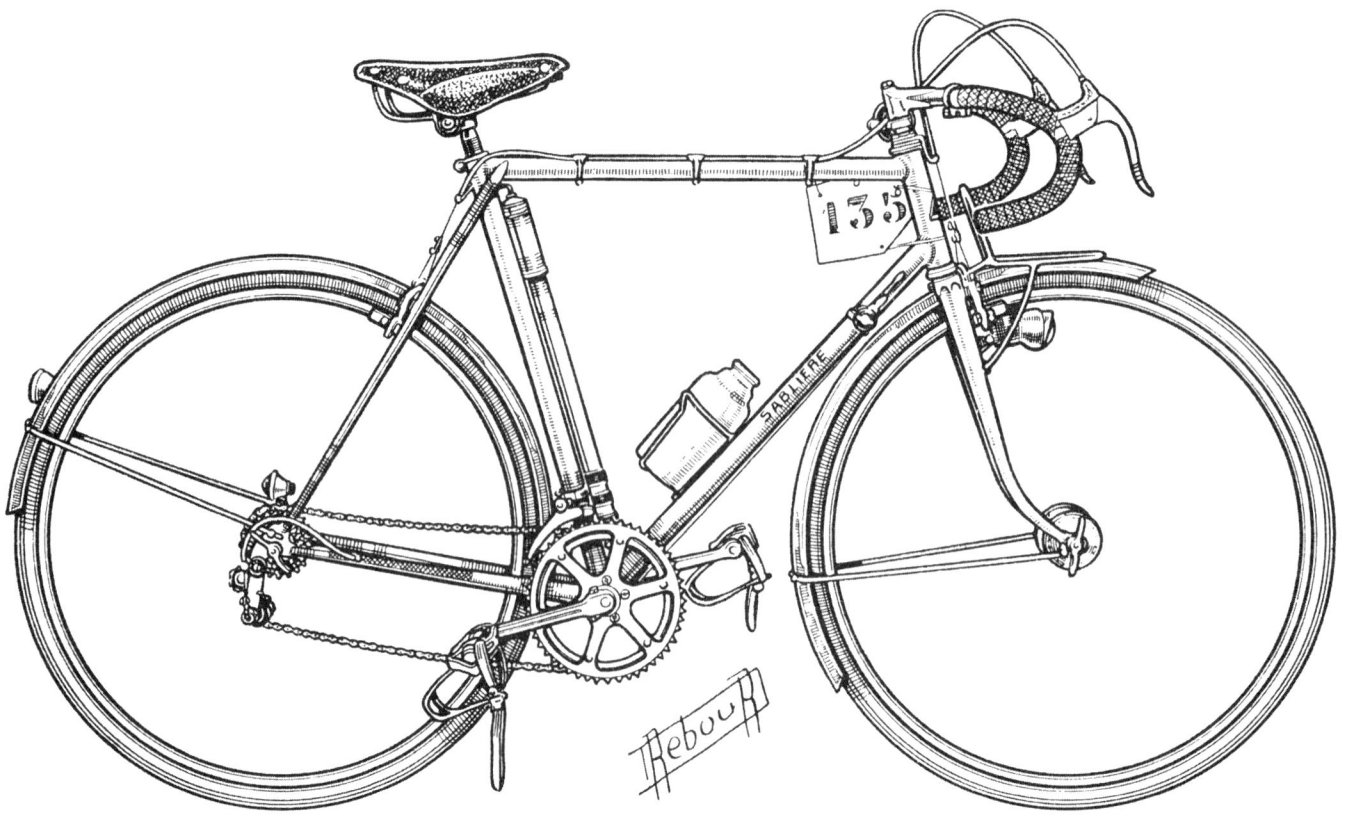

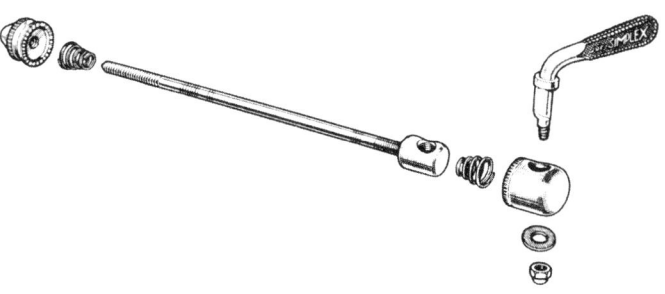
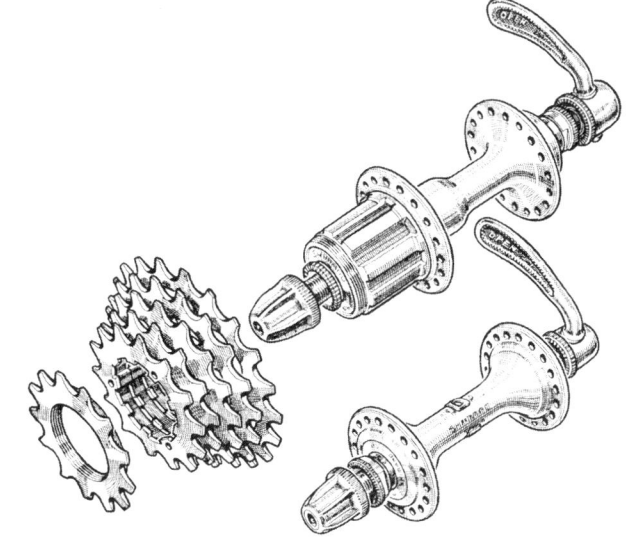

Above: Exploded view of Simplex quick-release. *Cycles de Compétition et Randonneuses.*

Right: 1980 Shimano Dura-Ace hubs with 6-speed freewheel cassette on the rear "Freehub." 1980 Milremo catalogue.

Below: Campagnolo Record high-flange hubs, still for screwed-on freewheel. 1981 Milremo catalogue.

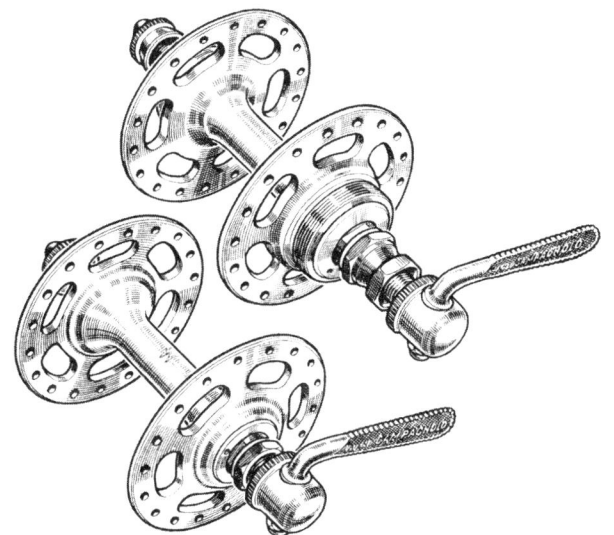
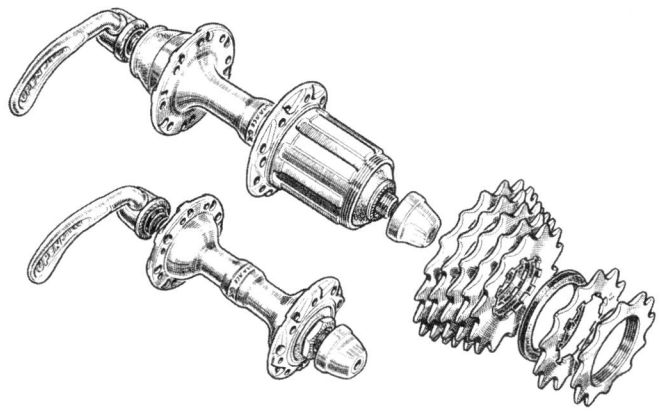

Above right: Shimano Dura-Ace hubs, with rear 7-speed freewheel cassette. 1981 Milremo catalogue.

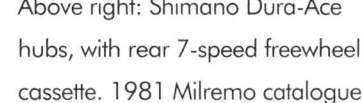

Left: Pélissier 2000 hubs for screwed-on freewheel. 1983 Milremo catalogue.

Right: 1983 Shimano Dura-Ace conventional hubs, for screwed-on freewheel. At this time, Shimano made both cassette-hubs and hubs for screwed-on freewheel. 1983 Milremo catalogue.

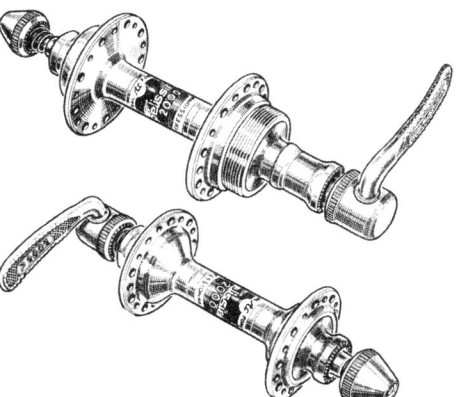
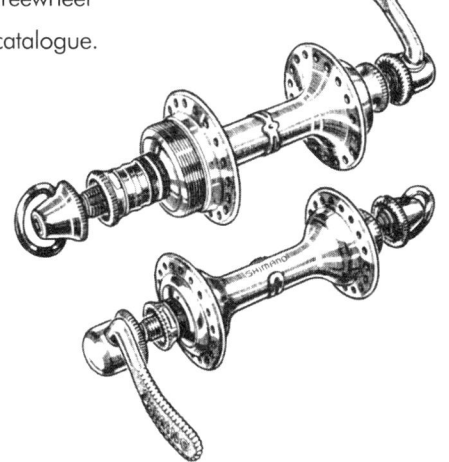

Chapter 8. Gear and Brake Hubs

This chapter is devoted to special wheel hubs. Although these were not as common in France, where Rebour worked, as in some other countries, he did draw a fair number of gear hubs, hub brakes, and even some disk brakes. Also included in this chapter are some of Rebour's drawings of hybrid gearing systems, which typically combine a rear derailleur and a hub gear to eliminate front derailleur shifting.

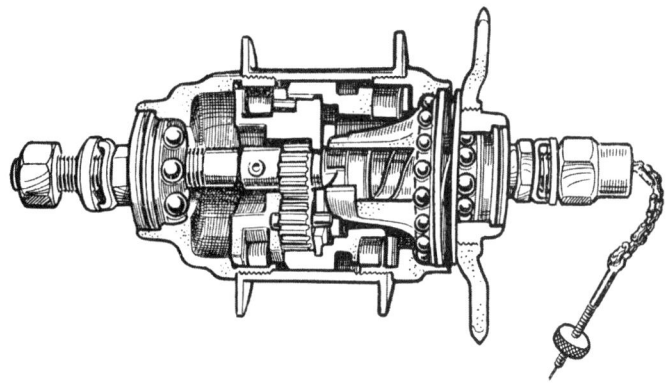

Above: Cut-away view of a typical three-speed hub gear. *Pratique du Vélo*.

Below: The Helyett bicycle of Pavard, the first-placed professional in the 1959 Poly de Chanteloup technical trials. *Le Cycle*, 16 May 1959.

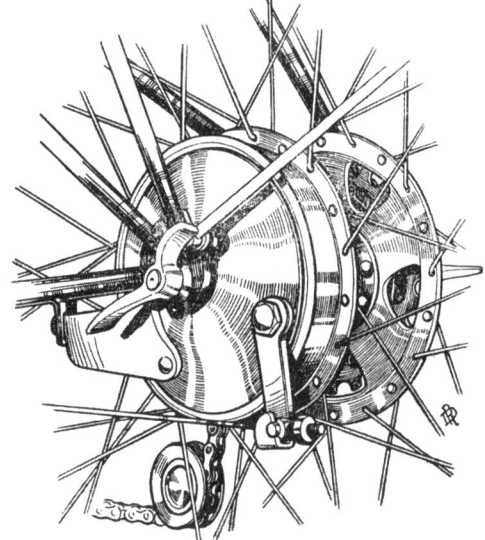

Left: Maxi-Car drum brake with rod-operation, installed on a randonneuring tandem. *Le Cycle*, 16 February 1946.

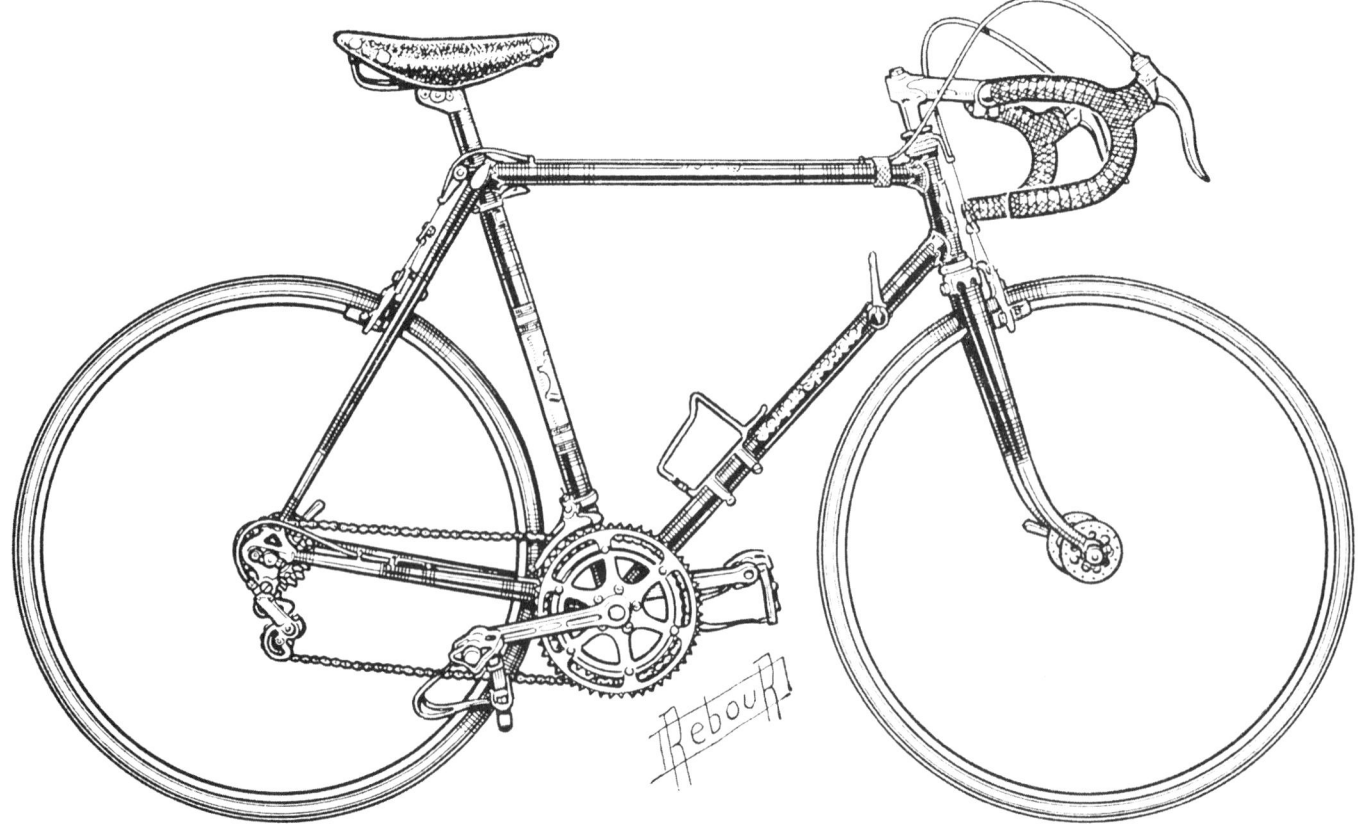

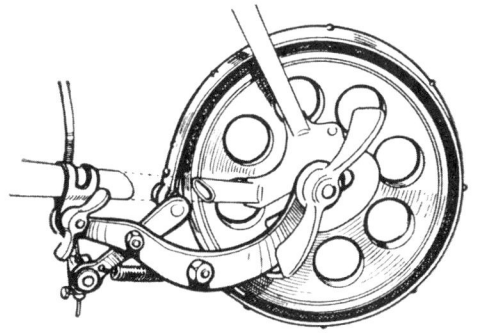
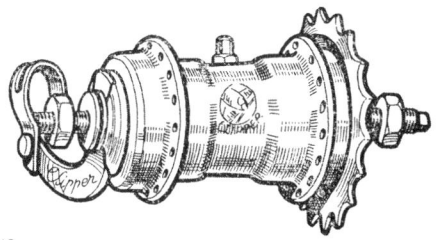

Left: Blocdur band-brake, a type that is more common in Asia than in Europe, with cable-control. *Le Cycle*, 6 December 1947.

Right: Clipper back-pedaling-operated coaster brake. *Pratique du Vélo*.

Below: Torpedo back-pedaling-operated coaster brake. Note the reinforcing between the seatstays and chainstays of the frame. *Le Cycle*, 16 March 1946.

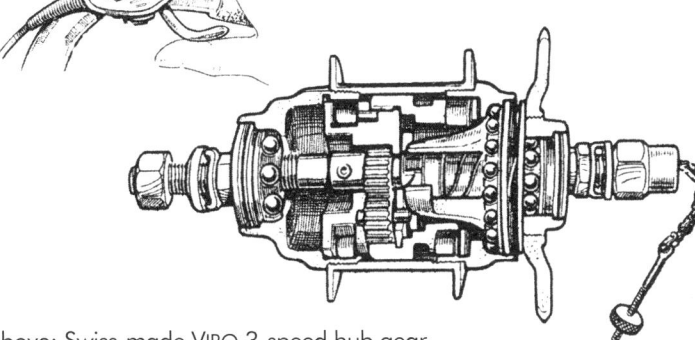

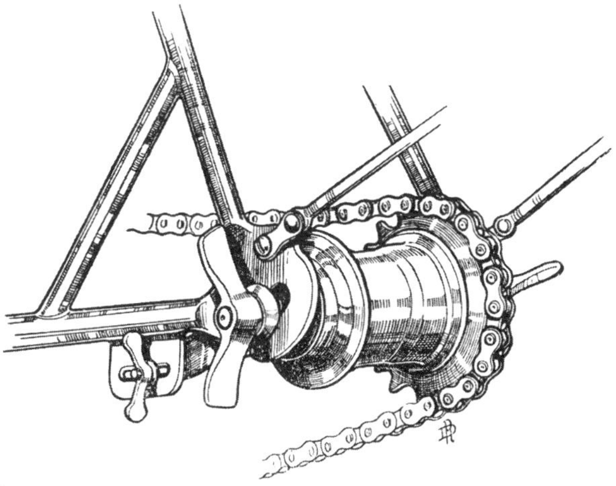

Above: Swiss-made VIBO 3-speed hub gear and shifter. *Le Cycle*, 22 March 1947.

Below: René Herse Randonneur bicycle ridden by Jean Fouacé in the 1959 Poly de Chanteloup technical trials. Although the bike has dynamo lighting, Rebour left out the wiring. *Le Cycle*, 16 May 1959.

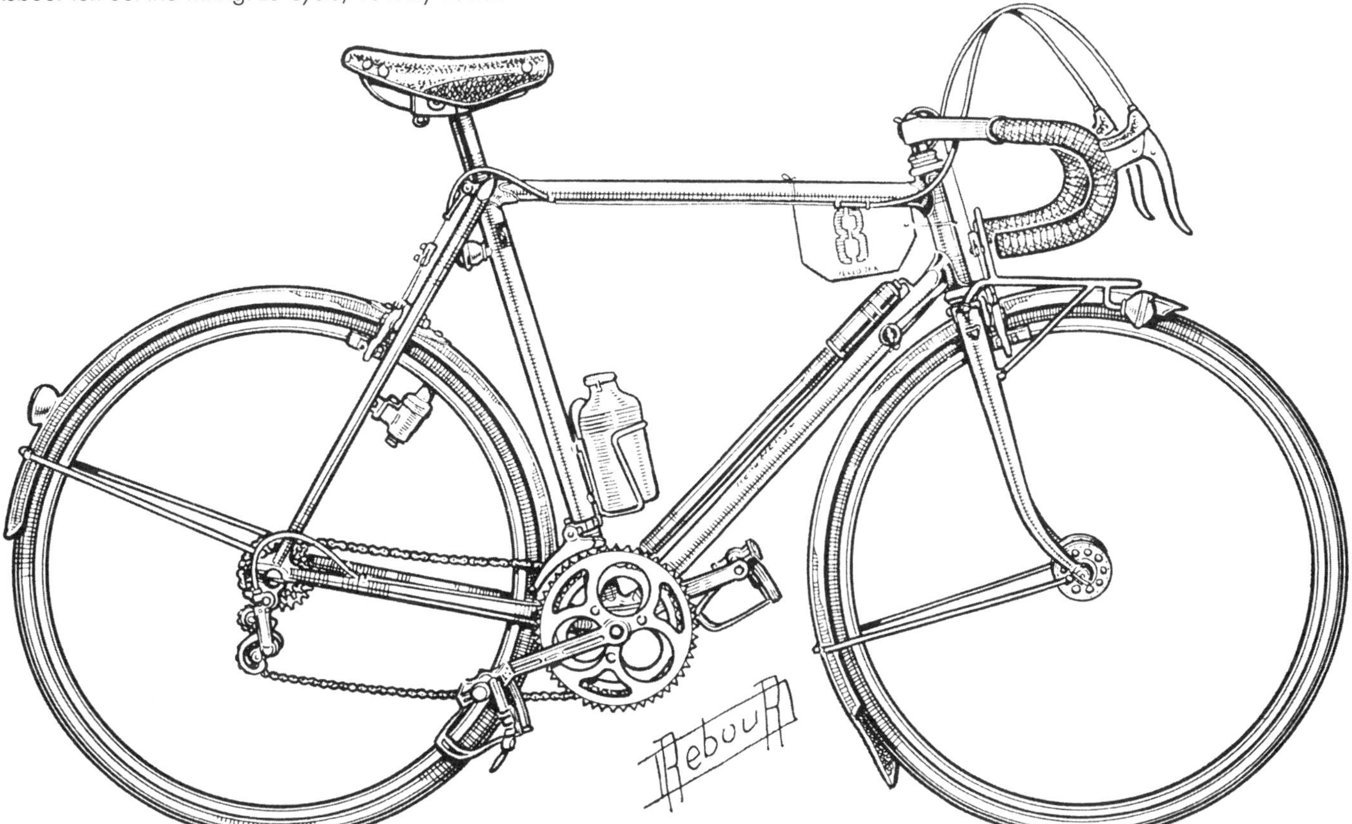

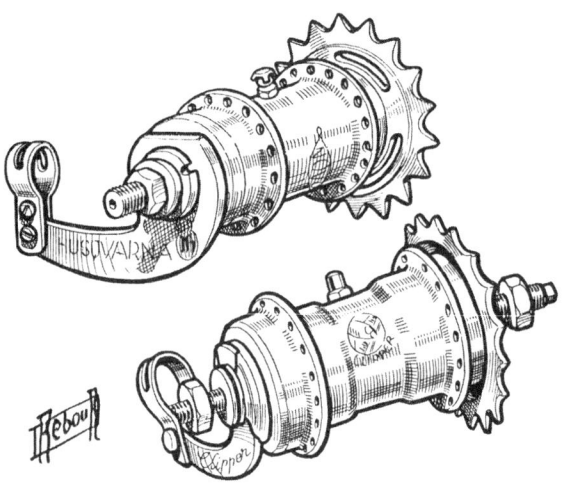
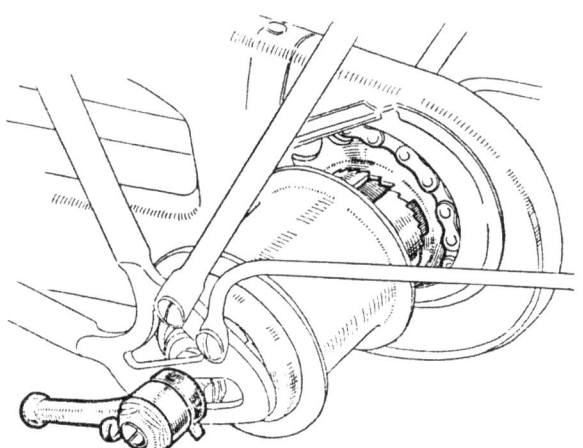

Right: Partially exposed view of a Titan split-axle multi-speed hub installed on a bicycle with fully enclosed chainguard. *Le Cycle*, 6 May

Above: Husqvarna and Clipper coaster brake hubs, shown at the Brussels bicycle trade show. *Le Cycle*, 12 February 1949.

Right: Cut-away view of BSA front drum brake. *Le Cycle*, 6 October 1951.

Below: Fédérico Bahamontès rode this Coppi bicycle to victory in the 1959 Tour de France. *Le Cycle*, 25 July 1959.

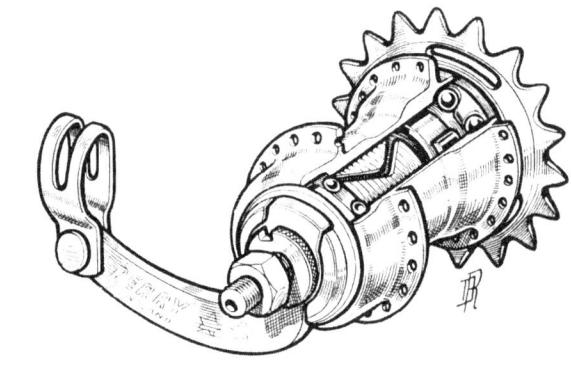

Above: Cut-away view of an English Perry coaster brake hub. *Le Cycle*, 25 March 1950.

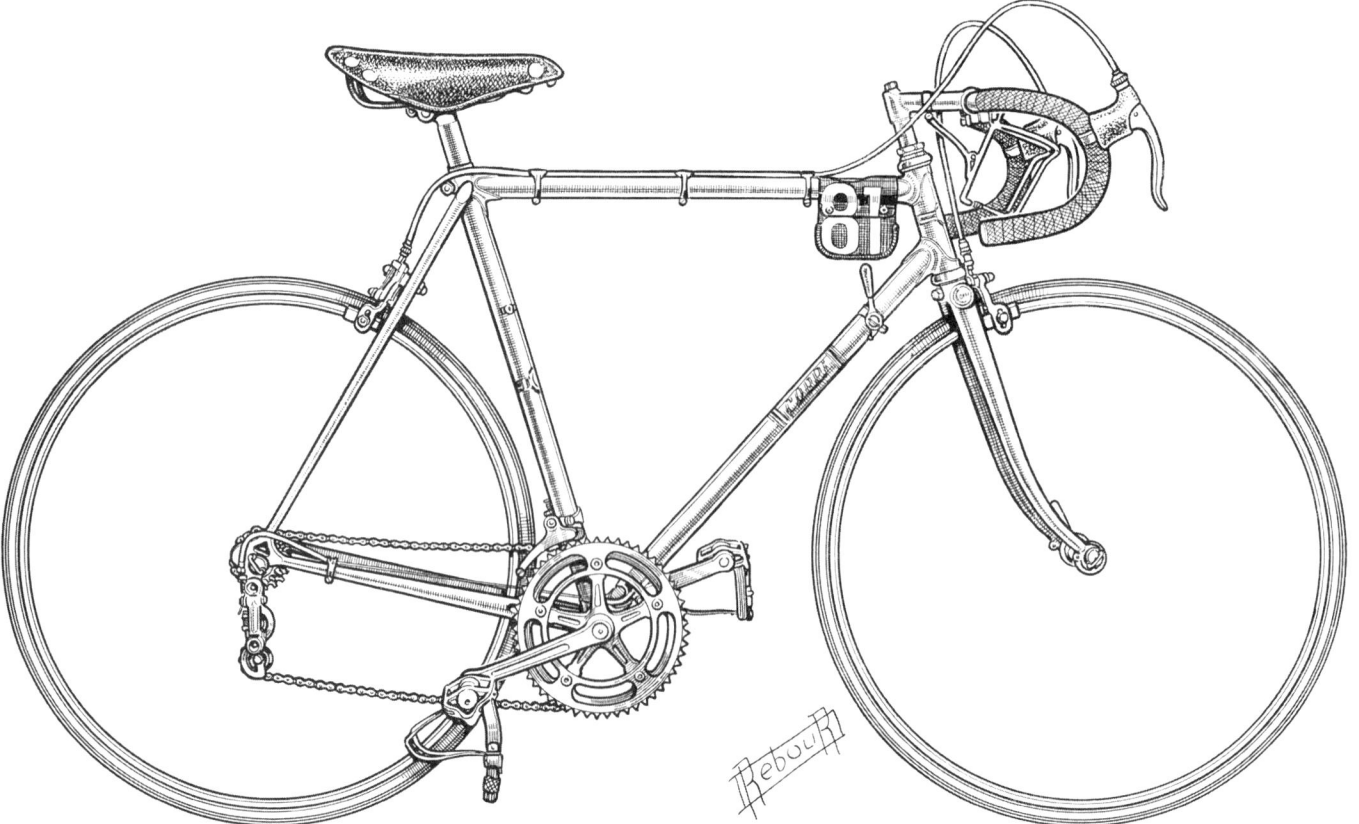

Chapter 8. Gear and Brake Hubs

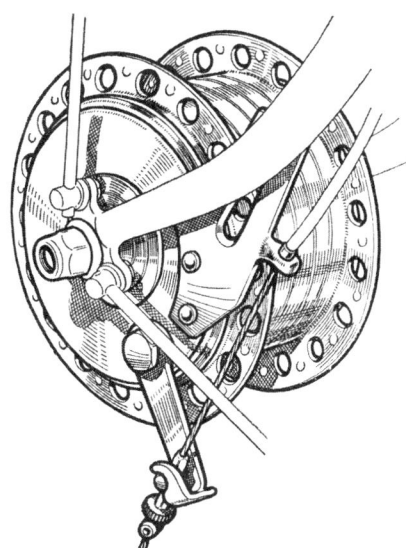

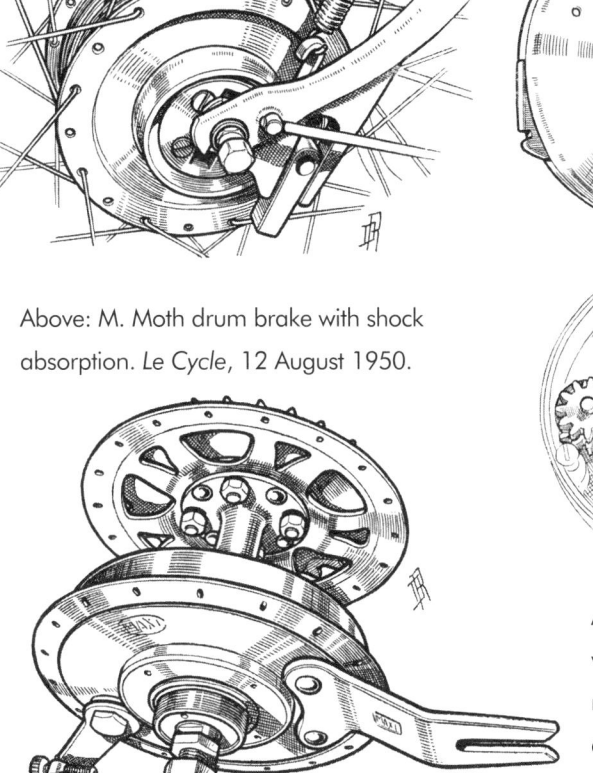

Above: M. Moth drum brake with shock absorption. *Le Cycle*, 12 August 1950.

Above: NMW full-width drum brake. *Le Cycle*, 10 March 1951.

Right: Maxi-Car drum brake, rated the highest quality by French randonneurs. *Le Cycle*, 10 March 1951.

Below: Henri Anglade placed second in the 1959 Tour de France on this Liberia bicycle. *Le Cycle*, 25 July 1959.

Above: Installed and exposed views of Vexlo epicyclic mechanism, which is typical for almost all hub gears. *Le Cycle*, 6 October 1951.

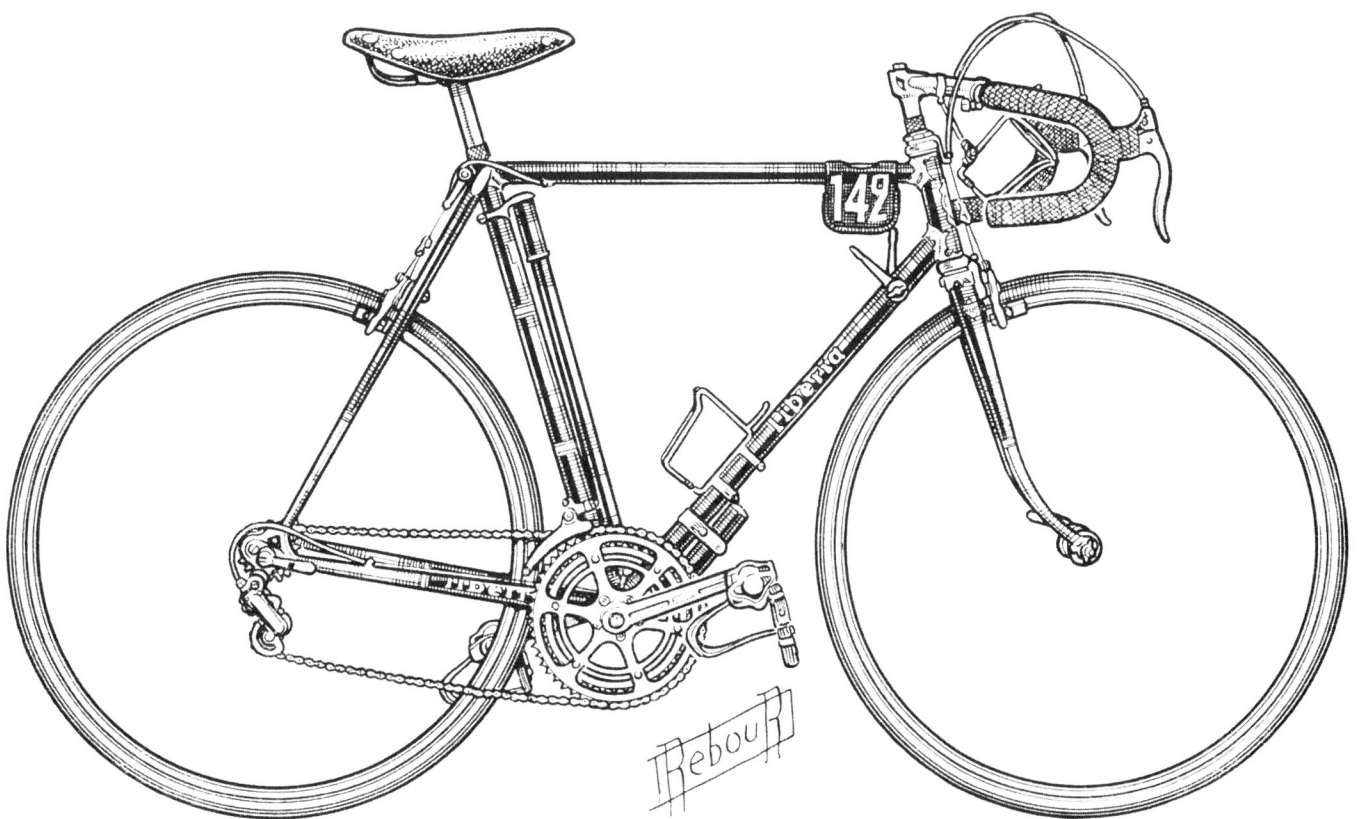

133

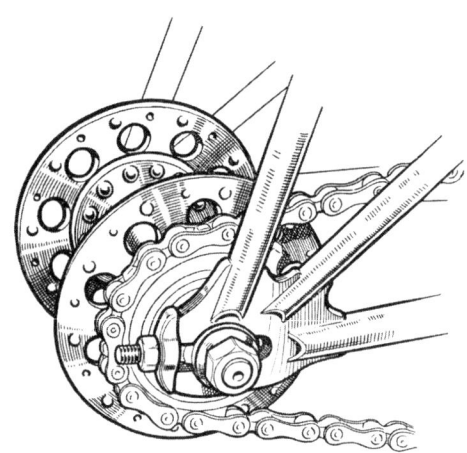
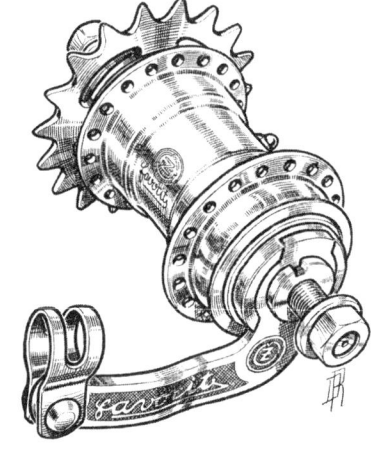
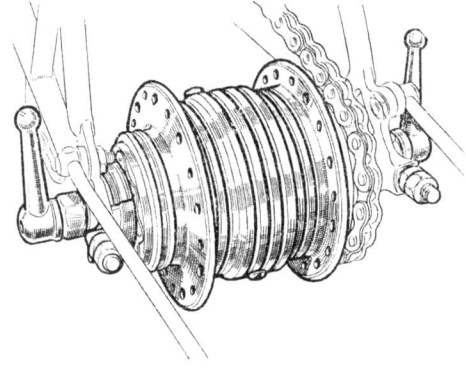

Above: Maxi-Car direct-drive hub installed on the track racing tandem built by René Herse for the Saarbrücken world championships in 1952. *Le Cycle,* 17 January 1953.

Above center: CZ Favorit coaster brake, from Czechoslovakia. *Le Cycle,* 4 October 1952.

Below: Peugeot bicycle at the 1960 Poly de Chanteloup technical trials. *Le Cycle,* May 1960.

Above: Renard coaster brake, installed with solid-axle quick-release wing nuts. *Le Cycle,* 23 May 1953.

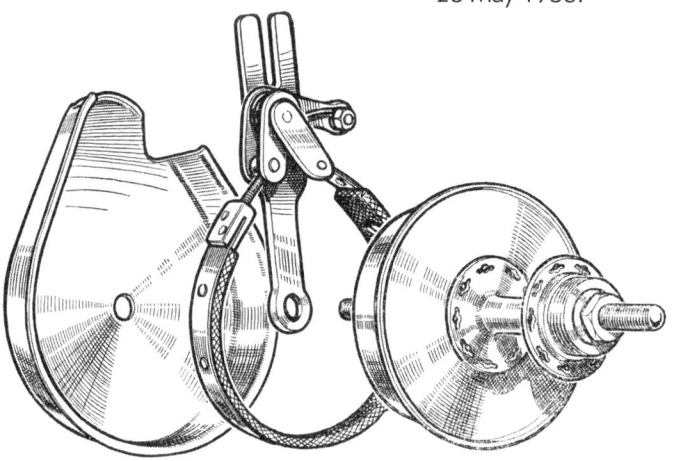

Left: Exploded view of Tourbillon-Stop band brake hub. *Le Cycle,* 4 October 1952.

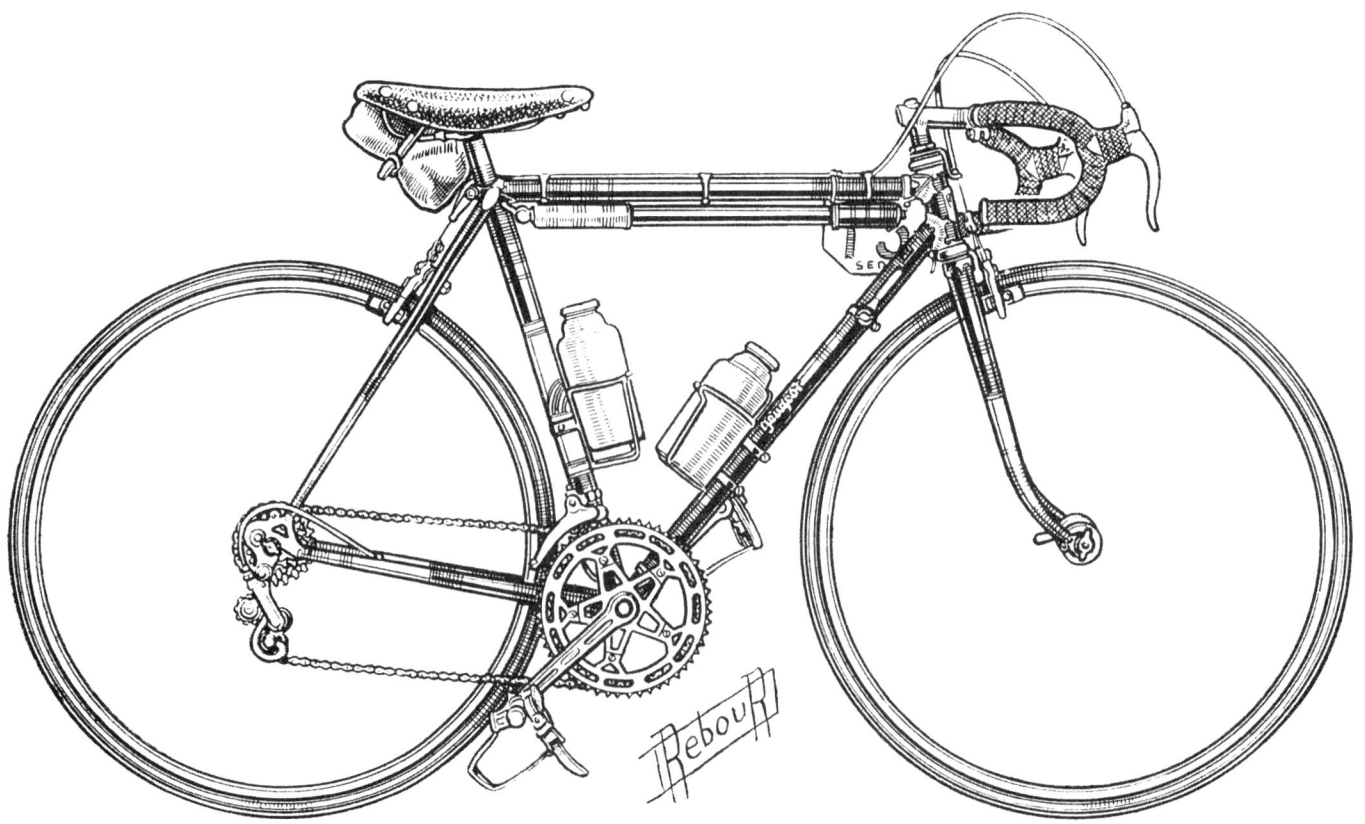

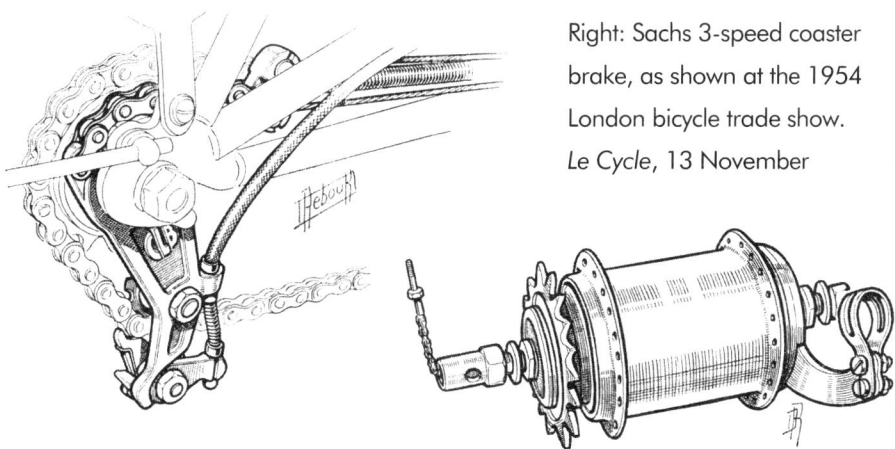

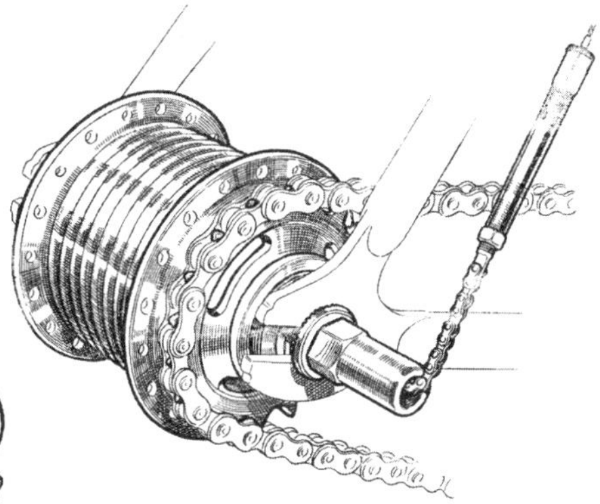

Right: Sachs 3-speed coaster brake, as shown at the 1954 London bicycle trade show. *Le Cycle*, 13 November

Above: CLB freewheel clutch that acts as a hub brake. *Le Cycle*, 24 April 1954.

Above center: Sturmey-Archer TCW 3-speed hub gear. *Le Cycle*, 1 Oct. 1953.

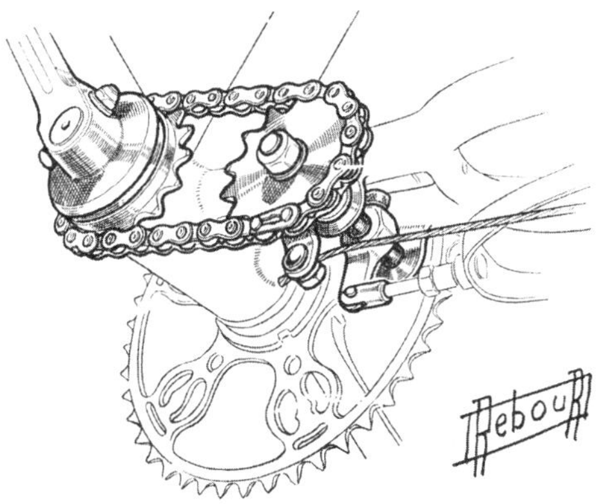

Below: René Herse bicycle at the 1960 Poly de Chanteloup technical trials. *Le Cycle*, May 1960.

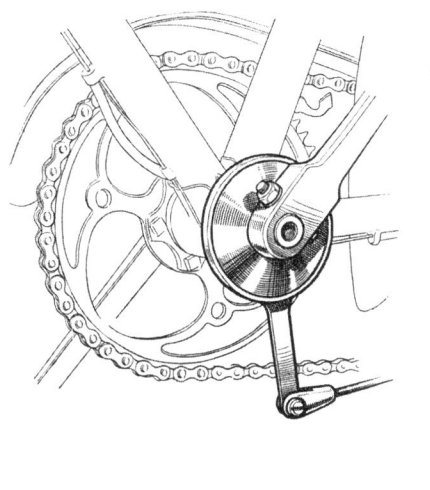

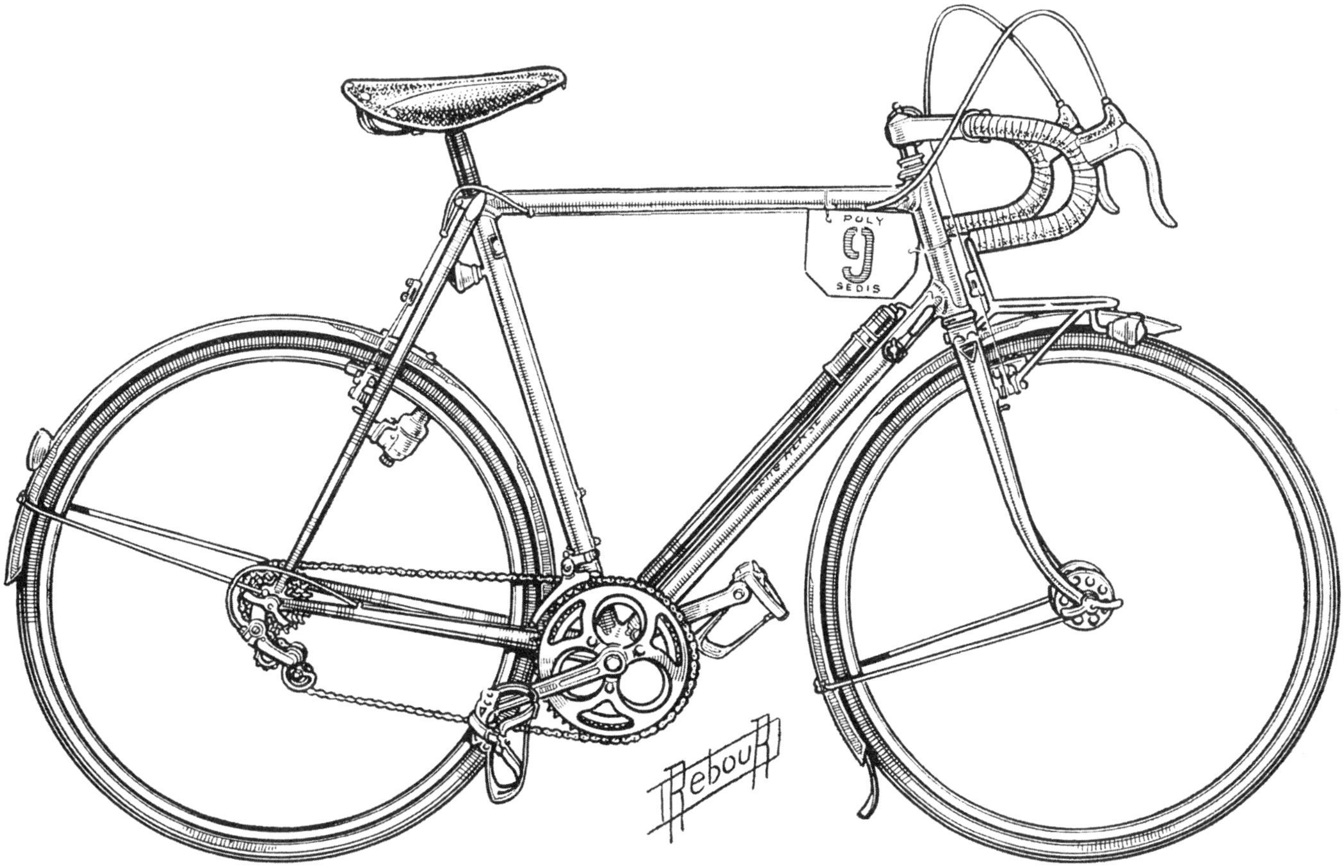

Below: Back-pedal-operating adaptations on bicycles with rod-operated brakes. *Le Cycle*, 23 May 1953.

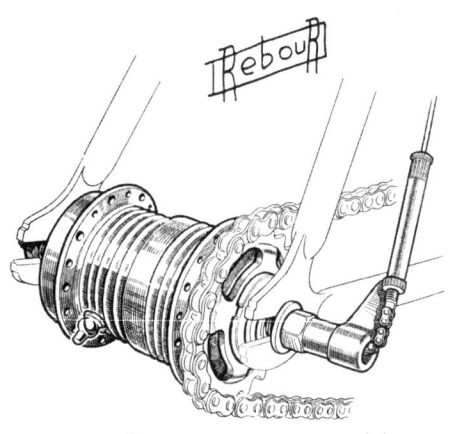
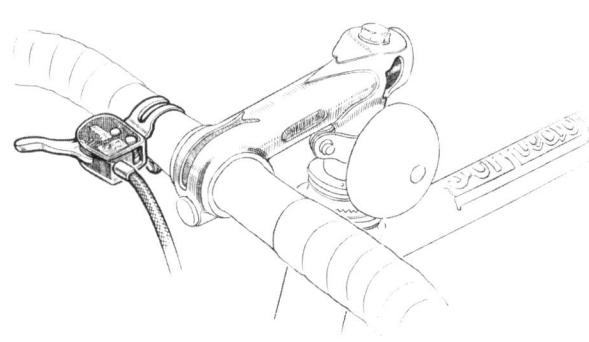

Left: Sachs Torpedo 3-speed hub gear without coaster brake. *Le Cycle*, 24 March 1956.

Right: Handlebar-mounted Sturmey-Archer shifter on Sauvage randonneur bike. *Le Cycle*, June 1962.

Below: Exploded view of Sturmey-Archer SW 3-speed wide-range hub gear and shifter. *Le Cycle*, 11 January 1958.

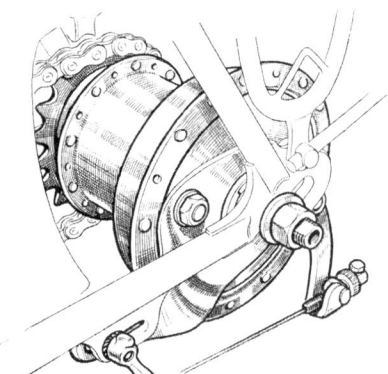
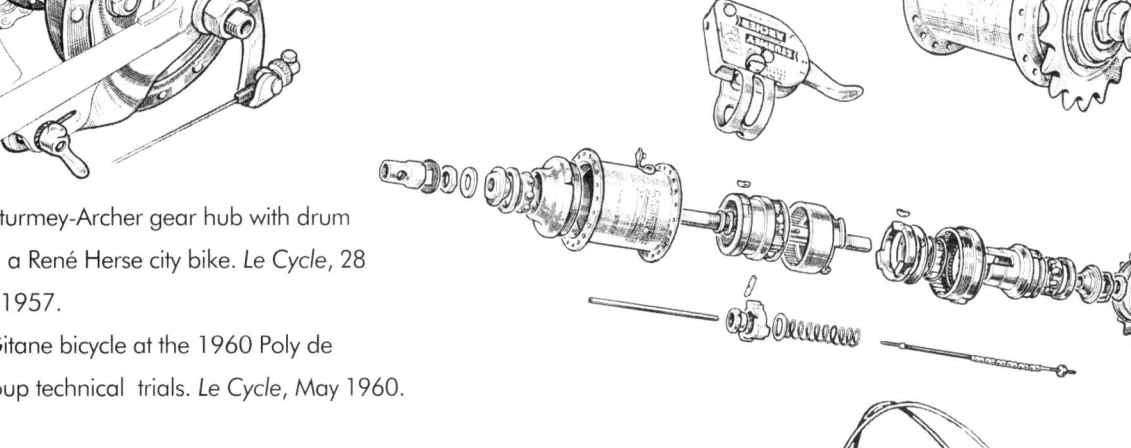

Above: Sturmey-Archer gear hub with drum brake on a René Herse city bike. *Le Cycle*, 28 October 1957.

Below: Gitane bicycle at the 1960 Poly de Chanteloup technical trials. *Le Cycle*, May 1960.

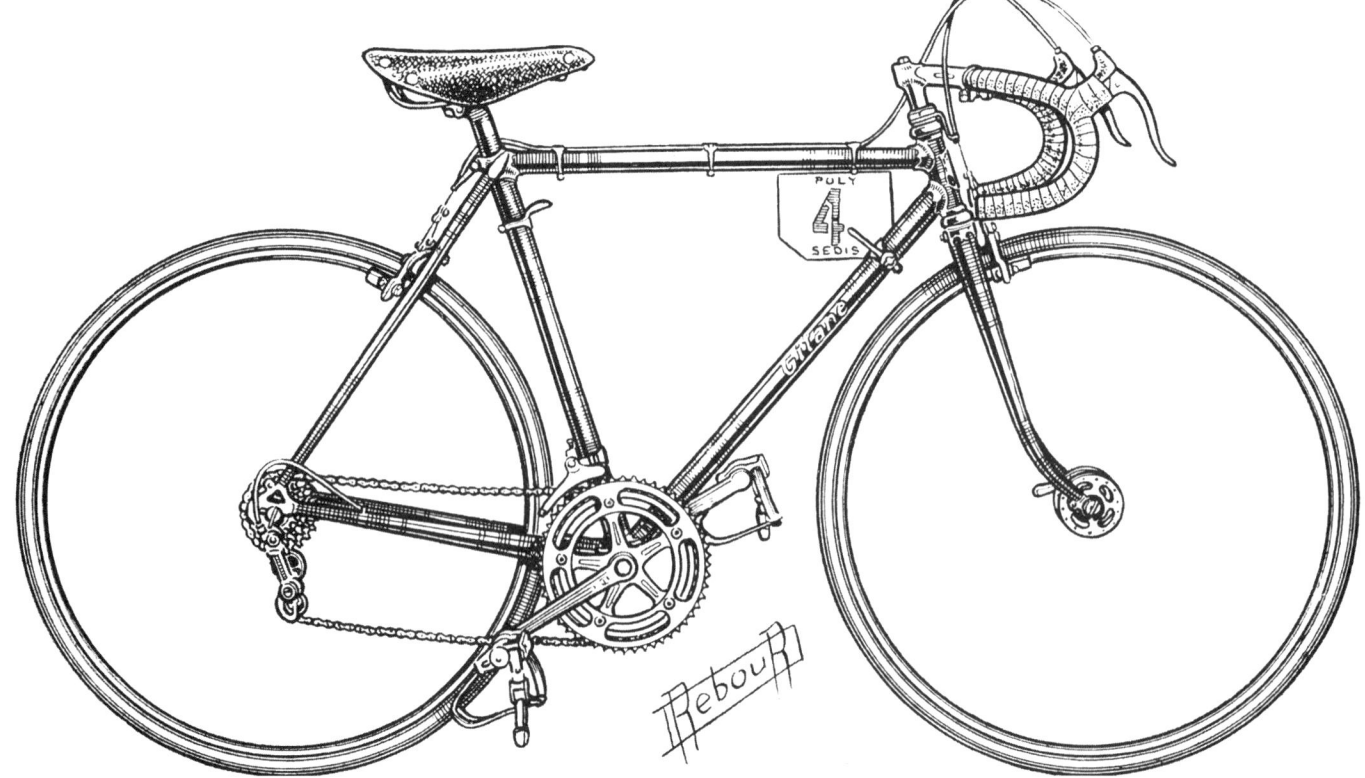

Chapter 8. Gear and Brake Hubs

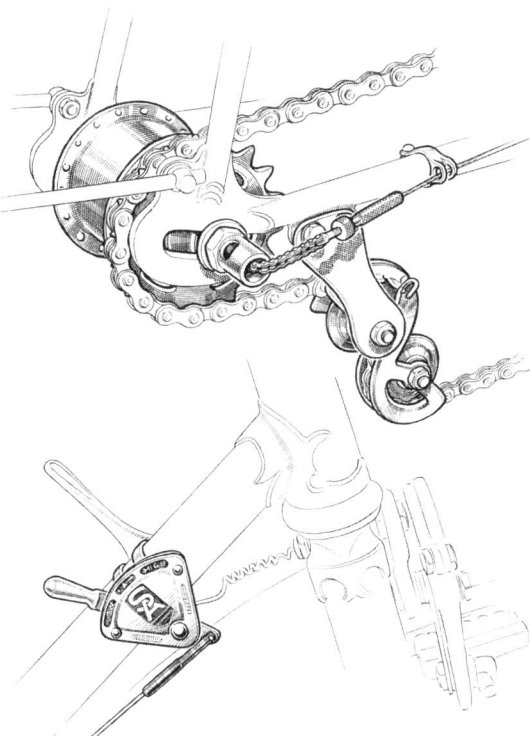
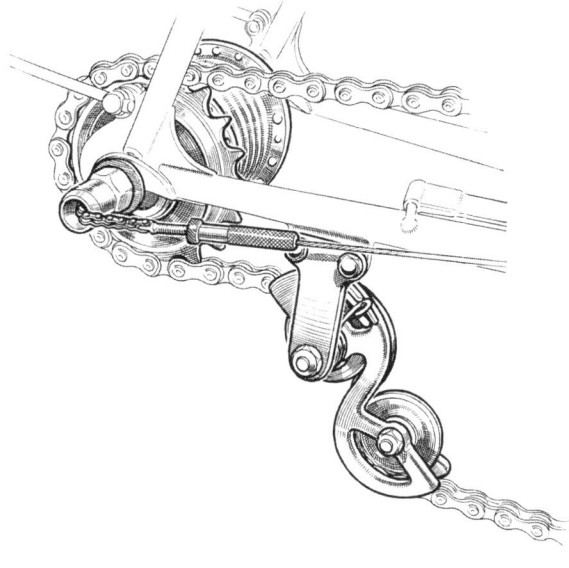

Left: Hybrid gearing with Sturmey-Archer hub gear and front derailleur shifting at the 1962 Poly de Chanteloup technical trials.
Right: Another hybrid gearing system, this one using a Torpedo hub gear, at the same event.
Both images from *Le Cycle*, June 1962.

Right: Shimano cable-operated disk brake for the rear wheel, shown at the 1972 Milan bicycle trade show. *Le Cycle*, December 1972.

Far right: Campagnolo double-disk brake, installed on a suspension fork, presumably intended for moped use. *Le Cycle*, December 1966.

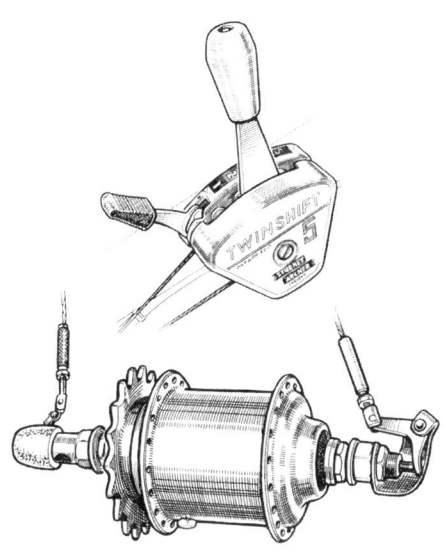
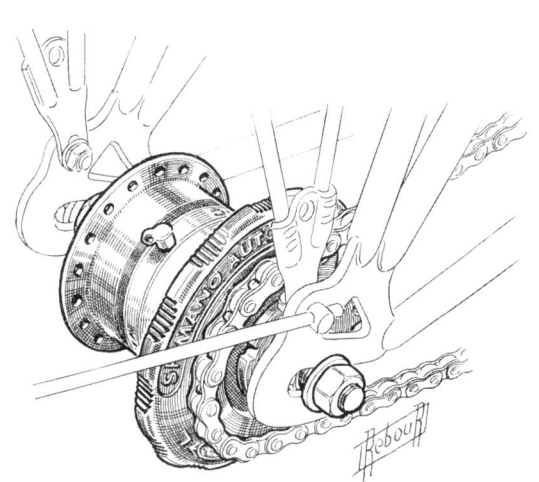

Left: Sturmey-Archer 5-speed hub and 2-lever trigger shifter introduced at the 1968 Brussels bicycle trade show. *Le Cycle*, March 1968.

Right: Shimano automatic-shifting 2-speed hub shown at the Motobécane product introduction for 1970. *Le Cycle*, October 1969.

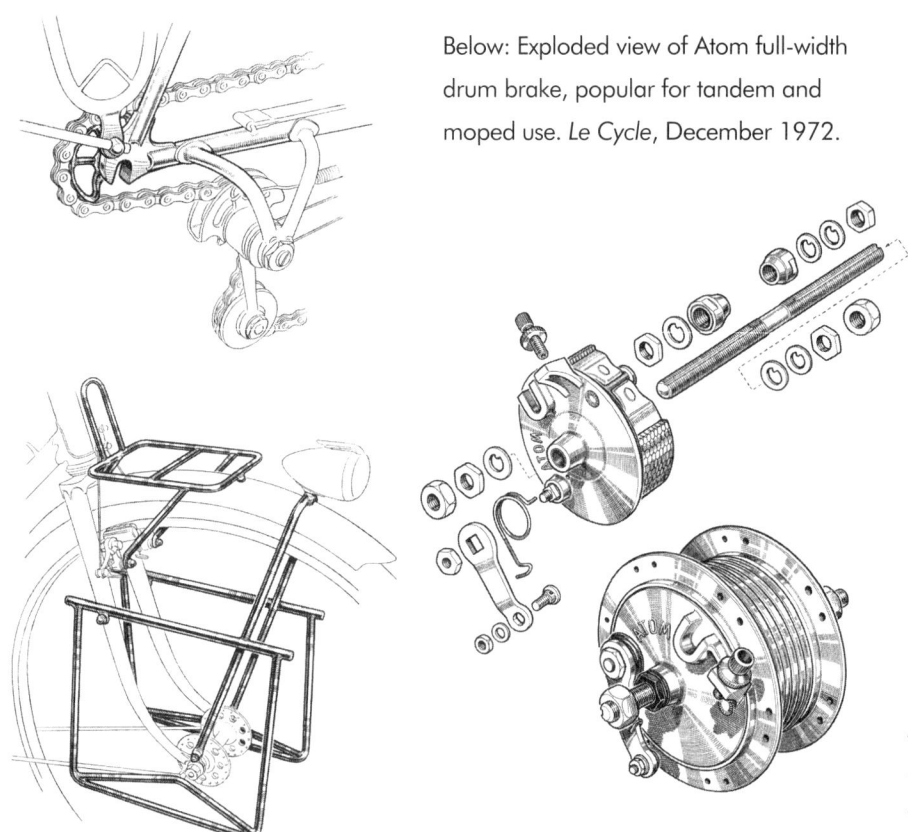

Below: Exploded view of Atom full-width drum brake, popular for tandem and moped use. *Le Cycle*, December 1972.

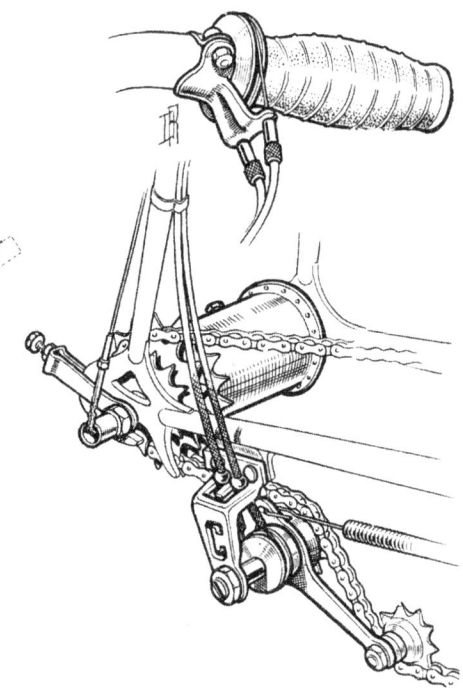

Above: English hybrid gearing set-up, combining a Cyclo Belenux rear derailleur with a Sturmey-Archer 3-speed. The derailleur is shifted with the twin-cable twist-grip shown, and the hub with the customary Sturmey-Archer trigger shifter (not shown). *Le Cycle*, October 1949.

Below and above and top left: René Herse loaded-touring bicycle shown at the May 1960 Concours Plain Air, with details of derailleur mounted on chainstay and front racks. *Le Cycle*, May 1960.**

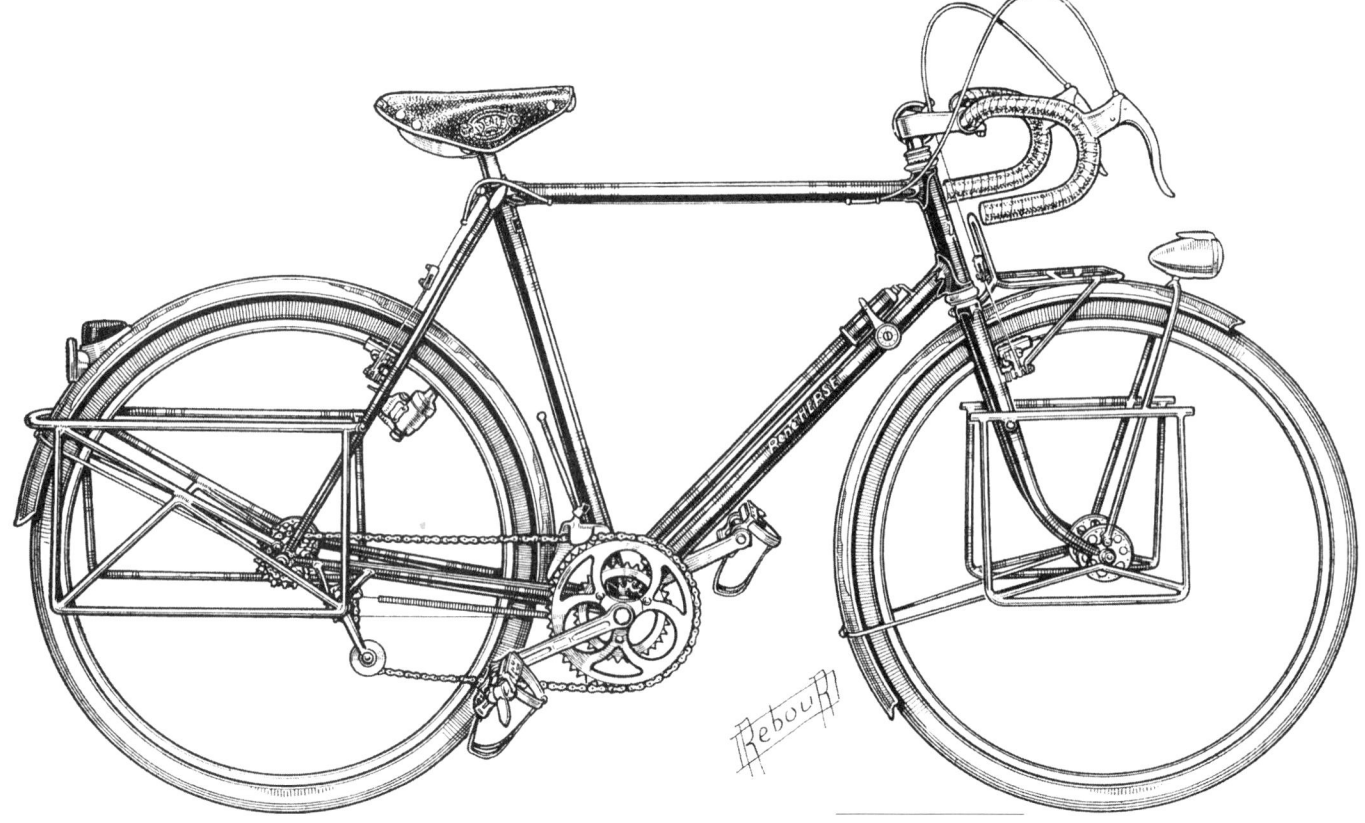

** See pages 269–271 for expanded caption text.

Chapter 9. Rims, Tires, and Spokes

This chapter is devoted to drawings of the other wheel components, not covered in the two preceding chapters 7 and 8. Rebour made quite a number of drawings of such seemingly simple things as rims, tires, and even spokes, clearly showing the subtle differences between various makes and models of even such minor components.

Right: Aluminium Sprint-type rim, i.e. the type designed for the installation of tubular, or "sew-up," tire. *Pratique du Vélo*.

Below: Helyett bicycle of Jean Graczyk, winner of the green jersey in the 1960 Tour de France. *Le Cycle*, July-August 1960.

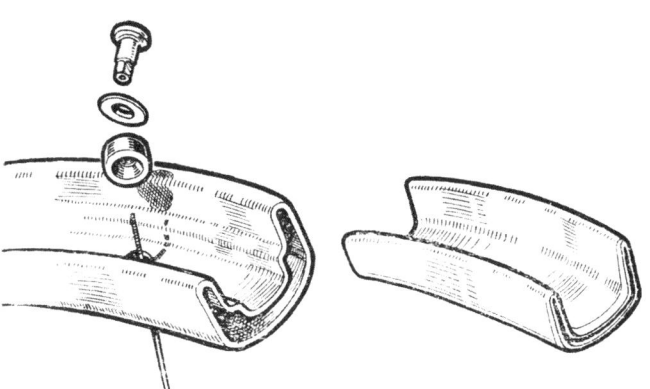

Left: Details of Integra alloy rim for wired-on, or "clincher," tires. *Le Cycle*, 18 October 1947.

Below: Fox rim and tube-protector insert detail. *Le Cycle*, 23 October 1948.

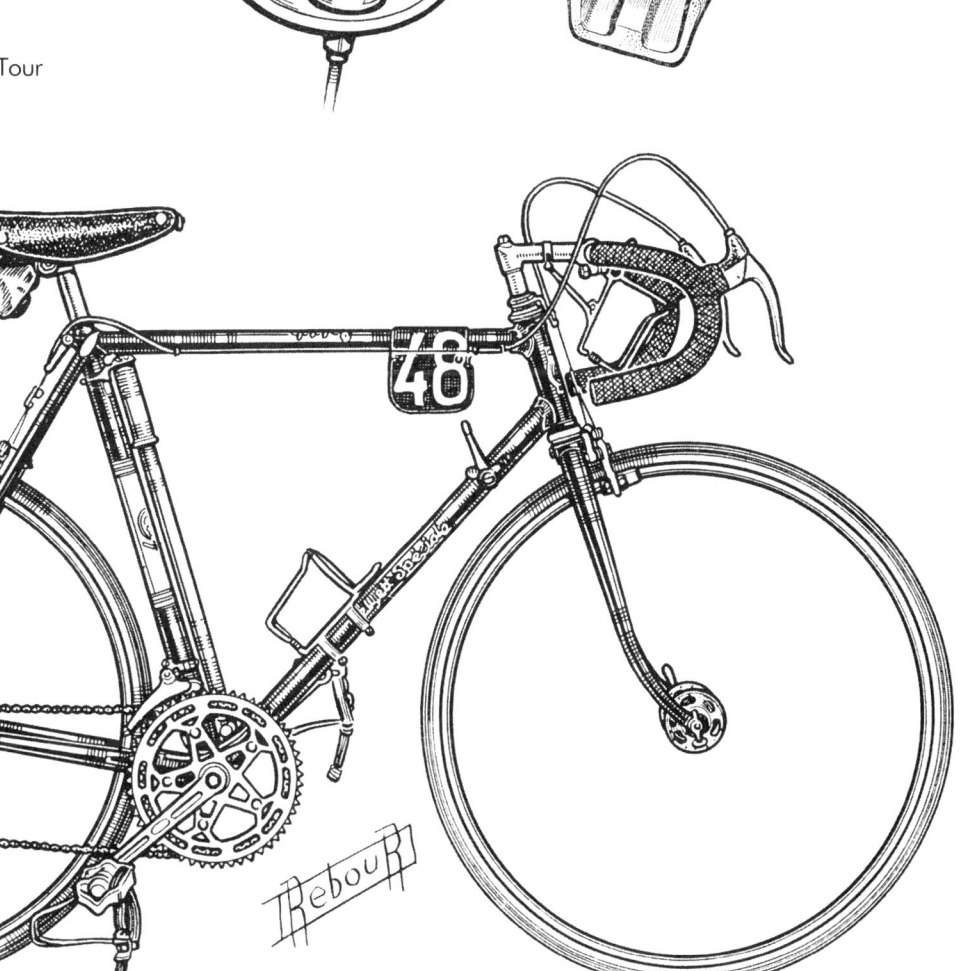

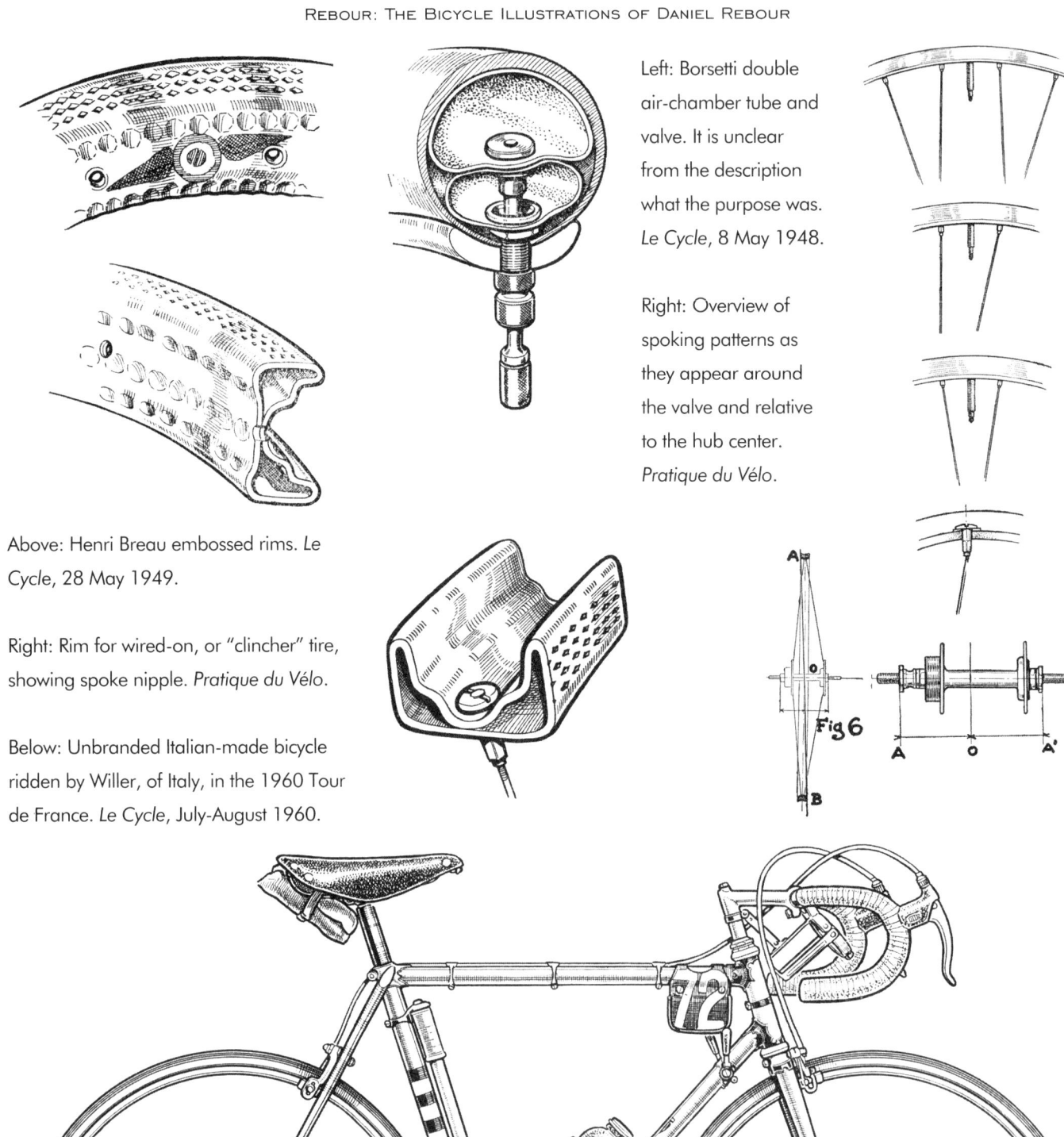

Above: Henri Breau embossed rims. *Le Cycle*, 28 May 1949.

Right: Rim for wired-on, or "clincher" tire, showing spoke nipple. *Pratique du Vélo*.

Below: Unbranded Italian-made bicycle ridden by Willer, of Italy, in the 1960 Tour de France. *Le Cycle*, July-August 1960.

Left: Borsetti double air-chamber tube and valve. It is unclear from the description what the purpose was. *Le Cycle*, 8 May 1948.

Right: Overview of spoking patterns as they appear around the valve and relative to the hub center. *Pratique du Vélo*.

Chapter 9. Rims, Tires, and Spokes

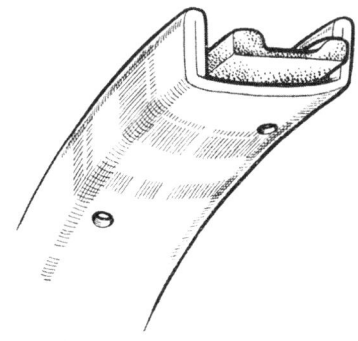
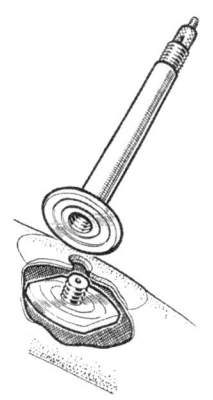
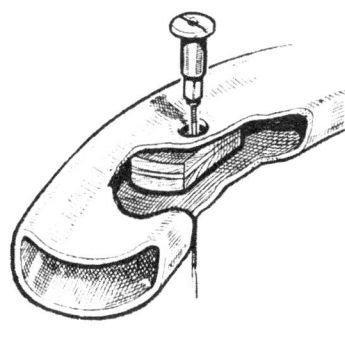

Left: Léfol Dural (aluminium alloy) rim with protector strip. *Le Cycle*, 11 June 1949.

Right: Chinchavaud valve detail. *Le Cycle*, 7 January 1950.

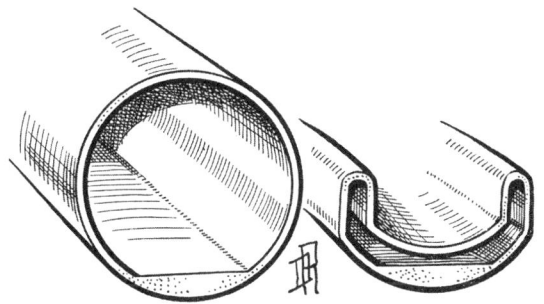
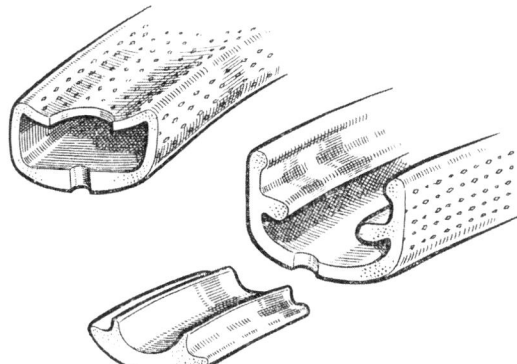
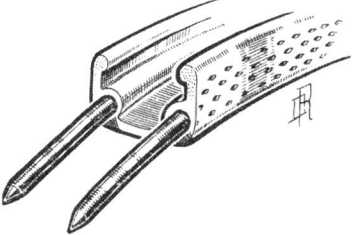

Top right: Maravel Sprint rim, for tubular tire, with wooden reinforcing blocks at the spoke nipples. *Le Cycle*, 5 November 1949.

Above: Production stages of Nieddu reinforced rim, starting as a tube, then rolled into the rim shape. *Le Cycle*, 7 January 1950.

Below: Mercier bicycle of the first-placed professional at the 1961 Poly de Chanteloup technical trials. *Le Cycle*, June 1961.

Above: Hook-edge rim end joining detail. *Le Cycle*, 21 February 1953.

Left: Ruban-Bleu Record rims for tubular tire and for wired-on tire, with protective insert for the latter. *Le Cycle*, 24 February 1951.

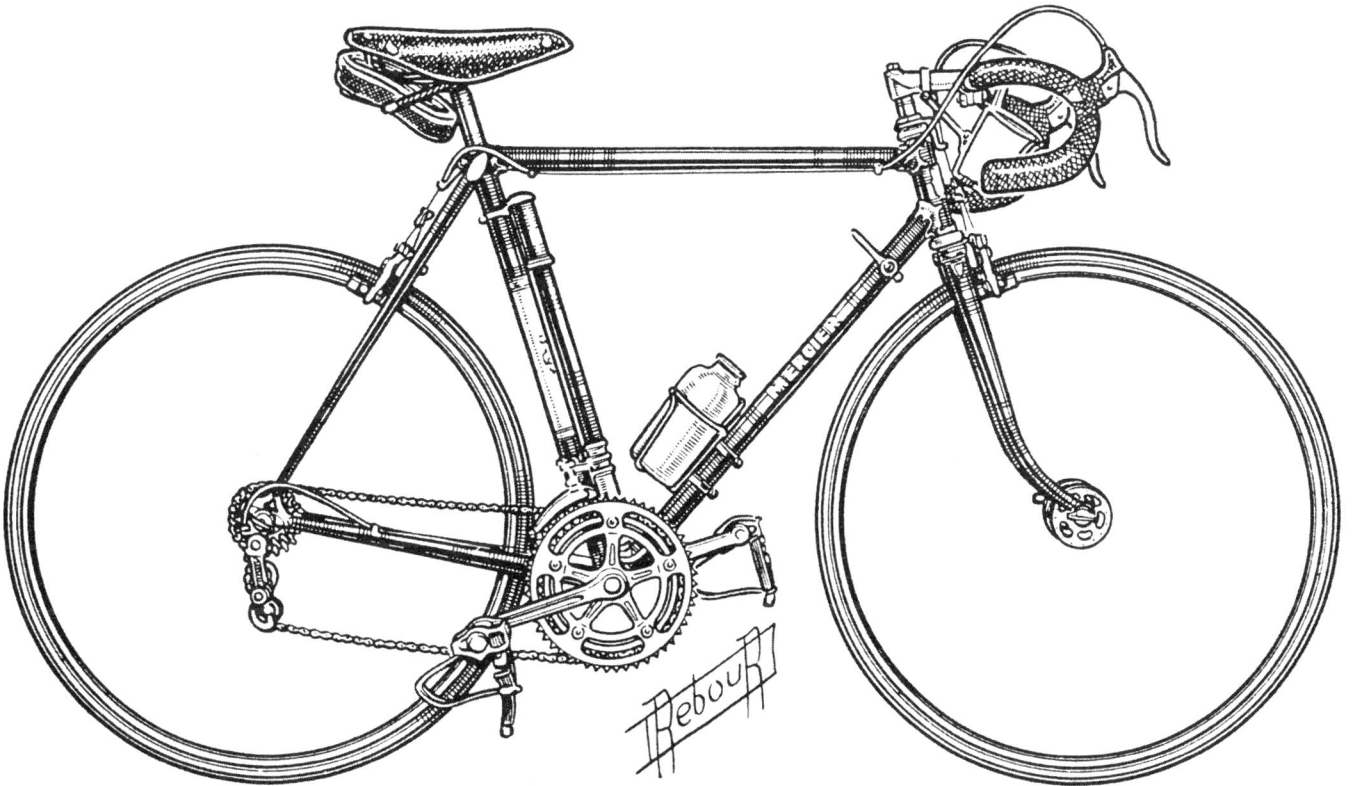

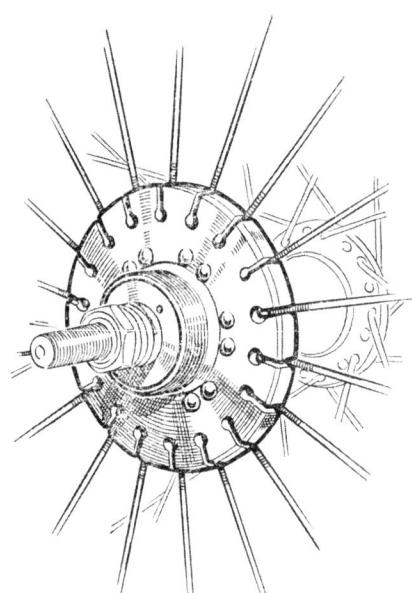

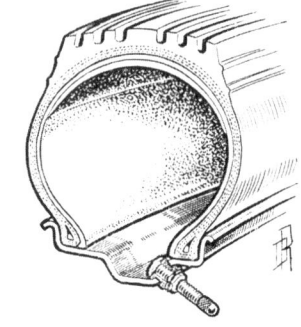

Right: Cut-away view of Dunlop tubeless tire, rim, and valve. *Le Cycle,* 25 July 1953.

Below: Mavic heavy-duty rim profile. *Le Cycle,* 16 October 1954.

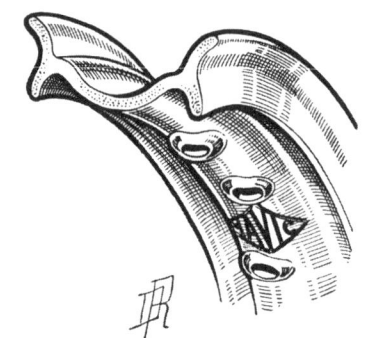

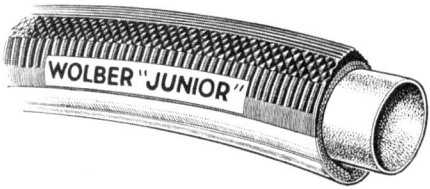

Above: Ducret straight spokes, threaded into the special hub designed for straight radial spoking on one side of the wheel and tangent-spoking on the other side. *Le Cycle,* 30 November 1952.

Below: First-place randonneur bicycle at the 1961 Poly de Chanteloup technical trials. *Le Cycle,* June 1961.

Above: Wolber Junior tubular tire, intended for training, being heavier than tires for racing. *Le Cycle,* April 1964.

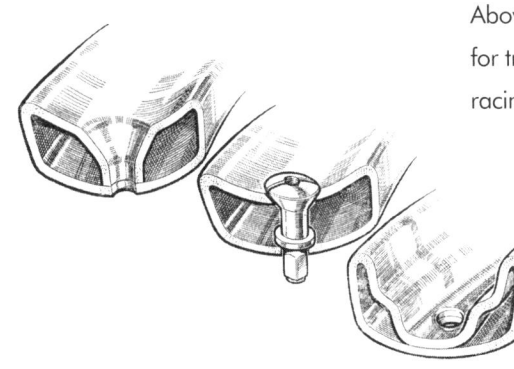

Left: KIK reinforced rims. *Le Cycle,* 13 March 1954.

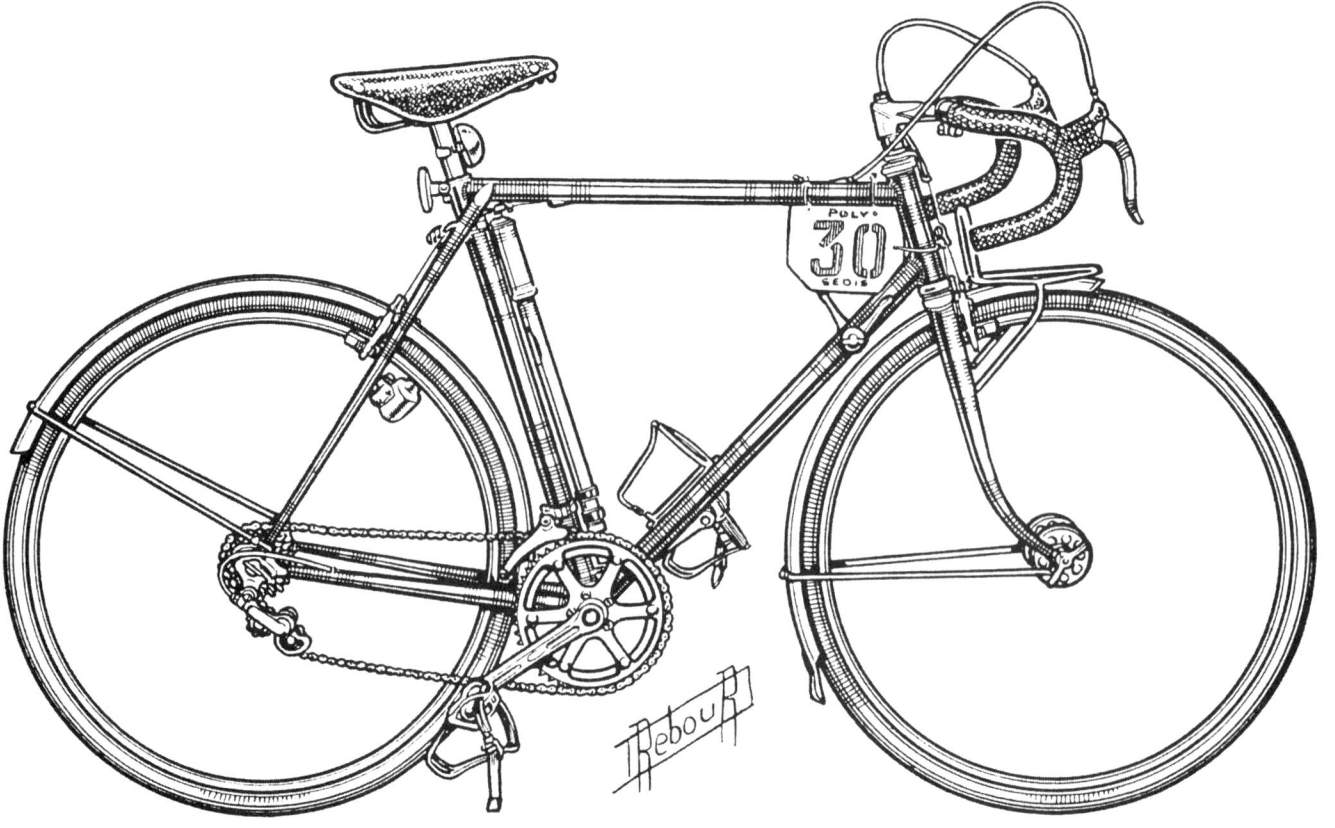

Chapter 9. Rims, Tires, and Spokes

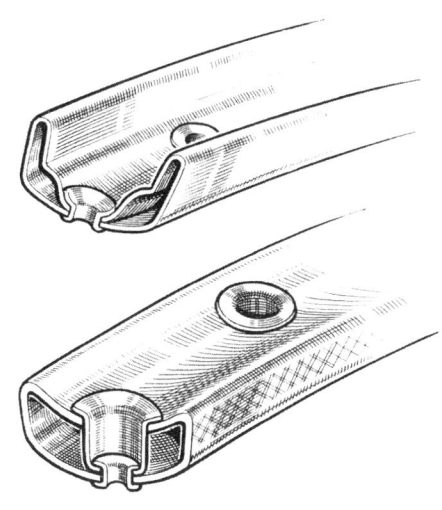

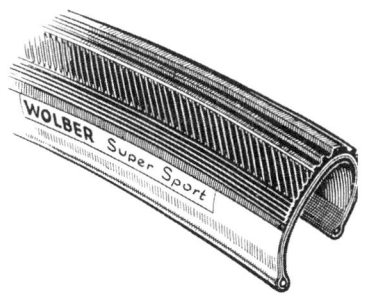

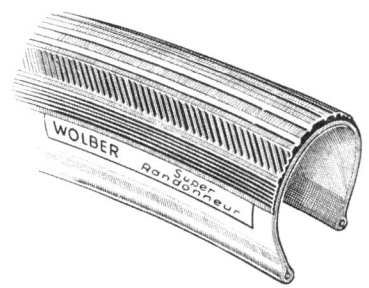

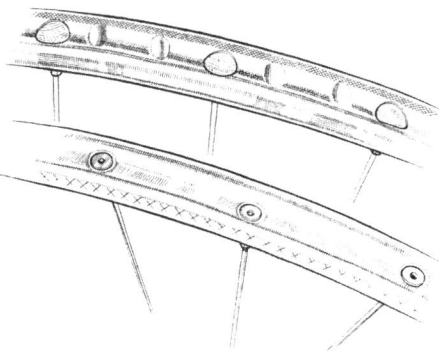

Above: Wheel details of Tour de France rims. *Le Cycle*, 11 July 1959.

Left and upper left: Wolber wired-on tires for high-pressure (top) and randonneuring. *Le Cycle*, September 1960 and February 1961.

Above: Mavic rims with reinforced nipple holes and valve hole for wired-on and tubular tires. *Le Cycle*, September 1962.

Right: V-profile, or "aero" Sprint rim, for tubular tire. 1983 Milremo catalogue.

Below: 1961 Tour de France winner of the points classification, André Darrigade's Alcyon bicycle, *Le Cycle*, July-August 1961.

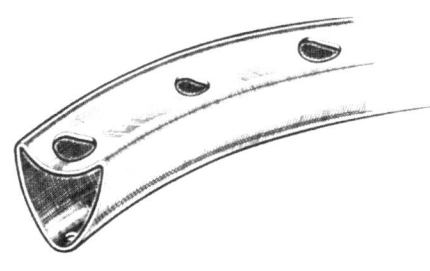

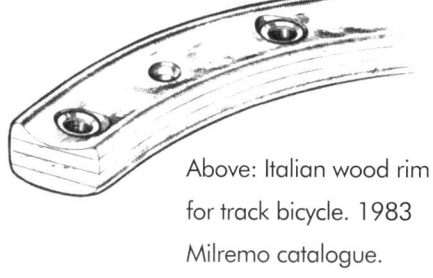

Above: Italian wood rim for track bicycle. 1983 Milremo catalogue.

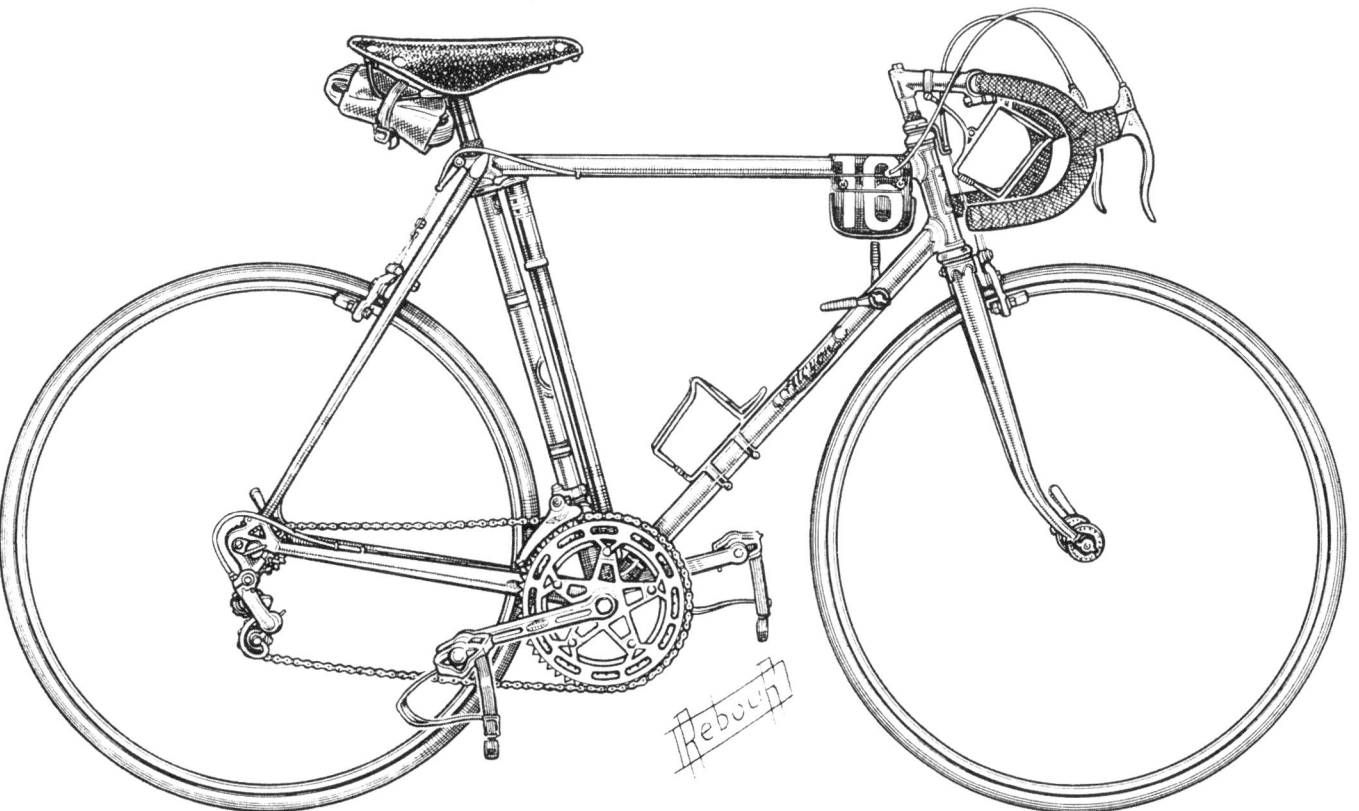

143

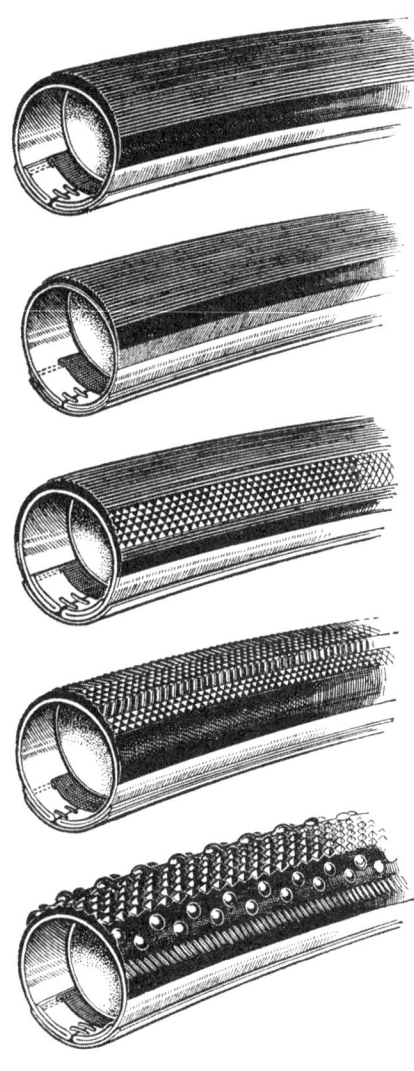

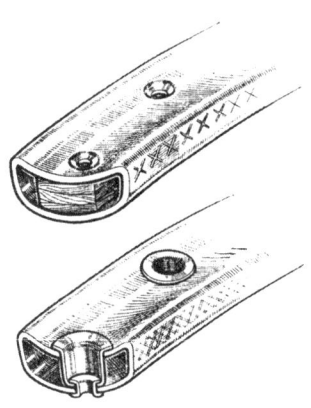

Above: Sprint rims, for tubular tires, from Mephisto and Mavic. *Cycle: Compétition, Cyclotourisme.*

Below: Mavic rims for tubular tires. 1983 Milremo catalogue.

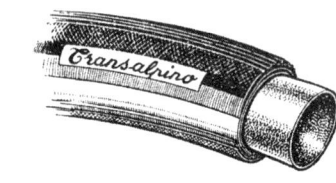

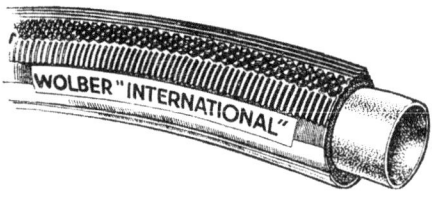

Above: Two heavy-duty, or training, tubular tires from Wolber.

Below: Two high-pressure wired-on tires from the same manufacturer.

Both images from *Cycle: Compétition, Cyclotourisme.*

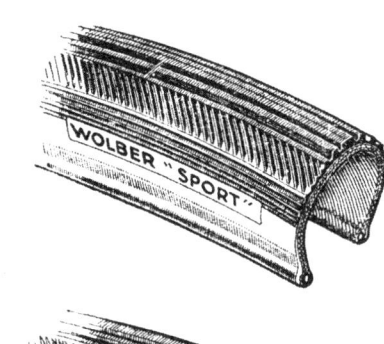

Above: Assortment of Canetti tubular tires. *Cycle: Compétition, Cyclotourisme.*
Below: Rigida channel-reinforced rim. *Le Cycle,* October 1972.

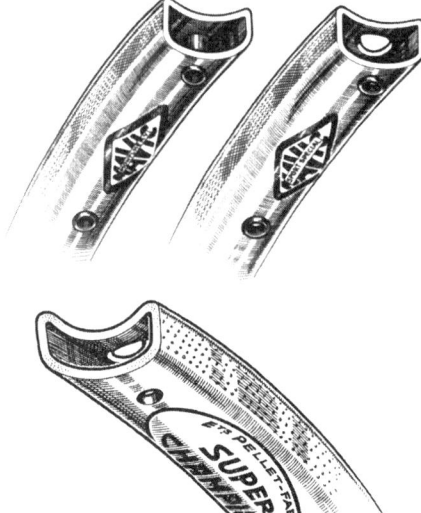

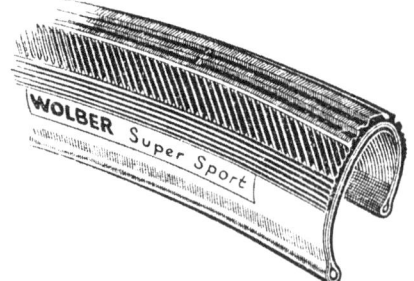

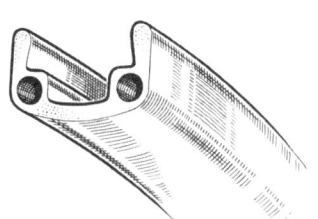

Above: Super Champion Sprint rim, for tubular tires. *Cycle: Compétition, Cyclotourisme.*
Bottom right: Mavic Sprint rims with single and double reinforcing eyelets. *Le Cycle,* December 1970.

Right: Detail of Sprint rim, for tubular tire, with plugged spoke holes. *Cycle: Compétition, Cyclotourisme.*

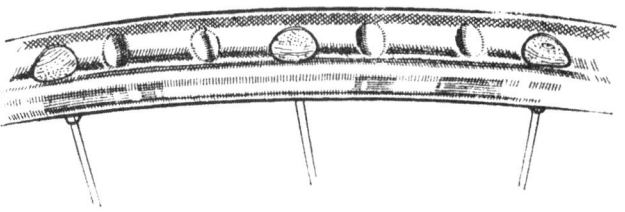

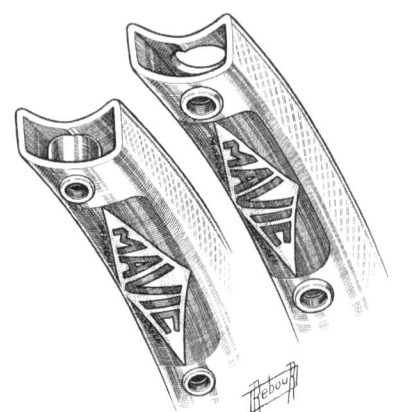

Chapter 9. Rims, Tires, and Spokes

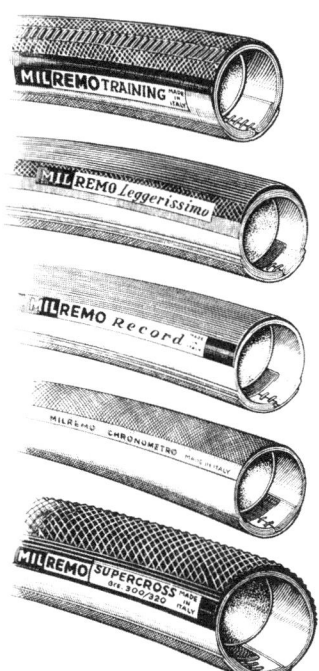

Above: Selection of Milremo tubular tires. 1976 Milremo catalogue.

Below: Jo Routens randonneur bicycle of Jean Fouace, winner of the 1961 Paris–Brest–Paris. *Le Cycle,* September 1961.

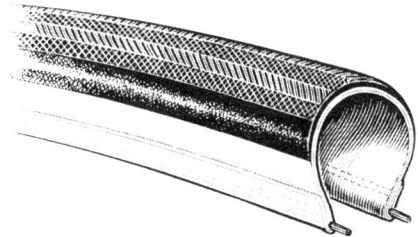

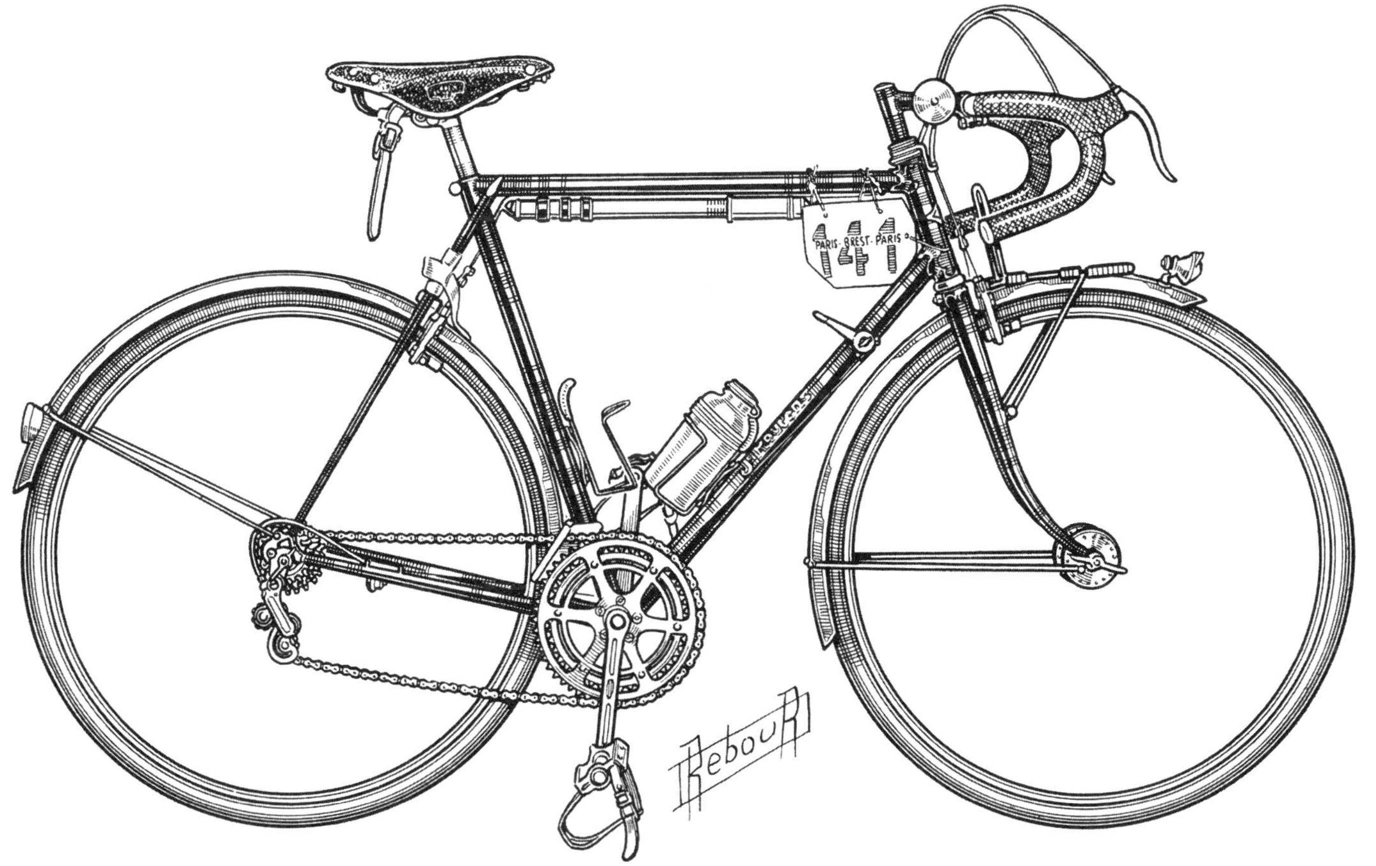

Above: Milremo 700-C hook-bead high-pressure wired-on, or "clincher," tire. 1976 Milremo catalogue.

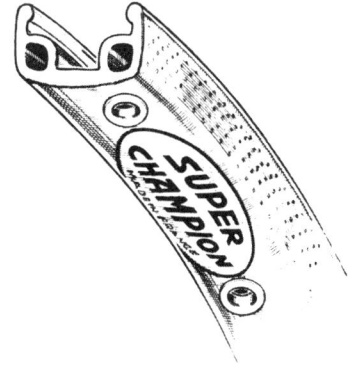

Above: Super Champion hook-edge rim, for high-pressure tires.

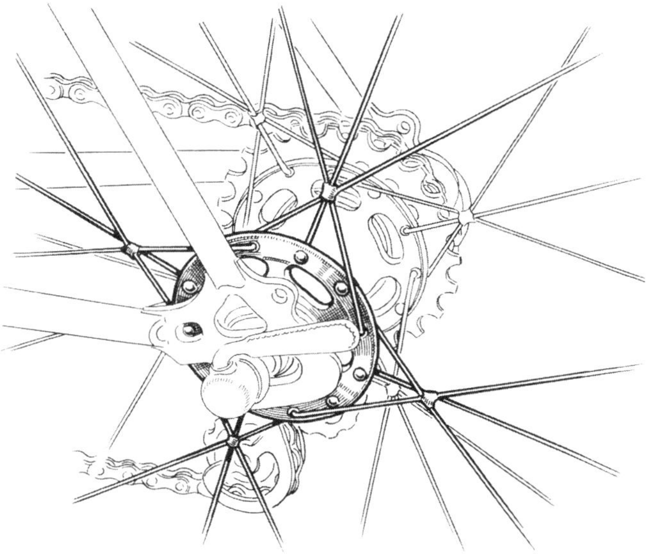

Left: Example of a wheel with grouped, tied, and soldered spokes, which was at the time believed to give a wheel greater strength.

Both images from *Cycles de Compétition et Randonneuses.*

145

Chapter 10. Steering Components

In the current chapter, we have collected a number of drawings of steering components. In addition to the handlebars themselves, we have included drawings of handlebar stems and headset bearings, as well as some of front forks (other illustrations of forks and fork components can be found in Chapter 2, under frame details).

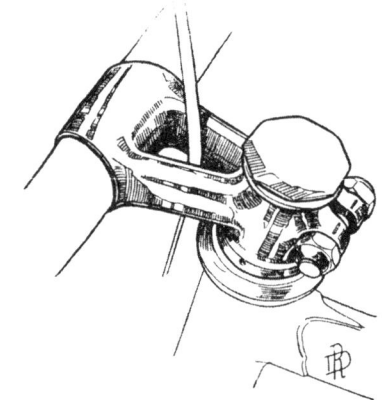

Left: Narcisse randonneur bike stem, clamped around an unthreaded steerer tube extension, similar to today's popular threadless headsets. *Le Cycle*, 20 April 1946.

Below left and right: Folding handlebar mechanism, used on early folding bicycles, also allowing adjustable handlebar angles. *Le Cycle*, 24 February 1947.

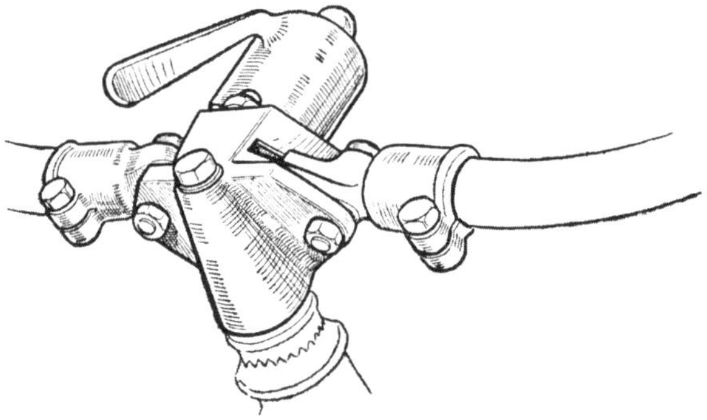

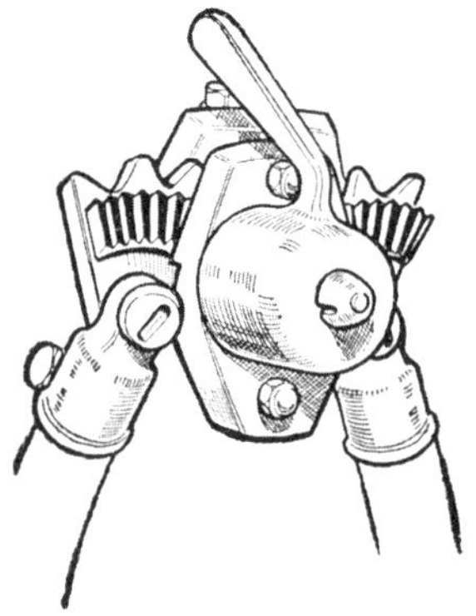

Below: 1961 Tour de France winner Jacques Anquetil's Helyett bicycle. The frame is built up with Reynolds 531 tubing and fork blades, using Nervex lugs. It is equipped with mostly French components: Simplex derailleurs, Stronglight crankset, Pivo rims, stem, and handlebars, Mafac brakes, Moyne freewheel, and Brampton chain. *Le Cycle*, July-August 1961.

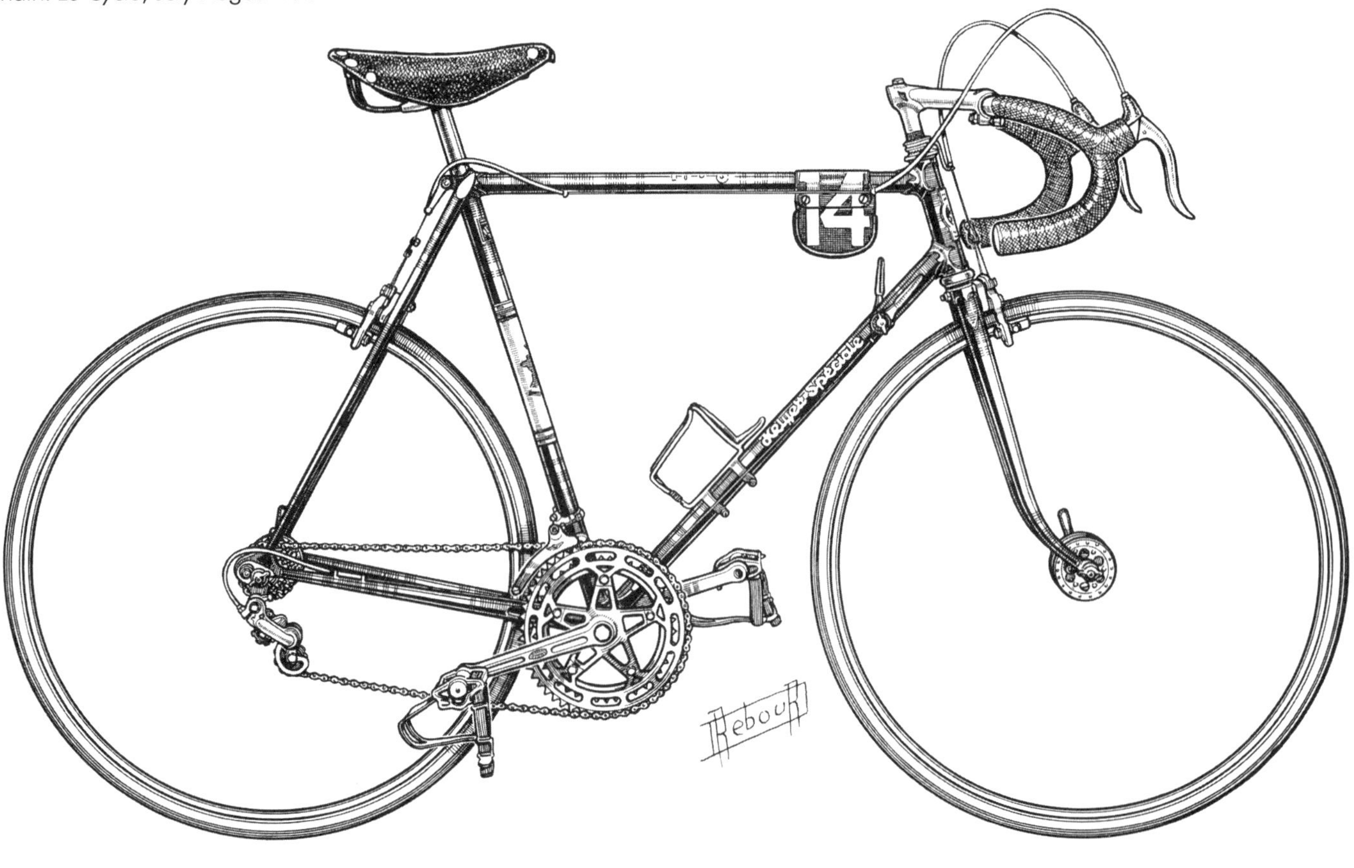

Chapter 10. Steering Components

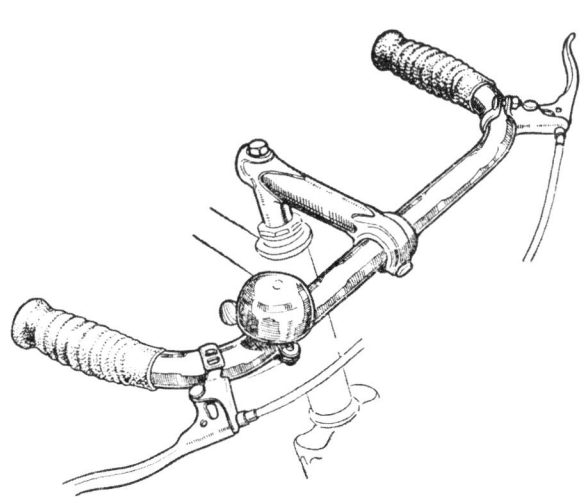

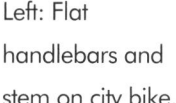

Left: Flat handlebars and stem on city bike.

Right: Drop handlebars and stem on touring or racing bike.

Both images from *Le Cycle*, 24 February 1947.

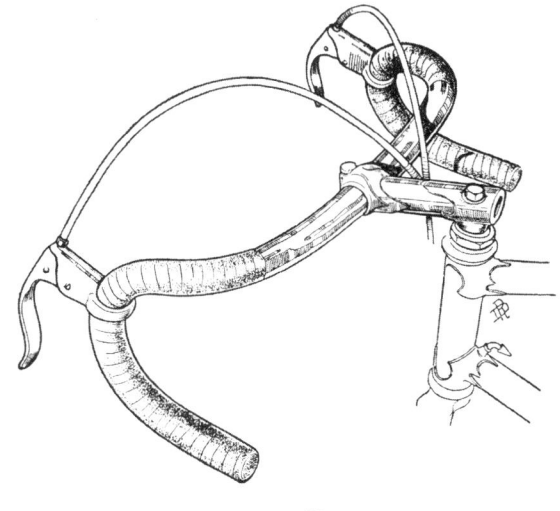

Right: Steering lock on an English roadster bicycle with rod-operated stirrup brakes. *Le Cycle*, 22 March 1947.

Far right: Guffanti steering lock. *Le Cycle*, 31 May 1947.

Below: Legnano bicycle of mountains classification winner Imerio Massignan, of Italy, in the 1961 Tour de France. *Le Cycle*, July-August 1961. **

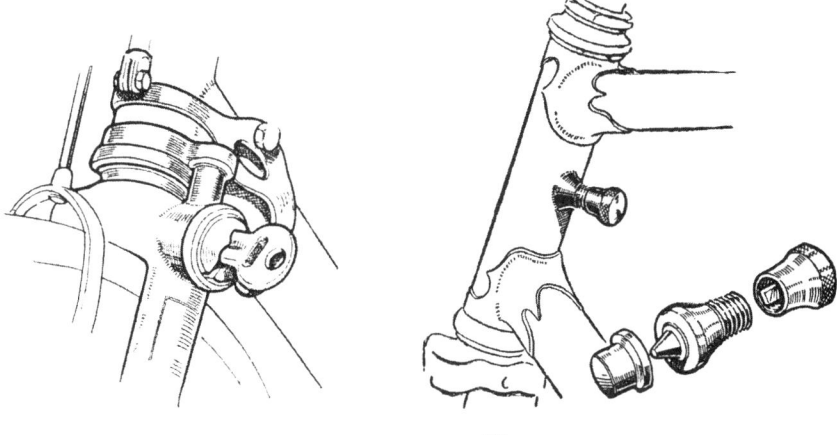

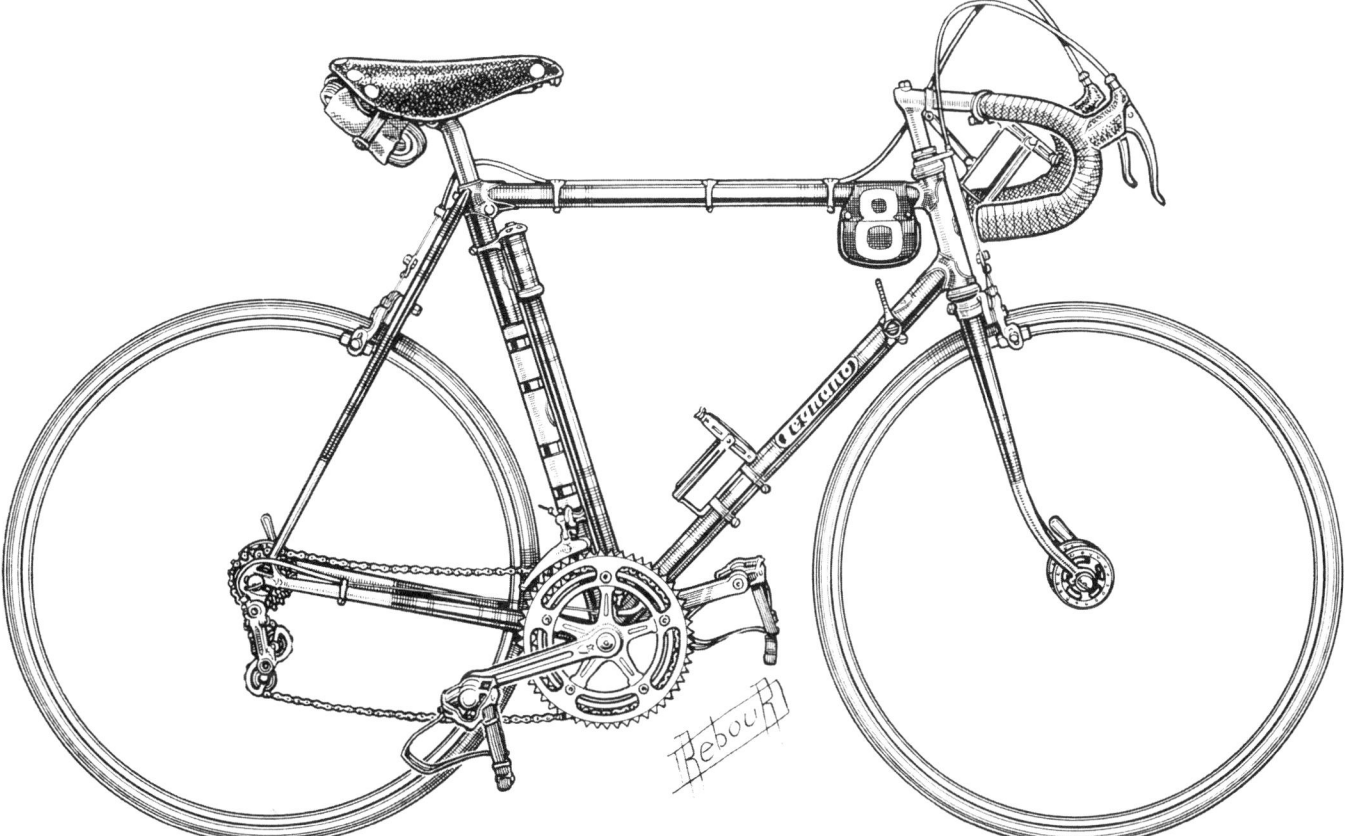

** See pages 269–271 for expanded caption text.

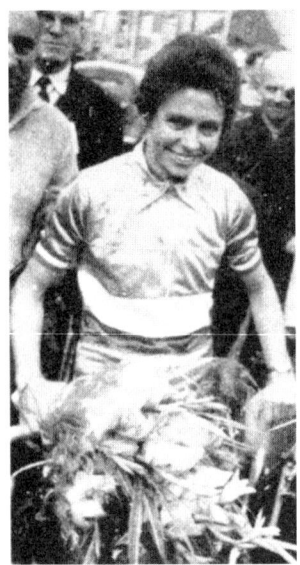

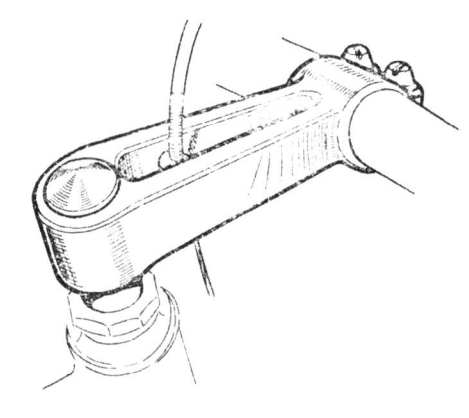

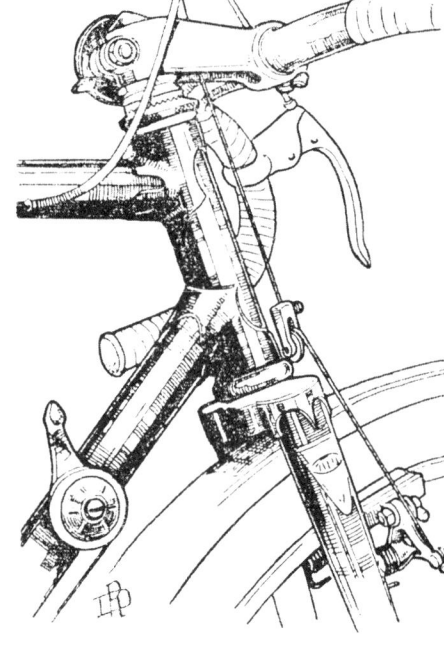

Lily Herse, René Herse's daughter, after winning the 1961 French women's road racing championship. *Le Cycle,* November 1961.

Above right: Detail of René Herse stem with brake cable stop for centerpull or cantilever brake, similar to the one on Lily's 1961 bike. *Le Cycle,* 10 January 1948.

Below: René Herse bicycle on which his daughter Lysette, or Lily, won the 1961 French women's road championship. *Le Cycle,* November 1961.

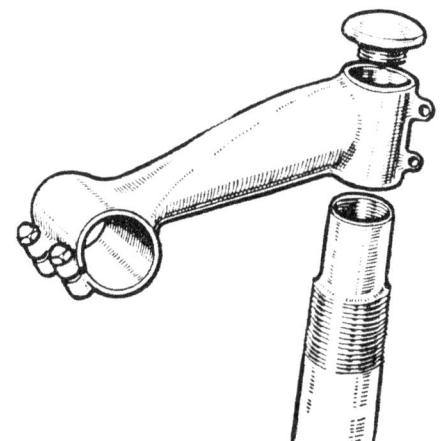

Above: Front end details of a René Herse randonneur bicycle, showing handlebars, clamp-on stem, headset, and fork. *Le Cycle,* 20 April 1946.

Left: Details of Vitus clamp-on stem and steerer tube with threaded and non-threaded sections. *Le Cycle,* 24 April 1948.

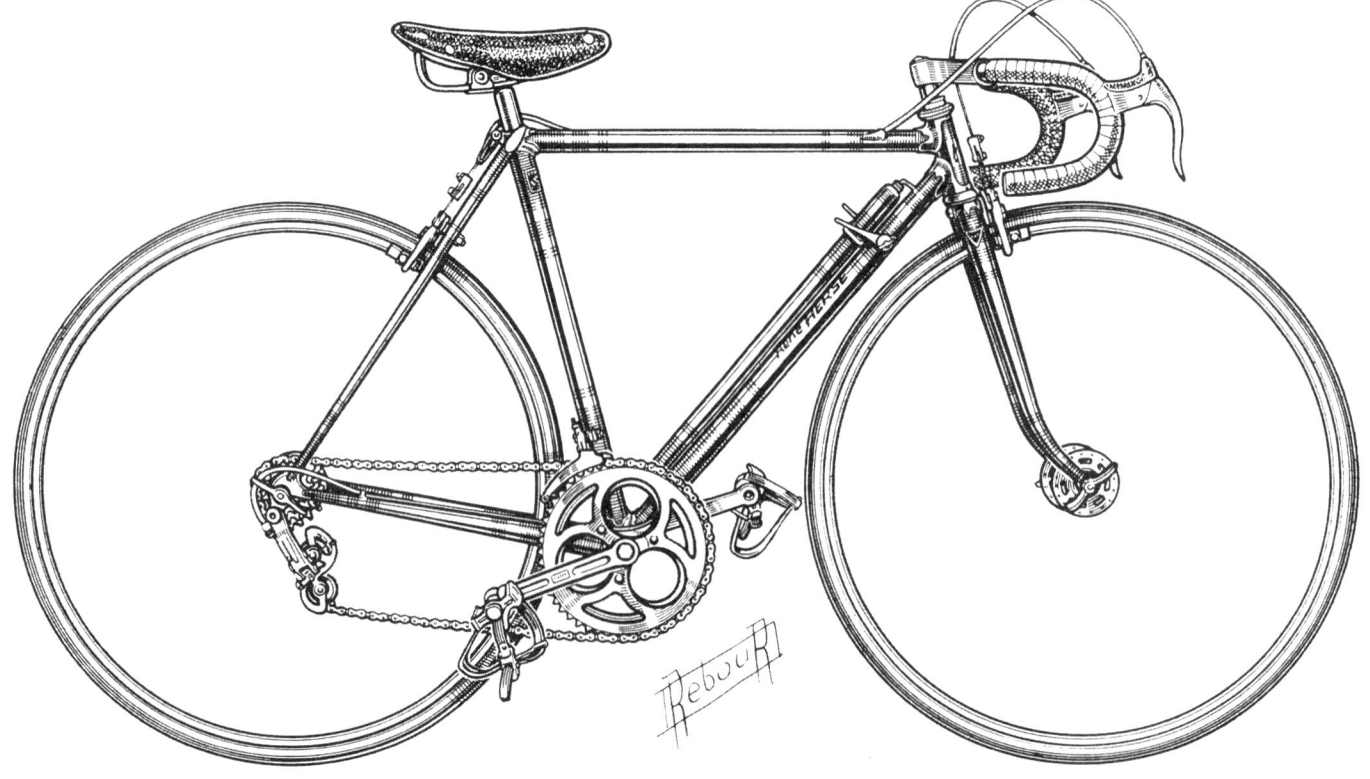

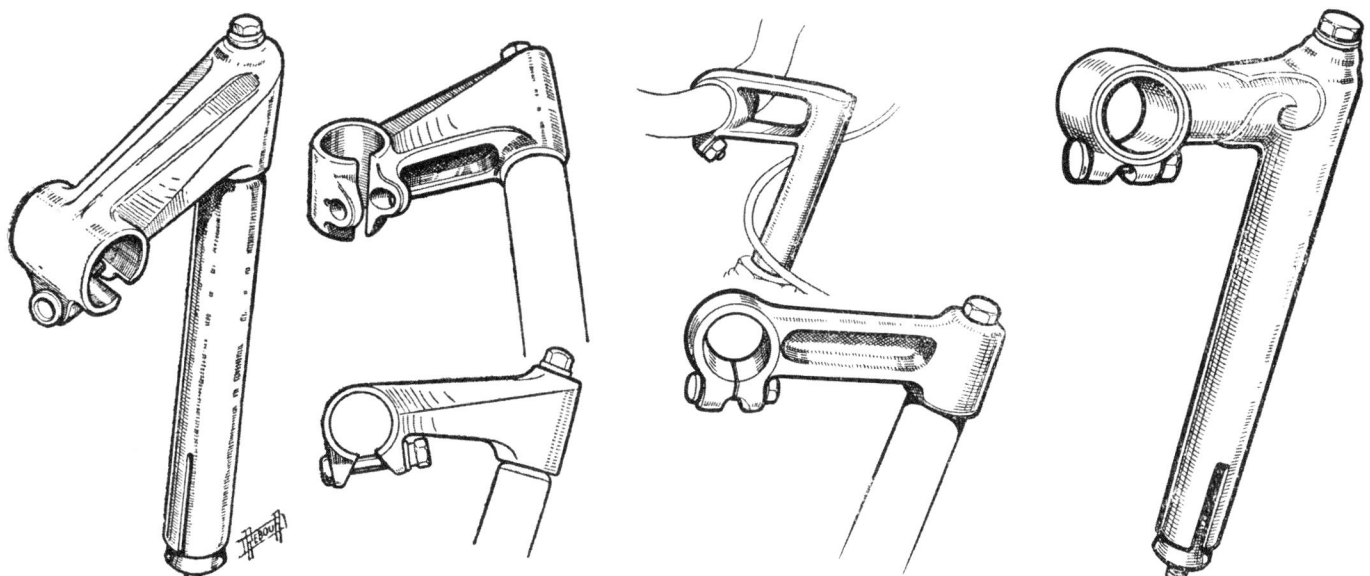

Above: Details of Tigra stems with steel post and aluminium alloy quills. *Le Cycle*, 27 September 1947.

Right: Quill-to-post clamping detail of a Tigra stem. *Le Cycle*, 9 October 1948.

Below: 1962 René Herse Diagonale randonneur bike. *Le Cycle*, January 1962.**

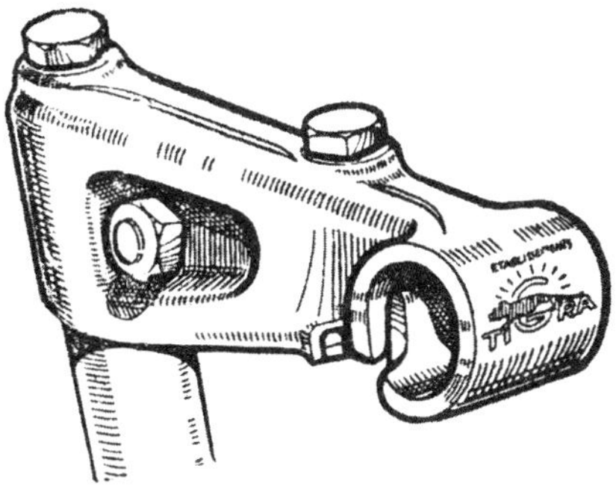

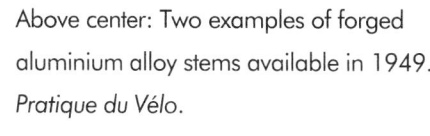

Above center: Two examples of forged aluminium alloy stems available in 1949. *Pratique du Vélo*.

Above right: English brazed steel stem. *Pratique du Vélo*.

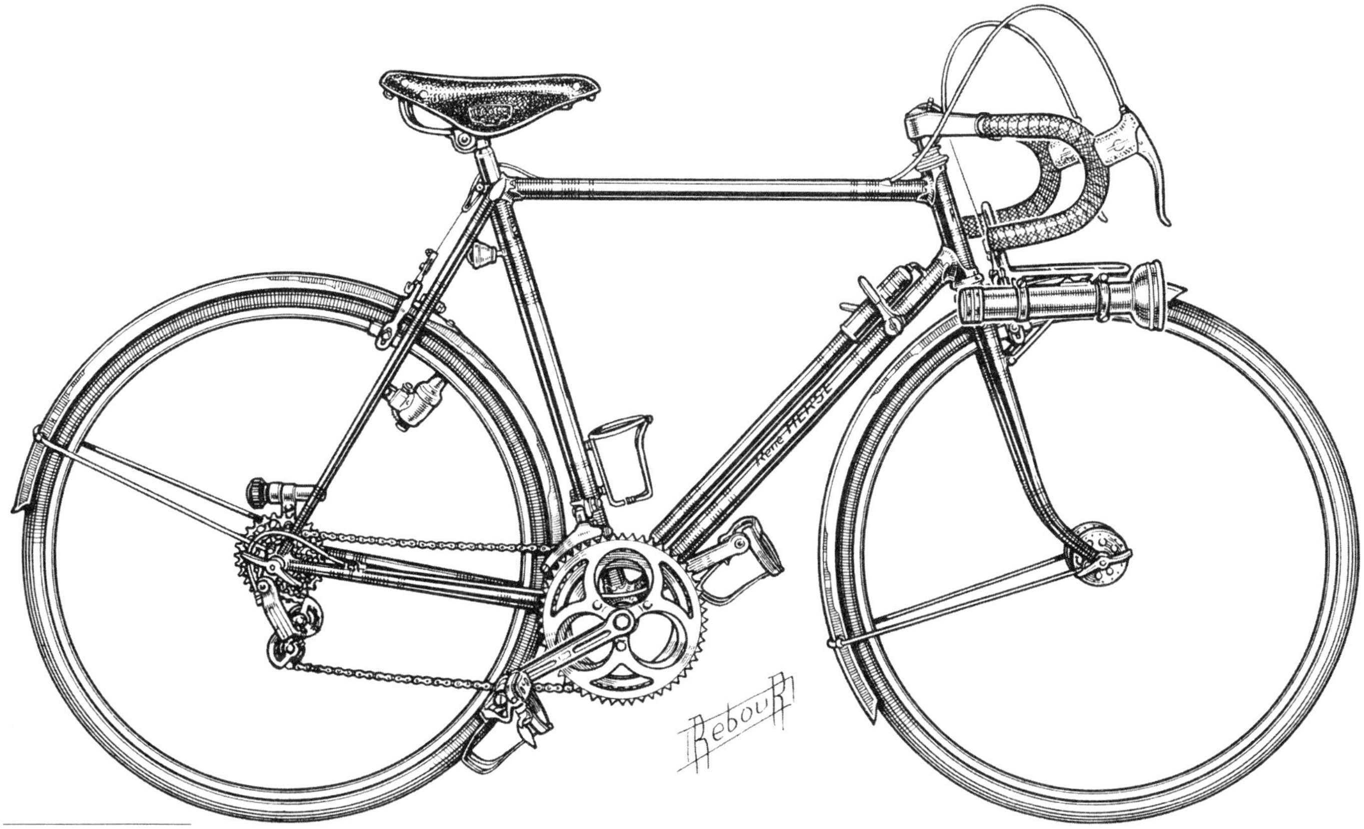

** See pages 269–271 for expanded caption text.

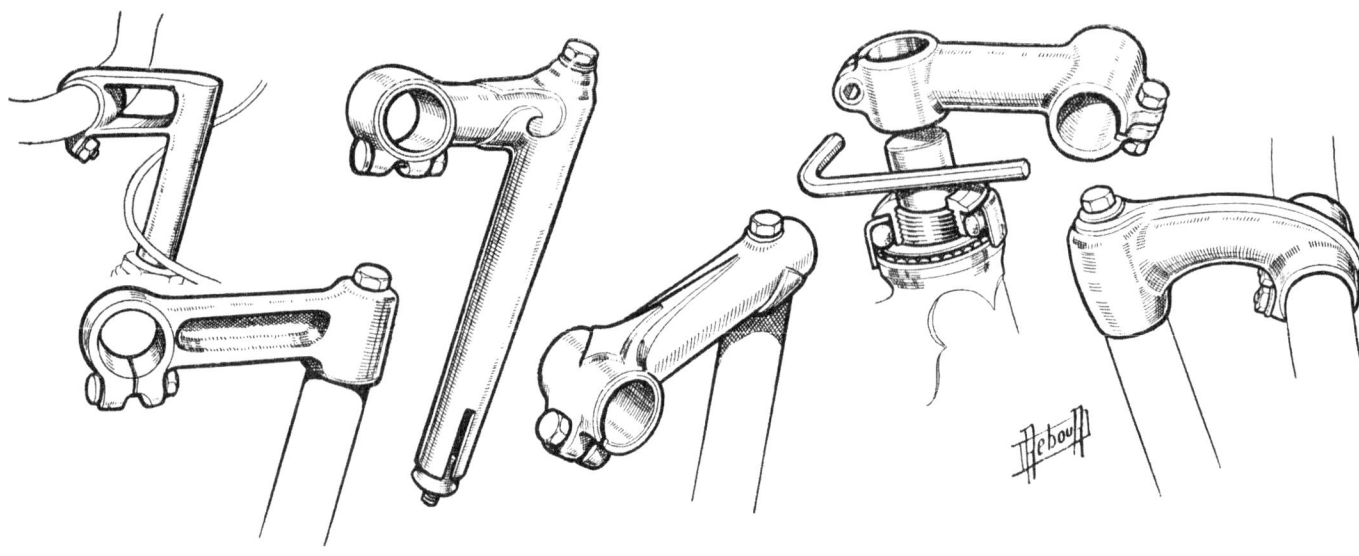

Above: Overview of stems available in England in 1948. *Le Cycle*, 4 December 1948.

Right: English welded stem. *Pratique du Vélo*.

Far right: Enlarged detail of the English clamp-on stem and headset shown above. *Pratique du Vélo*.

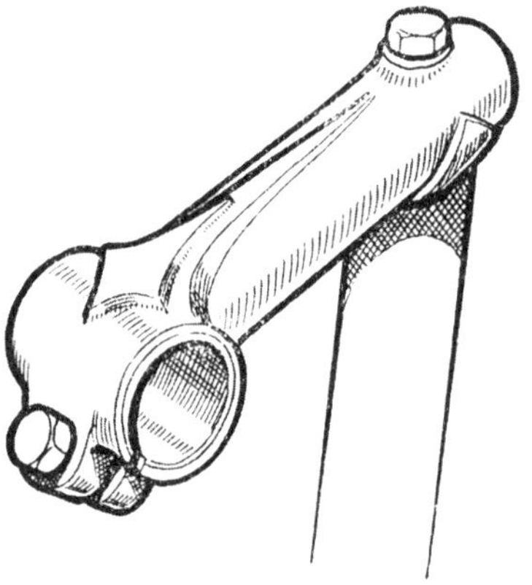

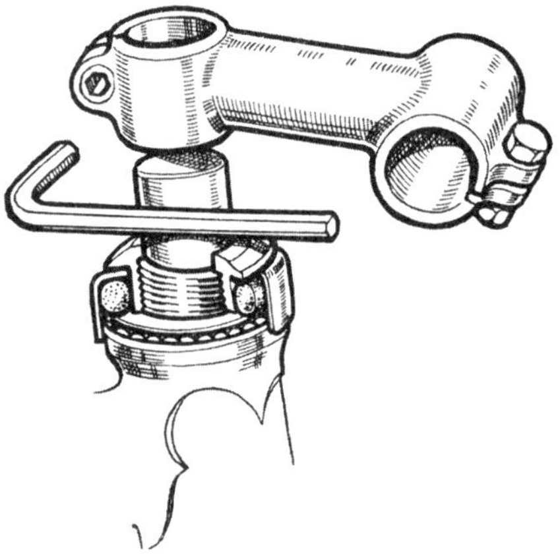

Below: Gitane bicycle of the first-placed woman in the 1962 Poly de Chanteloup technical trials. *Le Cycle*, June 1962.

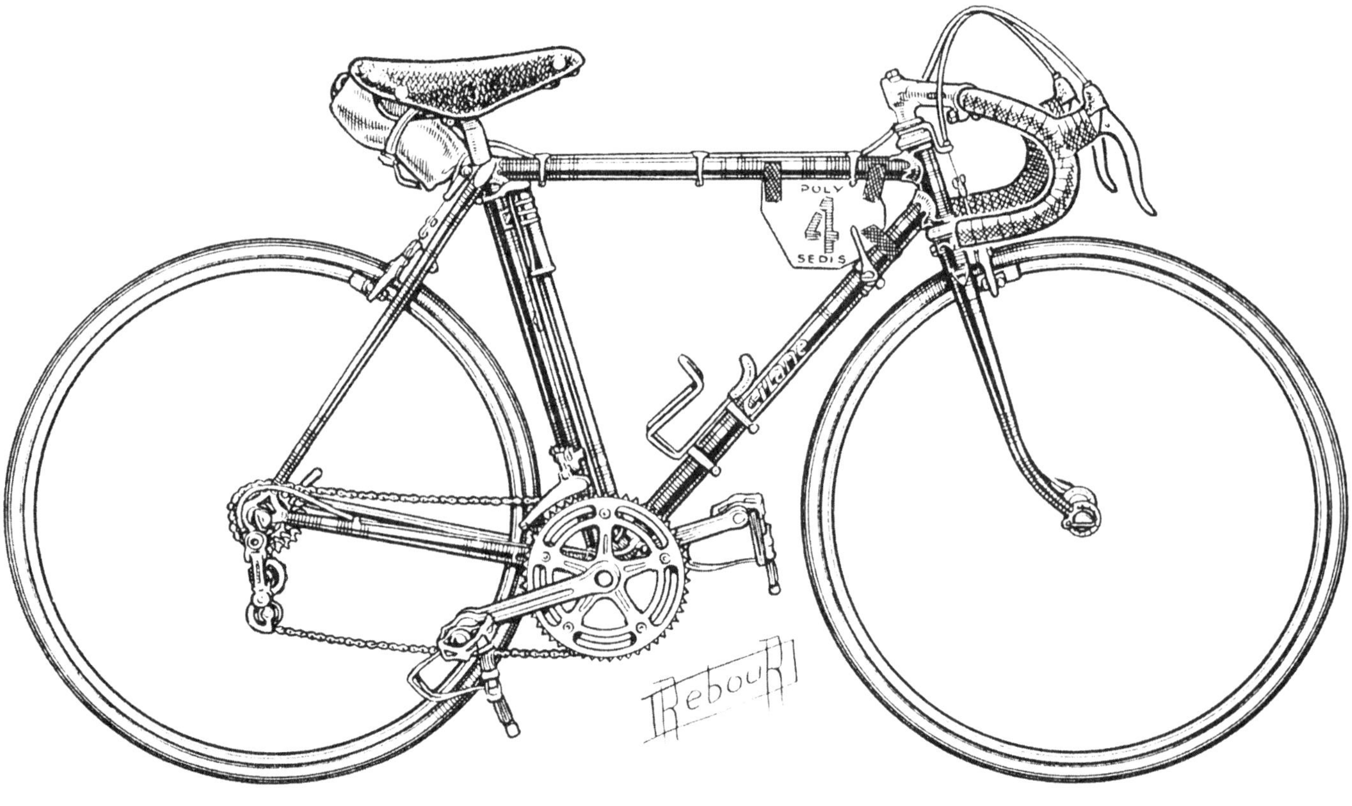

Chapter 10. Steering Components

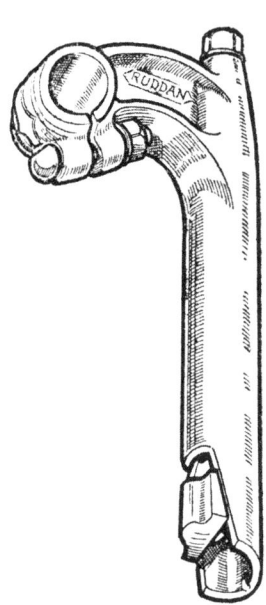

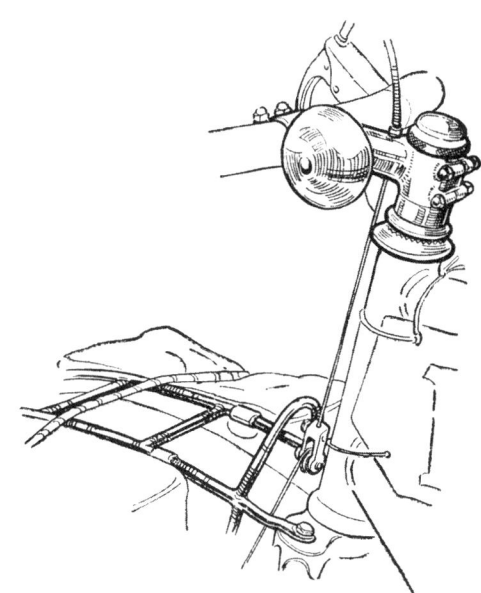

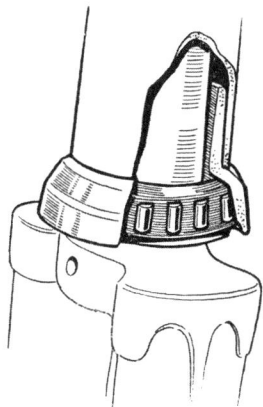

Left: Overview of front end of a touring bicycle with clamped-on stem. *Pratique du Vélo*.

Right: Bottom headset with needle bearings. *Pratique du Vélo*.

Below: Overview of flat handlebars and stem on a French city bicycle. *Pratique du Vélo*.

Above: Ruddan forged aluminium alloy stem with wedge-type clamp, as opposed to the conventional cone-type clamps commonly used at the time. *Le Cycle*, 8 May 1948.

Below: Helyett bicycle on which Jacques Anquetil won the 1962 Tour de France. *Le Cycle*, July-August 1962

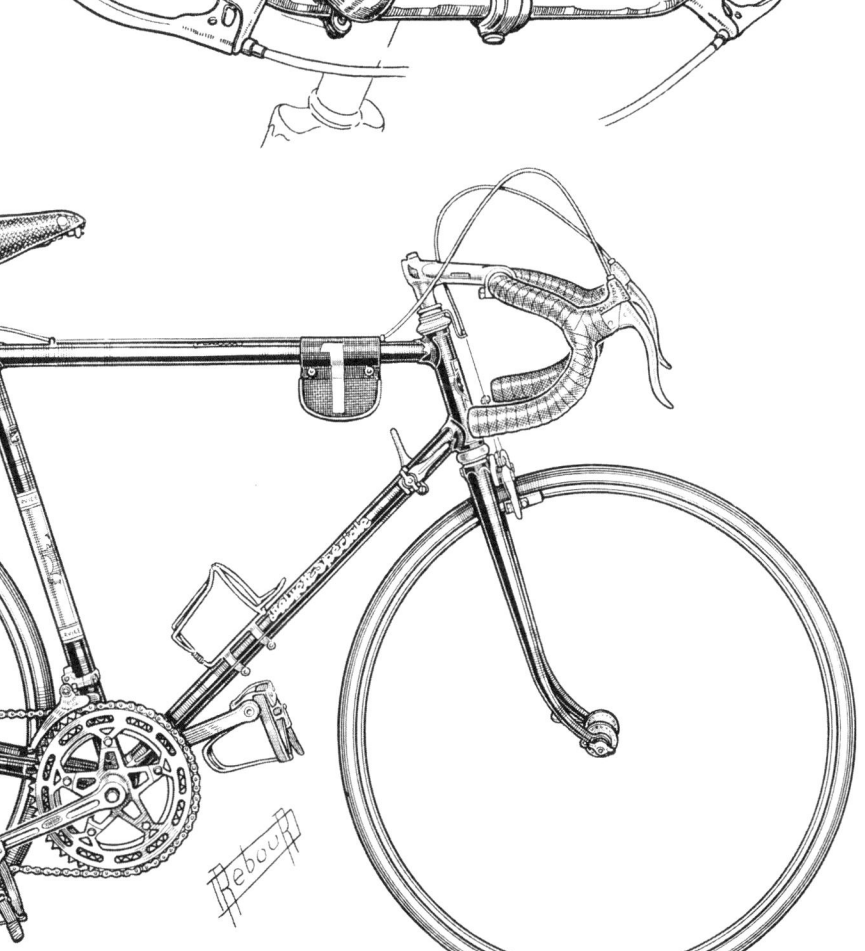

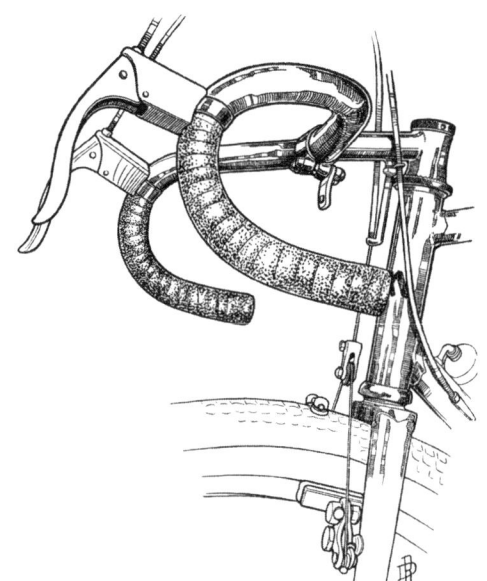

Right: Narcisse forged aluminium alloy stem and handlebars, with brake cable anchor in the stem. *Pratique du Vélo*.

Below right: Stronglight headset with toothed lockring, a feature of Stronglight headsets well into the 1990s. *Pratique du Vélo*.

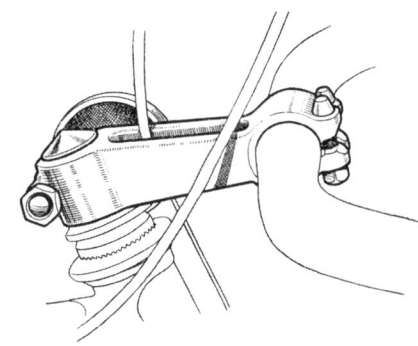

Above: Front end of Maury cyclo-cross bicycle with clamp-on stem. *Pratique du Vélo*.

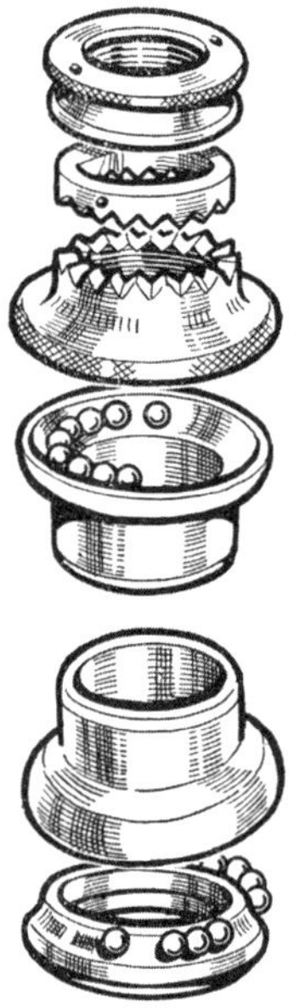

Right: Front end of touring bike, showing upswept randonneur-style handlebars. *Pratique du Vélo*.

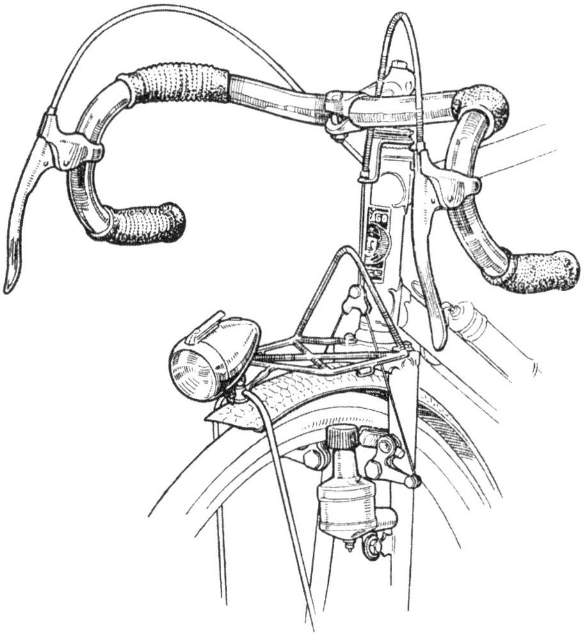

Below: Flandria bicycle of 1962 Tour de France 2nd-placed Jeff Planckaert, of Belgium. *Le Cycle*, July-August 1962.

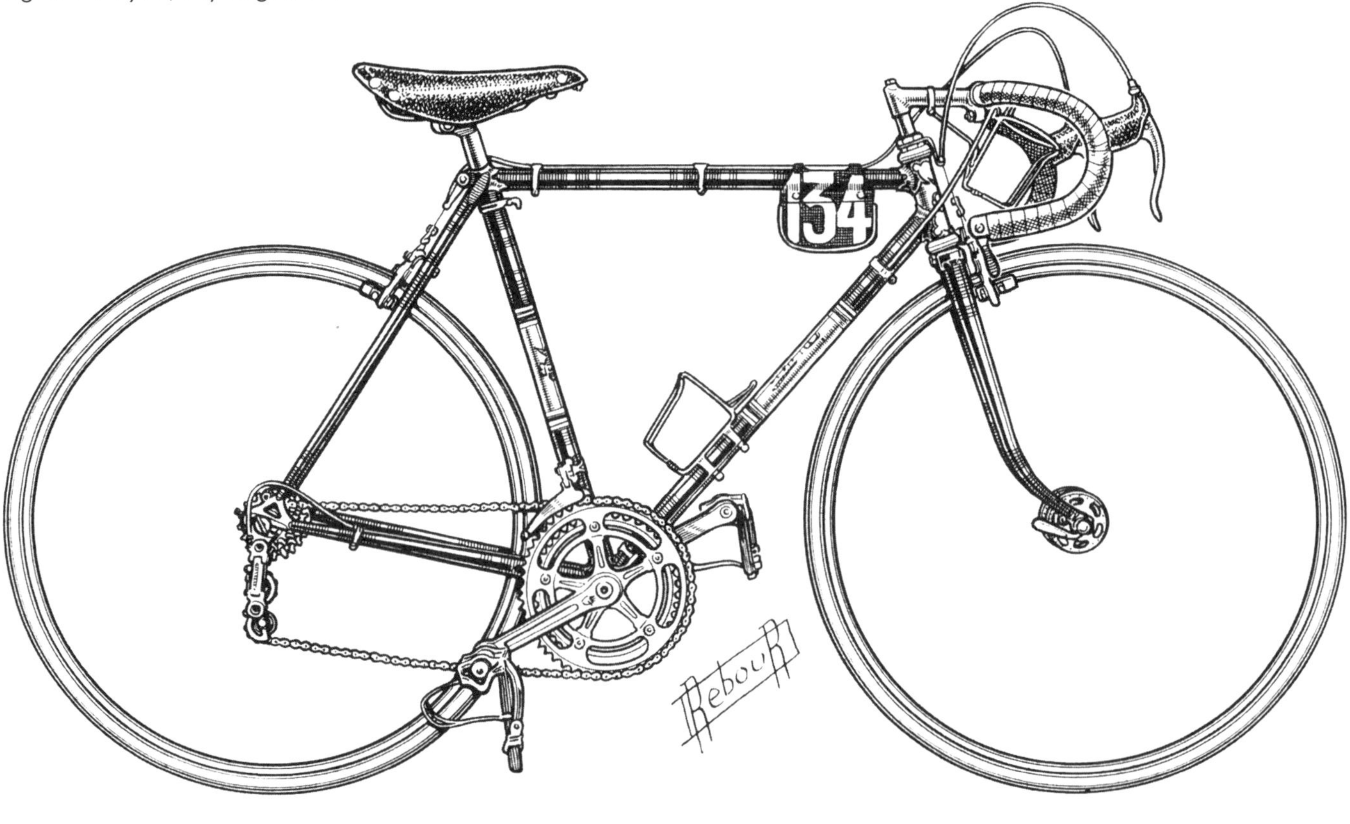

Chapter 10. Steering Components

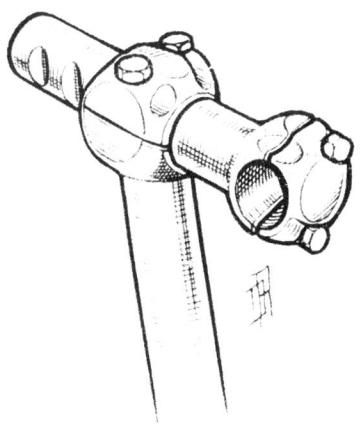

Right: Constrictor adjustable-reach handlebar stem. *Le Cycle*, 5 November 1949.

Below: Roland Wucher stems. *Le Cycle*, 7 January 1950.

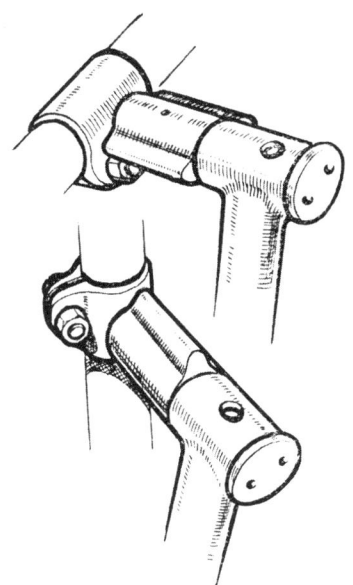

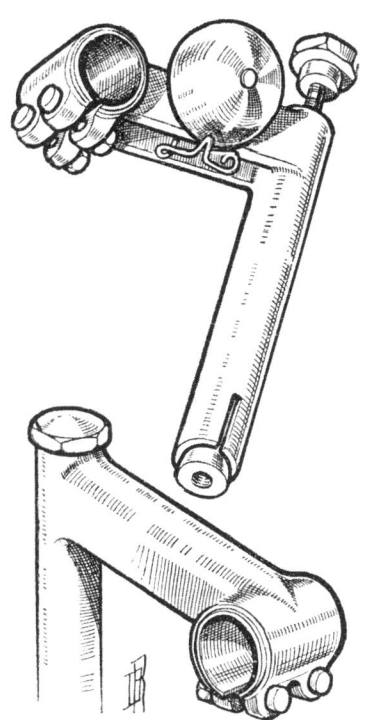

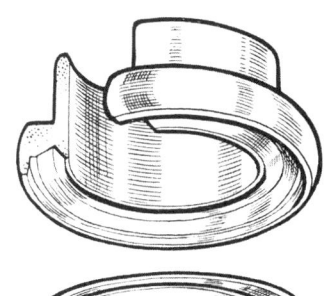

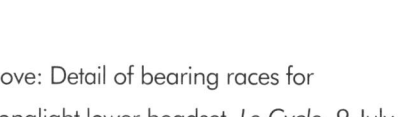

Above: English Shipway rotating stem, allowing the handlebars to be folded out of the way during transport of the bike. *Le Cycle*, 9 July 1949.

Below: Urago loaded-touring bicycle at the 1962 Paris bicycle trade show. Uncharacteristically, Rebour here even shows the spokes. The rear rack is forward-mounted. *Le Cycle*, September 1962.

Above: Detail of bearing races for Stronglight lower headset. *Le Cycle*, 9 July 1949.

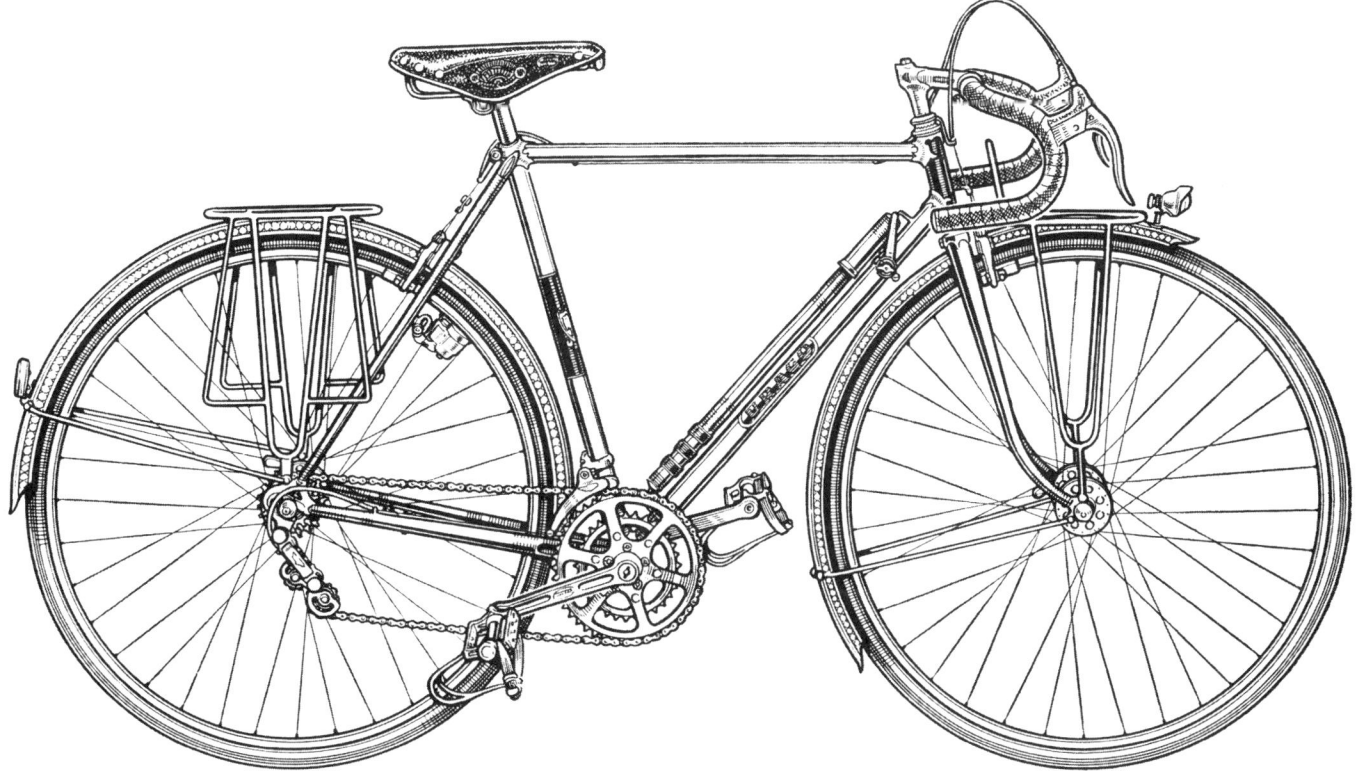

153

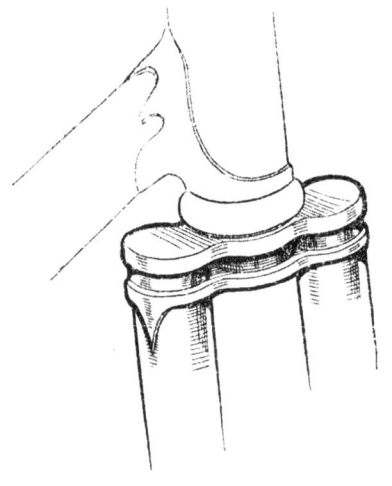
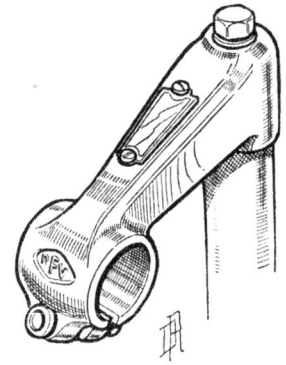

Above: PFV stem with name-plate. *Le Cycle*, 30 October 1950.

Above left: Double-plate fork crown and round fork blades. *Le Cycle*, 21 January 1950.

Right: Rare journal bearing headset, i.e. without ball bearings. *Le Cycle*, 12 January 1950.

Left: Ambrosio adjustable-reach stem. *Le Cycle*, 6 February 1950.

Below left: Fabrication and other details of pressed and welded stem construction. *Le Cycle*, 27 May 1950.

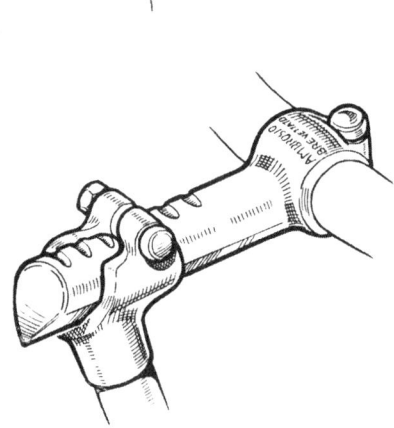
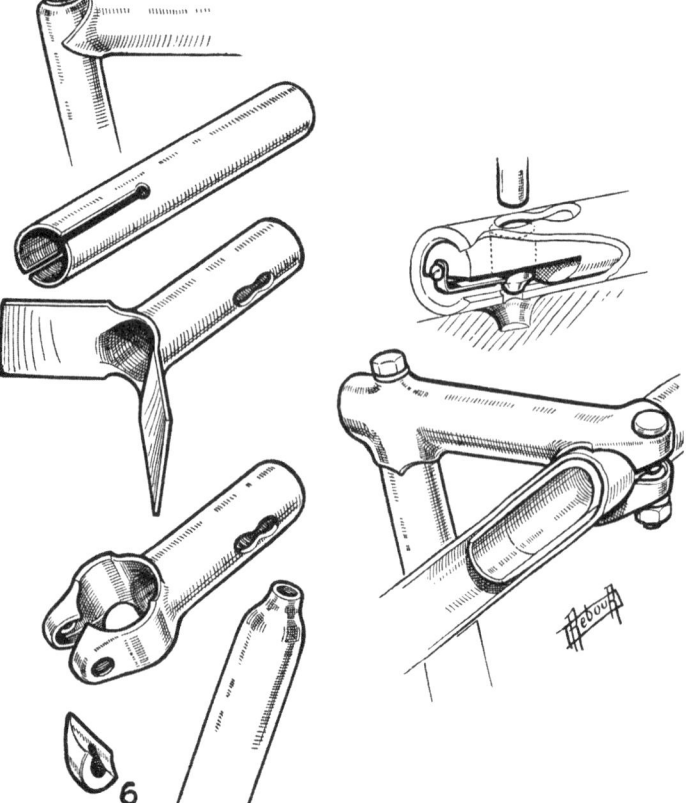
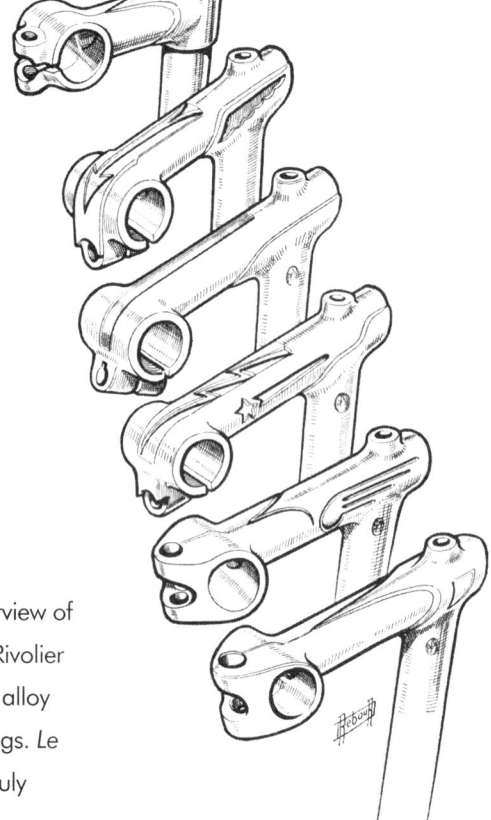

Right: Overview of Fonderies Rivolier aluminium alloy stem forgings. *Le Cycle*, 15 July 1950.

Chapter 10. Steering Components

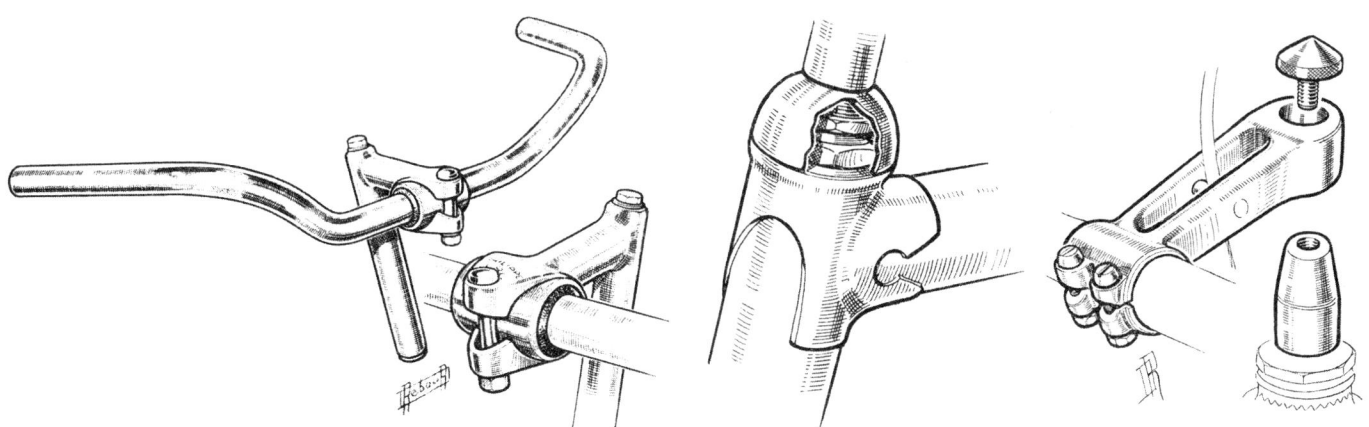

Above: Shock-absorbing handlebar stem. *Le Cycle*, 31 January 1953.

Above center: Coventry-Eagle covered headset. *Le Cycle*, 10 February 1951.

Right: Fork with round fork blades on the Friedrich bicycle ridden by Bauer in the 1959 Tour de France. *Le Cycle*, 22 August 1959.

Below: Winning the mountains classification once again, Fédérico Bahamontès rode this Paloma bicycle in the 1962 Tour de France. *Le Cycle*, July-August 1962.

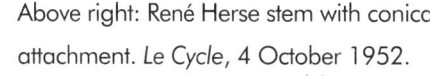

Above right: René Herse stem with conical attachment. *Le Cycle*, 4 October 1952.

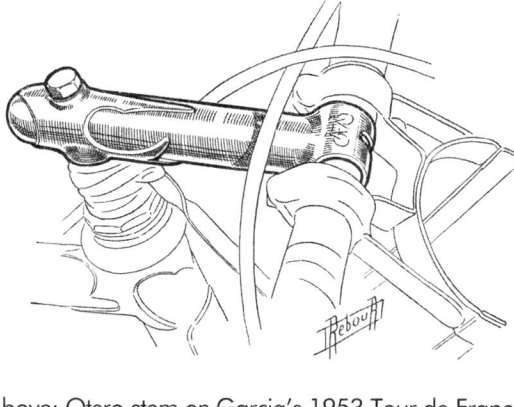

Above: Otero stem on Garcia's 1953 Tour de France bike. *Le Cycle*, 25 July 1953.

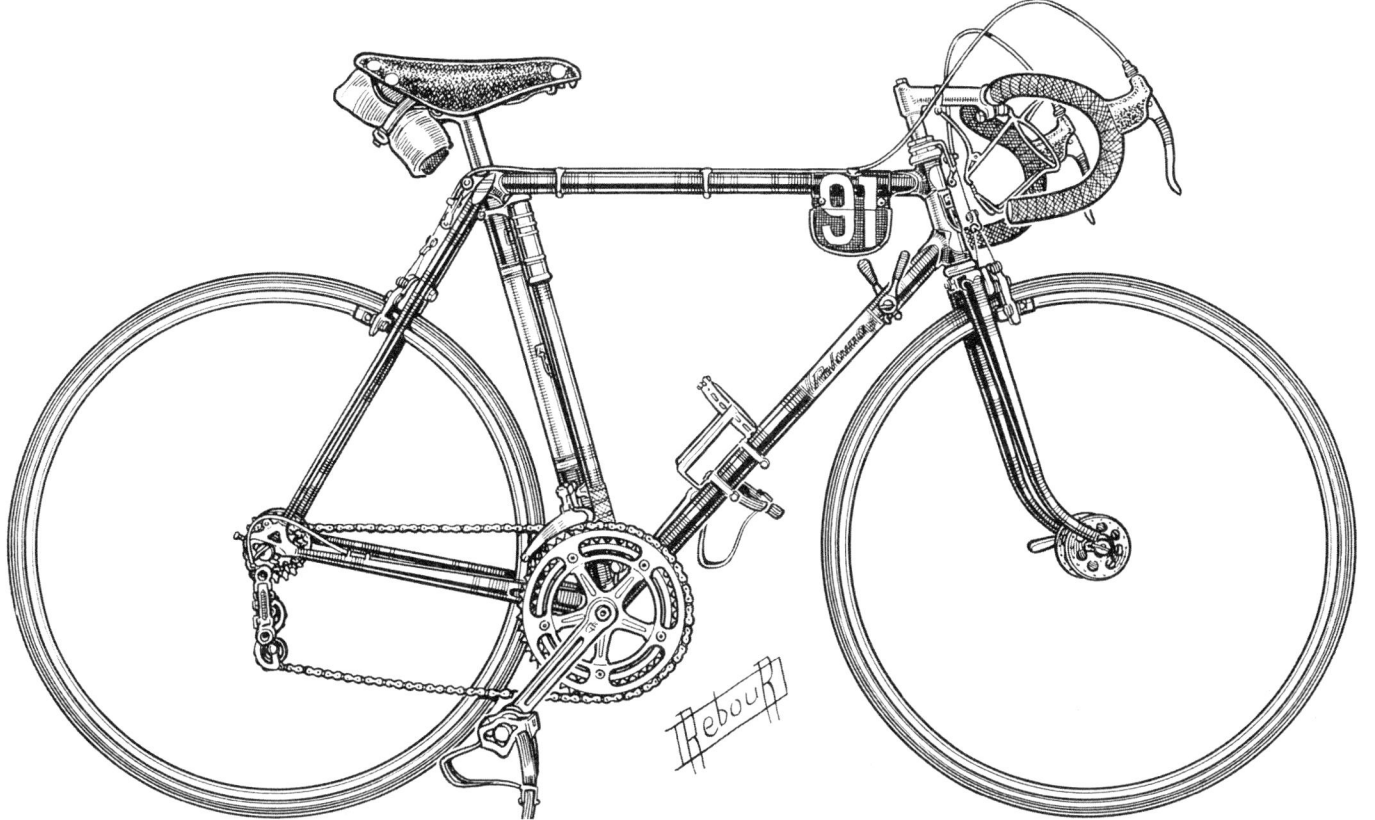

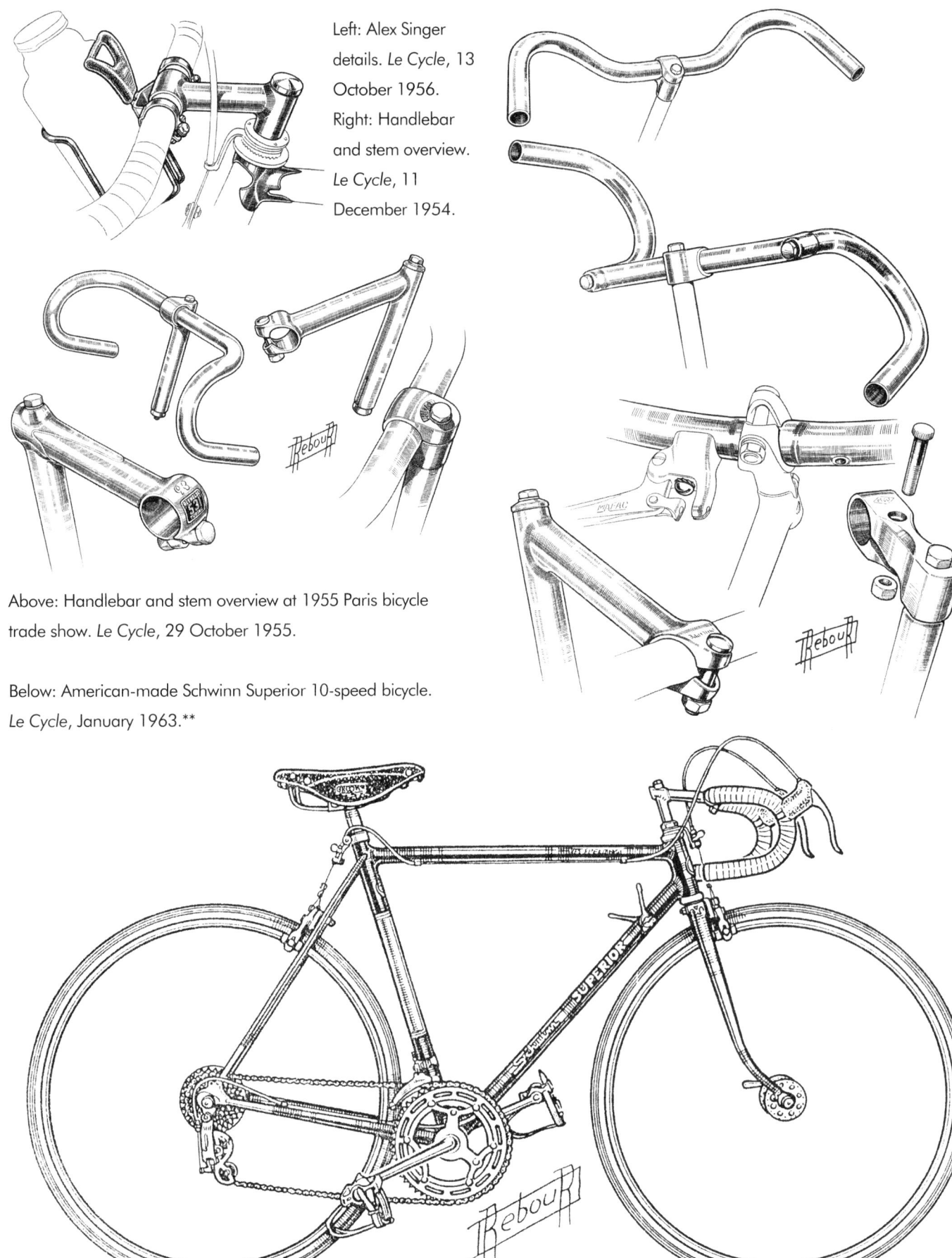

Left: Alex Singer details. *Le Cycle*, 13 October 1956.

Right: Handlebar and stem overview. *Le Cycle*, 11 December 1954.

Above: Handlebar and stem overview at 1955 Paris bicycle trade show. *Le Cycle*, 29 October 1955.

Below: American-made Schwinn Superior 10-speed bicycle. *Le Cycle*, January 1963.**

** See pages 269–271 for expanded caption text.

Chapter 10. Steering Components

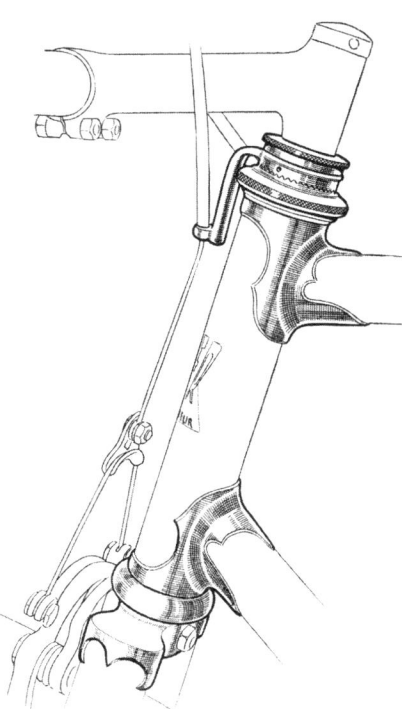

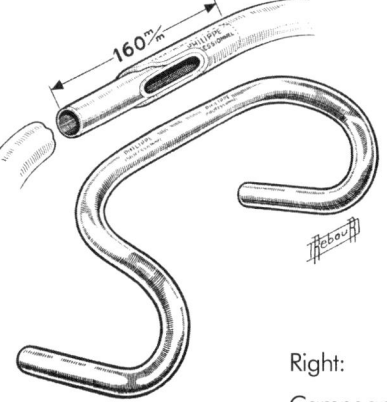

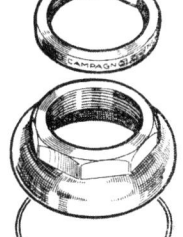

Left: Front end of Alex Singer randonneur bicycle. *Le Cycle*, 24 January 1959.

Right: Details of ATAX Philippe handlebar reinforcement. *Le Cycle*, 23 July 1955.

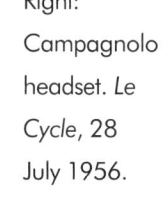
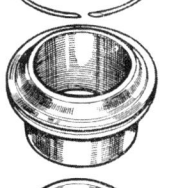

Right: Campagnolo headset. *Le Cycle*, 28 July 1956.

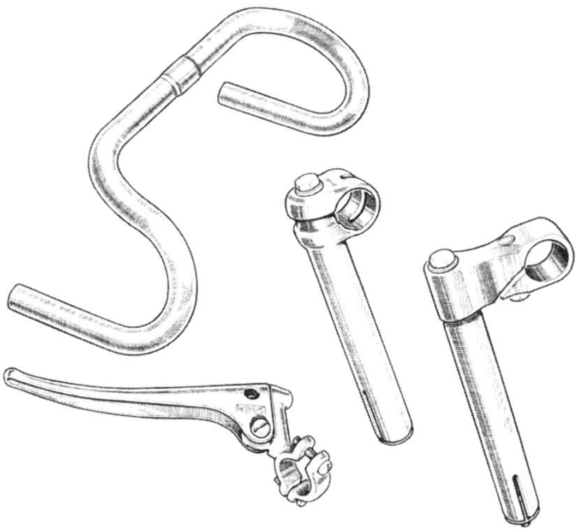

Left: Overview of Saker products. *Le Cycle*, February 1965.

Below: André Zimmermann, winner of the 1963 Tour de l'Avenir, for amateurs, rode this Messina bicycle. *Le Cycle*, August–September 1963.

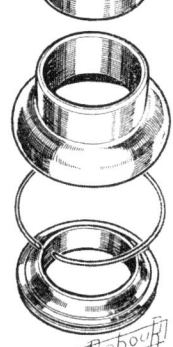

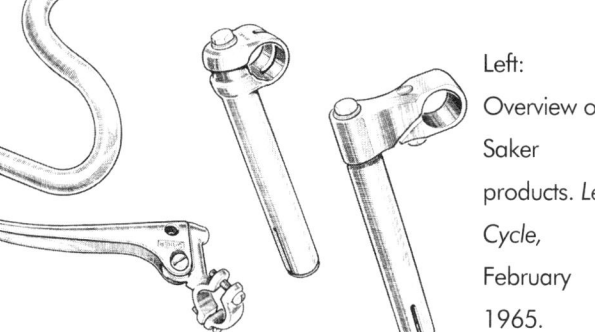

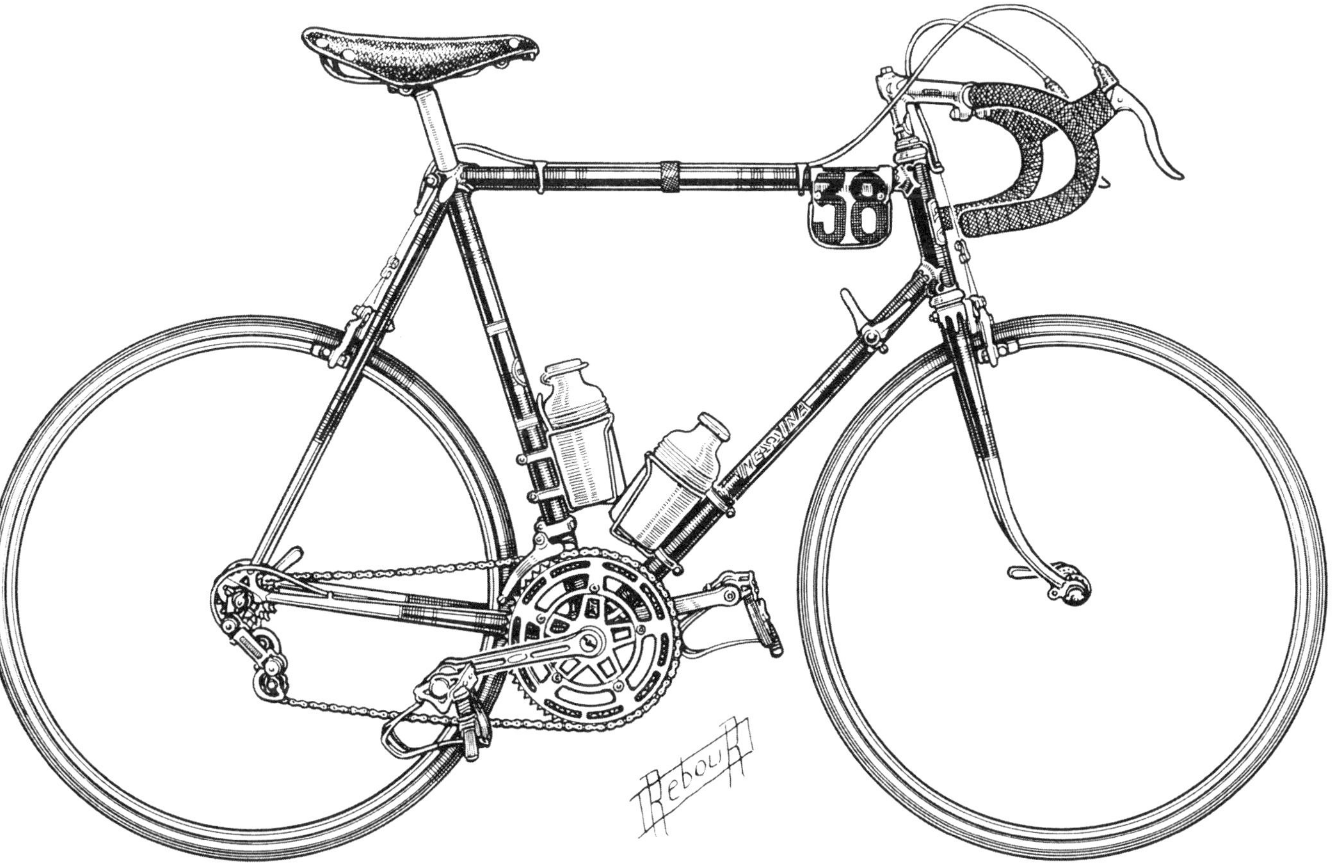

157

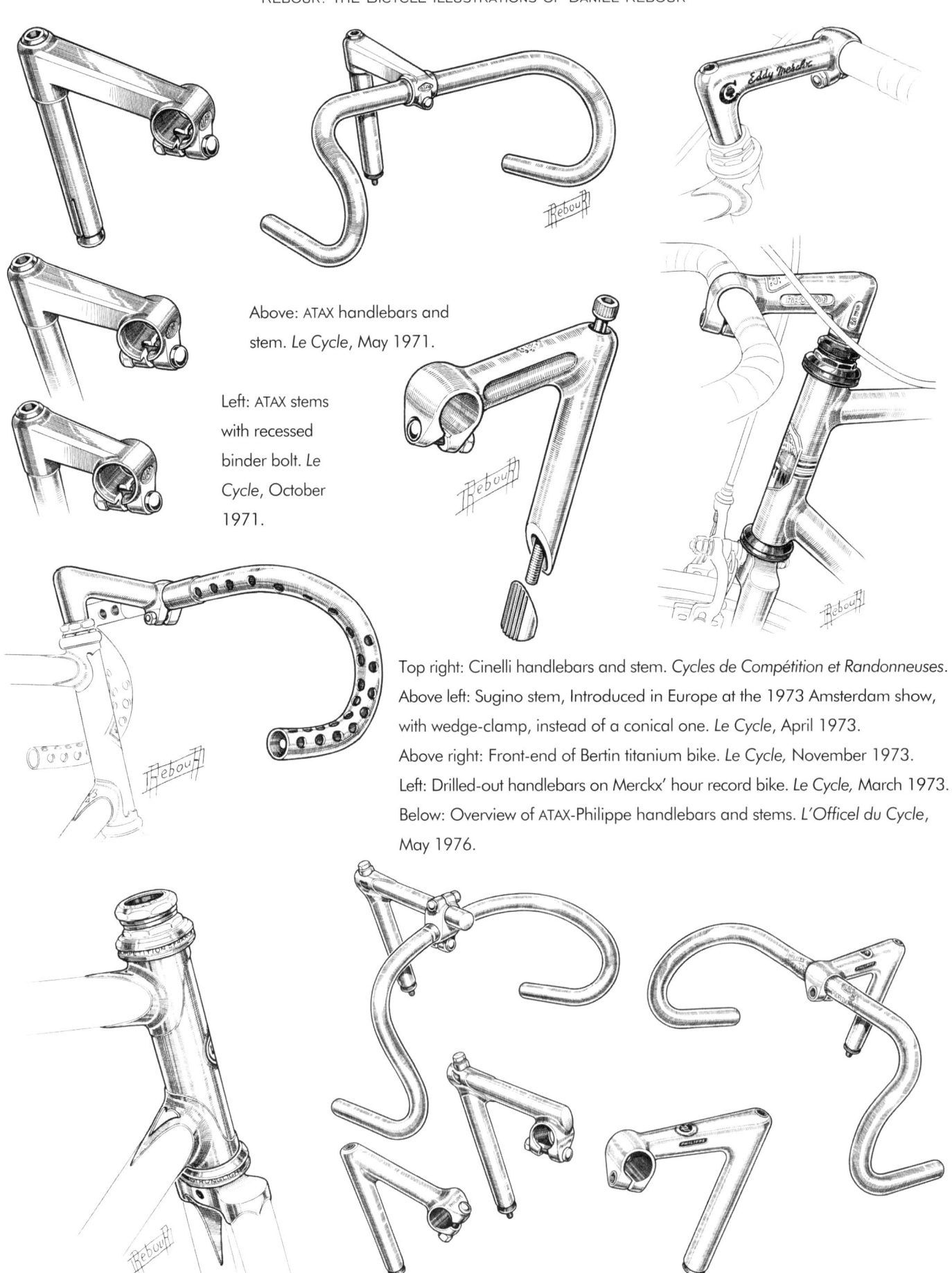

Above: ATAX handlebars and stem. *Le Cycle*, May 1971.

Left: ATAX stems with recessed binder bolt. *Le Cycle*, October 1971.

Top right: Cinelli handlebars and stem. *Cycles de Compétition et Randonneuses*.
Above left: Sugino stem, Introduced in Europe at the 1973 Amsterdam show, with wedge-clamp, instead of a conical one. *Le Cycle*, April 1973.
Above right: Front-end of Bertin titanium bike. *Le Cycle*, November 1973.
Left: Drilled-out handlebars on Merckx' hour record bike. *Le Cycle*, March 1973.
Below: Overview of ATAX-Philippe handlebars and stems. *L'Officel du Cycle*, May 1976.

Chapter 10. Steering Components

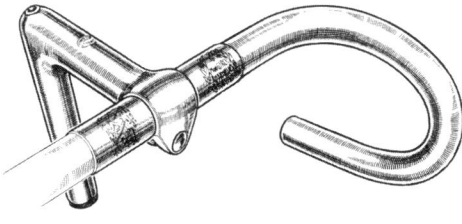

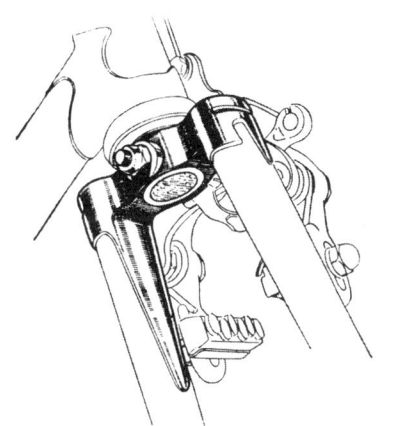

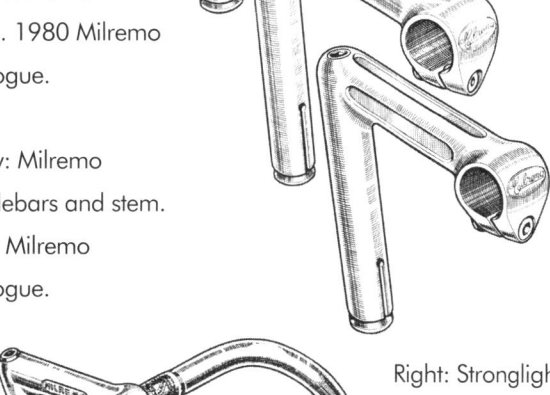

Left: Cinelli handlebar reinforcing. *Cycles de Compétition et Randonneuses.*

Right: Milremo stems. 1980 Milremo catalogue.

Below: Milremo handlebars and stem. 1980 Milremo catalogue.

Above: Cork inserted in the bottom of the fork's steerer tube to prevent corrosion. *Cycles de Compétition et Randonneuses.*

Below: Points classification winner Rik Van Looy rode this Libertas in the 1963 Tour de France. *Le Cycle*, August-September 1963.

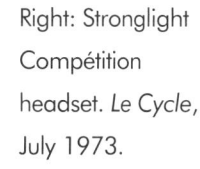

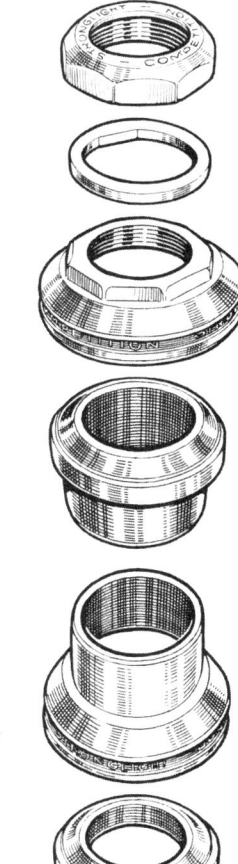

Right: Stronglight Compétition headset. *Le Cycle*, July 1973.

Left: Milremo stem and handlebars. 1980 Milremo catalogue.

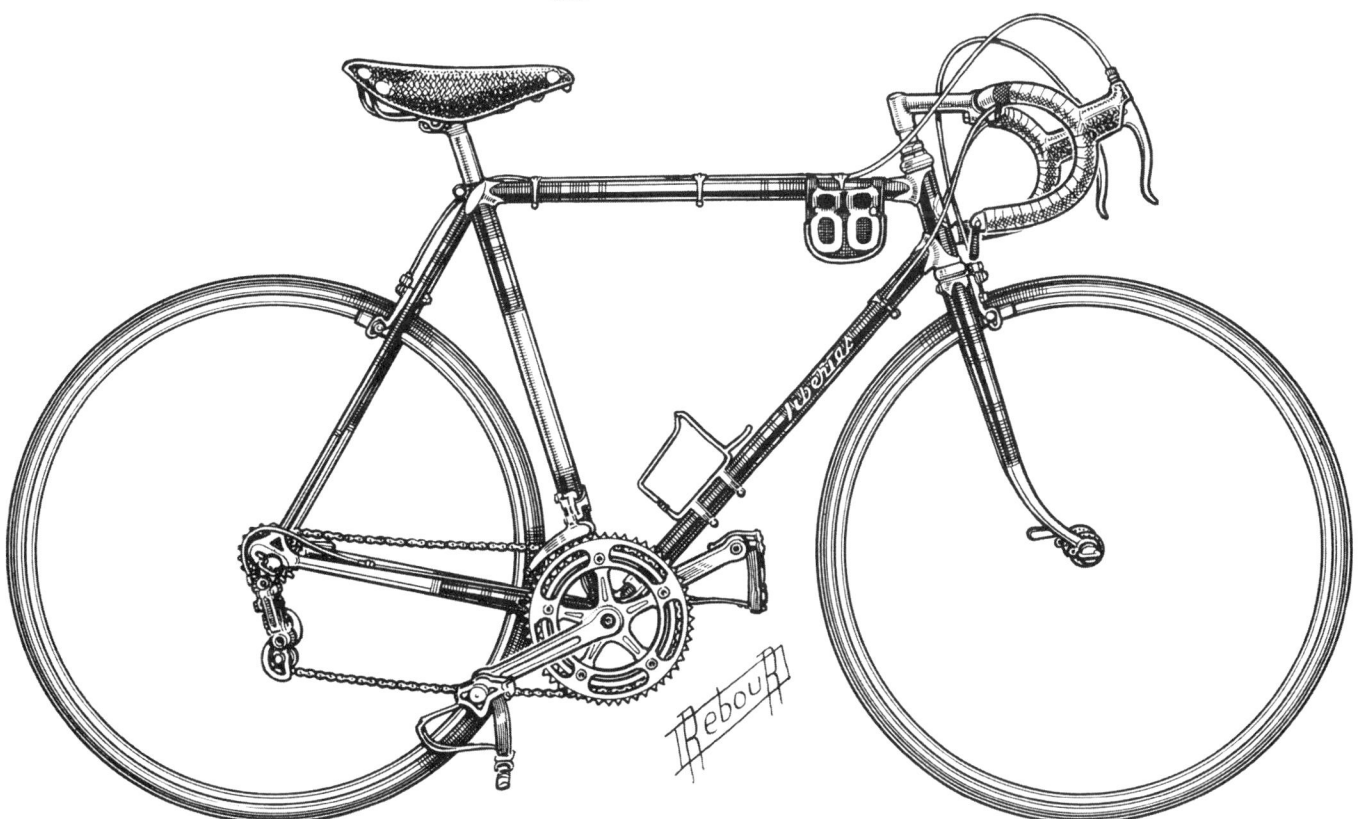

159

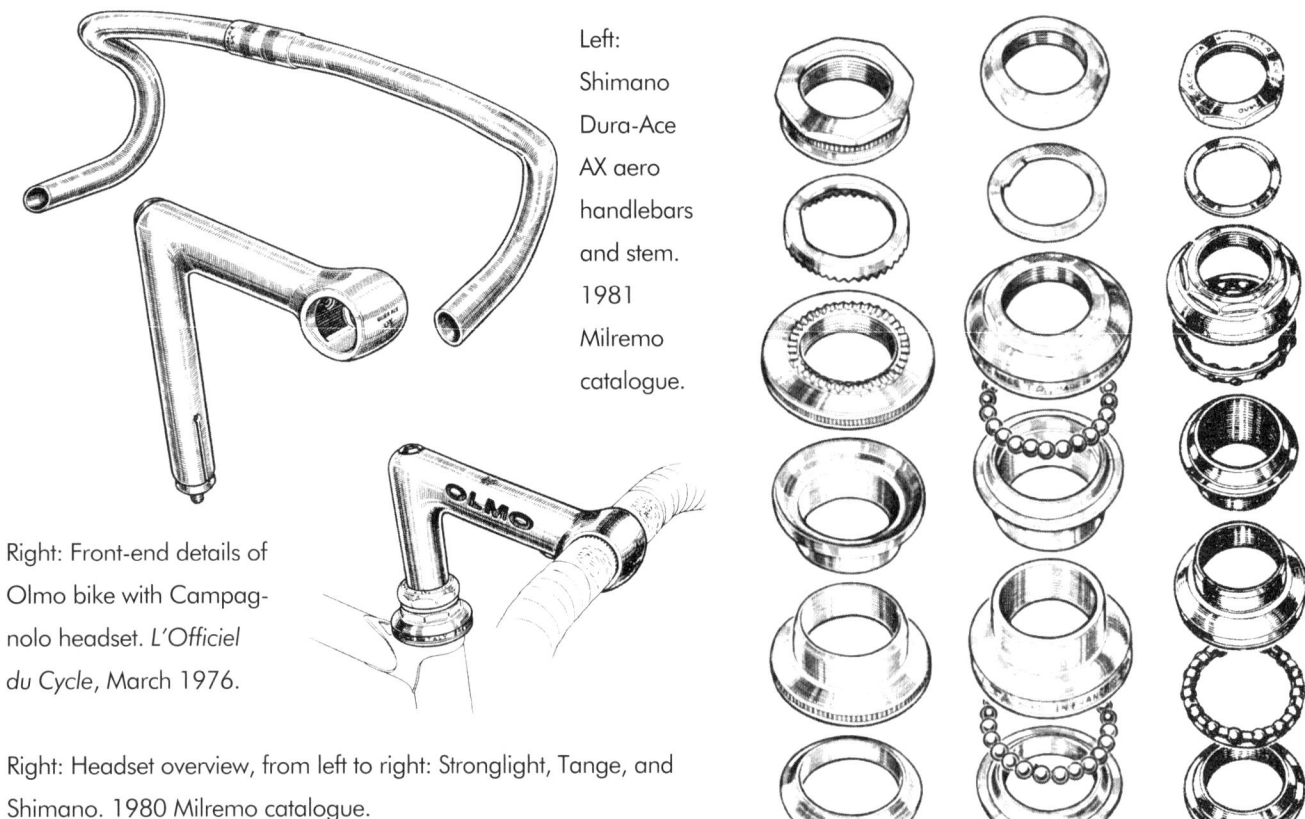

Left: Shimano Dura-Ace AX aero handlebars and stem. 1981 Milremo catalogue.

Right: Front-end details of Olmo bike with Campagnolo headset. *L'Officiel du Cycle*, March 1976.

Right: Headset overview, from left to right: Stronglight, Tange, and Shimano. 1980 Milremo catalogue.

Below: Fédérico Bahamontès won the mountains classification and 2nd place overall in the 1963 Tour de France, once again riding a Paloma bicycle. *Le Cycle*, August-September 1963.

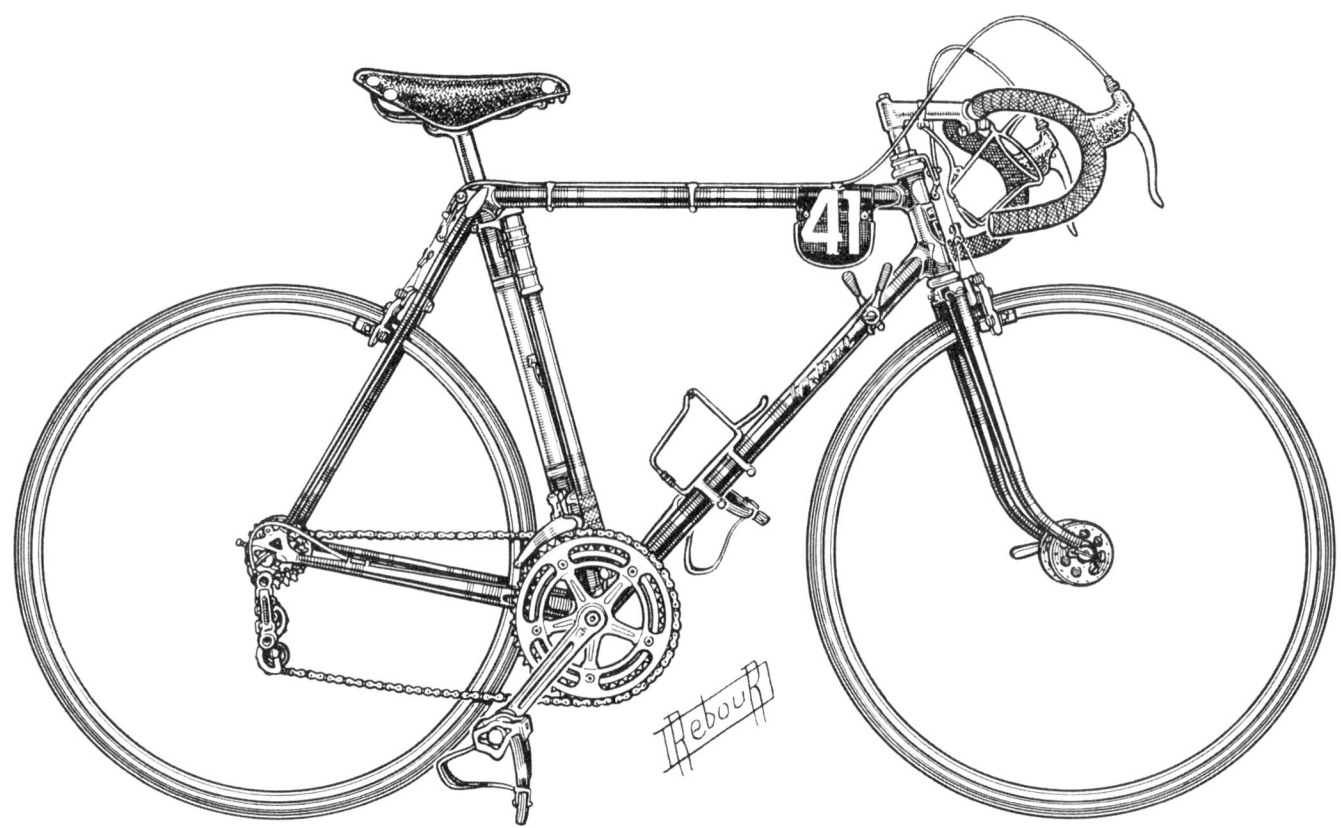

Chapter 11. Saddle and Seatpost

Rebour appeared to have a special interest in bicycle saddles. He introduced a method of pre-softening leather saddles, which was marketed by the French manufacturer Idéale, and when he did a series of articles on his visit to Raleigh in England, in 1961, he devoted an inordinate amount of space to a tour of the Brooks saddle factory. In this chapter, we have collected some of his drawings of saddles and seatposts.

Below: Jacques Anquetil won the 1963 Tour de France riding this Gitane bicycle. It is shown here equipped with Campagnolo derailleurs, hubs, and seatpost, though Anquetil usually used Simplex derailleurs. *Le Cycle*, August-September 1963.

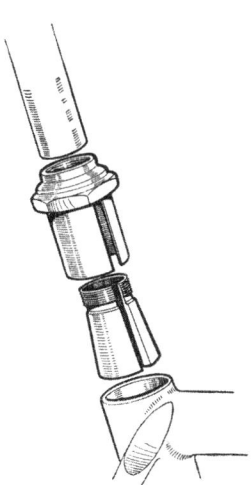

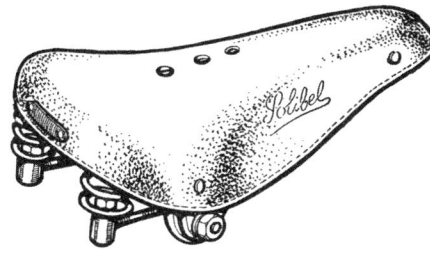

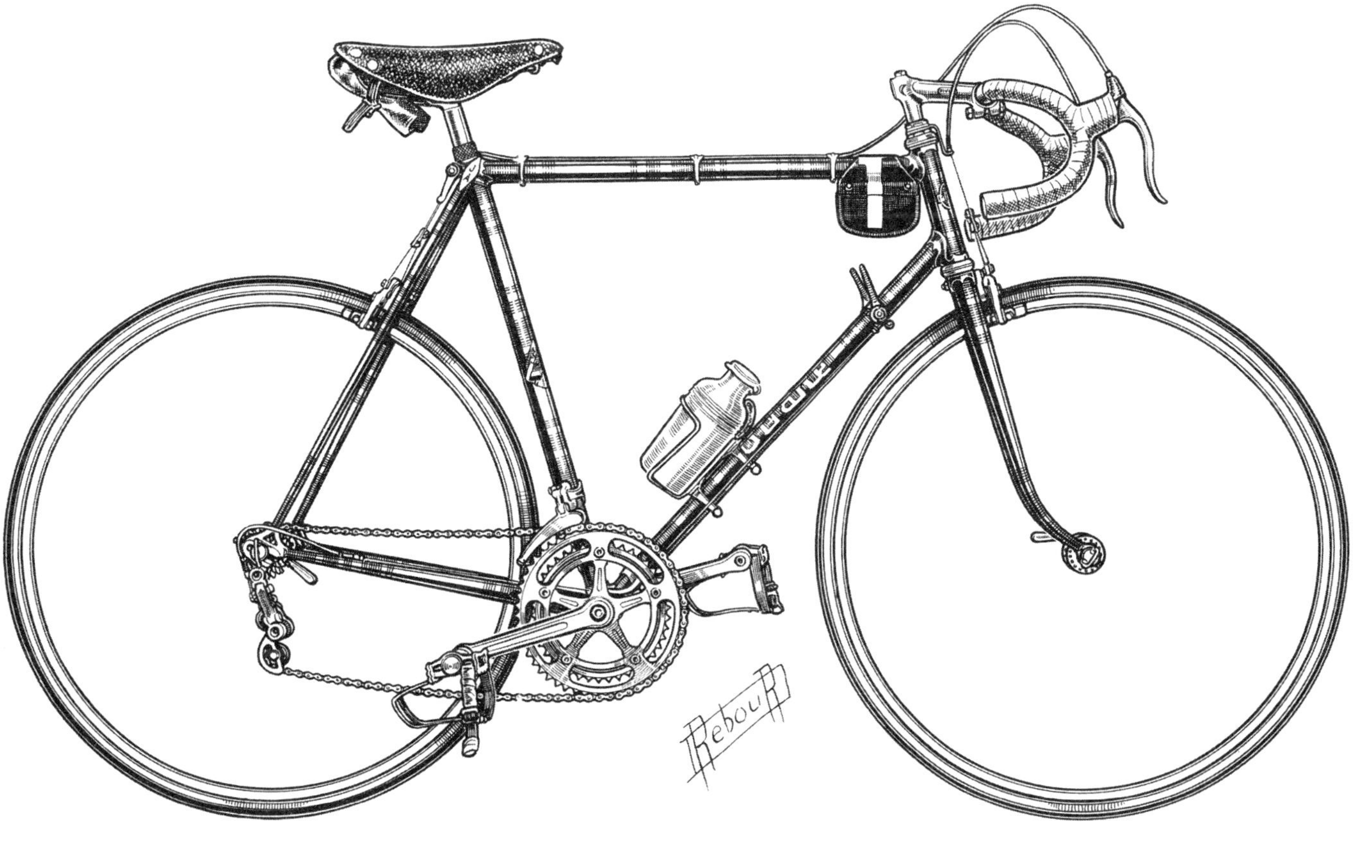

Right: Coil-spring-supported leather touring saddle. *Pratique du Vélo*.
Left: Asclip seatpost clamping detail. *Le Cycle*, 8

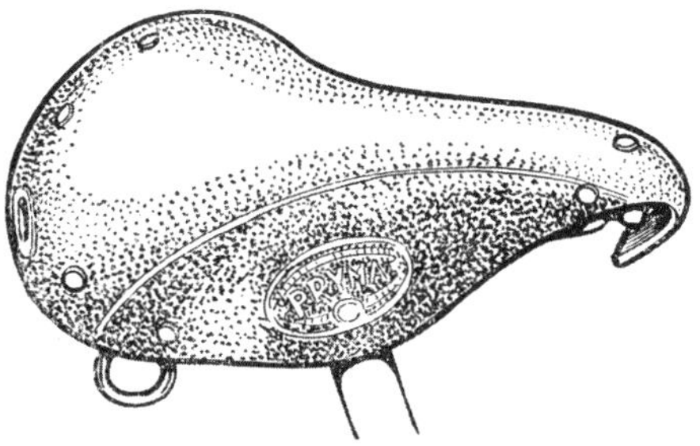

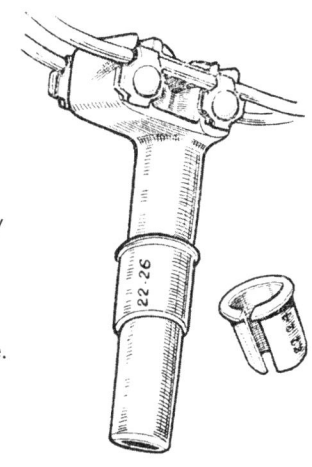

Right: Rudan seatpost and shim to fit seat-tube. *Le Cycle*, 21 July 1947.
Left: Leather ladies' saddle. *Pratique du Vélo*.

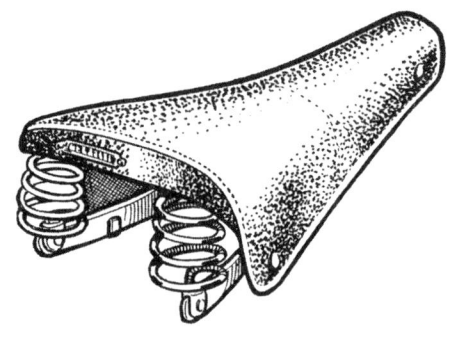
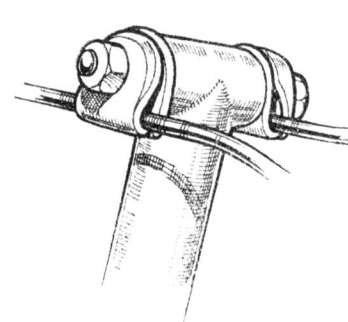
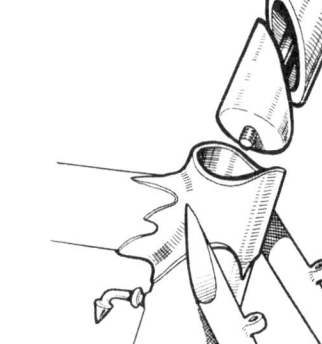

Left: Sprung city bike saddle. *Pratique du Vélo.*
Right: Seat clip detail on Alex Singer bike. *Le Cycle,* 26 January

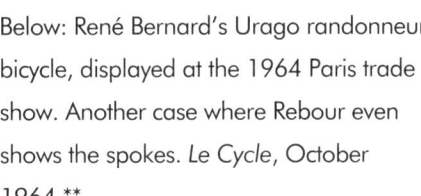

Left: Detail of fillet-brazed frame with integrated seat-post. *Pratique du Vélo.*
Right: Detail of seatpost wedge-clamp on Alex Singer bicycle. *Le Cycle,* 26 February 1949.
Below: Idéale 53 leather saddle. *Le Cycle,* 6 October 1951.
Below right: Detail of saddle nose for cyclo-cross bike. *Le Cycle,* 9 December 1950.

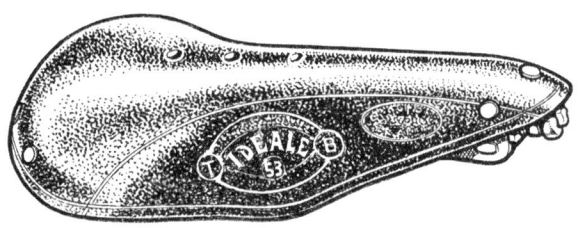
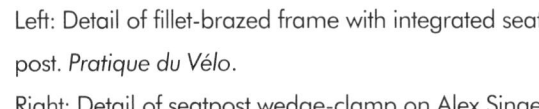

Below: René Bernard's Urago randonneur bicycle, displayed at the 1964 Paris trade show. Another case where Rebour even shows the spokes. *Le Cycle,* October 1964.**

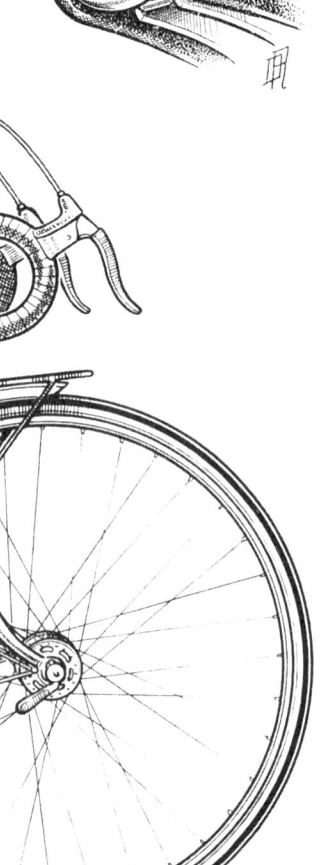

** See pages 269–271 for expanded caption text.

Chapter 11. Saddle and Seatpost

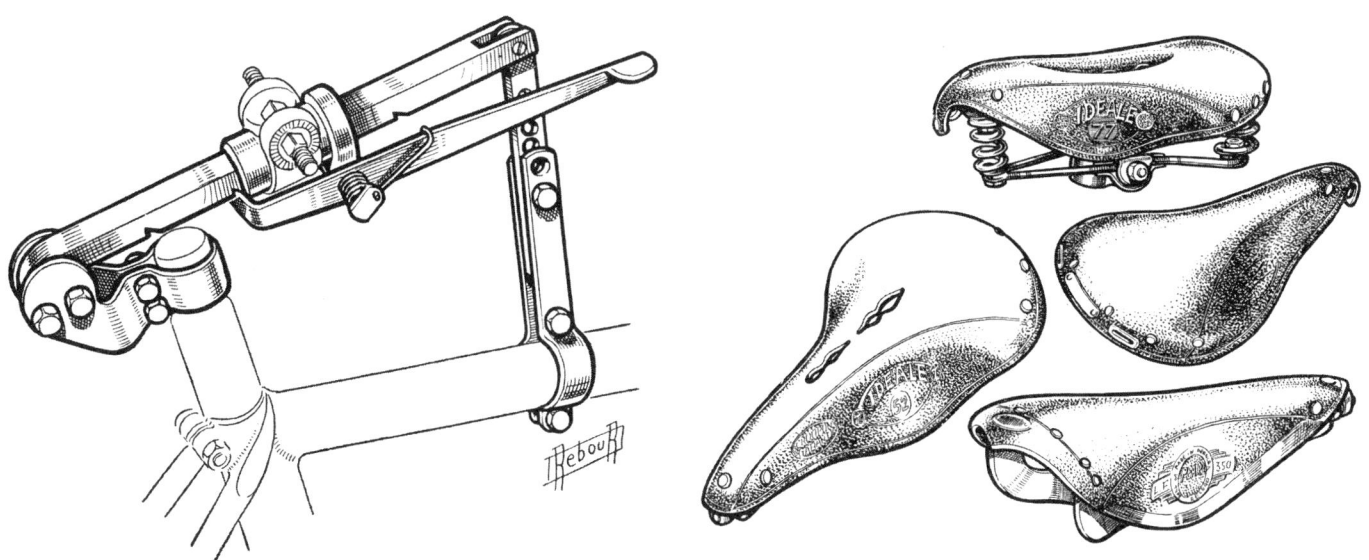

Above: Dr. Riffier's Grimpex seat adjusting device, designed to establish an optimal seat position. *Le Cycle*, 5 May 1951.
Right: Spanish BH saddle with continuous strap support. *Le Cycle*, 8 December 1951.

Below: Winner of the mountains classification in the 1965 Tour de France, Julio Jiménez' bicycle. *Le Cycle*, August-September 1965.

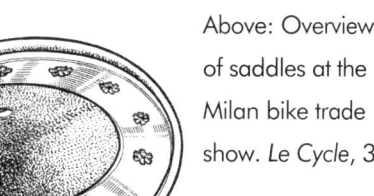

Above: Overview of saddles at the Milan bike trade show. *Le Cycle*, 3

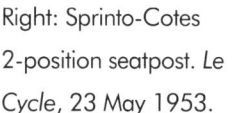

Right: Sprinto-Cotes 2-position seatpost. *Le Cycle*, 23 May 1953.

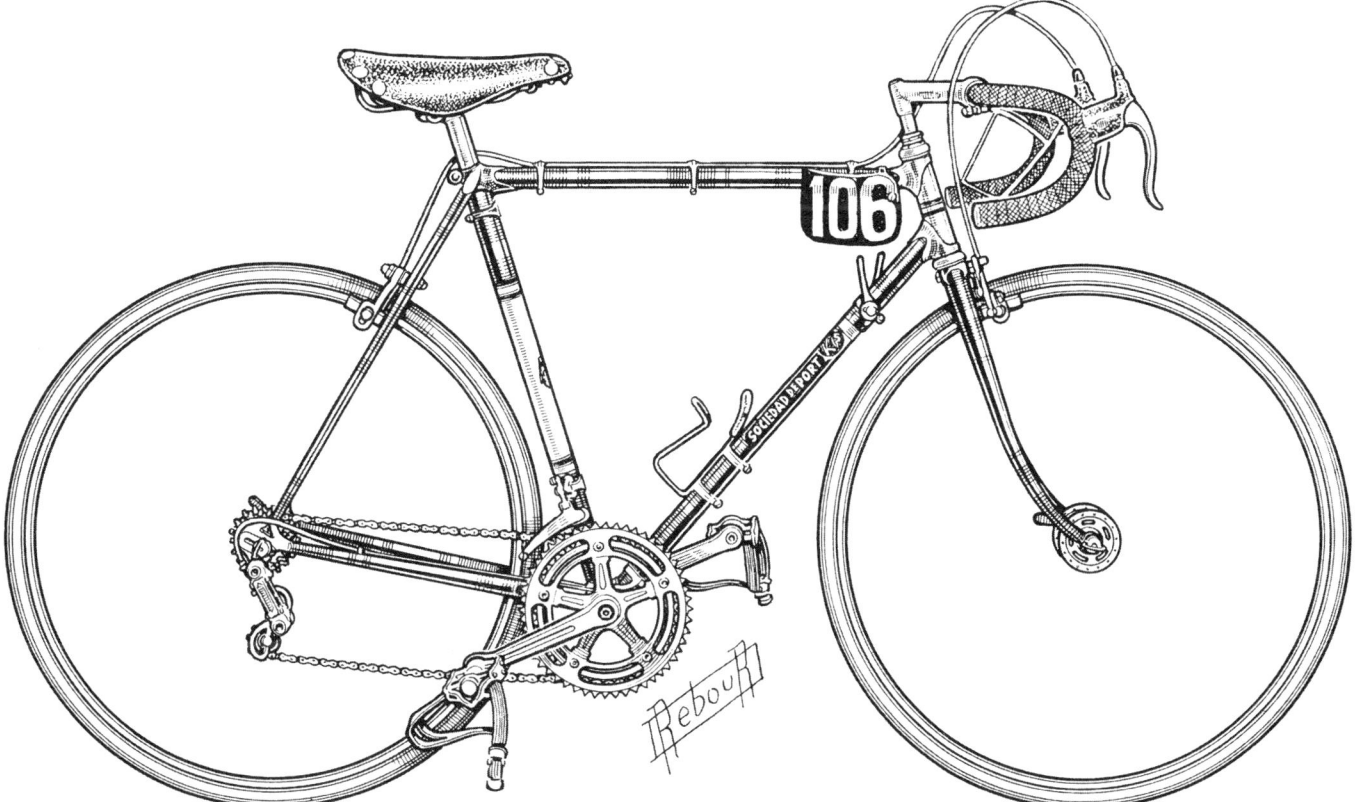

163

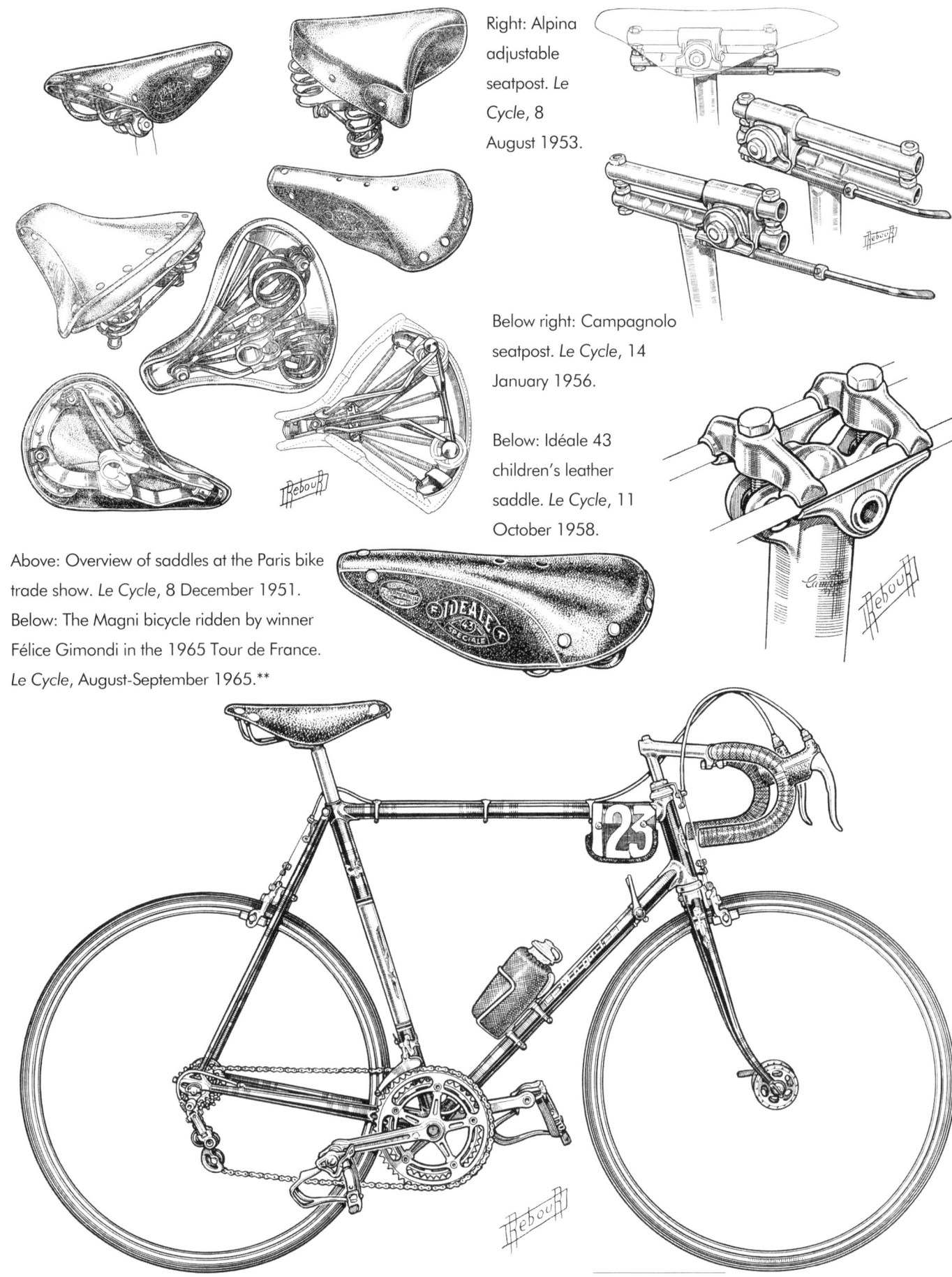

Right: Alpina adjustable seatpost. *Le Cycle*, 8 August 1953.

Below right: Campagnolo seatpost. *Le Cycle*, 14 January 1956.

Below: Idéale 43 children's leather saddle. *Le Cycle*, 11 October 1958.

Above: Overview of saddles at the Paris bike trade show. *Le Cycle*, 8 December 1951.
Below: The Magni bicycle ridden by winner Félice Gimondi in the 1965 Tour de France. *Le Cycle*, August-September 1965.**

** See pages 269–271 for expanded caption text.

Chapter 11. Saddle and Seatpost

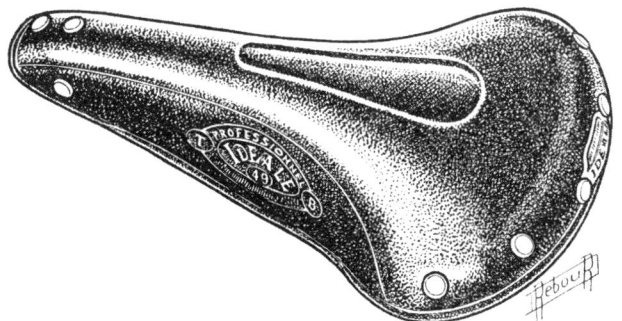

Idéale 49 women's leather saddle, with recess to prevent pressure in a sensitive area. *Le Cycle*, 7 October 1954.

Right: Campagnolo seatpost details. *Le Cycle*, 28 July 1956.

Below: Simplex adjustable seat clip. *Le Cycle*, 11 October 1958.

Below right: Brooks leather saddle, seen from below. *Le Cycle*, October 1961.

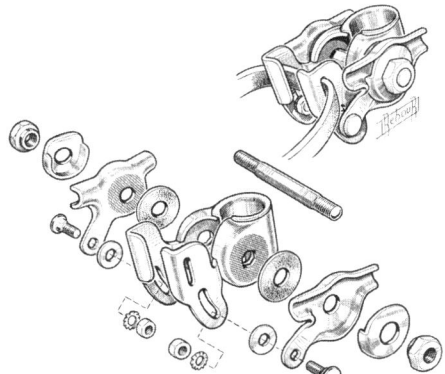

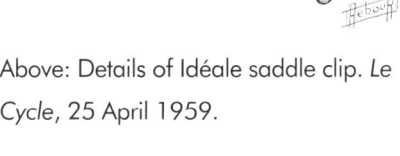

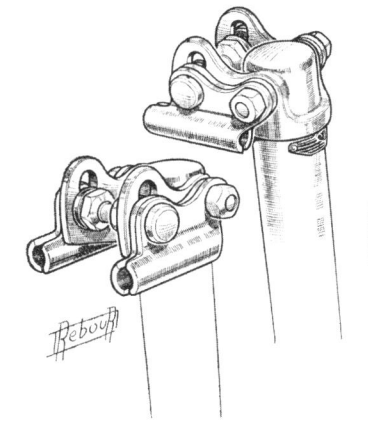

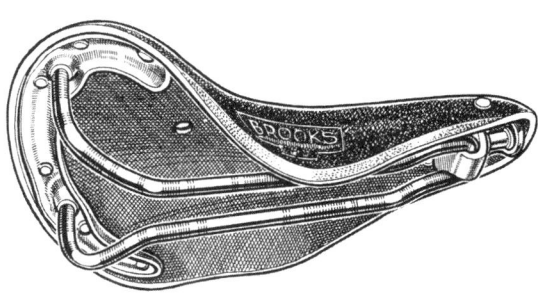

Above: Details of Idéale saddle clip. *Le Cycle*, 25 April 1959.

Below: 1965 Tour de France second-placed Raymond Poulidor's Mercier bike. *Le Cycle*, August-September 1965.**

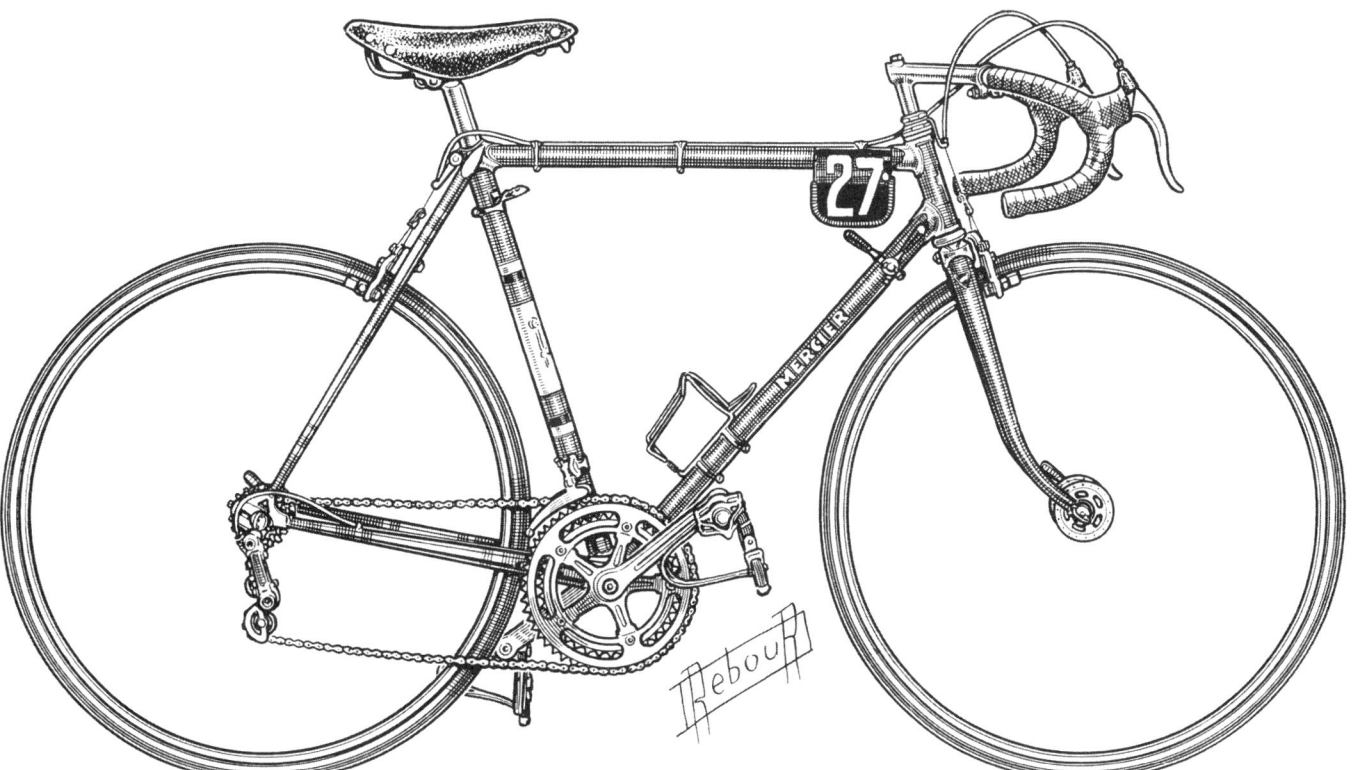

** See pages 269–271 for expanded caption text.

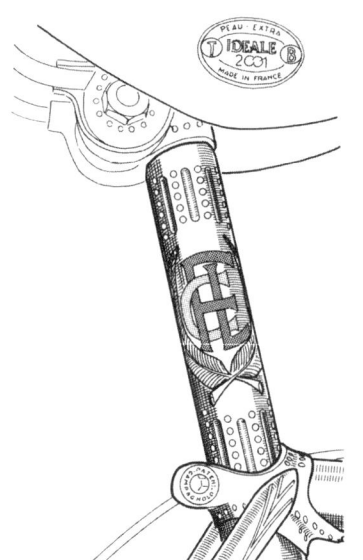
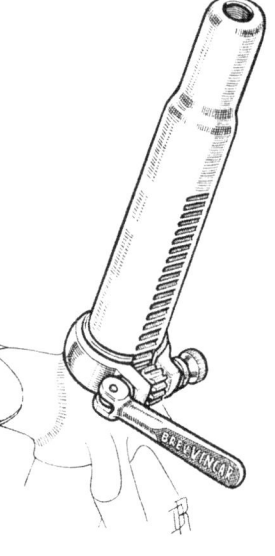
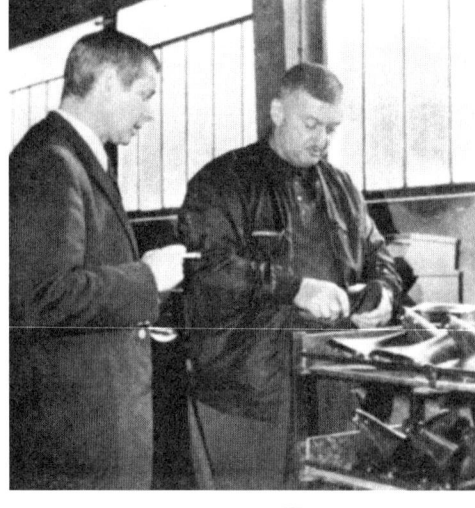

Above left: France-Loire lightened seatpost detail. *L'Officiel du Cycle*, December 1975. Above right: Vincar ratchet-adjustable seatpost. *Le Cycle*, 28 August 1954.

Right and below: Daniel Rebour's signature appeared on Idéale leather saddles softened following his proprietary technique, which he demonstrates in the photo. *Le Cycle*, December 1968 (photo) and May 1969 (drawing).

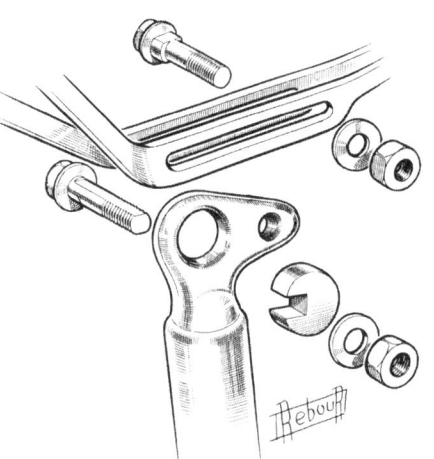

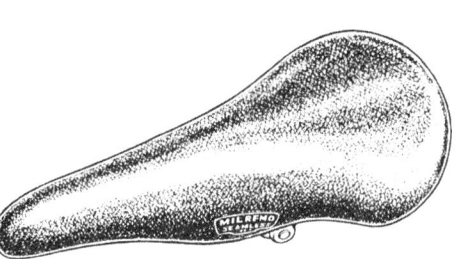

Left: Unica saddle adjusting detail. *Le Cycle*, Sept. 1960. Right: Milremo plastic saddle. 1976 Milremo catalogue.

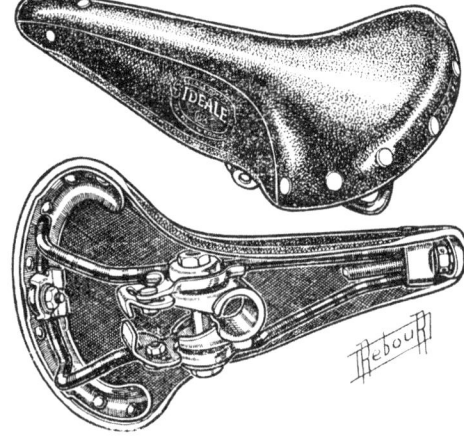

Left: Idéale 88 leather touring saddle. *Cycles de Compétition et Randonneuses*.

Right: Nittor adjustable seatpost. *Le Cycle*, June 1962.

Right: 3-TTT saddle with thin leather cover over plastic base. *Cycles de Compétition et Randonneuses*.

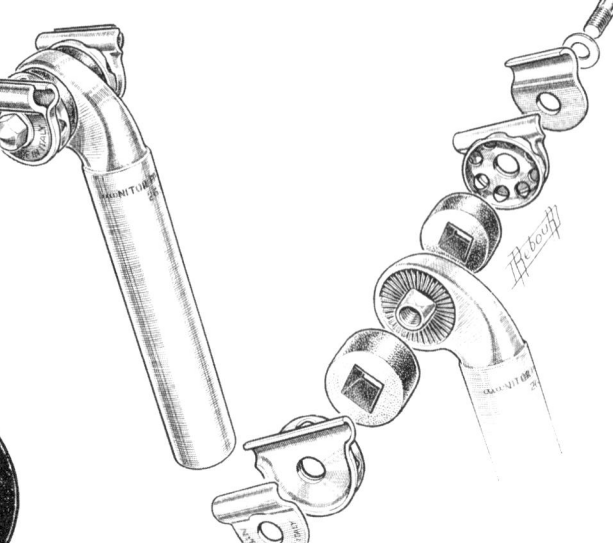

CHAPTER 11. SADDLE AND SEATPOST

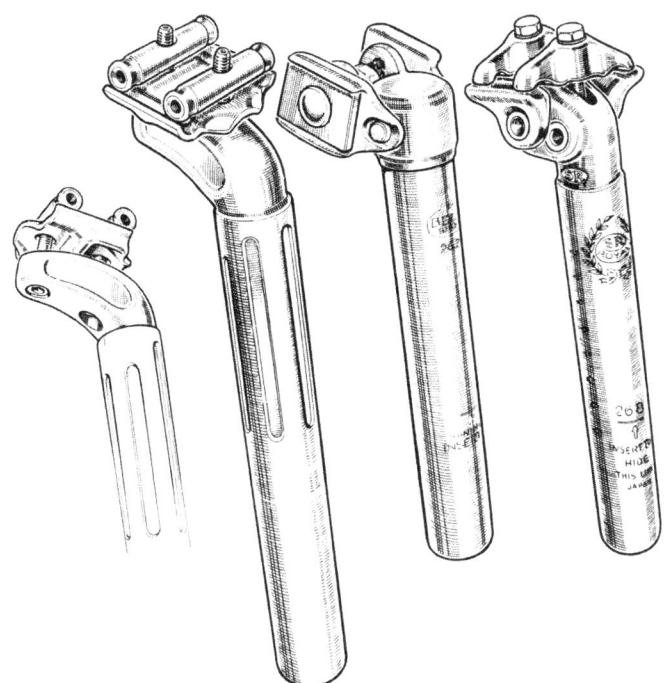

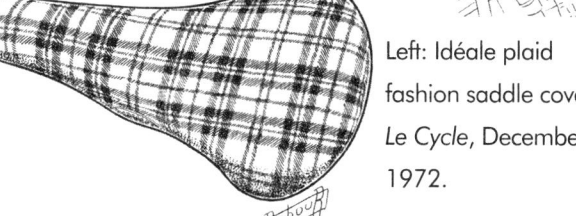

Right: Ladies' saddle designed to be used with a tight skirt, as was not uncommon in Amsterdam, where this Lemmer Rok saddle was introduced. *Le Cycle*, March 1964.

Left: Idéale plaid fashion saddle cover. *Le Cycle*, December 1972.

Above: Assortment of micro-adjustable seatposts available in 1975. *Le Monde de Daniel Rebour*.

Right: Brooks Professional leather saddle, with big brass rivets. *Le Monde de Daniel Rebour*.

Below: Sauvage-Lejeune machine of 1965 Tour de France points classification winner Jan Janssen. *Le Cycle*, August-September 1965.

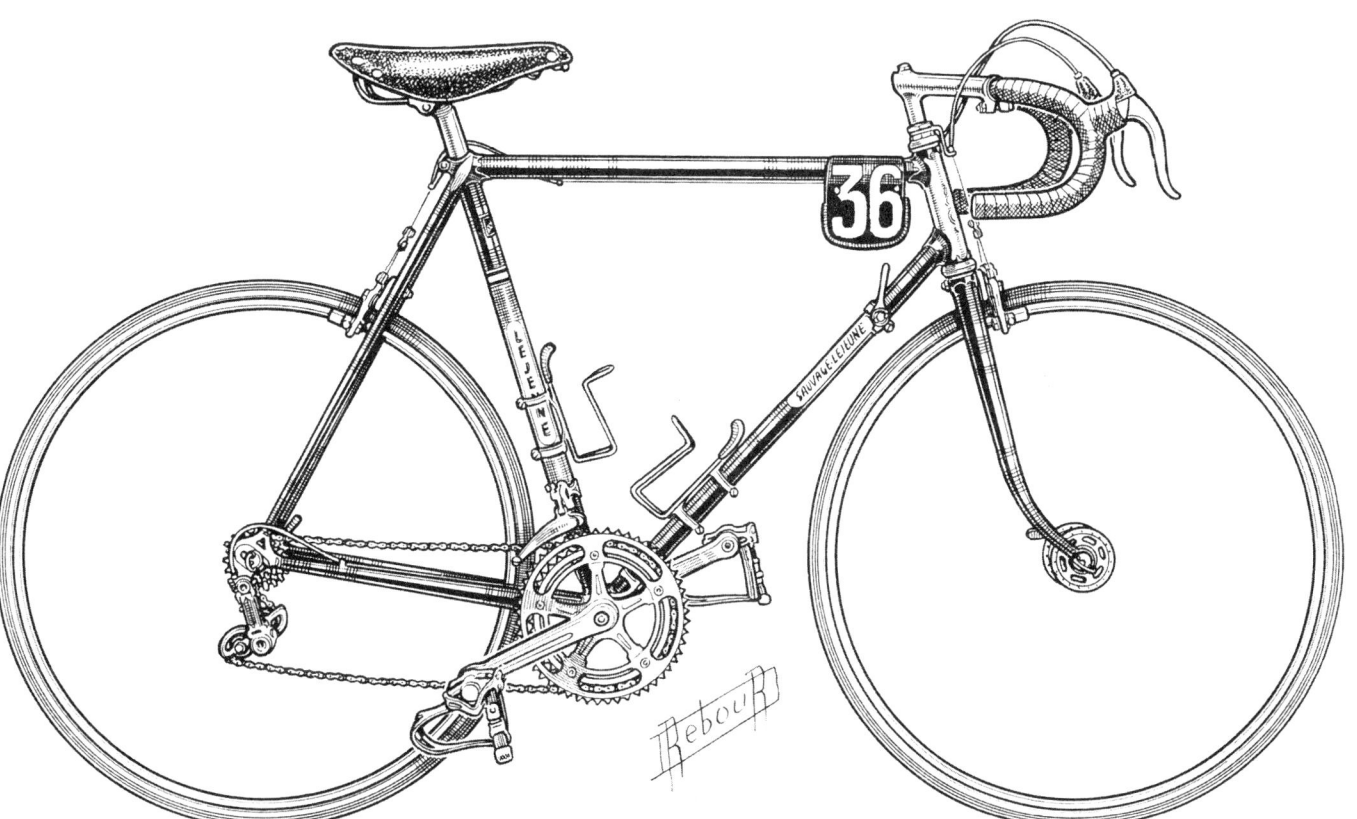

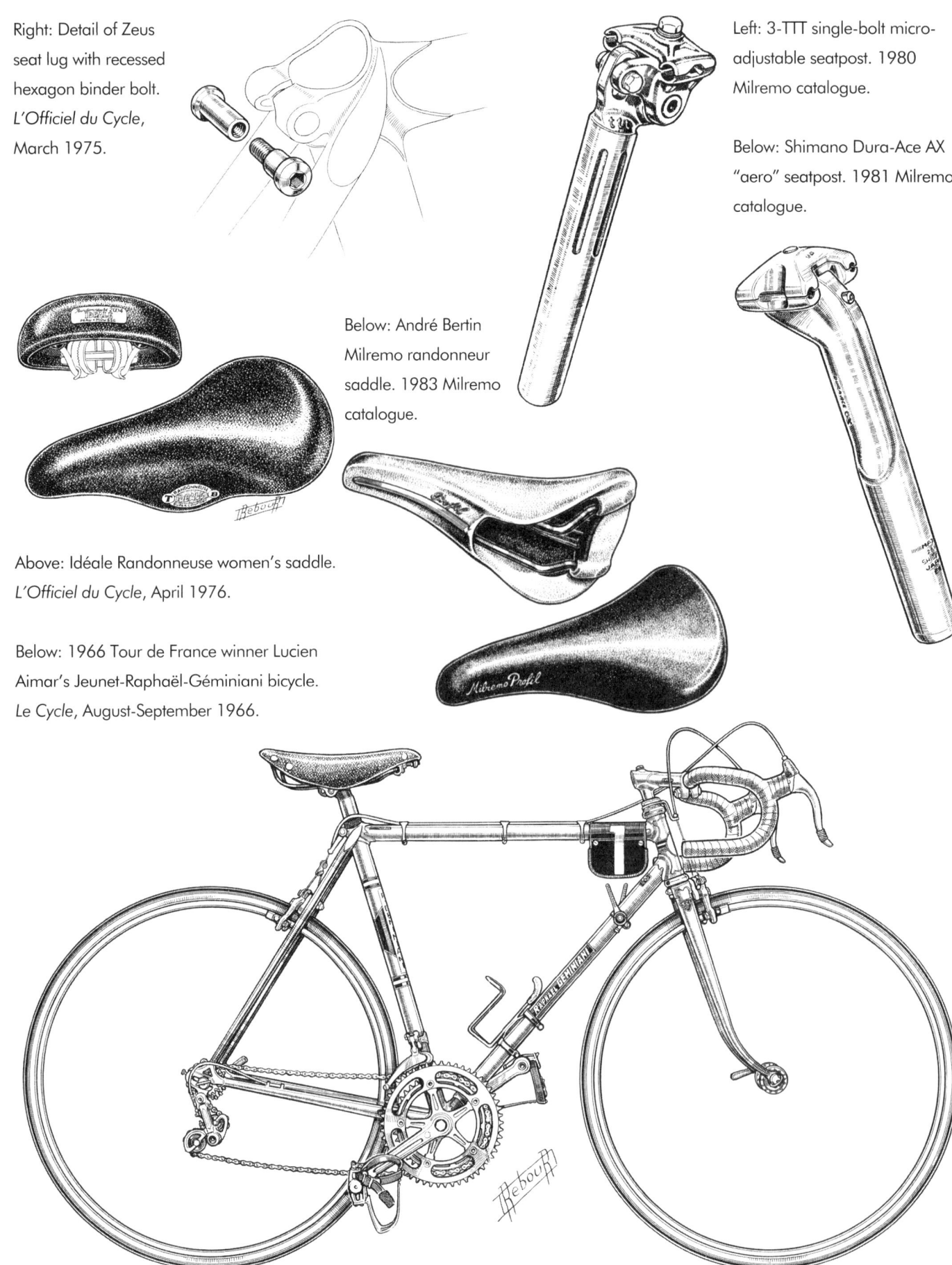

Right: Detail of Zeus seat lug with recessed hexagon binder bolt. *L'Officiel du Cycle*, March 1975.

Left: 3-TTT single-bolt micro-adjustable seatpost. 1980 Milremo catalogue.

Below: Shimano Dura-Ace AX "aero" seatpost. 1981 Milremo catalogue.

Below: André Bertin Milremo randonneur saddle. 1983 Milremo catalogue.

Above: Idéale Randonneuse women's saddle. *L'Officiel du Cycle*, April 1976.

Below: 1966 Tour de France winner Lucien Aimar's Jeunet-Raphaël-Géminiani bicycle. *Le Cycle*, August-September 1966.

Chapter 12. Component Gruppos

The concept of component groups seems to have been first introduced by the Italian manufacturer Campagnolo, and that's why, at least in the U.S., they're often referred to by the Italian term *gruppo*, rather than the English term group-set. Whereas other manufacturers tended to specialize in a limited number of component types, Campagnolo decided to offer a more complete package. Soon, other manufacturers followed suit (and some combined forces with other specialists). In this chapter, we have collected some of the drawings of complete groups of such components.

Right: Shimano Keirin track component gruppo with 10 mm pitch chain. 1979 Milremo catalogue.
Below: 1966 mountains classification winner Julio Jiménez, riding for the same team as Aimar, also rode a Raphaël-Géminiani-branded Jeunet bicycle, with a complete Campagnolo gruppo. *Le Cycle*, August-September 1966.

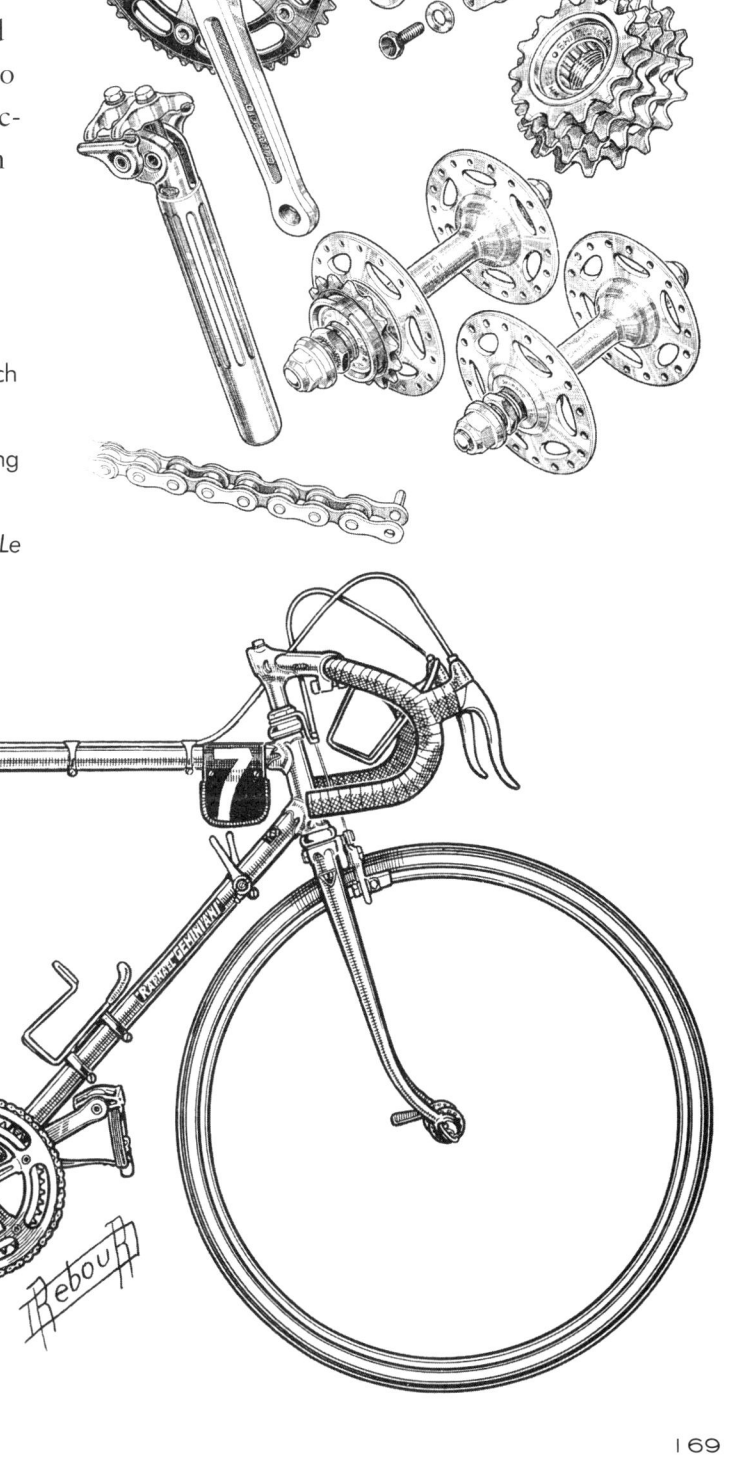

This page: Campagnolo Record product overview in Campagnolo advertisement. *Le Cycle*, December 1966.

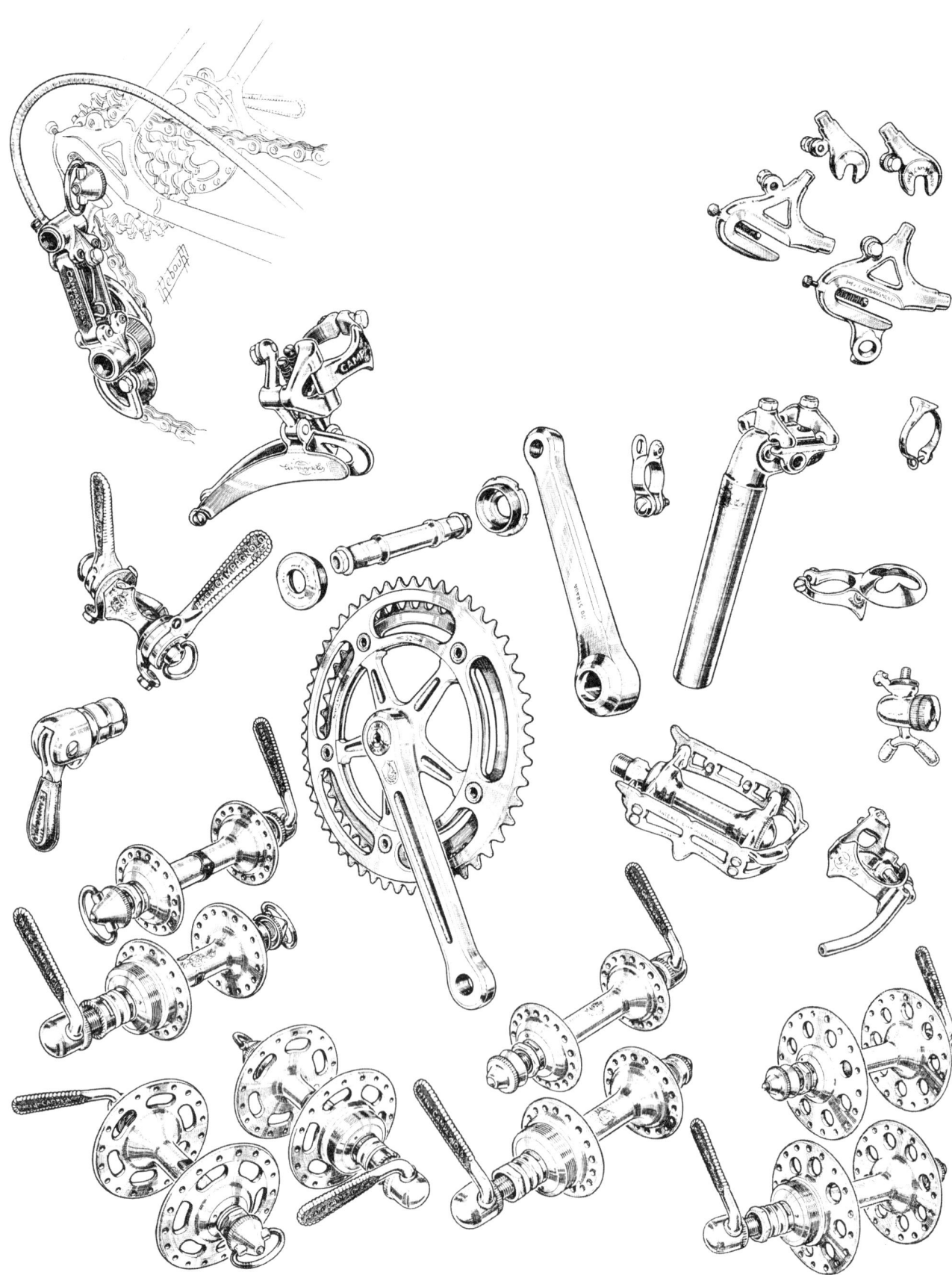

Below and right: 1975 product gruppo overview in Shimano advertisement. *L'Officiel du Cycle*, May 1975.

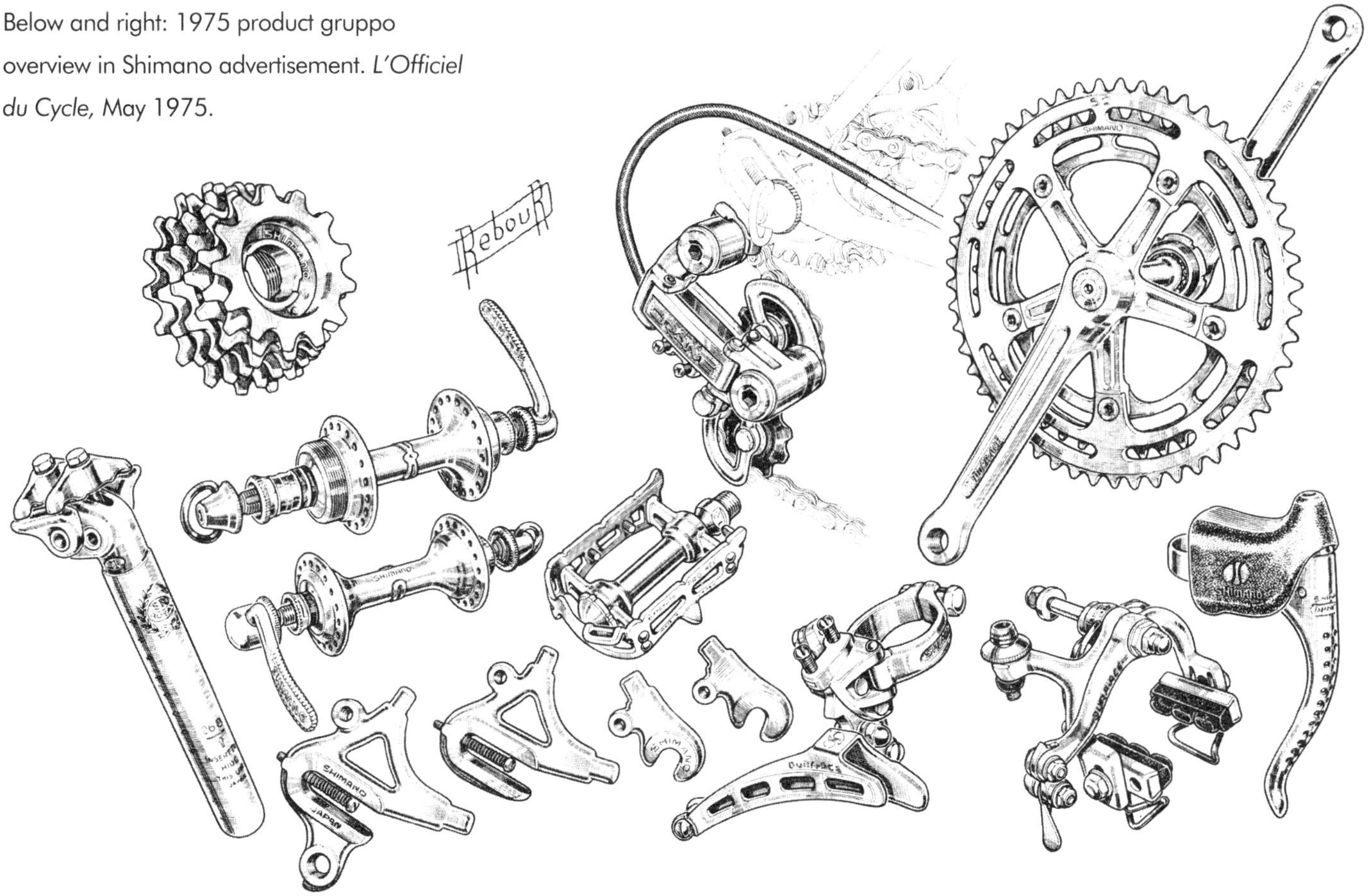

Below: In the 1966 Tour de France, "eternal second" Raymond Poulidor didn't come second but third, riding this Mercier bicycle. At least this French bike still uses a French Stronglight crankset, Mafac brakes, and Simplex derailleurs. *Le Cycle*, August-September 1966.

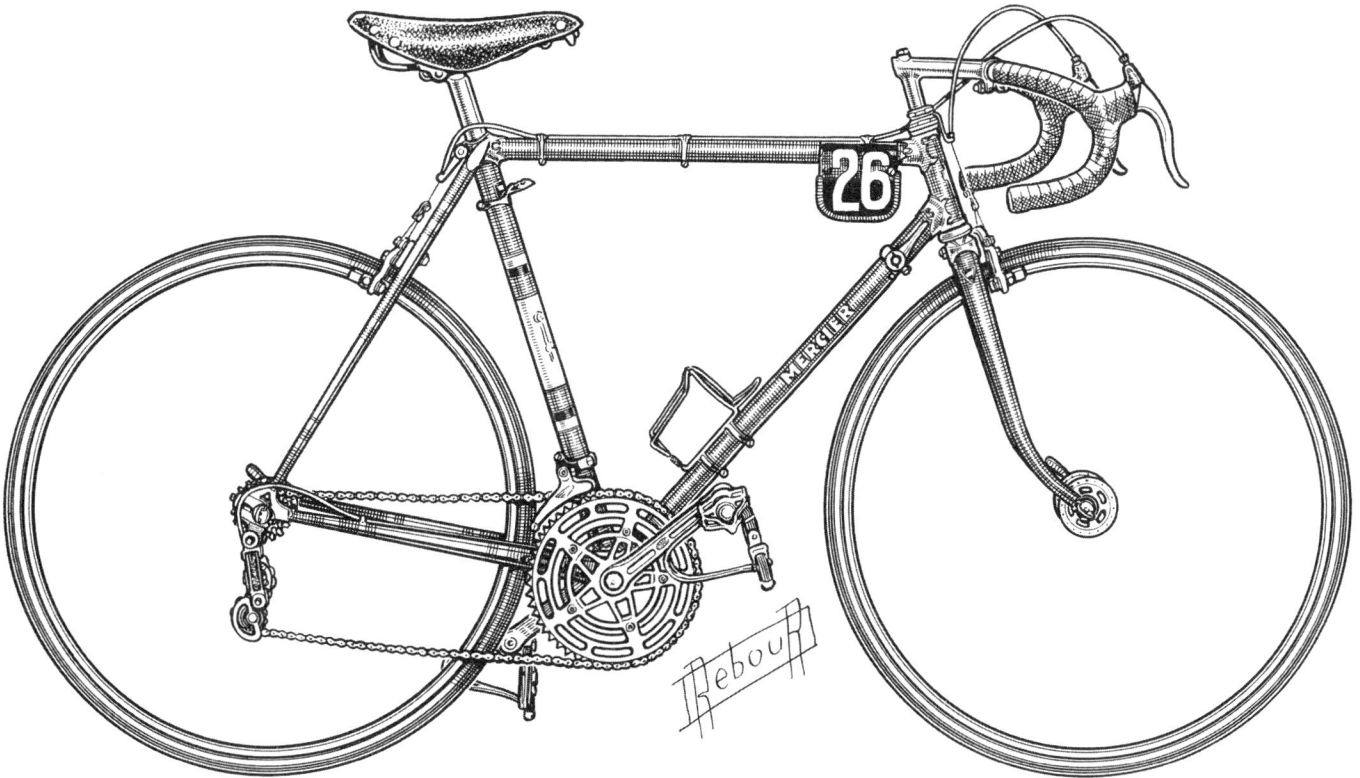

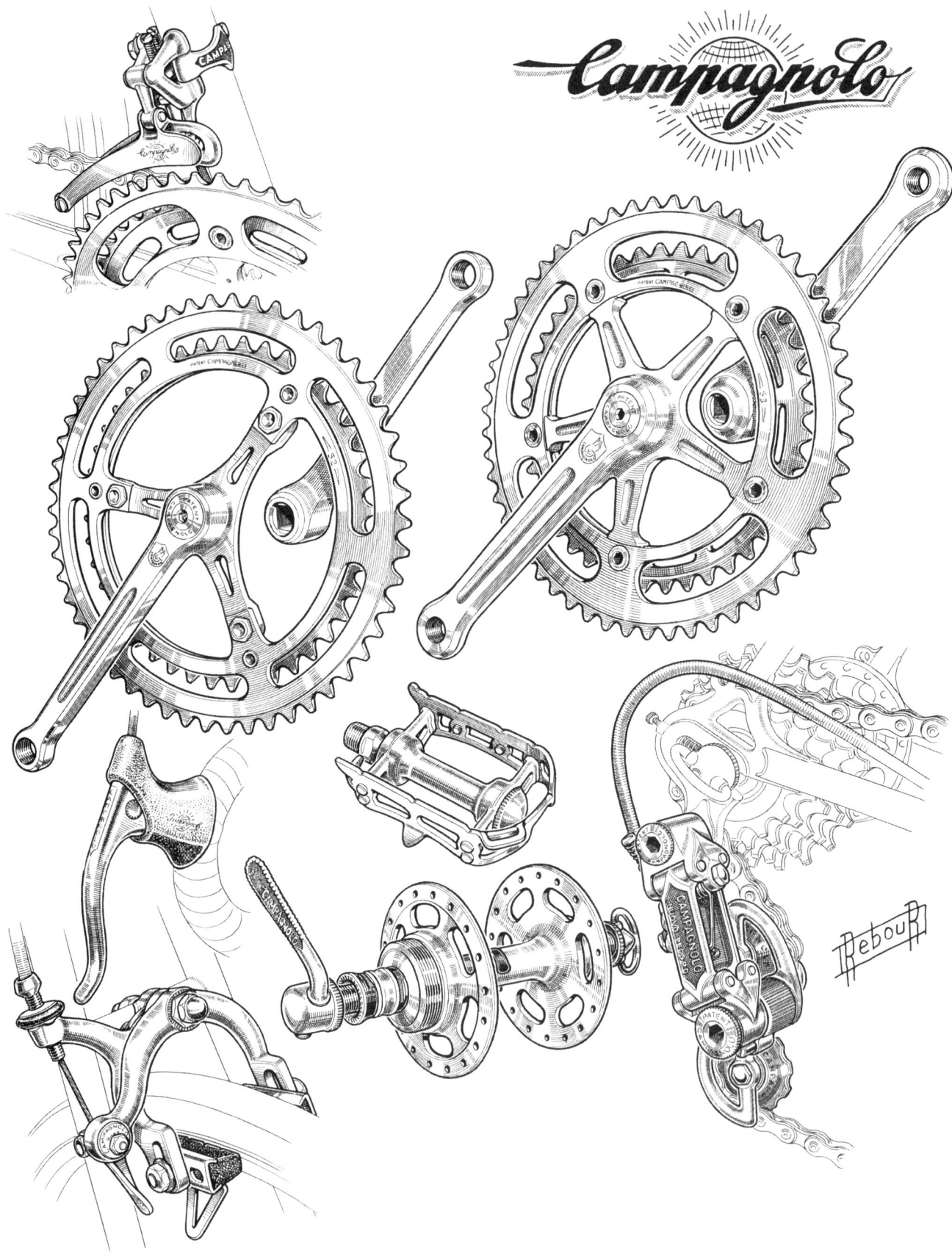

This page: Campagnolo product overview, including 3-arm Sport crankset as well as the 5-arm Nuovo Record version. Campagnolo advertisement in *Le Cycle*, October 1973.

Chapter 12. Component Gruppos

Below and right: The first Shimano 600 component gruppo, as drawn for Shimano advertisement in *L'Officiel du Cycle*, October 1976.

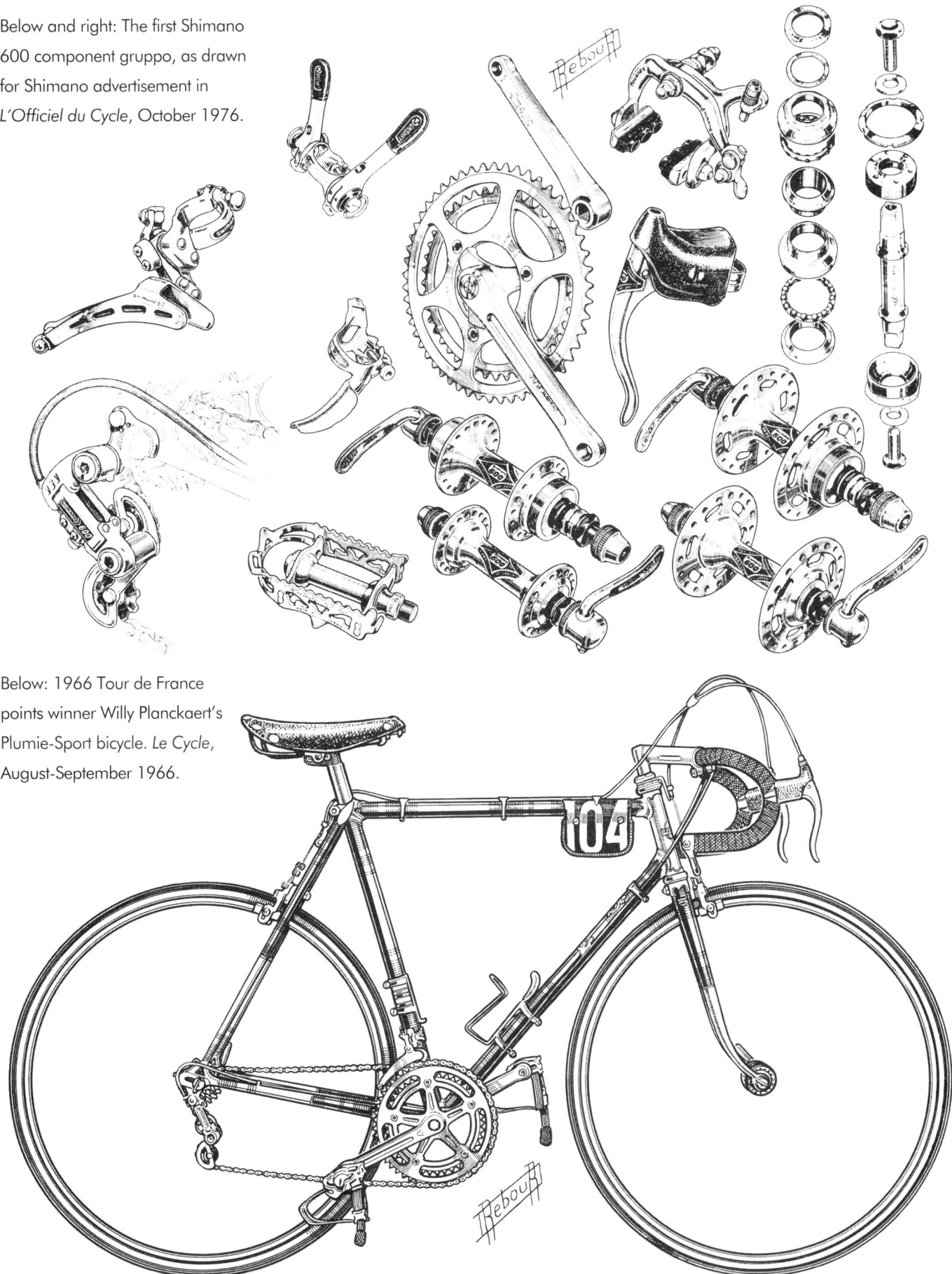

Below: 1966 Tour de France points winner Willy Planckaert's Plumie-Sport bicycle. *Le Cycle*, August-September 1966.

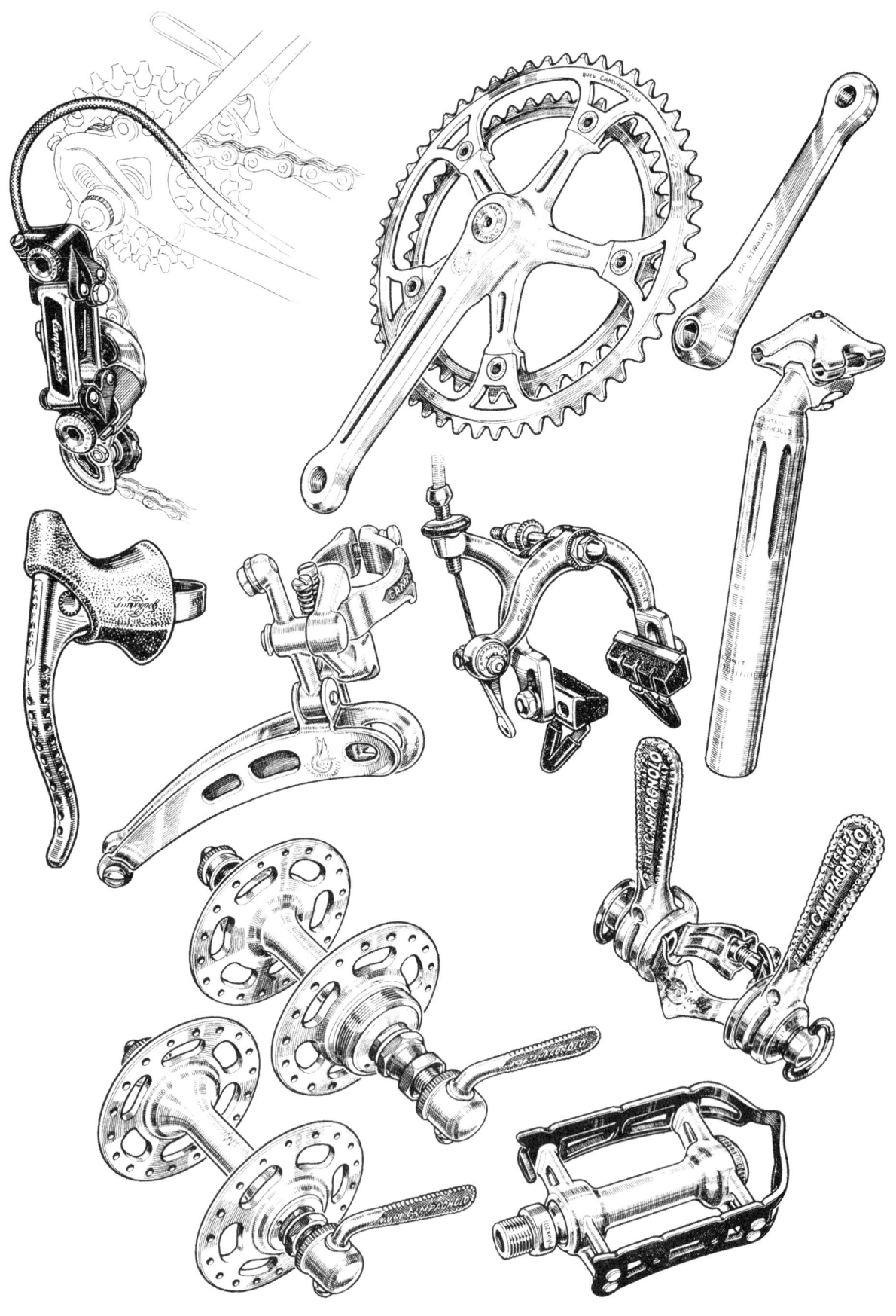

Campagnolo Super-Legere, or "super-light," component gruppo, including titanium minor parts. 1981 Milremo catalogue.

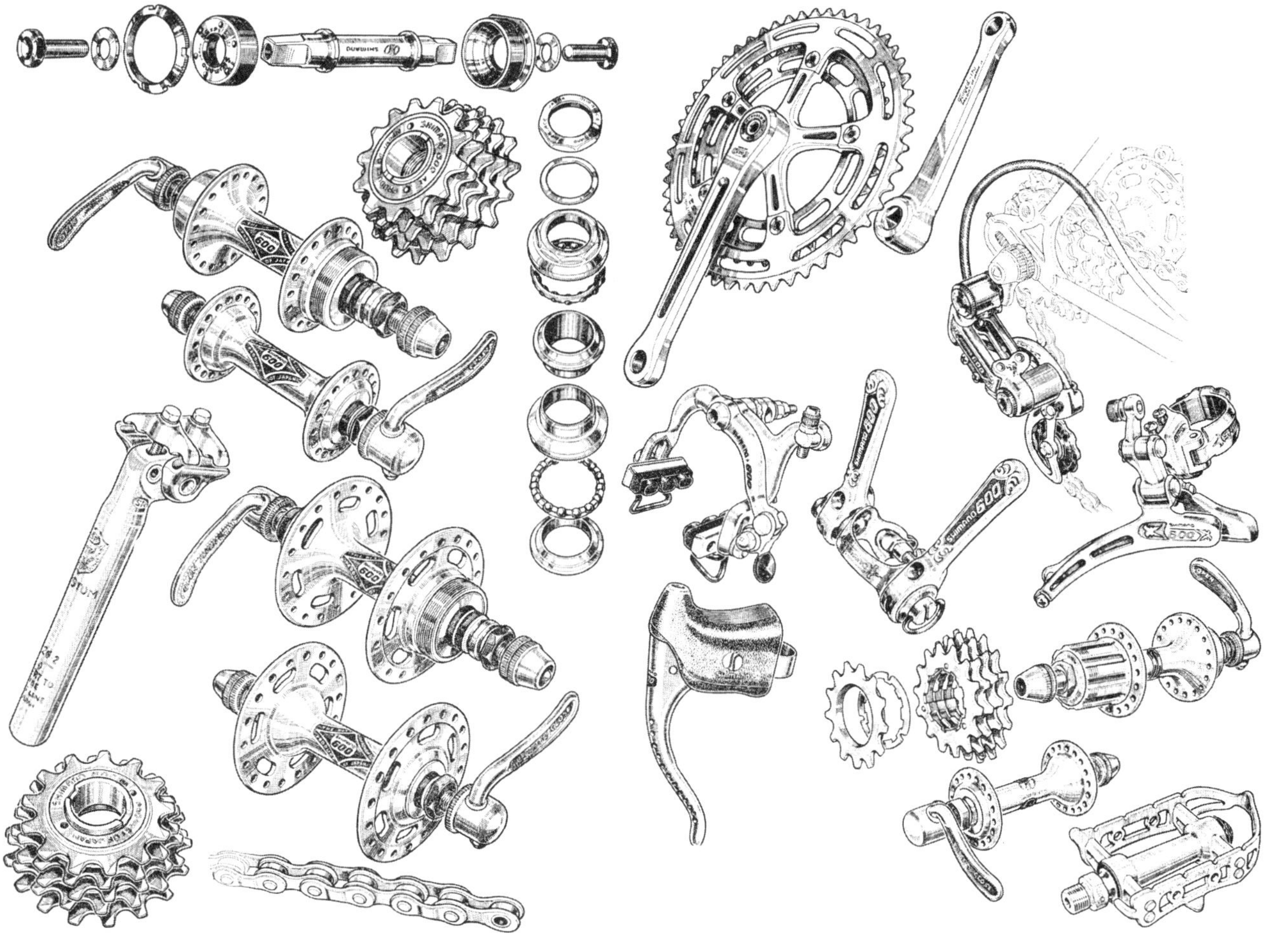

Above: Shimano 600 EX component gruppo. 1980 Milremo catalogue.

Below: Jan Janssen, second in the 1966 Tour de France, rode this Sauvage-Lejeune machine. *Le Cycle*, August-September 1966.

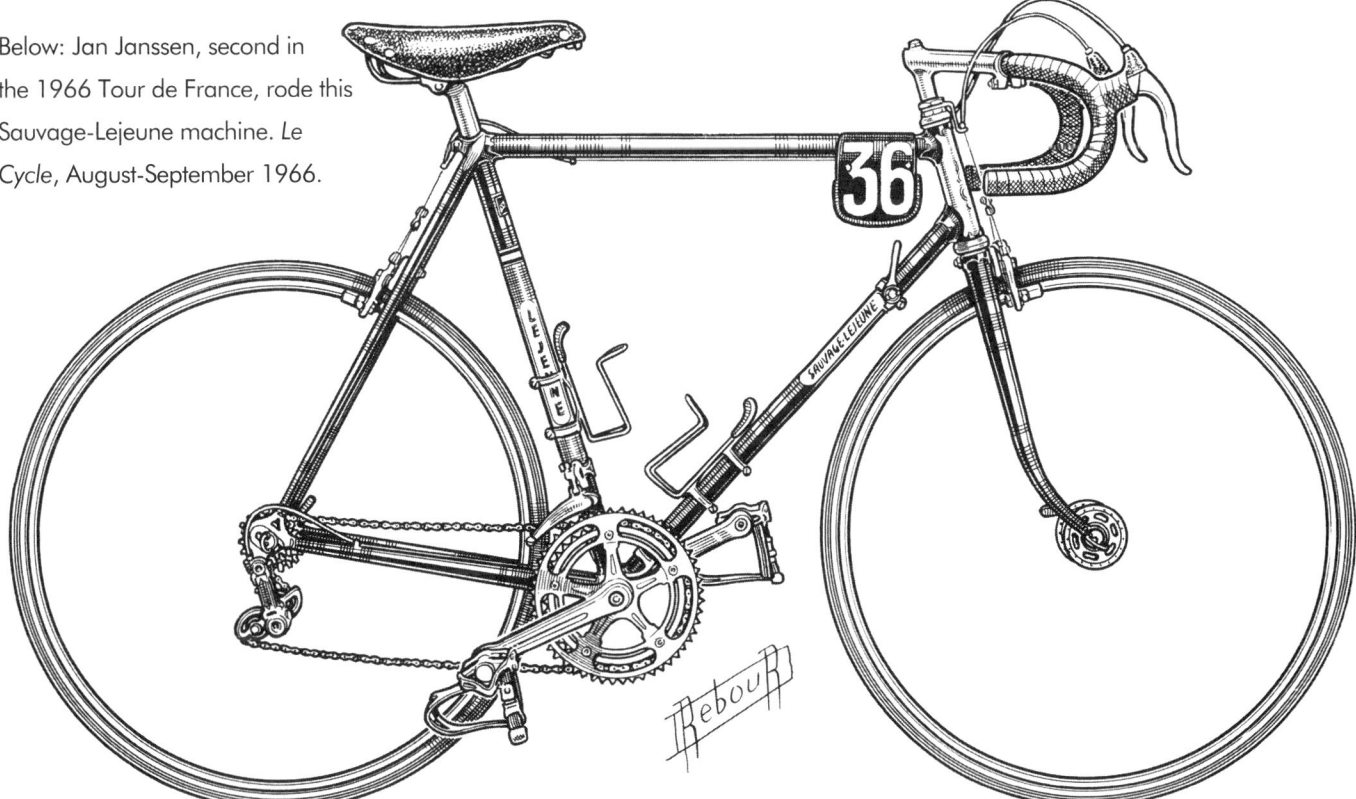

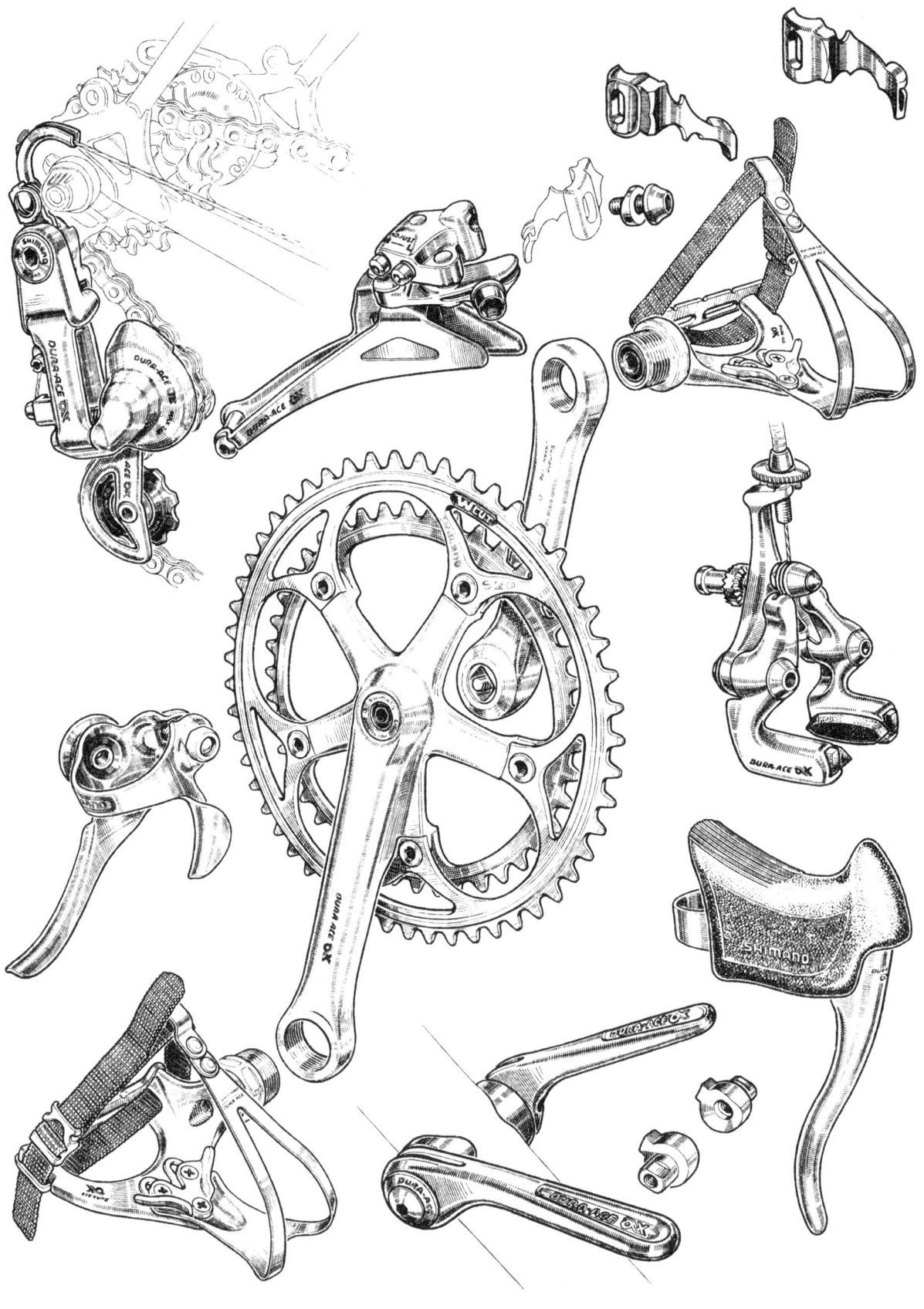

Chapter 12. Component Gruppos

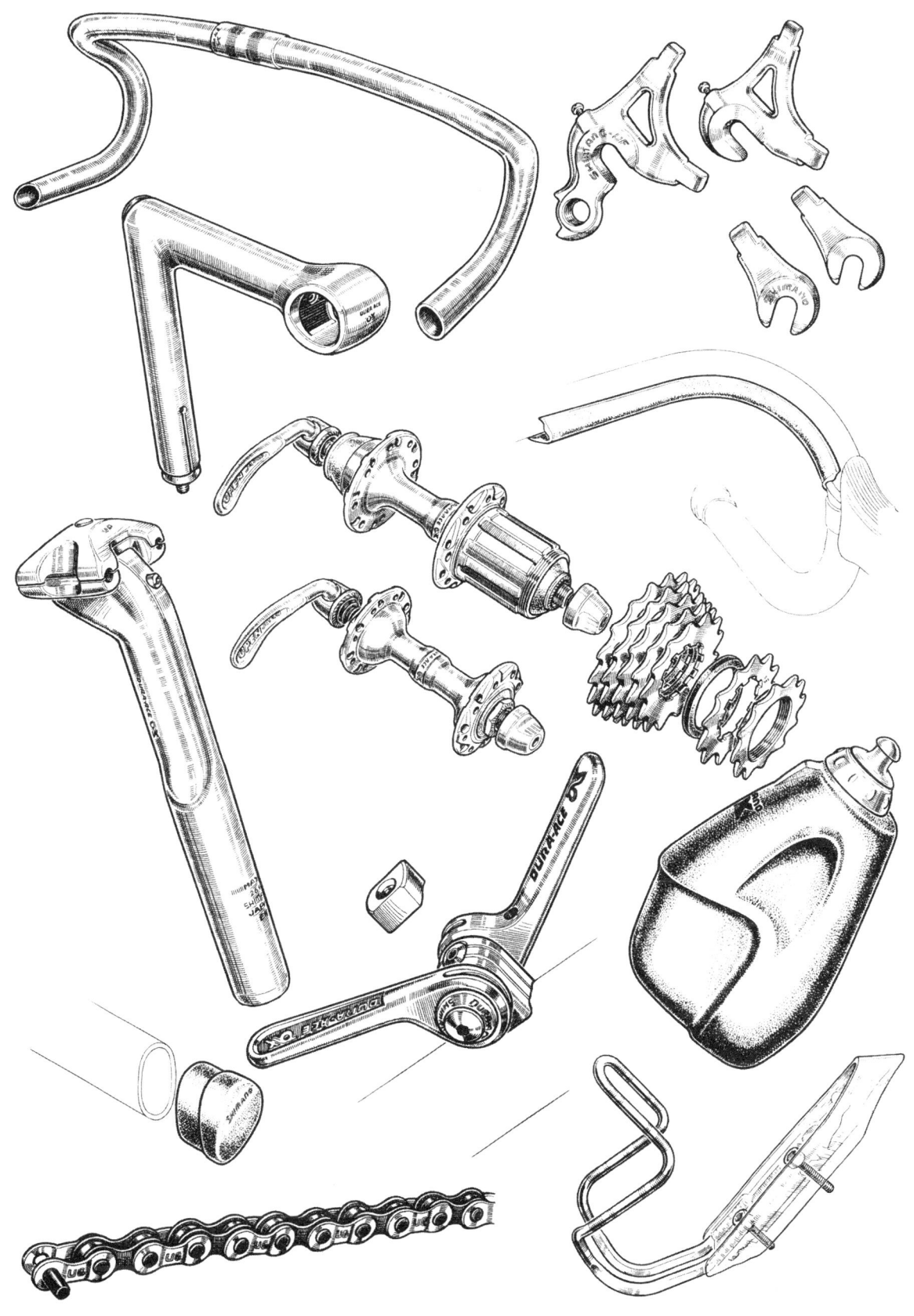

This page-spread (pages 176 and 177): Shimano Dura-Ace AX aerodynamic gruppo. 1981 Milremo catalogue.

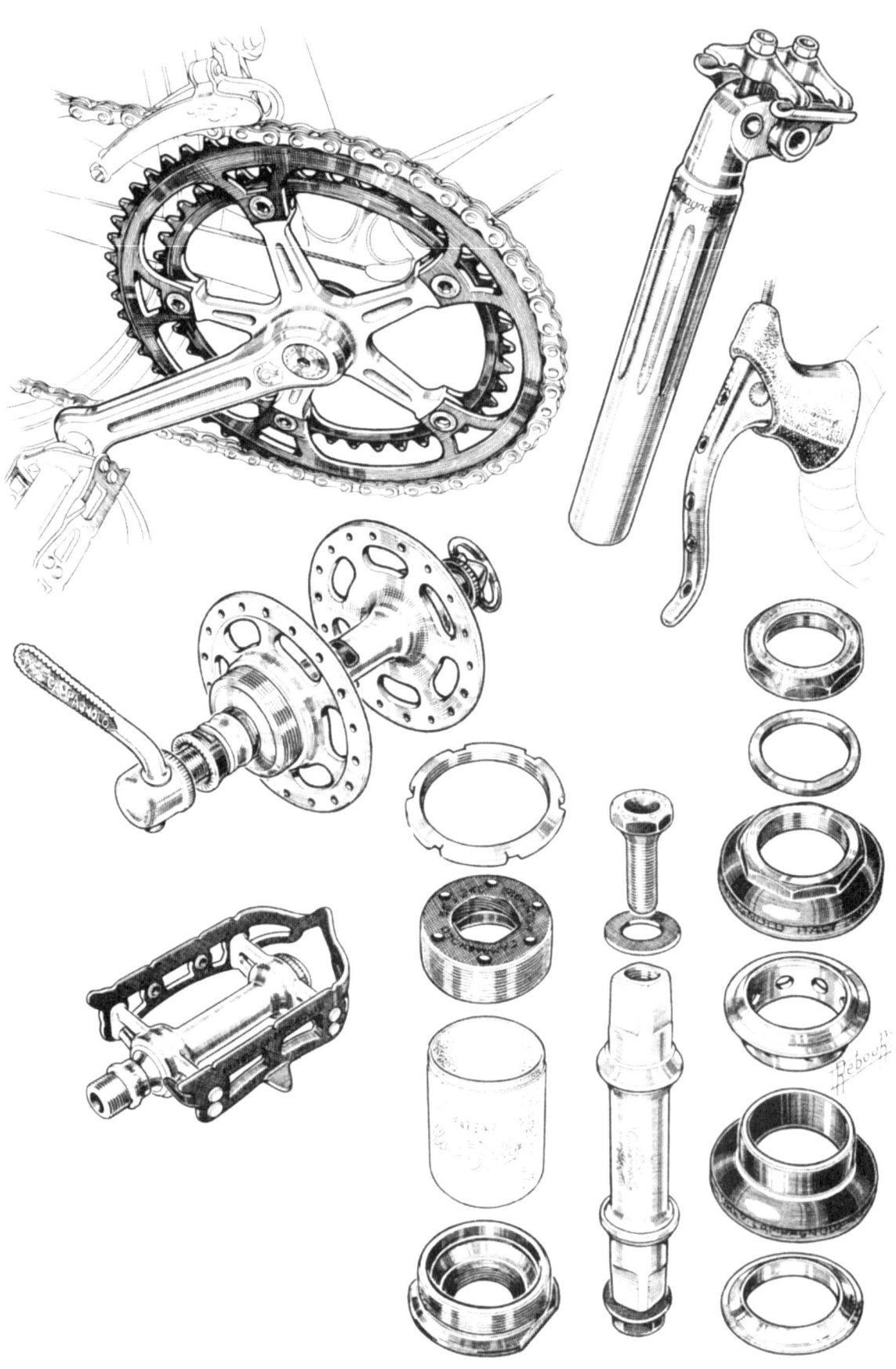

Components from the 1983 Campagnolo Record Super-Legere gruppo. 1983 Milremo catalogue.

Chapter 12. Component Gruppos

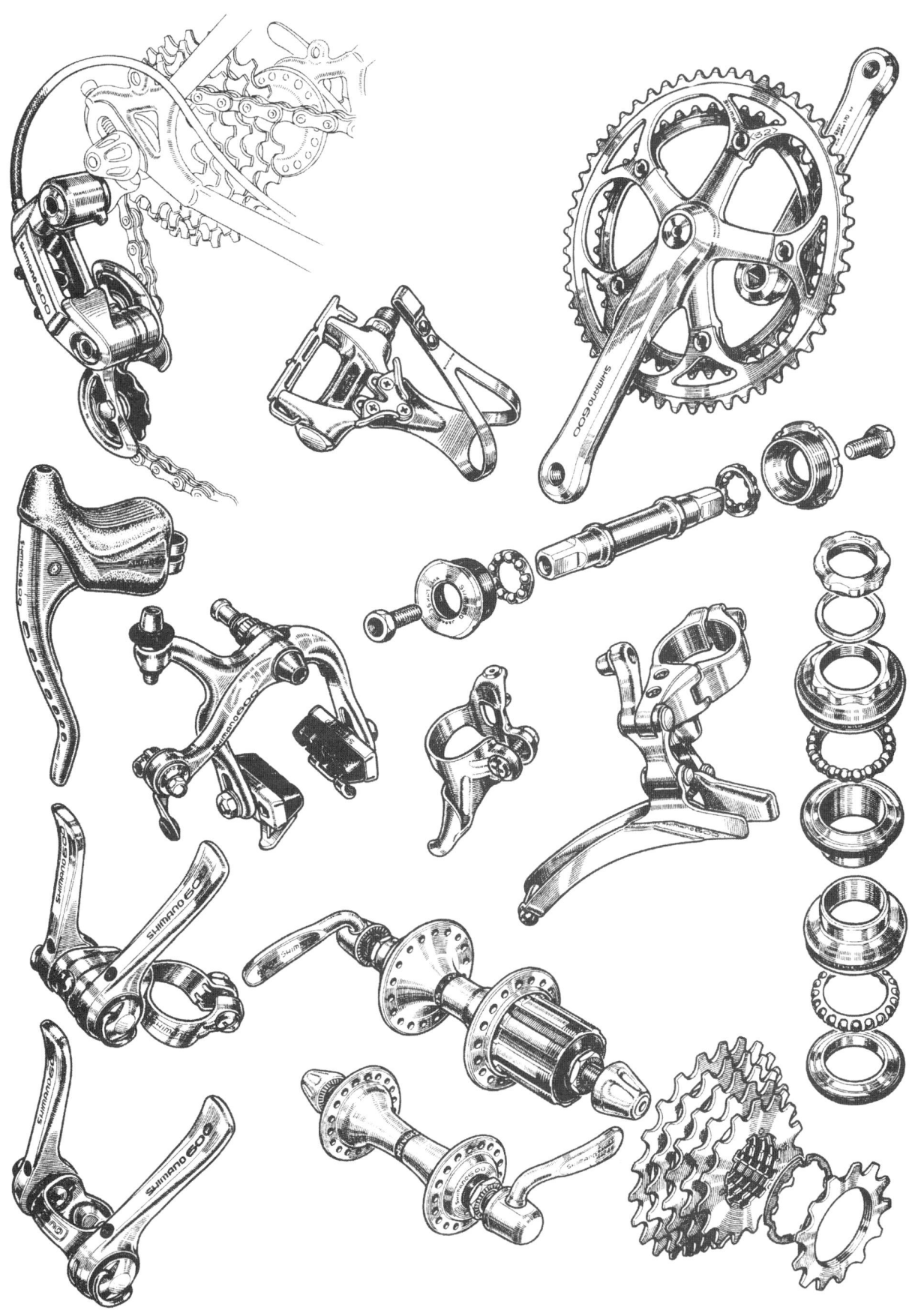

1983 Shimano 600 EX component gruppo. 1983 Milremo catalogue.

Chapter 13. Luggage Carrying Equipment

Especially in the early days of *Le Cycle*, bicycle touring and camping were still quite popular in France, as they were in other European countries after the war. Consequently, Rebour has produced numerous drawings of various ways to transport luggage. This chapter includes drawings of some of those contraptions as far as they are directly mounted on the bicycle. In addition, there are a number of solutions involving trailers, and even side-cars, some of which will be covered separately in Chapter 21.

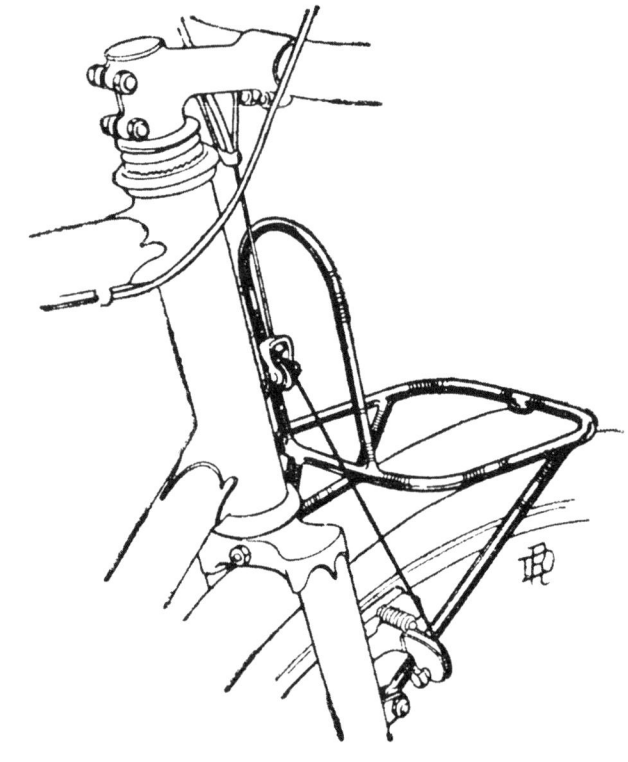

Right: Alex Singer front rack for handlebar bag support. *Le Cycle*, 20 April 1946.

Below: René Herse randonneur bicycle entered in the 1967 Poly de Chanteloup technical trials. Randonneurs typically carry only enough luggage to fill a handlebar bag, supported by the small front rack shown here. *Le Cycle*, June 1967.

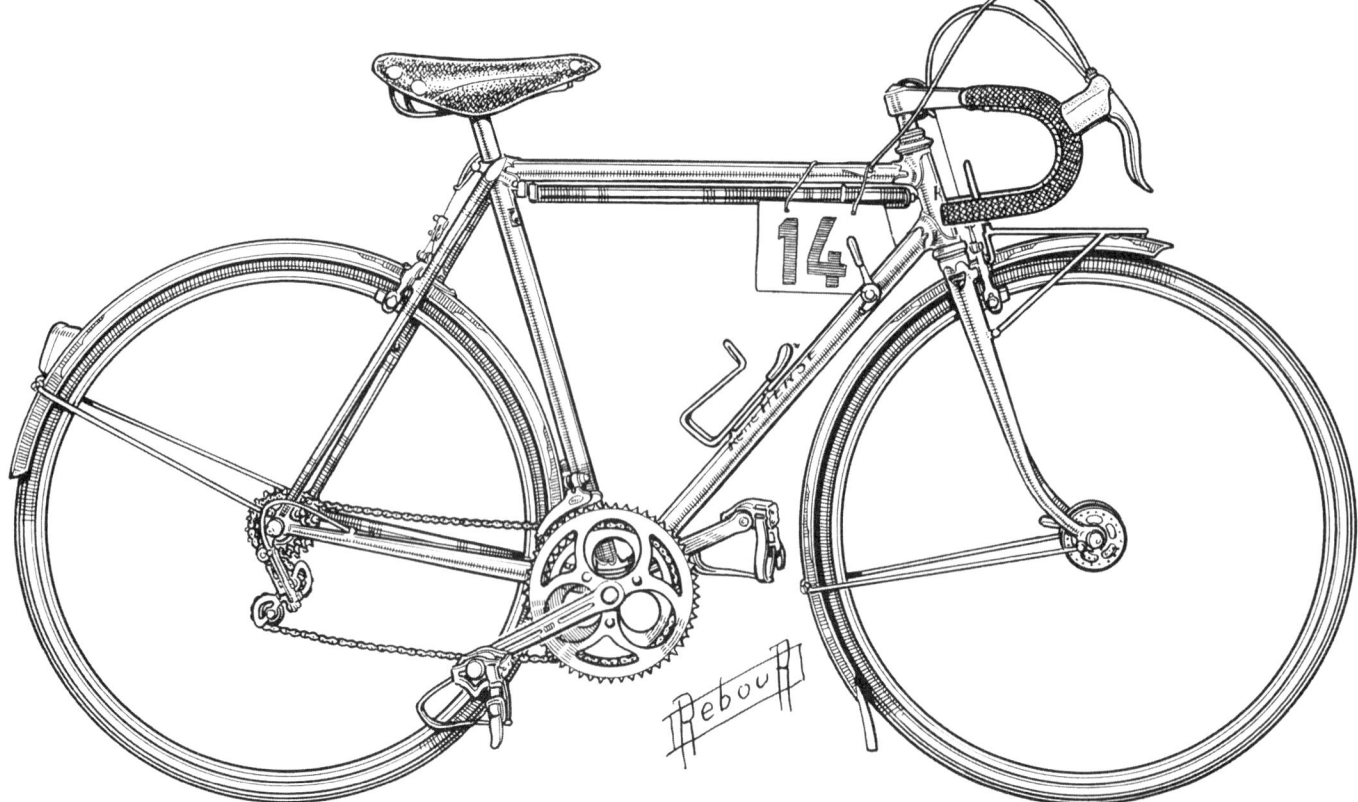

Chapter 13. Luggage Carrying Equipment

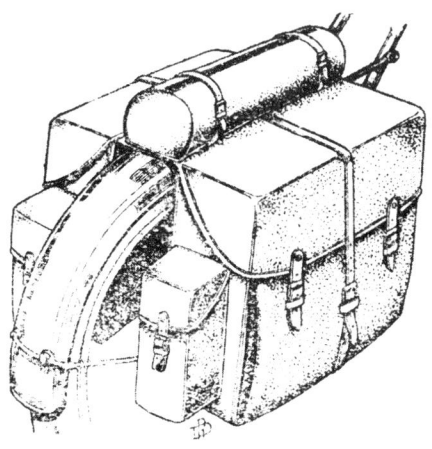

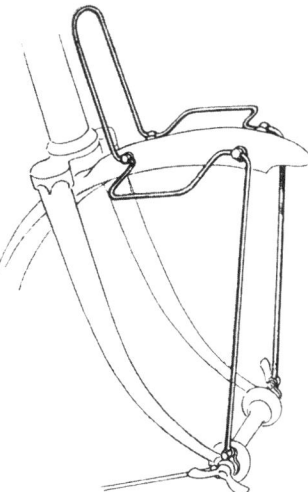

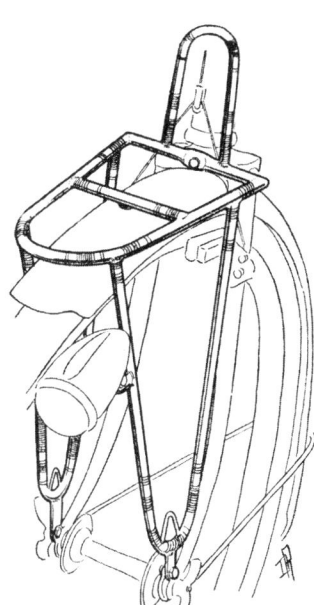

Far left: Rear pannier bags. *Le Cycle*, March 1946.
Left: Ducheron handlebar bag support. *Le Cycle*, 26 January 1947.
Right: Loaded-touring front rack. *Le Cycle*, 28 December 1946.

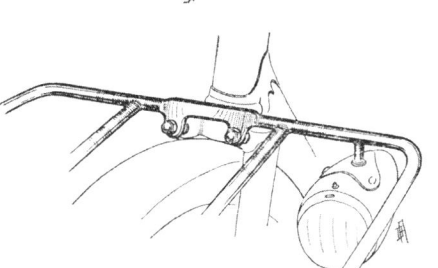

Below: Genty-Jolly front rack. *Le Cycle*, 26 January 1947.
Below right: Rear rack with luggage clamp for city bike. *Le Cycle*, 4 December 1948.

Above: René Herse large front carrier rack. *Le Cycle*, January 1948.

Below: Miro Denti, winner of the 1966 Tour de l'Avenir, for amateurs, rode this Bianchi bicycle. *Le Cycle*, September 1966.

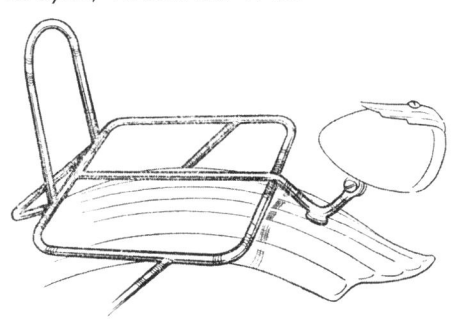

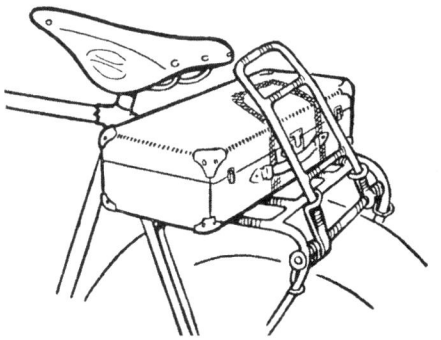

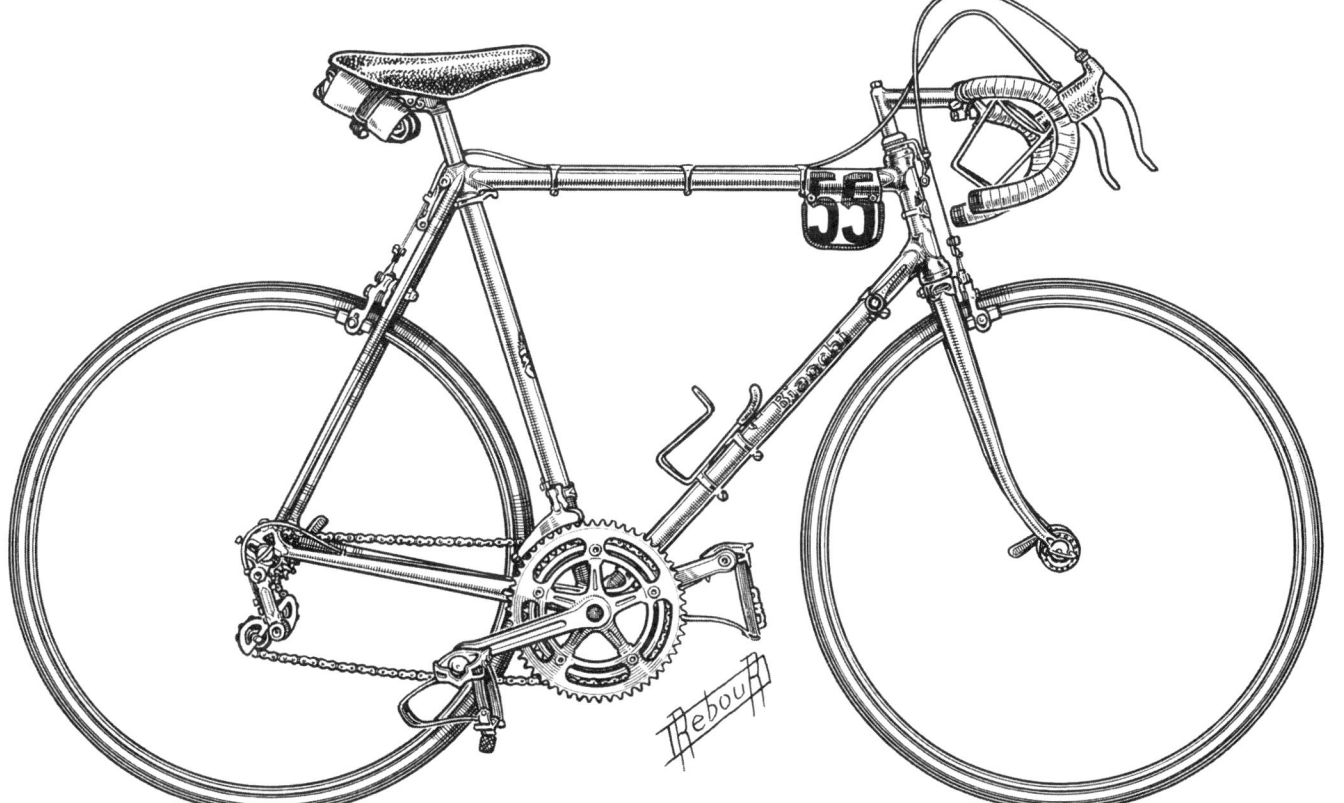

181

Right: Camille Daudon wheel wing-nut adapted to restrainning a front pannier bag. *Le Cycle*, 28 August 1948.

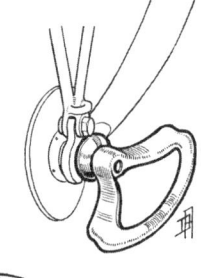

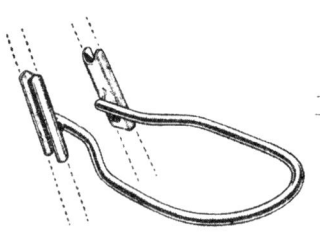

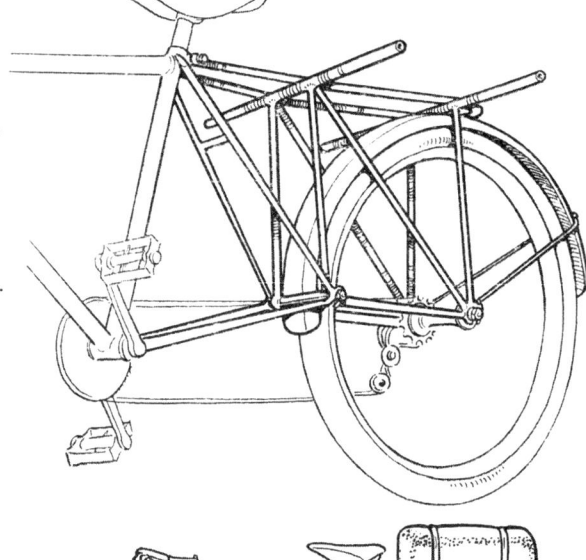

Above: Seat-stay-mounted clip-on support for saddle bag. *Le Cycle*, January 1948.
Left: Rack attachment for bag. *Le Cycle*, 10 March 1948.
Below: Brans compact saddle bag. *Le Cycle*, 28 August 1948.

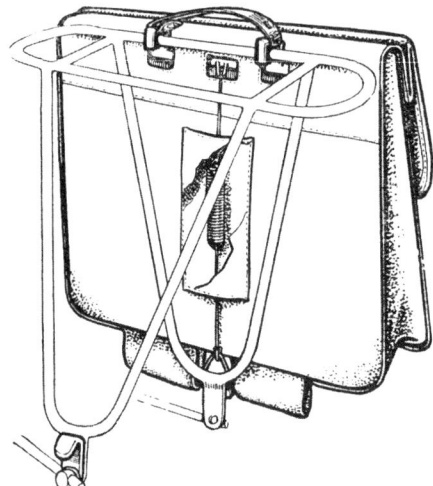

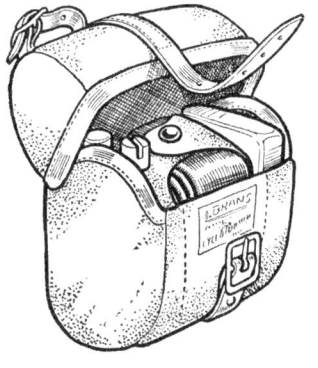

Below: Raphaël-Géminiani-badged Jeunet bicycle of Julio Jiménez, winner of the 1967 Tour de France mountains classification, used in the Poly de Chanteloup technical trials. *Le Cycle*, June 1967.

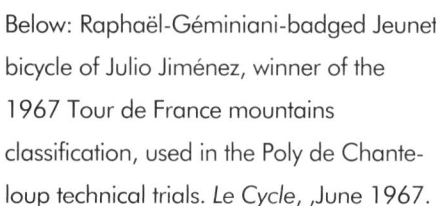

Above: Frame extension to increase the bicycle's wheel base, in order to carry more luggage. *Le Cycle*, 29 March 1947.**

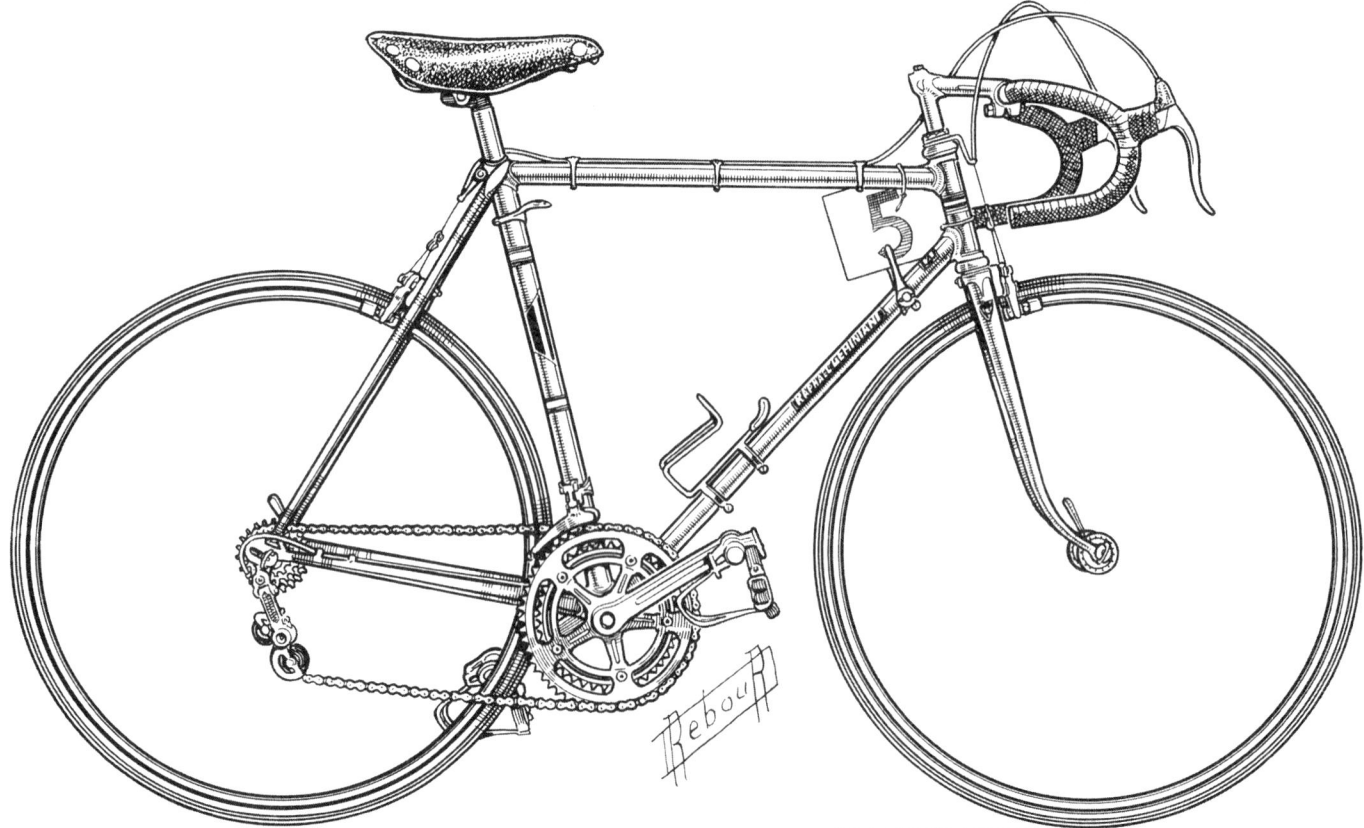

** See pages 269–271 for expanded caption text.

Chapter 13. Luggage Carrying Equipment

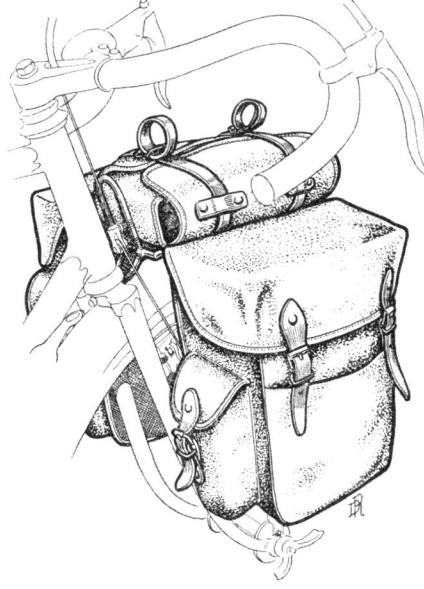

Right: Front panniers and rack top bag with high-mounting front rack. *Pratique du Vélo.*

Lower right: Lightweight front rack to serve as handlebar bag support, supported off the cantilever brake pivot bolts. *Pratique du Vélo.*

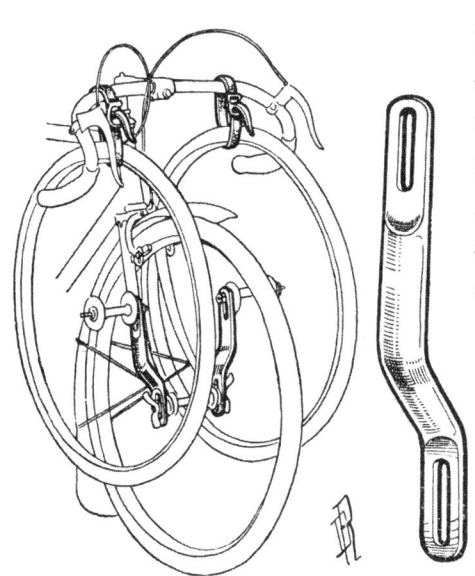

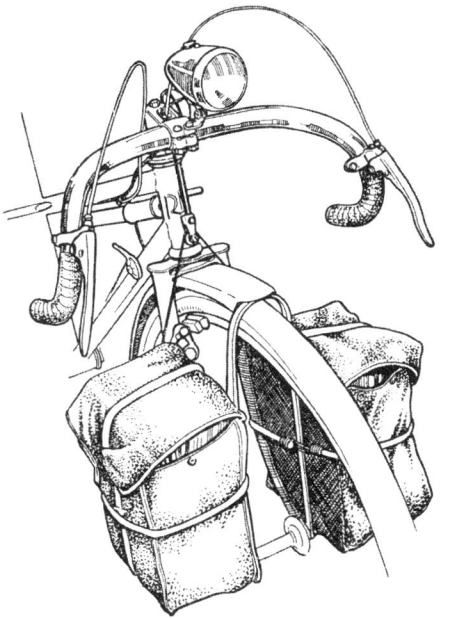

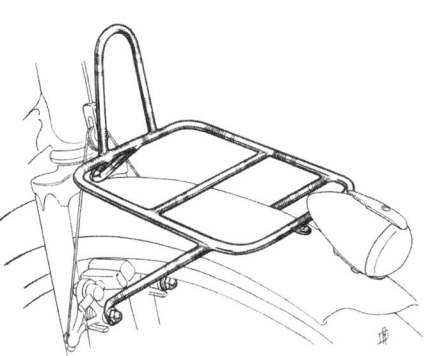

Above: Bracket for carrying racing wheels to the start of the race. *Le Cycle,* 4 December 1948.

Right: Front panniers on low-rider rack. *Pratique du Vélo.*

Below: 1967 Tour de France winner Roger Pingeon's Peugeot bicycle. *Le Cycle,* August-September 1967.**

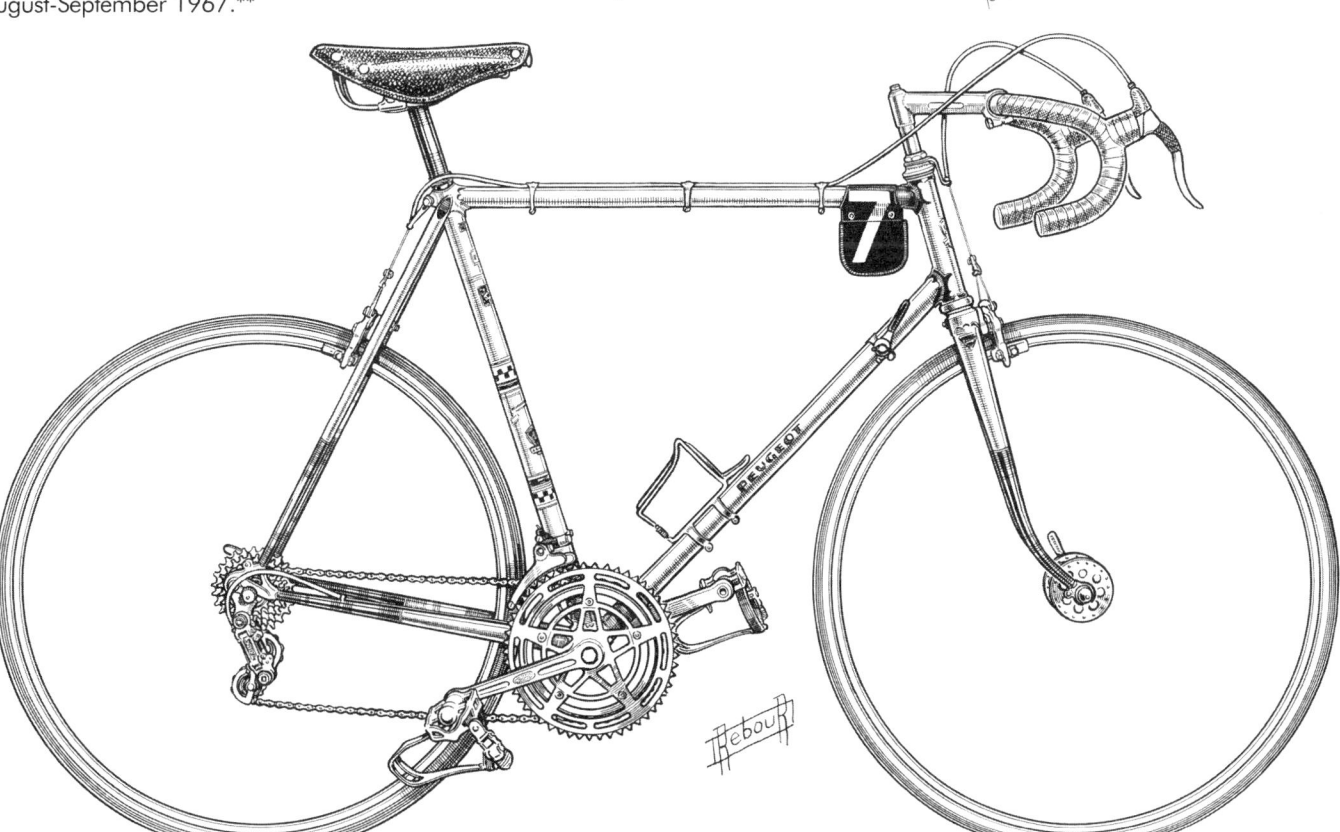

_____
** See pages 269–271 for expanded caption text.

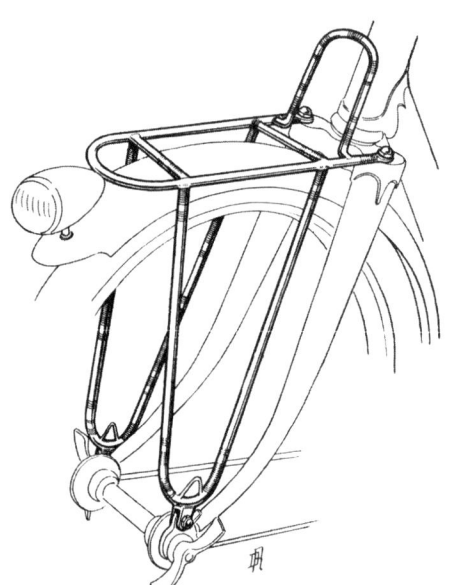
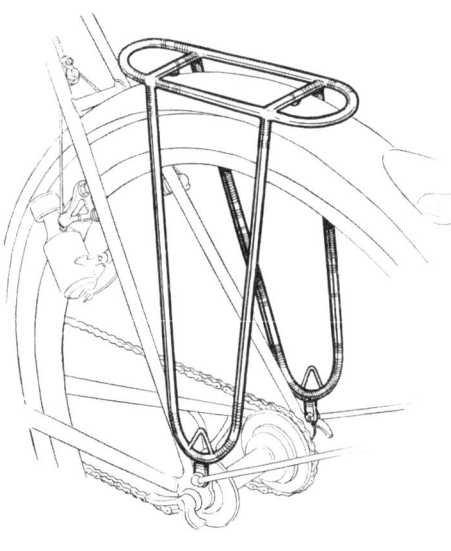

Above: Handlebar bag. *Pratique du Vélo.*
Above center: Small rear luggage rack. *Pratique du Vélo.*
Below: Lightweight rack mounted on rear mudguard. *Le Cycle,* 26 February 1949.

Above: Front rack supported at the fork-ends and braze-ons on the fork crown. *Pratique du Vélo.*
Right: Large double rear pannier bags. *Pratique du Vélo.*

Below: René Herse randonneur bicycle entered in the 1968 Poly de Chanteloup technical trials. *Le Cycle,* June 1968.**

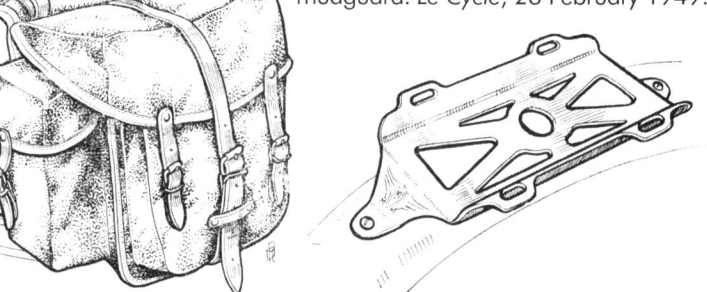
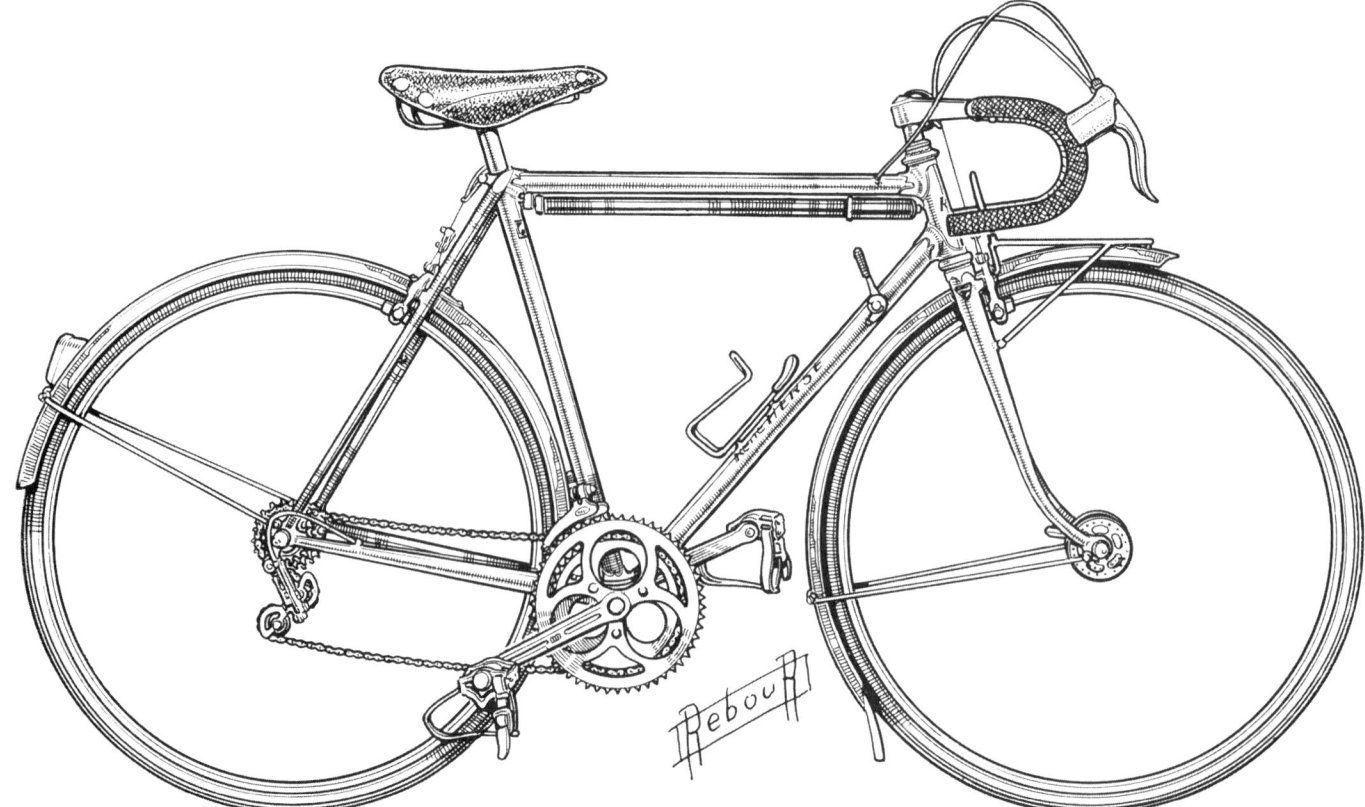

** See pages 269–271 for expanded caption text.

Chapter 13. Luggage Carrying Equipment

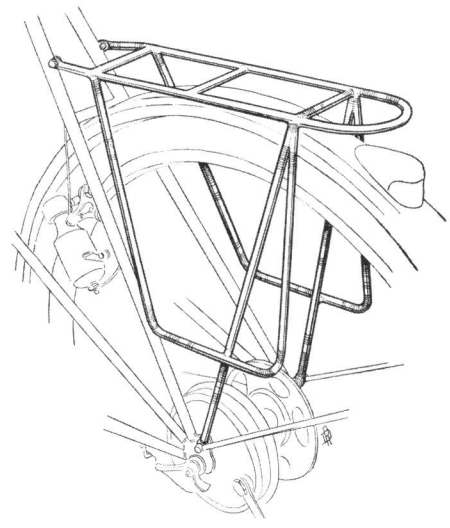

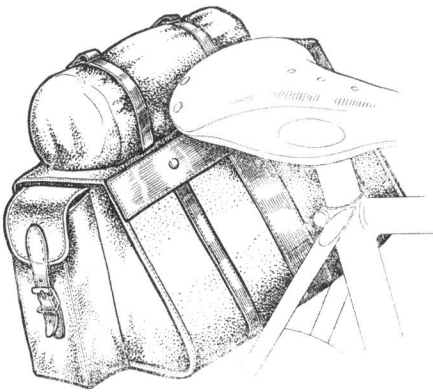

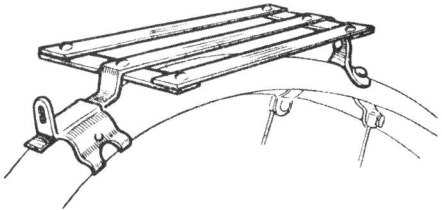

Above: Ivorrette Carriguard, attached to rear mudguard, from England. *Le Cycle*, 10 September 1949.

Above left: English saddle bag, attached to saddle eyelets. *Pratique du Vélo*.

Below: Goëland rack. *Le Cycle*, 9 September 1949.

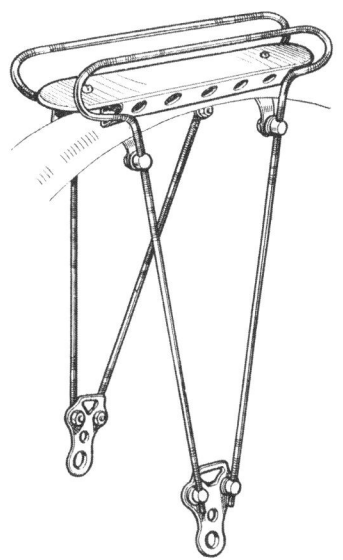

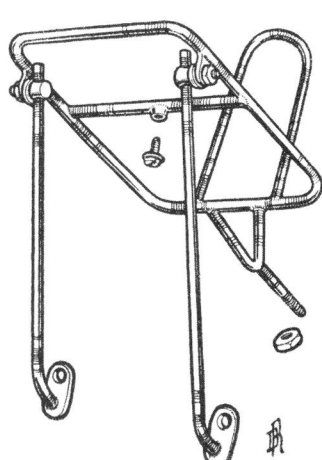

Above: Tubular steel rear luggage rack with lower bag restraints. *Pratique du Vélo*.

Right: Genor Supersport rear rack with solid platform integrated in the rear mudguard. *Le Cycle*, 12 February 1949.

Below: Jan Janssen, winner of the points classification of the 1967 Tour de France, rode this Sauvage-Lejeune machine. *Le Cycle*, August-September 1967.

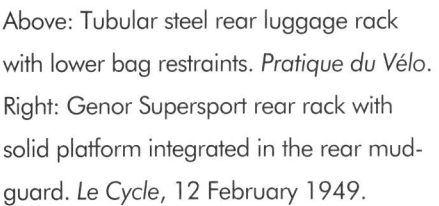

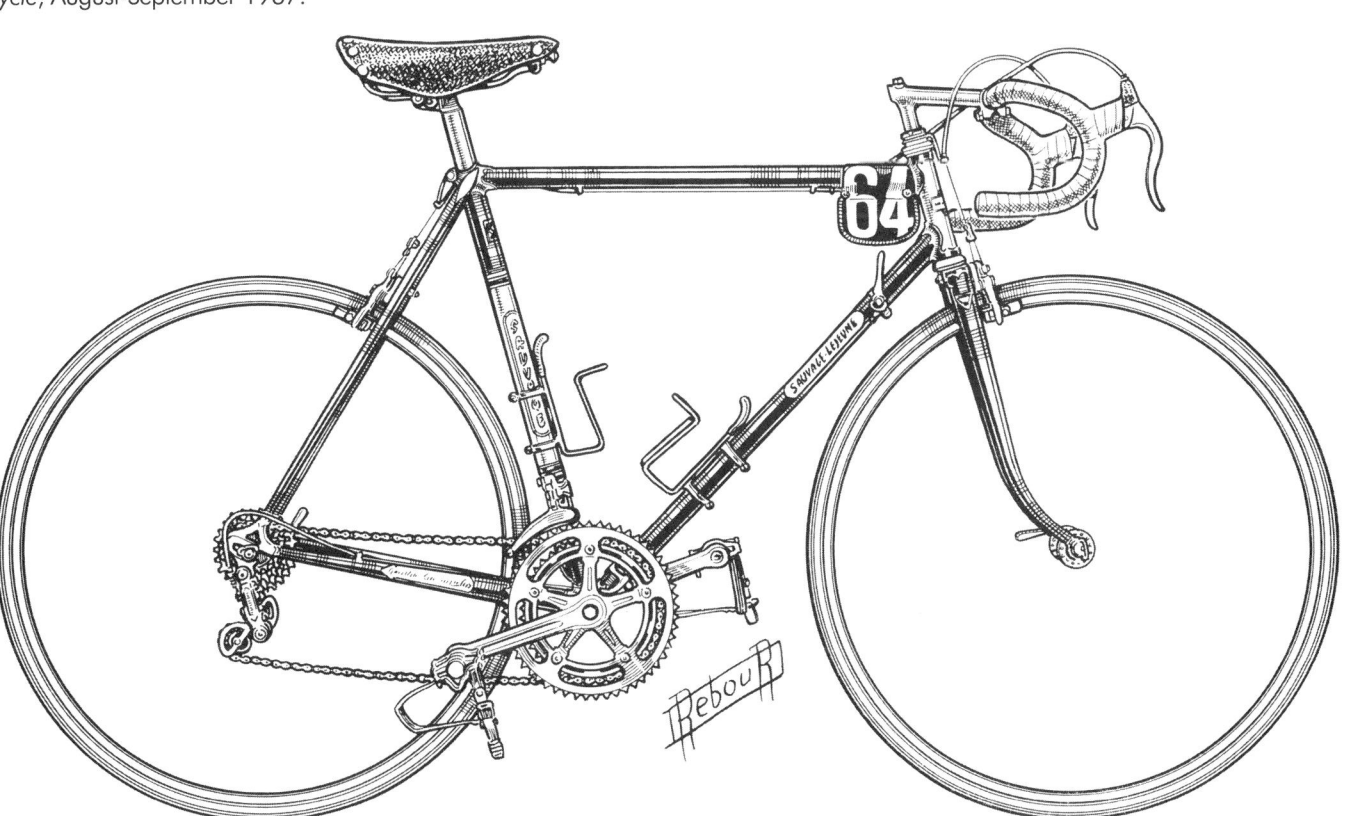

185

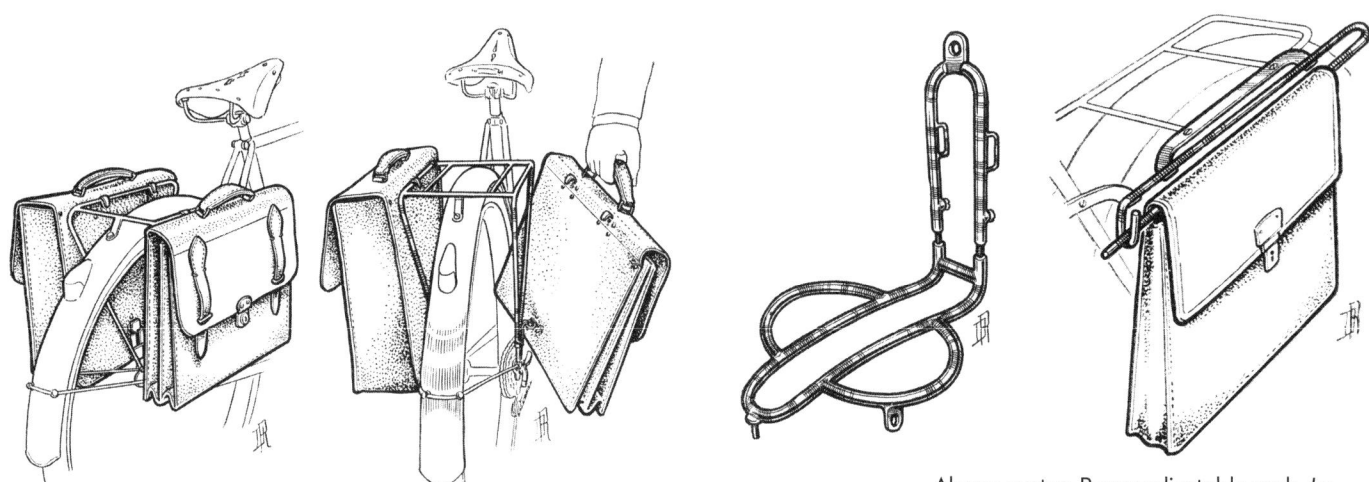

Above: Vélosac system of bags, including a briefcase, that clip to the luggage rack. *Le Cycle*, 5 November 1949.

Right: Special luggage rack and bag attachment at 1951 Paris bicycle trade show. *Le Cycle*, 24 November 1951.

Below: Raphaël-Géminiani-branded Jeunet bicycle of Julio Jiménez, 1967 Tour de France second overall and winner of the mountains classification. *Le Cycle*, August-September 1967.

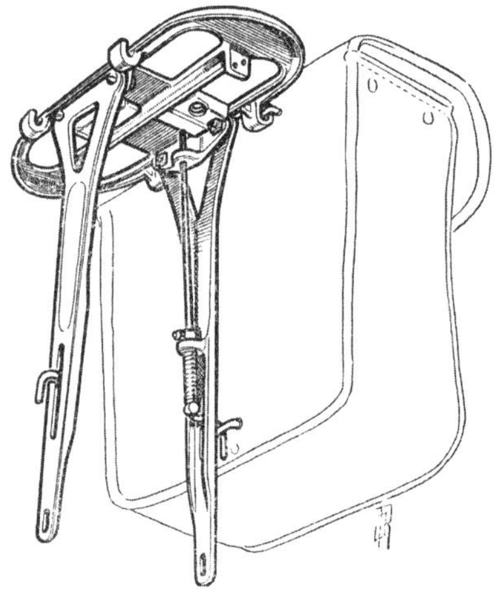

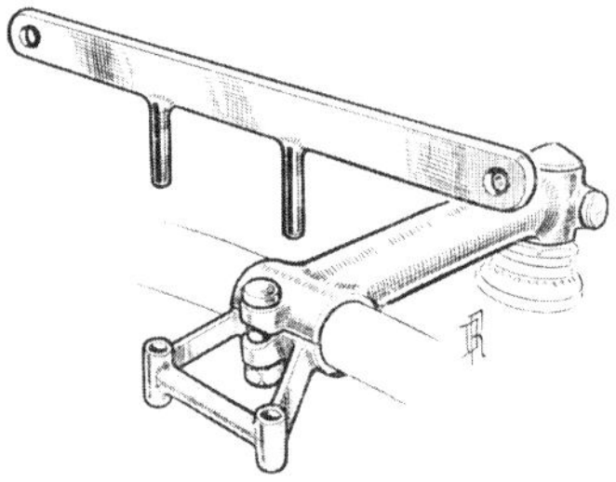

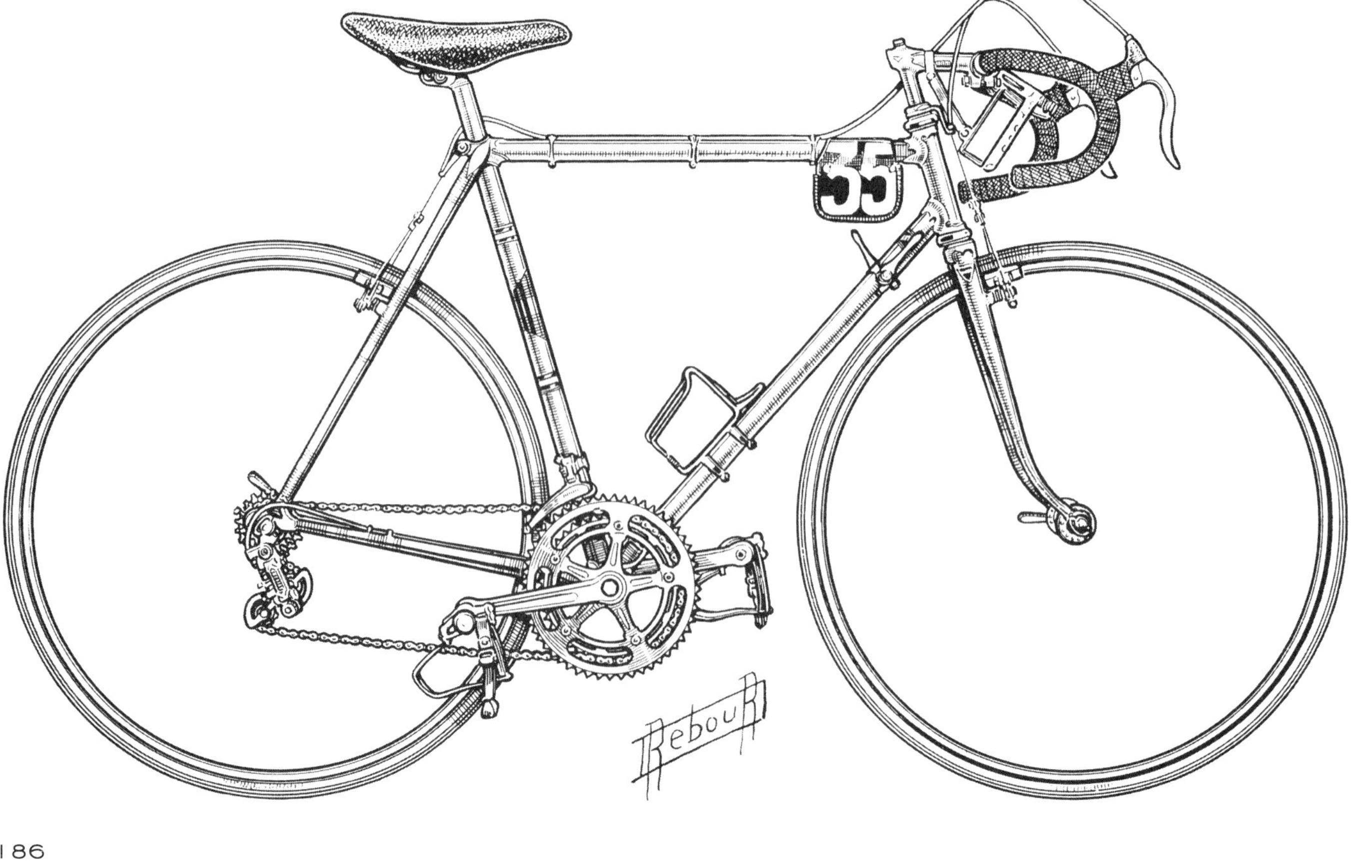

Above center: Remy adjustable rack. *Le Cycle*, 26 May 1951.

Above right: Briefcase support clip on Dutch city bike. *Le Cycle*, 27 May 1950.

Below: Handlebar bag support on special stem. *Le Cycle*, 23 August 1952.

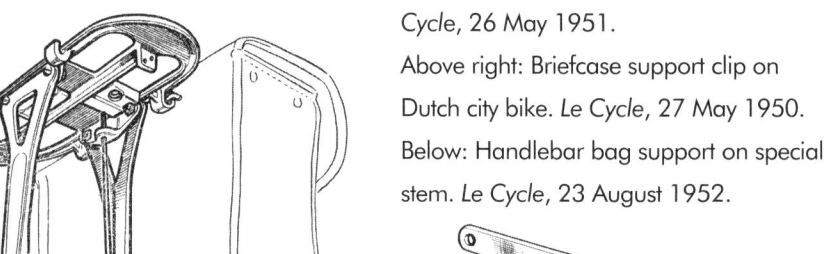

Chapter 13. Luggage Carrying Equipment

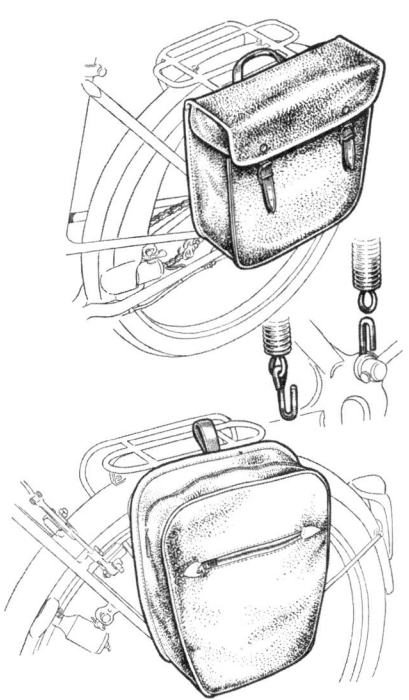

Above: Peugeot bag and rear rack. *Le Cycle*, 23 August 1952.

Below: With a final time-trial victory, Jan Janssen finally managed to win the 1968 Tour de France, riding this Lejeune machine. *Le Cycle*, August-September 1968.

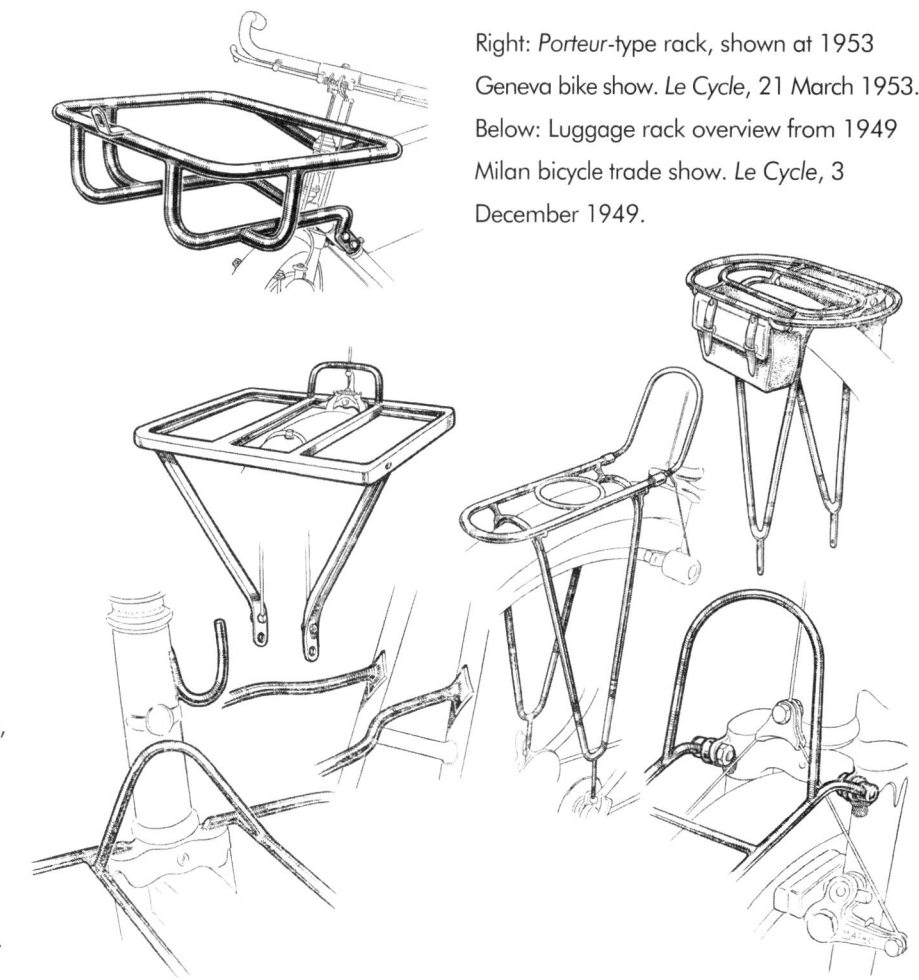

Right: *Porteur*-type rack, shown at 1953 Geneva bike show. *Le Cycle*, 21 March 1953.
Below: Luggage rack overview from 1949 Milan bicycle trade show. *Le Cycle*, 3 December 1949.

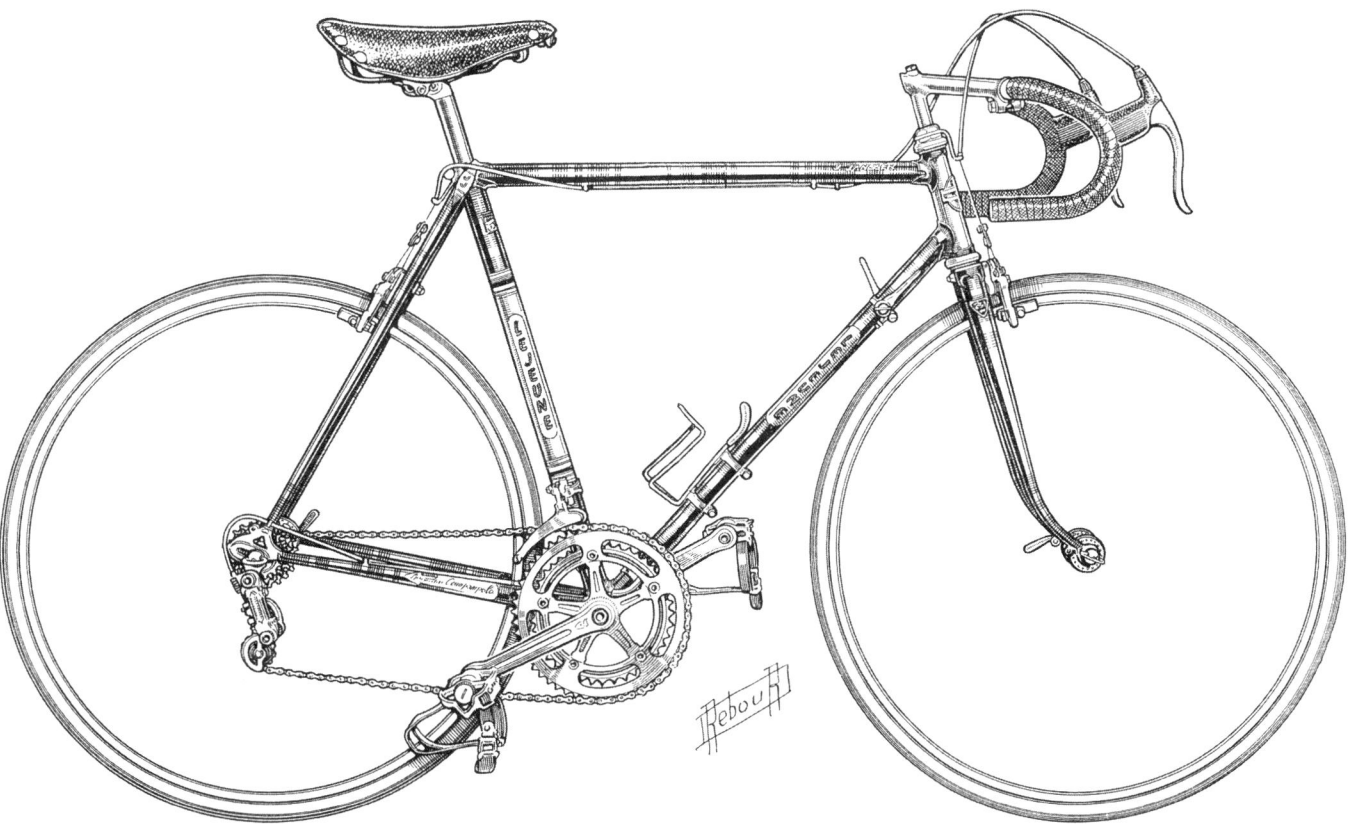

187

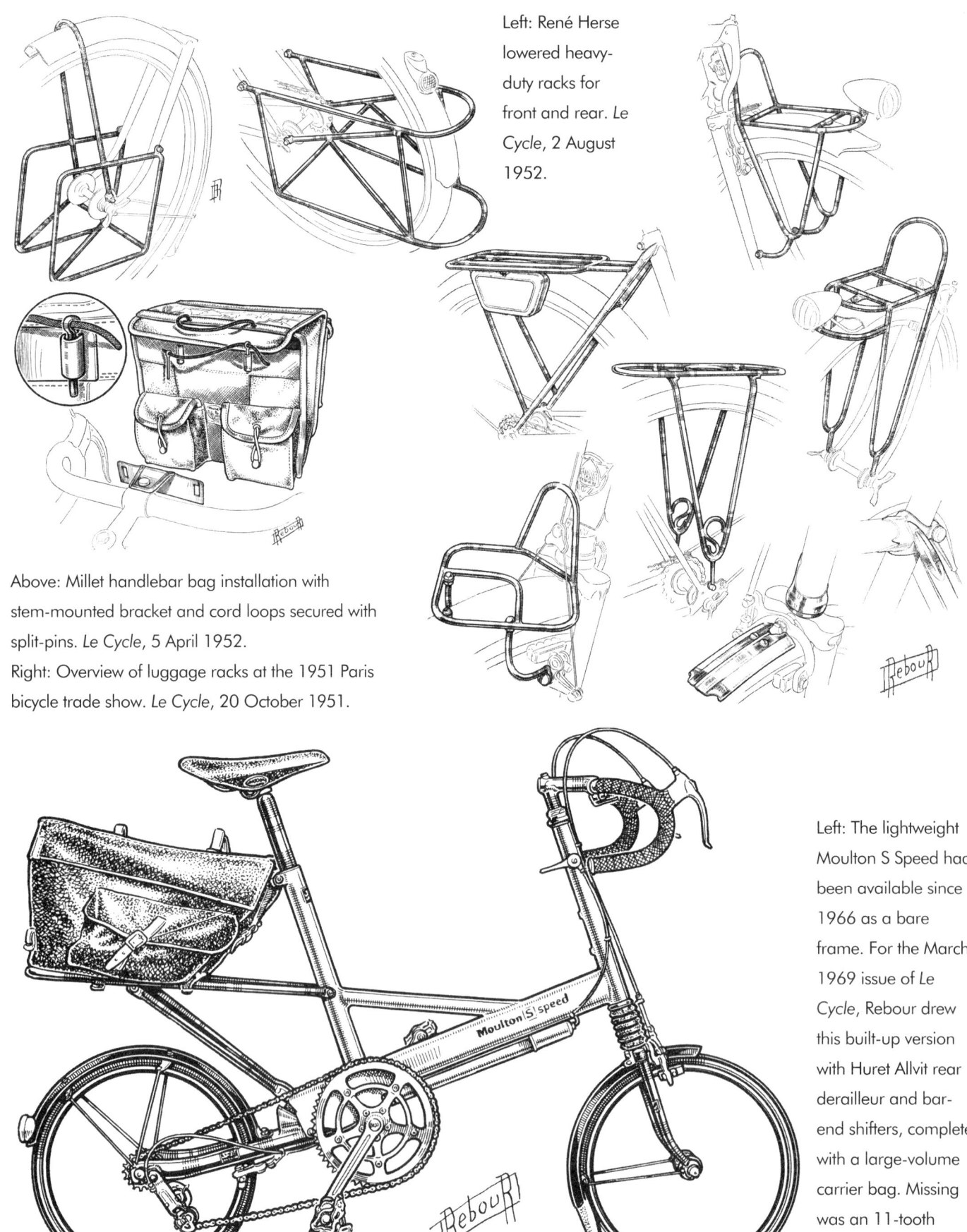

Left: René Herse lowered heavy-duty racks for front and rear. *Le Cycle*, 2 August 1952.

Above: Millet handlebar bag installation with stem-mounted bracket and cord loops secured with split-pins. *Le Cycle*, 5 April 1952.
Right: Overview of luggage racks at the 1951 Paris bicycle trade show. *Le Cycle*, 20 October 1951.

Left: The lightweight Moulton S Speed had been available since 1966 as a bare frame. For the March 1969 issue of *Le Cycle*, Rebour drew this built-up version with Huret Allvit rear derailleur and bar-end shifters, complete with a large-volume carrier bag. Missing was an 11-tooth sprocket to provide an adequate top gear.

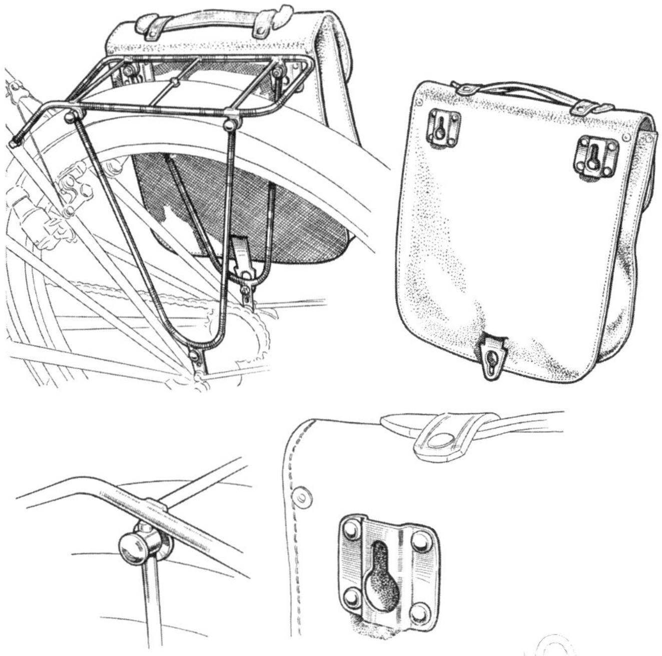

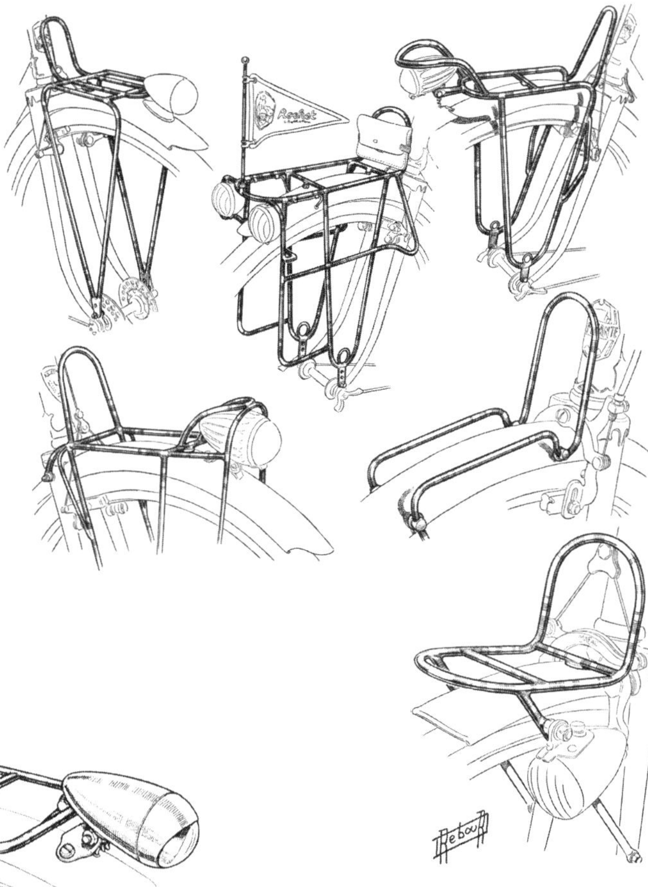

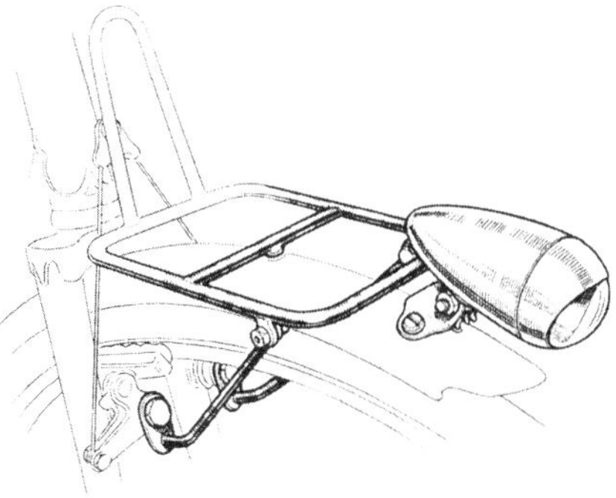

Chapter 13. Luggage Carrying Equipment

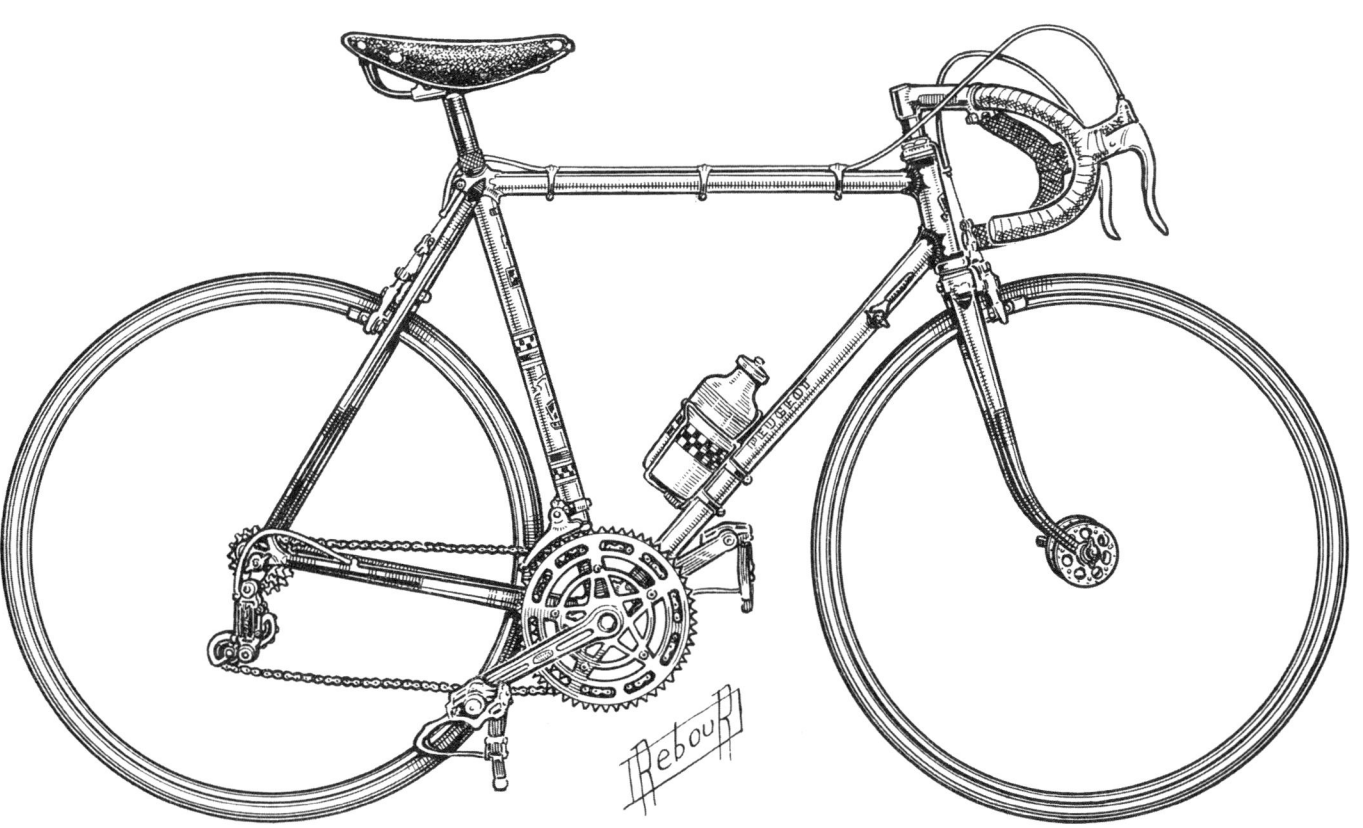

Above: Bourdel rack and bag with mounting details. *Le Cycle*, 23 August 1952.
Right: Goëland rack at Poly de Chanteloup technical trials. *Le Cycle*, 15 May 1954.

Below: Delisle's Peugeot bike at the 1969 Poly de Chanteloup. *Le Cycle*, May 1969.

Above: Overview of racks at the 1952 Paris bike trade show. *Le Cycle*, 18 October 1952.

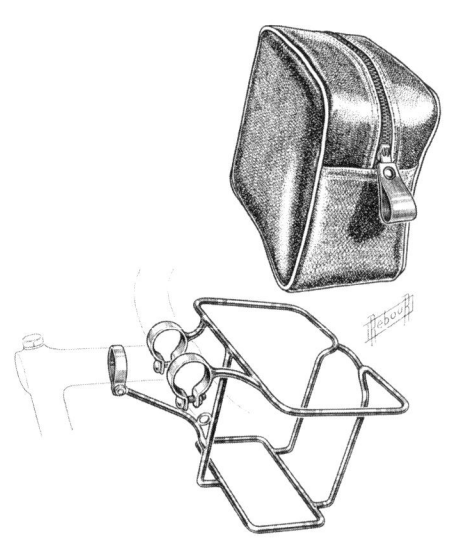
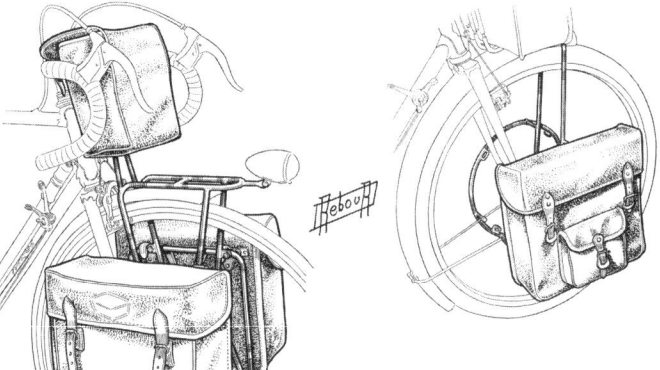
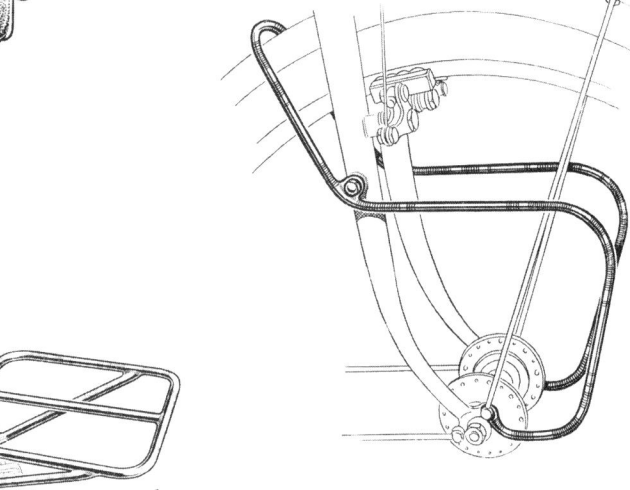

Left: Details of low-rider-style front racks and bags from Hergé and Remy. *Le Cycle*, 19 May 1952.

Above: Vito front bag and support mounted on handlebars. *Le Cycle*, October 1962.
Right: René Herse handlebar bag support. *Le Cycle*, 4 October 1957.

Below: Raymond Poulidor was third again in the 1969 Tour de France, riding this Mercier bicycle. *Le Cycle*, August-September 1969.

Above: Pittard low-rider front rack with connecting loop behind the front fork. *Le Cycle*, 23 May 1953.

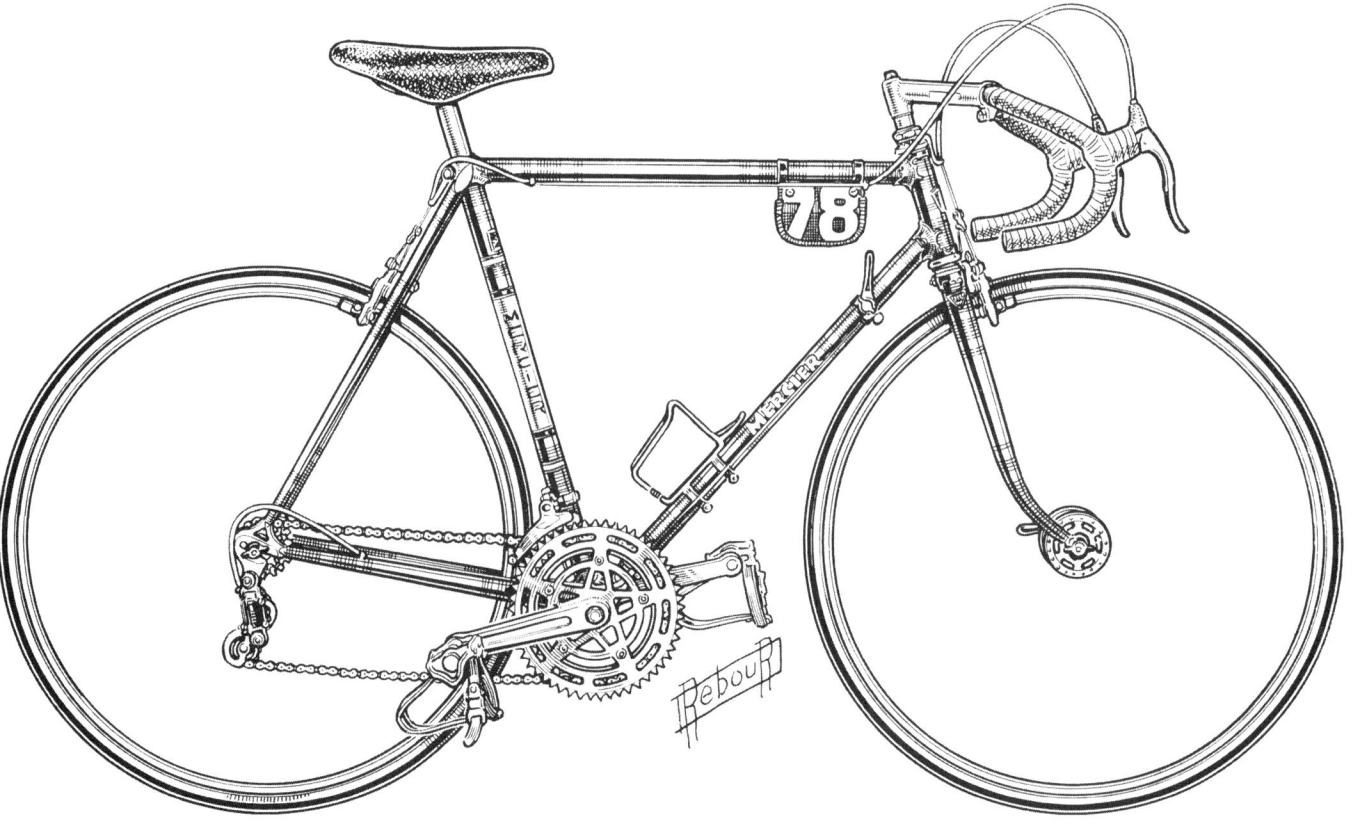

Chapter 13. Luggage Carrying Equipment

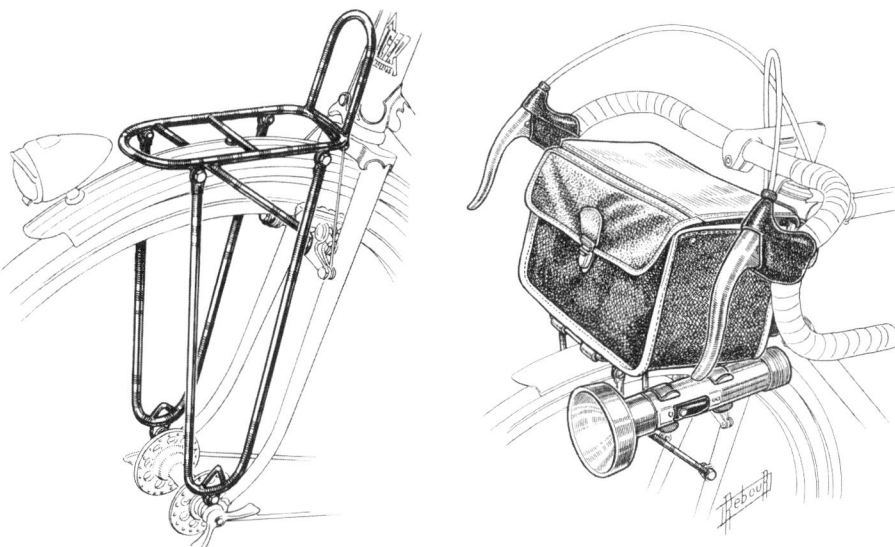

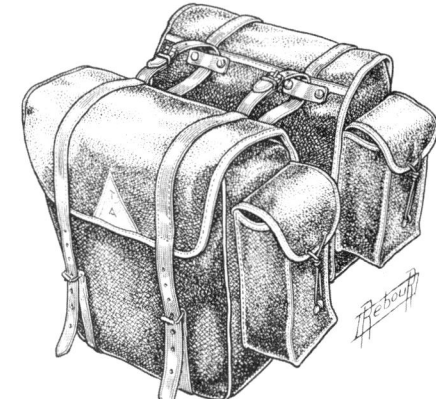

Left: Super Randonneur handlebar bag, support rack, and light at 1976 Motobécane house show. *L'Officiel du Cycle*, Dec. 1976.

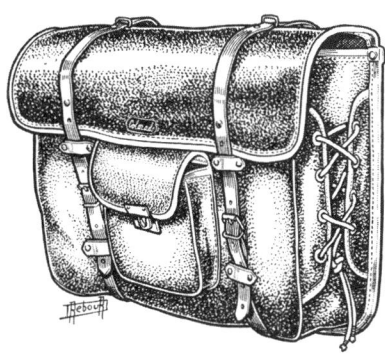
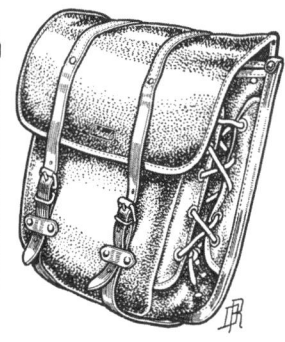
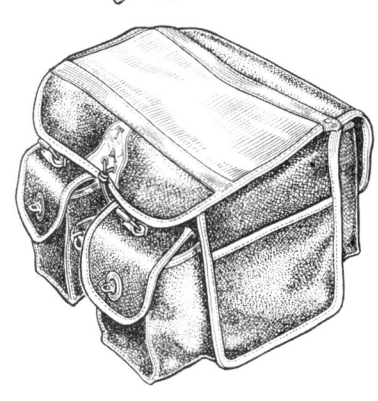

Above left: Front luggage rack. *Cycles de Compétition et Randonneuses*.

Right: TA pannier bags and large handlebar bag. *Le Cycle*, February 1972.

Above: Colorado pannier bags, from France, notwithstanding the American-sounding name. *Le Cycle*, 22 August 1953.

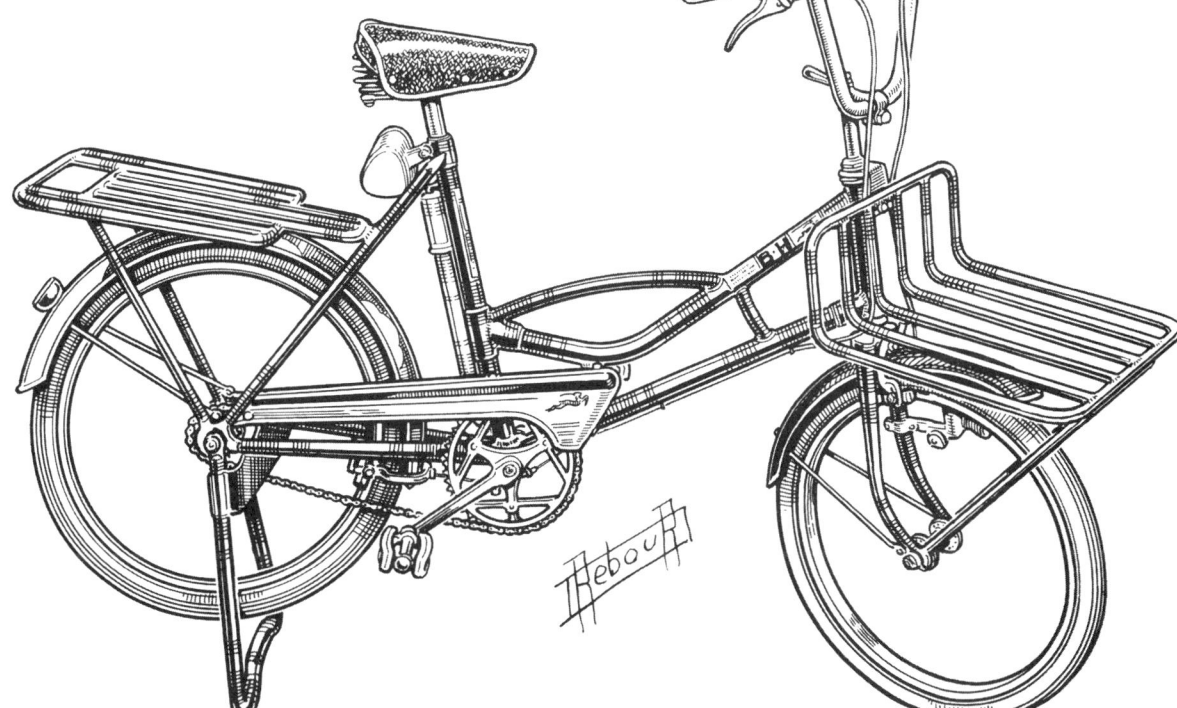

Right: Carrier bicycle made by BH, or Beistegui Hermanos, of Spain. *Le Cycle*, December 1969.

Chapter 14. Lighting Equipment

In this chapter we have collected a number of drawings of bicycle lighting components. These include both battery and dynamo, or generator, systems, as well as individual generators, battery packs, reflectors, and wiring details.**

Above right: Headlight built into a special handlebar stem. *Le Cycle*, 13 July 1946.
Right: Radios bloc-dynamo, i.e. a generator with the headlight attached. *Le Cycle*, 5 April 1946.
Far right: Two drawings showing details of internal wiring for dynamo lighting system. *Le Cycle*, 5 April 1946.

Below: 1969 Tour de France 4th place finisher Félice Gimondi's Chiorda bicycle. *Le Cycle*, August-September 1969.

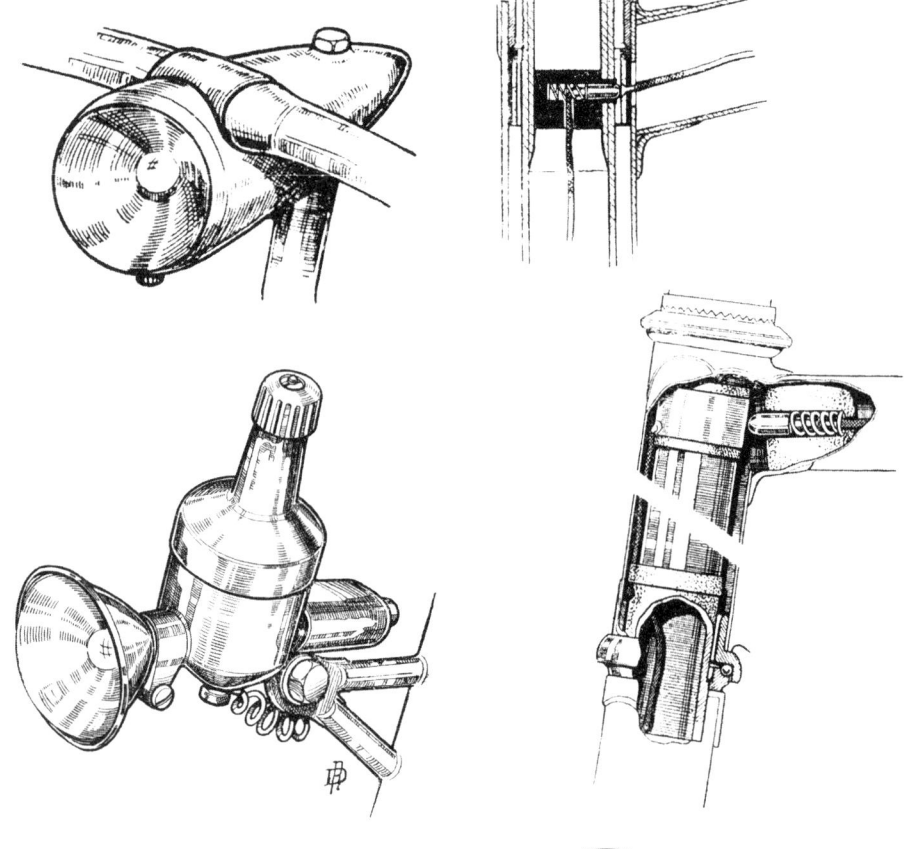

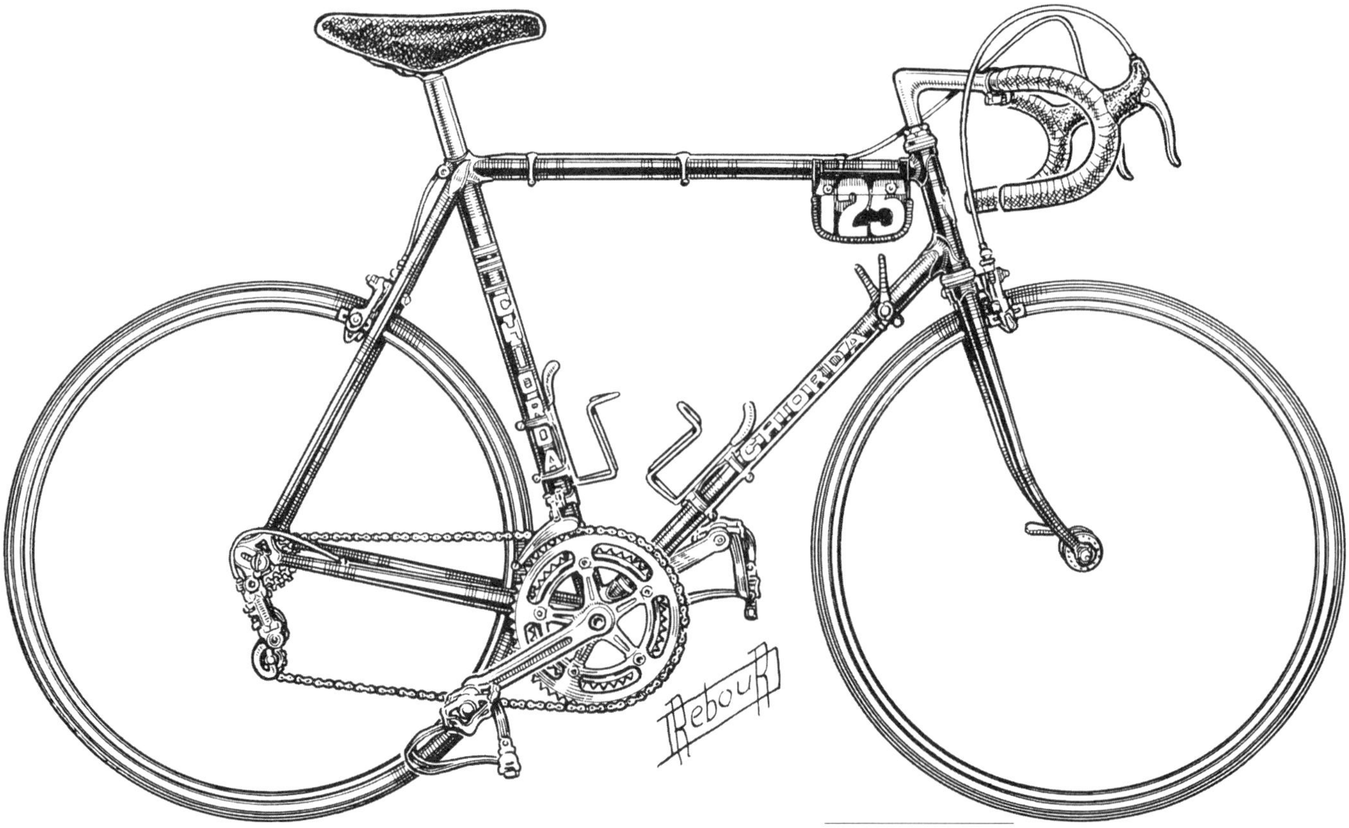

** See pages 269–271 for expanded caption text.

Chapter 14. Lighting Equipment

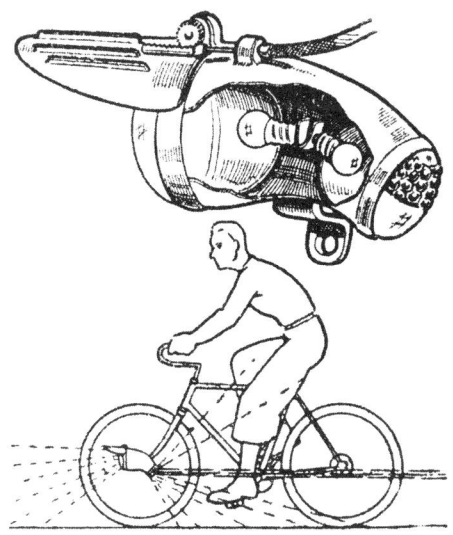

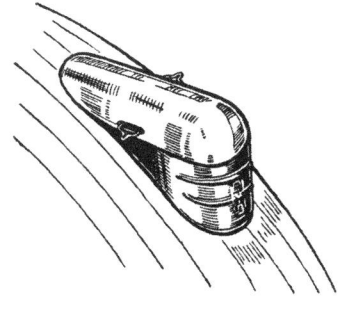

Above: PYB rear light mounted on mudguard. *Le Cycle*, 23 October 1948.

Below: Peugeot dynamo with a shroud over the roller. *Le Cycle*, 1 November 1947.

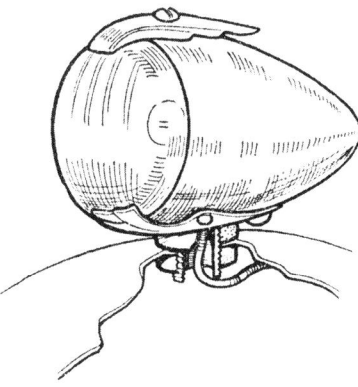

Above: Cable detail on headlight of a René Herse bicycle. *Le Cycle*, 26 January 1947.

Below: Headlight mounted on the front mudguard. *Le Cycle*, 18 December 1948.

Above: Combined head- and tail-light. Drawing the human figure was not Daniel Rebour's forté, so later he leaves those images to his brother Rodolphe. *Le Cycle*, 23 April 1947.

Below: Beginning his long streak of Tour victories, Eddy Merckx rode this Kessels bicycle to victory in the 1969 Tour de France. *Le Cycle*, August-September 1969.**

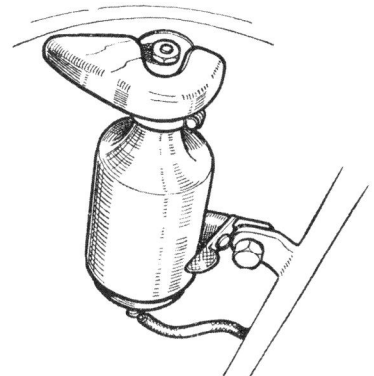

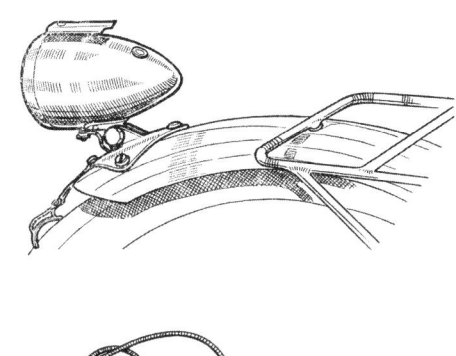

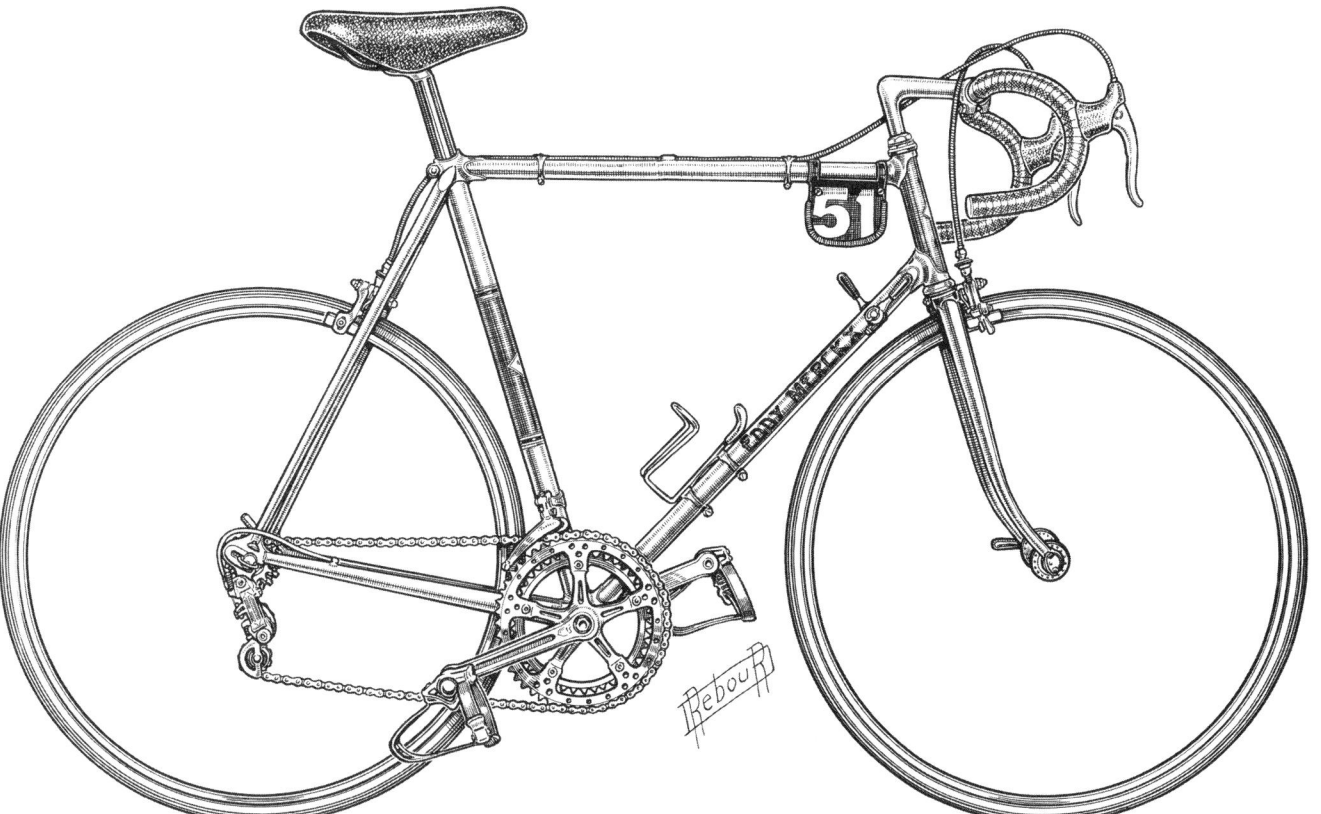

** See pages 269–271 for expanded caption text.

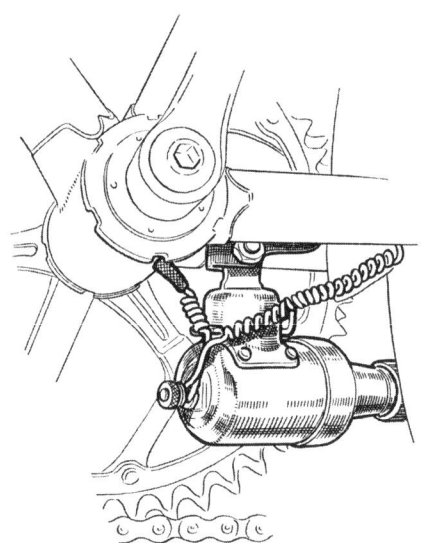

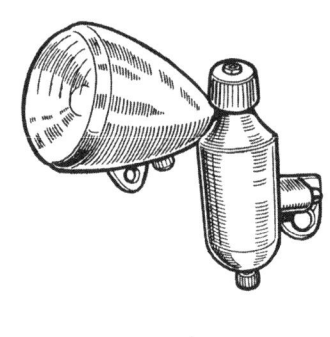

Right: Overview of lighting products at the 1949 Brussels bicycle trade show. *Le Cycle*, 12 February 1949.

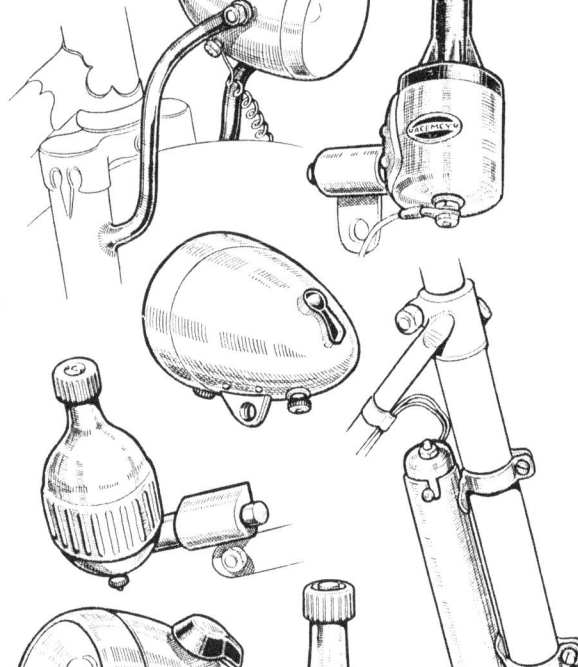

Above: Captivante dynamo mounting on chainstay. *Le Cycle*, 20 October 1951.

Above right: 1948 bloc-dynamo. *Pratique du Vélo*.

Lower right: Daudon internal wiring detail. *Pratique du Vélo*.

Below: 1969 Tour de France 2nd-placed Roger Pingeon's Peugeot bicycle. *Le Cycle*, August-September 1969.

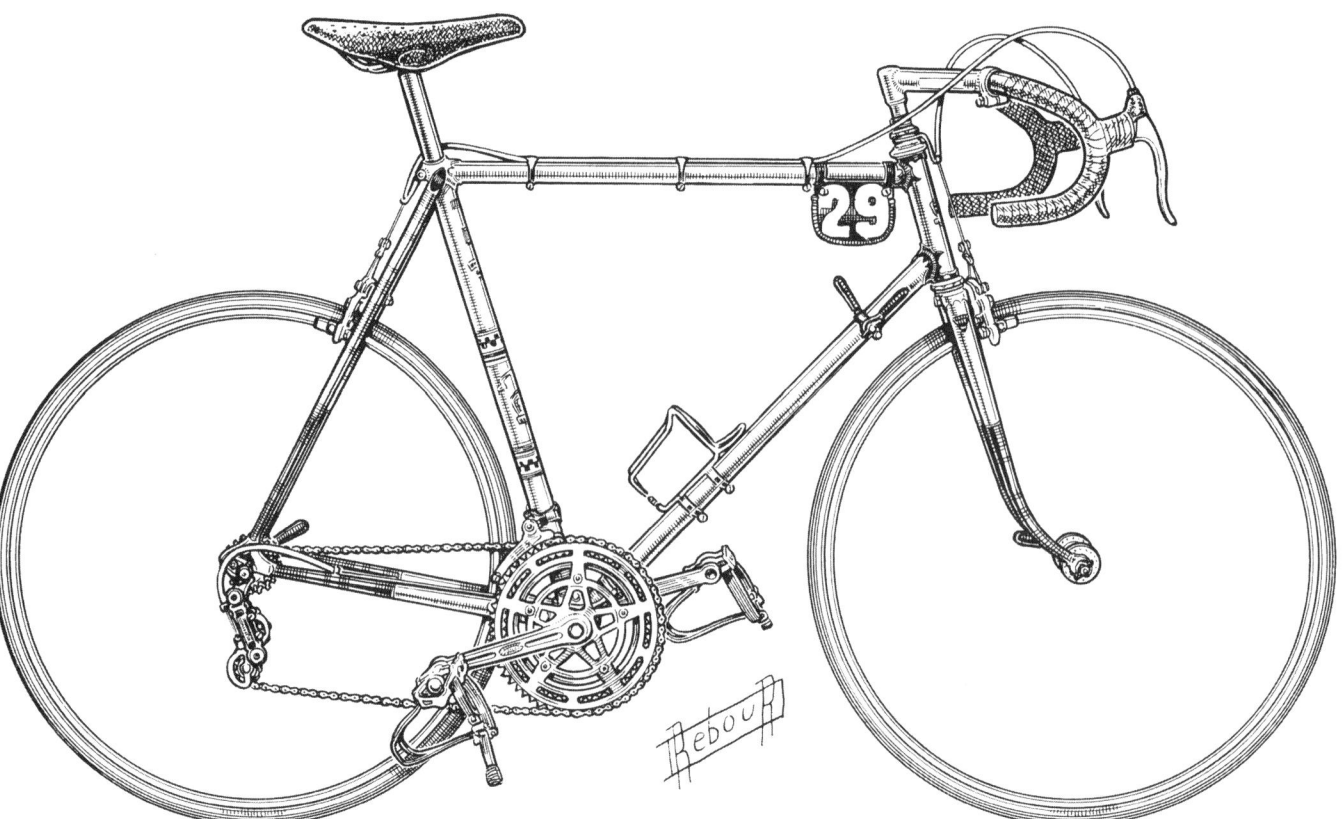

Chapter 14. Lighting Equipment

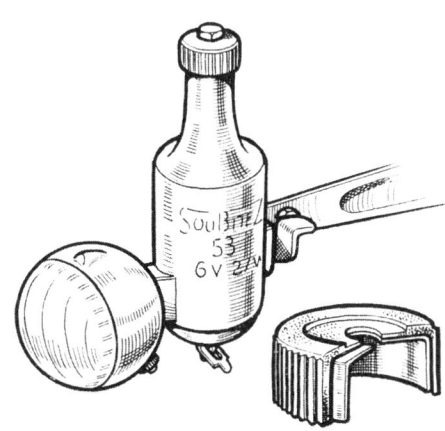

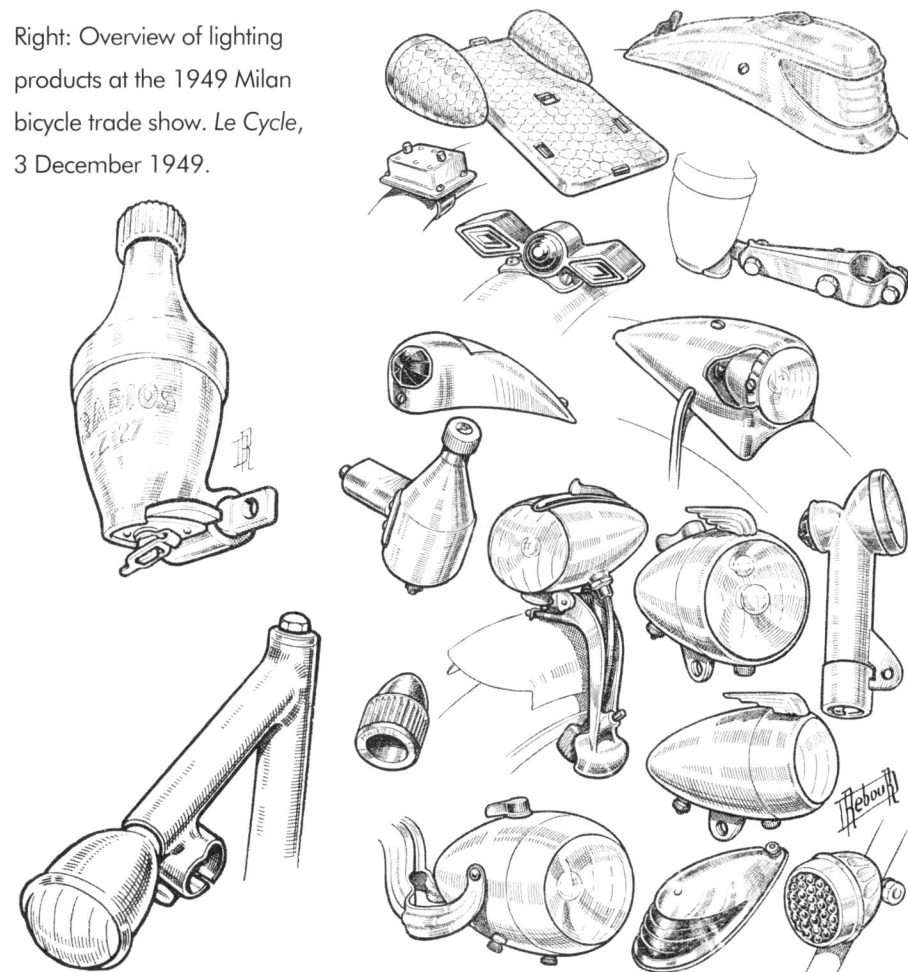

Right: Overview of lighting products at the 1949 Milan bicycle trade show. *Le Cycle*, 3 December 1949.

Above: Soubitez bloc-dynamo and rubber roller cap detail. *Le Cycle*, 9 October 1950.

Right: Radios dynamo. *Le Cycle*, 13 August 1949.

Lower right: Malecote stem-mounted mini-headlight. *Le Cycle*, 6 February 1950.

Below: Walter Godefroot finished second in the 1970 Tour de France on this Italian-made Chiorda bicycle. *Le Cycle*, August-September 1970.

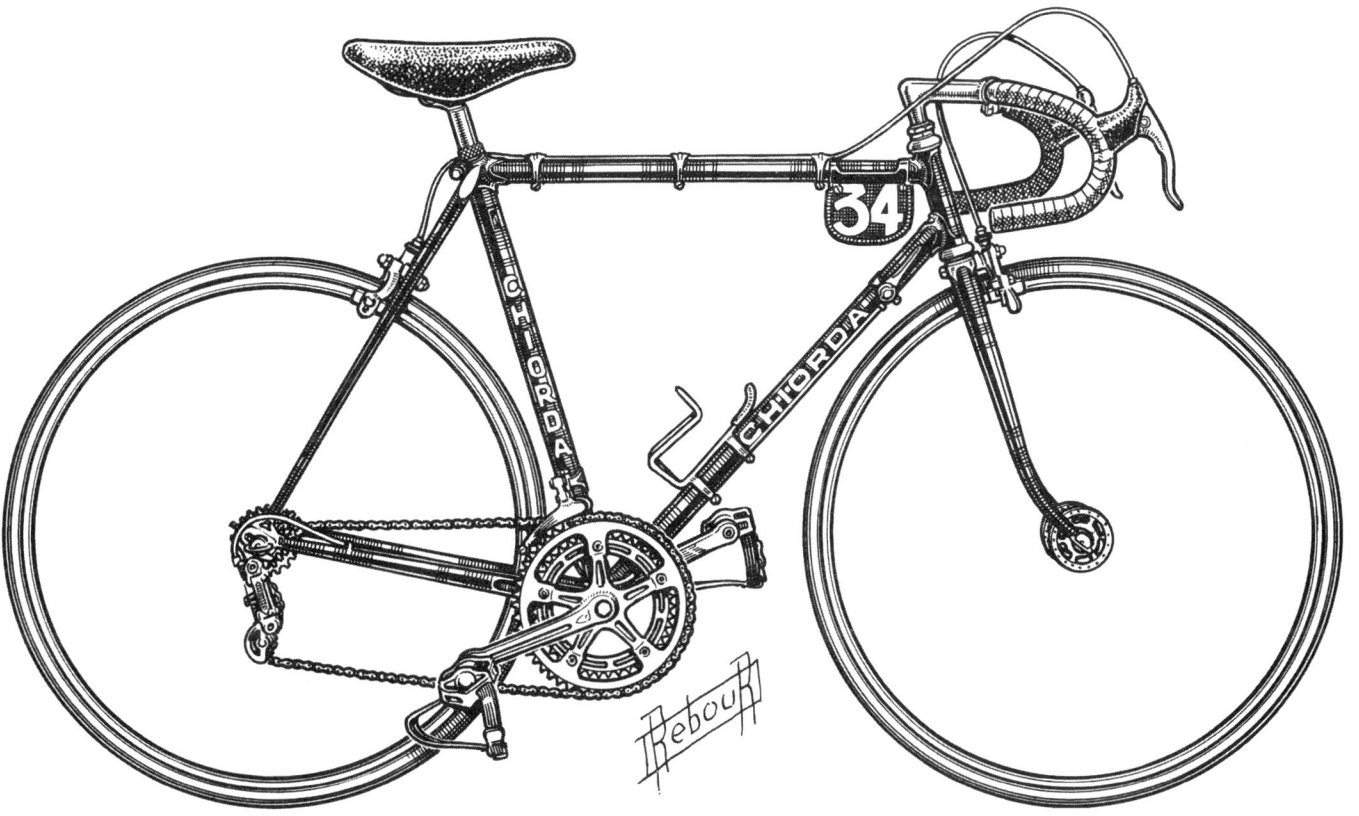

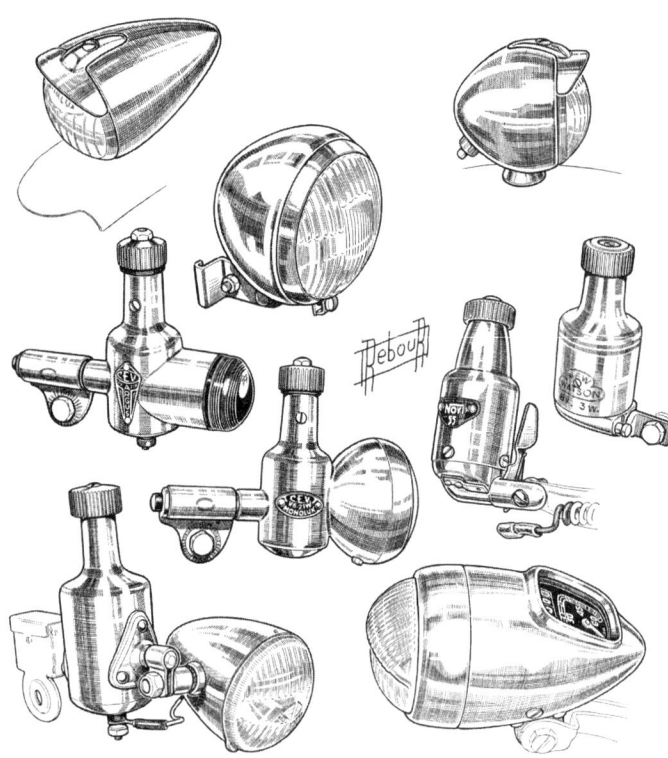
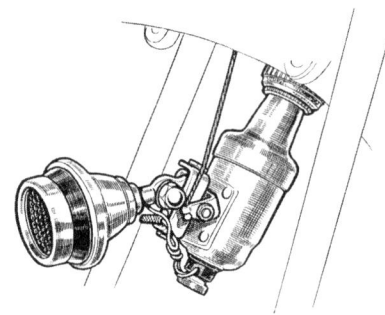
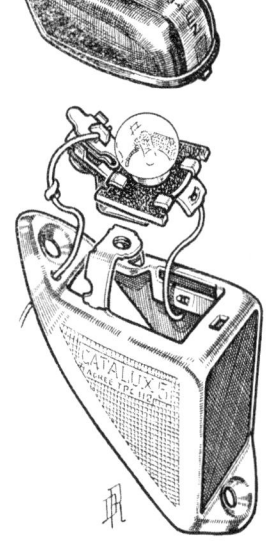
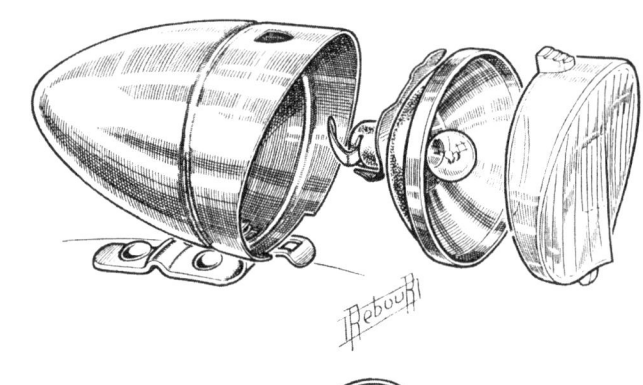

Above: cable-controlled JOS dynamo and rear light. *Le Cycle*, 24 Oct. 1953.
Right: Exploded view of Catalux rear light. *Le Cycle*, 27 June 1953.
Below: Exploded view of Soubitez headlight. *Le Cycle*, 1 November 1958.

Above: Overview of lighting products at the 1954 Paris bicycle trade show. *Le Cycle*, 30 October 1954.

Below: Flandria machine ridden by Joop Zoetemelk, 2nd in the 1970 Tour de France. *Le Cycle*, August-September 1970.**

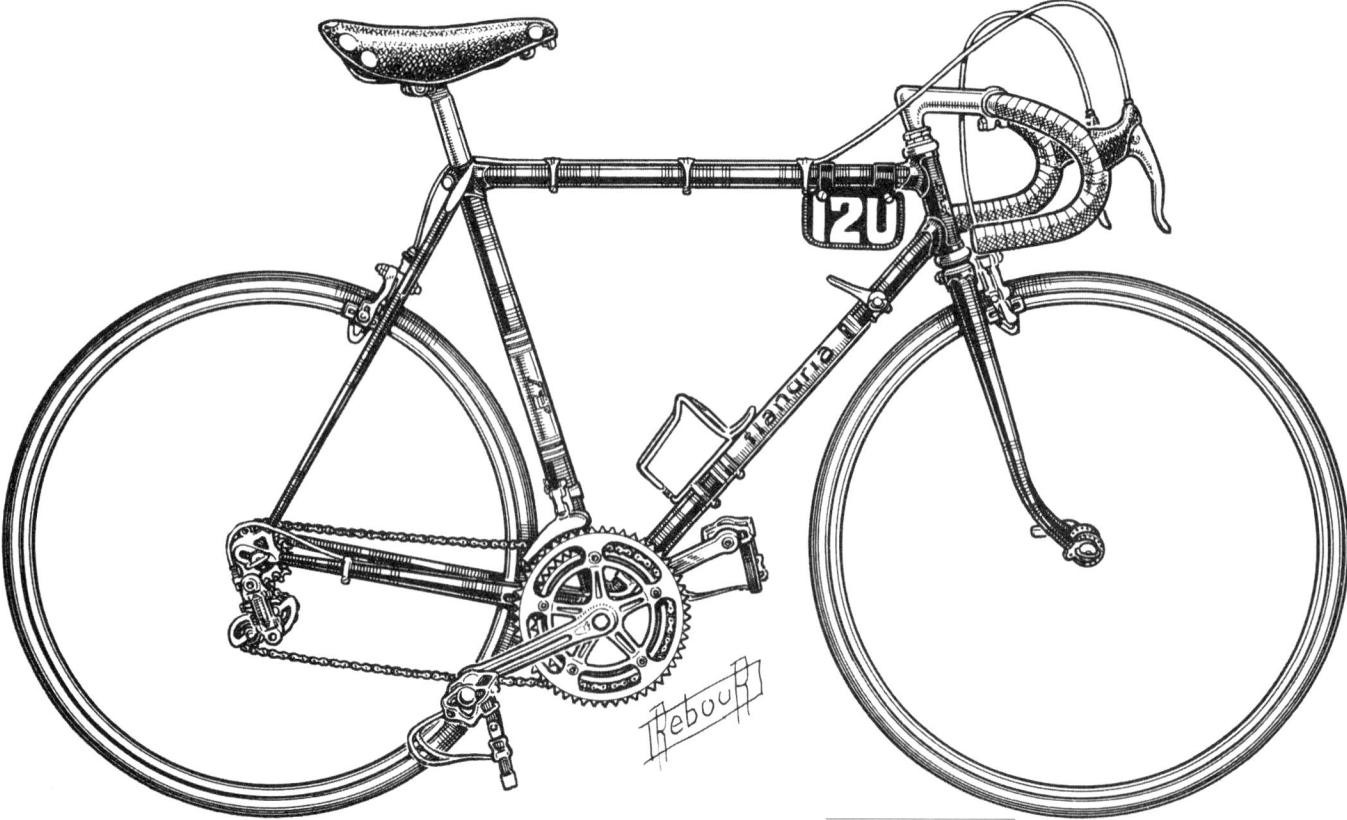

** See pages 269–271 for expanded caption text.

Chapter 14. Lighting Equipment

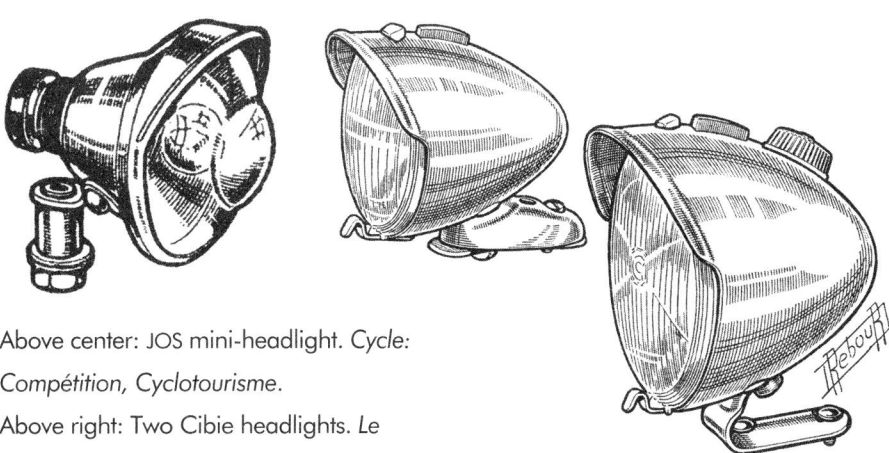

Above center: JOS mini-headlight. *Cycle: Compétition, Cyclotourisme.*

Above right: Two Cibie headlights. *Le Cycle,* October 1961.

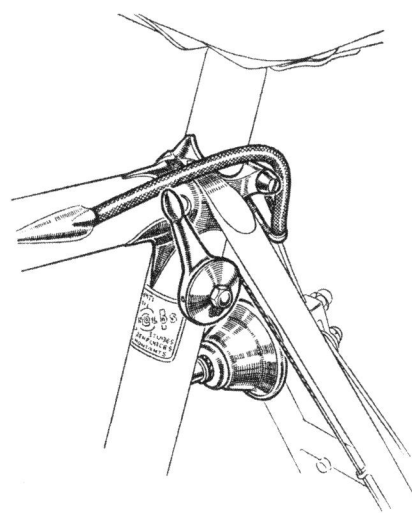

Above: Frame-mounted rear light and shifter used to activate the dynamo on a rondonneur bike. *Cycle: Compétition, Cyclotourisme.*

Right: JRC dynamo and 2-bulb headlight detail presented at the 1965 Brussels bicycle trade show. *Le Cycle,* April 1965.

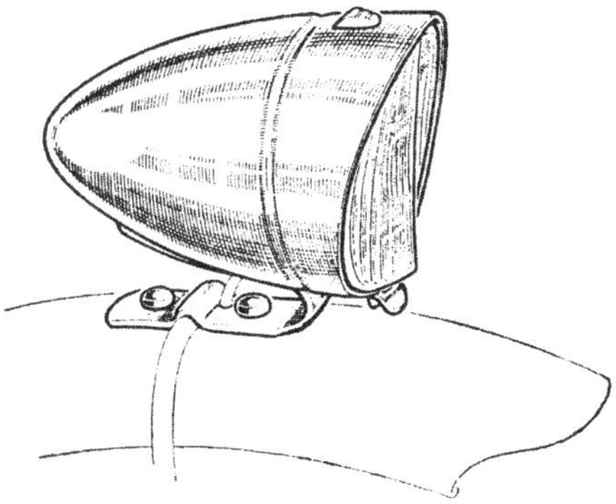

Below: Kessels bicycle ridden by Eddy Merckx, winner of the 1970 Tour de France. *Le Cycle,* August-September 1970.

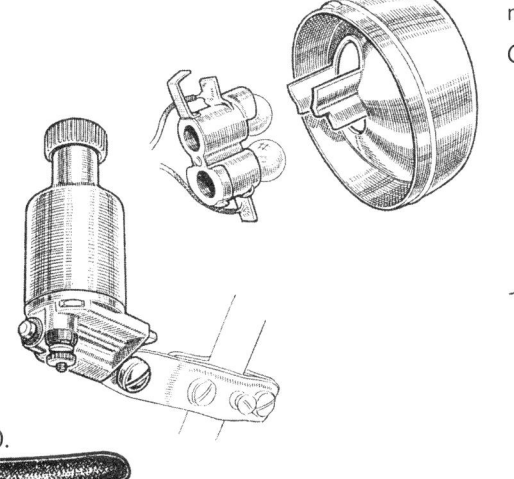

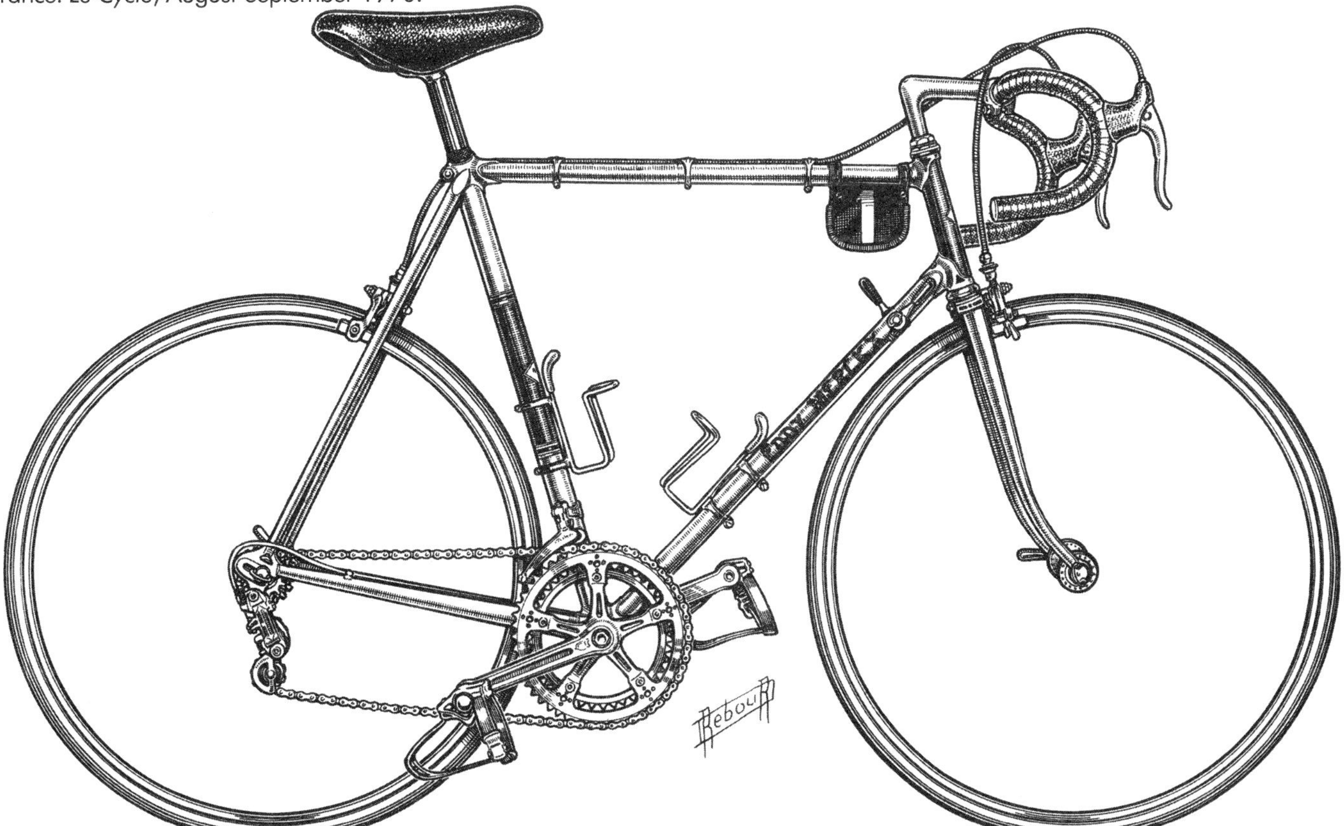

Below: Soubitez headlight with mudguard mounting. *Cycle: Compétition, Cyclotourisme.*

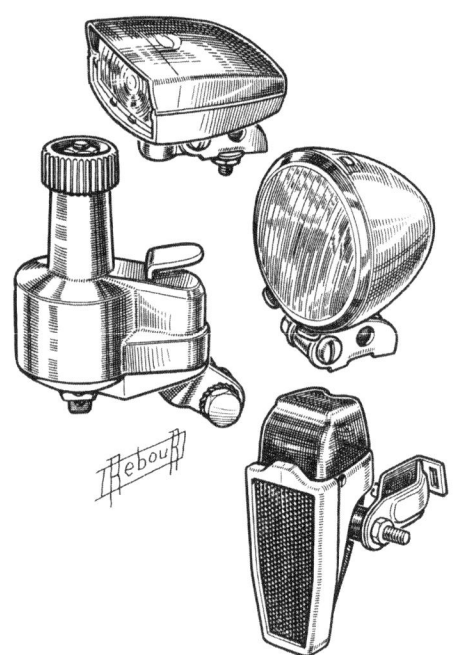
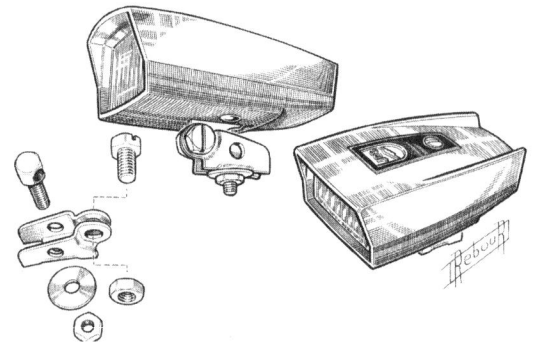

Left: Two views of a 1962 JOS headlight, and exploded view of mounting detail. *Le Cycle*, April 1963.

Below: Exploded view of Cibie headlight. *Cycles de Compétition et Randonneuses*.

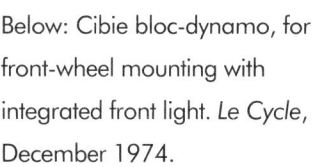

Below: Cibie bloc-dynamo, for front-wheel mounting with integrated front light. *Le Cycle*, December 1974.

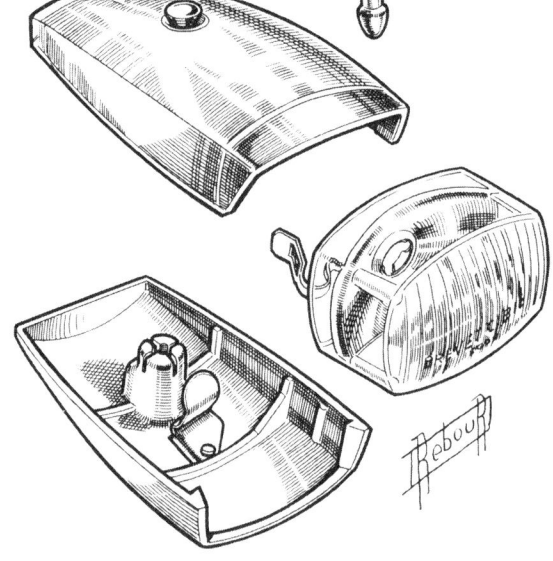

Above: Cibie dynamo lighting set, with rear light and two types of headlight. *Le Cycle*, October 1972.

Below: First amongst the French riders in the 1970 Tour de France was 7th-place finisher Raymond Poulidor. *Le Cycle*, August-September 1970.

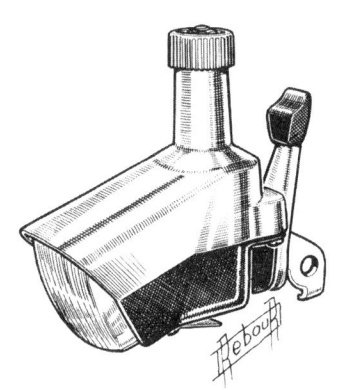

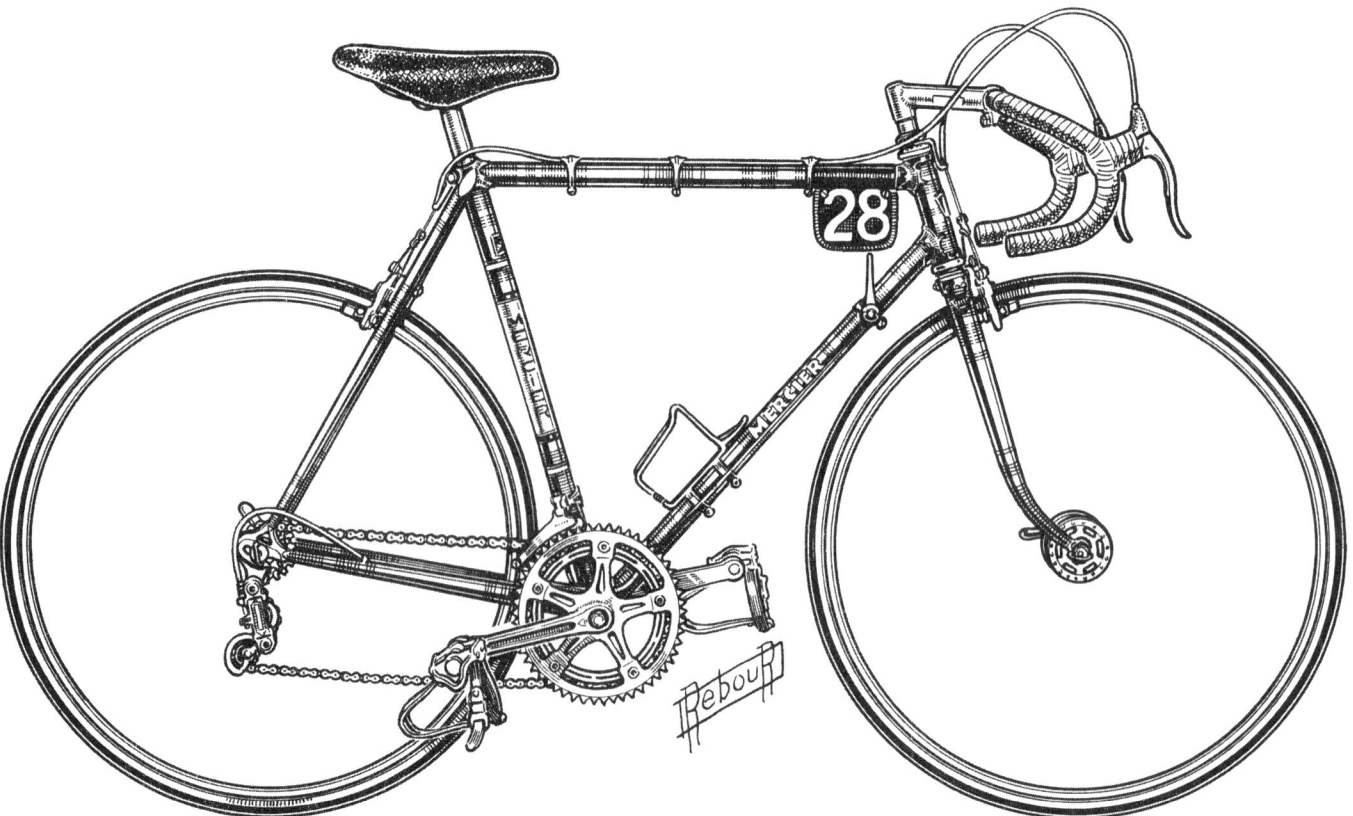

Chapter 14. Lighting Equipment

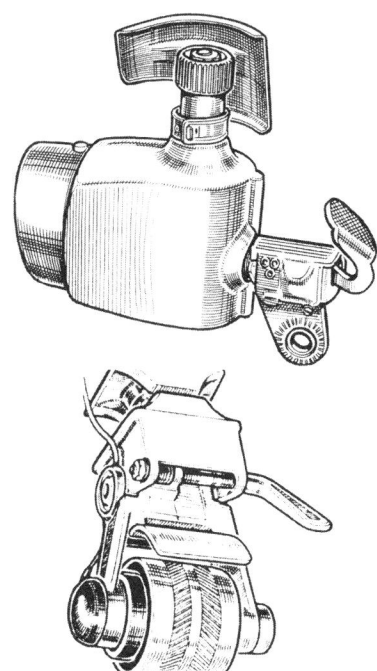

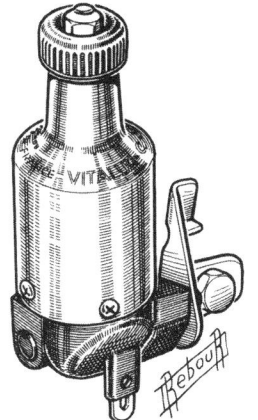

Left: Shrouded tire-sidewall dynamo, from Sanyo, of Japan. *Le Cycle*, March 1968.
Right: Cat-Eye battery light system, also from Japan. 1983 Milremo catalogue.

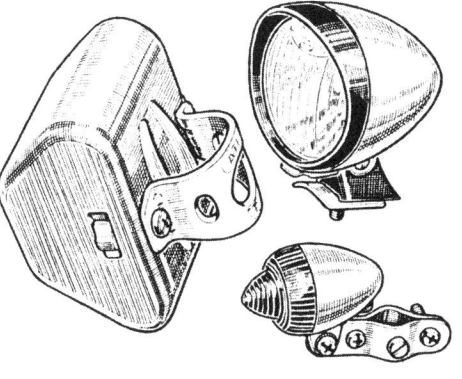

Left: Vitalux dynamo. *Le Cycle*, December 1974.

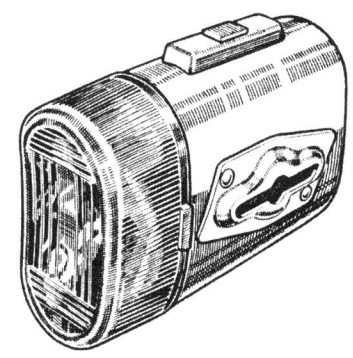

Above: Introduced in the late 1970s, this Japanese Sanyo roller-dynamo, installed behind the bottom bracket, rolled off the top of the tire, rather than the side. It tended to slip in the rain. 1980 Milremo catalogue.
Below: Peugeot machine ridden by Raymond Delisle in the 1970 Tour de France. *Le Cycle*, August-September 1970.

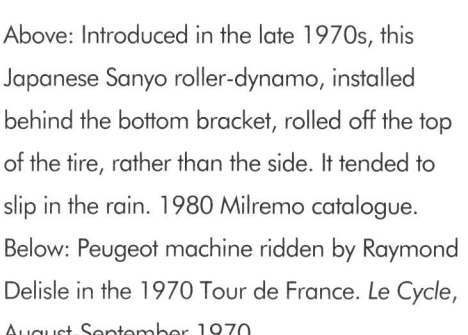

Left and above: These Berec front and rear battery lights, designed around the British Standard bicycle lighting specifications, were used by most British cyclists right up to the 1990s. 1983 Milremo catalogue.

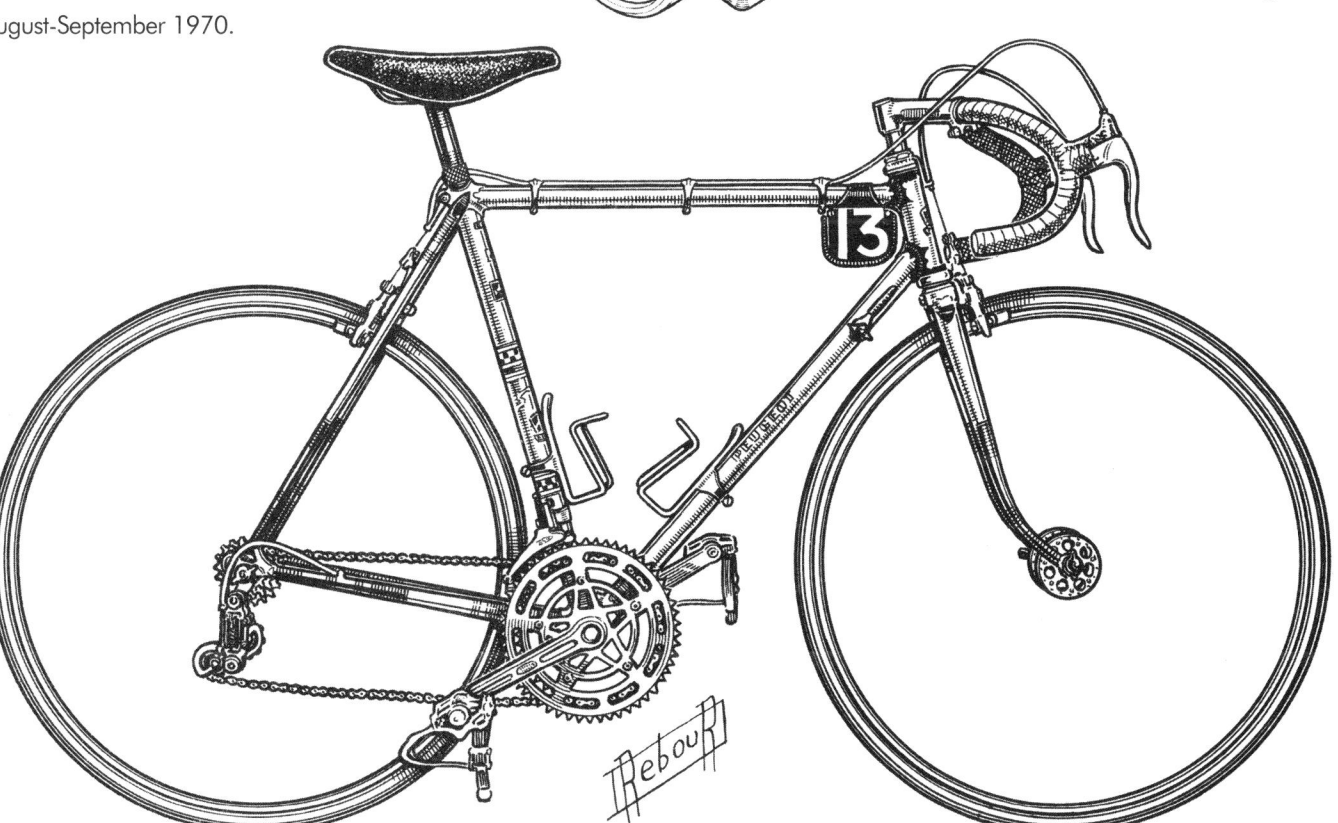

199

Chapter 15. Other Accessories

In this chapter, we have collected some images of other accessories, ranging from the humble water bottle to cyclometers, and from pumps to CO_2 inflators, which you may be surprised to note were available much earlier than generally perceived. Also included are some small tool kits. Other tools, together with professional workshop equipment, are covered separately in Chapter 25.

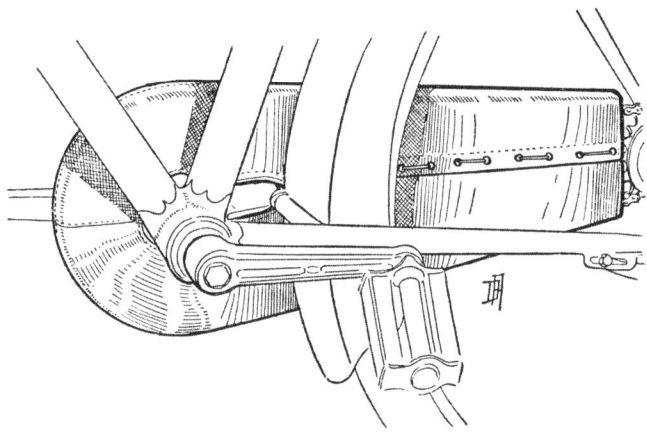

Above: Enclosed oil-cloth chainguard on a René Herse city bike. *Le Cycle*, 6 December 1947.

Below: Motobécane time-trial bike used by Luis Ocaña, of Spain, in the 1970 Tour de France. *Le Cycle*, February 1971.**

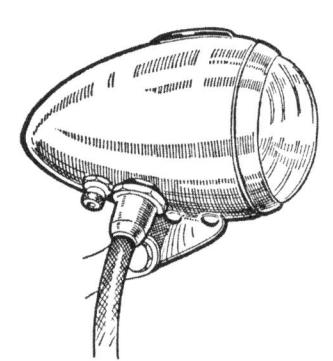

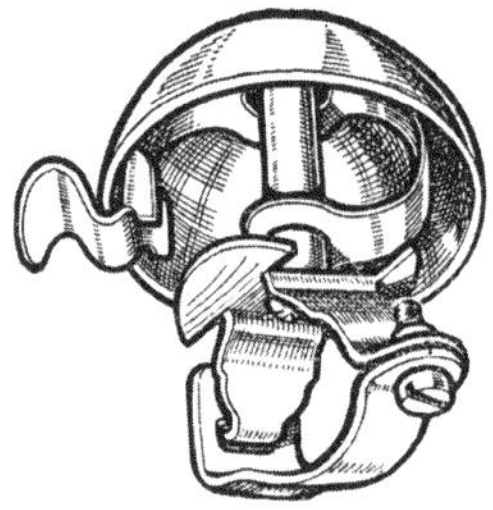

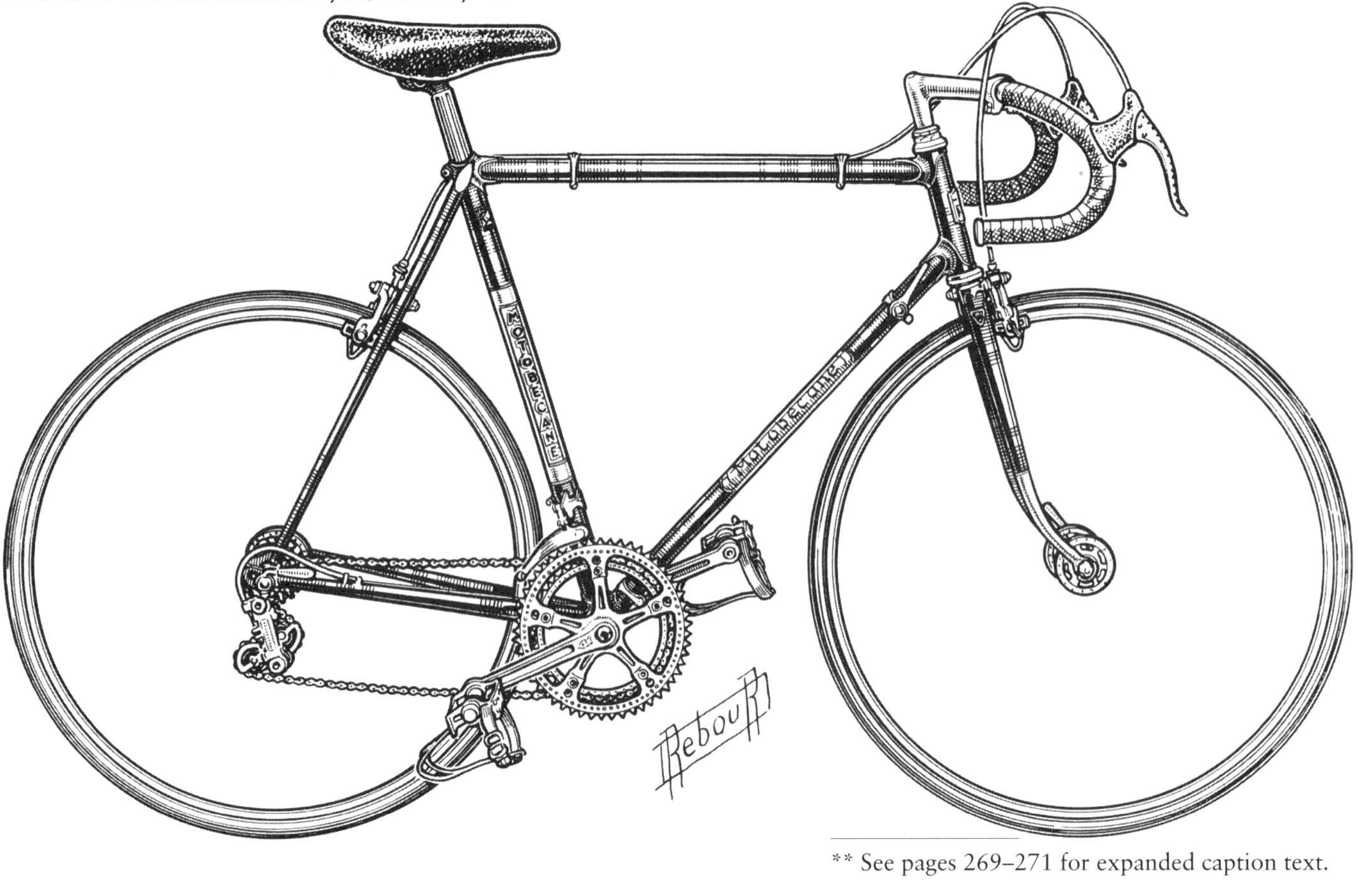

Above: TECLA single-ring bell. *Le Cycle*, 9 October 1948.

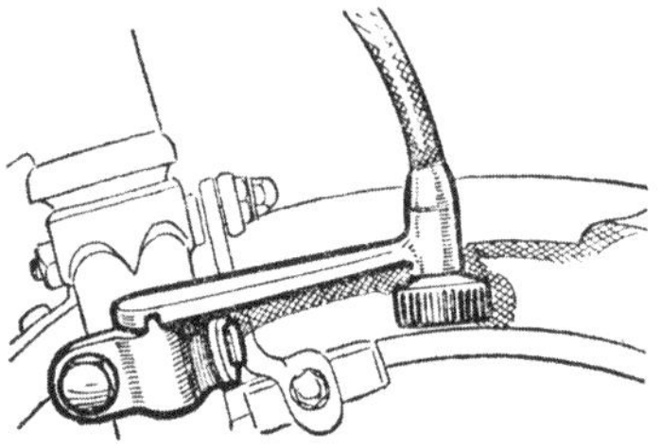

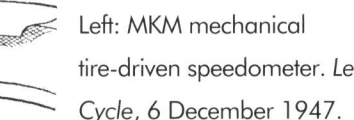

Left: MKM mechanical tire-driven speedometer. *Le Cycle*, 6 December 1947.

** See pages 269–271 for expanded caption text.

Chapter 15. Other Accessories

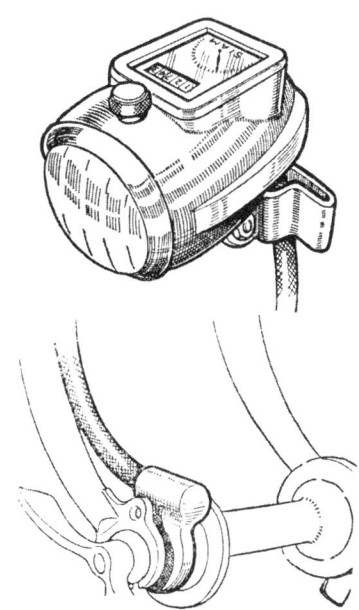

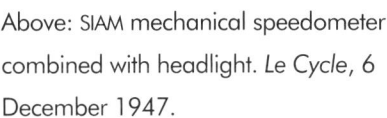

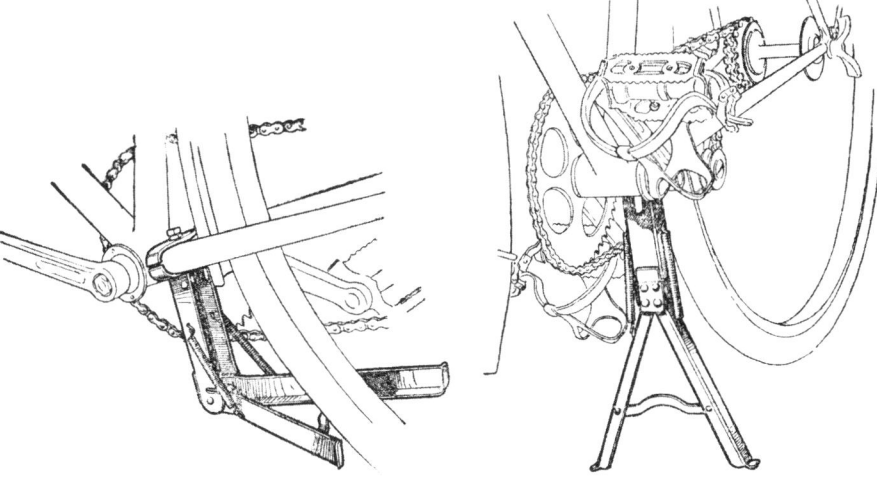

Above: SIAM mechanical speedometer combined with headlight. *Le Cycle*, 6 December 1947.

Right: Alcyon combined chainguard and front derailleur. *Le Cycle*, 11 November 1947.

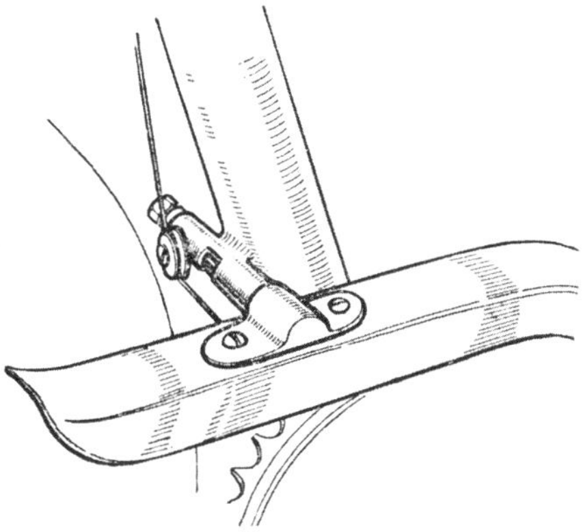

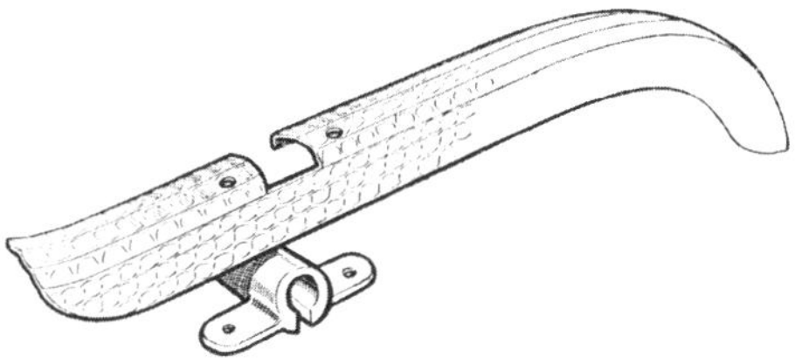

Below: Flandria bicycle of Joop Zoetemelk, second in the 1971 Tour de France. *Le Cycle*, August–September 1971.

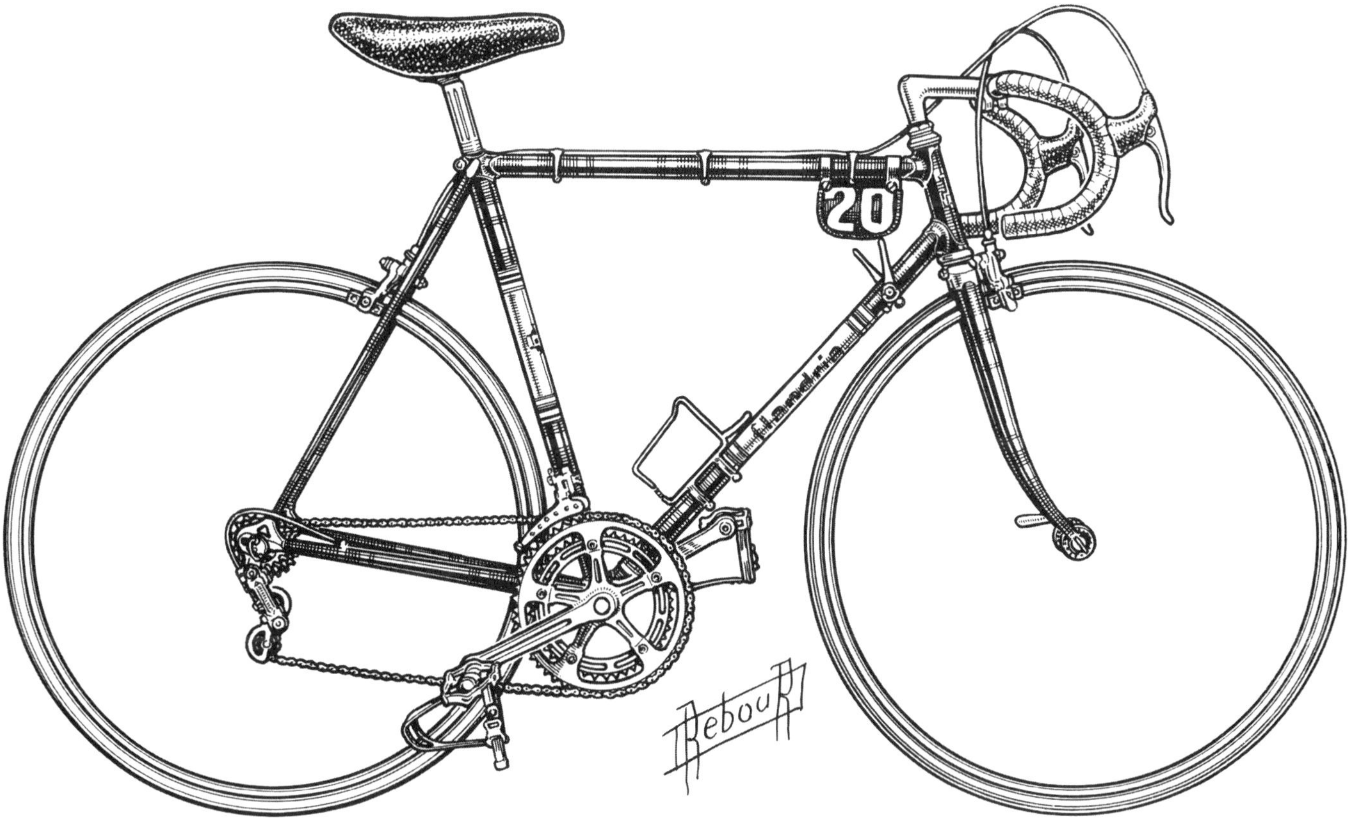

Above: AS2 heavy-duty prop stand. *Le Cycle*, 24 January 1948.

Below: Another version of the chainguard for use with a front derailleur. *Le Cycle*, 18 December 1948.

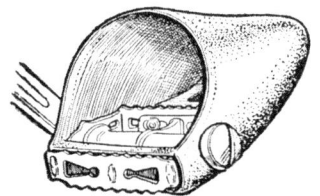

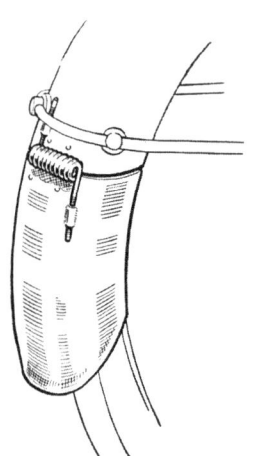

Above: Cold-weather shoe cover. *Le Cycle*, 24 March 1947.

Left: Spring-loaded mud-flap at bottom of mudguard. *Le Cycle*, 18 December 1948.

Below: Winning his third Tour de France in 1971, Eddy Merckx rode this machine bearing his own name, rather than the manufacturer's own Kessels brand name. *Le Cycle*, August-September 1971.

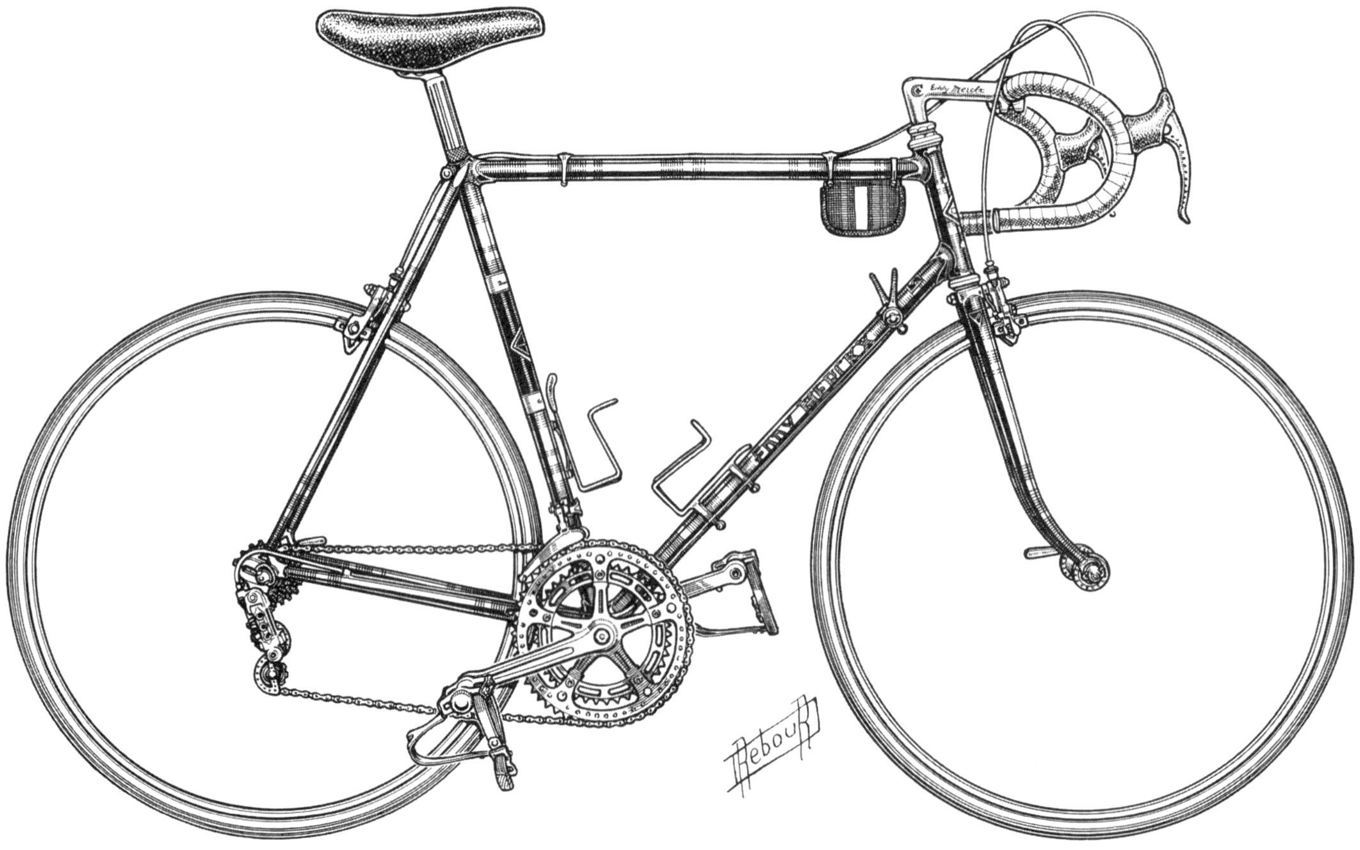

Right: Petitjean battery-powered direction-indicators for mudguard mounting. *Le Cycle*, 4 December 1948.

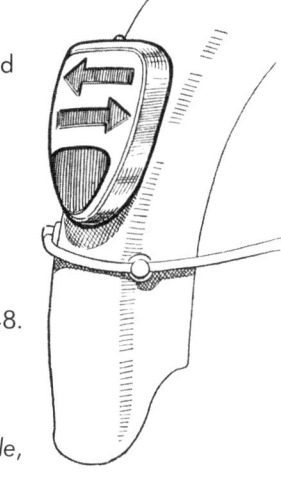

Below: CO_2 inflator. *Le Cycle*, 17 July 1948.

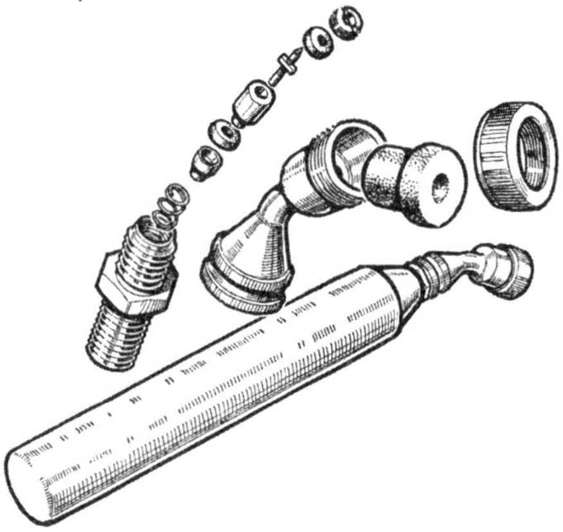

Below: Lightweight prop stand. *Le Cycle*, 18 December 1948.

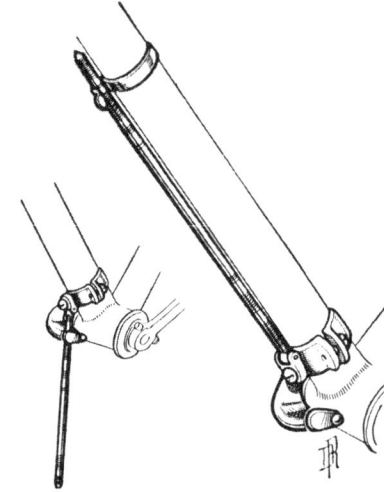

Right: Record hand rest for drop-handlebars with low-mounted brake levers. *Le Cycle*, 16 October 1948.

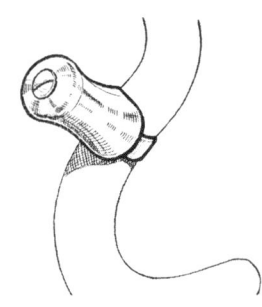

Chapter 15. Other Accessories

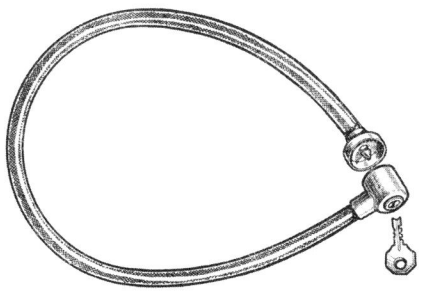

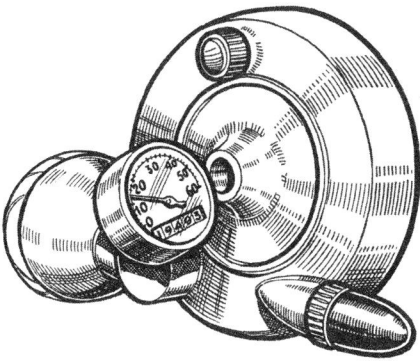

Above: Sirio electric unit with built-in batteries, headlight, rear light, and speedometer. *Le Cycle*, 26 March 1949.

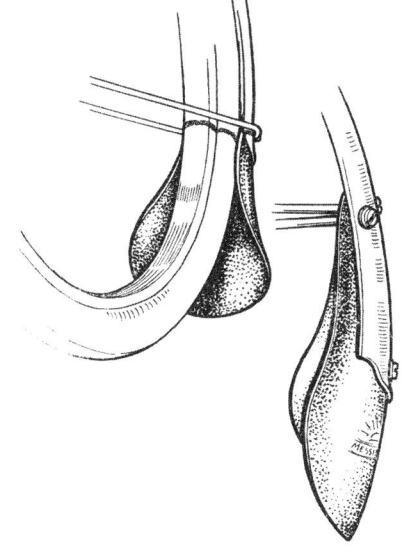

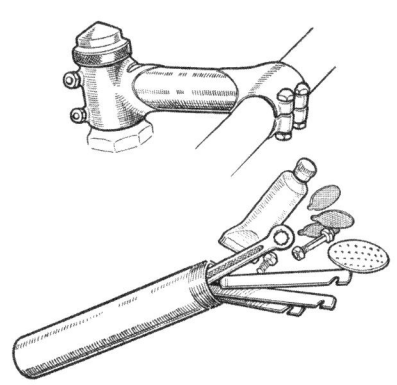

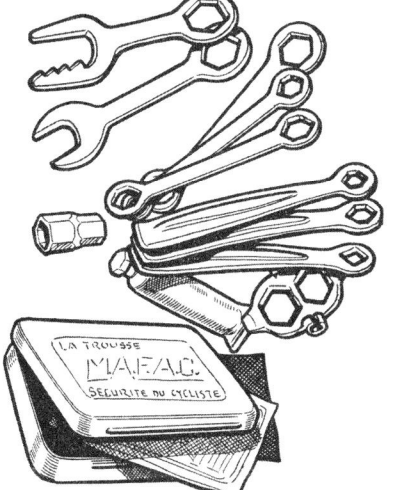

Above: Messidor mud-flap. *Pratique du Vélo*.

Below: Two views of a lightweight bell. *Pratique du Vélo*.

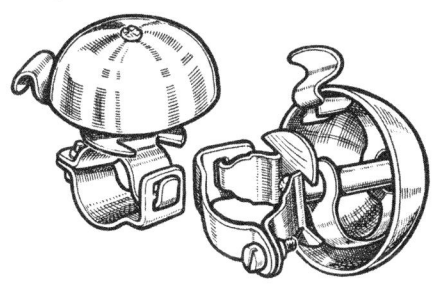

Top left: Cable lock. *Pratique du Vélo*.
Above: Tool kit hidden in the handlebar stem on a Daudon randonneur bike. *Pratique du Vélo*.
Right: Mafac mini tool kit. *Pratique du Vélo*.

Below: 1971 Lejeune bicycle of Lucien Van Impe. *Le Cycle*, August-September 1971.

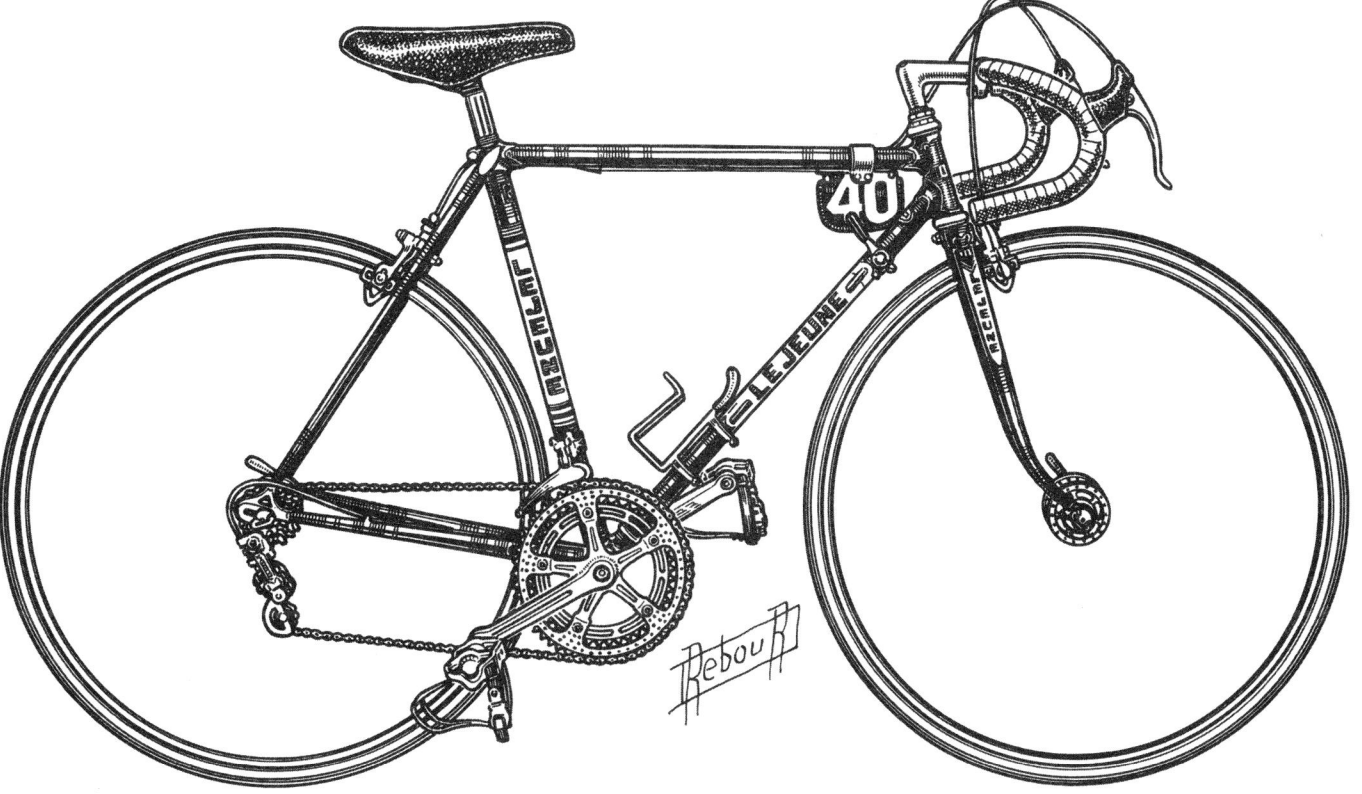

203

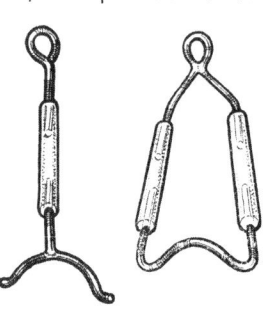

Left: Nupal device for leak-proofing an inner tube. *Le Cycle*, 10 September 1949.

Right: Carlton tire-protectors, or "nail-pullers." *Le Cycle*, 28 May 1949.

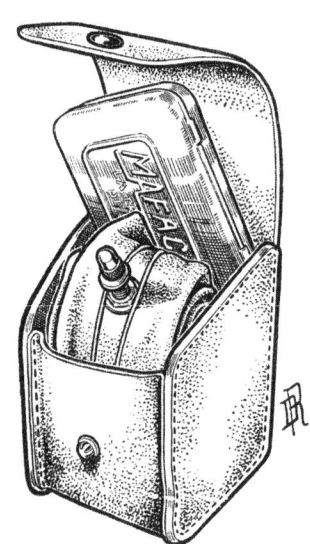

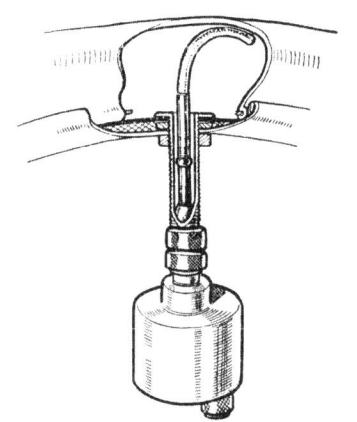

Below: Water bottle mounting detail on René Herse tandem bicycle. *Le Cycle*, 23 April 1949.

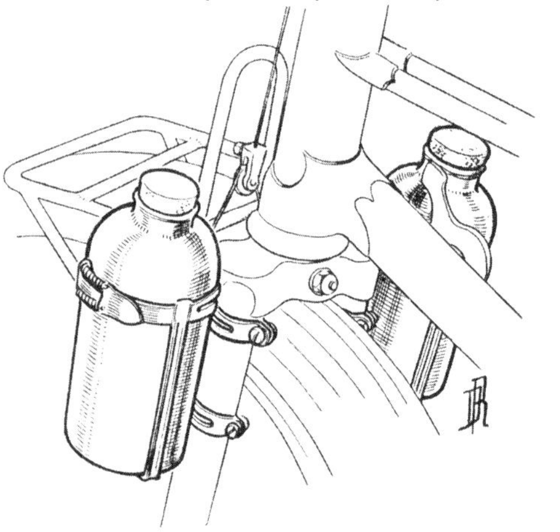

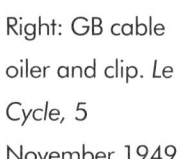

Left: AS steering lock. *Le Cycle*, 28 May 1949.

Above: Mafac pouch for a spare tube or tubular tire and a small repair kit. *Le Cycle*, 7 January 1950.

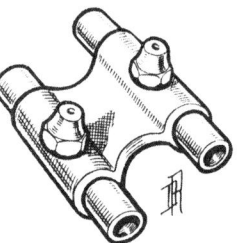

Right: GB cable oiler and clip. *Le Cycle*, 5 November 1949.

Below: Bernard Thévènet, the most promising young French rider in the 1972 Tour de France, rode this Peugeot bicycle. *Le Cycle*, August-September 1972.

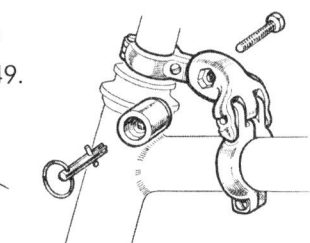

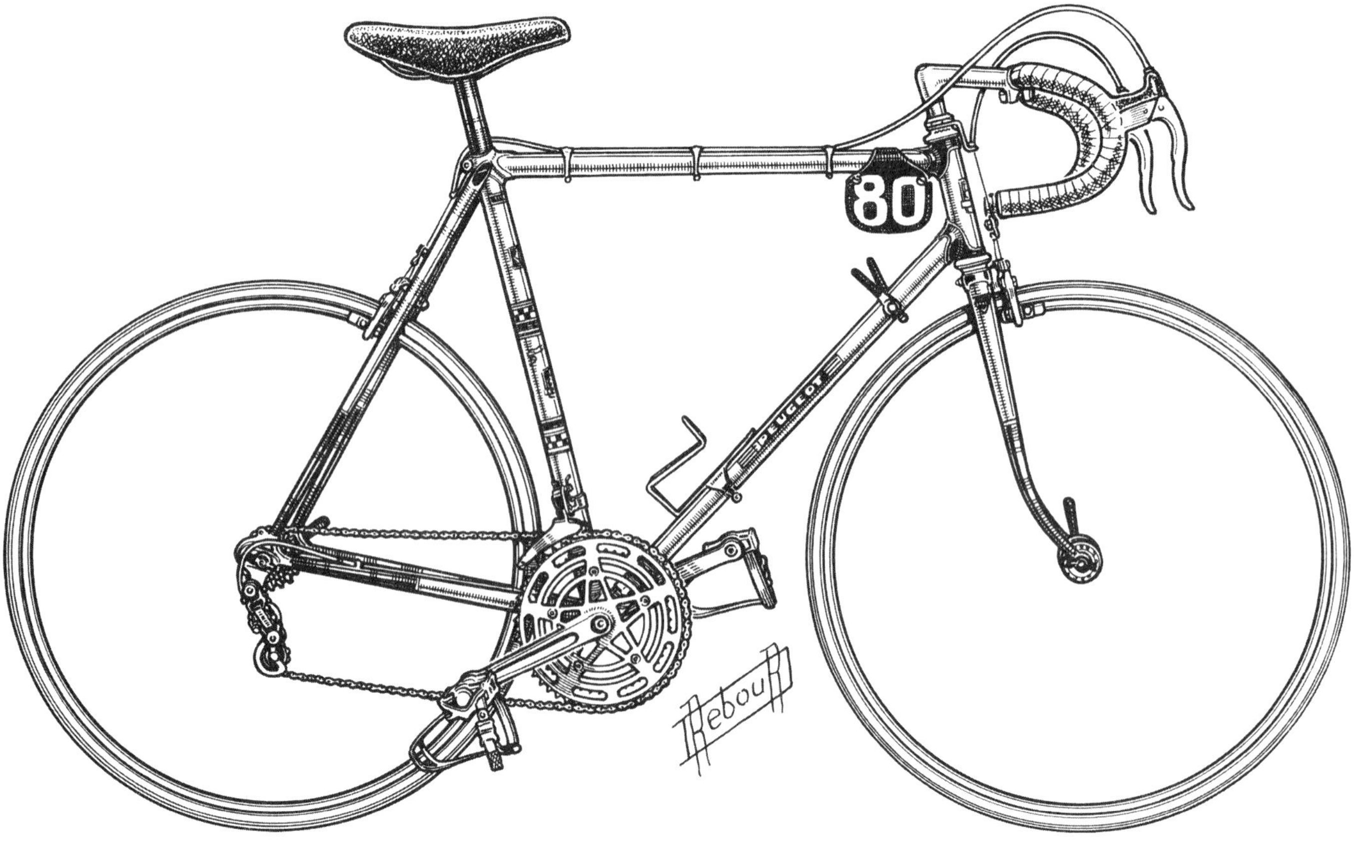

Chapter 15. Other Accessories

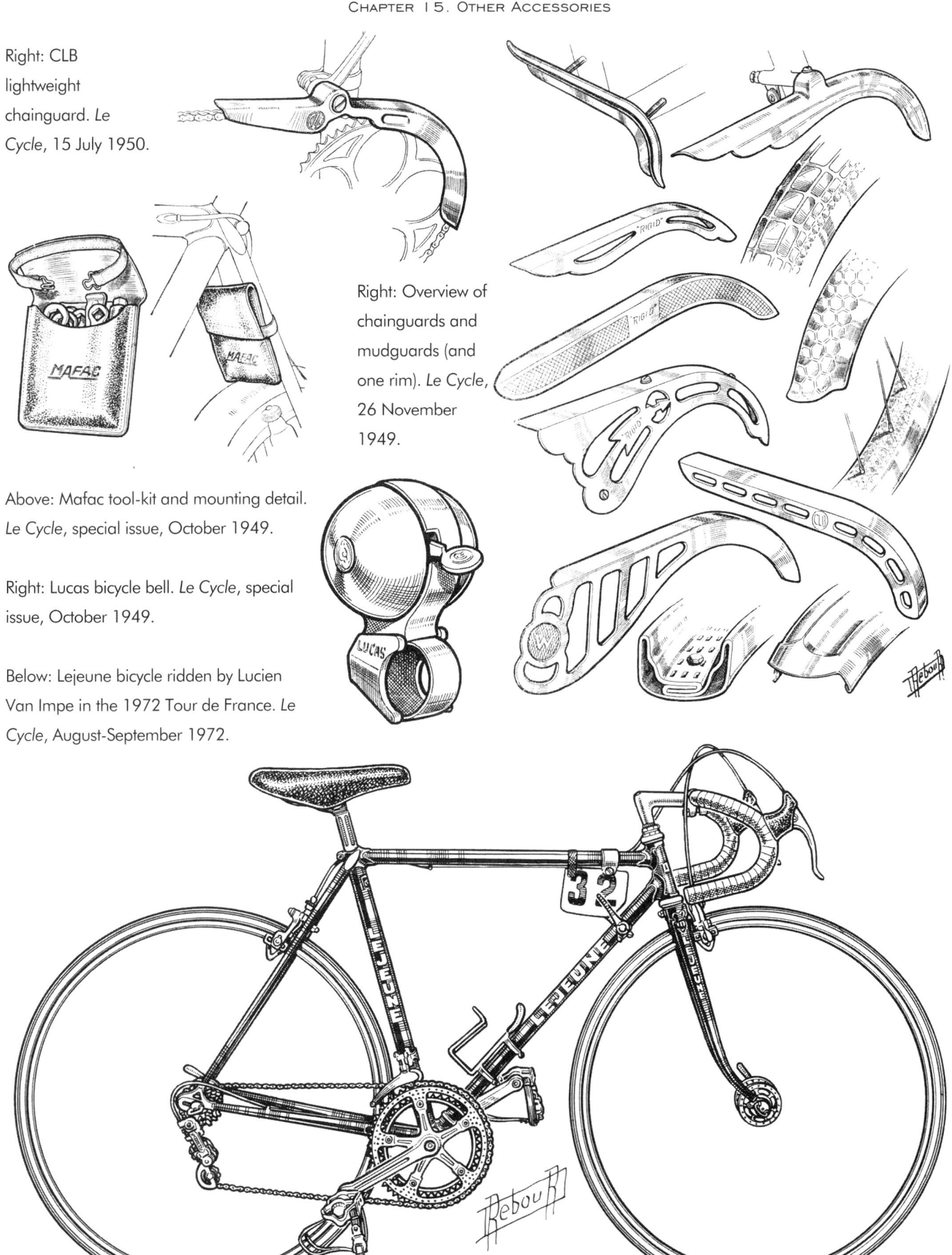

Right: CLB lightweight chainguard. *Le Cycle*, 15 July 1950.

Above: Mafac tool-kit and mounting detail. *Le Cycle*, special issue, October 1949.

Right: Lucas bicycle bell. *Le Cycle*, special issue, October 1949.

Below: Lejeune bicycle ridden by Lucien Van Impe in the 1972 Tour de France. *Le Cycle*, August-September 1972.

Right: Overview of chainguards and mudguards (and one rim). *Le Cycle*, 26 November 1949.

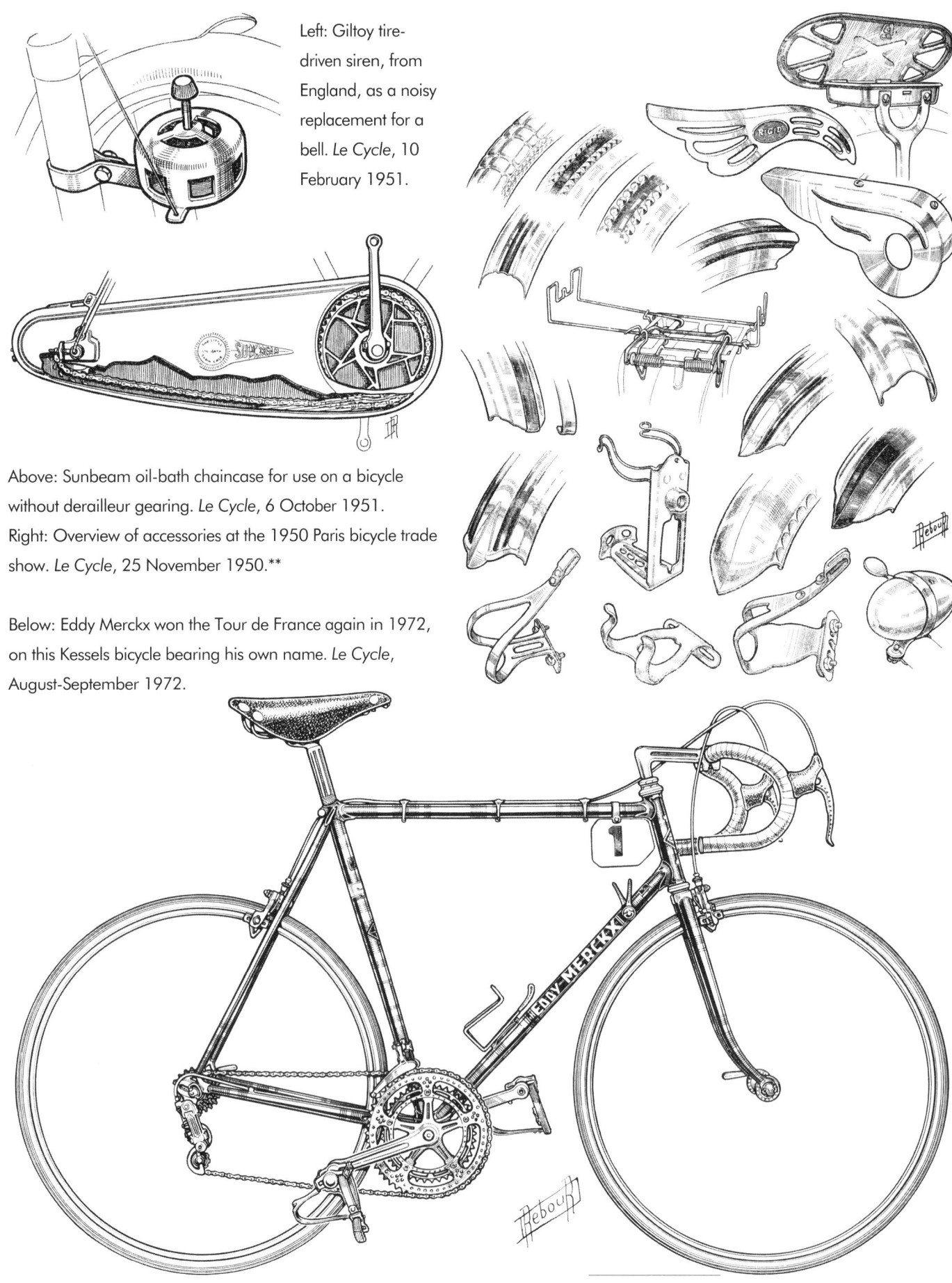

Left: Giltoy tire-driven siren, from England, as a noisy replacement for a bell. *Le Cycle*, 10 February 1951.

Above: Sunbeam oil-bath chaincase for use on a bicycle without derailleur gearing. *Le Cycle*, 6 October 1951.

Right: Overview of accessories at the 1950 Paris bicycle trade show. *Le Cycle*, 25 November 1950.**

Below: Eddy Merckx won the Tour de France again in 1972, on this Kessels bicycle bearing his own name. *Le Cycle*, August–September 1972.

** See pages 269–271 for expanded caption text.

Chapter 15. Other Accessories

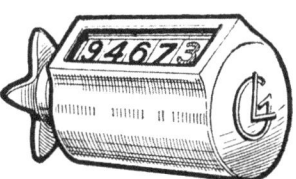

Above: Korean LG mechanical bicycle odometer. *Le Cycle*, 7 April 1951.

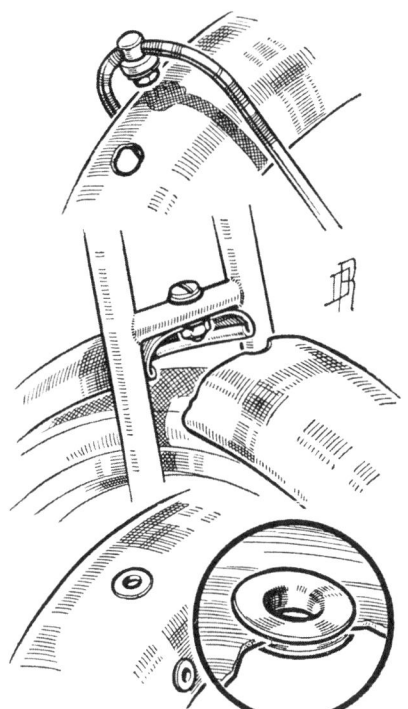

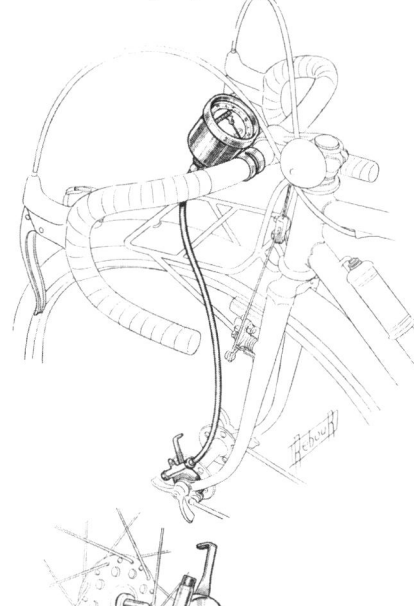

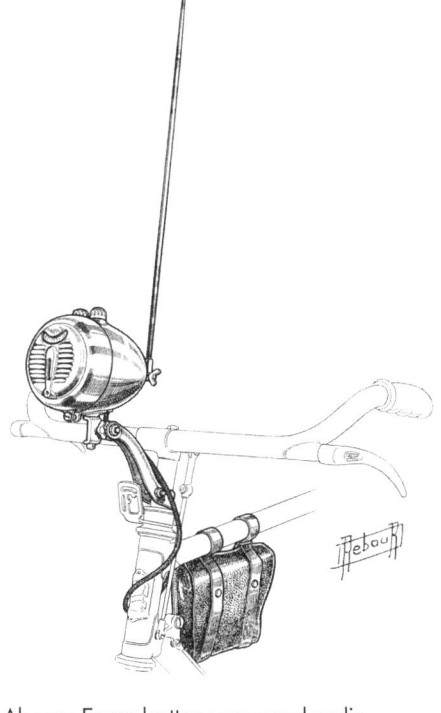

Above: Mudguard installation details, showing eyelets. *Le Cycle*, 19 April 1952.

Below: 1972 Tour de France 3rd-placed Raymond Poulidor rode this Mercier bicycle. *Le Cycle*, August-September 1972.

Above: Faras battery-powered radio disguised as a headlight on a Frejus bicycle at the 1955 Milan bicycle trade show. *Le Cycle*, 8 January 1955.

Above left: Huret hub-driven mechanical speedometer. *Le Cycle*, 9 June 1956.

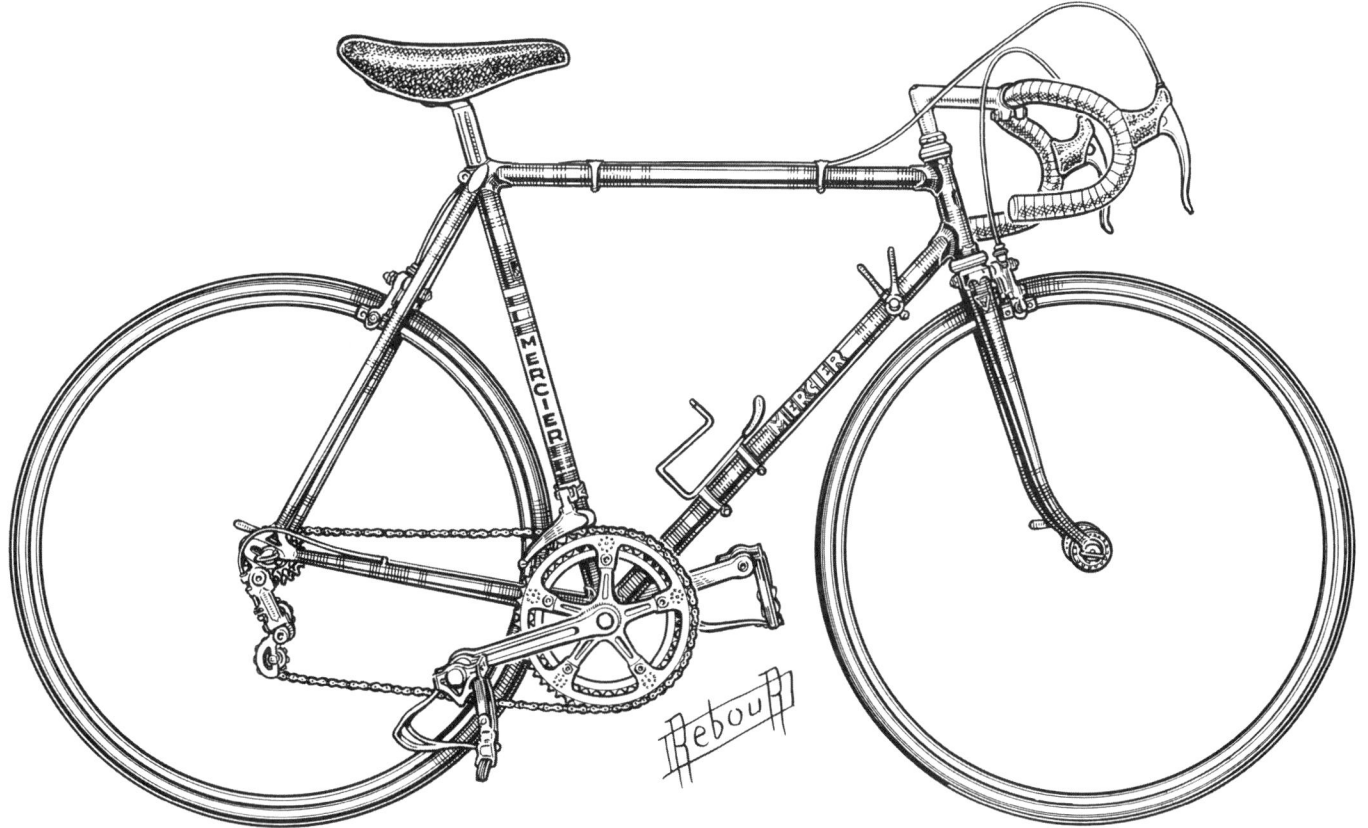

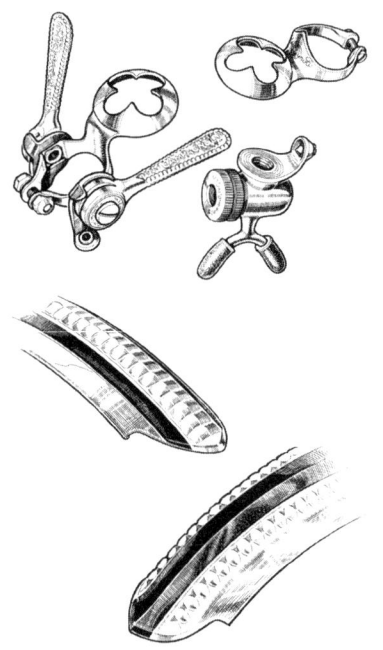
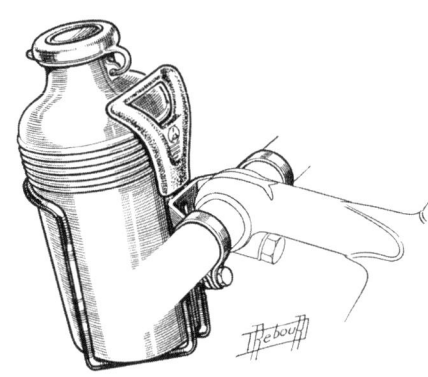
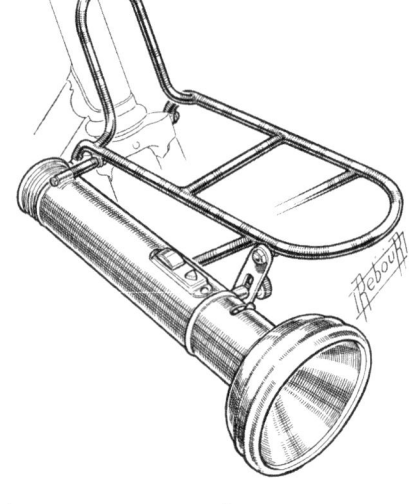

Left: Campagnolo pump parts and accessories. *Cycles de Compétition et Randonneuses.*

Below: TA water bottle installation detail. *Le Cycle*, 27 April 1957.

Above: Léfol mudguard details. *Le Cycle*, October 1961.

Right: Prunier CO2 inflator and mounting detail. *Le Cycle*, 23 March 1957.

Below: René Herse bicycle ridden to victory in the 1972 women's road world championship by Génèvieve Gambillon, of France. *Le Cycle*, October 1972.**

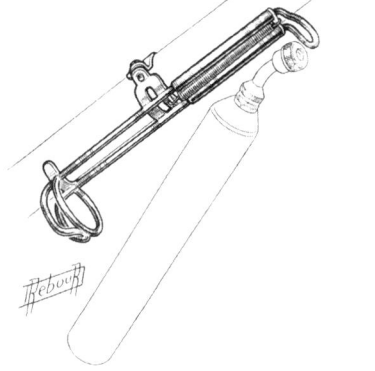
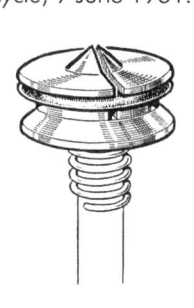
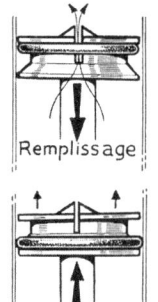

Above: René Herse rack and light detail. *Le Cycle*, February 1961.

Below: Zoe double-action pump detail. *Le Cycle*, 9 June 1961.

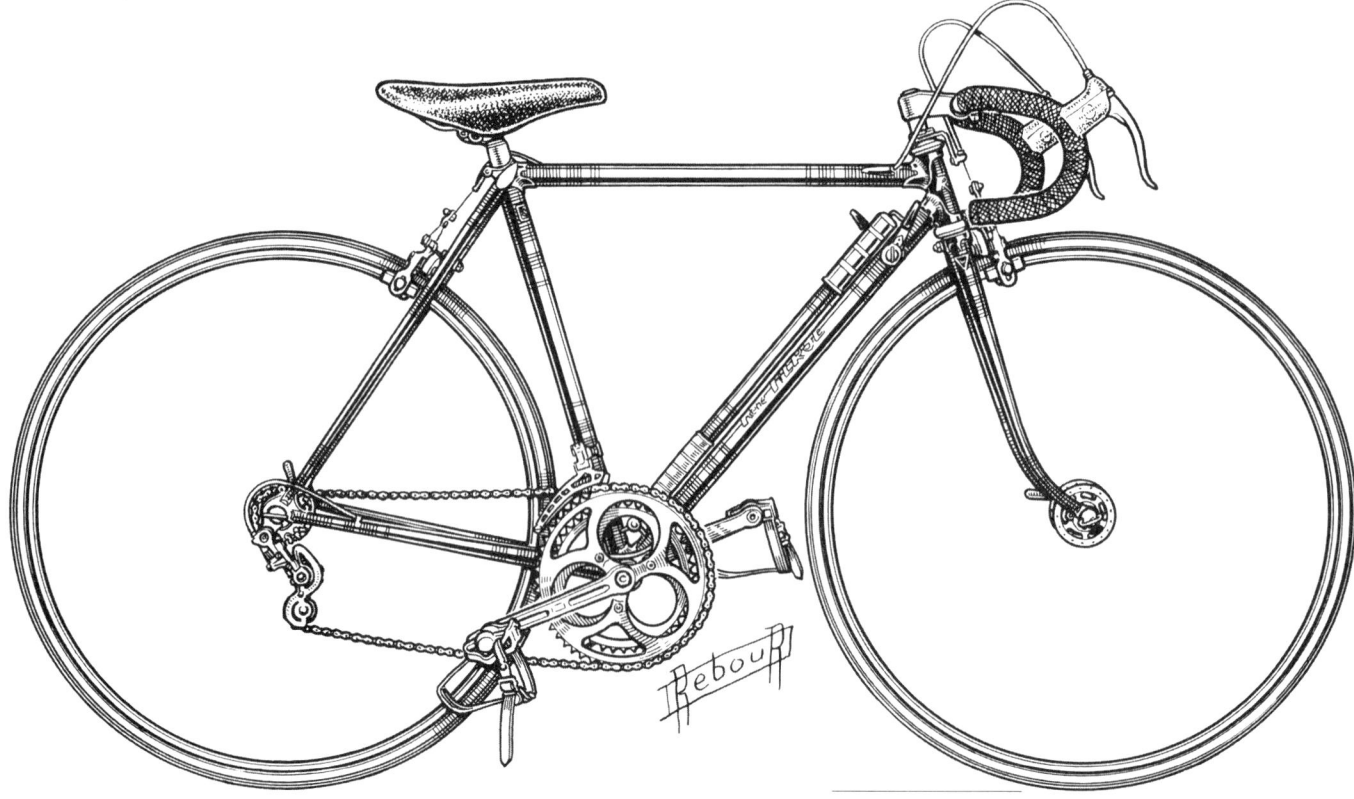

** See pages 269–271 for expanded caption text.

Chapter 15. Other Accessories

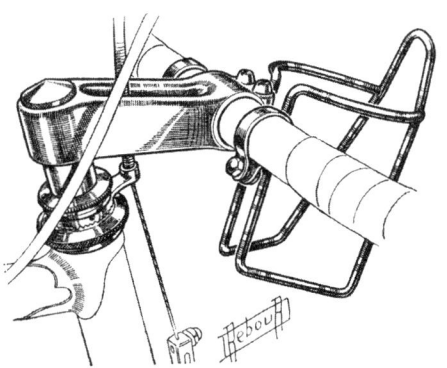

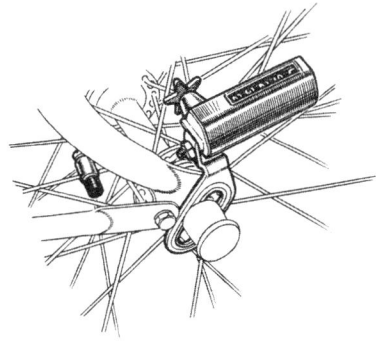

Above: CEV mechanical cyclometer, or odometer. *Le Cycle*, February 1966.
Top left: René Herse bottle cage. *Cycle: Compétition, Cyclotourisme*.

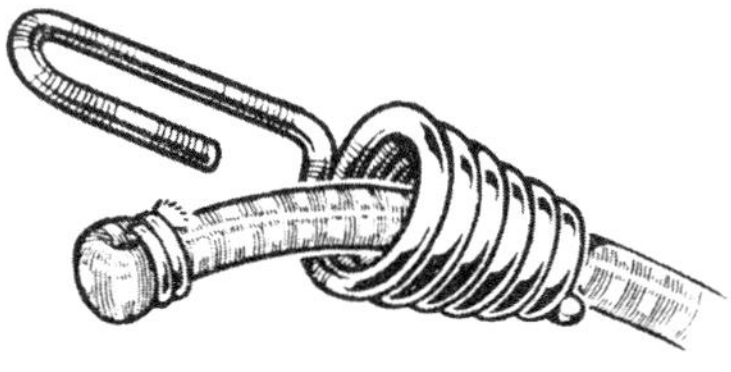

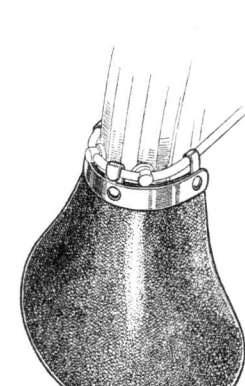

Above: 1957 novelty: the bungee cord. *Le Cycle*, 8 June 1957.
Right: Ruhier mud-flap. *Cycle: Compétition, Cyclotourisme*.

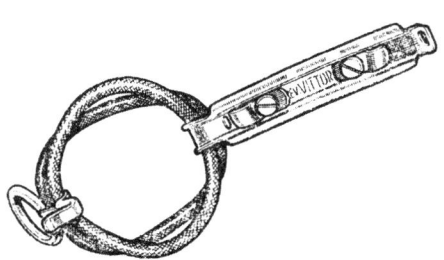

Above: Vittor spare tire attachment clip. *Cycle: Compétition, Cyclotourisme*.
Right: VAR tool and spare tube pouch. *Le Cycle*, December 1966.

Below: Bernard Thévènet's Peugeot bicycle in the 1972 Tour de France, where he placed 9th. *Le Cycle*, August-September 1972.

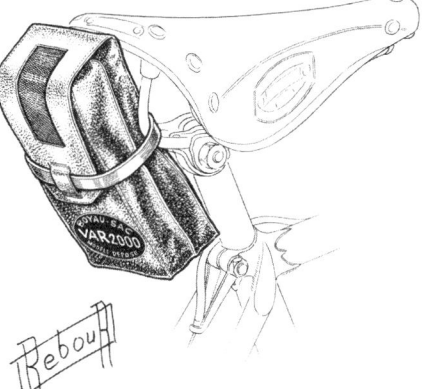

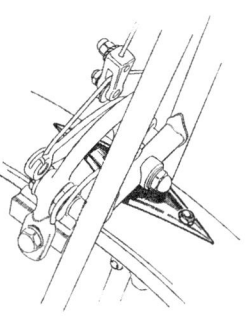

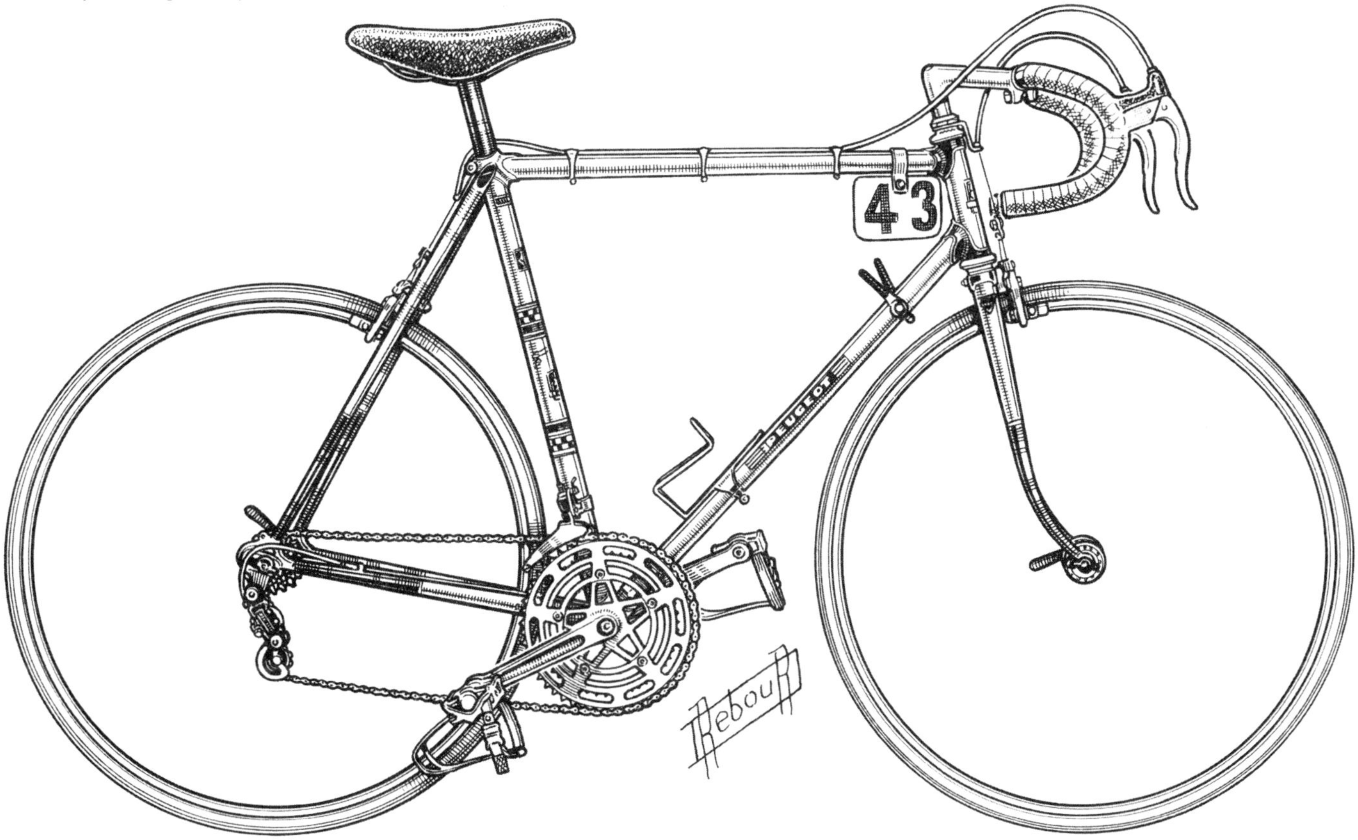

Right: René Herse reinforced mudguard attachment detail. *Cycle: Compétition, Cyclotourisme*.

209

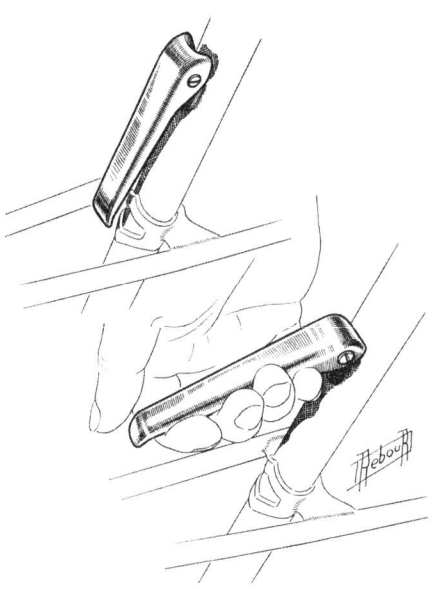

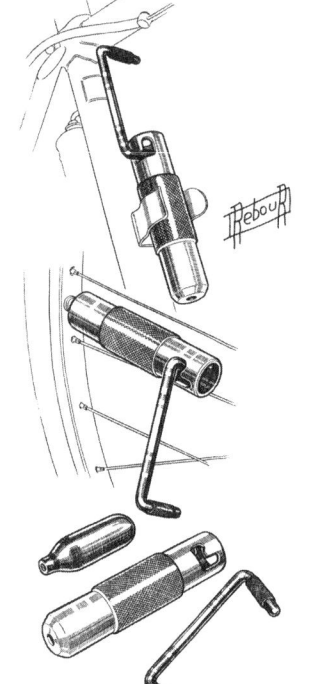

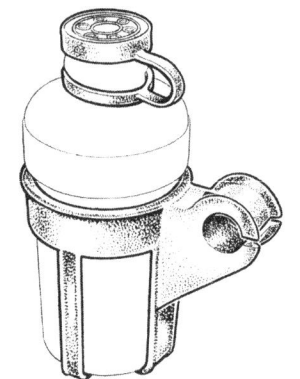

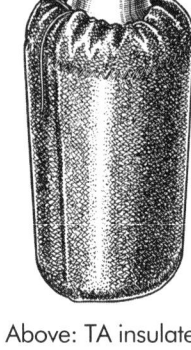

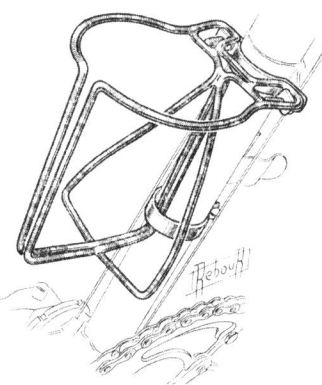

Below left: Details of a CO2 inflator on Jack Taylor bicycle at the 1955 London bicycle trade show. *Le Cycle*, 24 December 1955.

Above: TA insulated bottle. *Le Cycle*, October 1968.

Above: Bicycle carrying handle, shown here on a mixte frame at the 1960 Brussels bicycle trade show. *Le Cycle*, April 1960.

Below: Lejeune track bicycle ridden by Daniel Morélon, of France, winning the 1972 Olympic sprint. *Le Cycle*, October 1972.

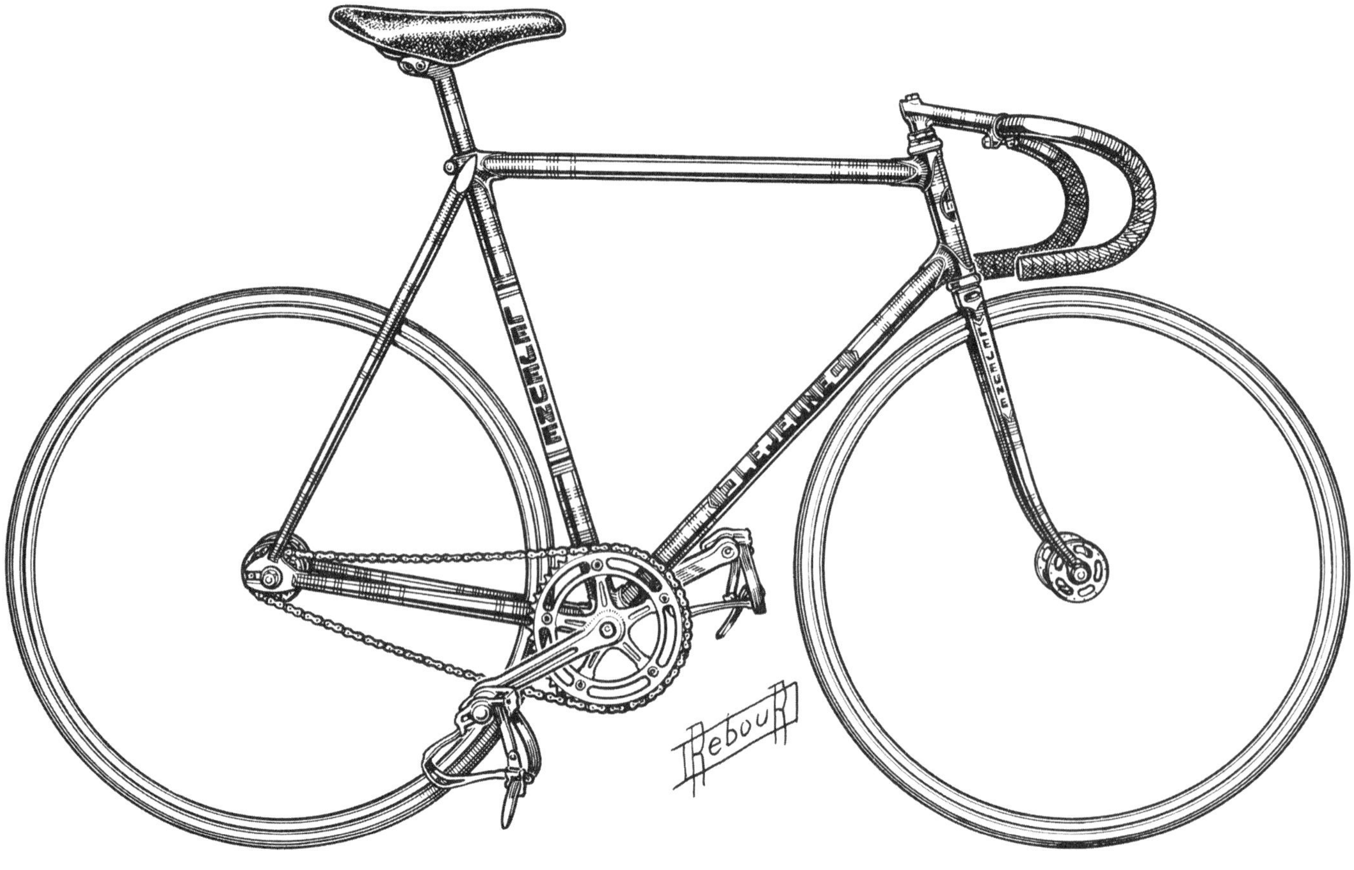

Above: Coloral plastic water bottle and plastic bottle-mount.

Right: Coloral metal bottle cage.

Both images from *Le Cycle*, 9 March 1957.

Chapter 15. Other Accessories

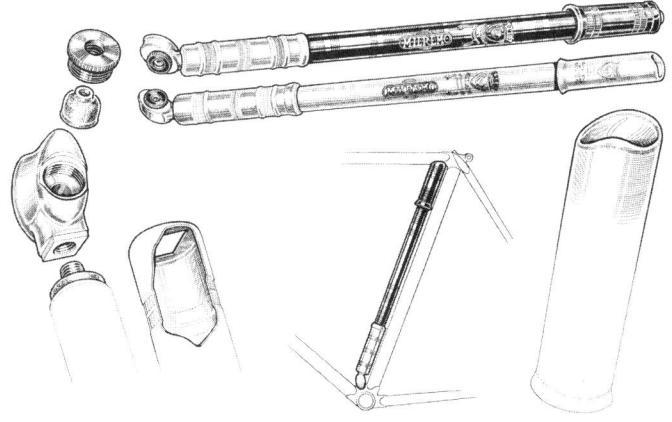

Left: Milremo frame-fit pump details. *Le Cycle*, April 1972.

Below: Zéfal high-pressure frame-fit pump. *Cycles de Compétition et Randonneuses.*

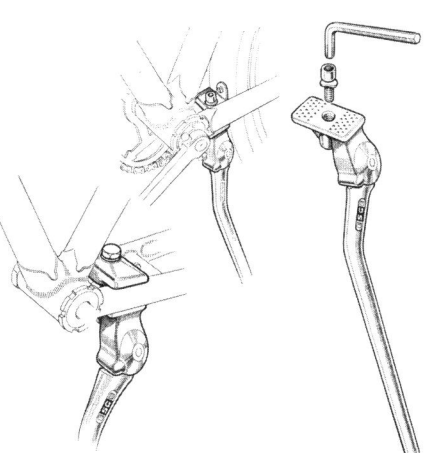

Above: ESGE prop-stand. *Le Cycle*, June 1967.

Below right: Plastic water bottle. *Cycle: Compétition, Cyclotourisme.*

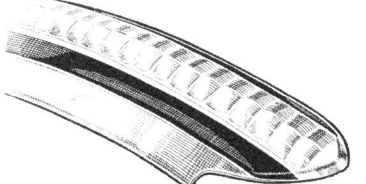

Above: Close-up of Gagnion aluminium mudguard. *Le Cycle*, October 1965.

Right: CLB center-mounted prop stand. *Le Cycle*, December 1967.

Below: 1972 Lejeune randonneur bike. *Le Cycle*, October 1972.

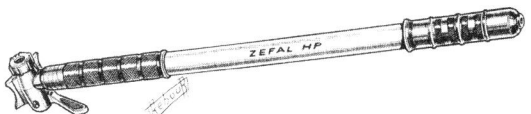

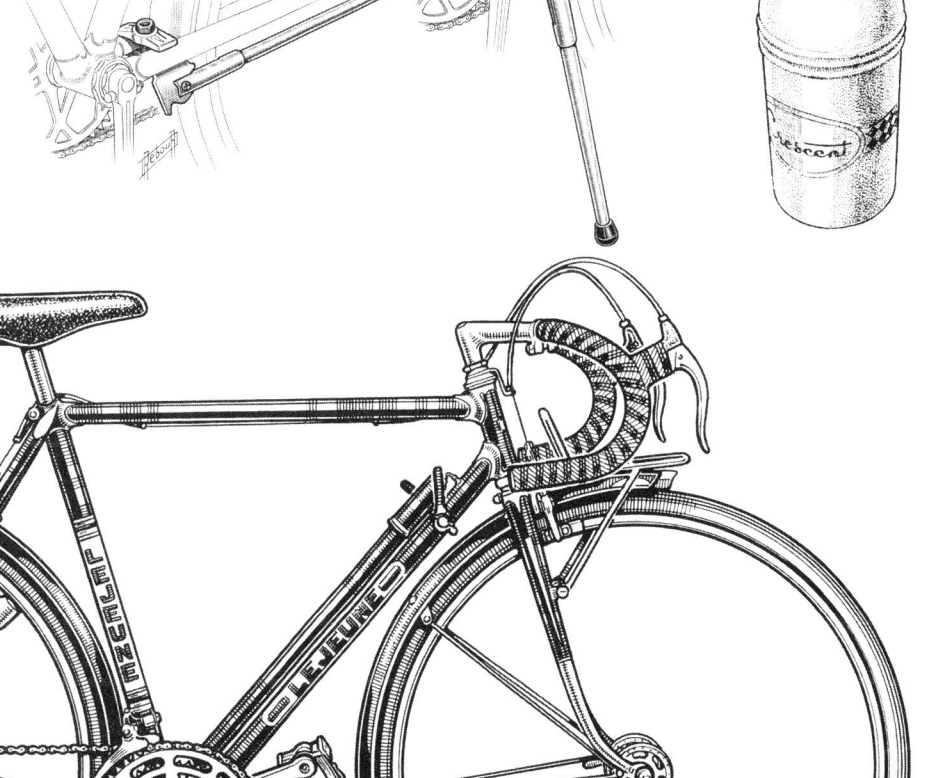

211

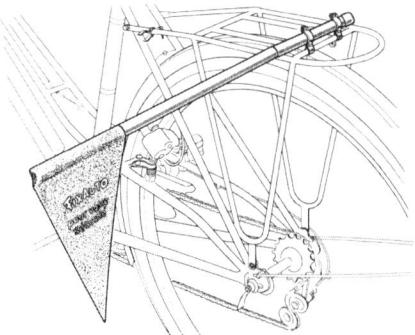

Left: Fix-Auto protruding flag to remind motorist to pass cyclists with generous clearance. *Le Cycle*, December 1974.

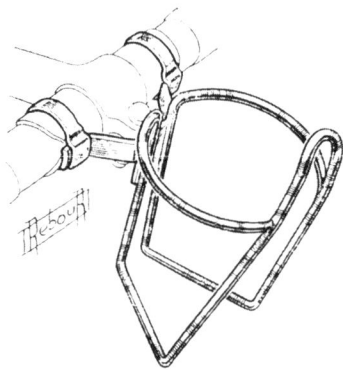

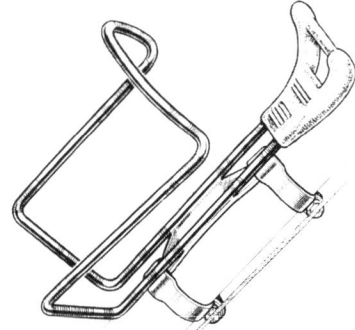

Above, left, and below left: Bottle cages for handlebar- and frame-mounting.
Below: Three plastic water bottles.
All images from *Cycles de Compétition et Randonneuses*.

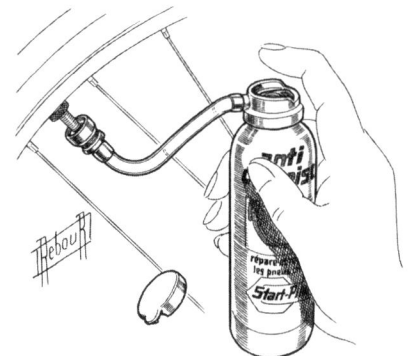

Above: Use of Star-Pilote tire-sealant ijnector. *Le Cycle*, October 1971.

Below: No, it's not the same bike as Morélon's, on page 210, but another Lejeune track bicycle. *Le Cycle*, April 1973.

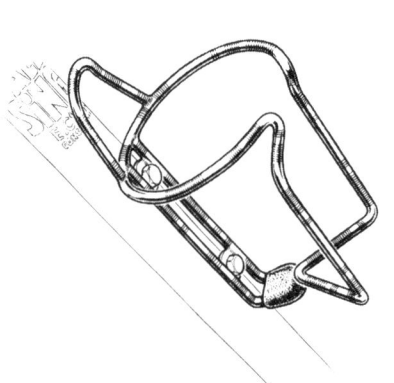

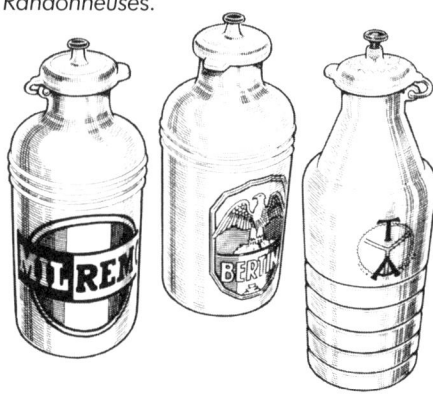

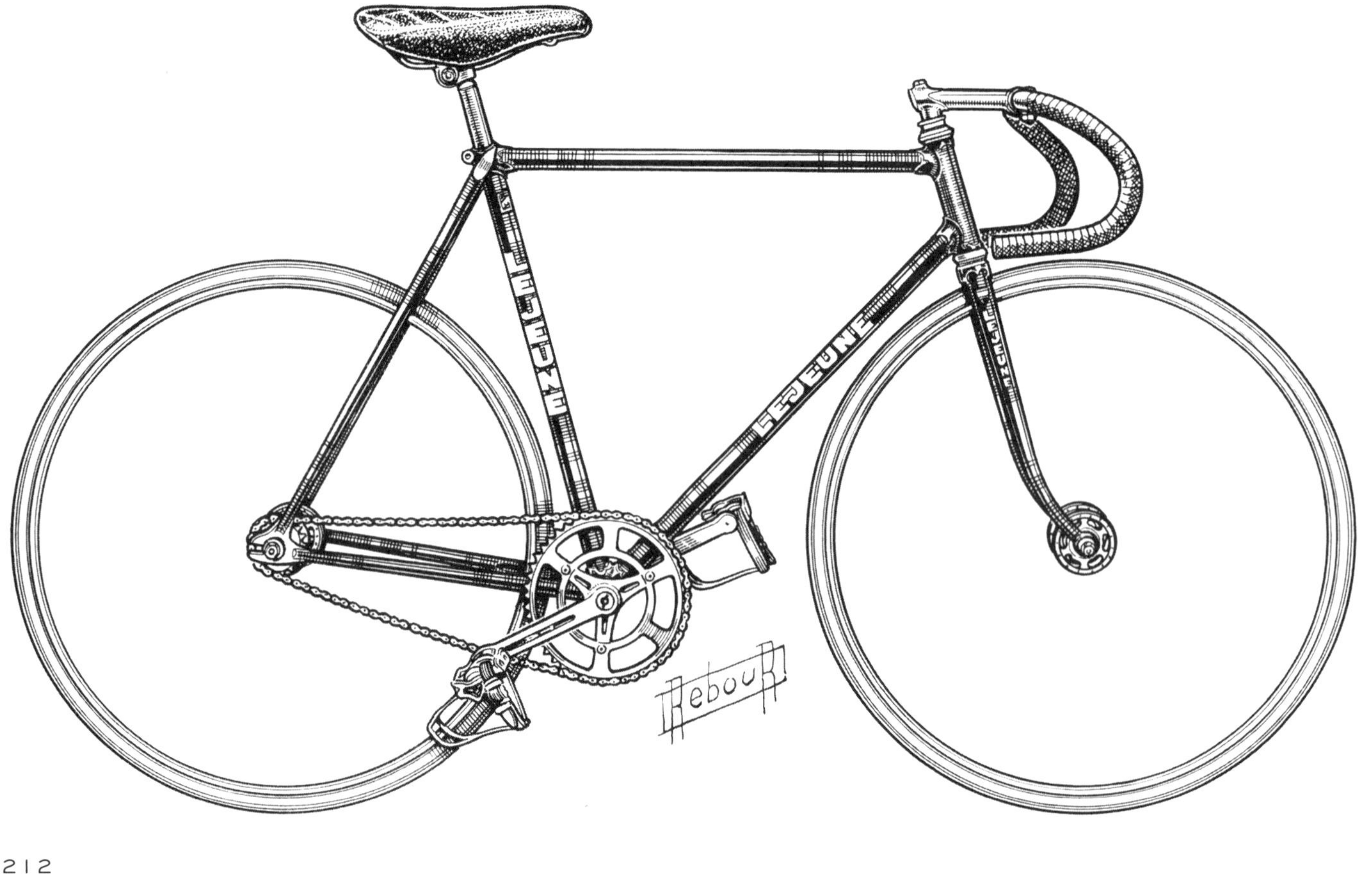

CHAPTER 15. OTHER ACCESSORIES

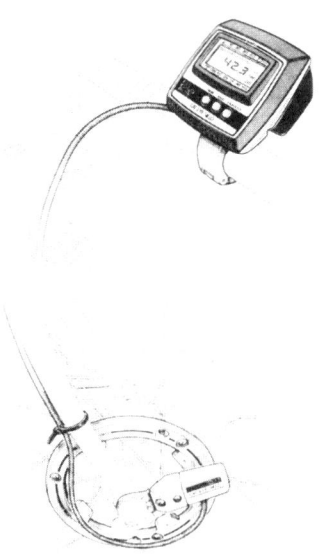

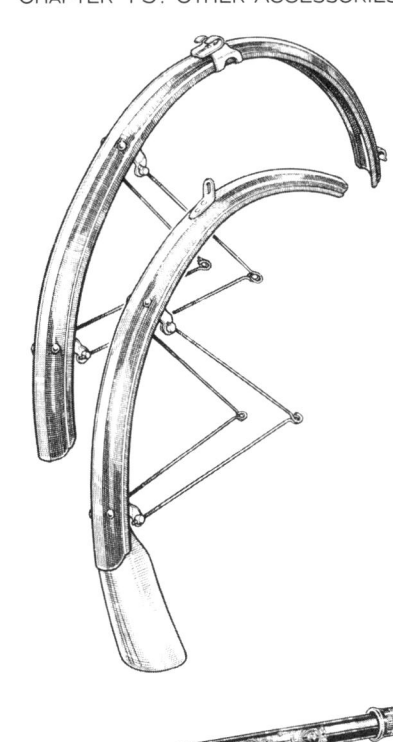

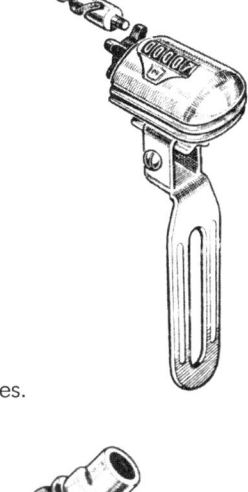

Left: Plastic mudguards.
Right: Matex mechanical cyclometer.
Below: Fast CO2 inflator.
All images from 1976–1983 Milremo catalogues.

Above: Cat-Eye bicycle computer, from Japan. 1983 Milremo catalogue.

Lower right: Selection of conventional frame-fit pumps. 1976 Milremo catalogue.

Below: Luis Ocaña's Motobécane bicycle, on which he won the 1973 Tour de France. *Le Cycle*, August–September 1973.

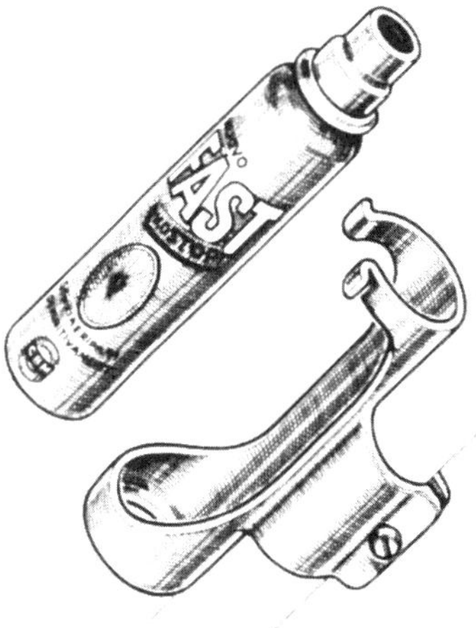

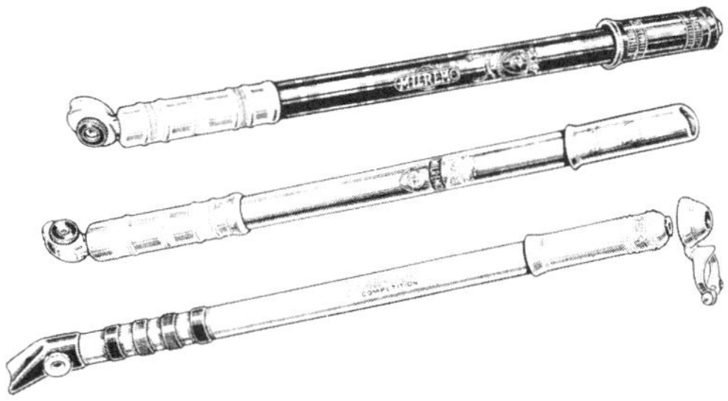

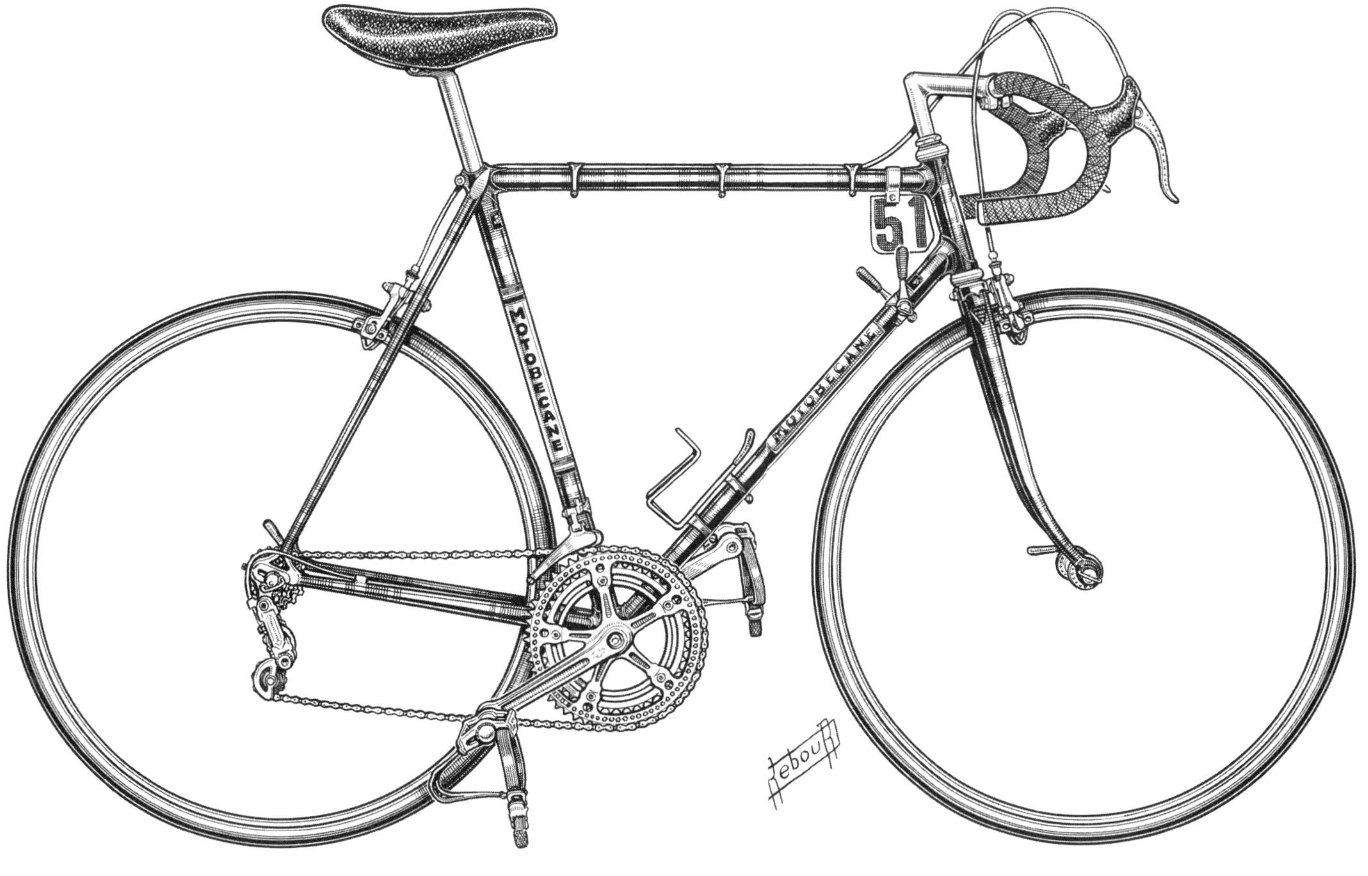

Chapter 16. Product Overviews

Rebour observed and illustrated products introduced at almost every major bicycle trade show, as well as those used at the annual Tour de France and at such events as the Poly de Chanteloup technical trials. In this chapter, we have included a tiny portion of those overview drawings. In some instances, we have had to reposition some of the individual details to make the overview fit the available space.

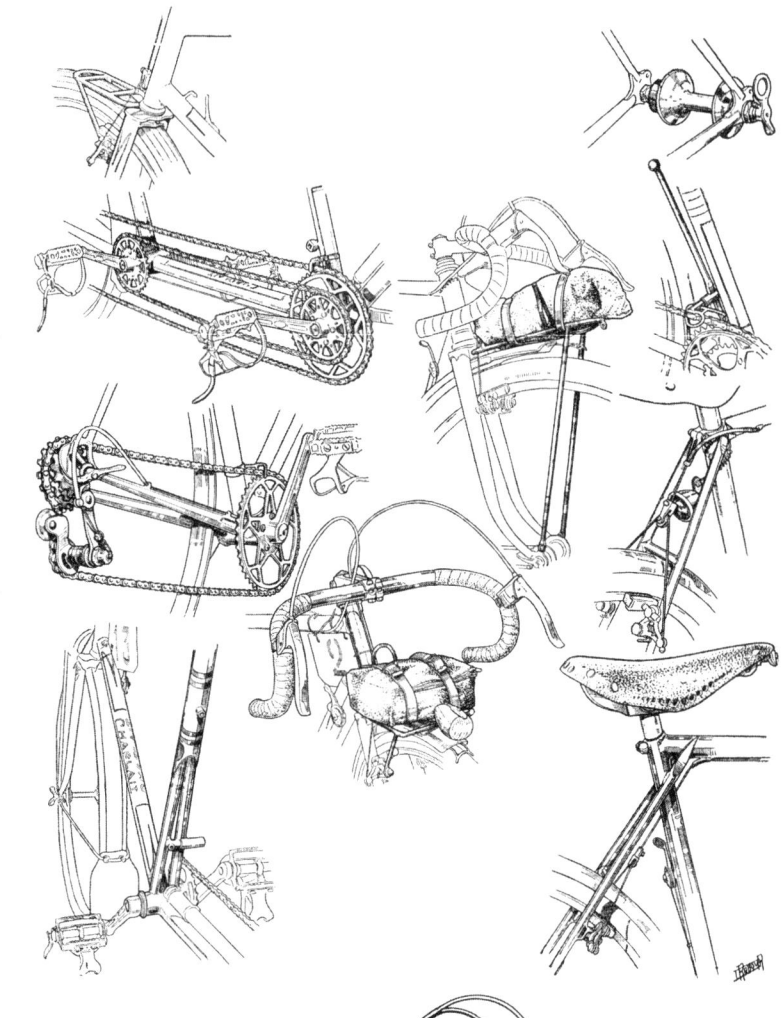

Right: Overview of products at the 1947 Poly de Chanteloup technical trials. *Le Cycle*, 23 April 1947.

Below: De Gibraldy bicycle ridden by Herman Van Springel, first in the points classification of the 1973 Tour de France. *Le Cycle*, August-September 1973.

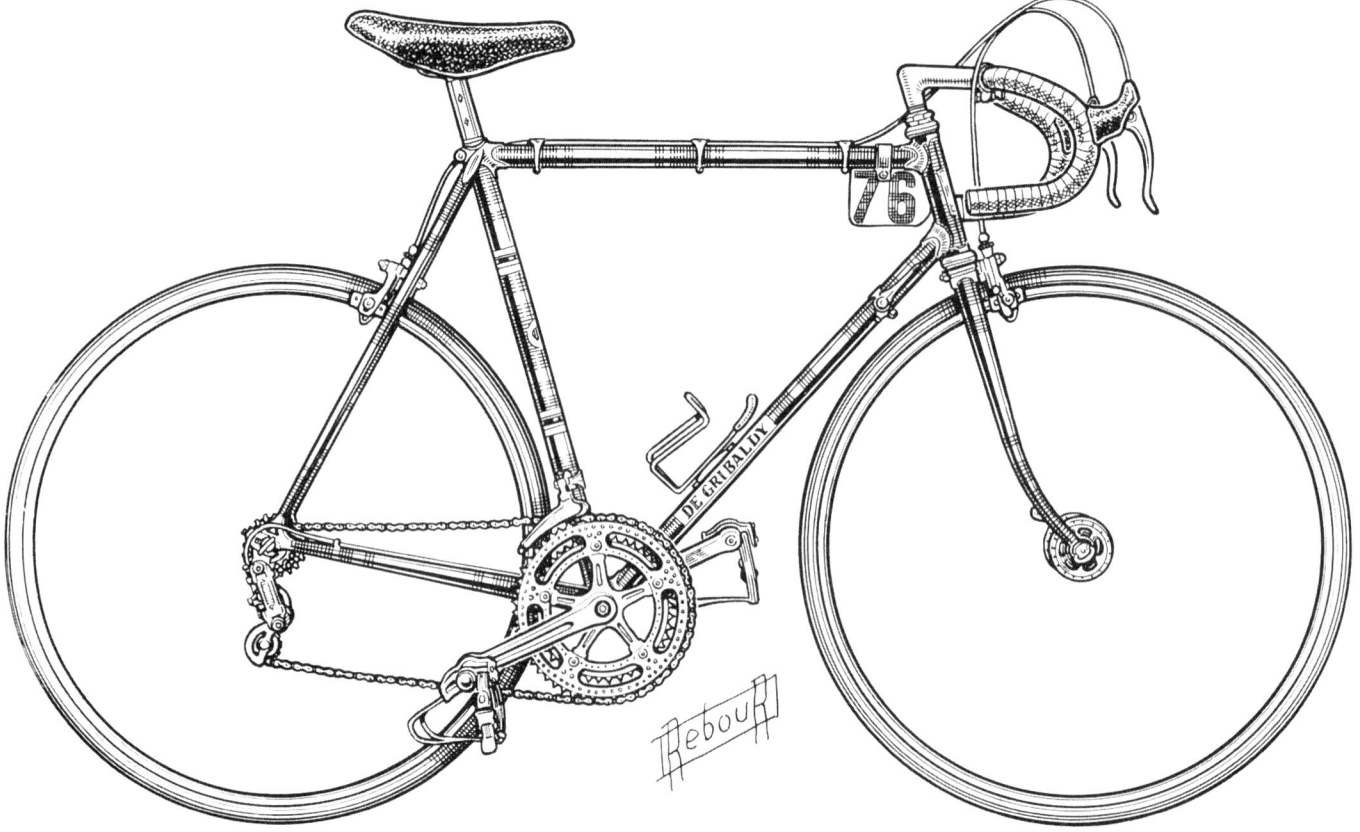

Chapter 16. Product Overviews

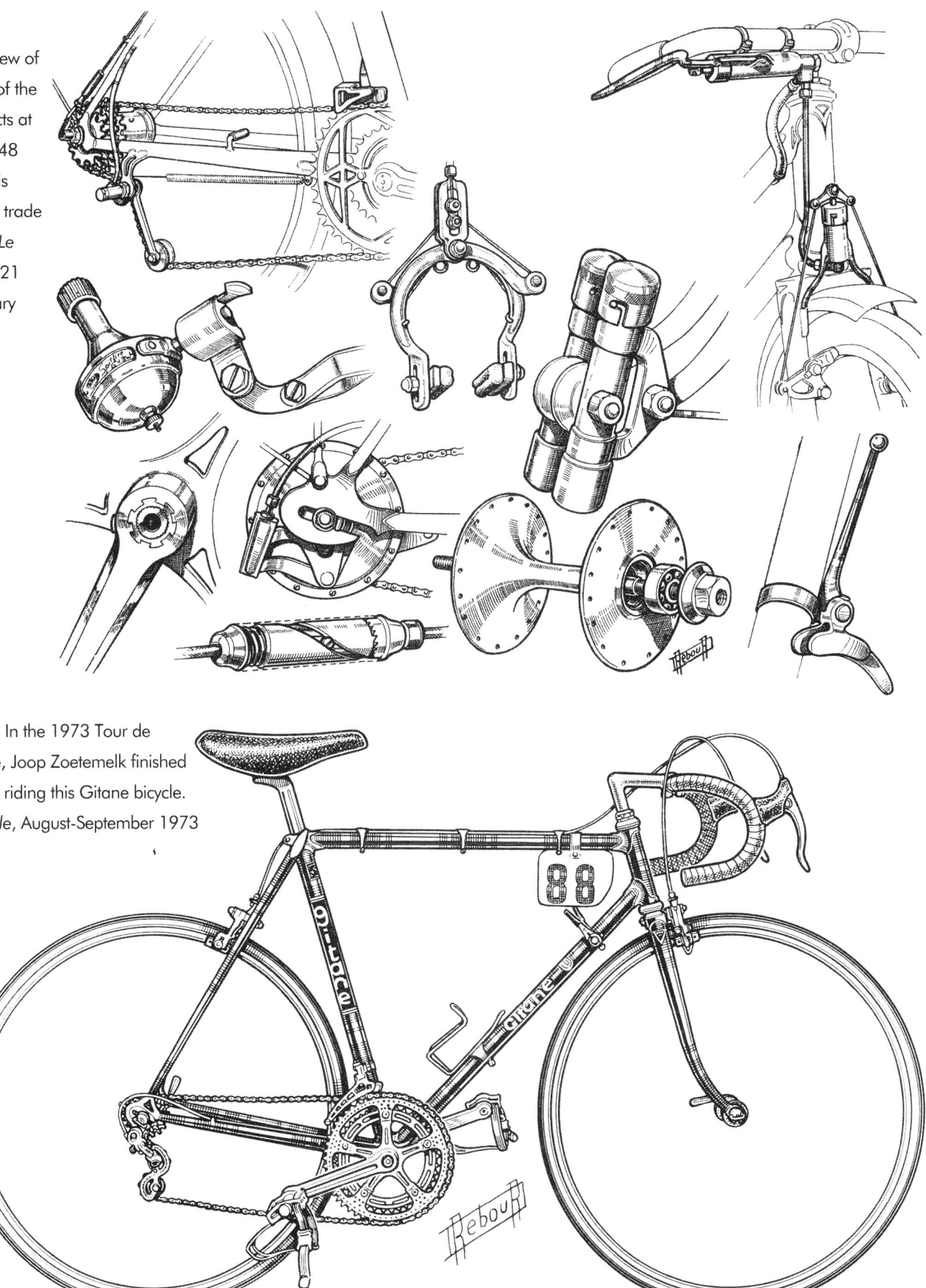

Right: Overview of some of the products at the 1948 Brussels bicycle trade show. *Le Cycle*, 21 February 1948..

Below: In the 1973 Tour de France, Joop Zoetemelk finished fourth, riding this Gitane bicycle. *Le Cycle*, August-September 1973

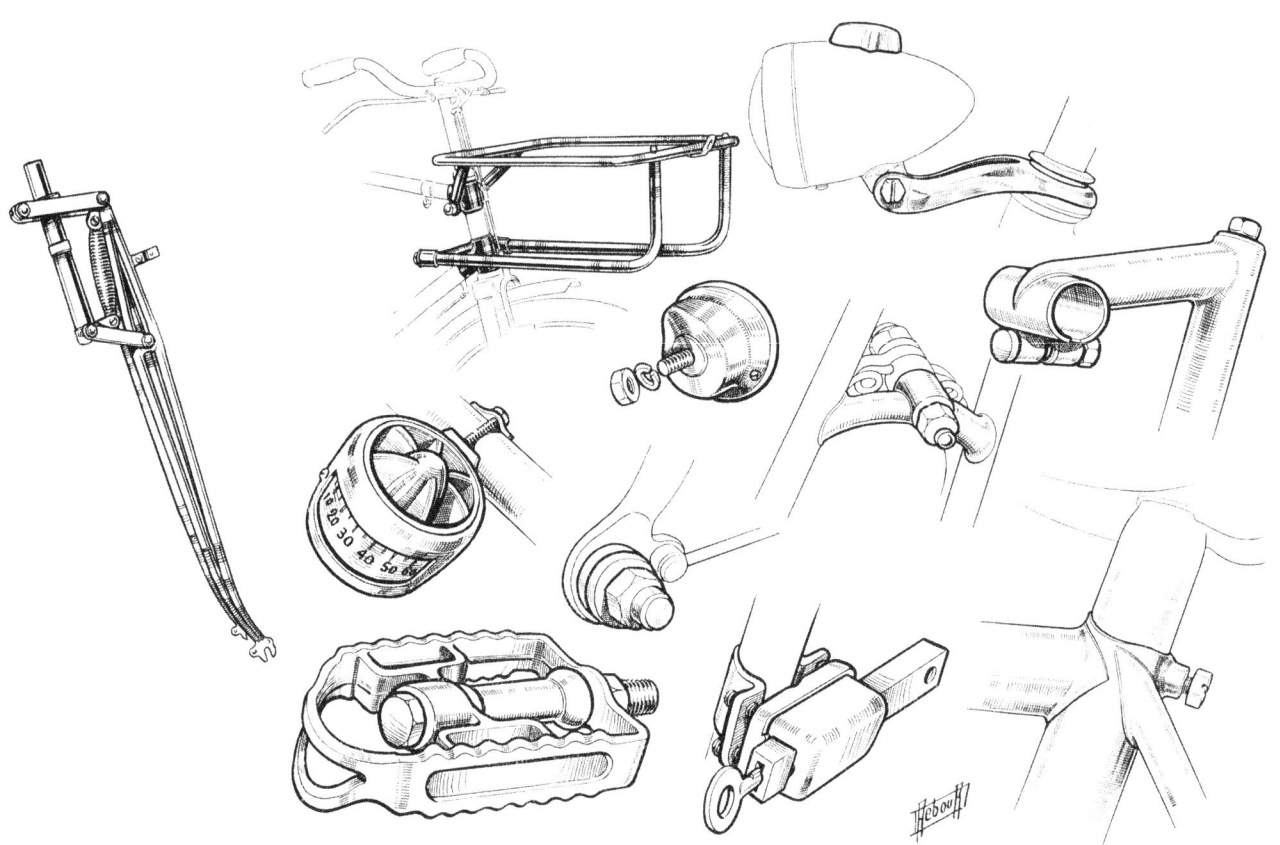

Above: Overview of products shown at the 1949 Geneva bicycle trade show. *Le Cycle*, 26 March 1949.

Below: Pedro Torès won the mountains classification of the 1973 Tour de France, riding this Bahamontès-branded machine. *Le Cycle*, September-August 1973.

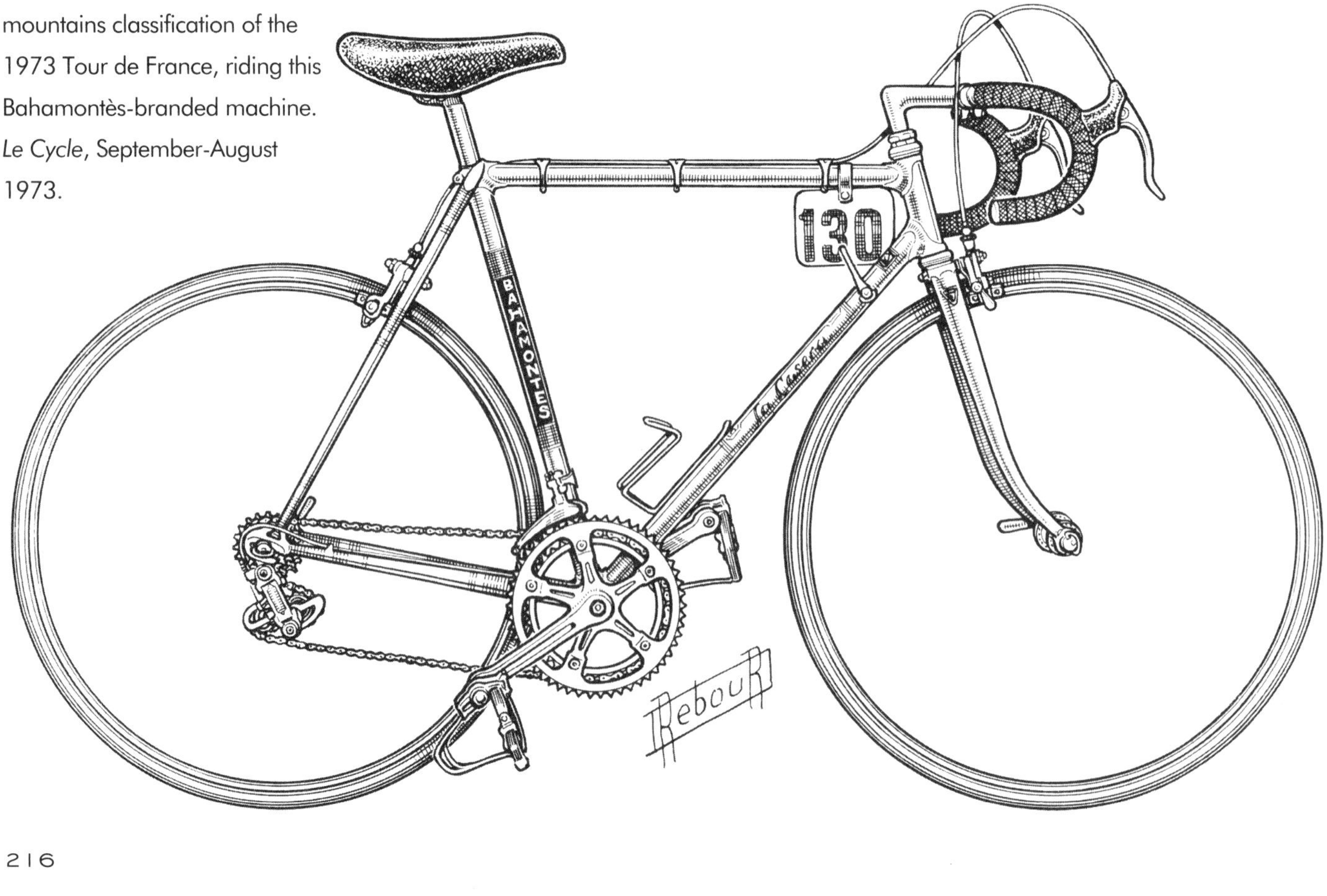

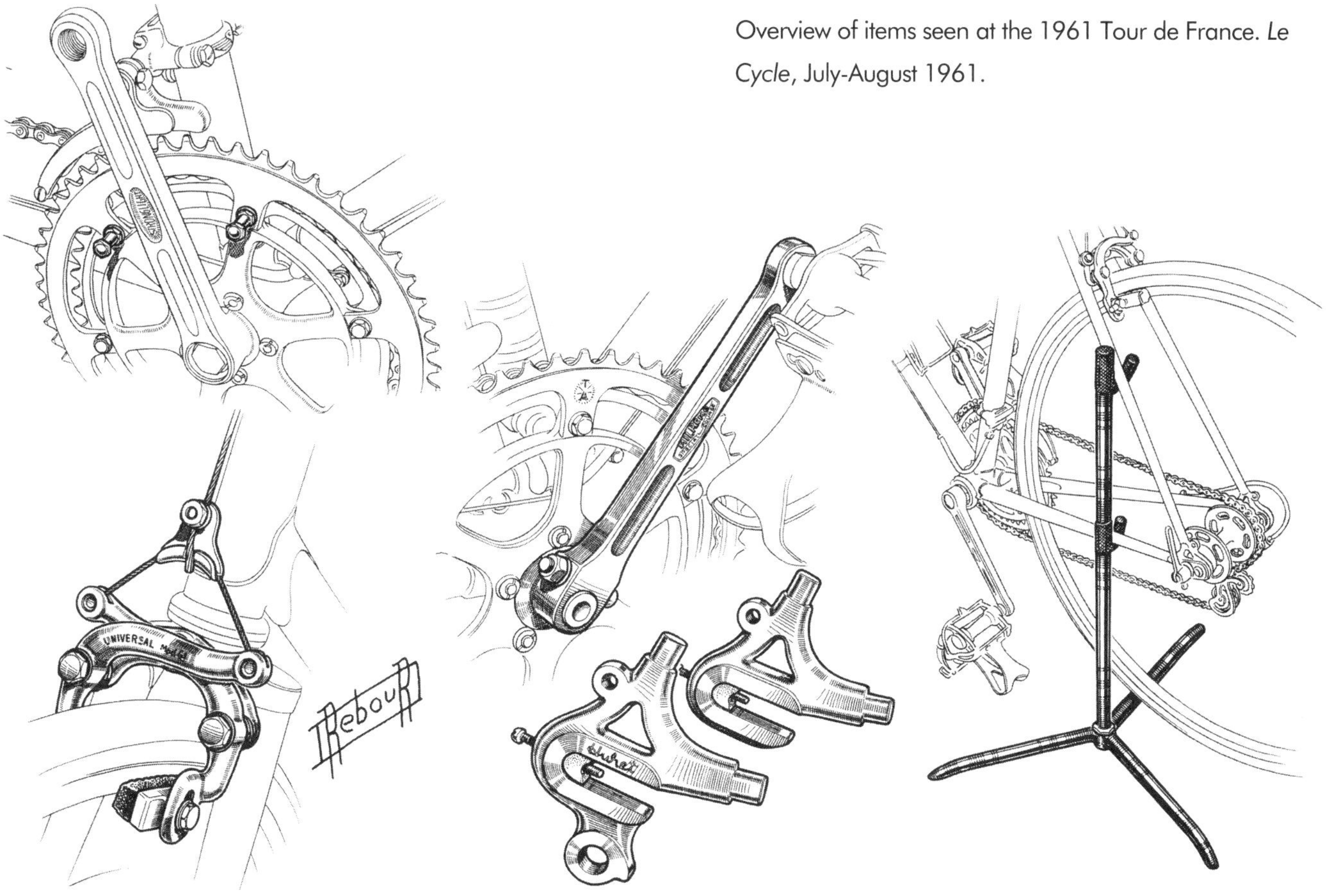

Chapter 16. Product Overviews

Overview of items seen at the 1961 Tour de France. *Le Cycle*, July-August 1961.

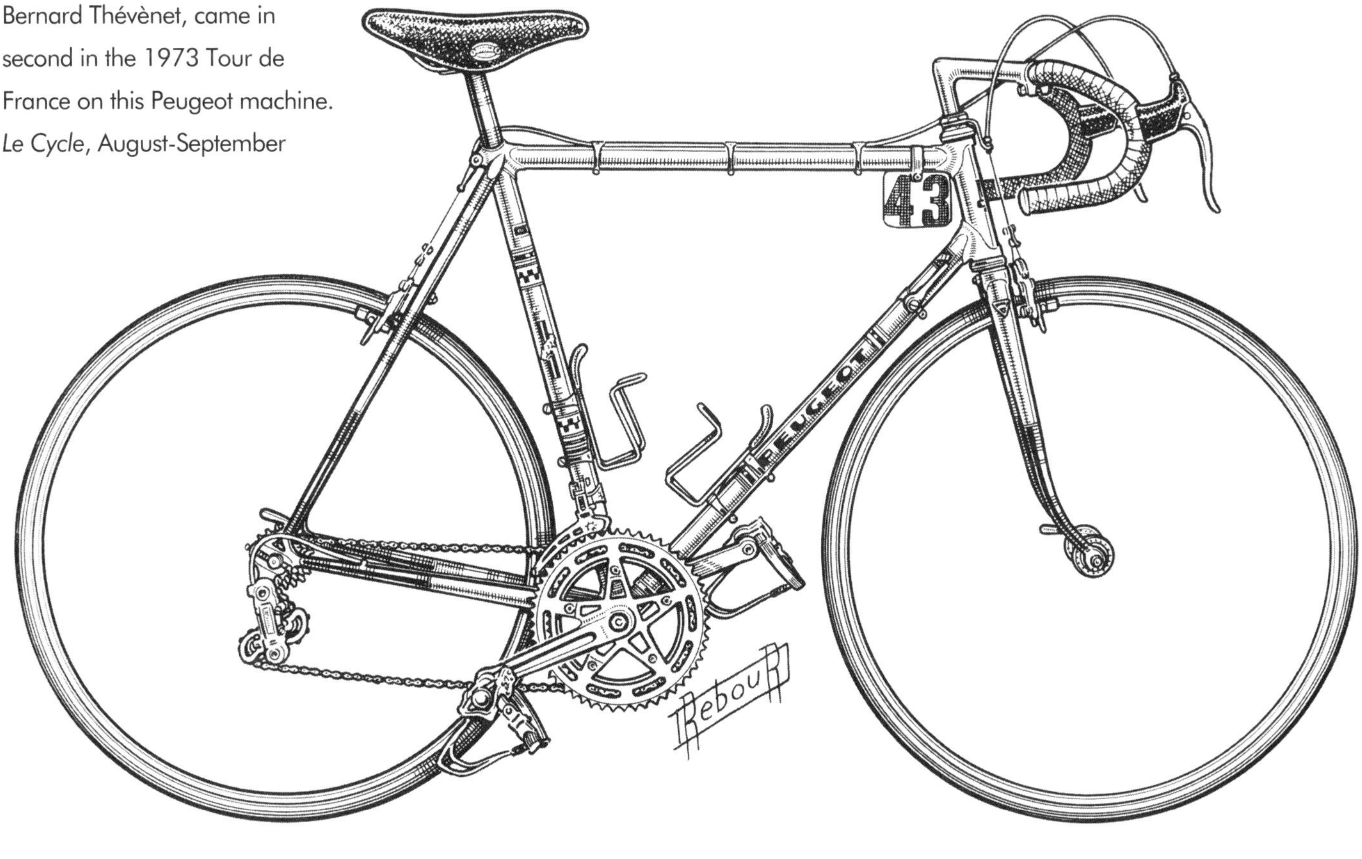

France's great new hope, Bernard Thévènet, came in second in the 1973 Tour de France on this Peugeot machine. *Le Cycle*, August-September

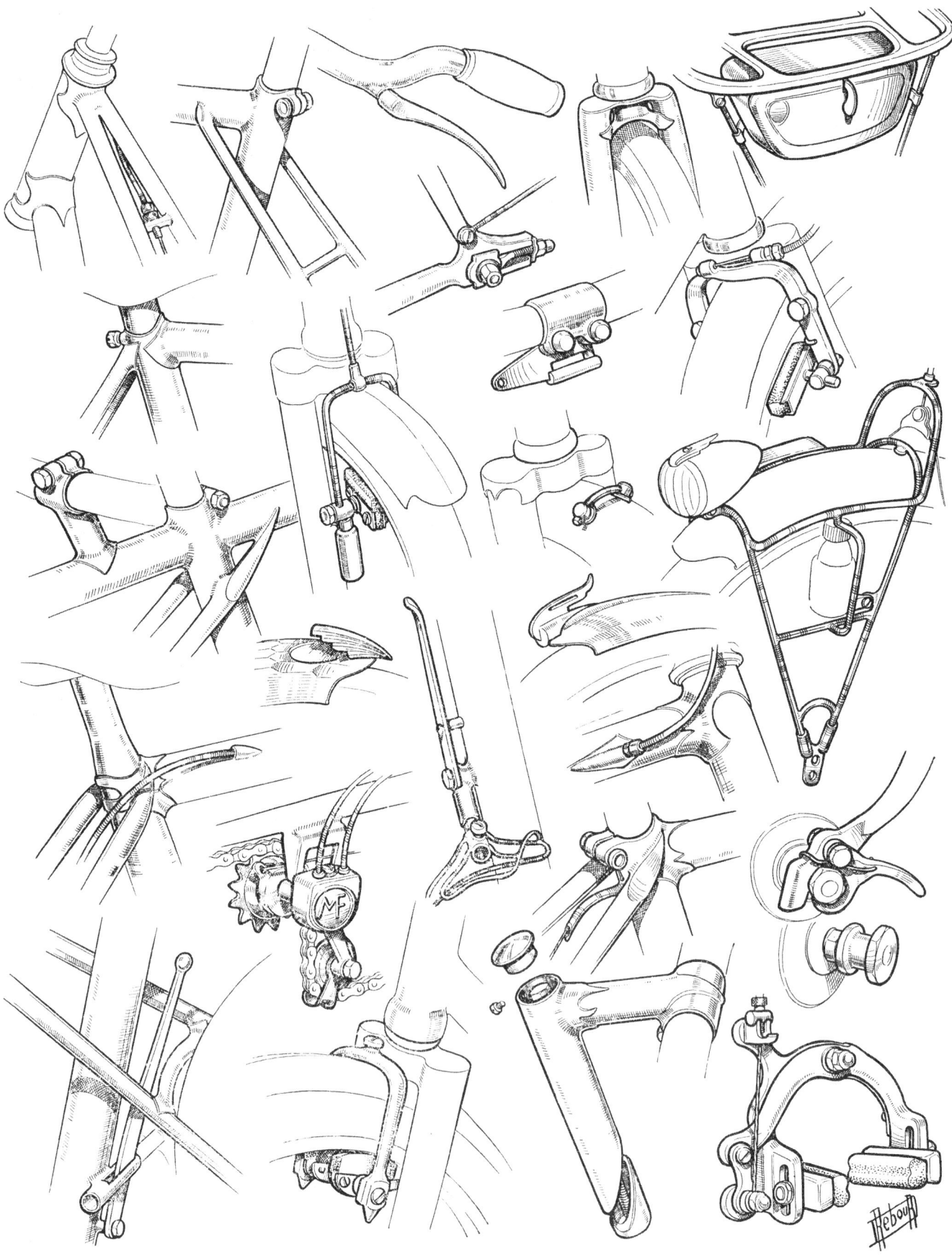

Above: Overview of products st the 1948 Paris bicycle trade show. *Le Cycle*, 16 October 1948.

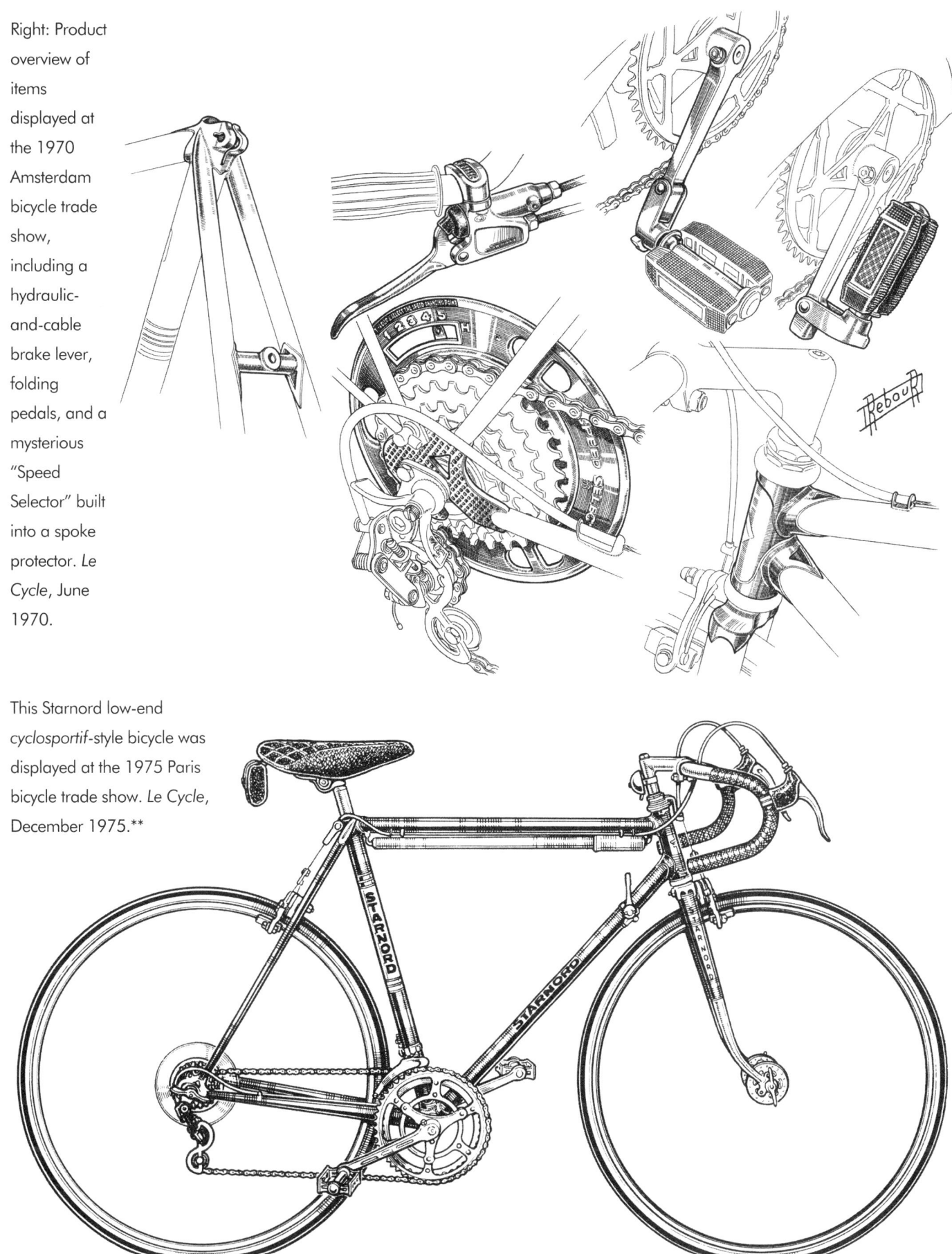

Right: Product overview of items displayed at the 1970 Amsterdam bicycle trade show, including a hydraulic-and-cable brake lever, folding pedals, and a mysterious "Speed Selector" built into a spoke protector. *Le Cycle*, June 1970.

This Starnord low-end *cyclosportif*-style bicycle was displayed at the 1975 Paris bicycle trade show. *Le Cycle*, December 1975.**

** See pages 269–271 for expanded caption text.

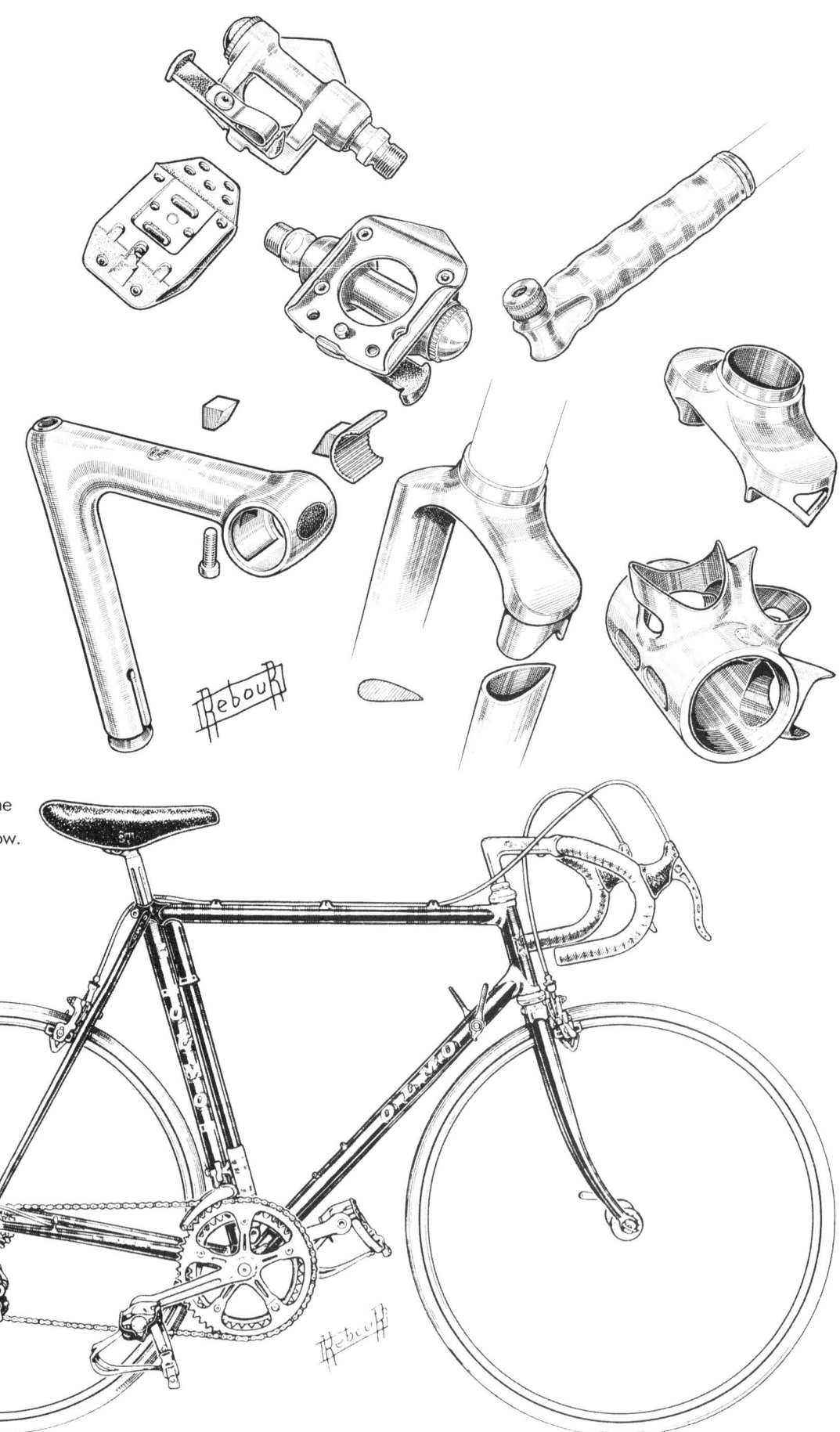

Right: Cinelli product overview, as displayed at the 1973 Milan bicycle trade show. Note the characteristic Cinelli investment-cast lugs and fork crown, the elegant forged aluminium alloy stem, as well as the F-71 "suicide" clipless track pedal. *Le Cycle*, December 1973.

Olmo bicycle, displayed at the 1975 Milan bicycle trade show. *Le Monde de Daniel Rebour.*

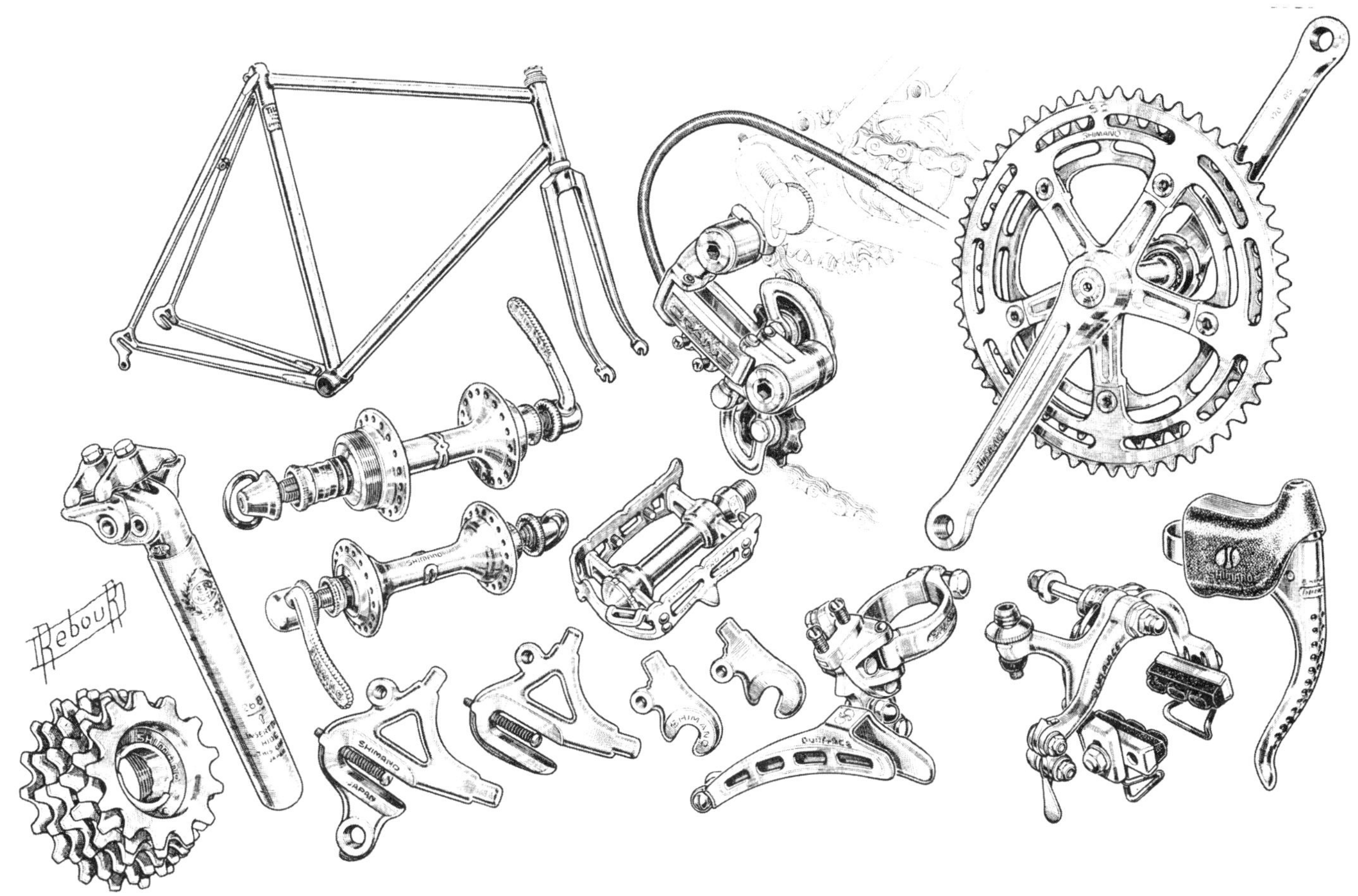

Above: 1975 overview of products, including Shimano and Speedwell. Milremo advertisement in *L'Officiel du Cycle*, July 1975.

Below: Left-side view of 1975 randonneur bike. *Cycles de Compétition et Randonneuses*.

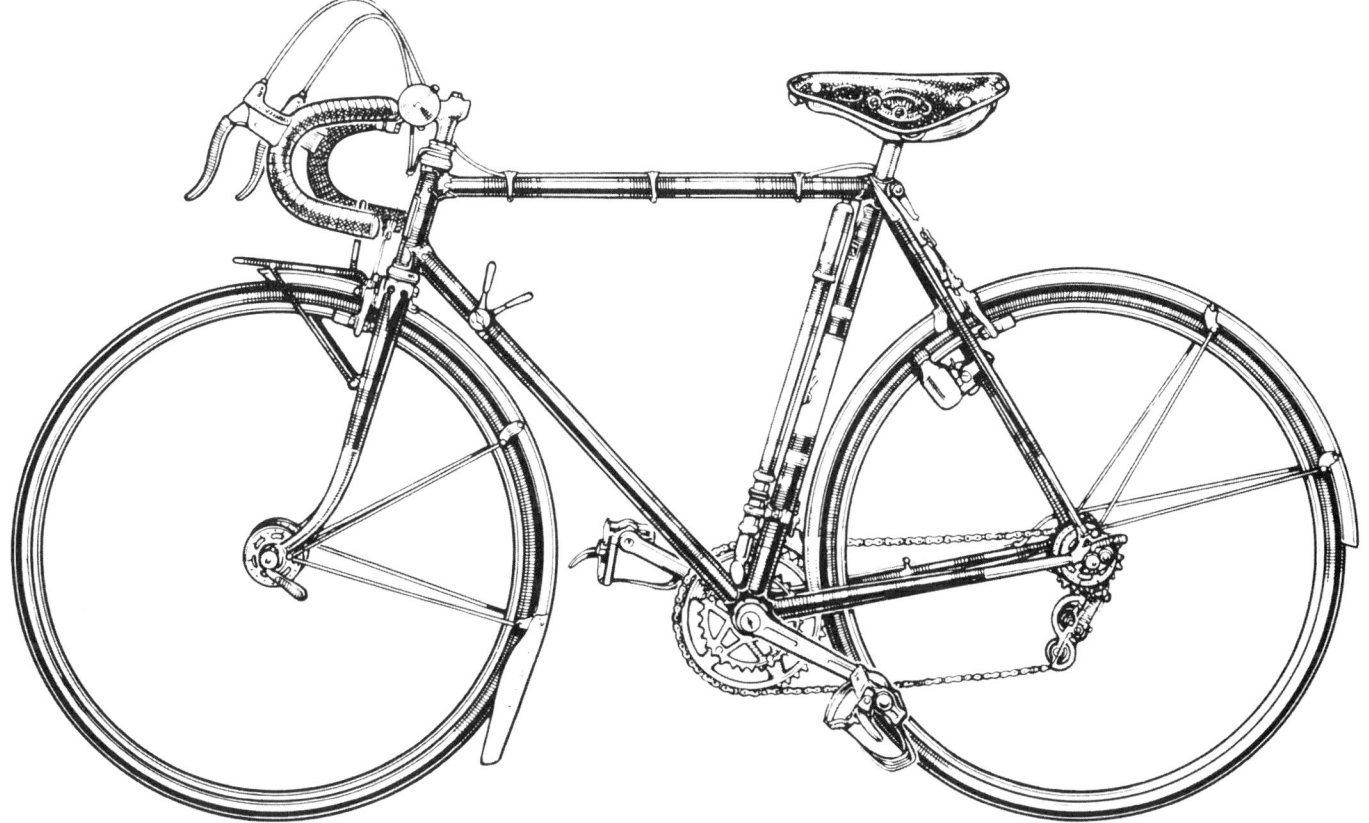

Chapter 17. Tandem Bicycles

During the first two decades after the Second World War, when cycle-touring was still quite popular in France, significant numbers of tandems were in use. Rebour himself often rode with his wife, Simone, and many others in his circle of friends rode tandems too. Although few of the major manufacturers offered high-end tandems on a regular basis, the specialist frame builders, such as Alex Singer, René Herse, Sabliere, and Jo Routens, built quite a few of these machines, as did André Bertin, who was not so much a specialist frame builder as a small-scale manufacturer and mail-order merchant of bicycle products.

Probably the most successful tandem builder (in terms of results) was René Herse, and in these pages are depicted more of his creations than anyone else's. Herse had a secret promotional weapon: his daughter Lysette, also know as Lily. She rode numerous of his tandems to victory as stoker (rear rider on a tandem) with several different pilots, or captains (front riders), in events such as Paris–Brest–Paris.

In the mid-1960s, however, interest in tandem riding diminished, and none of the tandems depicted by Rebour post-date 1962. Not until the late 1980s was there a revival of tandem riding, but by then Rebour had retired, both from riding and from illustrating.

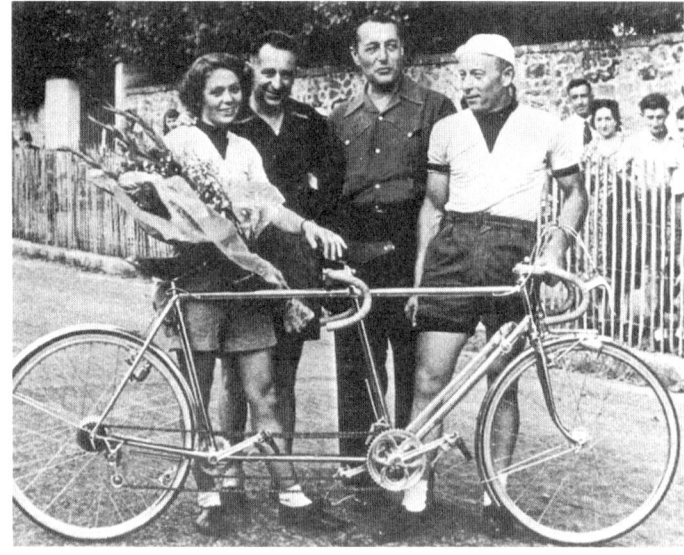

Lily Herse and Prestat, with father René and an unidentified third man, after winning the 1949 Poly de Chanteloup.

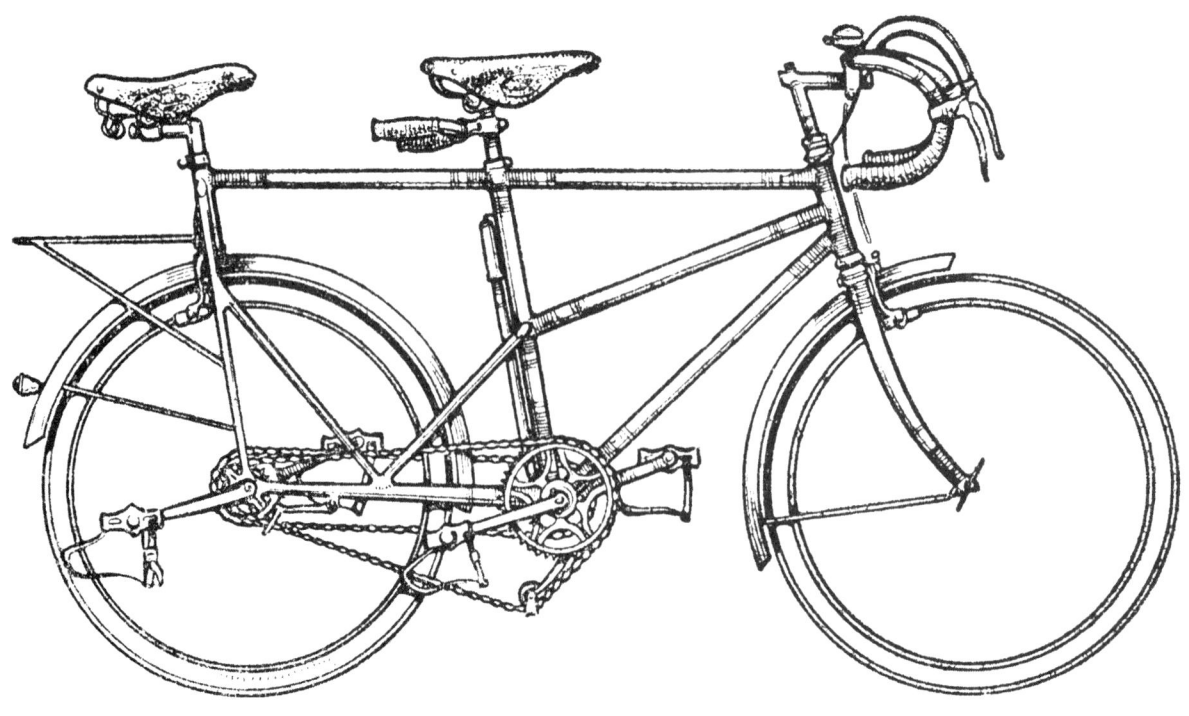

Left: A rare "compact," or short-wheel-base tandem, made by Gauthier, and illustrated in *Le Cycle*, 21 February 1948.

Right: Enclosed central timing chain on a Chauvin tandem that was first shown at the Poly de Chanteloup technical trials back in 1938. *Le Cycle*, 29 March 1947.

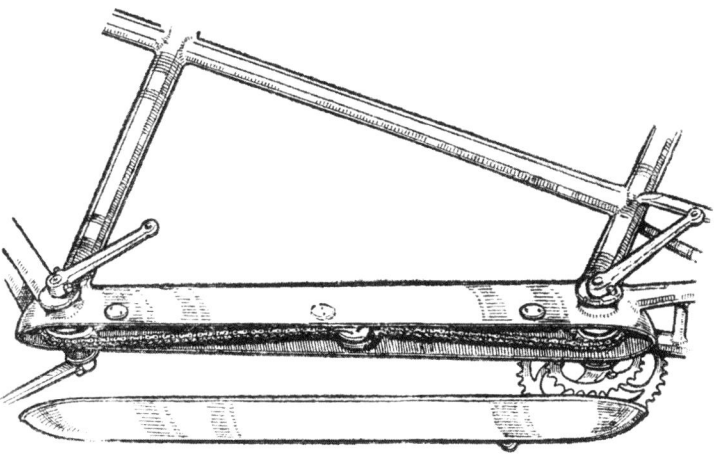

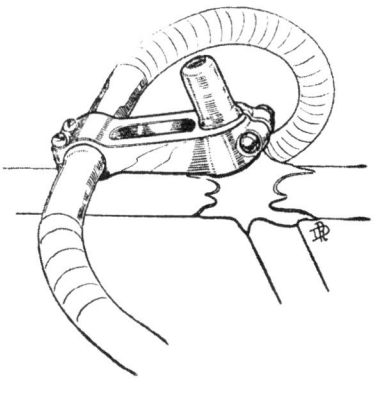

Above: René Herse stoker's stem, clamped around the pilot's seat post. *Le Cycle*, 1 December 1945.

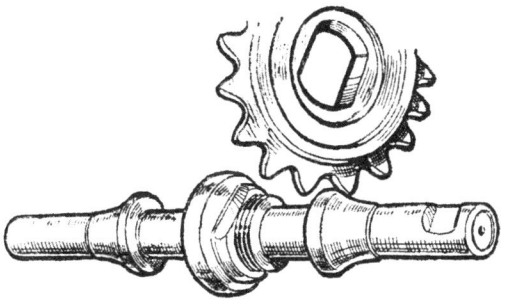

Below: Twin-tube arrangement on tandem with central timing chain. *Le Cycle*, 29 March 1947.

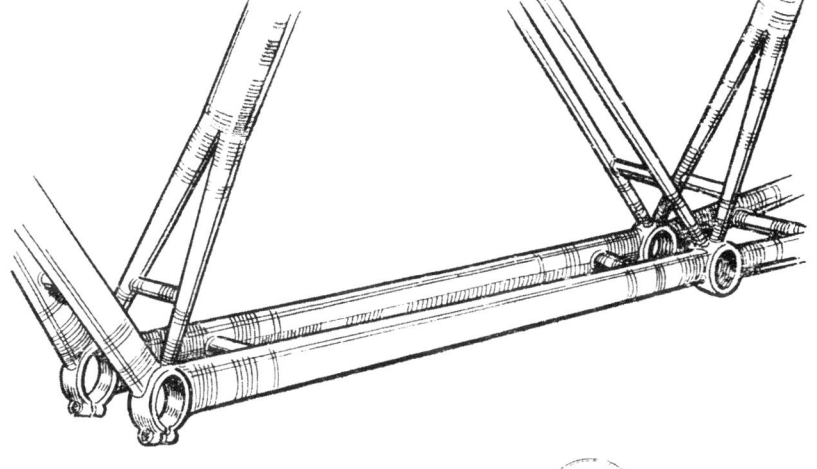

Above: 1947 reissue of the Chauvin bottom bracket spindle and central chainring for the central timing chain shown in the illustrations to the right and top center. *Le Cycle*, 29 March 1947.

Below: Circa 1948 René Herse open-frame, or marathon-style, tandem, depicted in *Pratique du Vélo*.

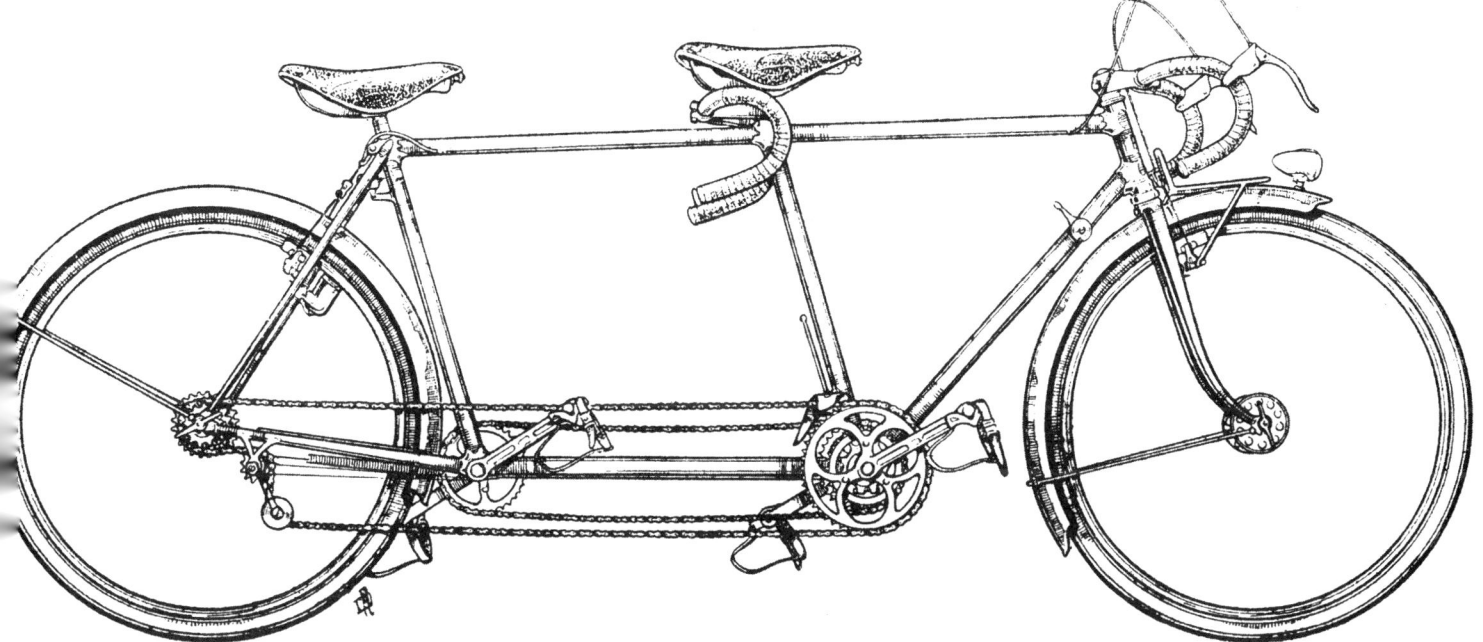

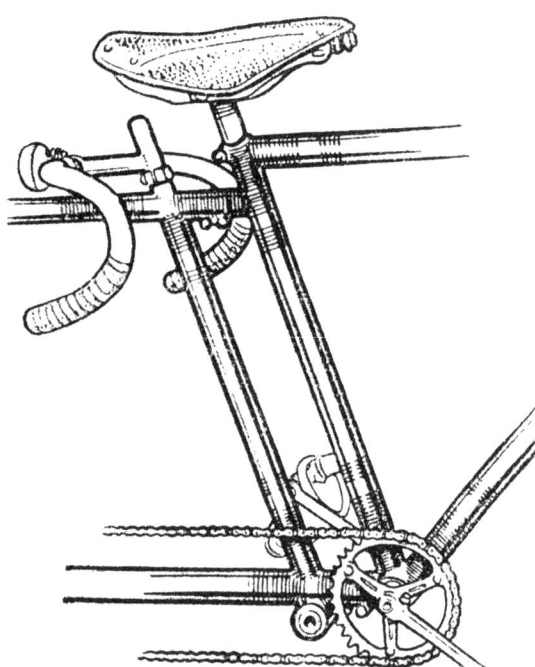

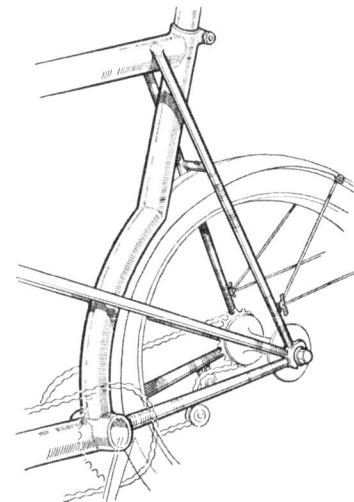

Right: Detail of curved rear seat tube on an English short-wheelbase tandem. *Le Cycle*, 4 December 1948.

Below: A triple, or "family tandem," with a middle seat for a child pedaling a raised crankset, referred to as "Kiddy Cranks" in English. *Le Cycle*, 24 January 1948.

Above: Detail of Léfol tandem laid out for a child stoker and plenty of horizontal clearance behind the pilot's seat. *Le Cycle*, 24 January 1948.

Below: René Herse track tandem with double twin-laterals. For the frame builder, it is easier to reinforce a tandem frame this way than it is to do so with single large-diameter tubing, although it does not seem to provide quite as much lateral stiffness. *Le Cycle*, 17 January 1953.

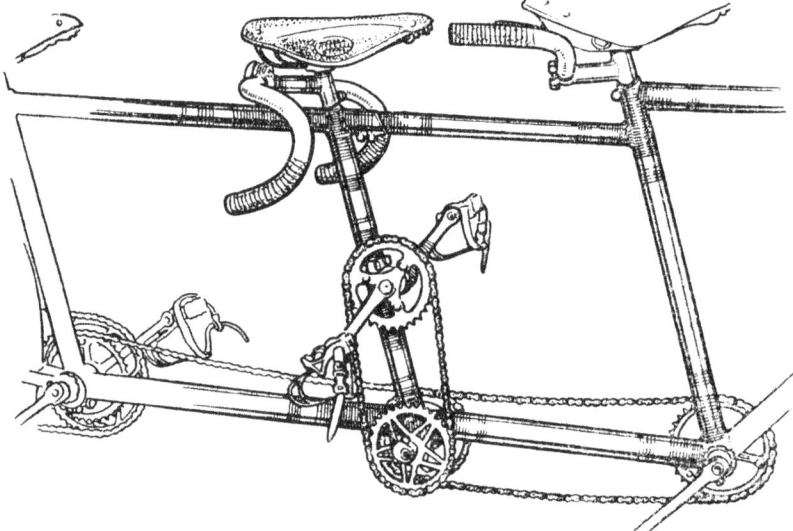

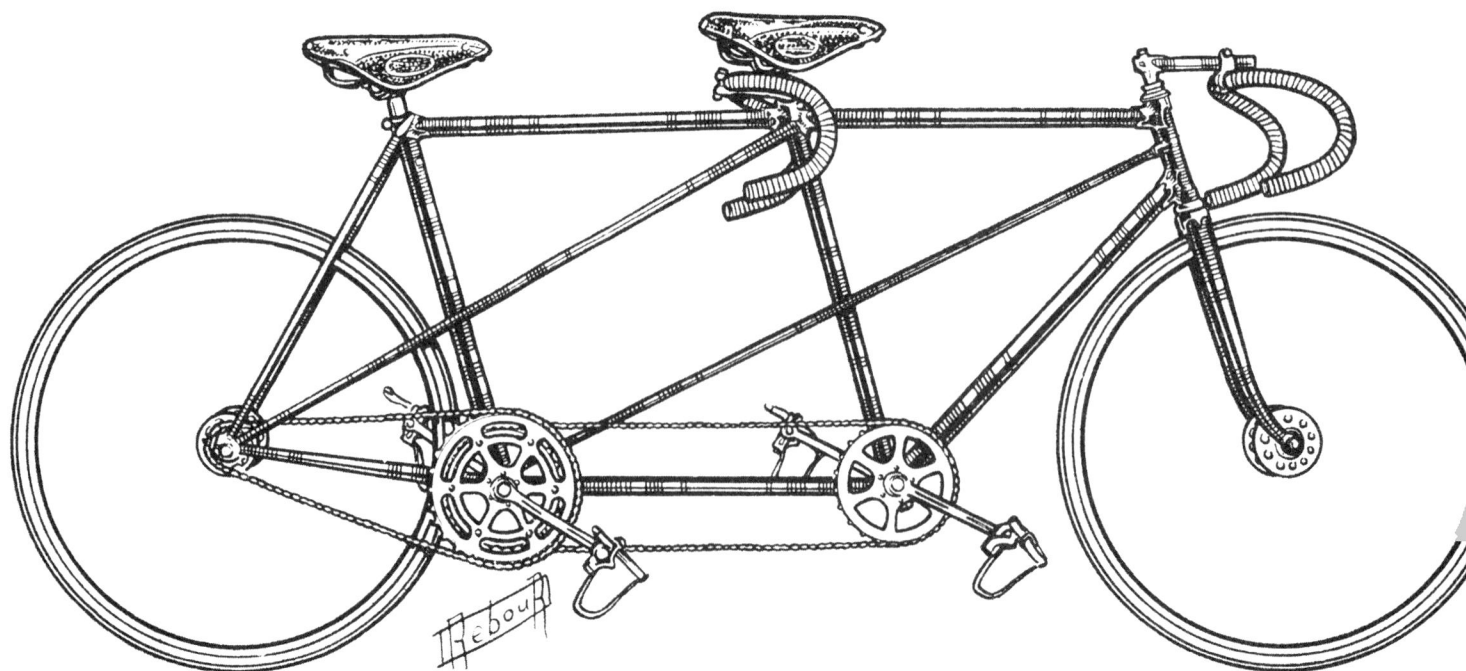

Chapter 17. Tandem Bicycles

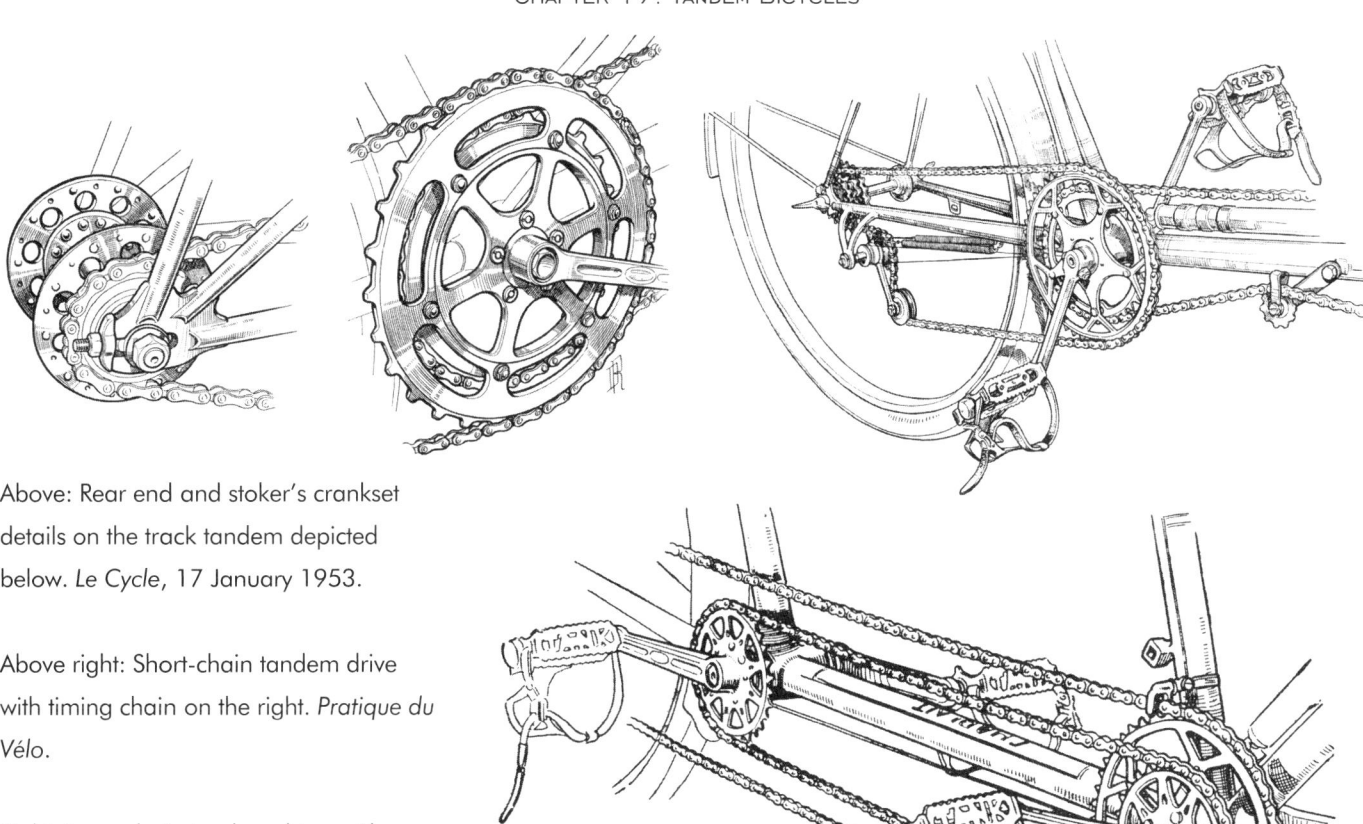

Above: Rear end and stoker's crankset details on the track tandem depicted below. *Le Cycle*, 17 January 1953.

Above right: Short-chain tandem drive with timing chain on the right. *Pratique du Vélo*.

Right: Long-chain tandem drive, with timing chain on the right, for easier gear changes but more complicated chain arrangement. *Pratique du Vélo*.

Below: Loaded-touring tandem, also with double twin-laterals, from *Pratique du Vélo*. Typical of French touring tandems of the period, it had wide tires, slack frame angles, and short trail, resulting in stable handling characteristics, according to *Bicycle Quarterly* test riders.

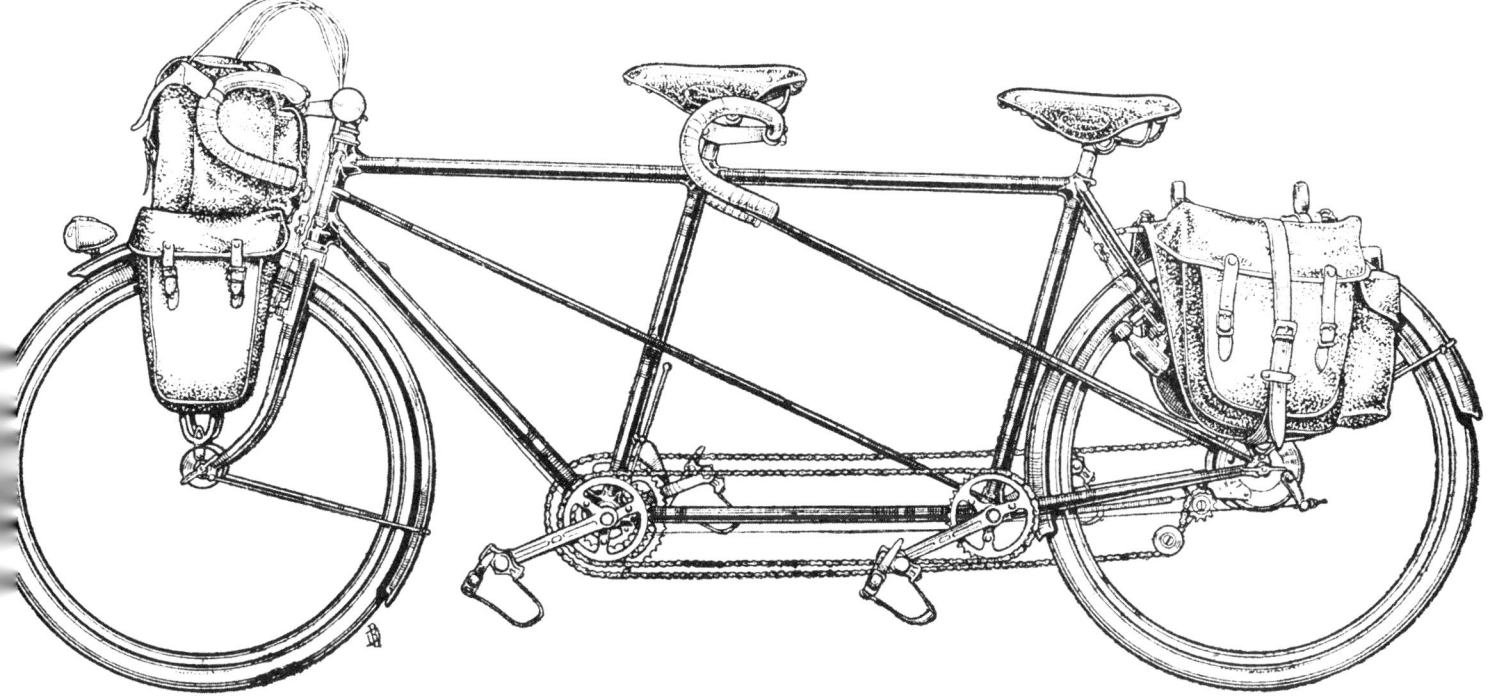

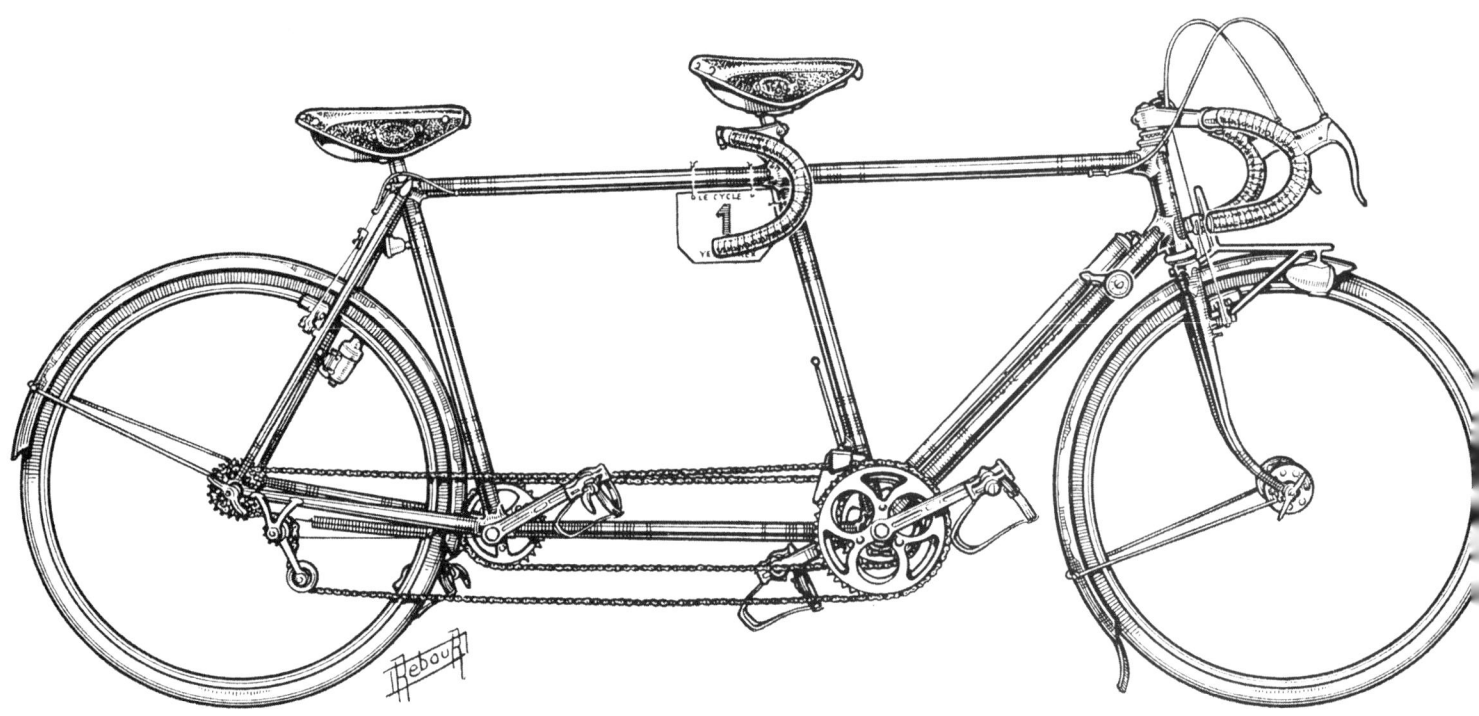

Above: Open-frame, or marathon-style, René Herse tandem ridden to victory by Lasne and Lily Herse at the 1955 Poly de Chanteloup technical trials. *Le Cycle*, 7 May 1955.

Below: The same tandem a year later. Can you tell the difference? There are new, more comfortable saddles for both riders. Although Rebour usually made each of his drawings new from scratch, it would appear that this one was merely a modified version of the drawing shown above. *Le Cycle*, 5 May 1956.

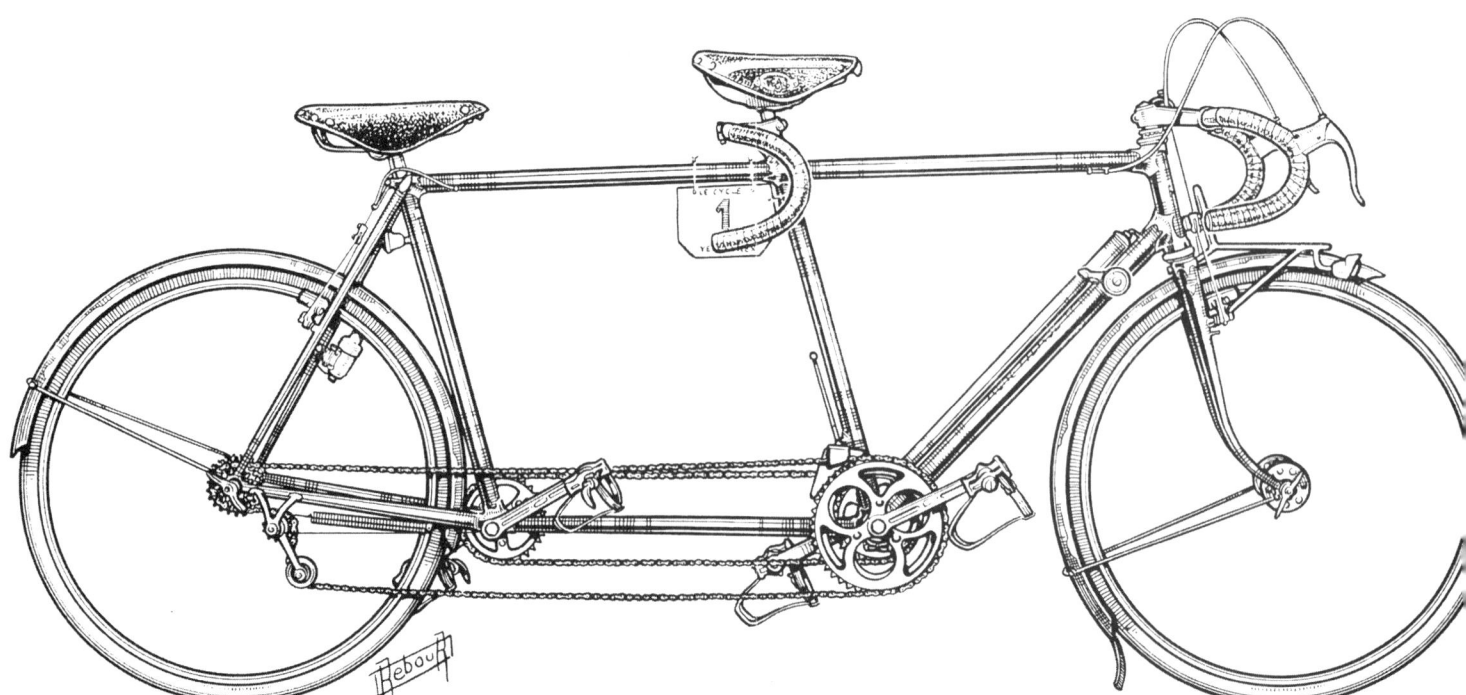

Chapter 17. Tandem Bicycles

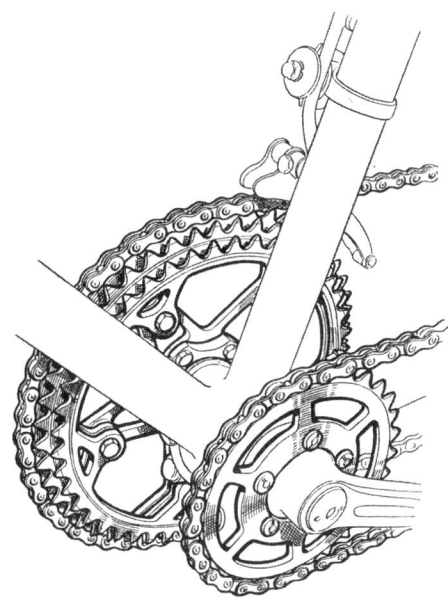

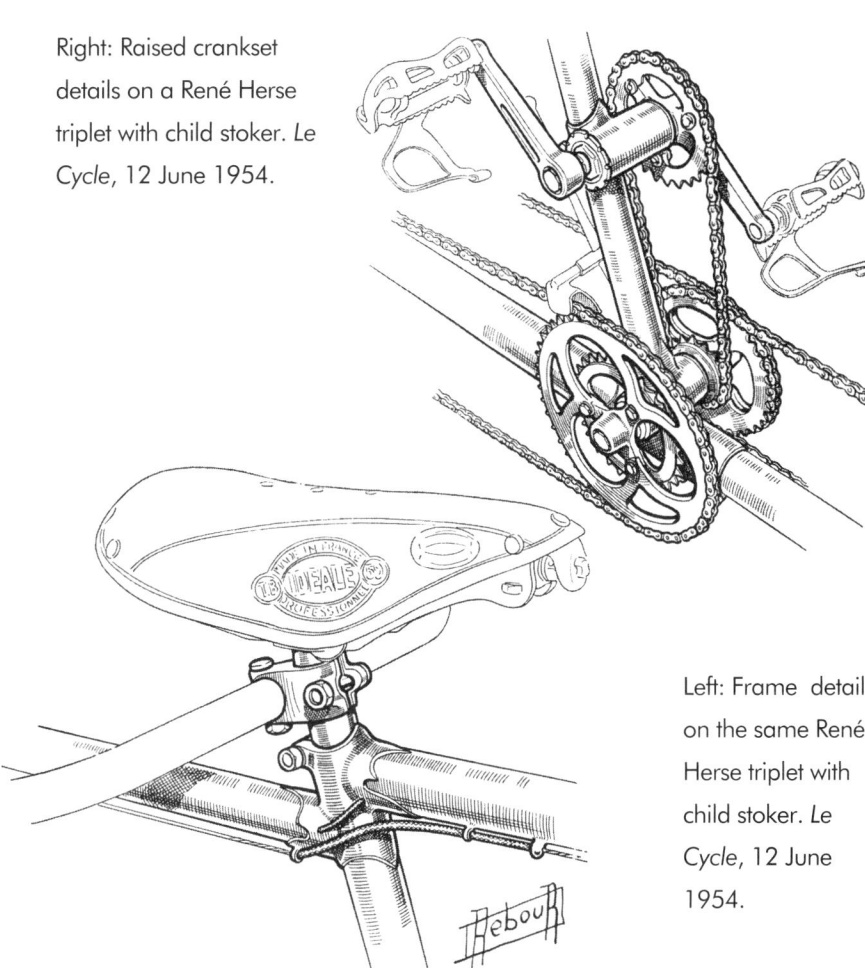

Right: Raised crankset details on a René Herse triplet with child stoker. *Le Cycle*, 12 June 1954.

Above: Central crankset with triple chainrings on the drive side and timing chain on the left side, on a Liberia tandem. *Le Cycle*, 18 October 1952.

Left: Frame detail on the same René Herse triplet with child stoker. *Le Cycle*, 12 June 1954.

Below: 1956 Paris–Brest–Paris marathon-style tandem built by René Herse. *Le Cycle*, 22 September 1956.

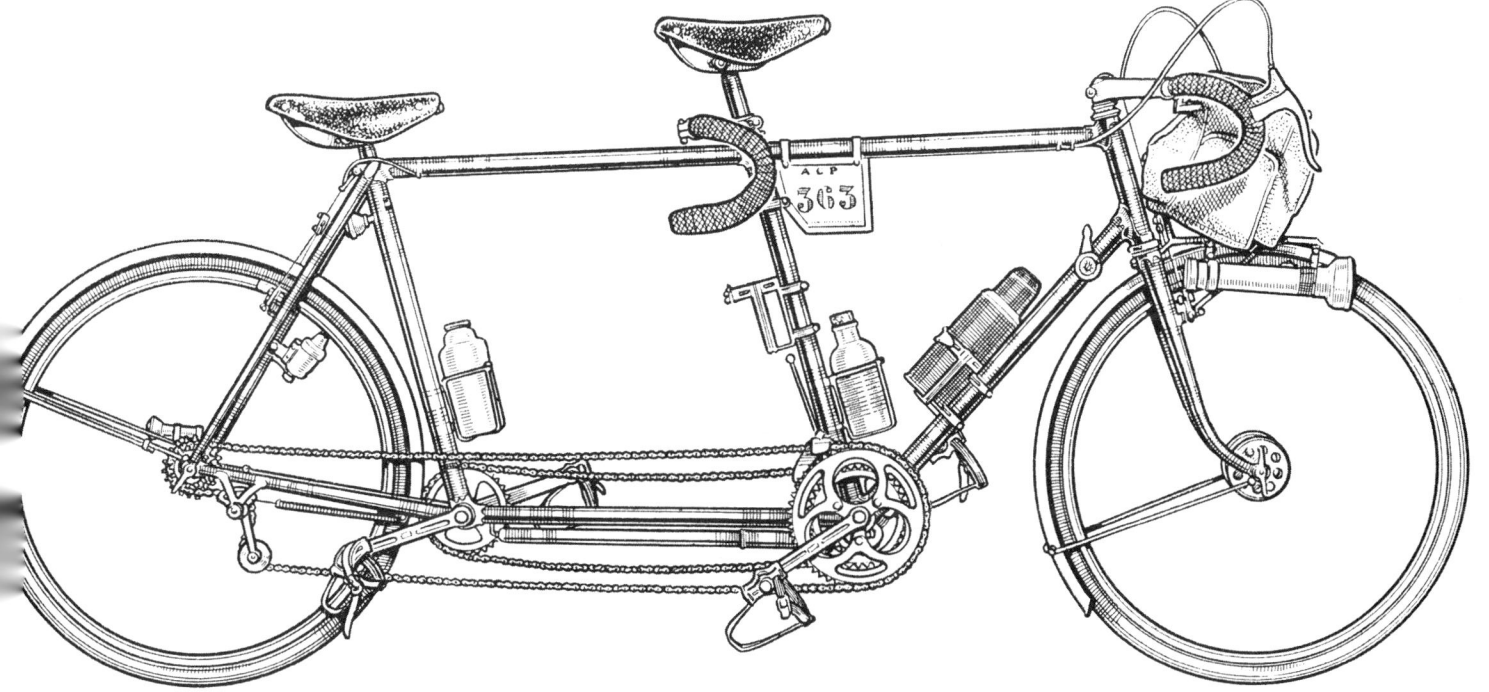

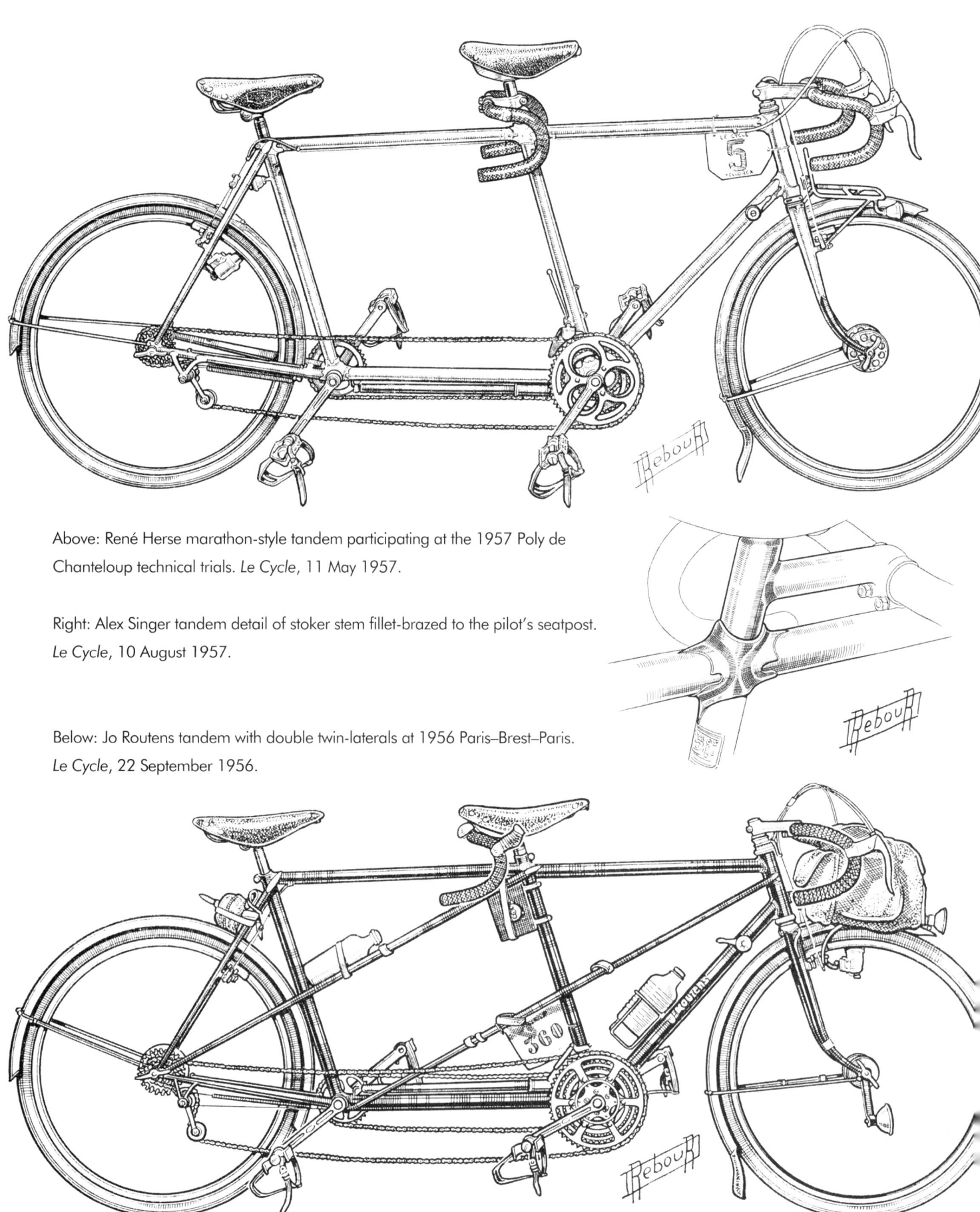

Above: René Herse marathon-style tandem participating at the 1957 Poly de Chanteloup technical trials. *Le Cycle*, 11 May 1957.

Right: Alex Singer tandem detail of stoker stem fillet-brazed to the pilot's seatpost. *Le Cycle*, 10 August 1957.

Below: Jo Routens tandem with double twin-laterals at 1956 Paris–Brest–Paris. *Le Cycle*, 22 September 1956.

CHAPTER 17. TANDEM BICYCLES

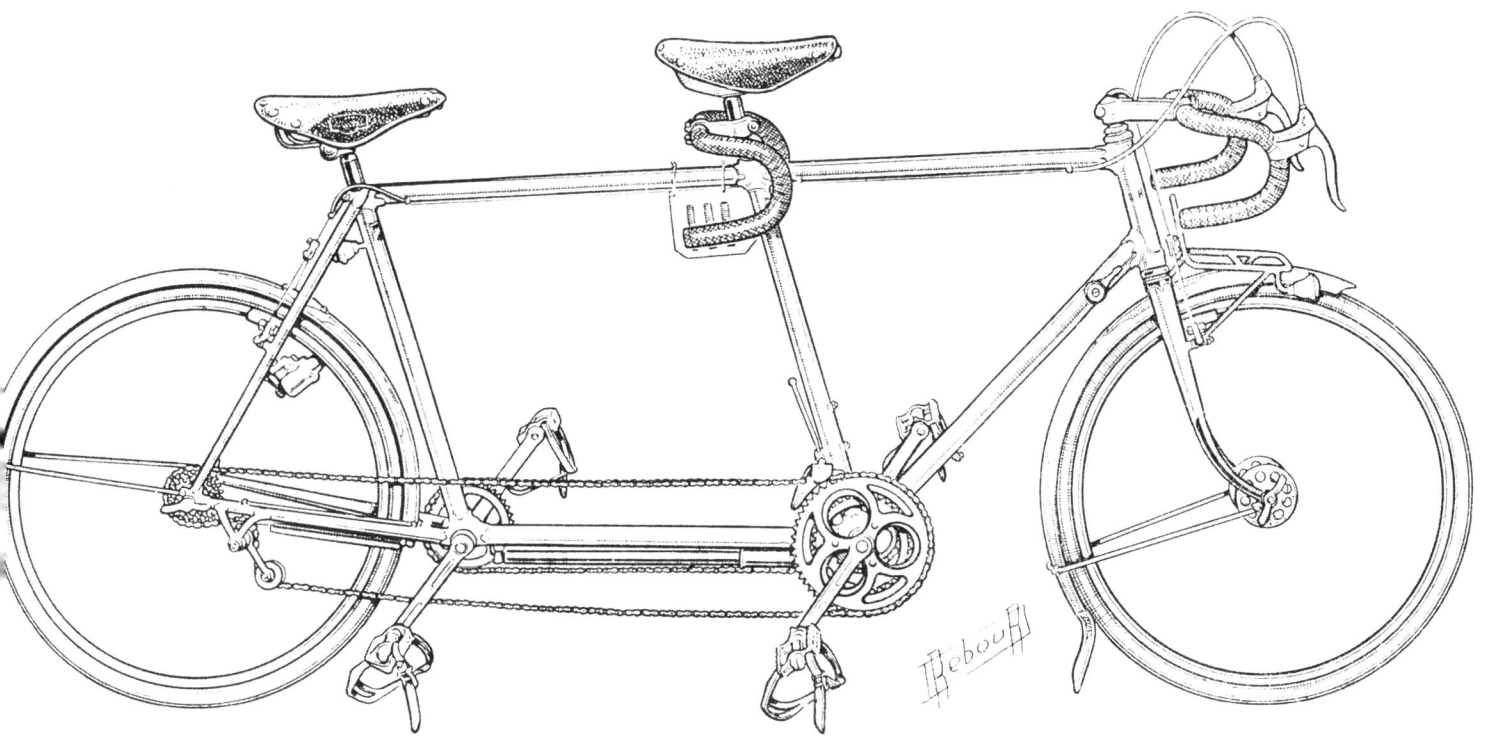

Above: 1957 René Herse randonneur tandem with marathon-style open frame. The use of oversize Reynolds tandem tubing allowed this configuration, which might have been too flexible with regular-size frame tubing. *Le Cycle*, 4 October 1957.

Below: Sabliere tandem participating at the Eastern regional technical trials, at Lyons, this one too of a marathon configuration. *Le Cycle*, 22 September 1956.

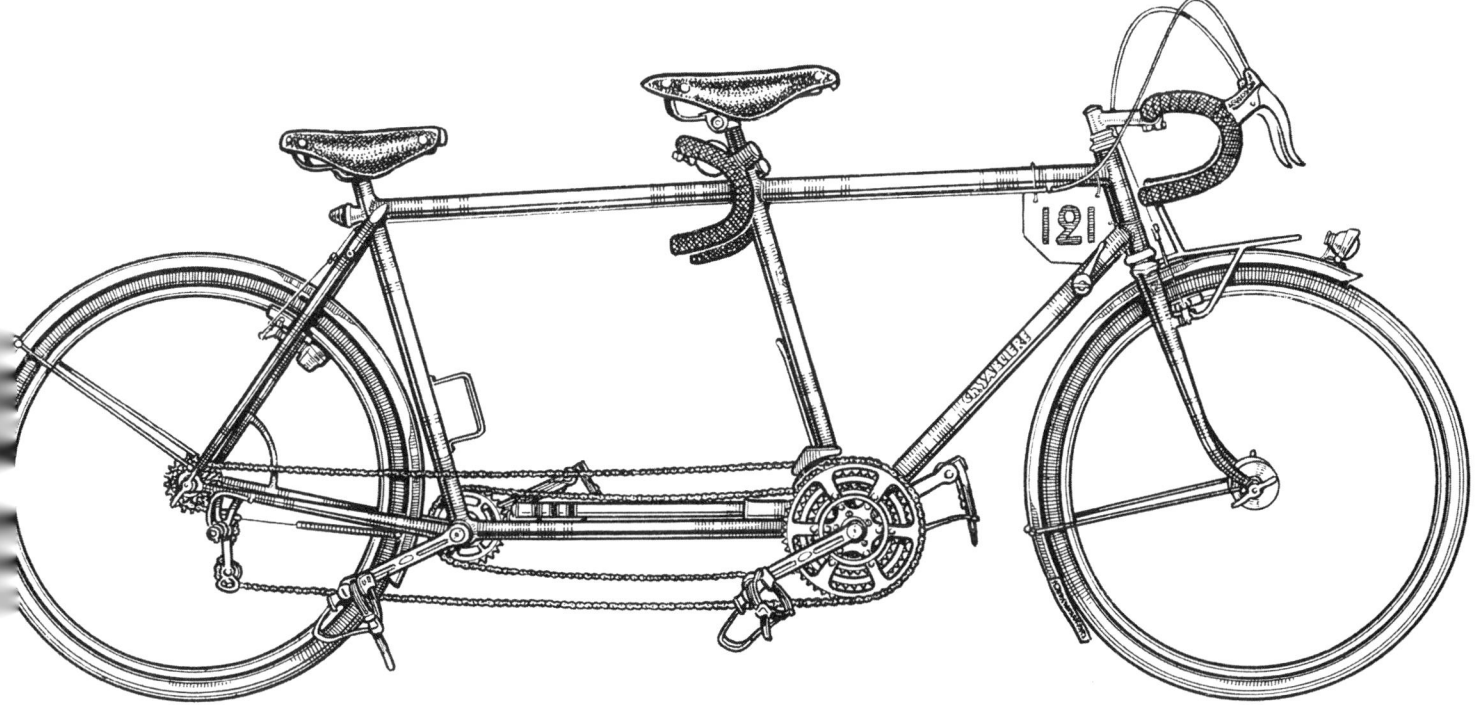

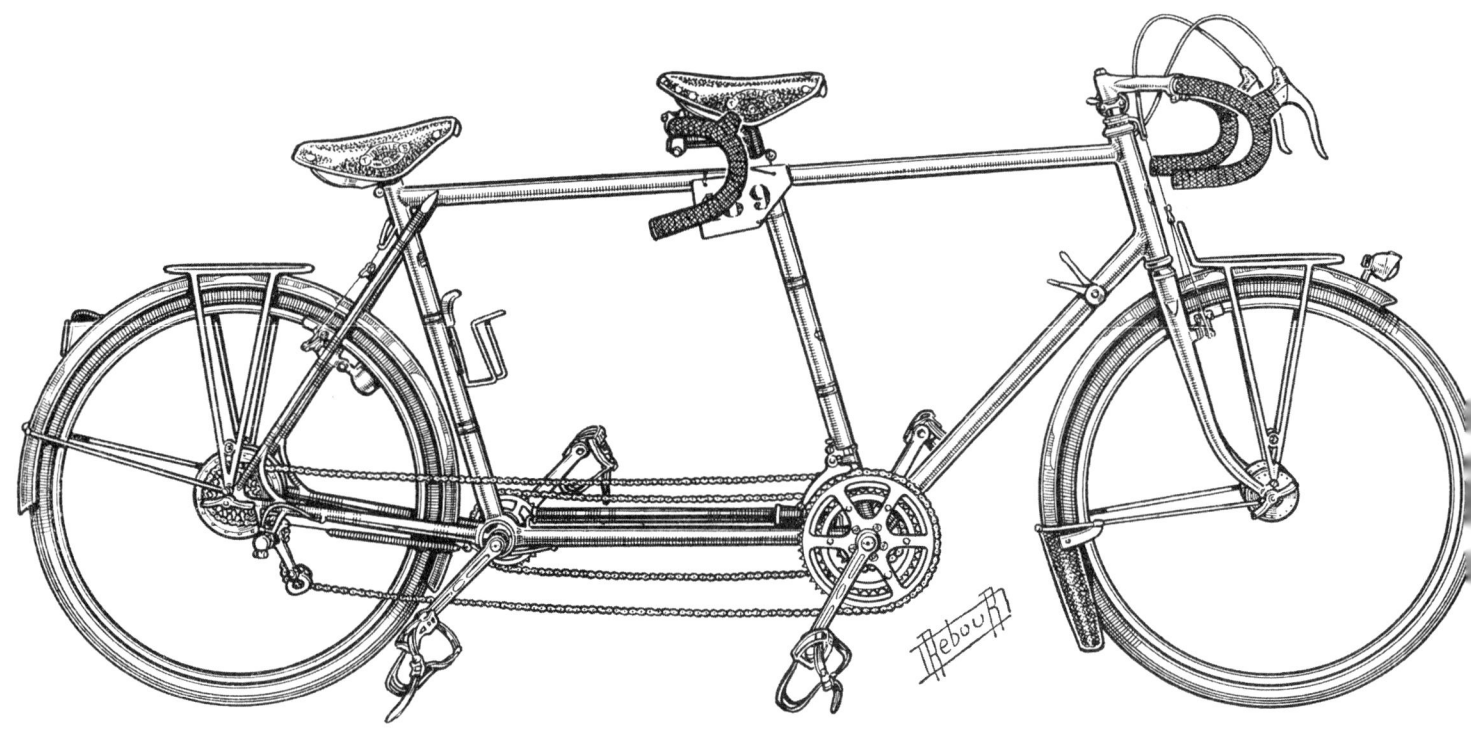

Above: First-placed tandem at the Eastern regional technical trials, at Lyons. *Le Cycle*, 20 September 1958.

Below: René Herse "English-style" short-wheelbase tandem at the 1958 Poly de Chanteloup technical trials. *Le Cycle*, 10 May 1958. Compare this image with the detail shown on page 224.

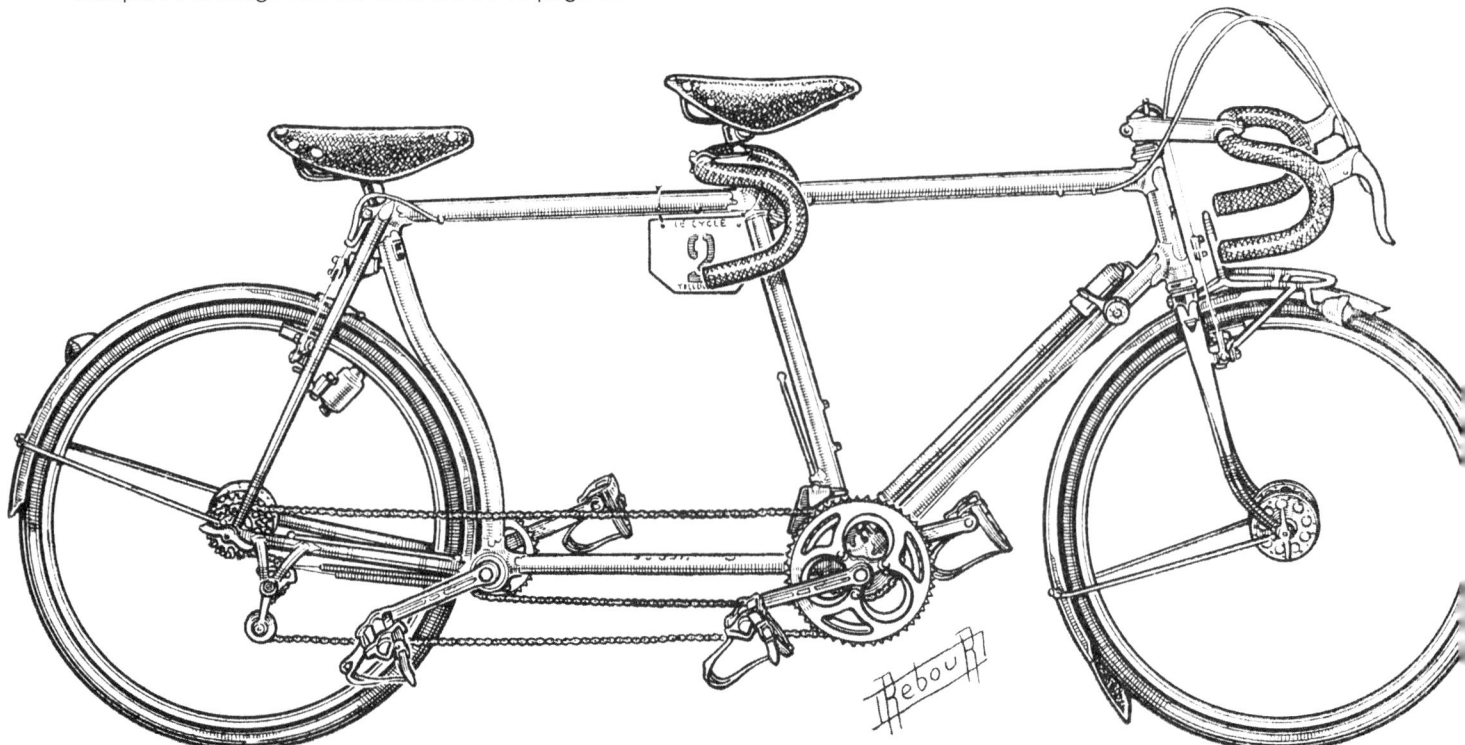

Chapter 17. Tandem Bicycles

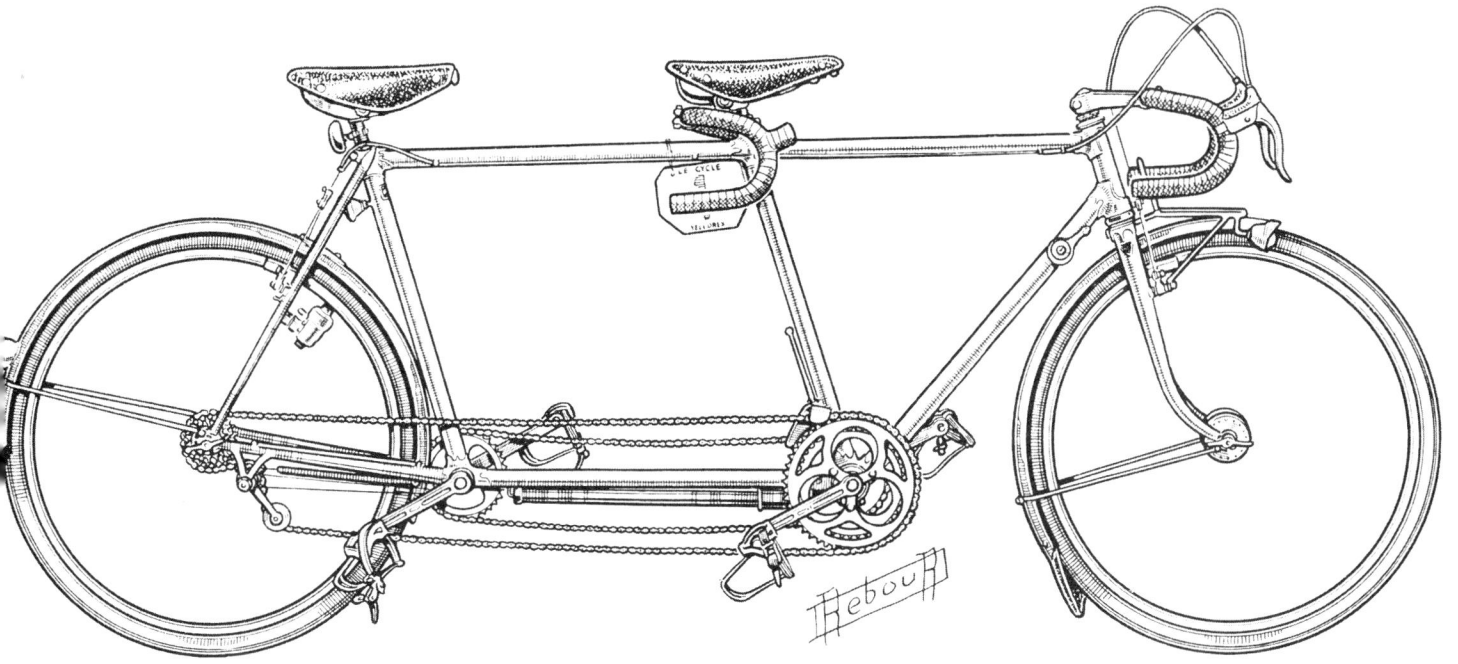

Above: René Herse tandem at the 1959 Poly de Chanteloup technical trials. *Le Cycle*, 16 May 1959.

Right: Eccentric bottom bracket, for adjusting the timing chain tension, on a René Herse tandem at the 1958 Poly de Chanteloup technical trials. *Le Cycle*, 24 May 1958.

Below: Sabliere tandem at the 1960 Poly de Chanteloup technical trials. *Le Cycle*, May 1960.

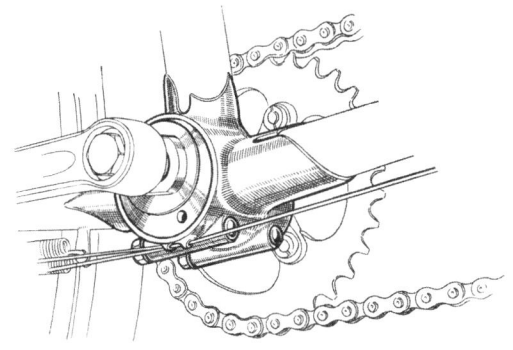

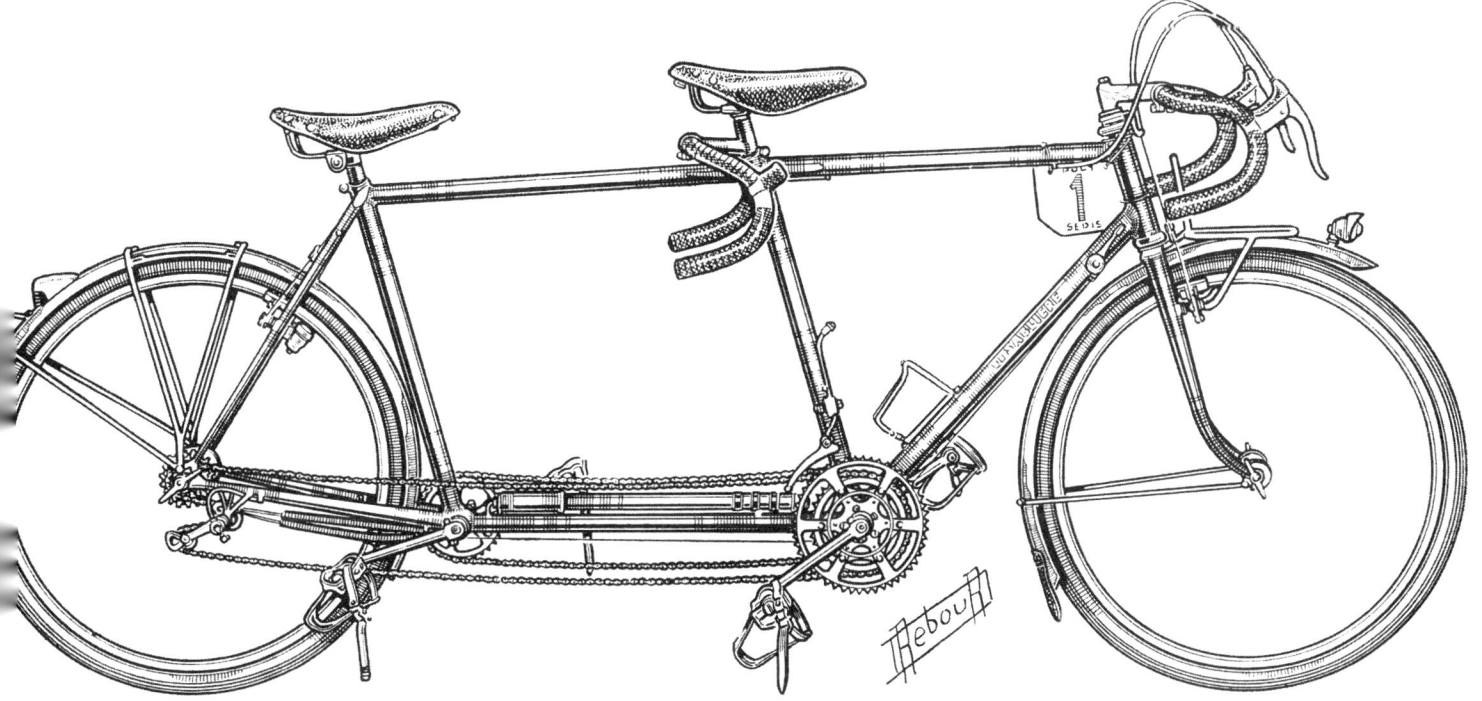

Right: Daniel Rebour and his wife Simone showing off their tandem with dual twin-laterals-reinforced frame, after winning the mixed tandem category in Paris–Brest–Paris. Rebour later mentioned he regretted not having used the wider *semi-ballon* tires. *Le Cycle*, 1948.

Below: Crankset and front derailleur details on a René Herse tandem at the 1962 Poly de Chanteloup technical trials. *Le Cycle*, June 1962.

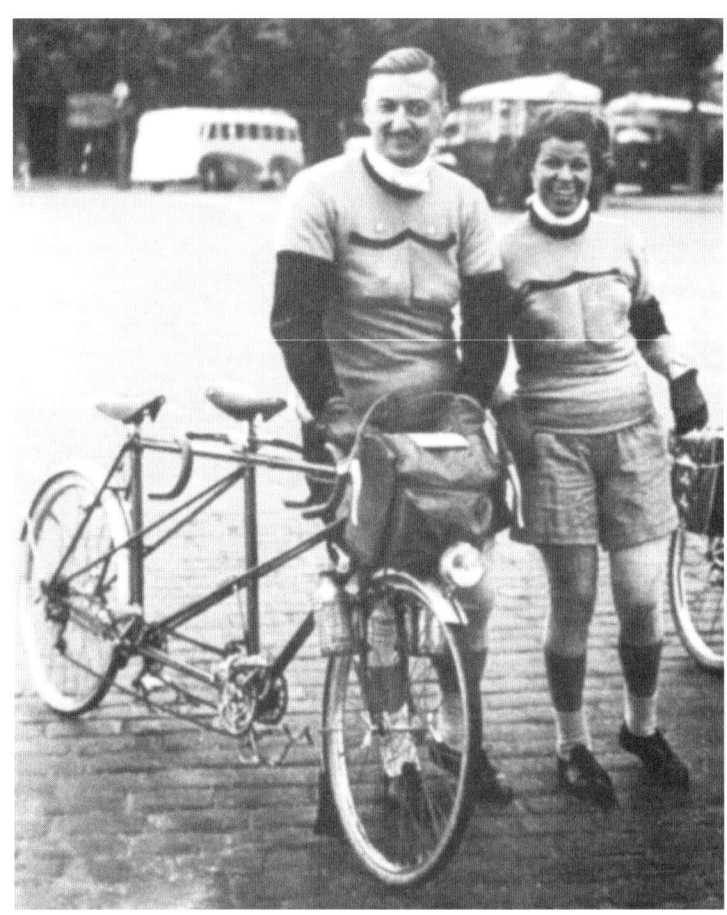

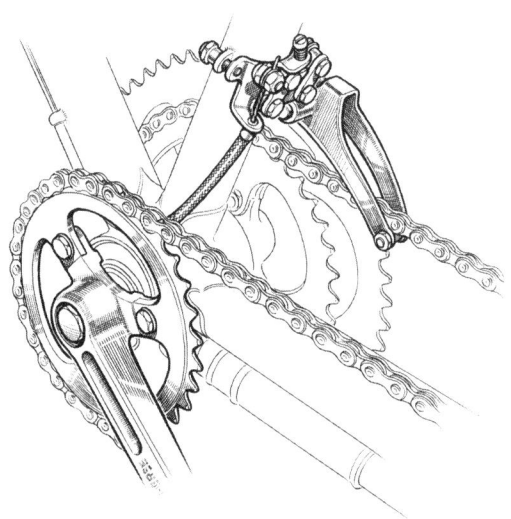

Below: One of the last complete Rebour tandem images published in *Le Cycle*, this is a René Herse tandem at the 1961 Poly de Chanteloup technical trials. *Le Cycle*, June 1961.

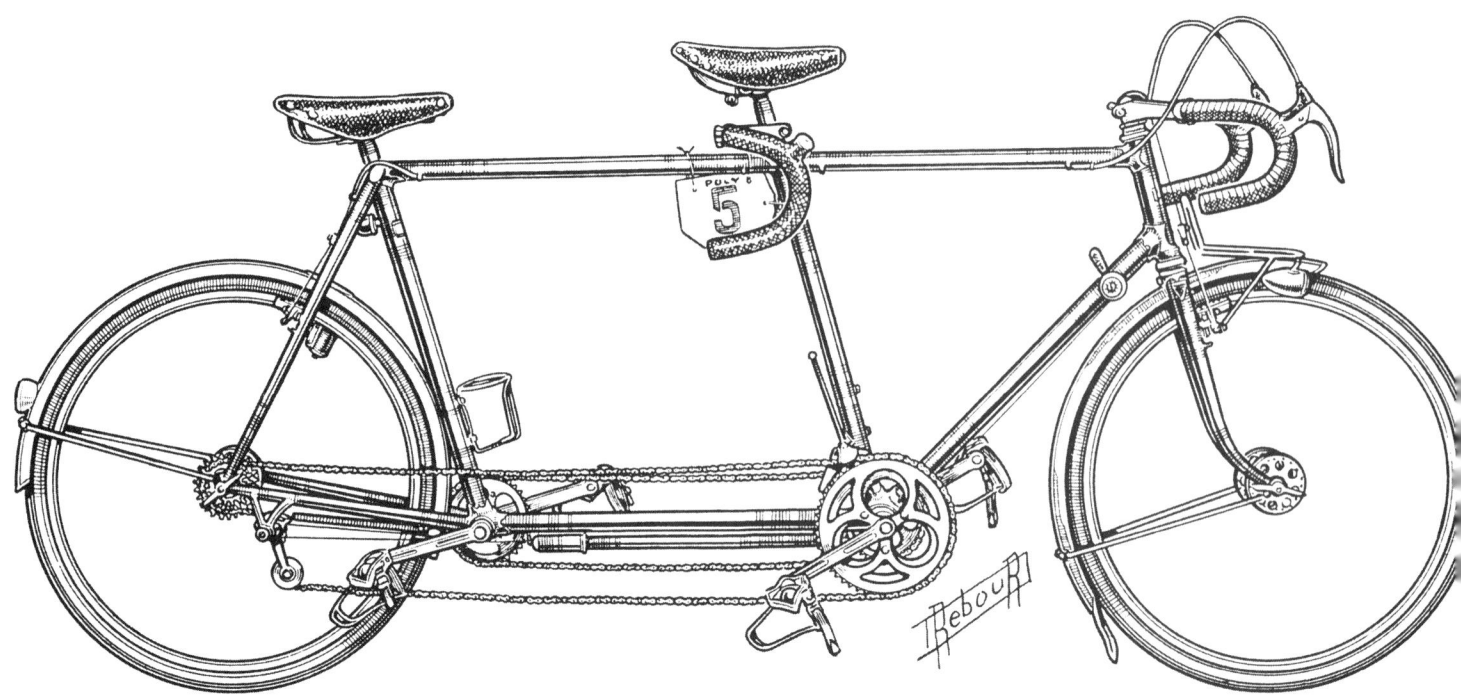

Chapter 18. Folding and Parting Bikes

Folding bicycles, and models that can be taken apart for easy transport, have been around for a long time. The best-known early examples are the French military bicycles introduced by Captain Gérard at the turn of the 20th century. Dating to the 2nd World War, another well-known example was the BSA paratrouper bike used by the English military.

The first post-war commercial bicycle of this kind appears to have been the Japanese Silk, which was developed from a wartime military folding machine. But the big push for folding bikes came when motorization began to get a firm hold in continental Europe, the last half of the 1950s, and at the 1956 Frankfurt IFMA trade show, a number of such machines were shown, all with small wheels (usually 18- or 20-inch), signaling the beginning of a trend in European bicycle usage that would last until the late 1970s.

This chapter presents some of the bicycles in this category, ranging from tiny-wheeled contraptions to the dismountable full-size bikes made by specialist frame builders such as René Herse. Also see page 188 for a drawing of the Moulton small-wheeler with suspension (and Chapter 20 for some details of the Moulton's suspension).

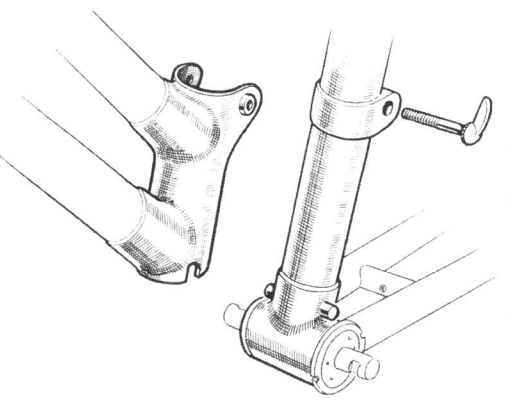

Left: Frame joint detail on a 1957 German parting bike. *Le Cycle*, 7 September 1957.

Right: Frame hinge on an English BSA folding bike based on the World War II BSA paratrouper machine. *Le Cycle*, 12 February 1949.

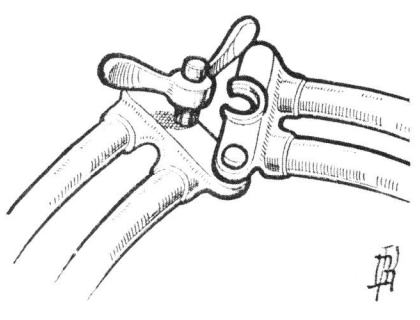

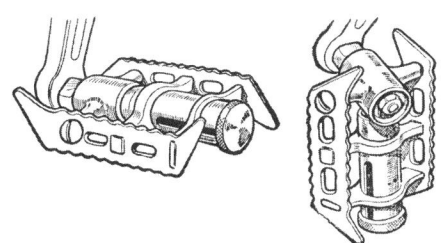

Above: This drawing of a folding pedal appeared before the first folding bicycle was depicted. *Le Cycle*, 20 February 1947

Right: Appropriately called Origami, this Japanese folding bicycle, with 18-inch wheels and fold-down handlebars, was presented at the 1951 Amsterdam bicycle trade show. *Le Cycle*, 7 April 1951.

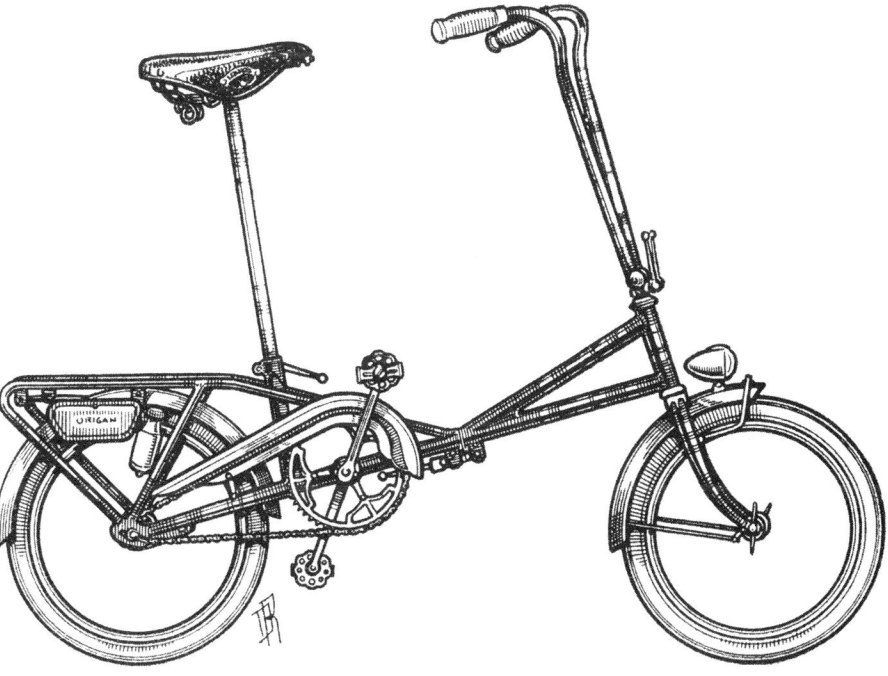

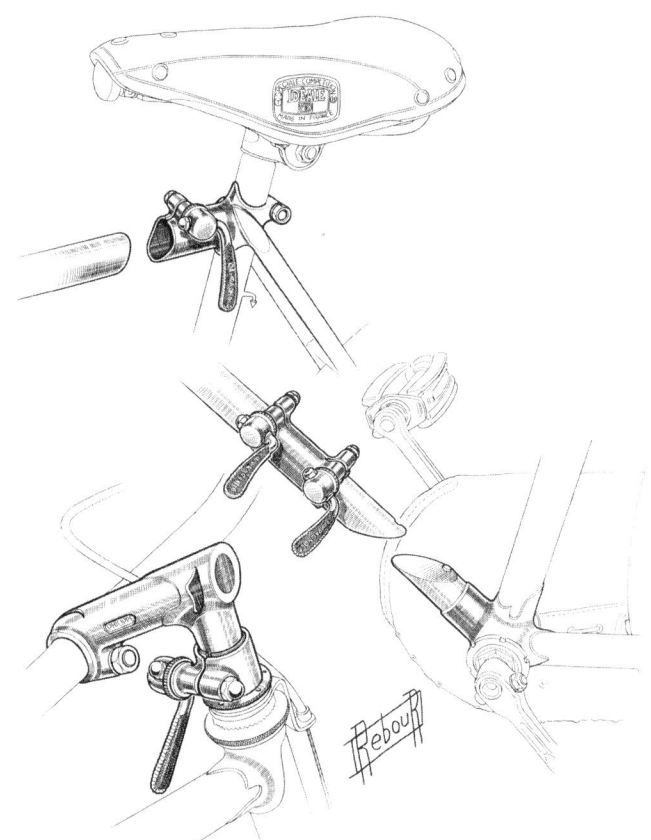
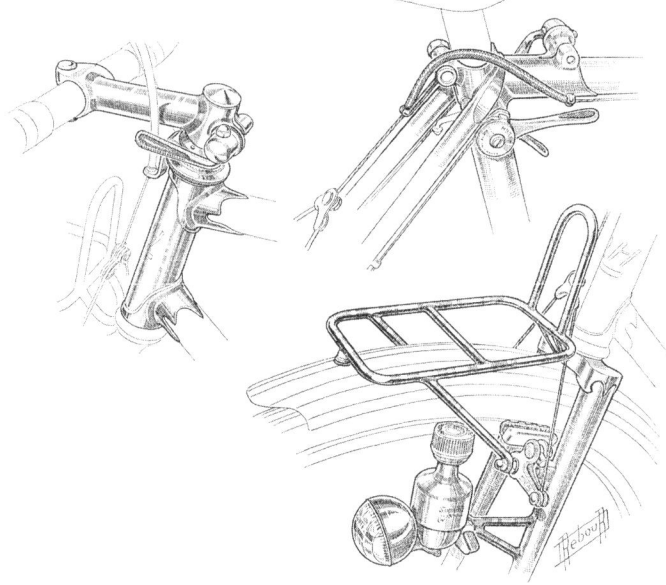

Right: ATAX folding handlebars for folding bikes. *Le Cycle*, November 1966.

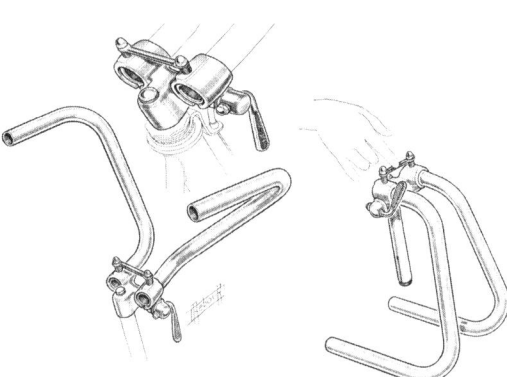
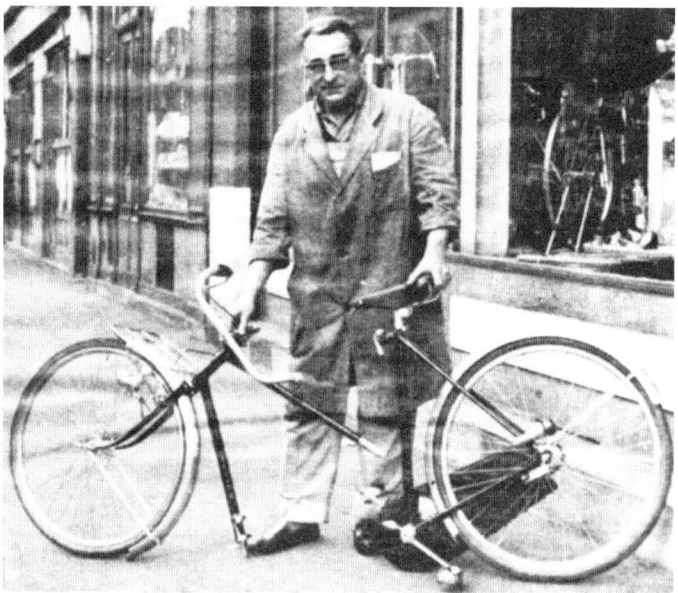

Above: Photo of René Herse demonstrating how his Démontable, or partitioning bike, works. *Le Cycle*, December 1962.

Left: And this is Rebour's drawing of the assembled Démontable.

Top left: Details of the same bike.

Top right: Details of the 1965 version of the Démontable. *Le Cycle*, May 1965.

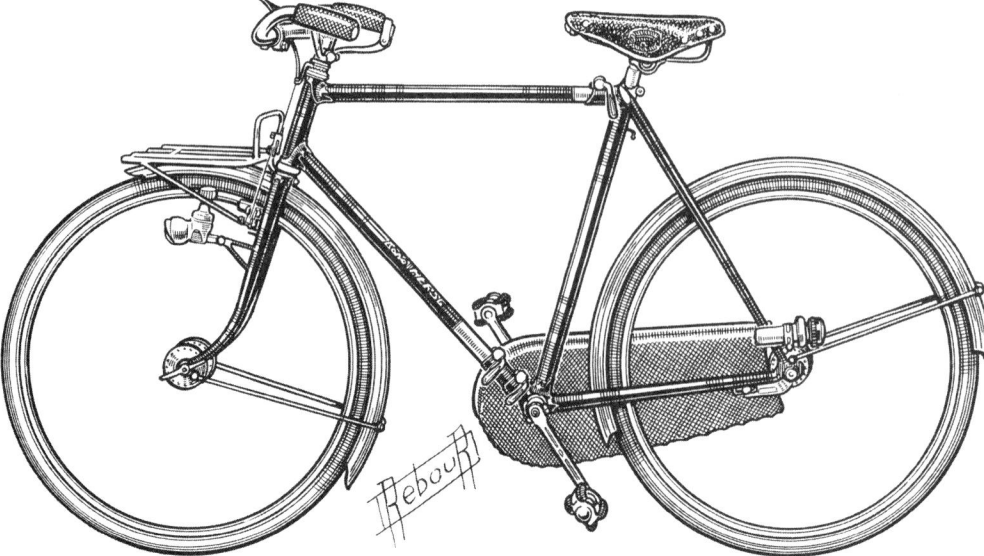

Chapter 18. Folding and Parting Bikes

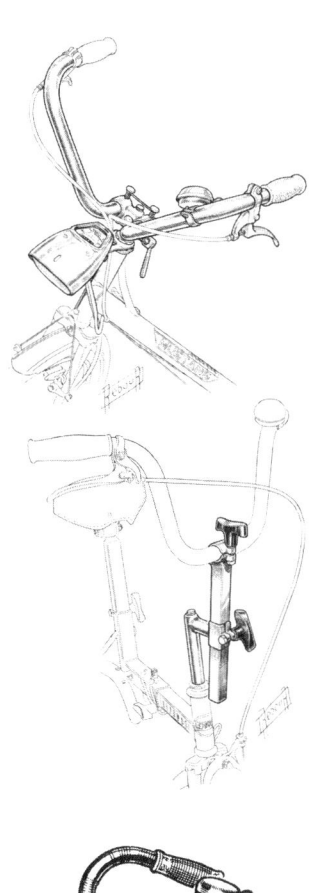

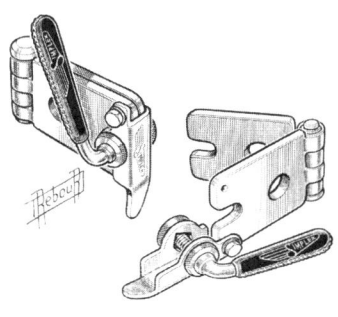

Above: Simplex hinge and latch for folding bikes. *Le Cycle*, January 1969.

Left: Folding handlebar detail. *Le Cycle*, November 1968.

Right: Silk folder, from Japan, and detail, as seen at the 1964 Amsterdam bicycle trade show. *Le Cycle*, March 1964.

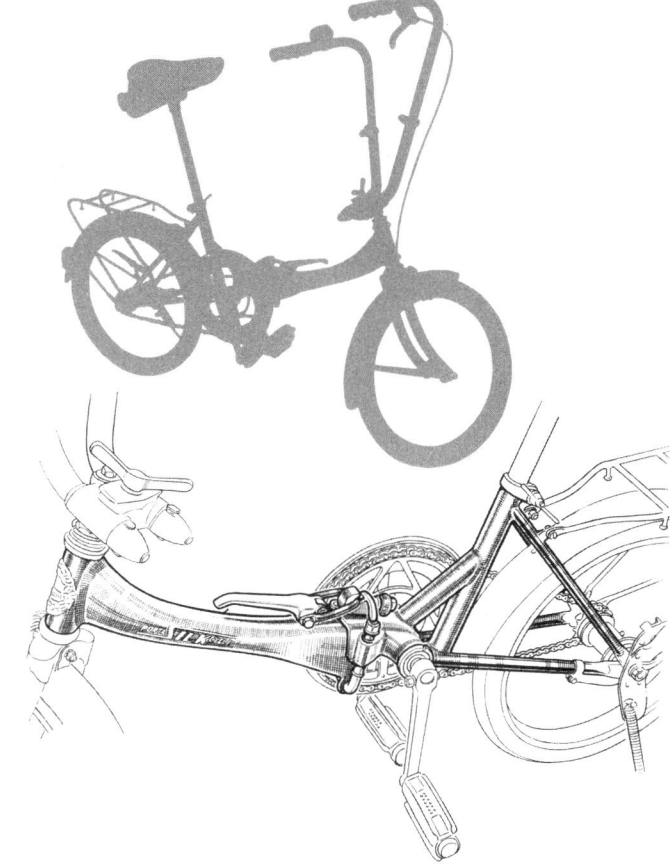

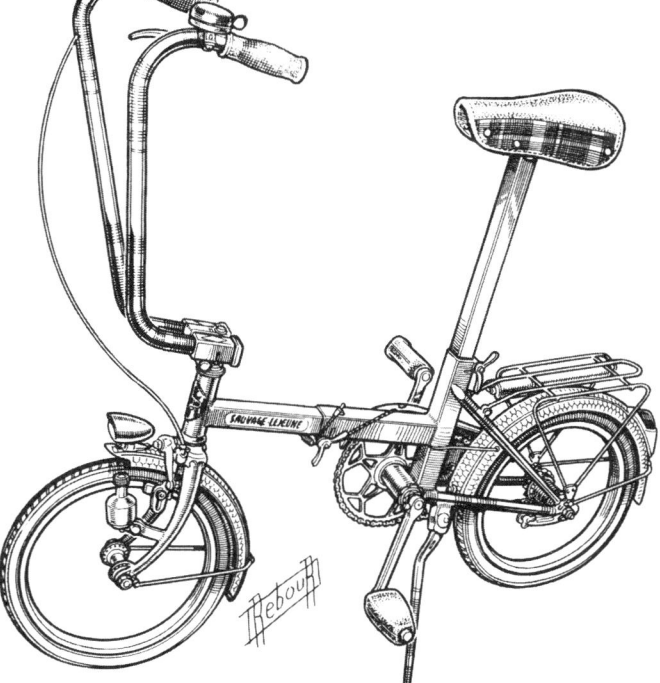

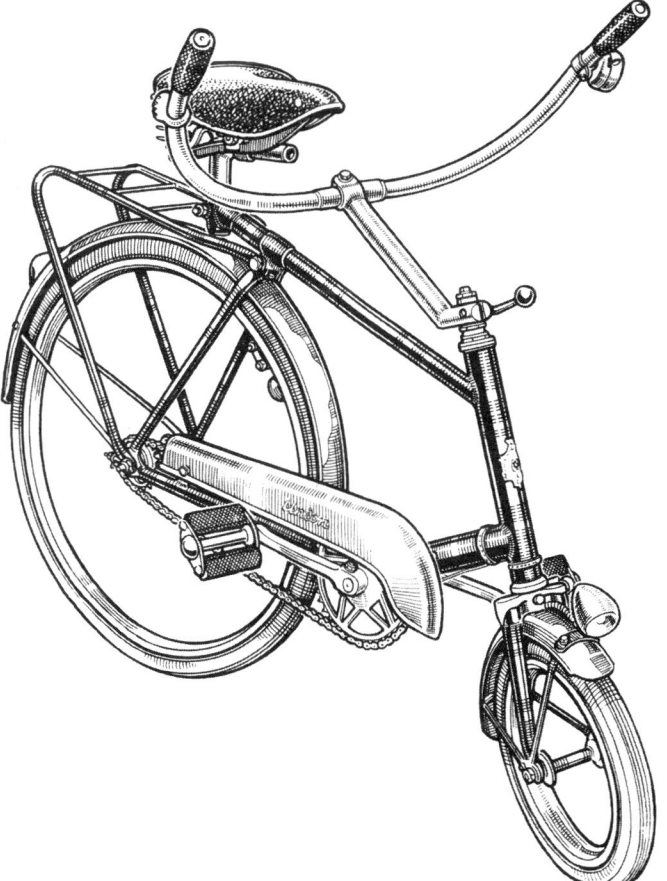

Above: Sauvage-Lejeune folding bike with folding handlebars, tiny 16-inch wheels, and square frame tubes, including a square seatpost. *Le Cycle*, November 1966.

Right: Though presented at the Amsterdam trade show as an original, this Dutch-made Union Strada was actually copied from the pre-war Italian Velocino design. *Le Cycle*, March 1964.

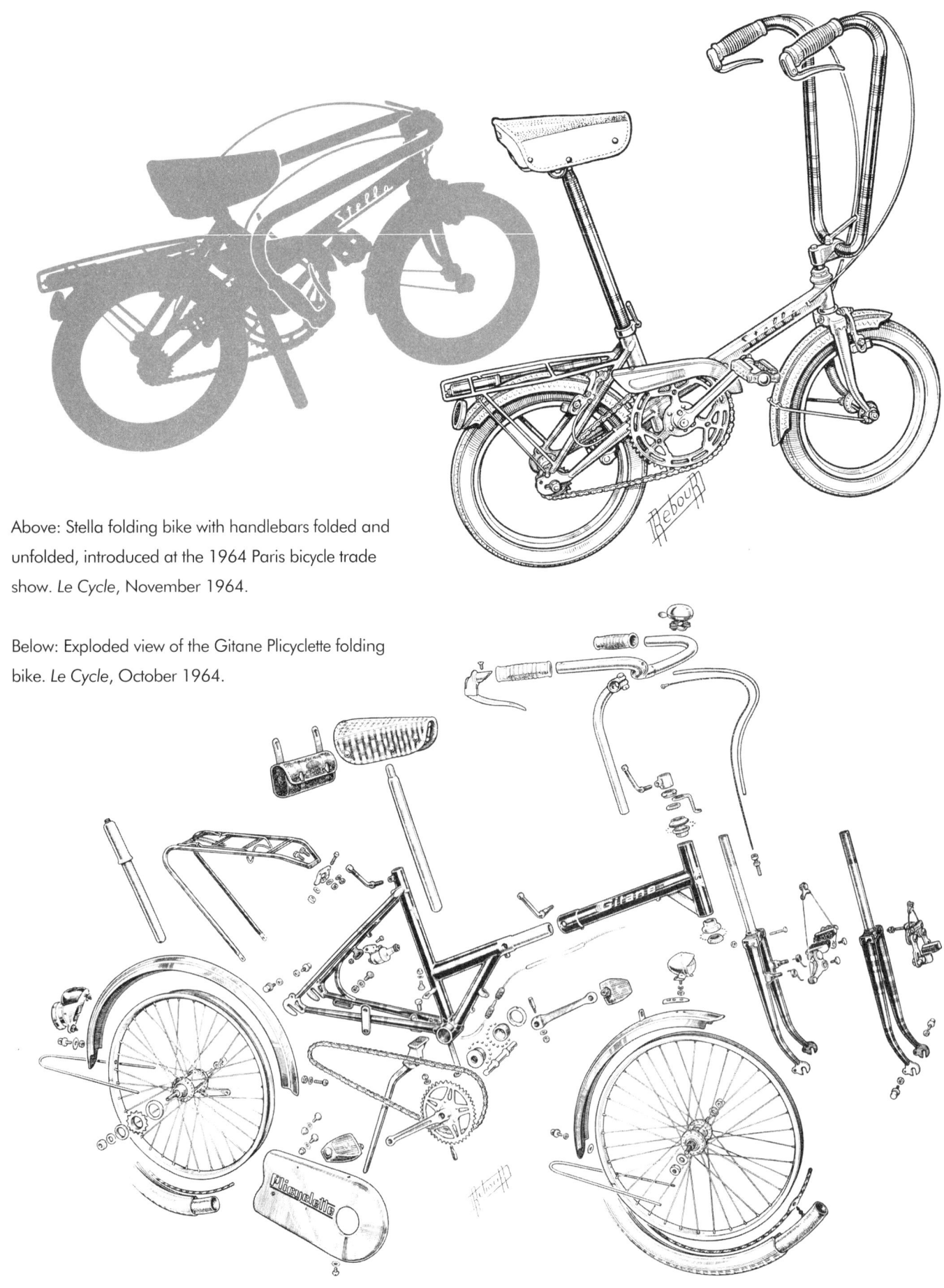

Above: Stella folding bike with handlebars folded and unfolded, introduced at the 1964 Paris bicycle trade show. *Le Cycle*, November 1964.

Below: Exploded view of the Gitane Plicyclette folding bike. *Le Cycle*, October 1964.

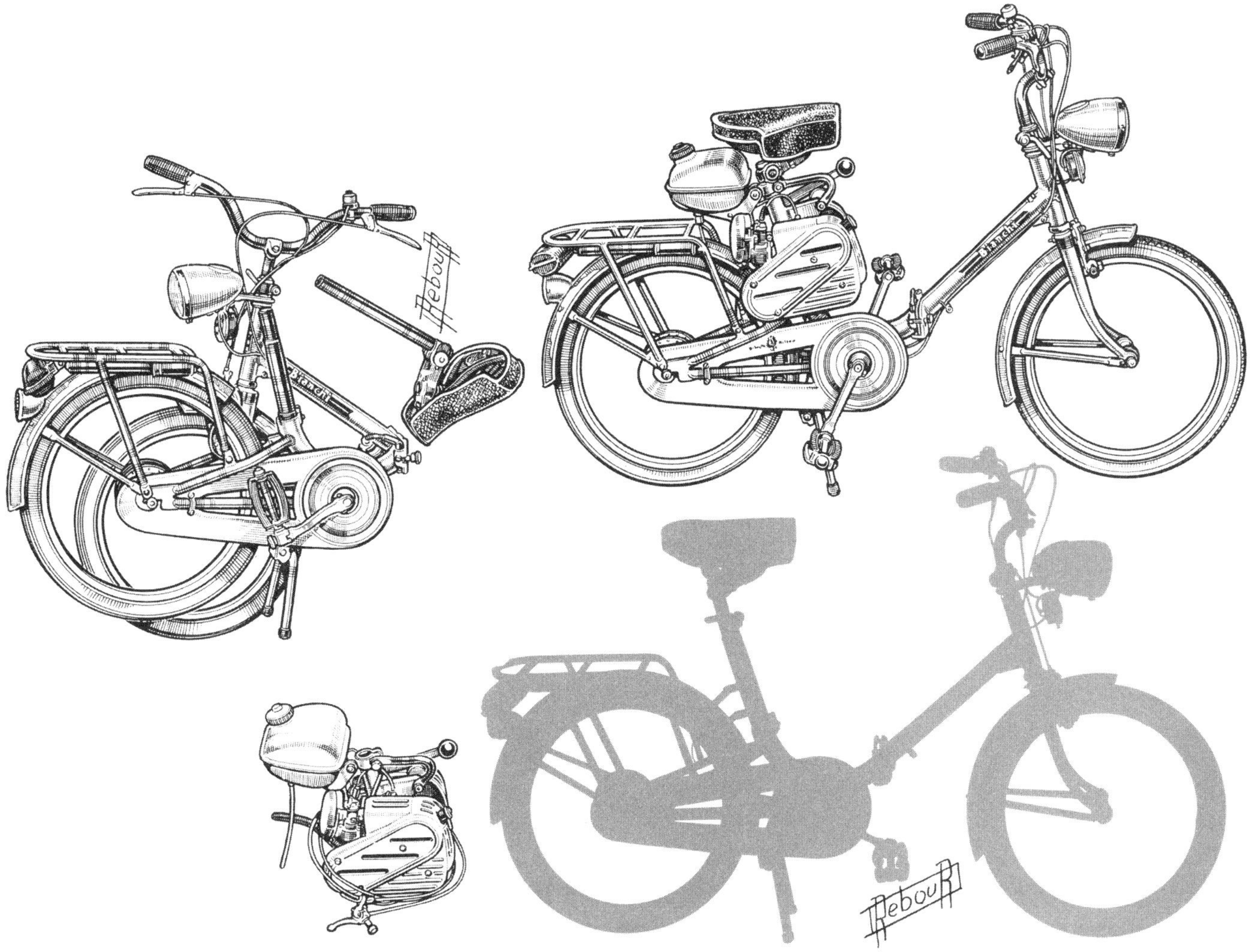

CHAPTER 18. FOLDING AND PARTING BIKES

Above: Shown at the 1966 Paris trade show, this Bianchi folding bike can be mated to an auxiliary motor to turn it into a foldable moped. *Le Cycle*, November 1966.

Below: Captivante folding bike, introduced at the 1966 Paris show, ready to ride and folded. *Le Cycle*, October 1966.

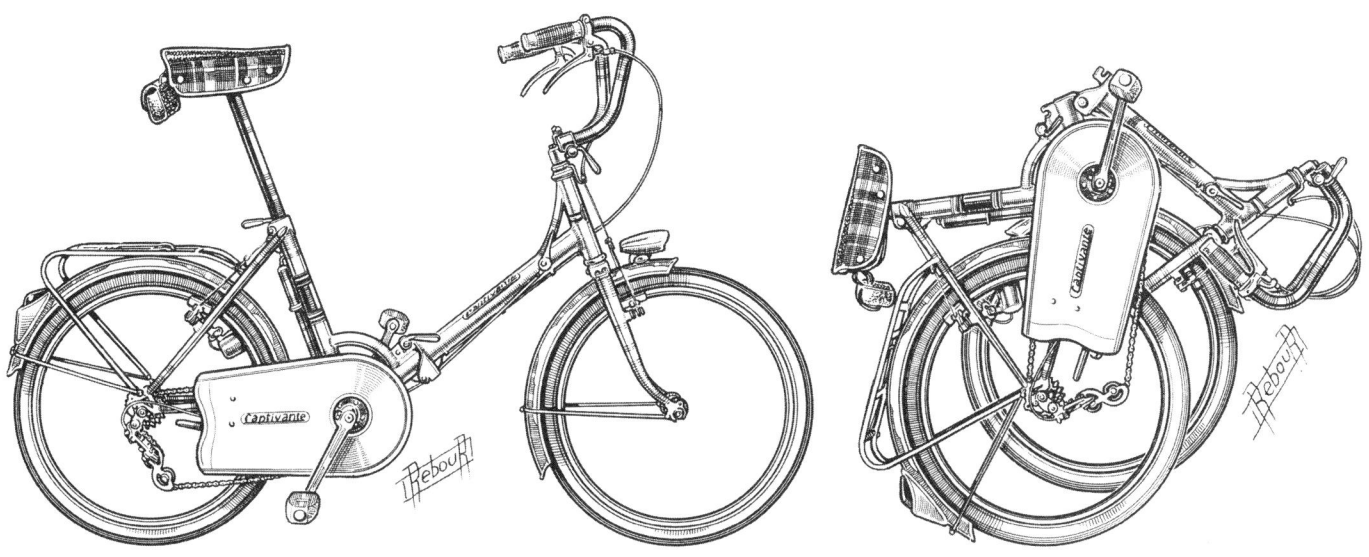

237

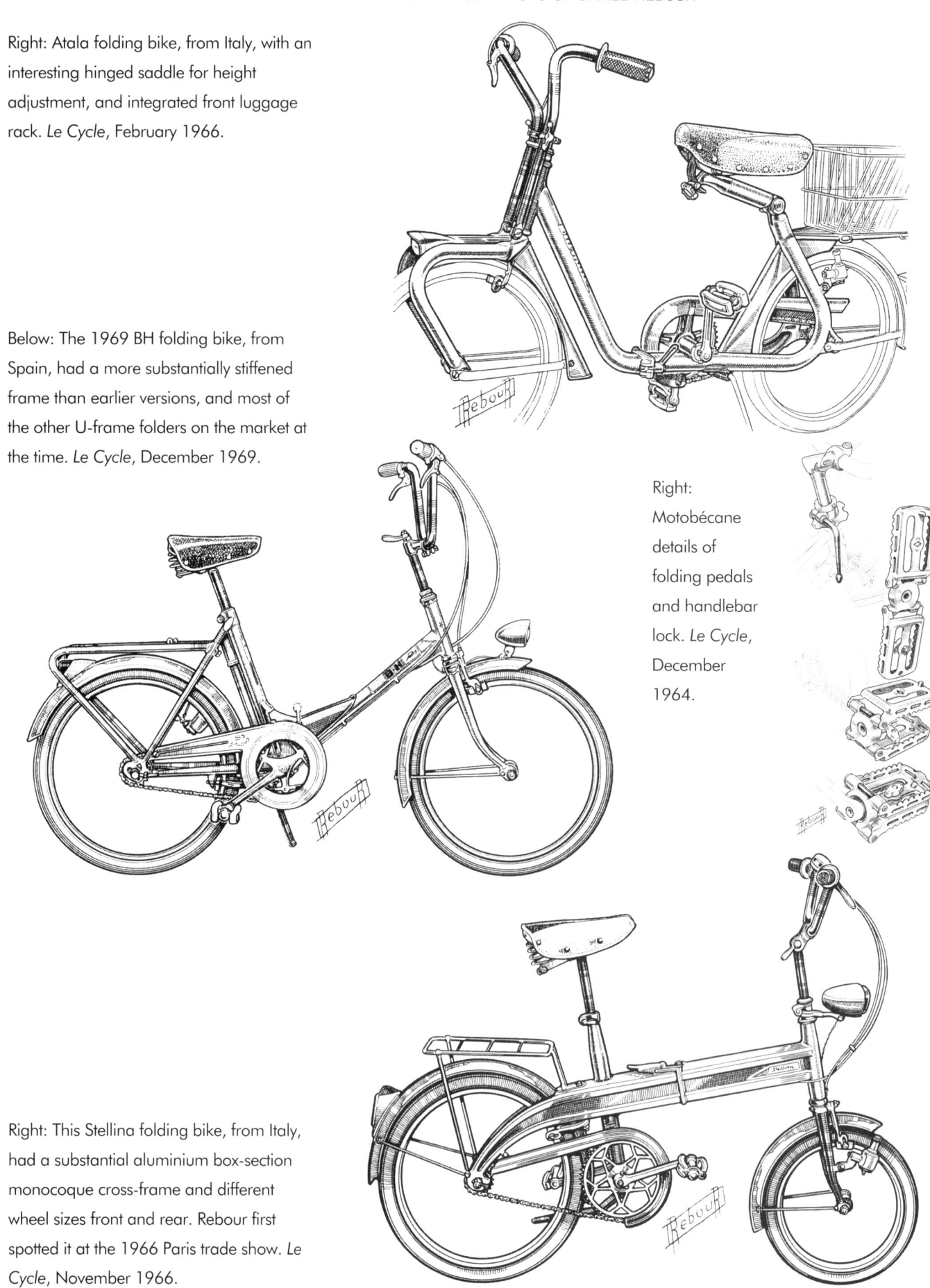

Right: Atala folding bike, from Italy, with an interesting hinged saddle for height adjustment, and integrated front luggage rack. *Le Cycle*, February 1966.

Below: The 1969 BH folding bike, from Spain, had a more substantially stiffened frame than earlier versions, and most of the other U-frame folders on the market at the time. *Le Cycle*, December 1969.

Right: Motobécane details of folding pedals and handlebar lock. *Le Cycle*, December 1964.

Right: This Stellina folding bike, from Italy, had a substantial aluminium box-section monocoque cross-frame and different wheel sizes front and rear. Rebour first spotted it at the 1966 Paris trade show. *Le Cycle*, November 1966.

Chapter 19. Children's Bikes

Although he never had children himself, Rebour was keenly aware of any developments in the realm of cycling for, and with, children. In the pages of *Le Cycle*, there are numerous illustrations of children's bikes, toy bikes, child seats, and other adaptations for cycling with children.

In addition to the various bicycle trade shows around Europe which Daniel Rebour mined for interesting development, he also attended the toy fairs, paying special attention to bicycles for children and juniors. This chapter contains some examples of that work.

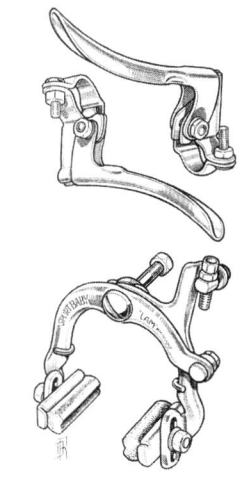

Right: LAM special brakes for children's bikes, with levers small enough, and close enough to the handlebars when mounted, to allow a child's small hands to operate them. *Le Cycle*, 19 September 1953.

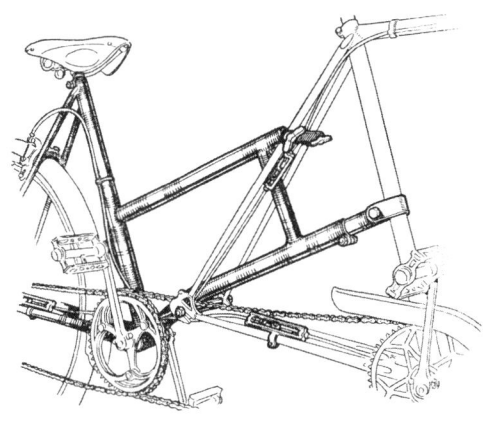

Right: Child extension, turning a standard bike into a tandem with child stoker. *Le Cycle*, 27 May 1950.

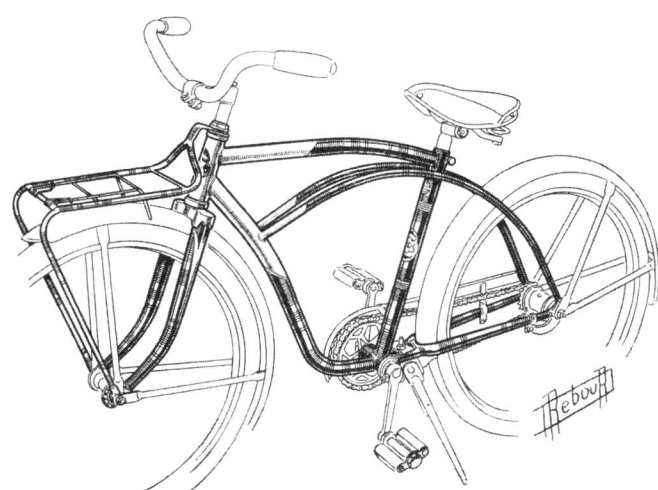

Above: "American-style" boy's bike from TSK, in Belgium. *Le Cycle*, 23 May 1958.

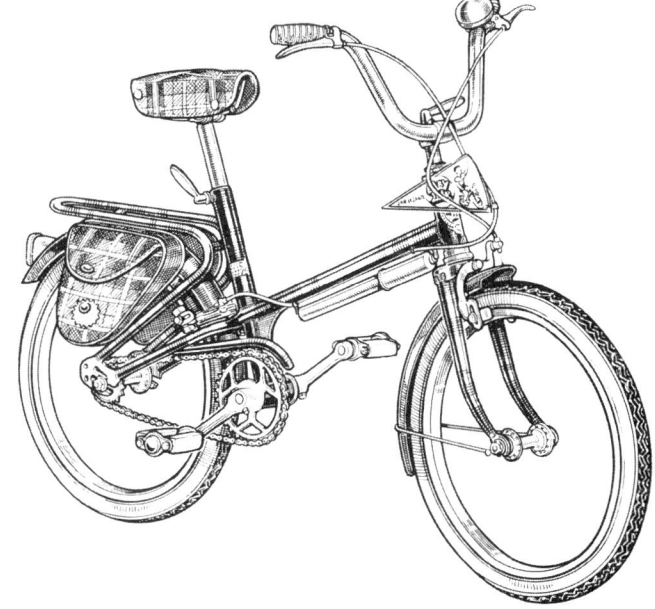

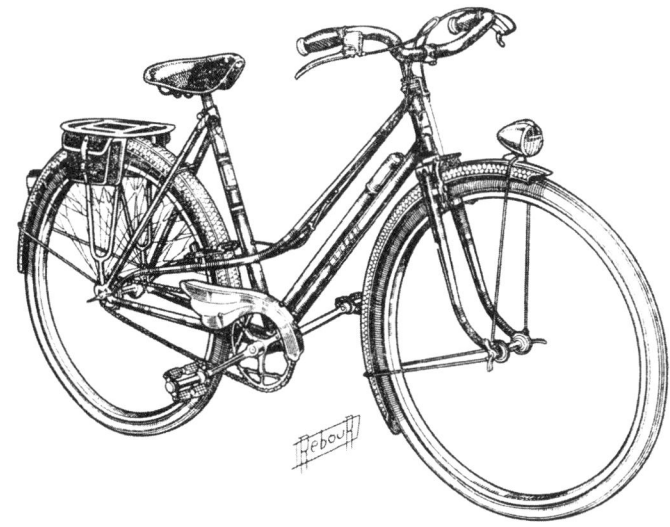

Above: Gitane Minijet G-50, with 20-inch wheels and cross-frame. *Le Cycle*, March 1966.

Left: Rochet girl's bicycle with 24-inch wheels. *Le Cycle*, 13 April 1965.

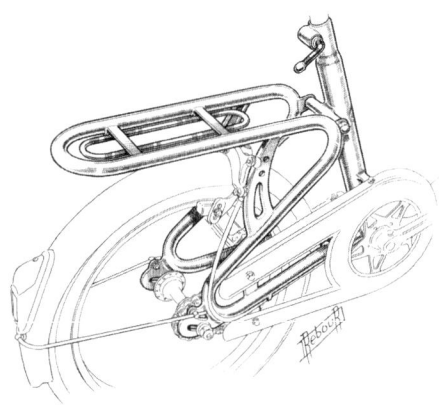

Left: Integrated luggage rack on a Gitane child's bike. *Le Cycle*, March 1968.

Right: Superia children's version of a traditional high-wheel bicycle, displayed at the 1966 Paris bicycle trade show. *Le Cycle*, December 1966.

Below: Baby-Star was a brand that specialized in toy tricycles and children's bicycles. These are their 24-inch wheel Alda models in boys' and girls' versions. *Le Cycle*, February 1967.

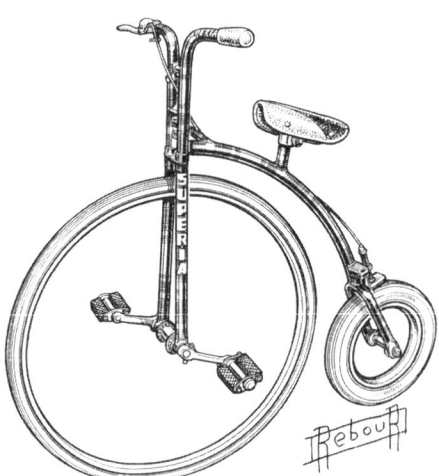

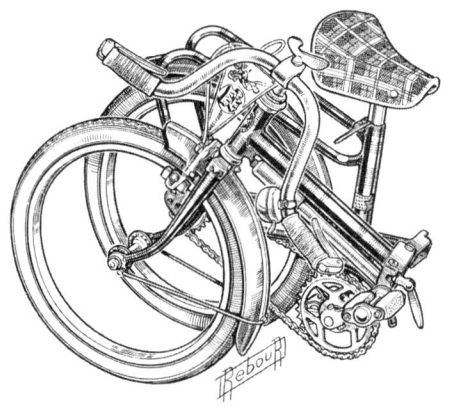

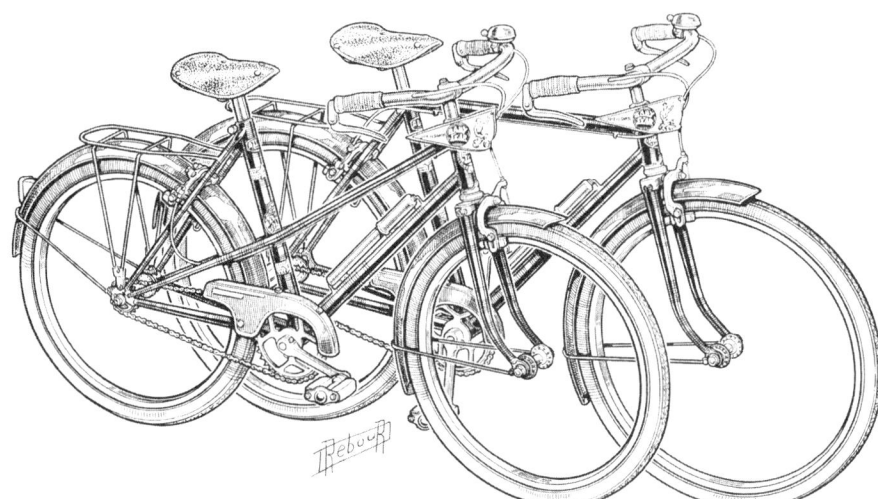

Above: Baby-Star brand Plicystar child's folding bike. *Le Cycle*, February 1967.

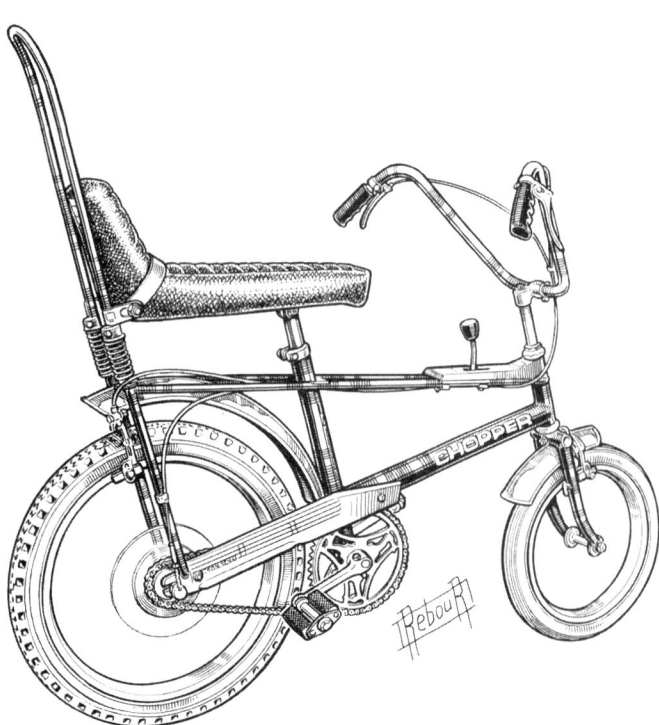

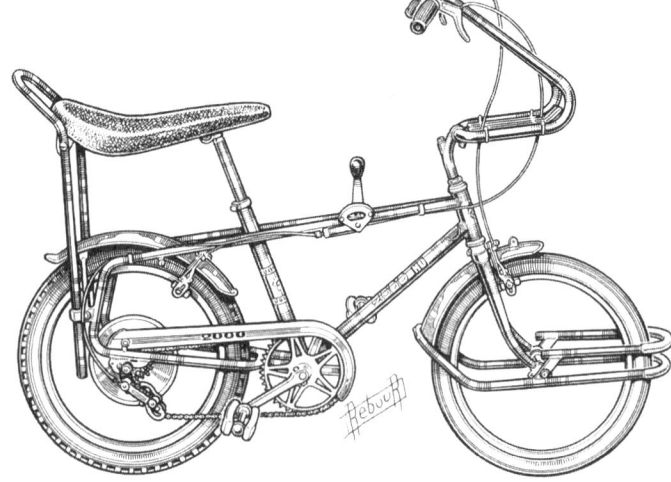

Two U.S.-inspired children's bikes on display at the 1970 Amsterdam bicycle trade show.

Left, the Raleigh Chopper was Raleigh's successful entry into the market created by the Schwinn Sting Ray.

Above: The chopper offered by Burgers, of Holland.

Both images from *Le Cycle*, June 1970.

Chapter 20. Suspension Systems

Bicycle suspension systems have been in use for many years, although they have not figured much in mass-production bicycles until the development of the mountain bike.

This chapter illustrates some of the suspension systems and their components developed during the years that Daniel Rebour's illustrations were created.

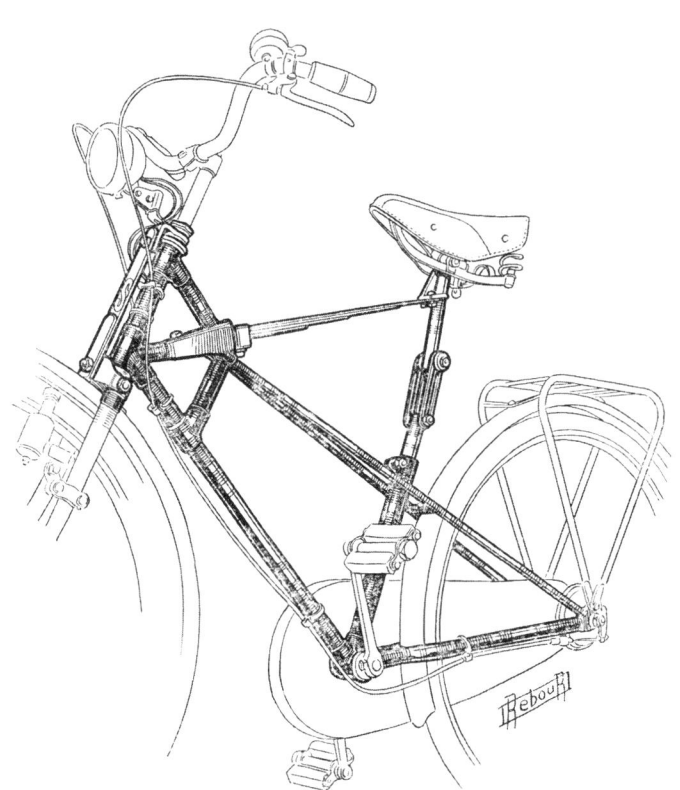

Right: Simplex "Zweeffiets," or glider bike, introduced by the Dutch Simplex bicycle company (not related to the French component maker). *Le Cycle*, 21 March 1953.

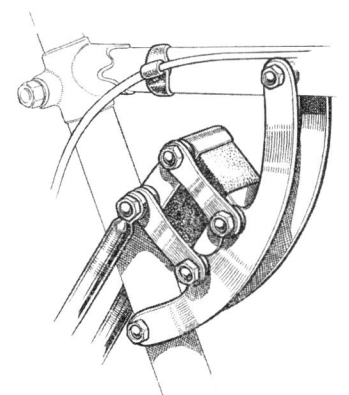

Below and left: English-made Phillips Swinglight, and its suspension detail. *Le Cycle*, 24 November 1951.

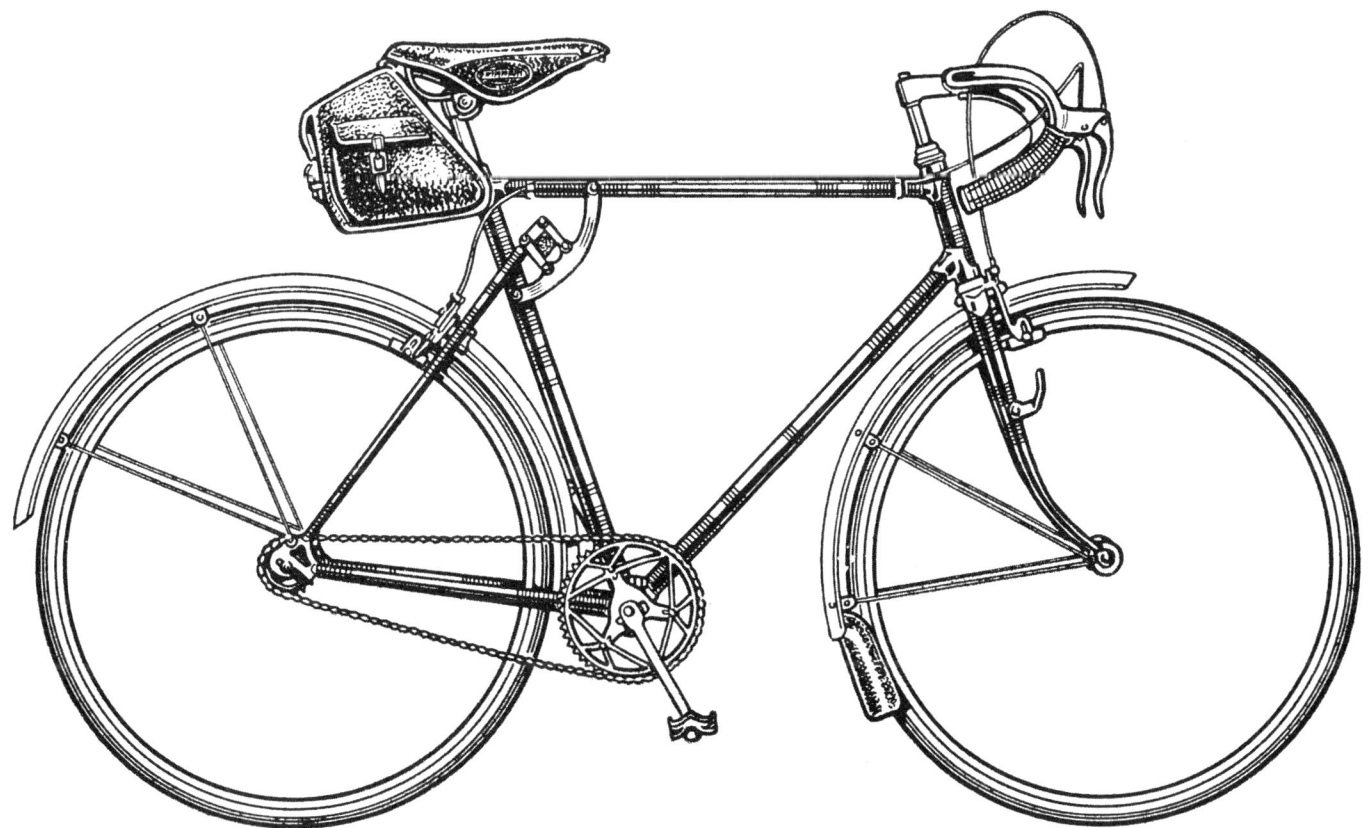

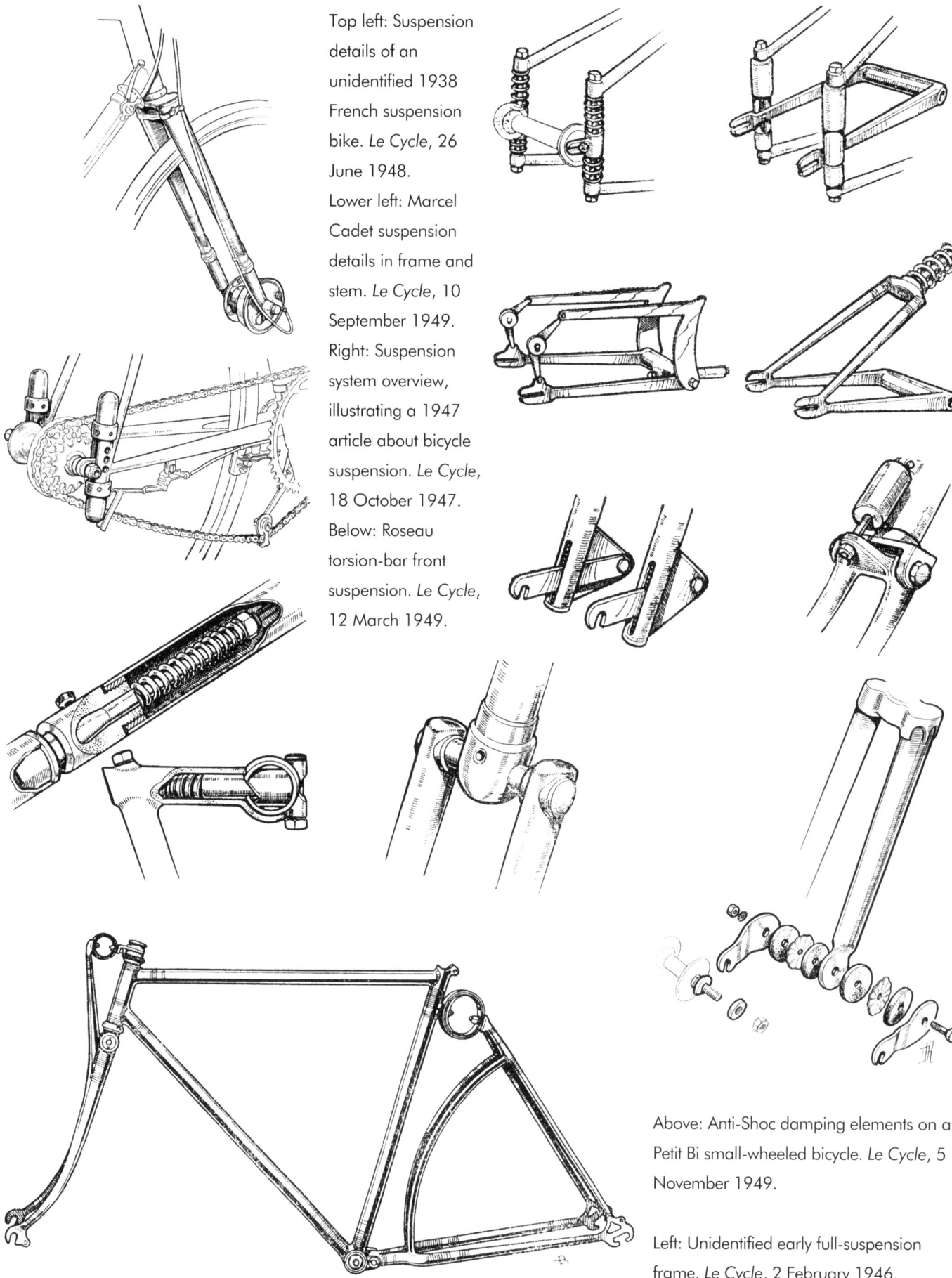

Top left: Suspension details of an unidentified 1938 French suspension bike. *Le Cycle*, 26 June 1948.

Lower left: Marcel Cadet suspension details in frame and stem. *Le Cycle*, 10 September 1949.

Right: Suspension system overview, illustrating a 1947 article about bicycle suspension. *Le Cycle*, 18 October 1947.

Below: Roseau torsion-bar front suspension. *Le Cycle*, 12 March 1949.

Above: Anti-Shoc damping elements on a Petit Bi small-wheeled bicycle. *Le Cycle*, 5 November 1949.

Left: Unidentified early full-suspension frame. *Le Cycle*, 2 February 1946.

Chapter 20. Suspension Systems

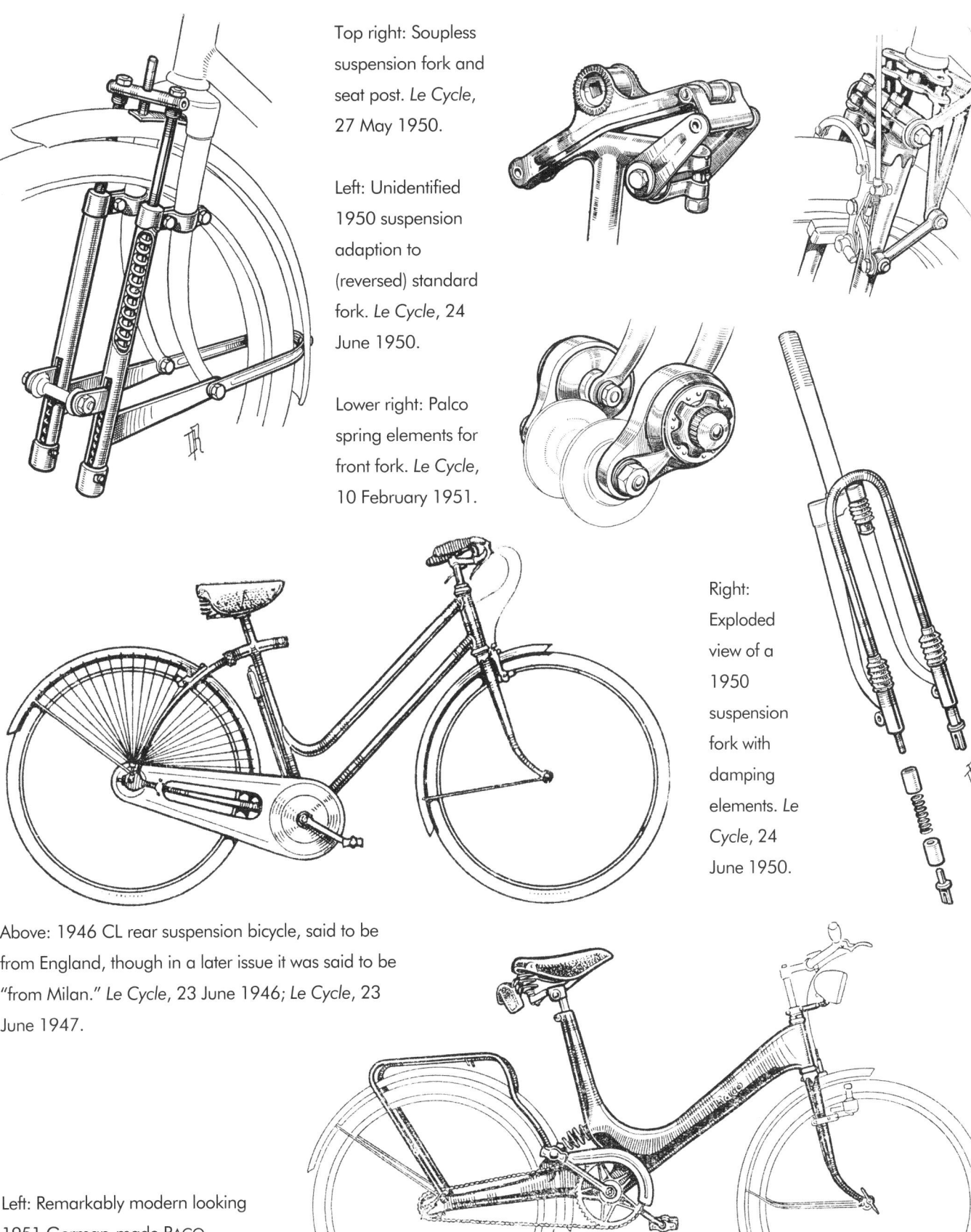

Top right: Soupless suspension fork and seat post. *Le Cycle*, 27 May 1950.

Left: Unidentified 1950 suspension adaption to (reversed) standard fork. *Le Cycle*, 24 June 1950.

Lower right: Palco spring elements for front fork. *Le Cycle*, 10 February 1951.

Right: Exploded view of a 1950 suspension fork with damping elements. *Le Cycle*, 24 June 1950.

Above: 1946 CL rear suspension bicycle, said to be from England, though in a later issue it was said to be "from Milan." *Le Cycle*, 23 June 1946; *Le Cycle*, 23 June 1947.

Left: Remarkably modern looking 1951 German-made RACO pressed-steel monocoque-frame bicycle with integrated rear suspension. *Le Cycle*, 10 November 1951.

243

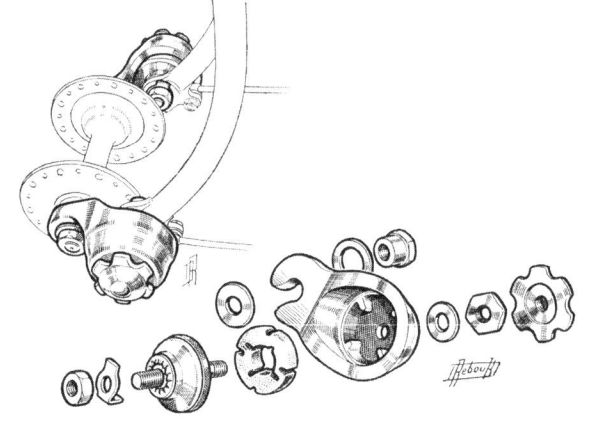

Left: Exploded view of Palco front suspension spring element. *Le Cycle*, 21 July 1951.

Right: Also from England, the Moulton S-Speed front suspension. *Le Cycle*, March 1969.

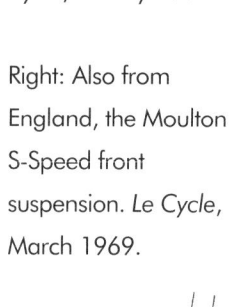

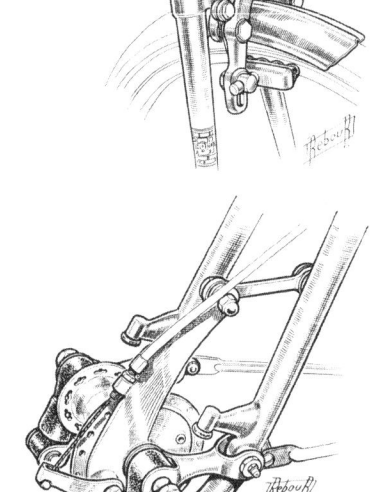

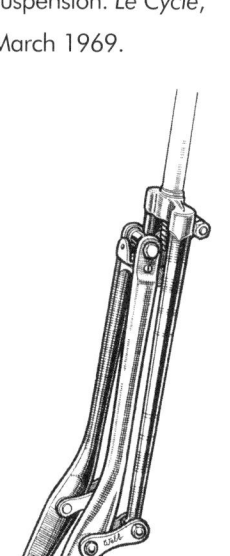

Above: 1954 Neimann suspension fork on Universal moped at Geneva trade show. *Le Cycle*, 24 April 1954.

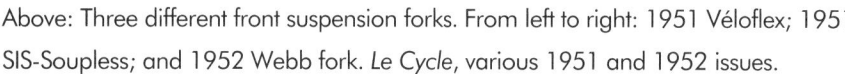

Above: Three different front suspension forks. From left to right: 1951 Véloflex; 1951 SIS-Soupless; and 1952 Webb fork. *Le Cycle*, various 1951 and 1952 issues.

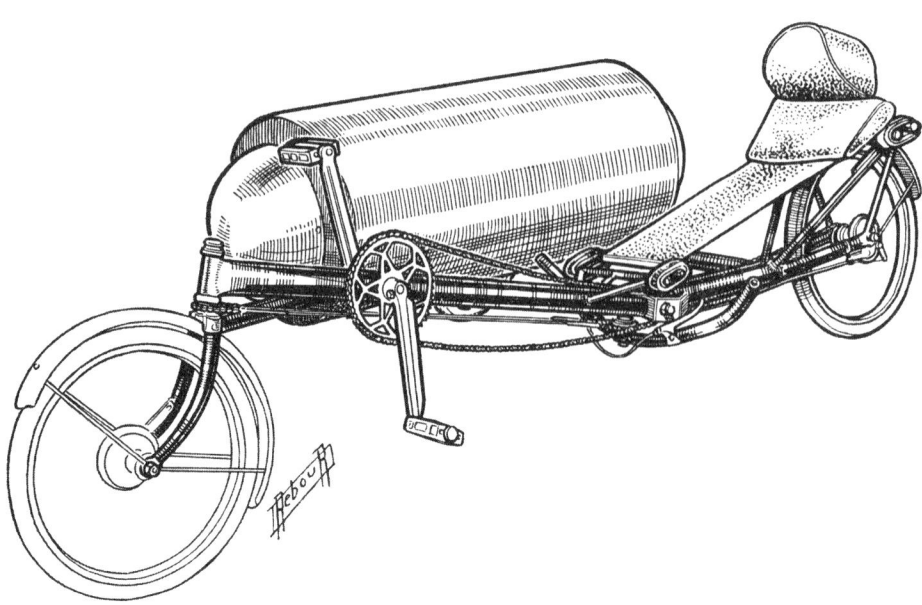

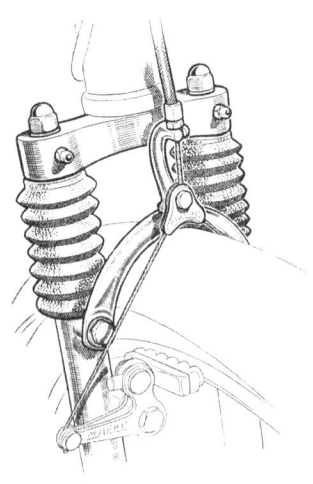

Above: 1953 Liberia telescoping front fork detail. *Le Cycle*, 9 October 1953.

Left: Danish-made enclosed recumbent bicycle with rubber-strap suspension system in the rear. *Le Cycle*, 7 February 1953.

Chapter 21. Trailers and Sidecars

Rebour made a number of drawings of trailers, sidecars, and other devices for carrying additional persons or luggage on bicycles. In this chapter you will find drawings of a few of these devices, which also include various forms of bicycle rickshaws.

Interesting though the latter were, most of those were curios, displayed at trade shows, and not really used in practice. Trailers and sidecars, on the other hand were widely used by bicycle campers, while carrier bikes were in use for deliveries of all sorts.

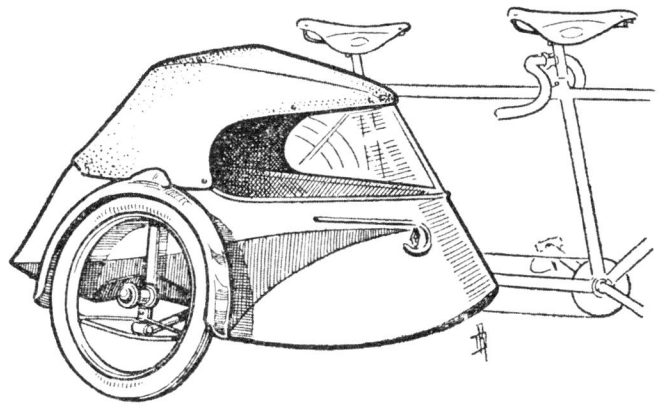

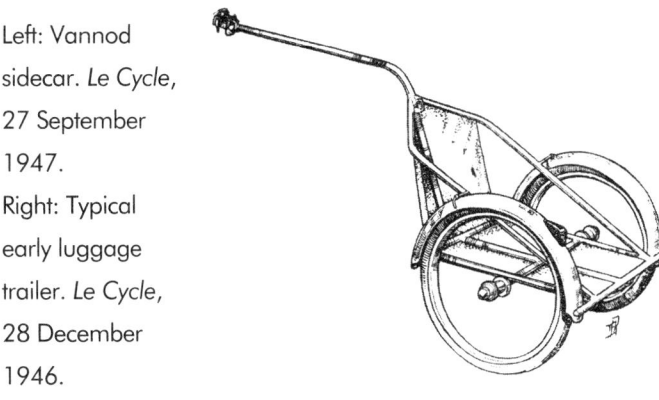

Left: Vannod sidecar. *Le Cycle*, 27 September 1947.

Right: Typical early luggage trailer. *Le Cycle*, 28 December 1946.

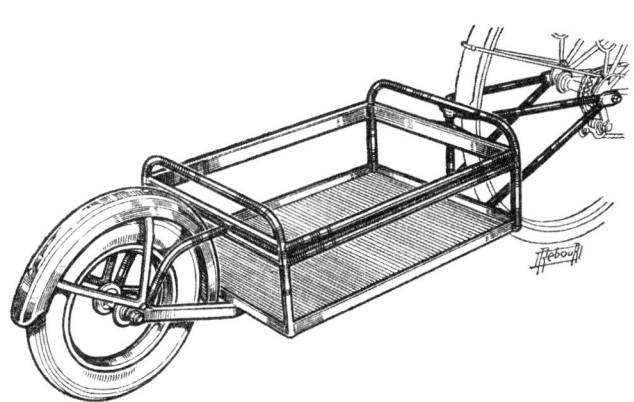

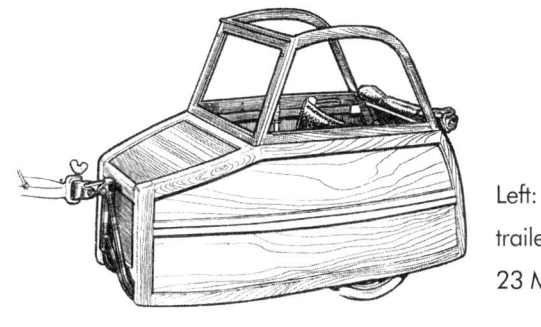

Left: Hergé child trailer. *Le Cycle*, 23 May 1953.

Above: CMDC-Monosport luggage trailer. *Le Cycle*, 9 May 1953.

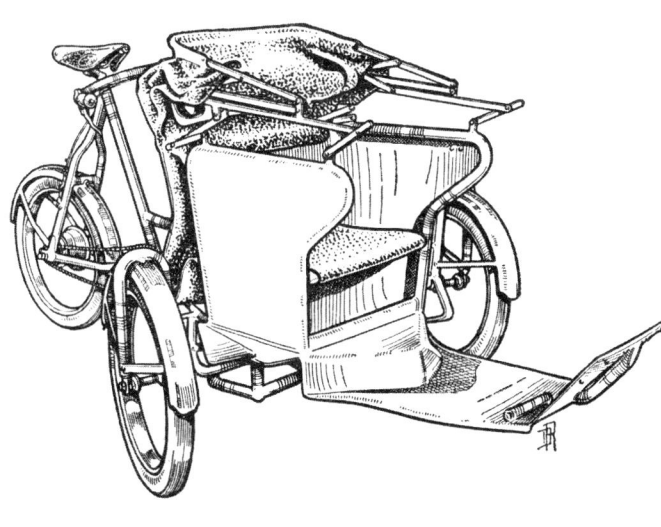

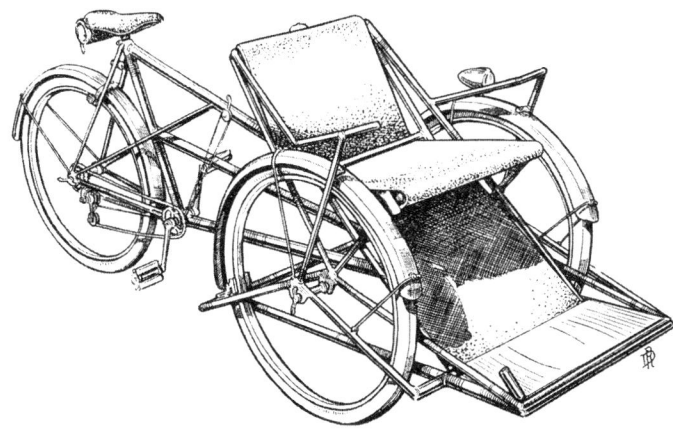

Above: Rebour's own design cycle carriage, dubbed Père-Maman (father-mother) cycle. *Le Cycle*, 18 May 1946.

Left: Cycle carriage, displayed at the 1948 Earls Court cycle show. *Le Cycle*, 13 November 1948.

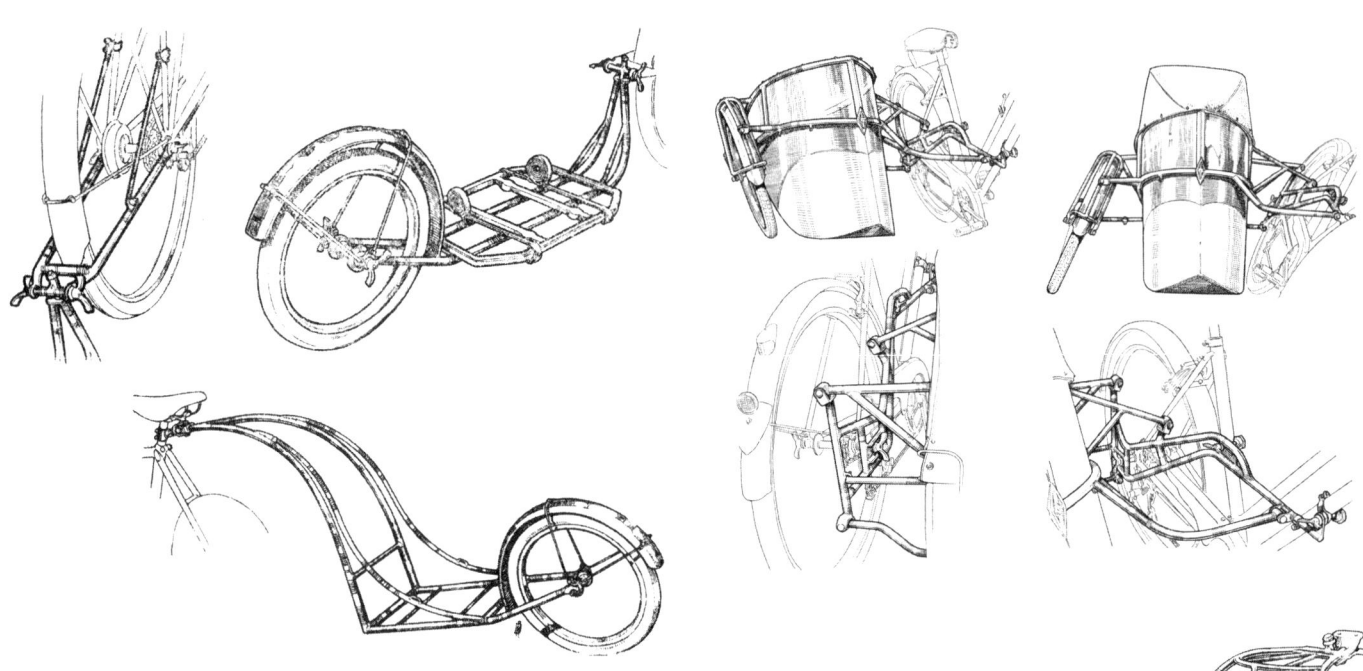

Above left: Vogue & Pittard trailers. *Le Cycle*, 8 May 1948.

Above right: Louis Vannod sidecar. *Le Cycle*, 29 July 1950.

Left: Fulgur-spring and rubber-strap trailer suspensions. *Le Cycle*, 30 November 1952.

Right: René Herse camping trailer. *Le Cycle*, 14 December 1957.

Lower right: René Herse luggage rack and trailer attachment. *Le Cycle*, 23 May 1953.

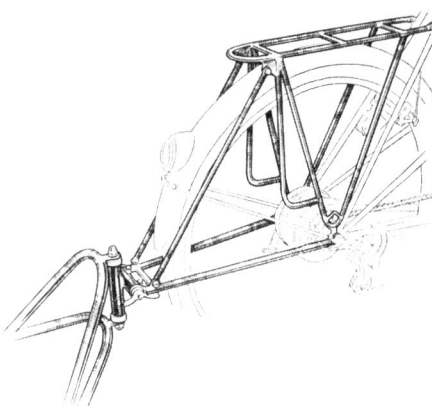

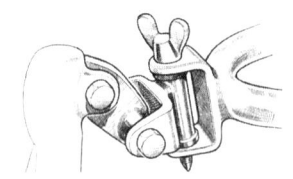

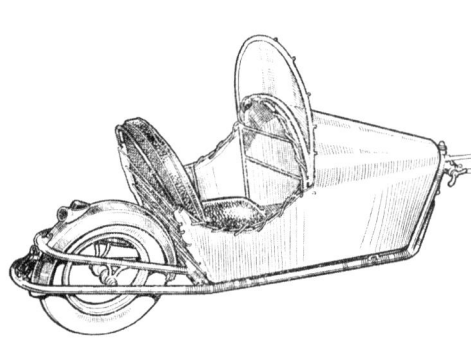

Above: Goëland trailer coupling. *Le Cycle*, 5 May 1956.

Left and right: Goëland child trailer. *Le Cycle*, 30 November 1952 and 25 July 1953.

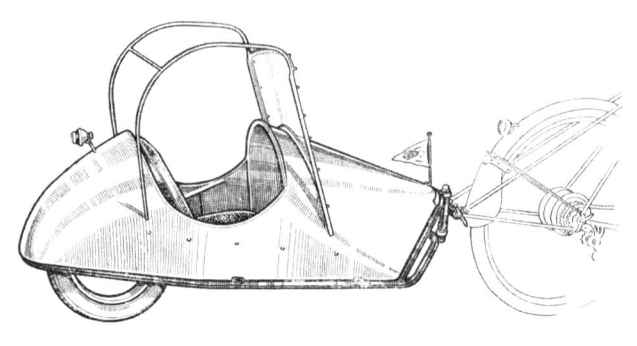

Chapter 22. Alternate Drives

Hope springs eternal in what may best be described as "alternative bicycle design." Not prepared to accept the status quo as the ultimate in bicycle technology, quite a few designers have come up with ideas to change the rules of physics and mechanics, offering various devices promoted as more efficient than the direct or geared chain-drive.

This chapter presents a number of such devices that were offered during the period covered by Daniel Rebour's drawing and writing career. Most of these images refer to designs regularly shown off by would-be inventors at the annual Concours des Inventors at Lépine, but a number of these actually went into production, invariably without success.

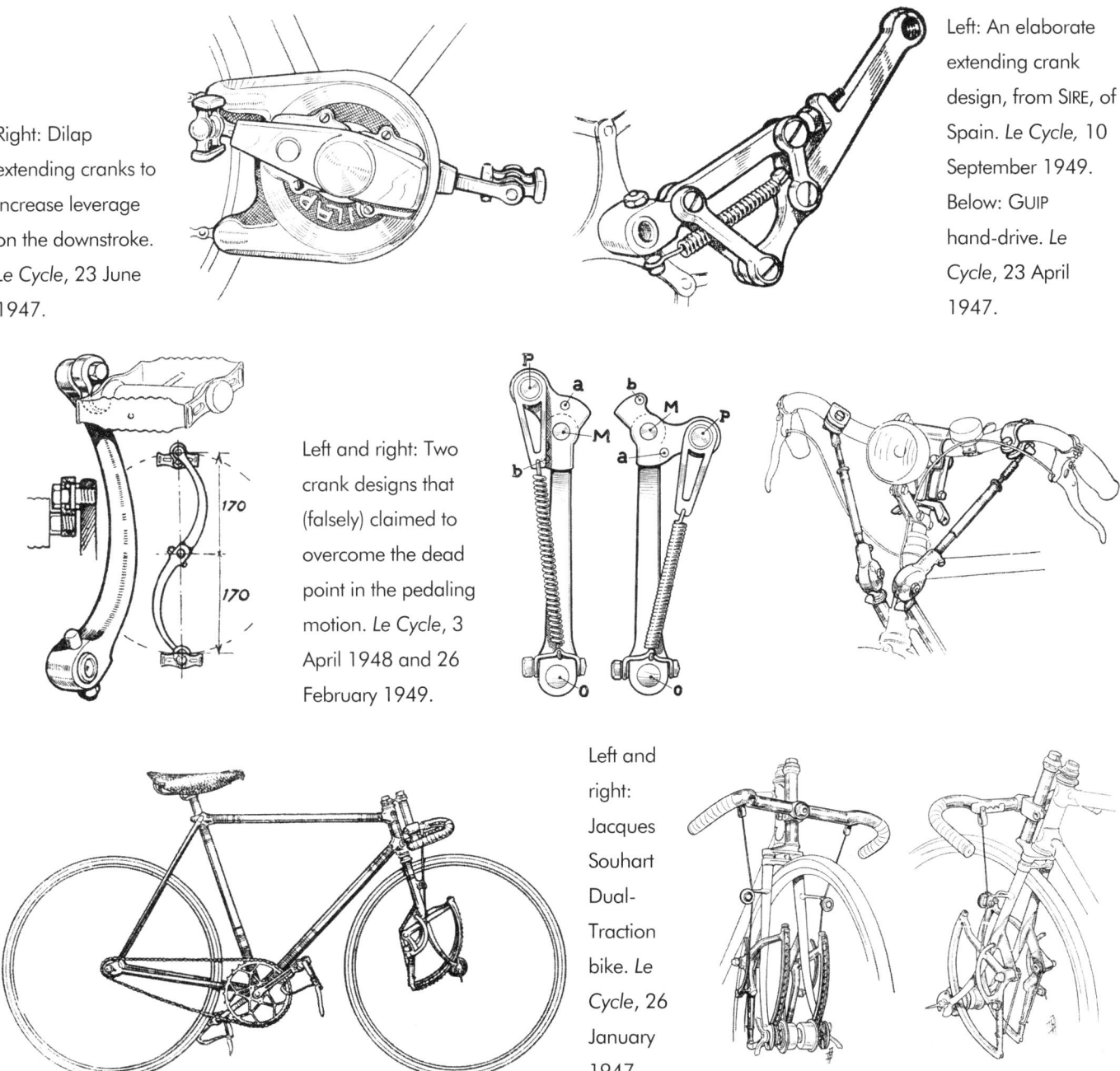

Right: Dilap extending cranks to increase leverage on the downstroke. *Le Cycle*, 23 June 1947.

Left: An elaborate extending crank design, from SIRE, of Spain. *Le Cycle*, 10 September 1949.
Below: GUIP hand-drive. *Le Cycle*, 23 April 1947.

Left and right: Two crank designs that (falsely) claimed to overcome the dead point in the pedaling motion. *Le Cycle*, 3 April 1948 and 26 February 1949.

Left and right: Jacques Souhart Dual-Traction bike. *Le Cycle*, 26 January 1947.

247

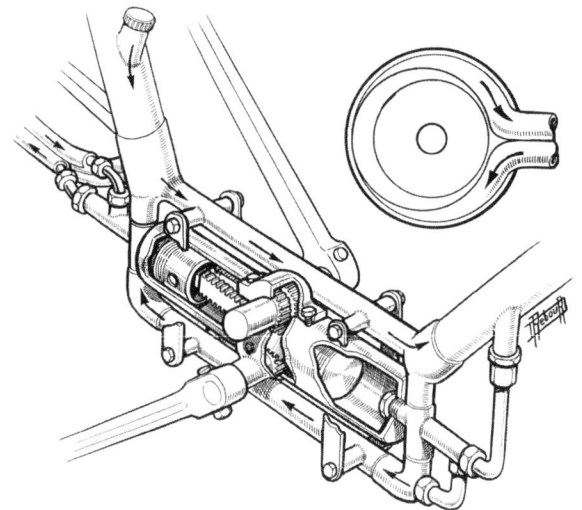
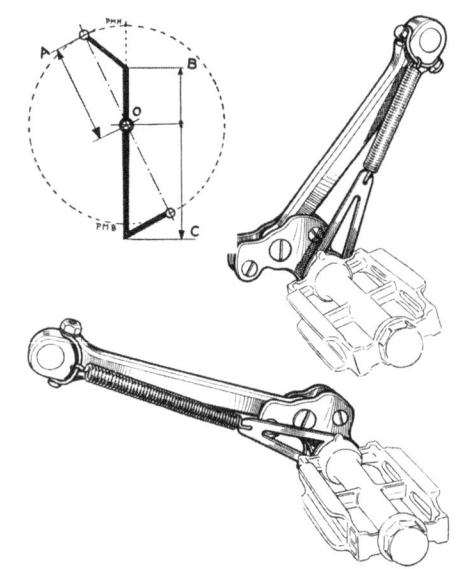

Left: Dunlop-designed hydraulic drive system, in an effort to replace the chain. No doubt it was much less efficient than a chain, and a lot more complicated. *Le Cycle*, 7 January 1950.

Right: Another expanding crank design, from Robert Josset. *Le Cycle*, 10 March 1951.

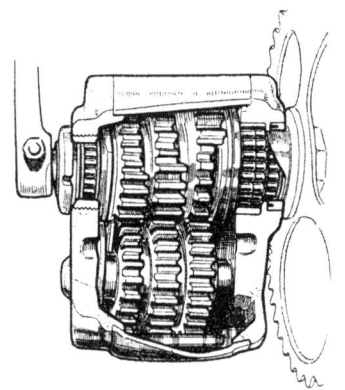

Above: Mutaped 3-speed bottom-bracket gear. *Le Cycle*, 22 March 1947.

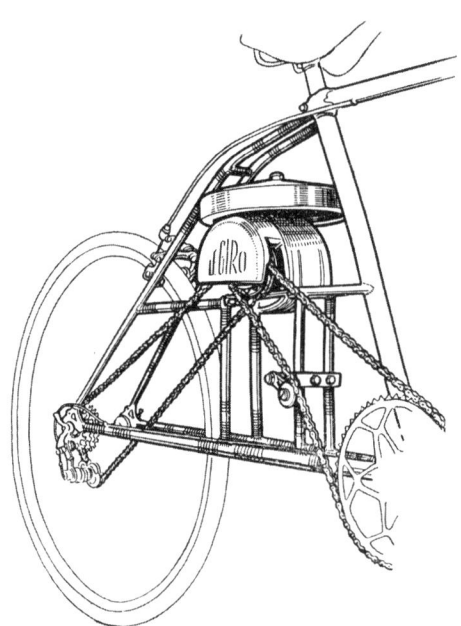
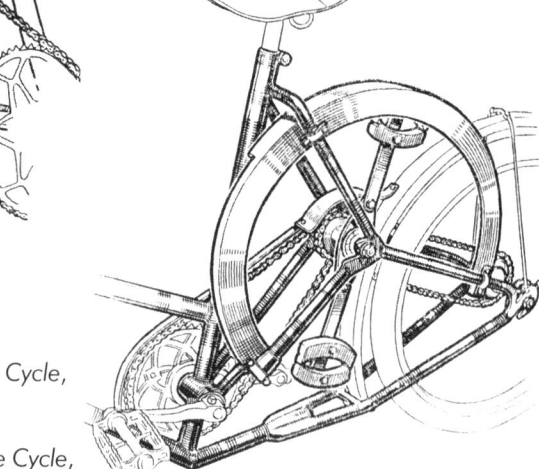

Left and below: Two types of gyroscopic energy-storage drivetrain designs. Left: Le Gyro. *Le Cycle*, 22 April 1950. Below: Gyro-Cycle. *Le Cycle*, 23 May 1952.

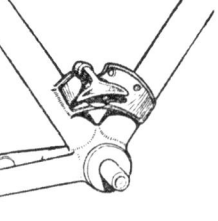

Left: Varia-7 expanding chainwheel design. *Le Cycle*, 18 October 1947.

Right and below: Buec bottom bracket gear. *Le Cycle*, 6 December 1947.

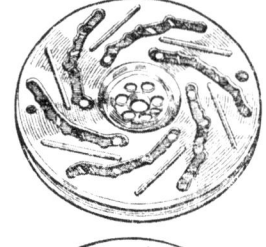
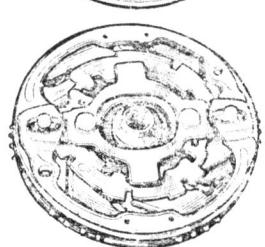
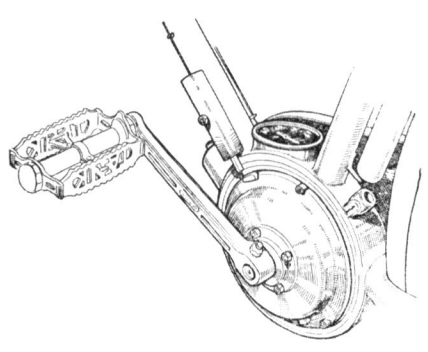
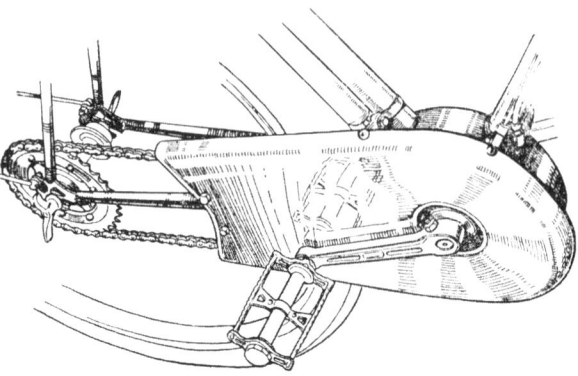

Chapter 22. Alternate Drives

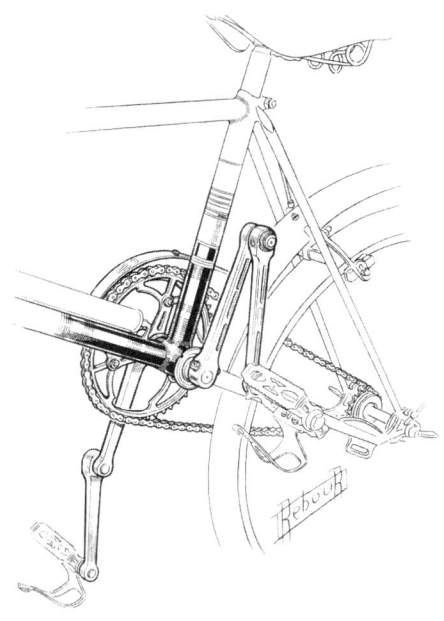
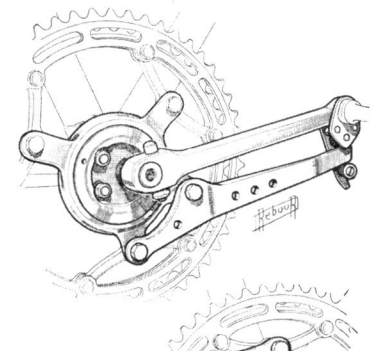
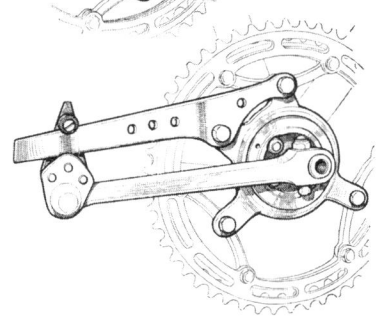
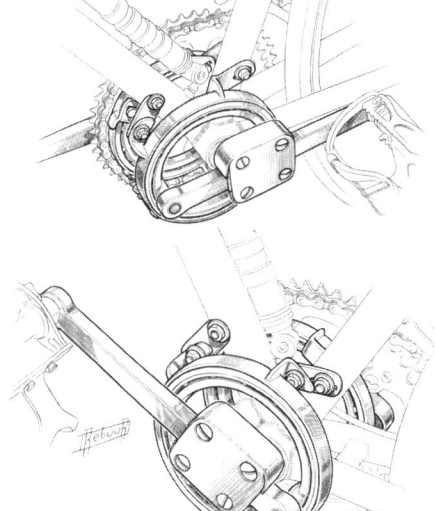

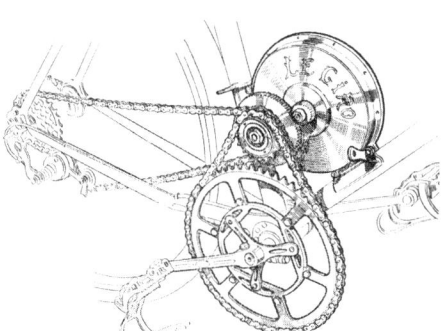

Above left and center, two presumed dead-point-overcoming devices: 1963 Delongmare and 1954 Poupard. *Le Cycle*, June 1963 and June 1954.

Above right: Unidentified 1964 expanding-crank-drive. *Le Cycle*, May 1954.

Left: Later development of Le Gyro gyroscopic drive. *Le Cycle*, 23 May 1953.

Right: Audoux lever drive. *Le Cycle*, 29 May 1954.

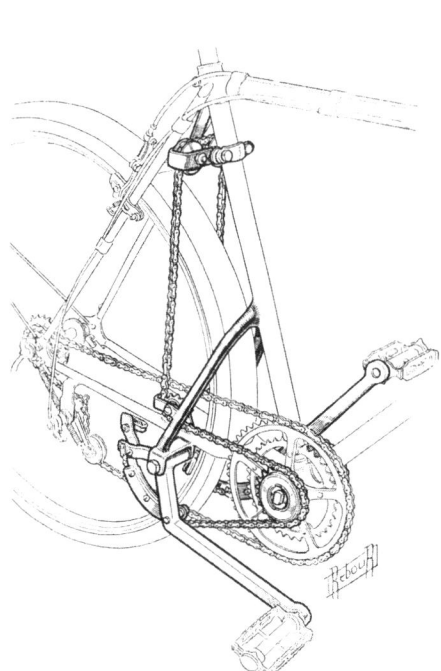

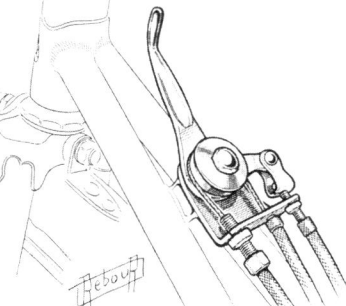
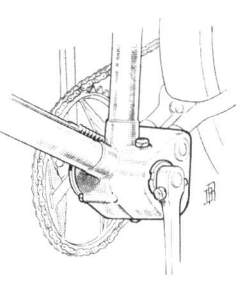
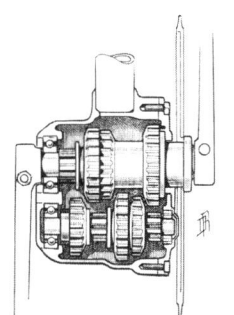

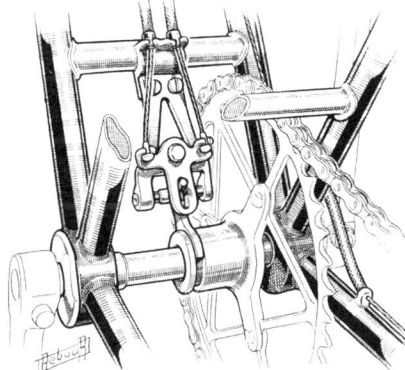

Above: Adler bottom bracket gear, from Germany. *Le Cycle*, 10 June 1950.
Left: Elswick-Hopper design to keep the chain aligned when shifting gears with the derailleur. *Le Cycle*, 10 December 1955.
Right: Elvish-Fontan shaft drive. *Le Cycle*, 15 October 1952.

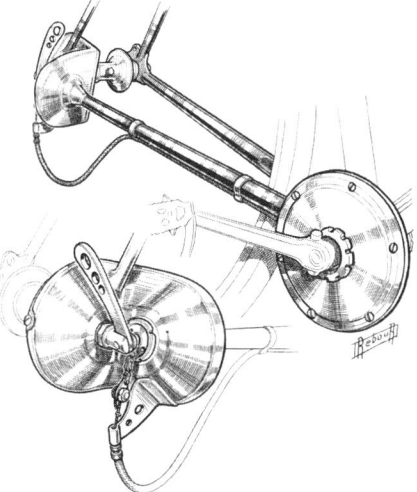

Chapter 23. Bicycle Derivatives

This chapter highlights some devices based on bicycle technology that aren't bicycles themselves. Like the alternate drivetrains, many of these were introduced at the Concours des Inventeurs at Lépine, but others were commercially available products that have proven somewhat practical, or at least commercially viable.

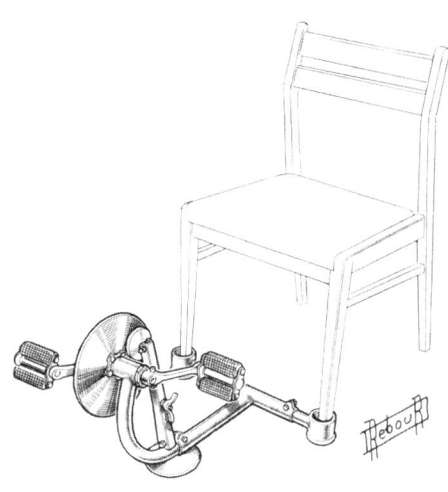

Right: It does not allow for a cycling stance, but it represents the ultimate simplicity in home-trainer design, introduced at a Brussels bicycle trade show. *Le Cycle* (date not recorded).

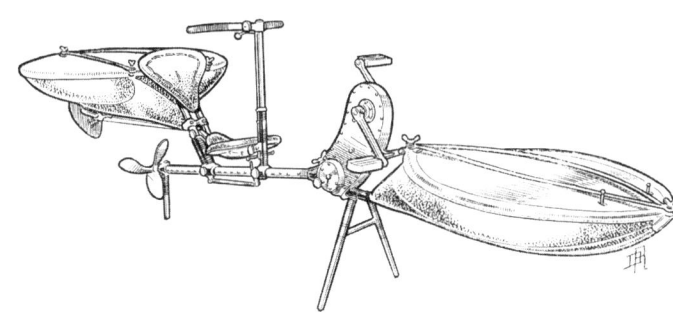

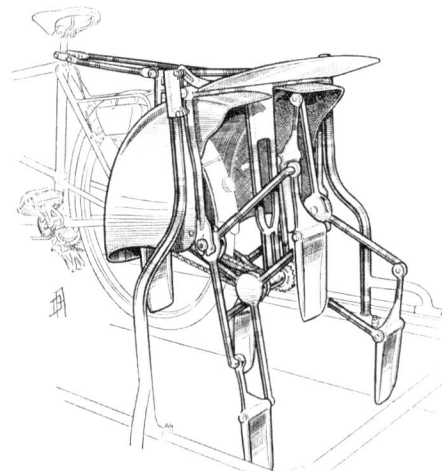

Above and left: Two types of water bikes shown at the 1962 Concours des Inventeurs, Lépine. Both images from *Le Cycle*, 29 June 1952.

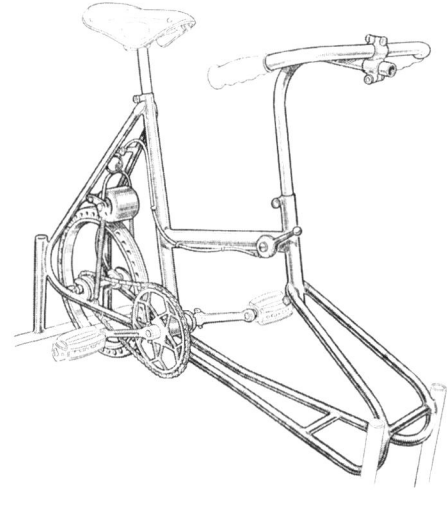

Left: Ducheron home trainer. *Le Cycle*, 23 May 1953.

Below: Manet bicycle-sizing device. *L'Officiel du Cycle*, April 1976.

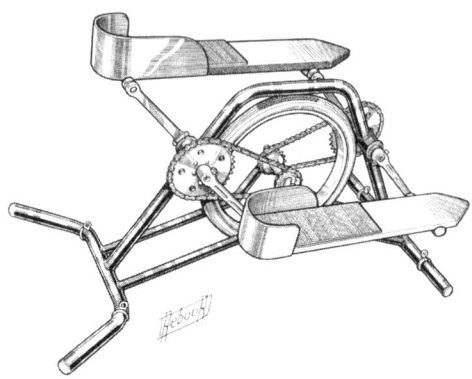

Right: Bicycle-based ski-exercise home-trainer. *Le Cycle*, 25 February 1956.

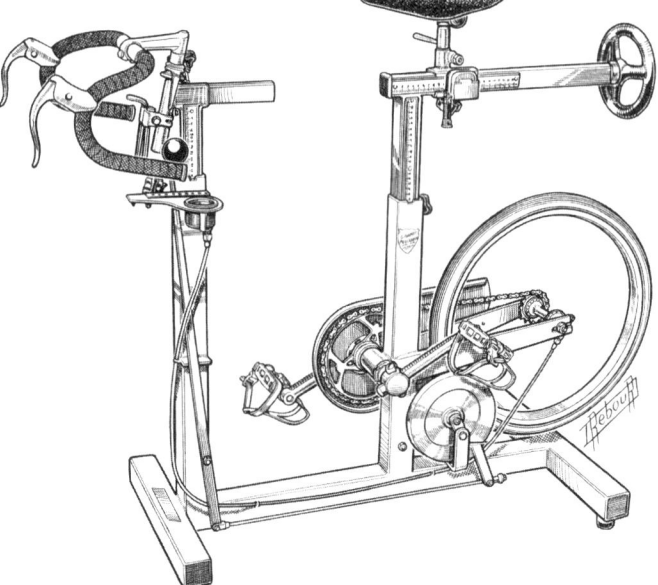

250

Chapter 23. Bicycle Derivatives

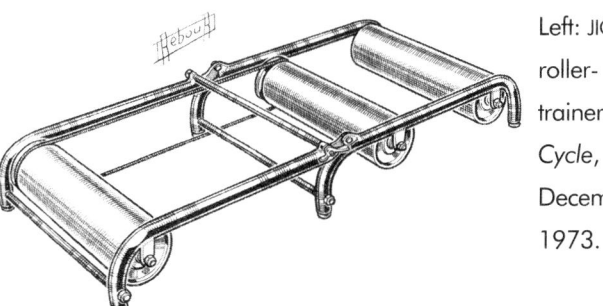

Left: JIC roller-trainer. *Le Cycle*, December 1973.

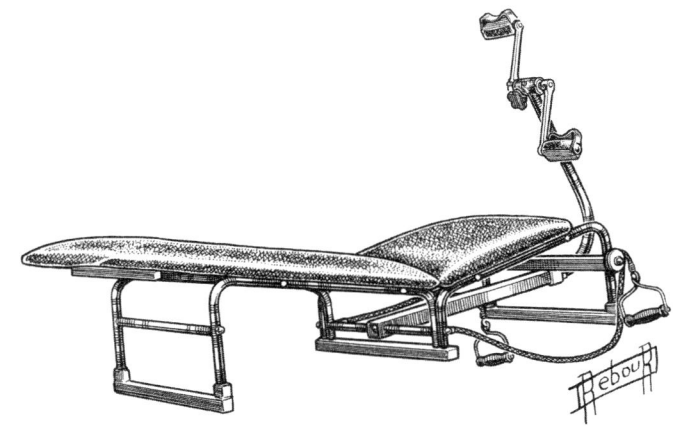

Above: Lejeune convalescence cycling exercise adaptation. *Le Cycle*, January 1969.

Left: Cazenave four-wheeler. *Le Cycle*, November 1968.

Below: Luciane-Oto pedal cart. *Le Cycle*, 27 April 1957.

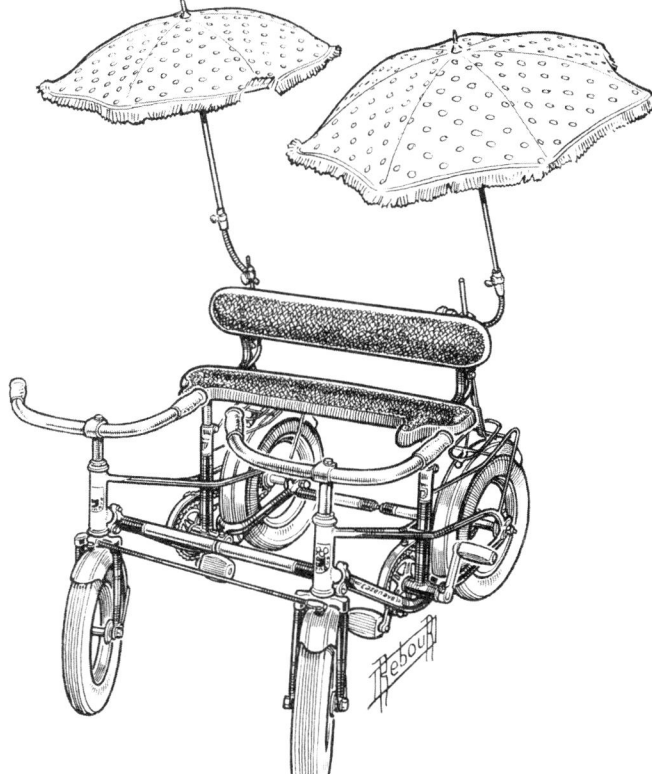

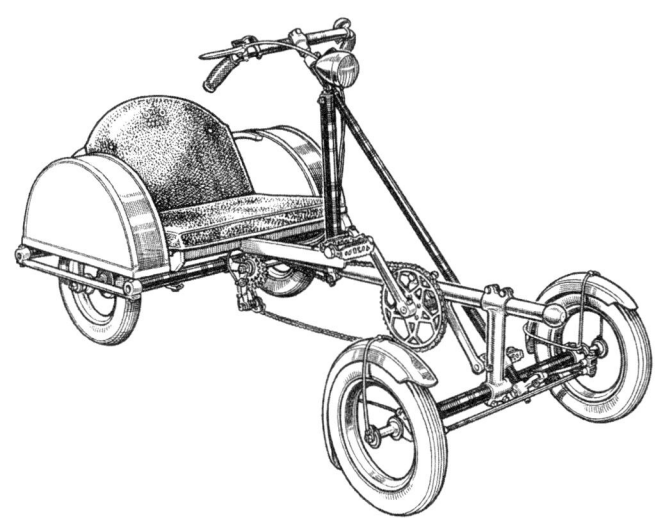

Chapter 24. Motorized Bicycles

The 1950s was the period of motorization in many European countries. In France, as in neighboring countries, the first stage of this process consisted of auxiliary motors to be installed on more or less standard bicycles, soon followed by purpose-built motor-assisted bicycles, known as "mopeds" in English, and as "*motorisées*" in French.

Since in France most of these vehicles were sold in bike shops, *Le Cycle*, catering as it did primarily to the bike trade, could not ignore them. Rebour, of course had no trouble churning out any number of drawings of motorized vehicles and their details—working for *Moto-Revue*, it had been his day job before the war. In this section, we've assembled a few examples of his work in this field during his time with *Le Cycle*.

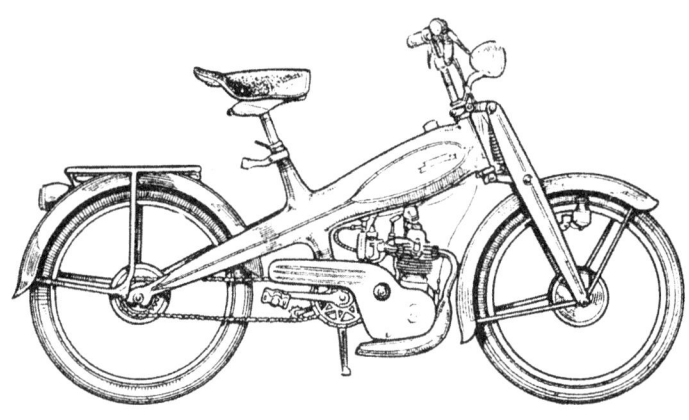

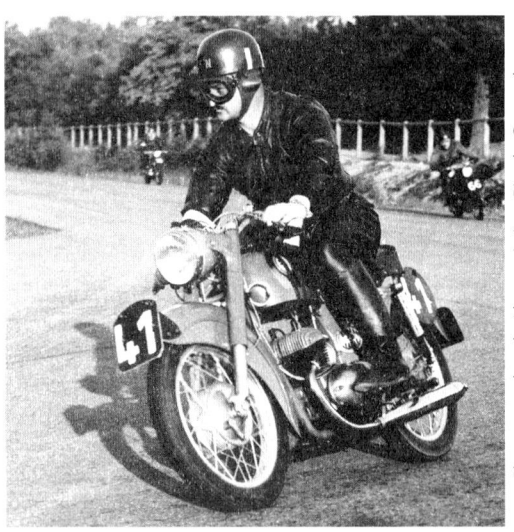

Rebour loved motorcycles too. A test rider for *Moto-Revue* in his pre-war job, he still participated in the Bol d'Or 24-hour endurance race in 1956, riding a Belgian 250 cc FN.

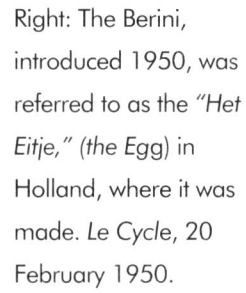

Photo reproduced with permission, Bicycle Quarterly

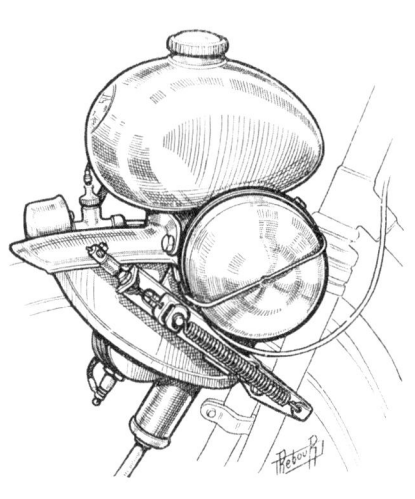

Above: 1947 Motom moped. *Le Cycle*, 22 March 1947.

Right: The Berini, introduced 1950, was referred to as the *"Het Eitje,"* (the Egg) in Holland, where it was made. *Le Cycle*, 20 February 1950.

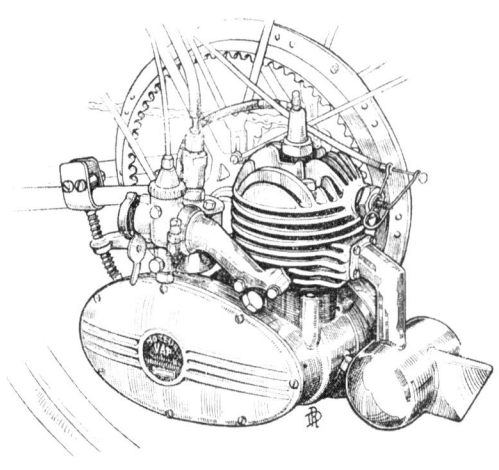

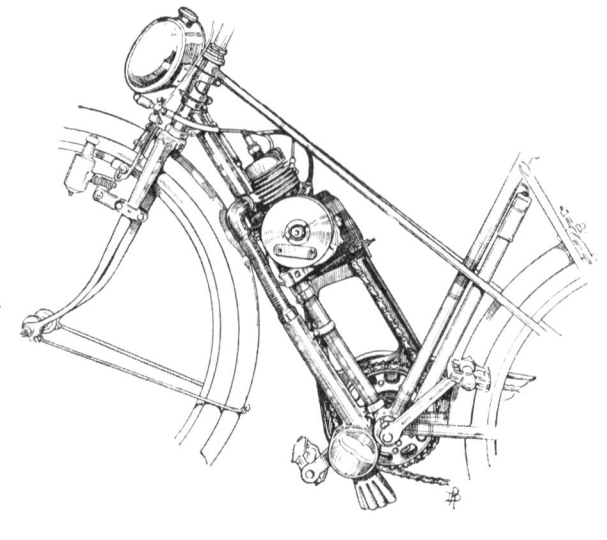

Left: Rebour's first motor drawings to appear in *Le Cycle*, in December 1945, included this one of the VAP auxiliary motor to be attached to the rear wheel (left) and the PNG, for installation into the frame of an existing bicycle (right).

Chapter 24. Motorized Bicycles

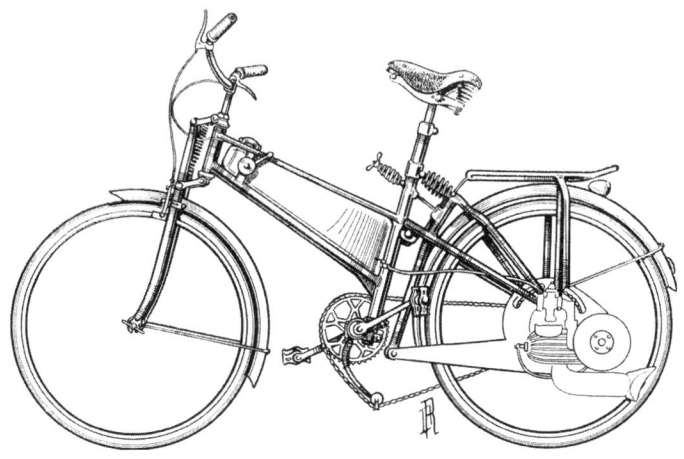

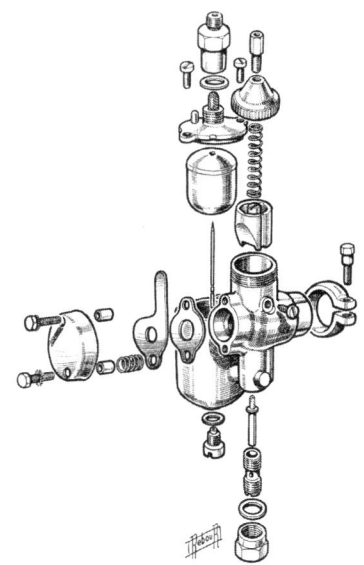

Left: One of the first full-suspension mopeds, with P. P. Roussey motor. *Le Cycle*, 18 December 1948.

Right: Exploded diagram of moped carburetor. *Le Cycle*, 24 February 1952.

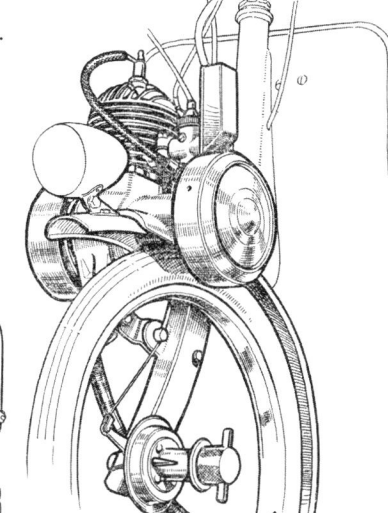

Left: 1947 Vélectrique electric auxiliary bicycle drive, much like today's E-bikes. *Le Cycle*, 22 June 1946.

Below left: Puch Electric bicycle, shown at the 1973 Amsterdam bike trade show. *Le Cycle*, April 1973.

Below center and right: 1950 VAP and Scoto Veloreve. *Le Cycle*, December 1949.

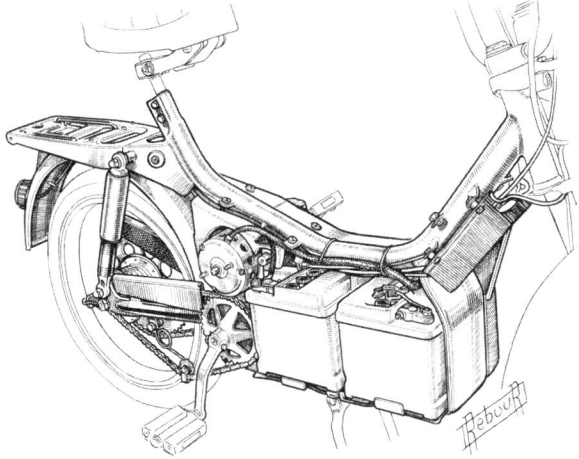

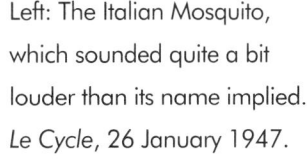

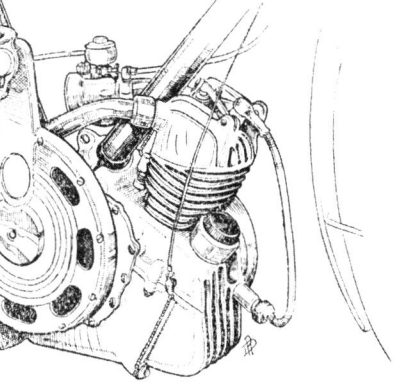

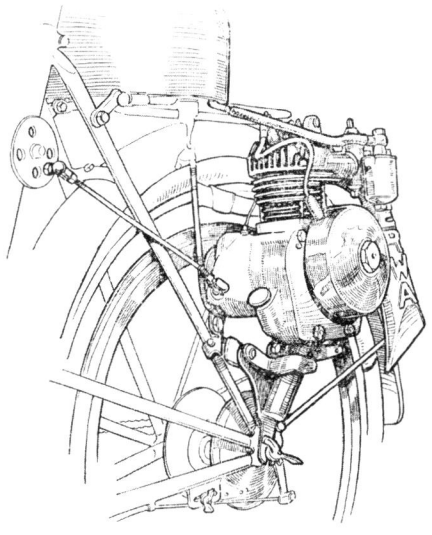

Left: The Italian Mosquito, which sounded quite a bit louder than its name implied. *Le Cycle*, 26 January 1947.

Right: Serwa auxiliary motor, which differed from most in that it was not a 2-stroke but a 4-stroke machine—more complex, but also more efficient and without need for premixing the fuel with oil. *Le Cycle*, 5 February 1946.

253

Right: Probably the simplest and most popular moped available in France was the Vélosolex, shown here with a purpose-built sidecar in a 1948 drawing, republished in *Pratique du Vélo*.

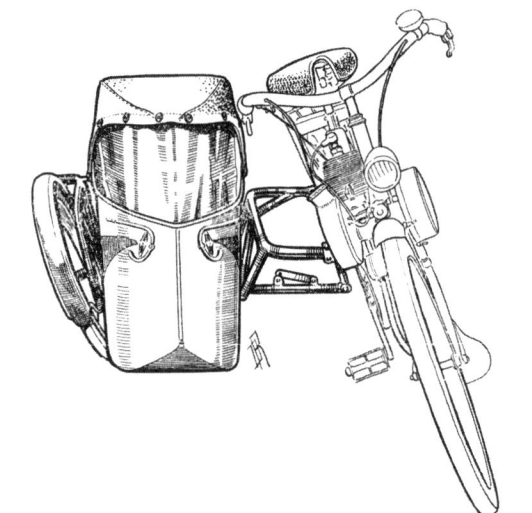
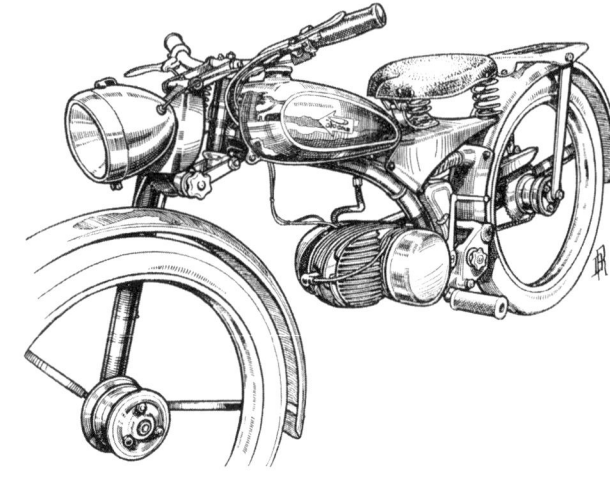

Above: Single-arm suspension front and rear on Golb 100 cc motorcycle. *Le Cycle*, 12 February 1949.

Left: Boerri Lambretta machine in the 1957 Monthléry Bol d'Or race. *Le Cycle*, 27 April 1957.

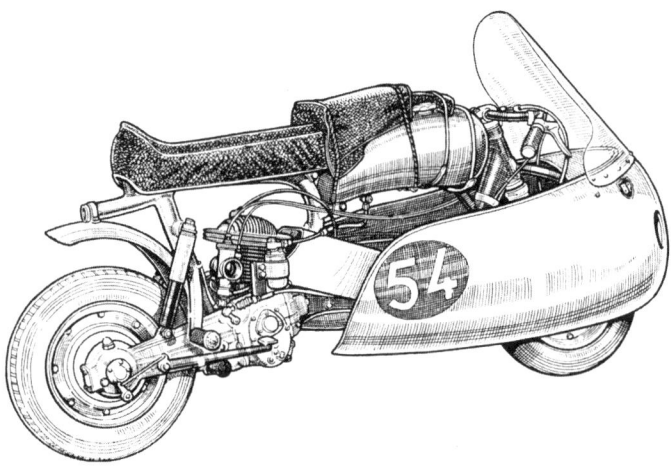
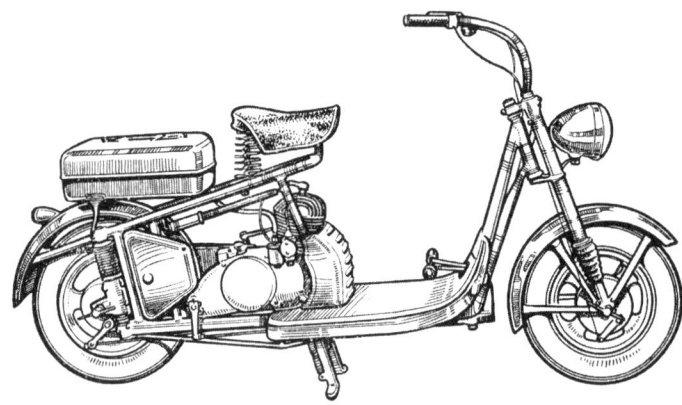
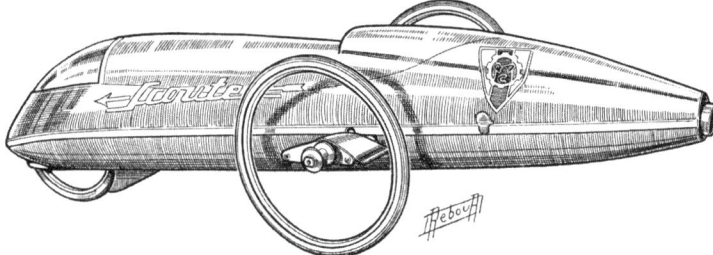

Above: 1948 AGF scooter, predating the enclosed types.
Left: 1955 Scoutex 50 cc record machine at Monthléry;
Bottom left: Dhagan-Ghome-Rhone Monthléry Bol d'Or race entrant.
Below: 1953 Messerschmidt motorized tandem-seat 3-wheeler.

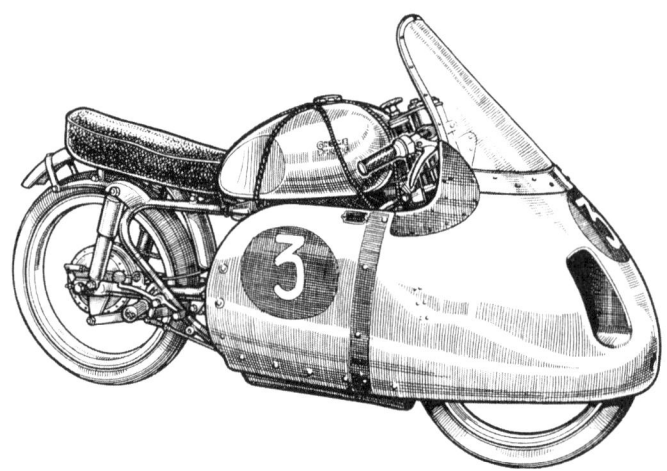
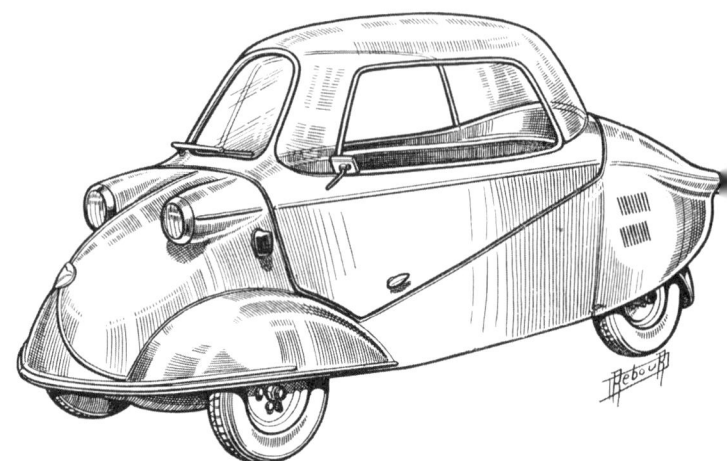

Chapter 24. Motorized Bicycles

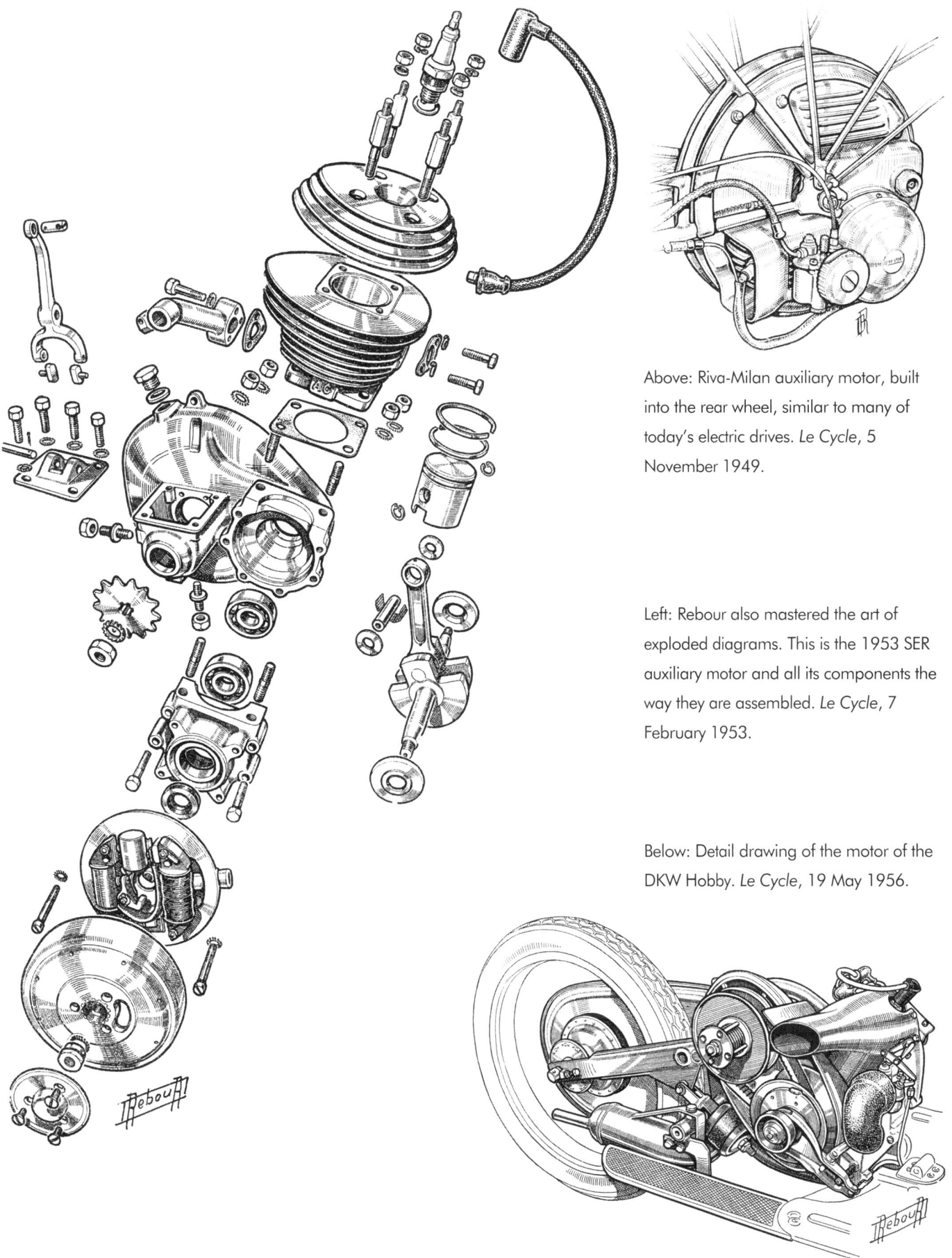

Above: Riva-Milan auxiliary motor, built into the rear wheel, similar to many of today's electric drives. *Le Cycle*, 5 November 1949.

Left: Rebour also mastered the art of exploded diagrams. This is the 1953 SER auxiliary motor and all its components the way they are assembled. *Le Cycle*, 7 February 1953.

Below: Detail drawing of the motor of the DKW Hobby. *Le Cycle*, 19 May 1956.

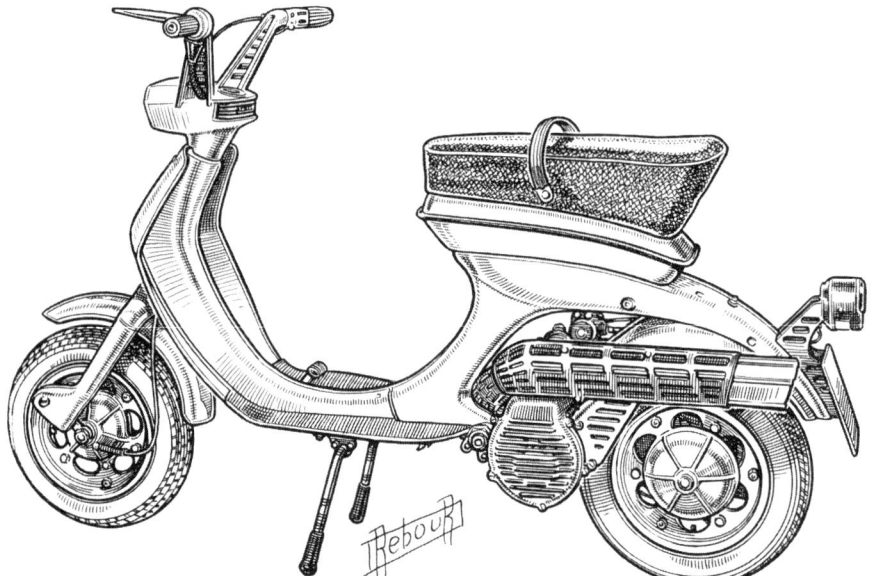

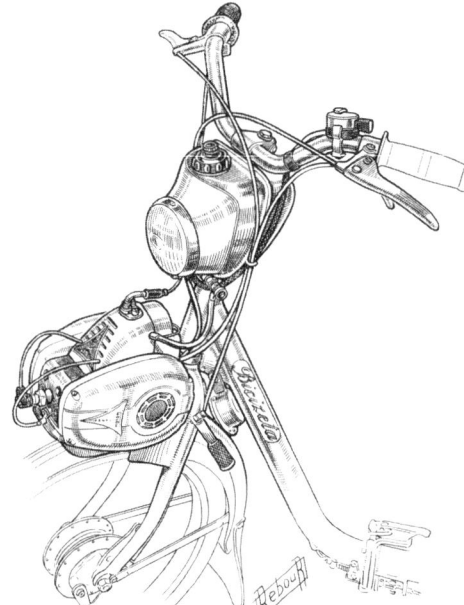

Below: Italian-made Bicizeta 50 cc auxiliary motor, installed on small-wheel folding bike. *Le Cycle*, March 1969.

Above: Lambretta Luna mini-scooter with 50 cc motor. *Le Cycle*, March 1969.

Below: Narcisse motorized tandem, on which the large-diameter diagonal tube served as the gas tank. One of many interesting designs included in a spacial issue of *Le Cycle* published in October 1949.

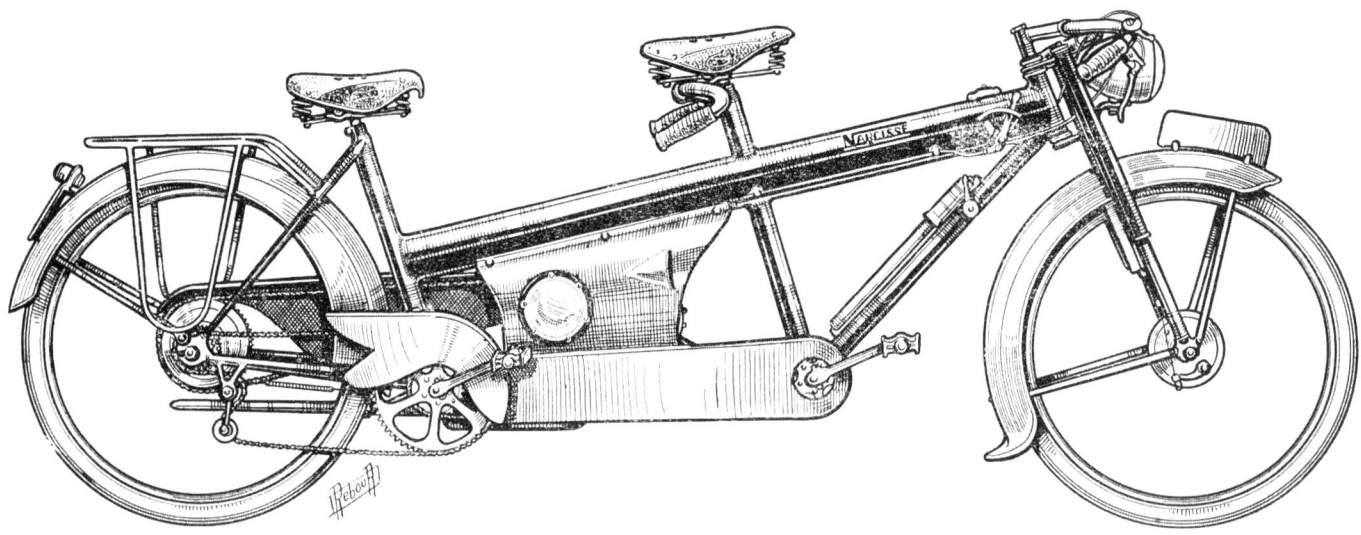

Chapter 25. Tools and Equipment

Over his career, Rebour drew thousands of tools. For many years, he provided the illustrations of all the tools introduced by the VAR tool company, which specialized in tools for the bicycle trade, although they also made other types of tools (not included here). This chapter provides a sampling of drawings made for VAR as well as other tool illustrations specifically drawn for *Le Cycle*.

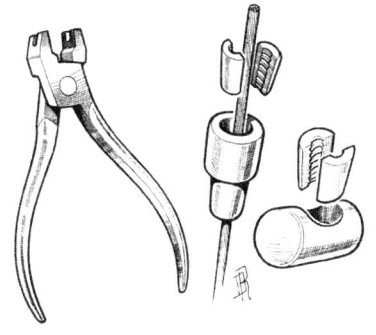

Above: Safety-S.A. cable nipple crimping tool and parts. Bertin catalogue, 1981.

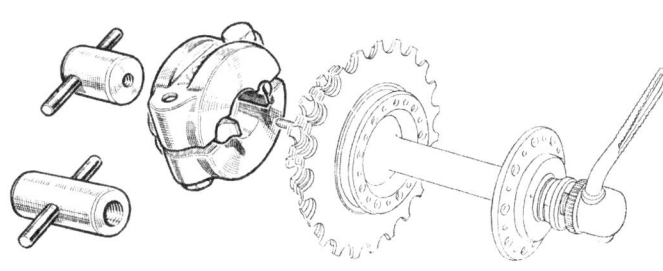

Left: VAR freewheel removal tool. *Le Cycle*, 11 December 1954.

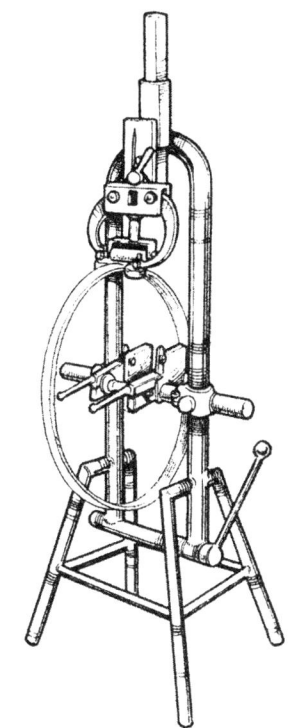

Right: G.C. wheel truing stand. *Le Cycle*, 22 March 1947.

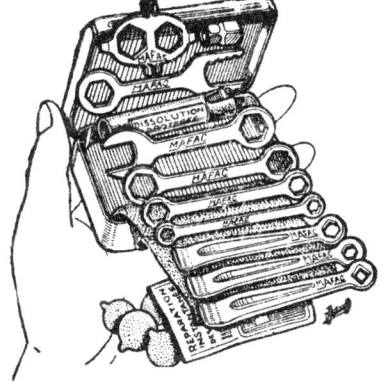

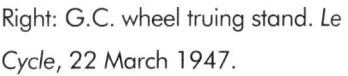

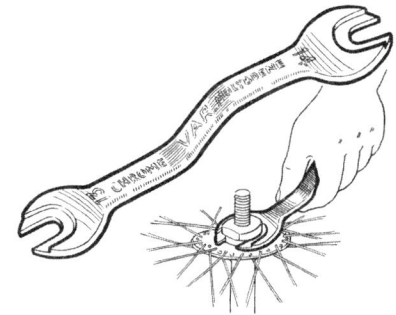

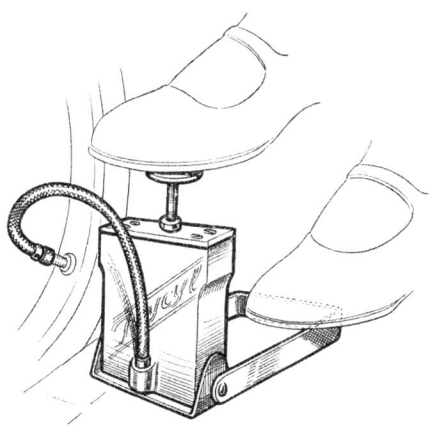

Above: VAR cone wrench. *Pratique du Vélo*.

Above left: Mafac cyclist's mini tool kit. *Le Cycle*, October 1949.

Above right: Trycyl compact foot-pump. *Le Cycle*, 10 February 1951.

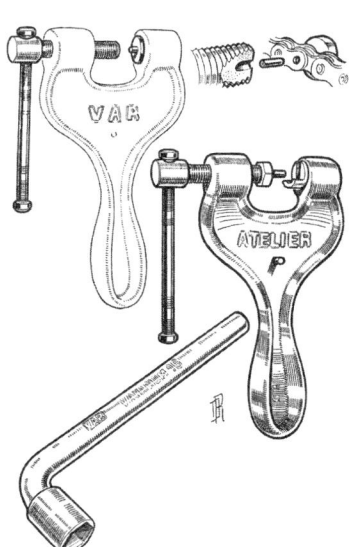

Left: VAR chain rivet extractors and crank bolt wrench. *Le Cycle*, 20 October 1951.

Right: Sterpress headset fitting tool. *Le Cycle*, 26 January 1947.

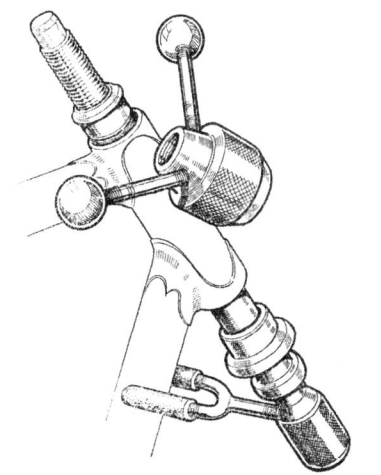

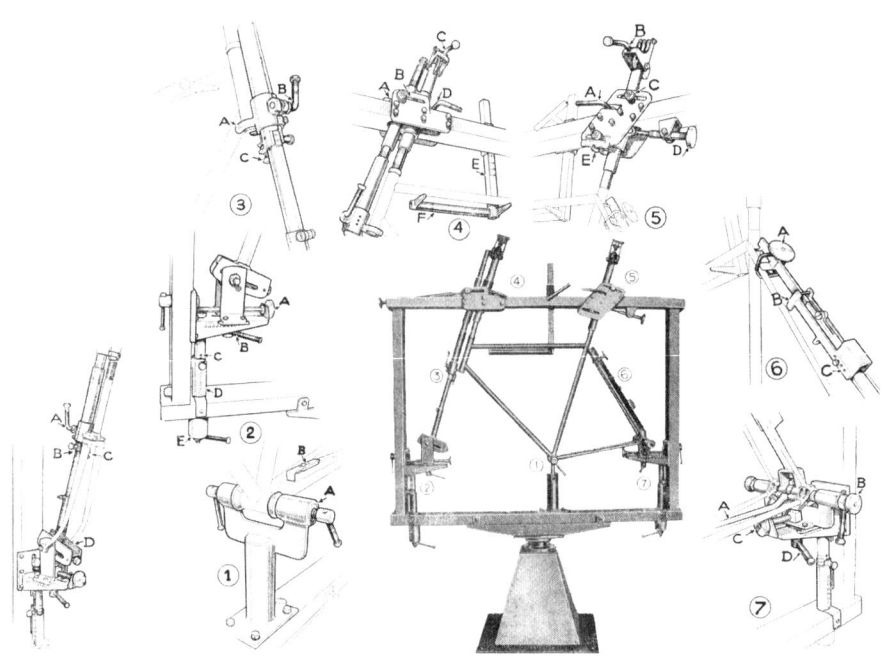
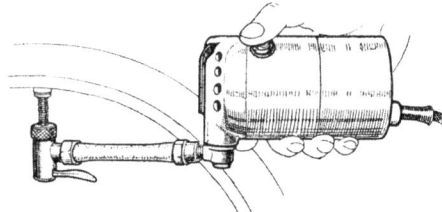

Above: Scintilla electric tire inflator. *Le Cycle*, 22 March 1947.

Left: Jegues frame-building jig, and operations that can be carried out using this equipment. *Le Cycle*, 30 July 1949.

Below: Some large workshop tools. *Le Cycle*, 30 October 1950.

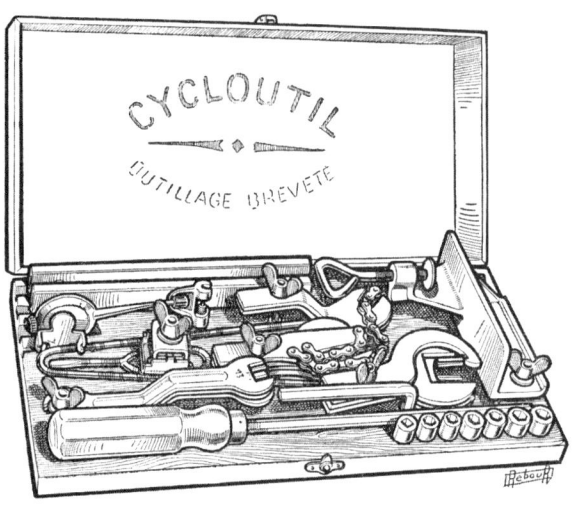

Above and below: Cycloutil boxed workshop tool set. *Le Cycle*, 5 and 26 May 1951.

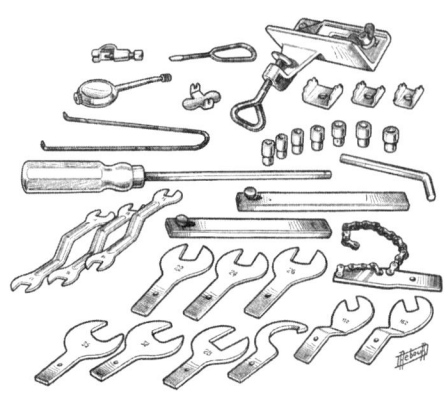
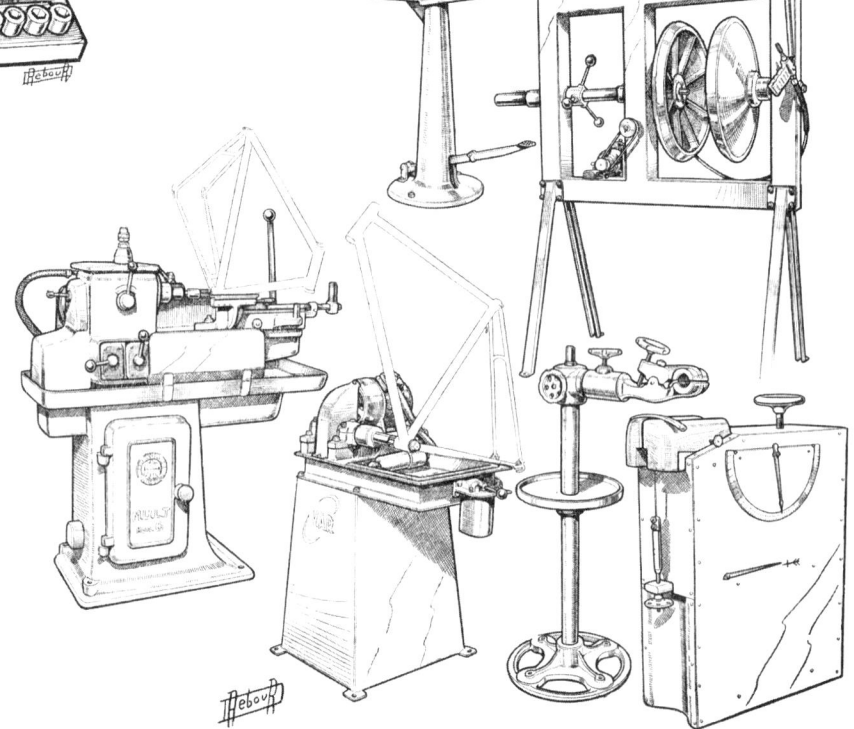

Chapter 25. Tools and Equipment

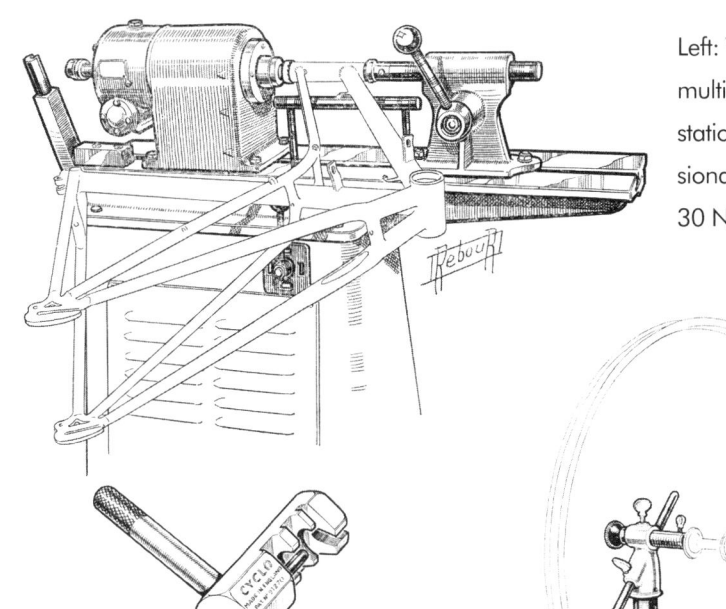

Left: VAR multifunction work station for professional use. *Le Cycle*, 30 November 1952.

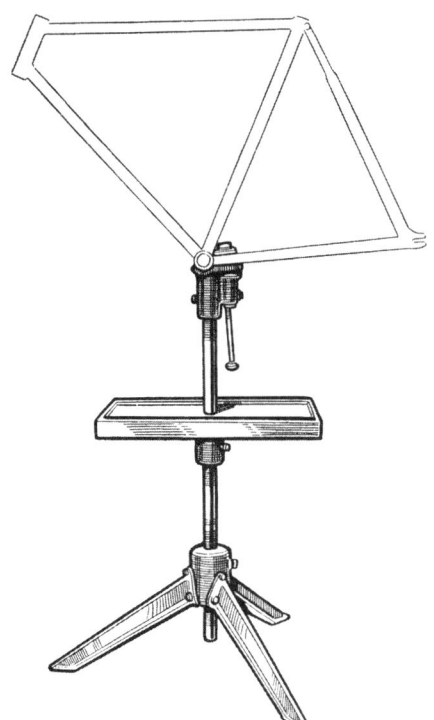

Above: Franz Diekman workstand. *Le Cycle*, 23 November 1953.

Above: Cyclo chain rivet tool. *Le Cycle*, October 1972.

Right: VAR wheel truing stand. *Le Cycle*, 4 October 1957.

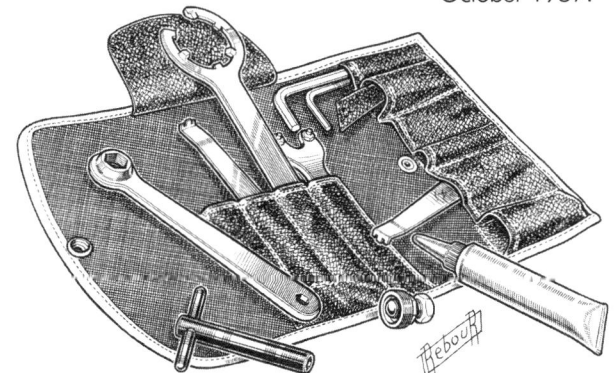

Above: TA crankset tool set, made by VAR. *Le Cycle*, December 1973.

Left: Flac tire patch kit. *Le Cycle*, December 1962.

Right: Milremo boxed freewheel and sprocket collection. 1980 Milremo catalogue.

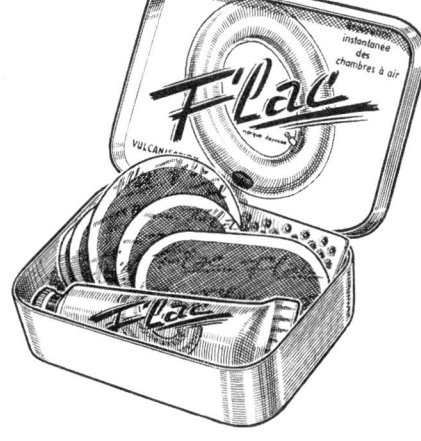

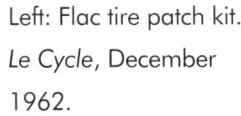

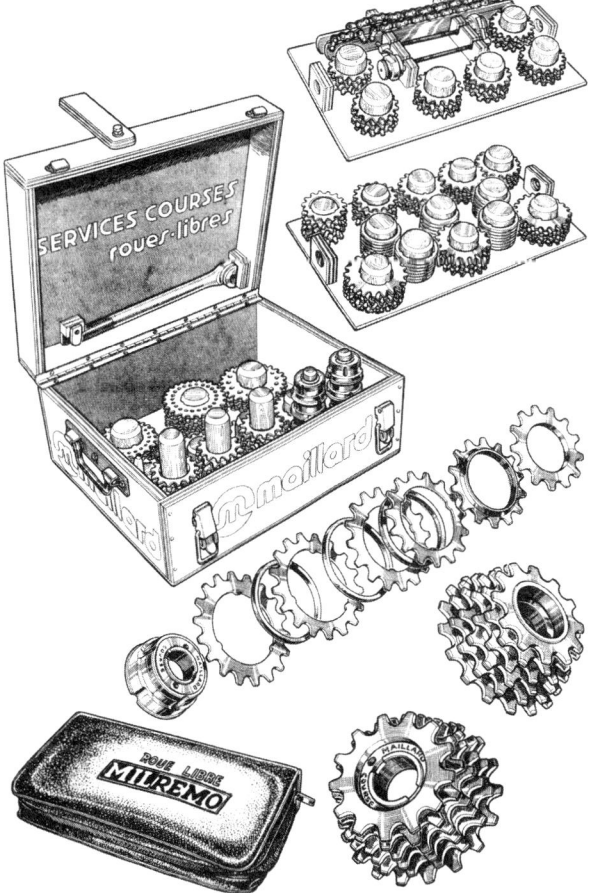

Chapter 26. Bicycle Clothing

Not the most intriguing subject perhaps, but Rebour did also make illustrations showing bicycle clothing. In this chapter, we have collected some of those drawings that appeared in *Le Cycle* or his various books.

Left: YAK rain poncho, offering rain protection for the touring cyclist. *Le Cycle*, 21 April 1951.

Top right: Satin & Maillet face shield, for the really hardy cyclist. *Le Cycle*, 3 October 1953.

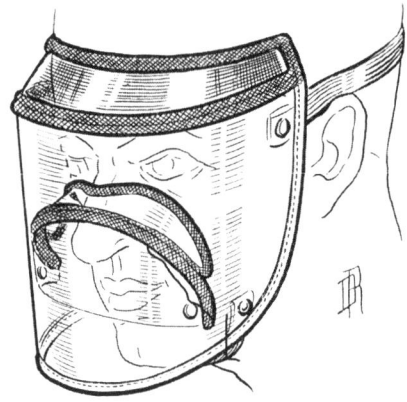

Center right: Cycling cap, for Eddy Merckx fans. *Cycles de Compétition et Randonneuses*.

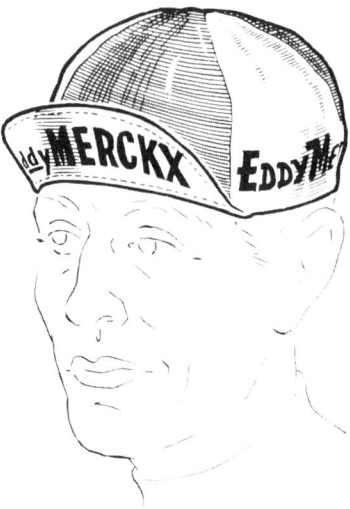

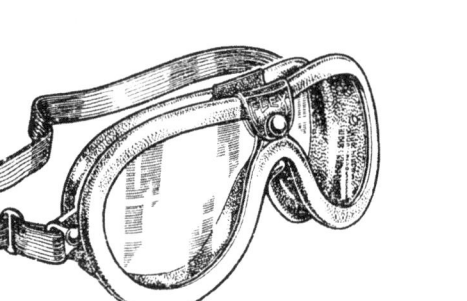

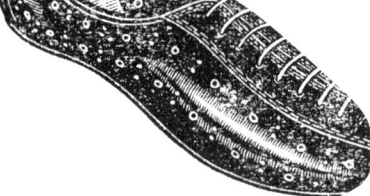

Above: Cycling shoe.

Left center: Cycling goggles for dusty roads.

Bottom left: sunglasses.

All three images from *Cycle: Compétition, Cyclotourisme*.

Below: Cycling gloves. *Le Cycle*, January 1969.

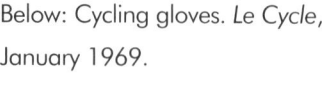

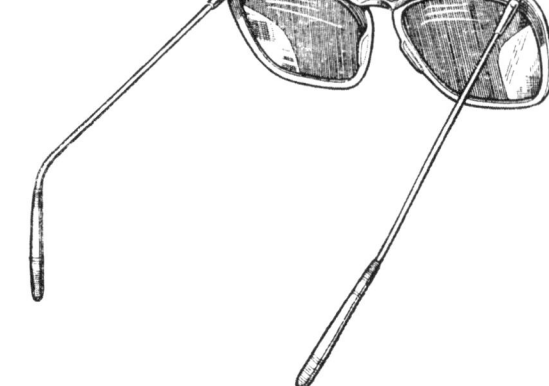

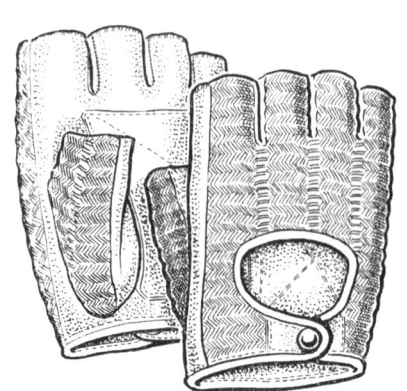

260

Chapter 26. Bicycle Clothing

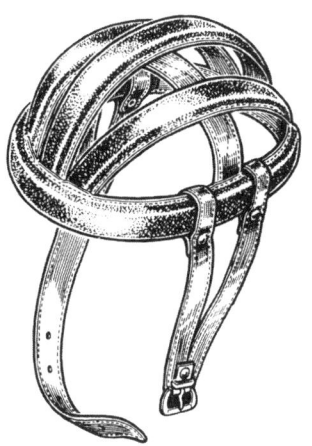

Left: Before the introduction of hard-shell helmets, which were available in the U.S. long before they were in France, the leather "hairnet" helmet, filled with horse hair, was the most common head protection for racers. *Cycles de Compétition et Randonneuses*.

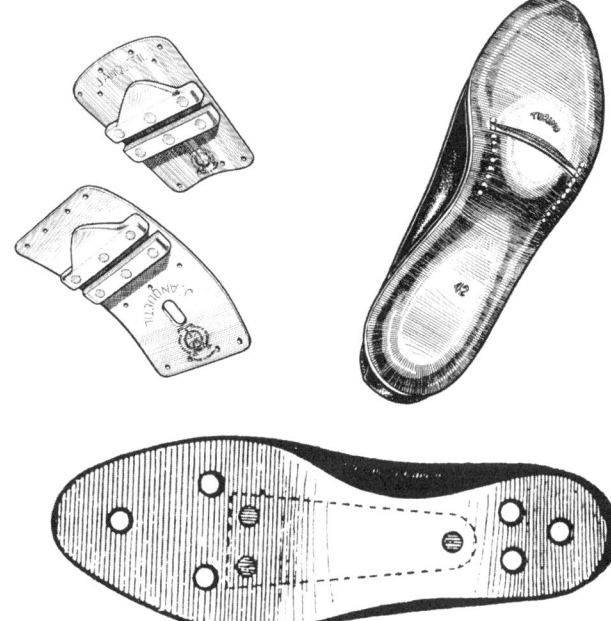

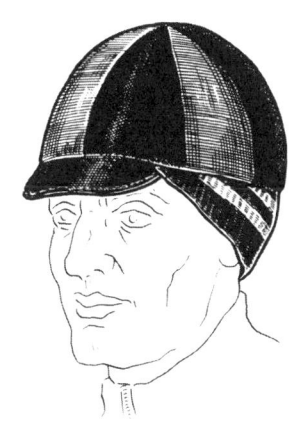

Right: Wool winter cycling cap. *Cycles de Compétition et Randonneuses*.

Above: Three images showing a cycling shoe and pedal cleats, and how to install them. Top right is a shoe with built-in cleat groove. All these predate the use of clipless pedals. All three images from *Cycles de Compétition et Randonneuses*.

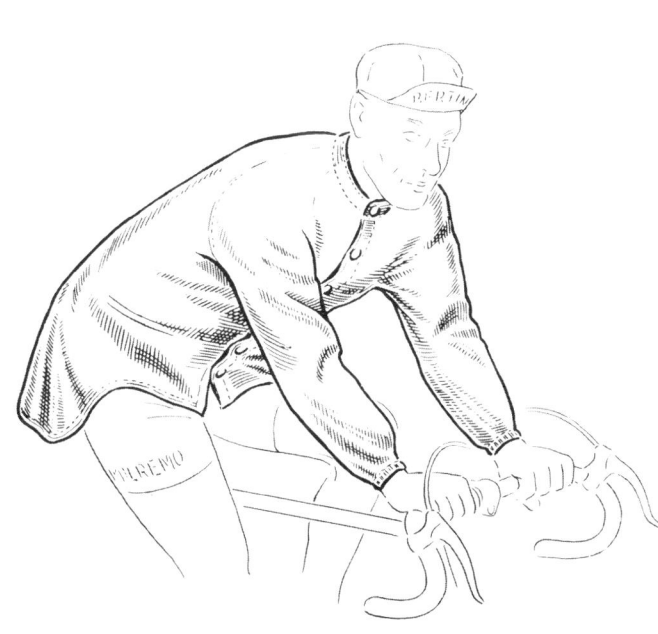

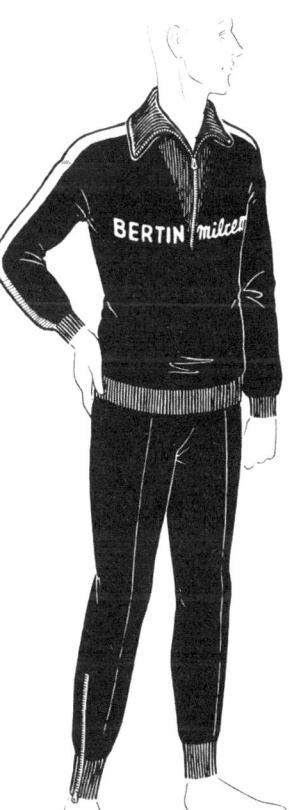

Above: Another image of a cycling shoe. *Cycle: Compétition, Cyclotourisme*.

Left and right: two images from the 1975 Bertin-Milremo catalogue: a windbreaker (left) and a cold-weather cycling and training suit (right). Similar images were used in Rebour's several books.

27. Scans of Original Illustrations

In this chapter, we have collected some of the original Rebour artwork. Unlike most of the images in the preceding chapter, these scans are made directly from Rebour's art boards, which were generously made available to us by David Herlihy, who had been given them by Daniel Rebour's brother Rodolphe during his 1991 interview.

The images in this chapter are all scanned at 1,200 dpi, and then reduced in size from their originals, some of which were amazingly large. Since many of these images are also represented in the preceding chapters, where they are captioned as to subject matter and date of publication, we have refrained from captioning them in this chapter.

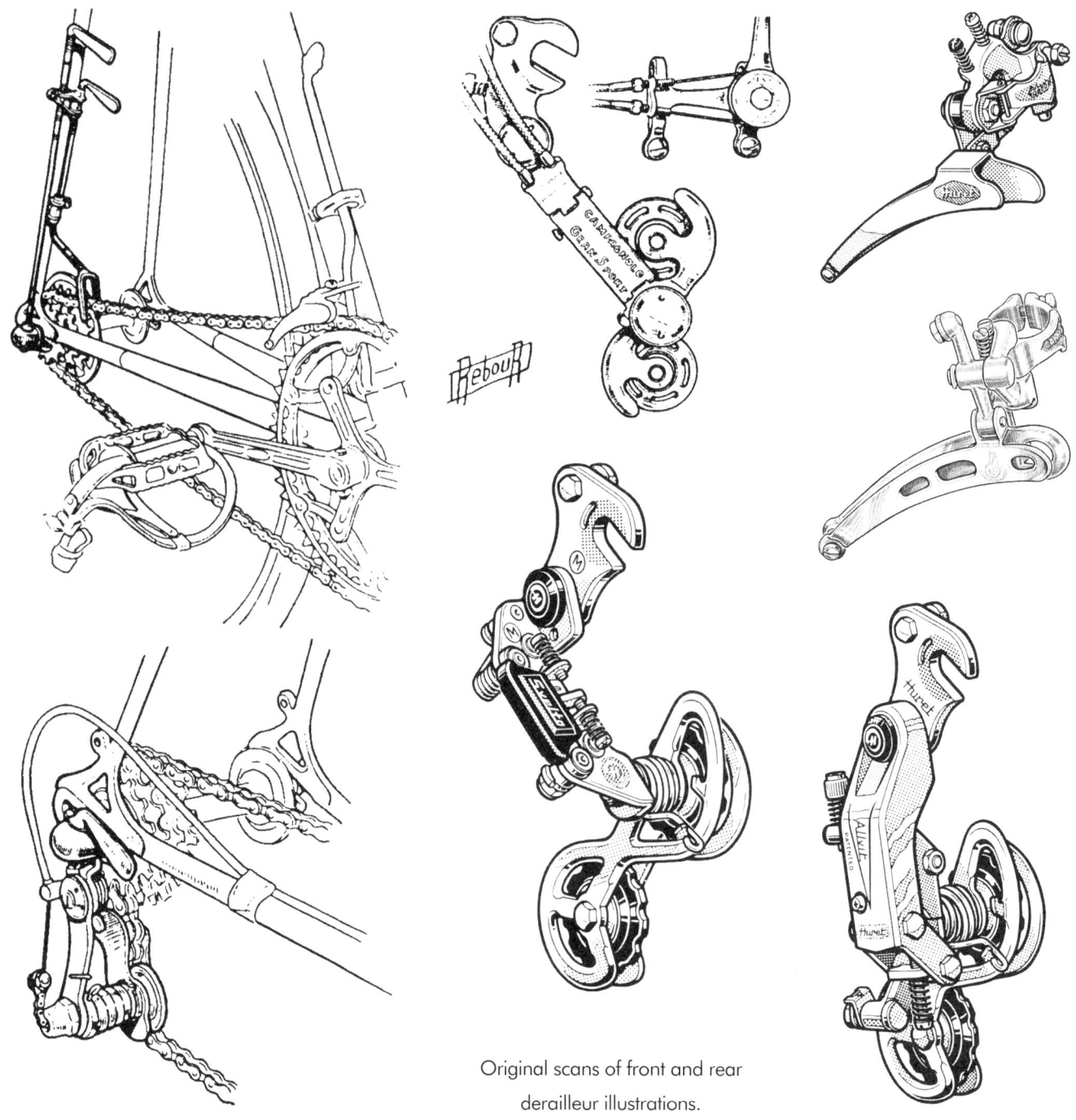

Original scans of front and rear derailleur illustrations.

27. Scans of Original Illustrations

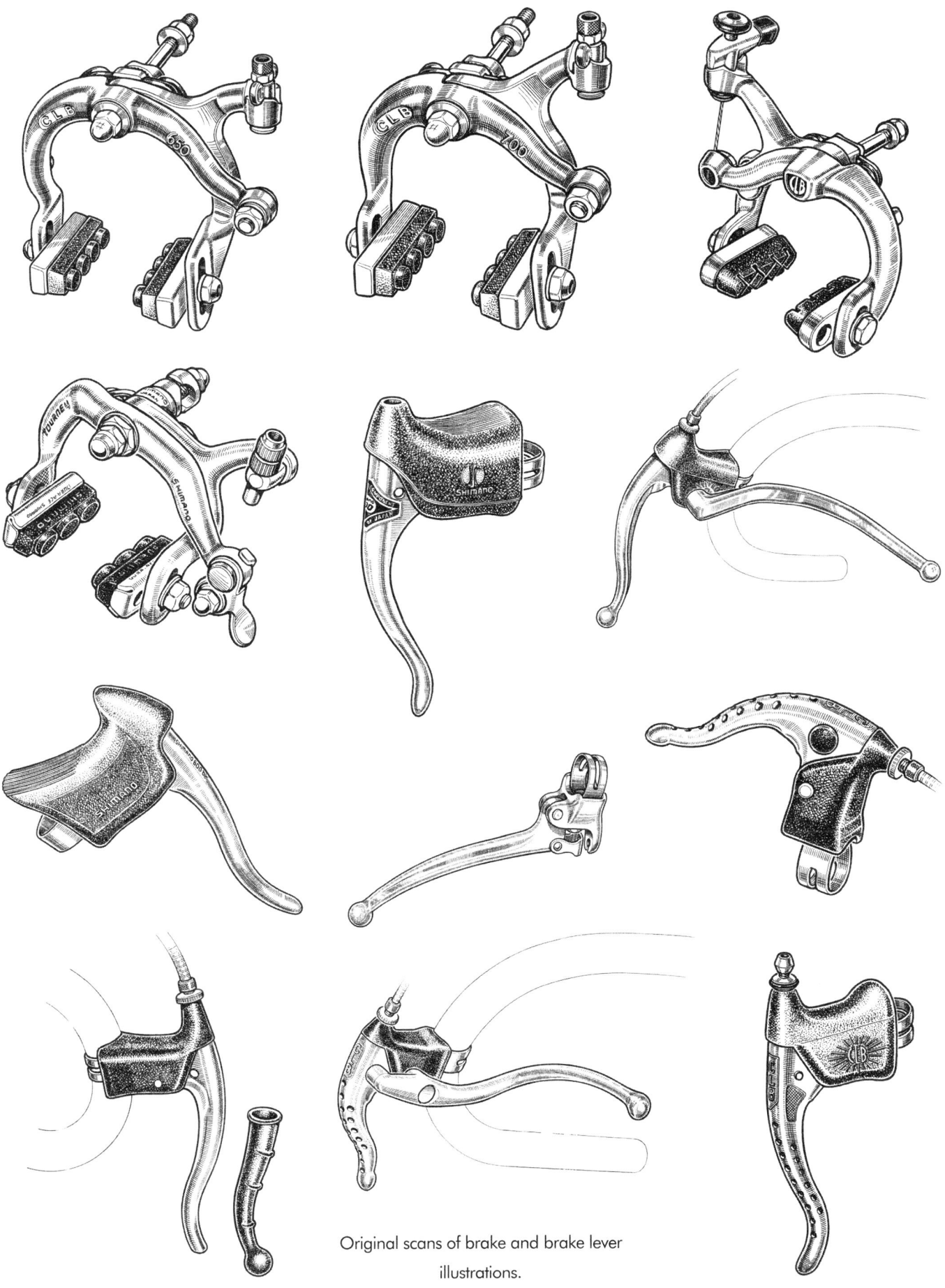

Original scans of brake and brake lever illustrations.

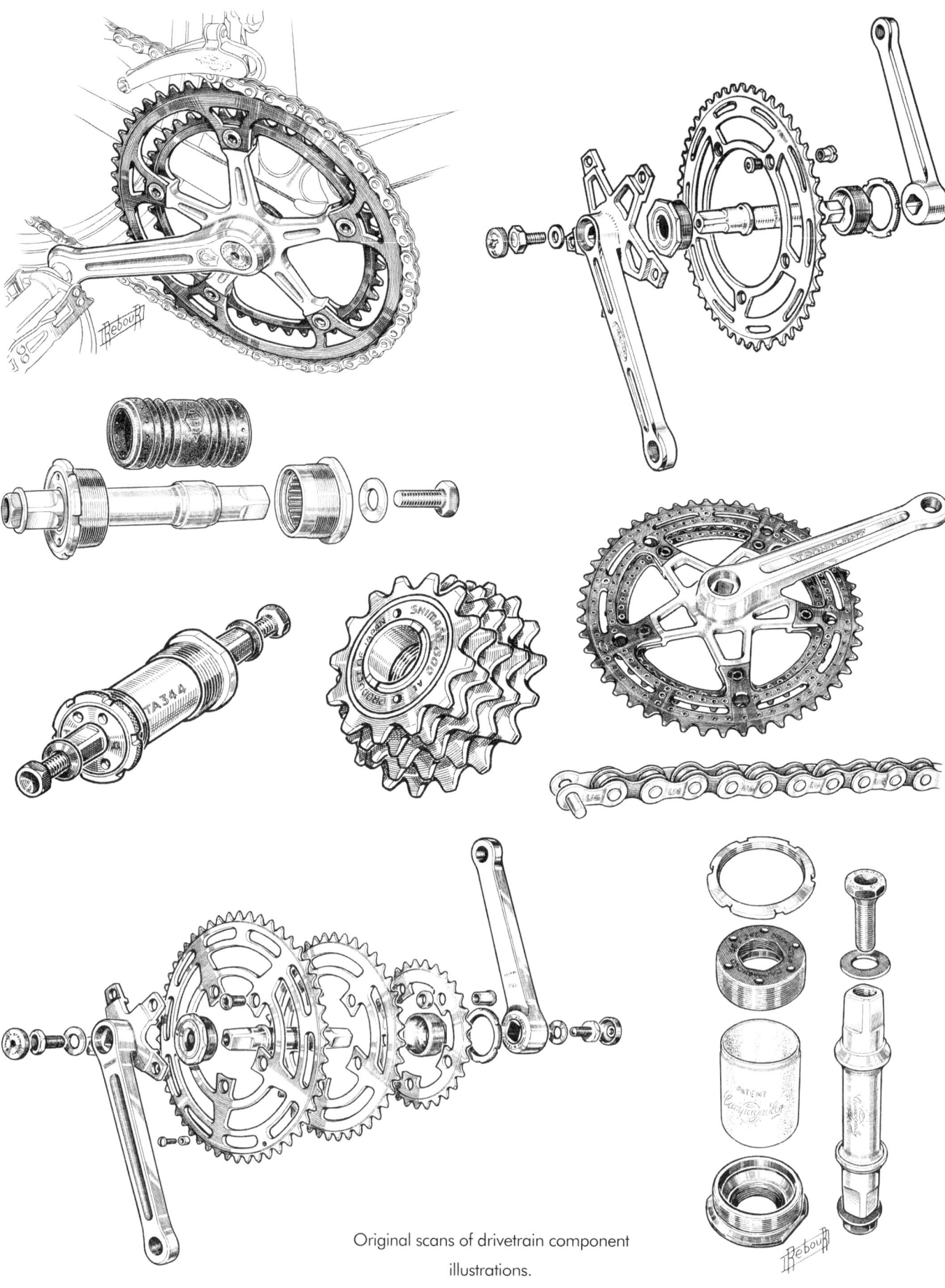

Original scans of drivetrain component illustrations.

27. Scans of Original Illustrations

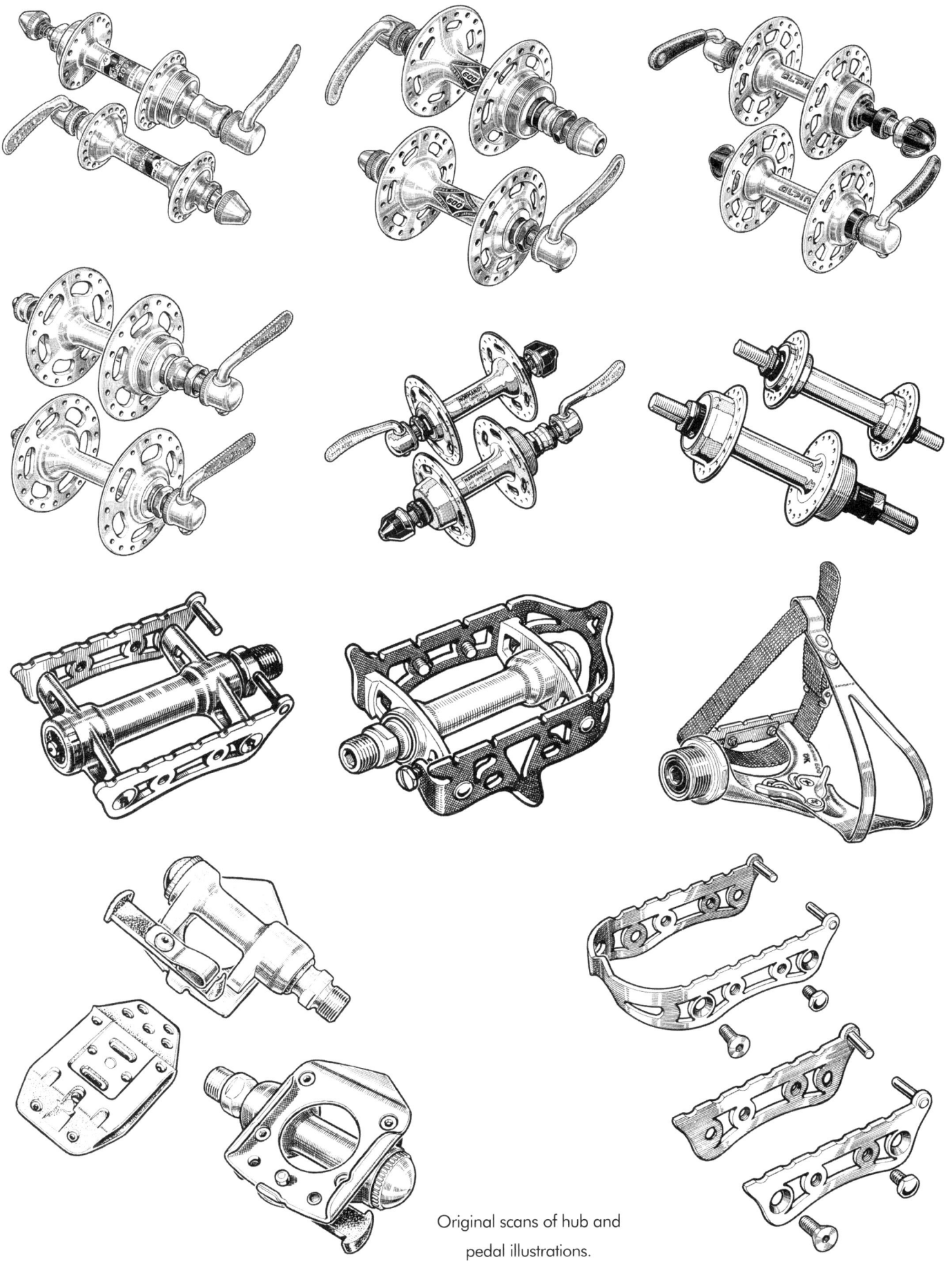

Original scans of hub and pedal illustrations.

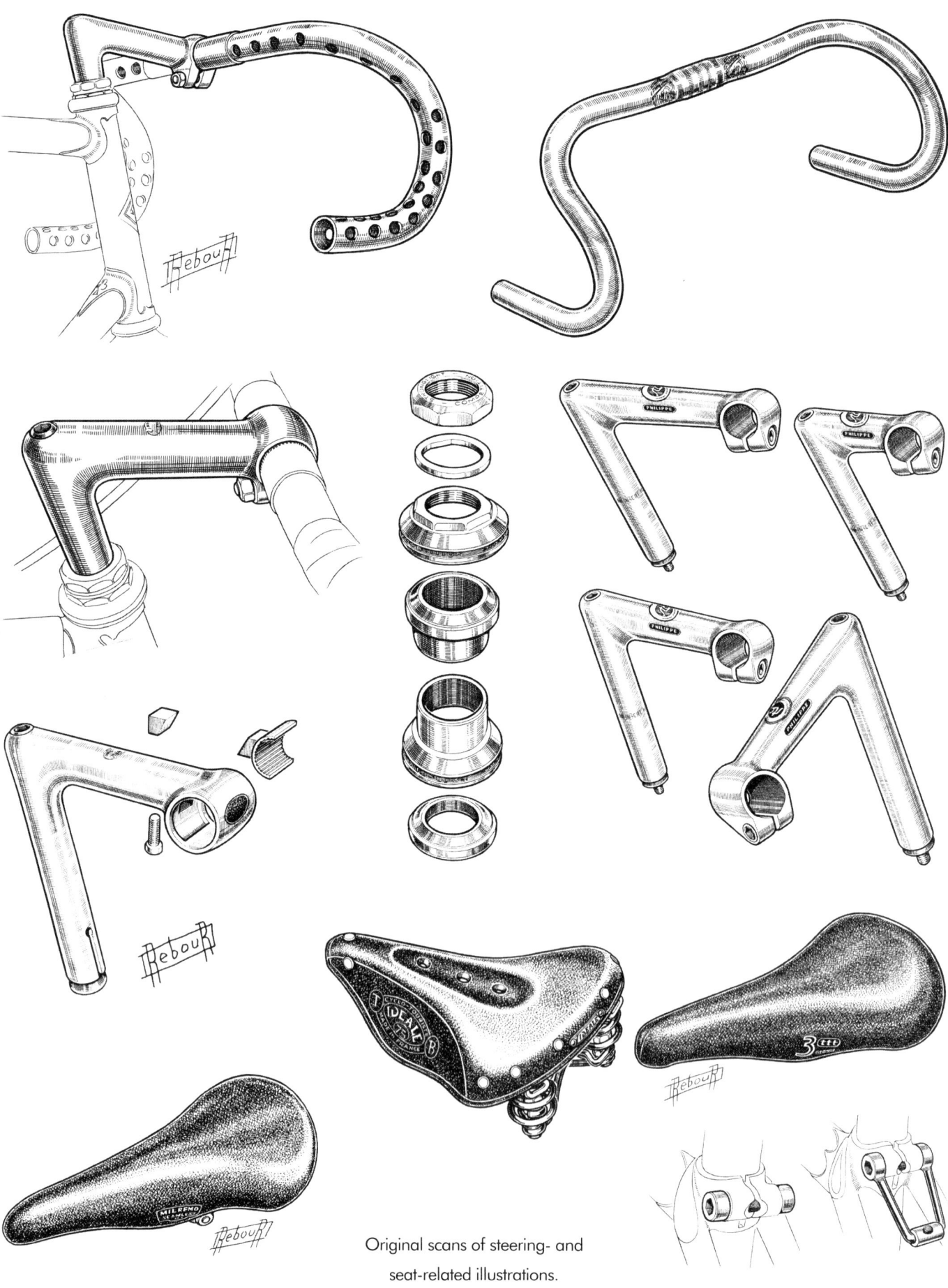

Original scans of steering- and seat-related illustrations.

27. Scans of Original Illustrations

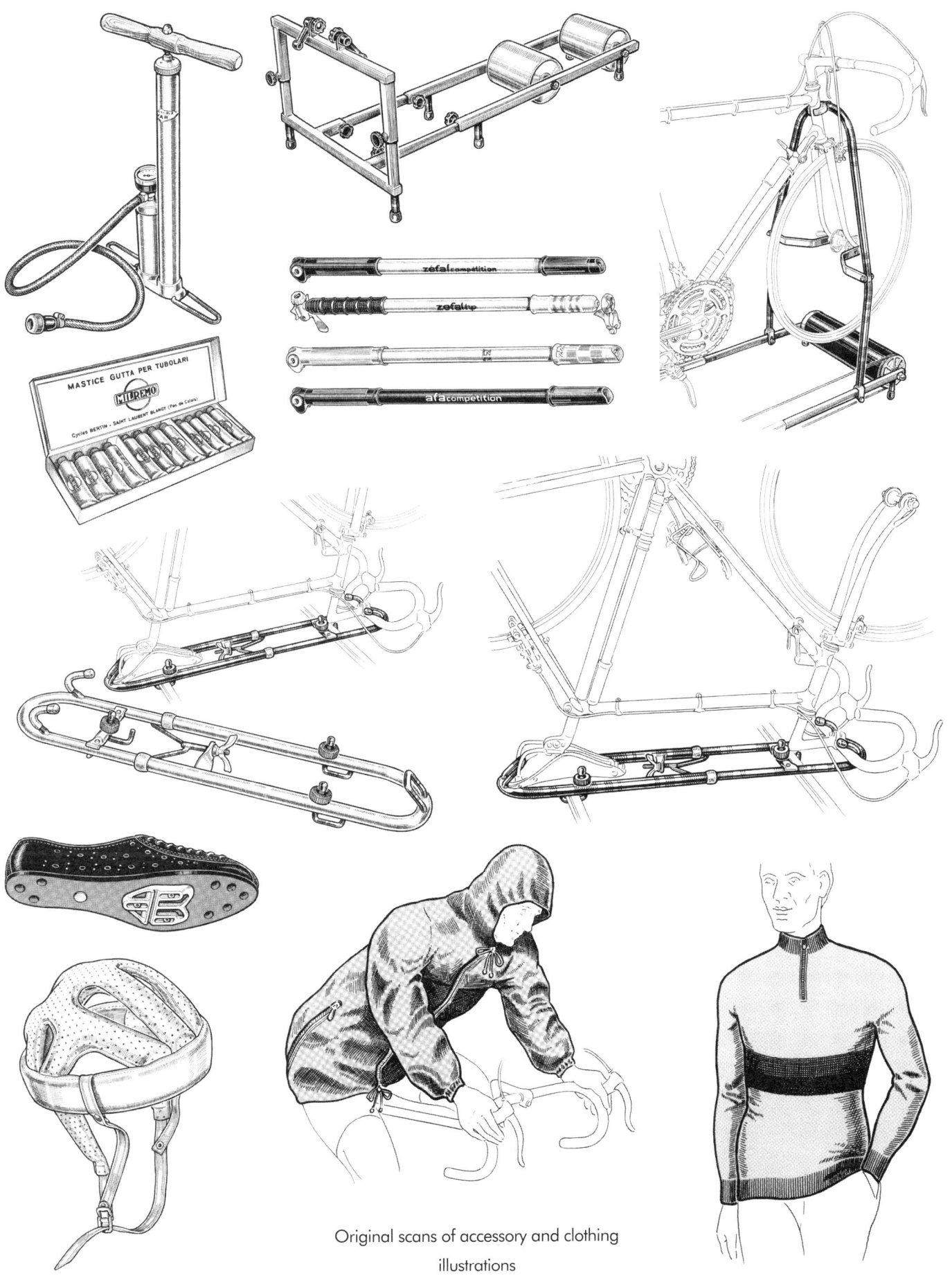

Original scans of accessory and clothing illustrations

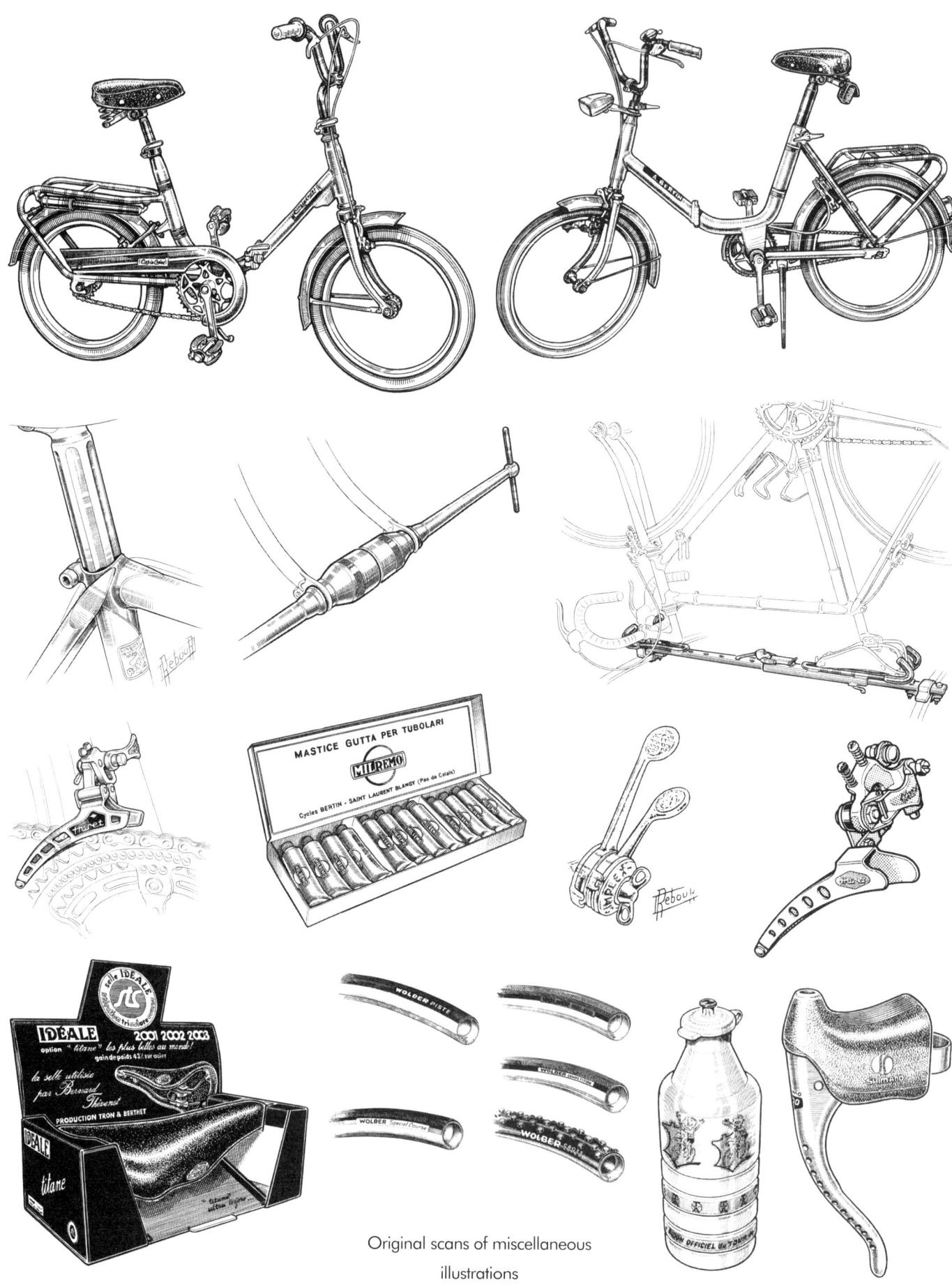

Original scans of miscellaneous illustrations

28. Selected Expanded Caption Texts

In this section, we provide more extensive descriptive texts for selected illustrations. In the body of the book, the relevant illustrations are marked with a footnote-style double-asterisk symbol (**) at the end of the caption, referencing to the information given below, arranged by page number on which the illustration appears.

Page 27: This bicycle geometry drawing contrasts with those of most bikes sold today. The longer chainstays, shallower angles and matching fork rake, and more generous clearances made for a bike that could be ridden comfortably for many hours without sacrificing efficiency.

Page 43: Kübler's bicycle had chrome-plated dropouts and was equipped with newly introduced Simplex rear derailleur and lever-operated front derailleur, close-geared Simplex 3-arm double chainrings and Magistroni cottered cranks, Ambrosio handlebars and stem, Babilla brakes with Vittoria hand-rests on the levers, high-flange solid-axle hubs with wingnuts, and, for the first time, an extra water bottle on the downtube.

Page 46, upper: Until the mid-1950s, most derailleur-geared bicycles had only a rear derailleur, and if a front derailleur was used, it was operated by means of a direct-mounted lever attached to the front derailleur itself. The passe-vitesse, or bar-end shifter shown in the lower illustration was initially used only to control the rear derailleur.

Page 46, lower: Although hailed as a "French bicycle" in *Le Cycle*, Koblet's 1952 La Perle machine was one of the first French bikes on which Campagnolo components were used extensively, including the rear dropouts and fork ends, hubs, and cable-operated front and rear derailleurs.

Page 49: Whereas for his 1949 Tour de France victory, Coppi's bike had been equipped with Simplex derailleurs (at least according to Simplex advertising), for his 1951 victory, Coppi's rode a Bianchi bicycle equipped with modern Campagnolo front and rear derailleurs. The other components were an eclectic mix: TA cottered steel cranks and aluminium alloy chainrings, FB hubs with Campagnolo quick-releases, an "English-type" headset, FOM pedals, Christophe toeclips, Ambrosio handlebars and stem, Universal brakes, Regina freewheel and chain, and Pirelli tubular tires.

Page 52 & 53: The three twistgrip shifters shown on these pages were amongst several instances of what is referred to as "Prior Art" in patent language, disclosed to successfully defend Shimano and SunRace-Roots against claims by SRAM that their products infringed the latter company's twistgrip patent, which presumably would not have been granted in the first place if the patent examiner had had access to publications like *Le Cycle*.

Page 55: Bobet's 1953 Stella bicycle was still largely equipped with French components: Vitus frame tubes, Huret front and rear derailleurs, TA cotterless cranks and chainrings, Pivo freewheel, Prior pedals, Mafac brake levers with Swiss Weinmann brakes. Only the hubs and quick-releases were from Campagnolo. Note that the front derailleur is still lever-operated (the second downtube lever does not control the front derailleur but the chain tension).

Page 71: Note the spare spokes tied to the front and rear mudguard stays on this bicycle at the Poly de Chanteloup technical trials. Apparently, the rider was worried about breaking spokes on the climb.

Page 82: Rebour criticized Jacquelin's 1956 Poly de Chanteloup entry for being too much of a racing bike, rather than a true *randonneur* machine, as which it was entered. Note the seat-tube-mounted front-derailleur-control lever (see also the note for pate 46).

Page 83: Anquetil's 1956 Hour-record bike, built by Masi, though with short chainstays and steep frame angles, is still a far cry from today's track bikes. The handlebars are not much lower than the saddle, and also in other respects it hardly differs from road bikes of the period (minus brakes and derailleurs). Rebour remarks that it would be less suitable on an outdoor track, such as the Milan Vigorelli track, than for the Paris Vél d'Hive track, where Anquetil did set the record.

Page 86: The bicycle presented to U.S. President Dwight Eisenhower by the French Cycling Federation (FFC) was delivered to the U.S. Embassy in Paris in July 1956. It was based on a frame made by M. Schmidely, blue-and-white enameled by Lapierre. The components included chrome-plated Simplex dropouts, Juy 543 derailleur, and quick-releases; Peugeot rack, fenders, and chainguard; Stronglight crankset; Mafac cantilever brakes; Lyotard pedals; Gauthier saddle; AVA handlebars and stem; Mistral pump; and Cibie dynamo lights. A special head badge in the shape of France was engraved "FFC au Président Eisenhower," and painted on the seat tube; and the initials "D.E." were on the top tube.

Page 87: Note the slack chain on Adriaenssens' Mercier bicycle in the 1956 Tour de France. At the time, many racers still believed that a taut chain would be less efficient (which is not true, because the tension in the lower chain run is offset by the much higher tension in the upper run).

Page 98: Baumann's René Herse bike was based on a large, 62 cm frame (measured center-to-center, which would translate to a 26-inch frame measured to the top of the seatlug, built with Reynolds tubing and round fork blades. Randonneurs used better derailleurs than did the racers at the time, as evidenced by the large-capacity chainstay-mounted Cyclo rear derailleur, though we still find a direct-lever-operated Cyclo front derailleur. Other components include TA chainrings with Stronglight cotterless cranks, and JOS dynamo lights combined with what looks like a standard front battery-torch-light.

Page 104: Nencini's Leo-branded 1957 Tour de France bike, made by Teodoro Carnielli, was largely equipped with Campagnolo components: derailleurs with bar-end controls, hubs with quick-releases, and micro-adjustable seatpost. The cotterless crankset is by Magistroni, and the brakes and levers are by Universal. Nencini kept his handlebars higher than most other riders.

Page 112: Considering he had to keep at it for 24 hours continuously, Leulhier's handlebar position was remarkably much lower than his seat, even if he may have spent a good amount of time with his hands on the handrests in a very stretched-out posture. His René Herse machine was geared 50 X 16, giving an 84-in gear, or 6.8 m development. It was equipped with Maxi-Car hubs, Mephisto rims, Robergel spokes, Herse proprietary crankset and chainring, Brambton chain, Lyotard pedals and Christophe toeclips.

Page 118: This bike is constructed of lugless brazed oversize Reynolds tubing, and is equipped with Cyclo rear derailleur and custom front derailleur, Stronglight crankset with TA triple chainrings, Mafac brakes, Maxi-Car hubs, and Moyne frictionless freewheel. Frame builder Jo Routens' signature design is seatstays overlapping the seat tube and joining the top tube, which is a form of stiffening the frame (see also the image of a Jo Routens bicycle on page 33). This same detail is currently used by mass-manufacturer GT, and has become essentially that company's signature as well.

Page 127: Of small stature, Gil, the winner of the professional category of the Lyons technical trials, had this special Urago bike made, which was reported to be perfectly suited to the climbing effort. It is equipped with Simplex derailleurs and a Stronglight steel cotterless crankset with TA chainrings.

Page 138: French cycle tourists and frame builders have long held that the load should be carried low. Tests conducted in the 1970s in America have demonstrated that this is a good idea for the front, though not for the back, where it is more important to carry the weight forward of the rear axle.

Page 147: Massignani's 1961 Legnano bicycle, which was reported to be very stable on fast descents, is pretty much an all-Italian bike, heralding a new era of Italian equipment dominance. Campagnolo provided hubs, derailleurs, cranks, pedals, headset, and seatpost. Also from Italy were the newly introduced Universal Type 61 centerpull brakes and levers.

Page 149: The term *"Diagonale"* refers to bikes designed for the French *cyclosportives*, fast touring cyclists, who like to ride all the 6 diagonal routes that connect the six extremities of their roughly hexagonal-shaped country. Since they do not carry significant luggage, these bikes are not equipped with heavy-duty racks but merely a handlebar-bag support. Like the bikes used in Paris–Brest–Paris, they always have lights.

Page 156: The American-made Schwinn Superior was one of very few derailleur bikes available in the US in the early 1960s, i.e. before the "10-speed boom." It had the same heavy "flash-welded" frame as the Schwinn Varsity, but was equipped with better components. It had a heavy forged-steel one-piece crankset, with triple chainrings, Huret front and rear derailleurs, Maillard hubs and freewheel, Sedis chain, Weinmann brakes, a Brooks leather saddle, Super handlebars and stem, and Wolber high-pressure tires.

Page 162: This 1964 Urago randonneur bicycle, ridden by Jean Bernard at the 1964 Vélocio Day event, is equipped with what are essentially typical French road racing components of the time: Stronglight cotterless crankset with half-step gearing, Huret Allvit derailleur, Mafac brakes, high-flange hubs with quick-releases, etc. However, the frame is built with adequate clearances for the installation of mudguards. The front rack suggests the use of a big handlebar bag, which may have impaired handling.

Page 164: Gimondi's bike, as the other Magni bikes ridden by his Salvarani team, were essentially all-Italian machines, with Campagnolo derailleurs, hubs, crankset, pedals, headset, and seatpost. Just the water bottle cage was made in France, by TA.

Page 165: Poulidor's Mercier bike, though nominally French-made, was also equipped with a full complement of Campagnolo components, just like Gimondi's Italian machine.

Page 182: To carry heavy and/or bulky loads in the back without negatively affecting the bicycle's handling, the load should be carried forward of the rear axle, which is achieved by this device. It is interesting to note that the currently available Xtracycle system works on the same principle, though it is unlikely the people who introduced it were aware of this historic precedent.

Page 183: The Peugeot bike ridden to victory in the 1967 Tour de France by Roger Pingeon was still mainly equipped with French components: Stronglight crankset with 52-42-tooth chainrings, Simplex derailleurs, Lyotard pedals, Perrin Exceltoo quick-release hubs, Mafac brakes, Mavic rims, and an Idéale leather saddle.

Page 184: By 1968, even supposed randonneur bikes started to look like road racing machines. Compared to earlier entries in the Poly de Chanteloup technical trials, this René Herse machine had very short chainstays and an upright geometry, and even the tires have become narrower. Perhaps good for climbing, but not for the long haul. The components on this bike include Herse's own chainrings with a Stronglight crankset, Huret derailleurs, and Mafac brakes.

Page 192: Unlike the English, French touring cyclists preferred to use generator-lighting rather than battery lights. It is also interesting to note how much attention was paid to the routing of wiring, often internally through the frame tubes. Bloc-dynamos were often used because they avoided the dangling wires from the generator to the front light.

Page 193: The Belgian manufacturer Kessels put Merckx' name on the bike. Note the drilled-out chainrings, which was to be a feature in coming years of component treatment to make them *look* lighter (though often they weren't). When he broke the World Hour record, in 1972, even the handlebars had been treated this way, making them weaker without any benefit. Also note that by now road racing bikes had shorter chainstays, steeper frame angles, and less fork rake.

Page 196: Joop Zoetemelk, unlike Merckx, did not believe in excessively light equipment and steep frame angles. His 1970 Flandria machine is essentially a standard bike as had been used 5 years earlier, with tested standard components and more relaxed frame geometry.

Page 200: More lightening craze: On Ocaña's time trial machine, the chainrings have not only lost their inner rings, but what's left has lots of unnecessary holes drilled in it.

Page 206: The fully enclosed chain case containing oil, or oil-bath chain case, was a feature of many English high-end roadsters, of which Sunbeam was the best-known exponent. It allowed constant lubrication of the chain, making it last practically forever and maintaining high drive-train efficiency.

Page 208: Génèvieve Gambillon's world championship bike shows a return to proven geometry by René Herse, as opposed to the short-wheelbase bike shown on page 184 (see note above).

Page 219: This Starnord bike was a late entry in a market that had already collapsed, namely that of the low-end bike for the American "10-speed boom," with its range of down-market components from various French manufacturers.

Appendix 1. Pierre-Georges Hugaud

Hugaud, who signed his work PGH, worked with Rebour at *Le Cycle* during the 1970s, and later went on to *L'Officiel du Cycle*. He was trained in Rebour's method of line illustrations, but also seemed to have picked up enough technical knowledge to eventually become technical editor of *L'Officiel du Cycle*.

Hugaud's style, though similar to Rebour's at first blush, can be distinguished from Rebour's in that he tended to use more mechanical aids, such as templates and straightedges, whereas Rebour was a true master of freehand drawing. Whereas Rebour's lines, whether straight or curved, would vary in thickness, Hugaud's lines tended to be more constant, and thus did not achieve the same degree of realistic representation of three-dimensional forms.

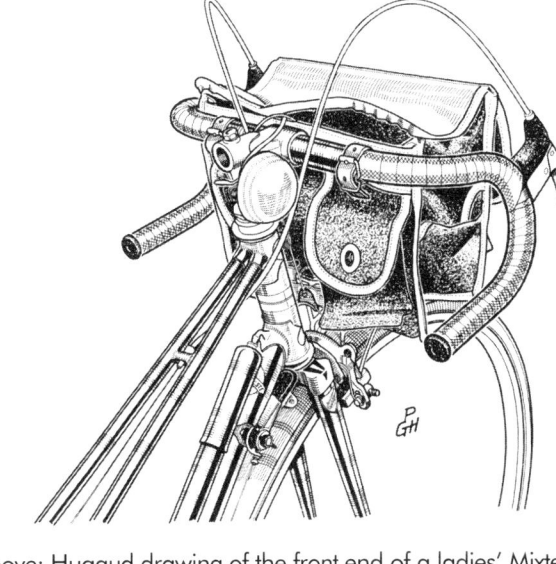

Above: Hugaud drawing of the front end of a ladies' Mixte randonneur bike with handlebar bag. *Le Cycle*, October 1973.

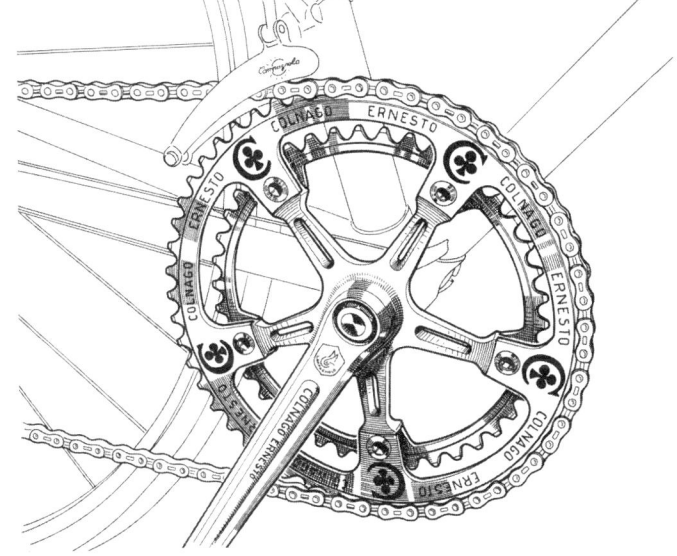

Left: Engraved Campagnolo crankset on Colnago bicycle. *L'Officiel du Cycle*, March 1976.

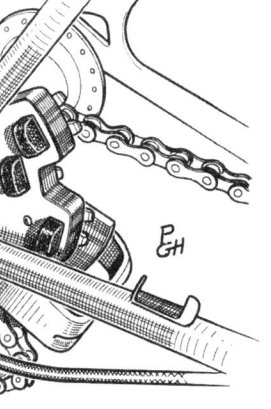

Left: American-made Tokheim expanding-chainwheel gear shifter on Stella bicycle. *Le Cycle*, December 1973.

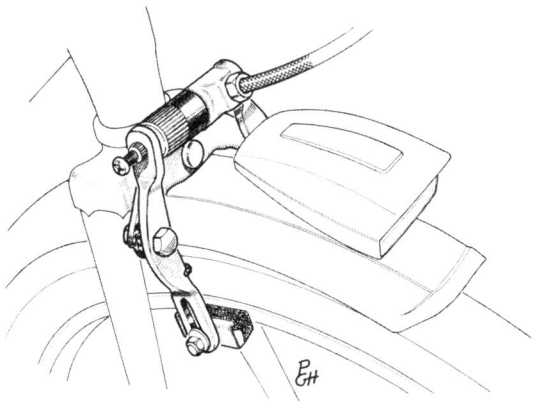

Right: Shimano hydraulic brake on Motobécane bicycle at the 1973 Paris bicycle trade show. *Le Cycle*, November 1973.

Appendix 2: Rodolphe Rebour

Rodolphe was Daniel's elder brother. Also trained at the same École National des Arts Décoratifs, he too became a respected illustrator. But unlike Daniel, Rodolphe specialized in freehand drawing and advertising. Indeed, many of the advertisements he designed appeared in *Le Cycle*. Quite often, Rodolphe's work was also featured on the covers of the magazine. Some examples of his work are shown on this page.

Rodolphe survived Daniel by several years, and bicycle historian David Herlihy did an interesting interview with him for *Bicycle Guide* magazine, which was published in 1995.

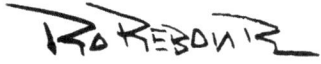 Left: Rodolphe Rebour signature.

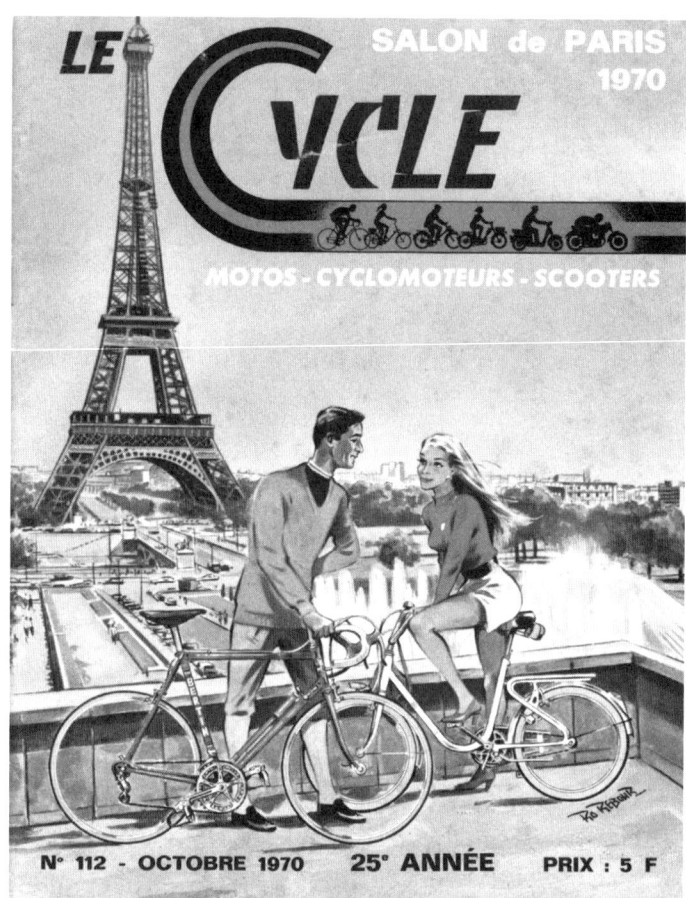

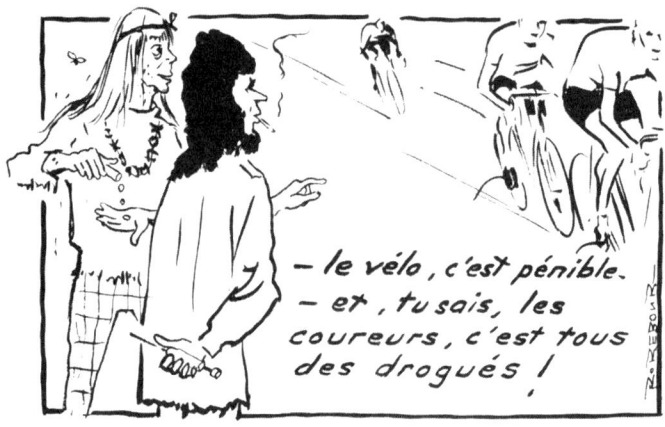

Above: Rodolphe Rebour illustration featured on the cover of the October 1970 issue of *Le Cycle*.

Left: "Bicycles, they're bothersome." "And you know, those racers, they're all on drugs." Rodolphe Rebour cartoon drawing that appeared in the October 1971 issue of *Le Cycle*.

Below: Rodolphe Rebour pagespread, undated Bertin catalogue. The technical drawings are attributed to his brother, Daniel Rebour.

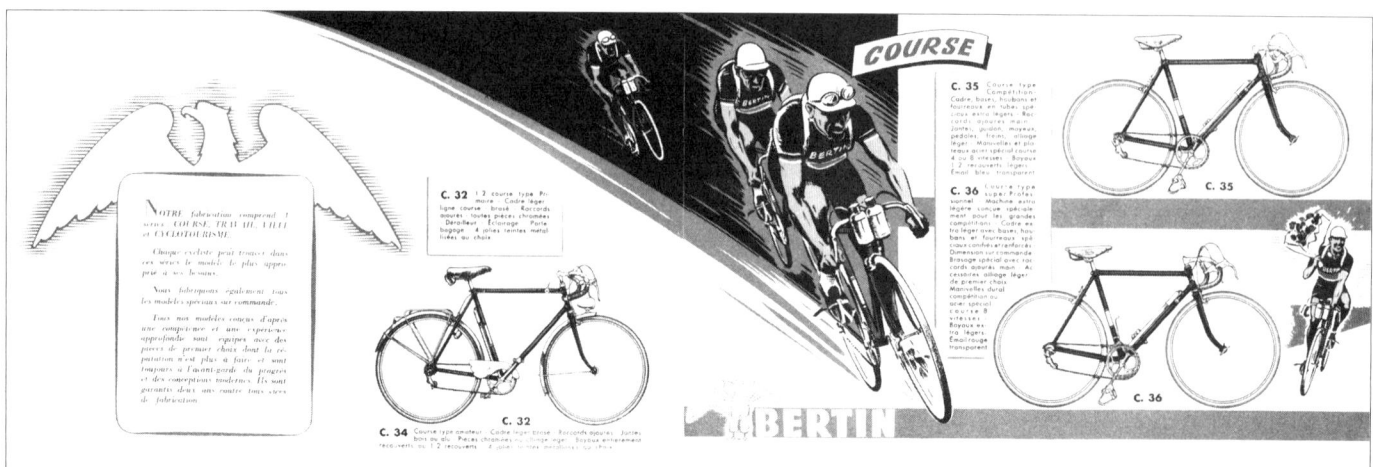

Appendix 3: George Retseck

The art of bicycle line-illustration did not die with Daniel Rebour's retirement. One prominent illustrator who followed in his footsteps is the American illustrator George Retseck.

He prepared many of the drawings that appeared in *Bicycling* magazine during the 1990s. In addition, he provided the "Rebour-like" line drawings for Bridgestone Bicycles' U.S. catalogues of the period, and more recently for Richard Sachs' frame lugs and Paul Component Engineering. Some examples of his work are shown on this page.

Although we know him mainly from his fine bicycle illustrations, George is by no means a one-trick pony. His technical illustrations regularly appear in such publications as *Scientific American*. And while in our context his line-drawing work is of most interest, he employs other media as well, as the project demands. Although most of his recent illustrations are made using computer software, George still loves working in pen and ink.

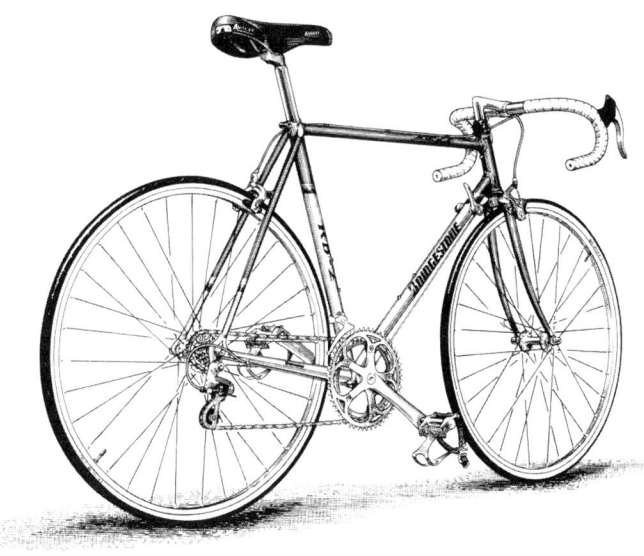

Above: George Retseck illustration for Bridgestone Bicycle's 1993 U.S. catalogue.

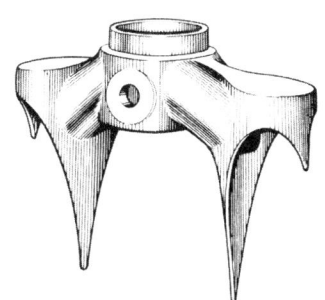 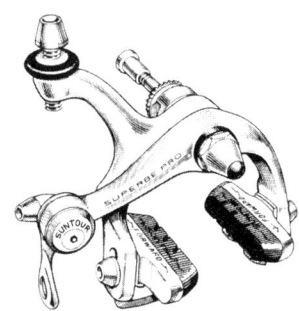

Above: Two detail illustrations for the 1993 Bridgestone catalogue, showing a fork crown and a Shimano sidepull brake respectively.

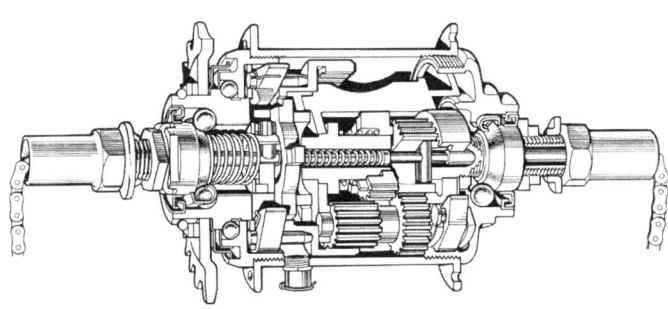

Above: Cut-away view of a Sturmey-Archer 5-speed hub gear, showing the working parts inside.

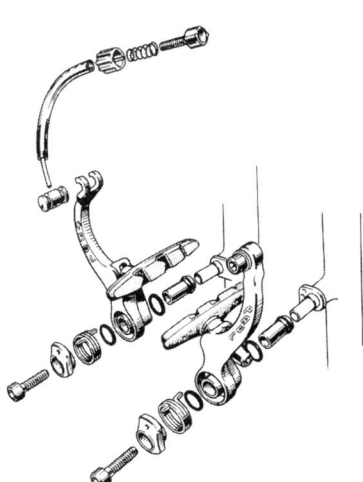

Left: Exploded view of Paul Component Engineering direct-pull brake. assembly.

BIBLIOGRAPHY

Berto, Frank. *The Dancing Chain: History and Development of the Derailleur Bicycle*. San Francisco: Cycle Publishing, 2000, 2005, 2009, 2012.

Le Cycle, various issues, 1945–1975.

Le Cycliste, various issues, 1946–1972.

L'Officel du Cycle, various issues, 1975–1983.

Henri, Raymond. "Daniel Rebour: Illustrative Genius of the Bicycle." *Proceedings of the 6th International Cycling History Conference*. San Francisco: Bicycle Books, 1996.

Herlihy, David. "Daniel Rebour: A Name Etched in Hardware History." *Bicycle Guide*, March 1995.

—. "Daniel Rebour: Illustrator." 1993 U.S. Bridgestone Bicycle catalogue.

Lawrence, Mark, and Ken Taylor. "Daniel Rebour's Technique." *Bicycle Quarterly*. Summer 2009.

Pradères, Jean-Pierre. "Daniel Rebour—The Life Behind the Illustrations." *Vintage Bicycle Quarterly*, Summer 2004.

Rebour, Daniel. *Cycle: Compétition, Cyclotourisme*. Paris: Technique et Vulgarisation, 1962.

—. *Cycles de Compétition et Randonneuses*. Paris: Technique et Vulgarisation, 1975, 1976.

—. *Le Monde de Daniel Rebour: irusuto ni yoru spo-tsu sha to buhin no hensen* (Illustrations of sports bikes and components). Tokyo: BERO SHUPPANSHA, 1976.

—. *La Pratique du Vélo: Technique, Choix, Entretien, Réparations, Entrainement, Cyclotourisme, Compétition, etc*. Paris: Technique et Vulgarisation, 1949.

'83 *The Data Book*. Osaka: Joto Ringyo Kaisha, 1983. Republished under the title *The Data Book: 100 Years of Bicycle Component and Accessory Design*. San Francisco: Cycle Publishing, 1998.

1946 André Bertin catalogue. Paris: Ets. André Bertin, 1946.

1946 Alex Singer catalogue (and subsequent undated catalogues).

Milremo catalogue. Paris: Ets. André Bertin, 1976, 1979, 1980, 1981, 1982, 1983.

Le Petit Livre Jaune: Catalogue des Utils VAR. Paris: Ets. VAR, 1972 (and subsequent years).

Index

A

AM chain, 80
AS steering lock, 204
AS2 prop-stand, 201
ATAX (see also Philippe), 157
    folding handlebars, 234
    handlebars and stem, 158
    stem, 158
Acatène, or chainless, bicycle, 17
accessories, 118–213, 267
    overview, 205
adjustable rack, 186
    seat clip, 165
    seat tube angle, 20
    seatpost, 164
    stem, 153–154
Adler bottom-bracket gear, 249
Adriaenssens, Jean, 87
aero components (see also individual component entries), 97, 104–105, 160, 168
    rim, 143
    seatpost, 168
Agrati fork crown, 26
Aimar, Lucien, 168
Alcyon bicycle, 143
    combined chainguard and front derailleur, 201
Alfredo Cardinali derailleur, 44
Alpina adjustable seatpost, 164
Altenburger brake, 113
    brake lever, 112
    Synchron brake, 114
    wing nuts, 125
alternate drives, 247–249
aluminium frame construction details, 32
    monocoque frame, 44
    mudguard, 211
Amadei Comfor shifter, 50
Amadel 3- to 5-pin chainring attachment converter, 78
Amalgam frame details, 26
Ambrosio adjustable-reach stem, 154
Amsterdam bicycle trades show, overview, 219
Anglade, Henri, 133
Anquetil, Jacques, 83, 103, 146, 151, 161
    track bike, 83
Anti-Shoc damping elements, 242
Asclip seatpost clamping, 161
Ashtabula cranks (see also Fauber, one-piece), 86
Astrua, Giancarlo, 58
Atala bicycle, 58, 119, 238
    folding bike, 238
Atom freewheel, 83, 87, 89
    quick-release, 125
    full-width drum brake, 138
    hub, 125
Audoux lever-drive, 249
Auto-Moto shift lever, 49
automatic-shifting 2-speed hub, 137
auxiliary motor, 252–255

B

BH (Beistegui Hermanos), 126, 163, 191, 238
    carrier bike, 191
    folding bike, 238
    hub, 126
    saddle, 163
BON derailleur, 43
BSA, 47, 99, 132, 99, 233
    derailleur, 47
    drum brake, 132
    folding bike, 233
    pedal, 99
Baby-Star children's bike, 240
back-pedal brake (see also coaster brake), 131
    adaptations, 135
bag restraints and supports, 183, 185
Bahamontès, Fédérico, 66, 122, 126, 132, 155, 160
Baldini, Ercole, 94
ball-bearing derailleur pulley, 61
band brake, 131, 134
Barbier, Paul, hub, 124
bar-end shifter (or passe-vitesse), 41, 45, 62
battery light, 192–199
Bauvin, Gilbert, 88
Beborex (or BeBo) brake, 112, 114
Belestibeau brake quick-release, 110
bell, 200, 203, 205
Berceau frame (see also mixte), 42
Berec battery lights, 199
Bergaud, Louis, 100, 116
Berini auxiliary motor, 252
Bernard, René, 162
Berthet pedal, 100, 101, 104
Bertin, André, 11
    pedals, 105
Berto, Frank, 10
Bianchi bicycle, 49, 181, 237
    folding bike, 237
    frame details, 31
Bicizeta auxiliary motor, 256
bicycle parts nomenclature, 24
bicycle computer, 213
bicycle derivatives, 250–251
bicycle rickshaws, 245
bicycle-based ski-exercise home-trainer, 250
bicycle-sizing device, 250
Bicycle Guide, magazine, 12
Bicycle Quarterly, magazine (see also Vintage Bicycle Quarterly), 12 and tandem testing, 225
binder bolt, recessed, 158
bloc-dynamo, 192, 194, 195, 198
Blocdur band-brake, 131
Blocpil cam-operated brake, 111
Bobet, Louison, 55, 64, 74
Borsetti dual air-chamber tube, 140
bottle cage, 208, 210, 212
bottom bracket gear, 248–249
bottom bracket, sealed bearings, 75
Bourdel rack and bag, 189
Bourgeois 3-cable brake lever, 110
Bowden plastic bicycle, 23
brakes, 106–119, 130–138, 264
    cable anchor, 24, 148
    centerpull, 110, 113, 116
    extension lever, 114, 264
    lever, 107, 112–119, 264
    lever orientation, 107
    overview, 109
    quick-release, 110, 116
brake-shift lever, 44, 219
Bridgestone, 275
Brisseay rear derailleur, 50
Brankart, Jean, 75
Brans saddle bag, 182
Brasobloc brazing method, 25
Breau, Henri, embossed rim, 140
    rubber pedal cleat, 101
Bridgestone catalogue, 12, 275
Briefcase support, 186
Brooks saddle, 161, 165, 167
Brussels bicycle trade show overview, 215
Buec bottom bracket gear, 248
bungee cord, 209
Burgers chopper-style children's bike, 240
bushingless chain, 77

C

CEV cyclometer, 209
CL suspension bicycle, 243
CLB, 108, 113, 118, 135, 205, 211, 264
    brake, 118, 264
    brake lever, 108, 264
    brake quick-release, 113
    chainguard, 205
    freewheel clutch, 135
    CLB laminated brake pad, 114
    prop-stand, 211
CMDC-Monosport luggage trailer, 245
CO_2 inflator, 208, 210, 212–213
cable guides, 63
cable nipple crimping tool, 257
cable oiler, 204
Cadet suspension details, 242
cam-operated brake, 106, 111, 119
Campagnolo
    Corsa derailleur, 47, 263
    front derailleur, 83, 263
    Gran Sport derailleur, 48, 53, 263
    Gran Turismo derailleur, 64, 71
    Nuovo Record hub, 128
    Record components, 119

Record brake, 117
Record brake lever, 117
Record front derailleur, 65
Record gruppo, 170
Record hub, 123, 129
Record pedal, 98, 105
Sport hub, 128
Super Record bottom bracket, 94, 97, 264
Super Record brake, 117
Super Record crankset, 95–96
Valentino derailleur, 65
bar-end shifter, 61
braze-on shifters, 56
crankset, 83, 93, 273
disk brake, 137
downtube shifters, 73
dropouts, 29
early derailleur system, 47
dropouts, 32, 37
front derailleur, 62
headset, 157, 160, 265
hubs, 125, 127, 266
pedals, 101, 265
product overview, 172
pump, 208
seatpost, 39, 164
shifters, 65
steel cotterless crankset, 93
track chainrings, drilled-out, 90
track pedal, 103
triple crankset, 85
camping trailer, 246
Canetti frame, 32, 33
tubular tires, 144
cantilever brake, 107–110
captions, expanded, 262–264
Captivante dynamo mounting, 194
folding bike, 237
carburetor, 253
Cardinale bicycle, 104
Cardinali, Alfredo, derailleur, 44
Carlton tire-protectors, 204
Carri-Guard rack, 185
carrier bicycle, 191
Carrot Preference cassette-type freewheel hub, 78
carrying handle, 210
cartridge bearing bottom bracket, 87

pedal, 101
hub, 121
cast aluminium frame, 30
cassette hub (see also Shimano), 120, 121
Cat-Eye bicycle computer, 213
Catalux rear light, 196
Cazenave four-wheeler, 251
centerpull brake, 110, 113, 115, 116
Centrix wheel axle stop, 24
Centro Sports pressed aluminium monocoque cross-frame, 31
chain, 96–98
chain alignment, 249
rivet tool, 257, 259
with external pins, 80
chainguard, 200, 205
enclosed, 206
chainless (see acatène)
chainring attachment converter, 78
Chanteloup (also Poly de Chanteloup, technical trials), 58, 59, 71, 72, 80, 82, 99, 100, 102, 116, 118, 130, 131, 134, 135, 136, 137, 141, 142, 150, 180, 182, 184, 189, 214, 222, 223, 226, 228, 230, 231, 232
product overview, 214
Chauvin, tandem with central timing chain, 223
children's bikes and accessories, 239–240
attachment, 239
brake and lever, 239
stoker, 224
trailer, 245–246
saddle, 164
Chioda hub, 120, 122
bicycle, 192, 195
Chinchavaud valve, 141
Chioda split rear hub, 122
Christian, Adolf, 106
Christophe toeclips, 103
Cibie headlight, 197
bloc-dynamo, 198
dynamo lighting, 198
Cinelli F-71 clipless pedal, 98, 103, 265
handlebars and stem, 158, 159, 266

lugs, 220
product overview, 220
city bike, 30, 151
clamp-on stem, 148
Clipper coaster brake, 131
clamp-on stem, 148
coaster brake, 132
clothing, 260–261, 267
cold-weather cycling wear, 261
Colnago frame details, 36, 273
Colorado pannier bag, 191
Coloral water bottle and cage, 210
Columb touring bicycle, 29
combination light, 193
component gruppos (or group-sets), 169–179
Concours des Inventeurs Lépine, 26
cone wrench, 257
convalescence bicycle adaptation, 251
Coppi, Fausto, 26, 49
bicycle, 106, 132
Corbelleta solid-axle quick-release, 128
cottered cranks, 77
cotter pin, 81
Coventry Eagle, frame details, 28
headset, 155
crank attachment, spliced and splined, 76
crank tool, 257, 259
cross-frame, 44, 114
Cross freewheel, 79, 93
curly rear stays, 25
cycle carriage, 245
Cycle Trading crankset, 81
Cycle: Compétition Cyclotourisme (book), 10
Cycles de Competition et Randonneuses (book), 10, 12
cycling clothing, 260–261
cap, 260–261
gloves, 260
goggles, 260
helmet, 261
shoes, 260–261
Cyclo (English) double-nut cotter pin, 81
pedal guide, 102
Benelux derailleur, 52
Benelux shifter, 60

Cyclo Compétition freewheel, 82
derailleur, 52, 53, 65
derailleur for use with coaster brake, 54
freewheel, 80
front derailleur, 56
shift lever, 49
Rapid hub, 124
cyclo-cross chainring, 85
saddle, 162
cyclocampeurs, 13
cyclometer, 200, 207, 209, 213
cyclosportifs, 13
cyclotouristes, 13
Cycloutil boxed workshop tool set, 258

D

DID chain, 96
DKW Hobby motor, 255
Dagedur aluminium alloy frame, 32
damping elements, 242–243
Dancing Chain: History and Development of the Derailleur Bicycle (book), 10
Dante Gianello derailleur, 44
Dardenne front derailleur, 43
Darrigade, André, 143
Data Book: 100 Years of Bicycle Component and Accessory Design (book), 10
Daudon brake, 109
front derailleur, 41, 48
internal wiring, 194
special wing-nut, 182
dead point in pedaling motion, 247, 249
De Gibraldy bicycle, 214
DeLange carrier bike, 53
Delay, Paulo, 26
Delisle, Raymond, 199
Delongmare dead-point drive, 249
Denti, Miro, 181
derailleur gearing, 41–73, 263
overview, 60
Derche front derailleur, 43
sealed bearing bottom bracket, 78

Dhagan-Ghome-Rhone racing moped, 254
Dilap extending cranks, 247
Dil Claudio bicycle, 25
direct-drive hub, 134
direction-indicators, 202
double-plate fork crown, 154
double air-chamber tube, 140
double-action pump, 208
Draisine, 16
    replica, built by Rebour, 14
drawing technique, Rebour's, 12
drilled-out components, 90, 93, 117, 158, 264, 265, 266
drivetrain components, 74–97, 265
drop-platform pedal, l99, 101
dropouts, 37–38, 40
    encased, 20
drum brake, 132–133
dual-pivot brake, 113, 114
Ducret straight spokes, 142
DuJee city bike, 44
Duban freewheel, 82
    freewheel, 81
Ducheron, Jean, 54
    bag support, 181
    home trainer, 250
Dunlop hydraulic drive system, 248
    tubeless tire, 142
Dunoiset brake lever, 112
Durax crank, 74
D'Allessandro split rear hub, 127
dynamo (or generator) lighting, 192, 193

E

eccentric bottom bracket, 231
École Nationale Supérieure des Arts Décoratifs, 9
ESGE prop-stand, 211
Eisenhower, Dwight, bicycle presented to, 86
electric bicycle, 253
    tire inflator, 258
    unit, 203
Elswick-Hopper chain-aligning gear-shifter, 249

Elve-Peugeot (see also Peugeot) bicycle, 75, 79
Elvish-Fontan shaft drive, 249
encased rear dropout, 20
English derailleurs, 48
epicyclic mechanism, 133
Everest Superlight chain, 96
Exceltoo hub, 121
    quick-release, 122
expanding chainwheel, 248
    cranks 247–249

F

face shield, 260
Faras radio, 207
Fast CO_2 inflator, 213
fastback seat lug detail, 36
Fauber-type one-piece crankset, 86
Favero, Vito, 119
Favorit coaster brake, 134
Ferdinand lugless frame,
Fichtel & Sachs derailleur, 61
fifth cog on 4-speed freewheel, 76
Fix-Auto protruding flag, 212
Flandria bicycle, 152, 196, 201, 215
    details, 88, l34
Fletcher front derailleur, 44
Flying Scott, frame detail, 35
folding and parting bikes, 233–238
    frame joint, latch, and hinge, 233, 235
    children's bike, 240
    handlebars, 146, 234–235
    pedals, 99, 233
Follis bicycle, 95
    brake, 107
    pedal, 101
Fonderies Rivolier stem, 154
foot-operated brake (see also coaster brake), 110
fork blades, 154–155
    crown, 154
    ends (see dropouts)
Forestier, Jean, 107
Fouacé, Jean, 145
four-wheeler, 251
fourth chainring, 94
Fox rim, 139

frame details, 19–40
    angles, 22
    building jig, 258
    extension, 182
    reinforcing, for coaster brake use, 131
    geometry, 22
    tubing, 19–20, 23, 35
France-Loire seatpost, 166
freewheel, 59, 74–84, 87, 89, 91, 93, 95, 97, 120, 121, 126, 129, 135, 257, 259
    and sprocket collection, 259
    tool, 89, 93, 257
    with frictionless roller engagement, 81
    with magnetic pawl engagement, 82
Frejus bicycle, 43
Frexel brake lever, 108
front luggage rack, 183, 191
    pannier, 183
    rack, 184
full-suspension frame (see also Moulton), 241–242
    moped, 253
full-width drum brake, 133

G

GB cable oiler, 204
    ergonomic wingnut, 121
GF scooter, 254
Gagnion aluminium mudguard, 211
Gambillon, Génèvieve, 208
Garin lugless frame, 28
Gasparetto derailleur, 45
Gaul, Charly, 76, 90, 123
Gauthier tandem, 222
Gautier, Bernard, 84
Geneva bicycle trade show, overview, 216
Géminiani, Raphaël (see also Raphaël-Géminiani), 45, 78
Genty-Jolly modified mixte frame, 22
    luggage rack, 181
Gérard, Captain, folding bike, 233
Giltoy tire-driven siren, 206
Gimondi, Félice, 192

Gitane bicycle, 136, 150, 161
    child's bike, 240
    frame, dropout details, 36
    lugless frame details, 35
    Minijet children's bike, 239
    Plicyclette folding bike, 236
Giu-Beste quick-release, 124
Gnutti spliced and splined crank attachment, 76
Godefroot, Walter, 195
Golb motorcycle, 254
Goëland child trailer, 246
    direct lever-operated front derailleur, 50
    rack, 185, 189
    trailer coupling, 246
Graczyk, Jean, 139
Graczyk, Louis, 120
Grimpex seat adjusting device, 163
group-sets (see component gruppos)
gruppos (see component gruppos)
Guffanti steering lock, 147
Guilleaume & Meyer, safety bicycle, 18
gyroscopic energy-storage drivetrain, 248–249
Gyro-Cycle, 248–249

H

hand rest, 202
hand-drive, 247
handlebars, 146–160, 266
    and stem overview, 158
    bag, 184, 188, 191, 263
    bag support, 186, 190
    reinforcing, 159
    stem (see also handlebar stem), 146, 266
    folding, 156
    drilled-out, 158
    flat, 147, 151
handlebar-controlled brake, 111
hanging pedal, 102
headset, 150–154, 155, 157, 159–160
    overview,160
    covered, 155
    with journal bearing, 154
    with needle bearing,151

Helyett (also Helyett-Essor) bicycle, 107, 120, 130, 139, 146, 151
Henri, Raymond, 12
Hercules (England) Herailleur derailleur, 52
  fiber-reinforced plastic frame tubing, 30
Hercules (Germany)
  monocoque cross-frame bicycle, 114
Hergé child trailer, 245
Herlihy, David, 11, 262
Hernandez self-energizing brake, 112
Herse, Lysette (or Lily), 148, 222, 226
Herse, René, 11, 113, 222
  Démontable parting bike, 12, 234
  bicycle, 98–99, 131, 135, 148, 208
  bottom bracket, 75
  crankset, 88
  frame with oversize tubing, 35
  handlebar bag support, 190
  headlight, 193
  ladies' bike, 34
  lever-operated front derailleur, 49
  lightweight frame details, 34
  mudguard, 209
  rack, 181, 188
  randonneur bicycle, 149, 180, 184
  stem, 148, 155
  tandem, 223, 224, 226–232
  touring bike, 39, 41, 138
  track bicycle, 112
  track tandem, 224
  trailer, 246
Hervé front derailleur, 49
Hetchins frame, 25
  frame details, 30
high-wheel bicycle, 16
historic bicycle drawings, 15–18
Hoffman (or cartridge) bearings, 121
home trainer, 250
hook-edge rim, 145
Hubs, 120–1387
hub brake, 130–138

hub gears, 130–138
  shifter, 131
Huet derailleur, 46
Hugaud, Pierre-Georges, 11, 273
Huot, Valentin, 72
Huret derailleur, 42, 47, 52, 56–57, 60–62, 64, 67, 263
  chainstay-mounted derailleur, 42
  combined twistgrip shifter and brake lever, 64
  direct-lever-operated front derailleur, 56
  double-cable-operated rear derailleur, 46
  front derailleur, 52, 56, 64, 67, 85, 89
  combined brake-shift lever, 114
  crankset and chainrings, 79
  cyclometer, 207
  hub nuts, 125
  quick-release solid-axle nuts, 121
  shifter, 52, 56, 61,64–65
  stem-shifters, 65
  stick-shift, 63, 65
  Allvit rear derailleur, 61–62
  Jubilee derailleur, 64
  Louison Bobet rear derailleur, 57
  Success front derailleur, 67
  Success rear derailleur, 67
  Svelto rear derailleur, 62, 263
  wing-nuts, 126
Husqvarna coaster brake, 132
hybrid gearing, 130, 137–138
hydraulic brake, 109
  drive, 248

I

ISO hanging platform pedal, 99, 102
Idéale saddle, 161
  children's saddle, 164
  leather saddle, 162
  saddle clip, 165
  touring saddle, 166
  women's saddle, 165, 168
indexed- shifting derailleur, 219
  shift lever, 56

Integra rim, 139
International Cycle History Conference, 12
integrated seatpost, 20, 162
internal wiring, 20–21, 108, 192, 194
Italian-style fork crown, 36
  head lug, 26

J

JIC roller trainer, 251
JOS dynamo and rear light, 196
  headlight, 197, 198
JRC dynamo, 197
James brake, 108
Janssen, Jan, 167, 185, 187
Janssens, Marc, 108
Jeay brake, 106
Jegues frame building jig, 258
Jeunet-Raphaël-Géminiani bicycle, 168–169
Jiménez, Julio, 163, 169, 182, 186
Joffre split-axle hub, 128
Joto Ringyo, 10
journal bearing headset, 154

K

KIK reinforced rim, 142
KIT spindle-operated brake, 111
Kangaroo-style bicycle, 15
Kaptein city bicycle, 32
Kessels bicycle, 197, 202
kick stand (see prop stand)
Koblet, Hugo, 46
KyoKuTo (KKT) pedal, 104
Kübler, Ferdi, 68

L

LAM brake, 106, 113, 239
LAM children's brake, 239
LDC pedal, 101
LG odometer, 207
La Perle bicycle, 46, 51
  ladies' saddle, 167
Lambretta scooter, 156
Lampo quick-release, 124

Lapize toestrap, 103
Lawrence, Mark, 12
leather saddle, 161–168
  ladies', 161
Le Chat front derailleur, 47
Le Cycle, magazine, 9–11
  demise of, 11
Le Cycliste, magazine, 10
Le Gyro gyroscopic drive, 248–249
Le Monde de Daniel Rebour, book, 9–10 13
Learco-Guerra bicycle, 90, 122, 123
Legnano bicycle, 94, 147
Lejeune bicycle, 187, 203, 205, 210–212
  Lejeune convalescence bicycle adaptation, 251
  Lejeune track bicycle, 210, 212
  track bike, frame detail, 38
Lepper saddle, 167
lever drive, 249
Lewis brake, 107
Liberia bicycle, 82, 111, 133
  frame detail, 28, 33
  front derailleur, 55
  telescoping front fork, 244
Libertas bicycle, 159
lighting equipment, 192–199
  overview, 194–196
Limongi frame detail, 37
loaded-touring tandem, 225
low-rider rack, 183, 190
Longoni frame, 28
Lucas bell, 205
Luciane-Oto pedal cart, 251
Ludy bushingless chain, 77
Lyotard pedal, 100–102
L'Officiel du Cycle, magazine, 11
Léfol mudguard, 208
  rim, 141
  tandem, 224
luggage carrying equipment, 180–191
luggage clamp, 181
  racks, 181–189
  rack overview, 187–189
  made of tubular steel, 185
lugless fame construction, 20, 21, 24, 27, 28, 35

M

MKM speedometer, 200
Mafac brake, 110, 115
   brake lever, 115
   self-energizing brake pads, 115
   spare tire pouch, 204
   tool kit, 203, 205
Magistroni crankset, 85
Magnat Debon bicycle, 76
magnetic pawl engagement, on freewheel, 82
Magni, Luigi, 164
Magura twist-grip shifter, 61
Maillard hub, 125
   freewheel, 89, 97
Malecote headlight, 195
Mallejac, Jean, 57, 70
Manet bicycle-sizing device, 250
Maravel rim, 141
Massignani, Imerio,
Matex cyclometer, 213
Maury brake, 108
   cyclo-cross bicycle, 152
Mavic rim, 142–144
Maxi-Car hub, 122, 130, 133–134
   direct-drive hub, 134
   drum brake, 130, 133
Mephisto rim, 144
Meral frame details, 33
Mercier bicycle, 74, 84, 87, 141, 165, 171
Merckx, Eddy, 14, 193, 197, 202, 206
   hour-record bike details, 93, 158
   with Rebour, 11, 14
Merlin-Garin & Debuit bicycle, 19
Messerschmidt motorized 3-wheeler, 254
Messidor mud-flap, 203
Messina bicycle, 157
Metevier-Laurent shifter, 43
Metropole bicycle, 45
Millet handlebar bag, 188
Milremo (see also Bertin)
   Milremo boxed freewheel and sprocket collection, 259
   brake, 113
   handlebars, 159
   hub, 128
   product overview, 221
   pump, 211
   saddle, 168
   stem and handlebars, 159
   toeclips, 105
Minimax brake lever, 108
mixte-frame bike (see also Berceau), 273
   frame, 34, 114
Mondia bicycle, 59
monobloc freewheel, 84
monocoque frame, 44, 114, 238, 243
monotube frame, 25
Monviso derailleur, 45
mopeds, 252–256
   suspension, 254
Morélon, Daniel, 210
Morin inverse linear-pull brake, 111
Mosquito auxiliary motor, 253
Moto-Revue (magazine), 9
Motobécane bicycle, 213
Motobécane folding details, 238
Motobécane time-trial bicycle, 200
Motom moped, 252
motorized bicycles, 252–256
Moulton S Speed bicycle, 188, 233
   S-Speed front suspension, 244
   carrier bag, 188
Moyne, J., monobloc freewheel, 84
mud-flap, 202, 203, 209
mudguard, 205 ,207–209, 213
   -mounted rack, 184–185
multifunction work station, 259
Mutaped bottom-bracket gear, 248

N

NMW drum brake, 133
Narcise road bike, 31
   stem, 146
   tandem with auxiliary motor, 256
Navet, Georges, integrated brake-shift lever, 44
Neimann suspension fork, 244
needle-bearing bottom bracket, 88, 265
headset, 151
pedal, 101–102
Nervar crankset, 56, 92, 94
New Star hub, 125
Nieddu, Thomasso, rim, 141
   Italsport derailleur, 51
Nittor adjustable seatpost, 166
Nivex chainstay-mounted derailleur, 41
Normandy hub, 127
Novy frame, with square tubing, 35
Nupal leak-proofing, 204
Nyuu Saikuringu, magazine, 13

O

Ocaña, Luis, 34, 200, 213
odometer, 207, 213
Olmo bicycle, 220
Olmo frame details, 39–40
one-piece crankset, 86, 88
Origami folding bike, 233
original scans, 262–267
Otero stem, 155
ovalized frame tubing, 23
oversize frame tubing, 33, 35

P

P.P. Roussey motor, 253
PFV stem, 154
PJ split rear hub, 123
PNG auxiliary motor, 252
PYB rear light, 193
Palco front suspension spring element, 243–244
Paloma bicycle, 155, 160
pannier bag, 181, 183–184, 191
passe-vitesse (see bar-end shifter)
Paratrouper bike, 233
Paris bicycle trade show overview, 218
Paris–Brest–Paris, 10, 27, 145
   Rebour's participation in, 10
Paul Component Engineering linear-pull brake, 275
pedals and toeclips, 98–105
   cart, 251
   cleat, 101, 261
   reflectors, 101
   rubber-block, 100–101
   screw-thread explanation, 100
   thread insert, 81–82
Pélissier hub, 129
Pelladini cassette hub, 76
Perry coaster brake, 132
Petitjean direction-indicators, 202
Peugeot (see also Elve-Peugeot), 50, 75, 80, 91, 108, 134, 183, 189, 194, 199, 204, 209, 217
   dynamo, 193
   rack, 187
Philippe handlebar (see also ATAX), 157
Phillips Swinglight suspension bike, 241
   derailleur, 60
Pingeon, Roger, 183, 194
Pioneer cross-frame safety bicycle, 15
Pittard front derailleur, 44
   low-rider rack, 190
Planckaert, Jeff, 152
Planckaert, Willy, 173
plastic water bottle, 210–212
Plumie-Sport bicycle, 173
Poly de Chanteloup (see Chanteloup)
Ponceblanc frame, 29
porteur rack, 187
Poulidor, Raymond, 165, 171, 198, 207
Poupard dead-point drive, 249
Poutrait-Morin toeclips, 103
Pratique du Vélo (book), 10, 15
Pradères, Jean-Pierre, 12
Préférence freewheel, 81
   split rear hub, 121
product overviews, 214–221
Promax Sansomax dropped platform pedal, 101
prop stand, 202, 208–211
Prunier CO_2 inflator, 208
Préférence spilt rear hub, 123
Puch Electric bicycle, 253
Père-Maman cycle, 245
pump, 208, 211, 213, 267
   overview, 213

Q

quick-release, 120, 122, 124–125, 129
   brake, 110, 116
   hub, 120, 122, 124–125, 129
   solid-axle, 121, 128

R

RACO suspension bicycle, 243
rack top bag, 183
radio, 207
Radios dynamo, 195
rain poncho, 260
Raleigh Chopper boy's bike, 240
   Rebour factory visit, 11, 161
   frame detail, 37
randonneurs, 13
   bicycle, 142, 221
   frame details, 21
   saddle, 168
Raphaël-Géminiani bicycle (see also Jeunet), 124, 182, 186
ratchet-adjustable seatpost, 166
rattrap pedal, 101–102
Ravat crankset, 79
Rebour, Daniel, background, 9–14
   as motorcycle tester, 252
   Draisine reconstruction, 14
   drawing technique, 12
   interest in saddles, 161, 166
   pedal design, 98
   Père-Maman cycle design, 245
   signature and initials, 10, 166
Rebour, Rodolphe, 11, 193, 274
Rebour, Simone, 9–11
recumbent bicycle, 244
Regina freewheel, 82, 87
Remy adjustable rack, 186
Renalb Lux derailleur, 45
Renard coaster brake, 134
Retseck, George, 275
Reynolds tandem tubing, 229
Rigida channel-reinforced rim, 144
Rigidex derailleur, 60
rims, 139–145, 205
   joint, 139, 141
   reinforced, 141–142
   wood, 143
rim brakes, 106–119
Riva Sport bicycle, 61
   Milan auxiliary motor, 255
Rivière, Roger, 115
roadster bicycle, 17
Rochet bicycle, 72
   cotterless cranks, 77
   girl's bicycle, 239
   touring bicycle, 102
rod-operated brake, 108, 130, 135
roller trainer, 251
Rosa double chainrings, 77
Roseau torsion-bar suspension, 242
Roto bottom bracket, 38
   fork crown, 38
Rouby-Lombardy frame detail, 27
Routens, Jo, 33, 96, 110, 118, 145, 222
   tandem, 228
Ruban-Bleu Record rim, 141
rubber-block pedal, 100–101
Rudan seatpost, 161
   stem, 151
Ruhier mud-flap, 209
Ruiz, Bernardo, 51

S

SER auxiliary motor, 255
SIAM speedometer, 201
SIS-Soupless, 244
SR (Sakae Ringyo), 11
   Raphaël-Géminiani bicycle, 92, 100
Sabliere randonneur bicycle, 128
   tandem, 222, 229, 231
Sachs 3-speed coaster brake, 135
   Torpedo hub gear, 136
   freewheel hub, 126
saddles and seatposts, 161–168, 266
   overview, 163–164
   women's 165, 266
saddle bag, 185
   bag support, 182
Sakae Ringyo (see SR)
Saker handlebars and stems, 157
Sanspeine brake, 110
Sanyo dynamo, 199
Sanyo roller-generator, 199
Sargent treadle-drive bicycle, 15
Sauvage Atomic bicycle, 63
Sauvage-Lejeune bicycle, 167, 185
   folding bike, 235
Schaer, Fritz, 59
Schulz, Jacques, 28
Schwinn Superior bicycle, 88, 156
Scintilla electric tire inflator, 258
Scoto Velorève auxiliary motor, 253
Scoutex 50 cc record machine, 254
seats and seatposts, 161–168
sealed bearing (see also Hoffman bearing), 78, 121–122
seat clip, 162
seat position, 163
seatposts, 161–168
   overview, 167
   integrated, 20, 162
   two-position, 163
Sedis chain, 93
self-energizing brake, 112, 115
semi-ballon tires, 41
Serwa auxiliary motor, 253
shaft drive, 249
shaped sprocket teeth, 77
shim, for seatpost, 161
Shimano, 11
   10 mm pitch Keirin (track) components, 95, 169
   105 crankset, 95
   600 derailleur, 69, 73, 173
   600 gruppo, 173
   600 pedals, 104
   600 shifters, 69, 71
   Altus shifters, 70
   brake, 264
   DeOre touring pedal, 105
   Parapull brake, 119
   Positron derailleur, 68
   Ultra-Glide chain, 97
   aero brake lever, 119, 264
   automatic shifting 2-speed hub, 137
   brake lever, 117–118, 264
   Crane derailleur, 66
   disk brake, 137
   dropouts, 40
   headset, 160
   hydraulic brake, 273
   shifters, 66, 69–70, 72
Shimano Dura-Ace, 71, 73, 96, 97, 117
   AX derailleurs and shifters, 71
   AX handlebars, 160
   AX pedals, 104
   AX seatpost, 168
   EX crankset, 96
   EX derailleurs and shifters, 70
   bottom bracket, 97
   cassette hub, 129
   derailleur, 66
   freewheel and cassette, 95, 265
   front derailleur, 72
   hub (with screwed-on freewheel), 129
   pedals, 104
   shifters, 72
Shipway rotating stem, 153
shoe covers, 101
short-wheel-base tandem, 222, 230
sidecar, for moped, 254
sidepull brake, 112, 117, 119
single-arm suspension, 254
siren, 206
shock-absorbing stem, 155
shoe covers, 202
sidecars (see trailers and sidecars)
Silk folding bike, 233, 235
Simplex Delrin plastic shifters, 63
   Juy-Record hub, 124
Simplex Juy 543 derailleur, 59
Simplex LJ derailleur, 65, 67
   adjustable seat clip, 165
   ball-bearing derailleur pulley, 61
   bar-end shifter, 62
   chainrings, 90
   derailleur range, 69, 72–73
   double-cable derailleur, 48
   dropouts, 27, 38
   folding bike hinge and latch, 235

front derailleur, 56, 67, 85
Gran Tourisme derailleur, 57
hub, 125–126
overview, 62
quick-release, 120, 125, 129
stem-mounted shifter, 73
stick-shift, 63
twist-grip shifter, 52
Simplex (Netherlands)
Zweeffiets suspension bike, 241
Singer, Alex, 222
2-part chainring, 75
brake, 107
wing nut, 125
4-th chainring on TA crankset, 94
luggage rack, 180
seat clip, 162
steering details, 157
stem, 156
tandem, 228
single pulley derailleurs, preference for, 50
Sirio electric unit, 203
softened saddle cover, 166
soldered spokes, 145
solid-axle hub nut, 125
Solex, (see Vélosolex)
solid-axle quick-release, 121, 128
solid-link brake control, 113
Soubitez bloc-dynamo, 195
headlight, 196–197
Souhart, Jacques, Dual-Traction bike, 247
passe-vitesse, or bar-end shifters, 41, 45
drop-platform pedal, 99
Soupless suspension fork and seatpost, 243
Spacelander bicycle, 23
spare tire clip, 209
Speedwell, titanium frame, 30–31, 36
Spirax derailleur, 53
indexed shift lever, 56
Splendid bicycle, 66
speedometer, 200, 201
split rear hub, 122, 123
spindle-operated brake, 111
splined and clamped crank attachment, 92
split rear hub, 127

split-axle hub gear, 132
spokes, 139–145
replacement, 121
patterns, 140, 145
Sprint rim (see also tubular tire), 144
Sprinto-Cotes 2-position seat post, 163
sprung saddle, 162
square frame tubing, 35
Star-Pilote CO_2 inflator, 212
Starnord *cyclosportif*-style bicycle, 219
stainless steel frame, 20, 112
steerer tube, 148
cork insert, 159
steering components, 146–160
Stella bicycle, 64
folding bicycle, 236
stem, 147, 149–152, 154–155
adjustable reach, 153
clamp-on, 148, 150–151
forged vs. welded vs. pressed, 149, 154
rotating, 153
shock-absorbing, 155
wedge-clamp vs. cone clamp, 151, 158
-mounted shifters, 65
steering components, 146–161
steering lock, 137, 204
Stella bicycle, 22, 55
Grossjean Aero bicycle, 22
Stellina folding bike, 238
stick-shift, 63
stirrup brake (see also rod-operated brake), 147
straight spokes, 142
Stronglight
93 crankset, 91
99 triple crankset, 93
cotterless bottom bracket, 83, 88, 94, 265
crankset and bottom bracket, 75–77, 80, 85, 89–90, 97, 265
double chainring, 81, 265
headset, 152–153, 159–160
needle-bearing bottom bracket, 88, 265
single crankset, 89
Super Compétition crankset, 85
triple crankset, 89

Sturmey-Archer 3-speed hub gear, 135–138
5-speed hub gear, 275
drum brake, 136
shifter, 136
Sugino stem, 158
"suicide pedal," 103
SunTour Cyclone derailleur, 68
Sunbeam oil-bath chaincase, 206
Super Champion derailleur, 50
rim, 144–145
Super Leader derailleur, 42, 55
Super Randonneur handlebar bag and rack, 191
suspension systems, 241–244
adaption, 243
fork, 137, 243–244
fork overview, 242, 244

T

TA brake cable anchor and seat binder bolt combination, 116
3-arm crankset, 91
chainring attachment detail, 80
chainrings, 79, 81, 89, 92
crankset, 74, 81–85, 93
cyclo-cross chainring, 85
double chainring, 84
insulated water bottle, 210
pannier bag, 191
pedal, 101–102
pedal cleat, 102
single crankset, 92
triple crankset, 84–85, 87, 89
water bottle cage, 208
TSK boy's bike, "American style", 239
tandems, 222–231
brake, 110
crankset, 227, 232
drive-train, 223, 225, 227, 232
stem, 223
timing chain, 223, 225, 227
eccentric bottom bracket, 231
short-wheel-base, 224
Tange headset, 160
Taylor, Ken, 12
technical trials, (see also Chanteloup), 58, 59

Terashima, Tsunezo, 10
Terrot bicycle, 57, 70
Thompson bottom bracket, 91
threadless headset, 146
three-cable brake lever, 110
three-speed hub gear, cut-away, 130
Through-axle split rear hub, 121
Thun crankset, 92
Thévènet, Bernard, 204, 209, 217
Tigra stem, 149
Tillet, Claude, 9
tires, 129–145
patch kit, 259
protector (or "nail-puller"), 204
tubeless tire, 142, 144
Titan split-axle hub gear, 132
titanium frame, 30
details, 31
toeclip, 100, 103, 105
toestrap, 103, 105
Tokheim expanding-chainwheel gear shifter, 273
tools and equipment, 257–259
tool kit (*or* tool pouch), 203, 205, 209, 257, 258
Torpedo coaster brake, 131
hub gear, 136–137
Torès, Pedro, 216
Tour de France bicycles, 16, 17, 26, 43, 45, 46, 47, 49, 50, 51, 54, 55, 58, 59, 60, 61, 64, 66, 67, 68, 74, 75, 76, 78, 79, 87, 91, 103, 106, 107, 108, 110, 119, 120, 122, 123, 124, 132, 133, 139, 140, 143, 146, 147, 151, 152, 155, 159, 160, 161, 163, 164, 165, 167, 168, 171, 175, 182, 183, 185, 186, 187, 190, 192, 193, 194, 195, 196, 197, 198, 199, 201, 202, 204, 205, 206, 207, 209, 213, 214, 215, 216, 217
Tourbillon-Stop band brake, 134
trailers and sidecars, 245–246
coupling, 246
suspension, 246
Transalpino derailleur, 55

tubeless tire, 142, 144
Trycyl compact foot-pump, 257
twist-grip shifter, 52–53, 64, 138
two-bulb headlight, 197
two-position seatpost, 163

U

Unica saddle, 166
Union Strada folding bike, 235
Union pedal, 101
Universal centerpull brake, 115
Urago bicycle, 42, 127, 162
    ladies' bicycle, 42
    loaded-touring bike, 153
    randonneur bicycle, 162
    road bike, 38

V

V-profile rim (*see also* aero components), 143
VAP auxiliary motor, 252
VAR tool company, 10, 11, 209, 257–259
    tool pouch, 209
VIBO 3-speed hub gear, 131
Van Geechten, Richard, 80
Van Impe, Lucien, 203, 205
Van Looy, Rik, 159
Van Springel, Herman, 214
Vannod sidecar, 245–246
Varia-7 expanding chainwheel, 248
Variateur hinged frame, 28
Vélectrique electric-assist bicycle, 253
Vélocio (*pen name of* Paul de Vivie), 10
Velocino, 235
Vélosac bag and support, 186
Vélosolex moped, 254
Véloflex, 244
Vexlo hub gear, 133
Viking track racing bicycle, 18
Vincar ratchet-adjustable seatpost, 166
Vintage Bicycle Quarterly, magazine, (*see also* Bicycle Quarterly), 12
Vitalux dynamo, 199
Vito front bag and support, 190
Vittor spare tire clip, 209
Vittoria derailleur, 56
    freewheel, 77
Vitus frame, 24
    tubing, 19, 24
    stem, 148
Volo ball-bearing derailleur pulley, 53Vogue & Pittard trailers, 246

W

Walkowiak, Roger, 92
water bikes, 250
water bottle, 200, 211–21
    mounts (*see also* bottle cage), 204
Webb suspension fork, 244
Weinmann Symmetric brake, 114
    brake lever, 116
wheels and wheel components, 120–145
    carrying bracket, 183
    details, 143
    truing stand, 257, 259
windbreaker, 261
wing-nut, 120–121, 125–126
Wolber tires, 142–144
Wucher, Roland, stem, 153

X

Xtracycle, 182

Z

Zeus 2000 freewheel, 91
    brake, 116–117
    brake lever, 117
    seat clamp, 168
Zimmermann, André, 157
Zoe double-action pump, 208
Zoetemelk, Joop, 196, 201, 215
Zéfal pump, 211

Notes

Notes